Teacher of Civil War Generals

Teacher of Civil War Generals

Major General Charles Ferguson Smith, Soldier and West Point Commandant

ALLEN H. MESCH

McFarland & Company, Inc., Publishers
Jefferson, North Carolina

This biography is based on official military records, unit histories, biographies, memoirs, and letters. Much of the information is from the Charles F. Smith collection at the United States Military Academy at West Point.

LIBRARY OF CONGRESS CATALOGUING-IN-PUBLICATION DATA

Mesch, Allen H.
Teacher of Civil War generals : Major General Charles Ferguson Smith, soldier and West Point commandant / Allen H. Mesch.
p. cm.
Includes bibliographical references and index.

ISBN 978-0-7864-9834-5 (softcover : acid free paper) ∞
ISBN 978-1-4766-2038-1 (ebook)

1. Smith, Charles Ferguson, 1807–1862. 2. United States—History—Civil War, 1861–1865—Biography. 3. Mexican War, 1846–1848—Biography. 4. United States Military Academy—Biography. 5. Generals—United States—Biography. I. Title.

E467.1.S68M47 2015   355.0092—dc23   [B]   2015021053

BRITISH LIBRARY CATALOGUING DATA ARE AVAILABLE

© 2015 Allen H. Mesch. All rights reserved

No part of this book may be reproduced or transmitted in any form or by any means, electronic or mechanical, including photocopying or recording, or by any information storage and retrieval system, without permission in writing from the publisher.

Front cover: Gen. Charles F. Smith, early 1860s
(Library of Congress)

Printed in the United States of America

*McFarland & Company, Inc., Publishers
Box 611, Jefferson, North Carolina 28640
www.mcfarlandpub.com*

To Helen I. Williams, who sparked my interest in the American Civil War; to Mrs. Francis Smith Oliver, who had the foresight to preserve her father's records and letters; and to Sharlyn K. Mesch, whose support in life and on this project was instrumental in its completion.

Acknowledgments

I became fascinated with Major General Smith during my studies of the American Civil War. As a student and educator, I felt that the influence of West Point instructors was not given as much credit as it deserved.

I would like to thank my mother-in-law, Helen I. Williams, for planting the seeds of interest in the American Civil War. From someone who had little interest in the conflict, I was transformed into a historian who has been to nearly 100 battlefields, taken more than 4,000 pictures, created a website and blog, taught classes at Collin College, and now authored this book.

During this writing journey, my wife of forty-eight years, Sharlyn Williams Mesch, has gathered books from numerous libraries, copied and photographed documents, assisted me through the perilous and difficult permissions, checked citations, edited drafts, and provided the emotional support that all writers need.

My special thanks to:

Eric A. Dubelier for permission to use material from his honors thesis at Tulane University, "Charles F. Smith: The Forgotten Soldier."

Jim Knight for permission to quote liberally from his book *The Battle of Fort Donelson*.

The staff of the United States Army Heritage and Education center for their help with my research.

Suzanne Christoff and her staff at the Archive Collection at United States Military Academy at West Point for providing access to the "Charles Ferguson Smith Family Papers 1840–1896" held in the Special Collections.

Sharon Doty, Joelle C. McGill, Alan Mesches, and Steve Strominger for reviewing and editing the book.

Fanny Smith Oliver who transcribed her father's letters, preserved documents and gave them to West Point. The letters are wonderful to read and reflect her father's affection, humor, and character.

Leslie A. Oliver, General Smith's grandson, who persisted in offering the collection of Major General Smith's correspondence and papers to the United States Military Academy. The collection contains "232 pieces of correspondence, 99 items relating to Smith's military career and eight volumes of letter books and journals."

Kurt Wille who provided information on the Smith family, historic news clippings, and kind words of support throughout the process.

Doug Richardson of the National Parks Service, James Vaughan, and Dave Stewart who reviewed my descriptions of the battles at Fort Donelson and Shiloh.

Betsy Miller who gathered information on the Smith family.

Librarians at Plano Public Library and Collin College Library who obtained books from around the state and country.

Table of Contents

Acknowledgments   vi
Preface: "Regular Army to the shoe-soles"   1

Part One
West Point to Texas: 1820–1845   5
1. "Grant him a warrant as a cadet"   6
2. "Thirteen years of service"   16
3. Commandant of Cadets   22
4. "At West Point always"   34
5. "Riot raging in Kensington"   40

Part Two
Corpus Christi to Mexico City: 1845–1848   45
6. "A tussle with the Mexicans"   46
7. "War at last sure enough!"   54
8. "The brilliant *coup de main*"   63
9. "A political war"   71
10. "Off for the far famed City of Mexico"   77
11. "This glorious army hoisted the colors"   86

Part Three
Between Wars: 1848–1861   93
12. "The most perfect soldier in the Army"   94
13. "Courage and Fidelity"   102
14. "A war must be waged"   111

Part Four
Disunion and Reunion: 1861–1862   131
15. "The storm will blow over"   132
16. "The war in Kentucky has commenced"   144
17. "Make demonstrations with your troops"   165

18.	The Incident at the Tilghman House	170
19.	"They are false in every particular"	177

PART FIVE
FORT HENRY AND FORT DONELSON: FEBRUARY 1862 ... 189

20.	"Take and hold Fort Henry"	190
21.	"I Shall take and destroy Fort Donelson"	201
22.	"You must take Fort Donelson"	211
23.	"Unconditional and immediate surrender"	224

PART SIX
TRIUMPH AND TURMOIL: MARCH–JULY 1862 ... 233

24.	"Take command of the expedition"	234
25.	"Hold his position"	243
26.	"Does not set easy on me yet"	250
27.	"The devils own day"	255
28.	"His great worth as a soldier and friend"	264

	Appendices	273
A.	*Biographical Sketch from the Cullum Register*	274
B.	*Notable Cadets During Smith's Term as Commandant*	277
C.	*Fort Donelson Union Order of Battle*	279
D.	*Chronology*	281

Chapter Notes	285
Bibliography	317
Index	323

"Battle is the ultimate to which the whole life's labor of an officer should be directed."—C. F. Smith[1]

Major General C. F. Smith (courtesy C. F. Smith Collection at U.S. Military Academy Library, Special Collections).

Preface: "Regular Army to the shoe-soles"

The American Civil War produced many famous generals. The names Lee, Grant, Jackson, and Sherman are well known. Many of the war's finest officers were brother cadets at the United States Military Academy at West Point. During their four years at the Academy, they formed friendships that would endure beyond the war. Like all students, their instructors would also shape their lives. This is a biography of one of their teachers: Major General Charles Ferguson Smith.

Smith served at West Point from 1829 to 1842 as Assistant Instructor of Tactics, Adjutant to the Superintendent, and Commandant of Cadets. He influenced many cadets, who became prominent Civil War generals, through formal instruction and personal conduct. As commandant, he was the faculty member responsible for teaching the cadets how to become soldiers and officers. According to Oliver E. Wood, "The Commandant of the Corps exercises a more important influence on the military character and opinions of the junior officers of the Army than any other individual."[1]

The following is a partial list of notable Civil War generals who were cadets during Smith's tenure as commandant.[2]

Bee, Barnard B. (1845), Confederate
Buckner, Simon B. (1844), Confederate
Buell, Don Carlos (1841), Union
Canby, Edward R. S. (1839), Union
Ewell, Richard E. (1840), Confederate
Gilmer, Jeremy F. (1839), Confederate
Gorgas, Josiah (1841), Confederate
Grant, Ulysses Simpson, (1843) Union
Halleck, Henry W. (1839), Union
Hancock, Winfield Scott (1844), Union
Hardee, W. Joseph (1838), Confederate
Hébert, Paul Octave (1840), Confederate
Hunt, Henry J. (1839), Union
Johnson, Bushrod Rust (1840), Confederate
Longstreet, James (1842), Confederate
Lyon, Nathaniel (1841), Union
McLaws, Lafayette (1842), Confederate
Ord, Edward O. C. (1839), Union
Pleasanton, Alfred (1844), Union
Pope, John (1842), Union
Porter, Fitz John (1845), Union
Reynolds, John Fulton (1841), Union
Richardson, Israel (1841), Union
Rosecrans, William Starke (1842), Union
Sherman, William Tecumseh (1840), Union
Smith, Edmund Kirby (1845), Confederate
Smith, G. Woodson (1842), Confederate
Smith, William F. (1844), Union
Stevens, Isaac I. (1839), Union
Sykes, George (1842), Union
Thomas, George Henry (1840), Union
Van Dorn, Earl (1842), Confederate

However, Smith was much more than an academic instructor. He continued to set an example for his former students during his distinguished service in the Mexican American War, where he was brevetted for bravery, and the Utah Expedition, or Mormon War. In *Duty, Honor, Country*, Stephen E. Ambrose included Smith in his list of able commanders who would make their reputation in the Civil War.³ Smith was instrumental in the capture of Fort Donelson. After the battle, his superior officer and former student General Henry W. Halleck said, "Brig. General Charles F. Smith, by his coolness and bravery at Fort Donelson when the battle was against us, turned the tide, and carried the enemy's outworks; make him a Major-General. You can't get a better one. Honor him for this victory and the country will applaud."⁴ General Ulysses S. Grant told his wife Julia "a better soldier or truer man does not live."⁵

When General Halleck removed Grant from command after Fort Donelson, Smith was placed in charge of coordinating the attack on the Confederate position at Corinth, Mississippi. During preparations for the advance, Smith sustained a severe gash in his leg when jumping into a small yawl after a meeting with General Lew Wallace. His health failed and he was forced to bed and relieved of his field command. His condition continued to decline, and he died on April 25, 1862.

General Halleck's Obituary Order said, "He combined the qualities of a faithful officer, an excellent disciplinarian, an able commander, and a modest, courteous gentleman. In his death the army has lost one of its brightest ornaments, and the country a general whose place it will be difficult to supply."⁶ In his letter to Mrs. Smith, Grant lamented, "Where an entire nation consoles with you in your bereavement no one can do so with more heartfelt grief than my self."⁷

In his *Personal Memoirs*, General Grant said: "In fact I regarded General Scott and Captain C. F. Smith, the Commandant of Cadets, as the two men most to be envied in the nation. I retained a high regard for both of them up to the day of their death" and "[Smith's] personal courage was unquestioned, his judgment and professional acquirements were unsurpassed, and he had the confidence of those he commanded as well as of those over him."⁸ Grant's son Frederick said that his "father had a more tender feeling for General Charles F. Smith than for any of the other officers of high rank with whom he was associated during his entire career, between 1860 and 1865." Grant also considered Smith to be "an ideal soldier" who "had every qualification necessary to make a man pre-eminent as a general."⁹ Another former cadet, William Tecumseh Sherman, said, "Had C. F. Smith lived Grant would have disappeared to history after Donelson."¹⁰

Smith was a positive influence on Grant at West Point, set an excellent example for Grant during the Mexican War, and mentored Grant while serving with him in the Civil War. Grant might not have achieved this success had not Smith helped his forces win at Fort Donelson. Smith's death forced Grant to mature into a capable field commander and to forge an alliance with William T. Sherman that would ultimately win the Civil War.

Brevet General George Cullum praised Smith in the summary prepared for the United States Military Academy Biographical Register.

> On the 25th of April, 1862, this brave and noble paladin, who was as intrepid as Ney, as chivalric as Murat, and as rock-fast as Macdonald, breathed his last. The Army could boast of no better general. His stately and commanding presence inspired his soldiers with respect and almost fear. In his rigid discipline, though severe, he was always just, requiring no greater subordination from inferiors than he was ready to yield to superiors. The call of duty was to him a magic sound for which he was always ready to make every sacrifice and endure any fatigue. He was the very model of a soldier, calm, prudent, and self-poised, yet, in the hour of danger, bold almost to rashness. Had he lived he would have held a high niche in the Temple of Fame, whose doors were already opened to him.¹¹

In his autobiography, General Lew Wallace said Smith "made no pretensions to civil attainments of any kind." Wallace believed "a reputation like Thomas's, and an esteem indistinguishable from glory, like Sherman's, had been his could he have lived to the end of the war." The author of *Ben Hur* was grateful to be able "to see an ideal friend in my ideal soldier, and venerate the hero even as I loved the man."[12]

Grant's personal physician, Dr. John H. Brinton, recalled Smith "to have been perhaps the handsomest man in the army, erect, six feet four[13] in stature. He was fond of the army, was universally esteemed, and left the reputation of a good and faithful soldier. In the execution of duty, he knew no friend, but duty over, he was a most genial commander."[14]

Perhaps Shelby Foote wrote the best and simplest epitaph in *From Donelson to Memphis*: "he was Regular Army to the shoe-soles."[15]

My goal in writing General Smith's biography is to recognize his contributions as a military educator and field commander. I especially want to acknowledge Smith's role in developing the Civil War's commanders.

In April 1885, Fanny Oliver, who was trying to gather information for a biography of her father to be written by General William F. Smith,[16] received a letter from his friend, Henry Robert Crosby. Crosby shared his memories of Smith, suggested others Mrs. Oliver might contact, and left her with the following advice:

> And now please let me say one word in this respect. Do not let it be done in a hurry. There is a good deal of ground to cover. Florida and Mexican War, service at the Military Academy and different posts in the West, special duty in the Utah Expedition as well as the Civil War. This information will take some time to collect.[17]

I hope that I have been true to both Mrs. Oliver's intent and Mr. Crosby's advice.

Part One

West Point to Texas: 1820–1845

"How vividly can I recall the tall, graceful, and handsome Lieutenant drilling our company of Cadets in marches and the manual of arms."—George W. Cullum[1]

The Plain at West Point, 1828, engraved from a painting by George Catlin (courtesy U.S. Military Academy Library, Special Collections).

1. "Grant him a warrant as a cadet"

"Seemed very cold, indeed half frozen"

A full moon illuminated the clear, bitter cold winter night. The rain had stopped and the snow had melted leaving the battlefield wet. As the soldiers rested and tried to sleep, their clothes froze to the ground. It must have been fifteen or twenty degrees below freezing.[1] The silence was interrupted occasionally by shots fired on the Union pickets who were stationed on the site of the former Confederate camp.[2] Unlike the previous night, fires were permitted to provide some warmth to the men and officers. Still it was much too cold for the old general to be out in the open field resting in bivouac with his men.

Smith leaned against an oak tree with his boots near the fire. Ice coated his white mustache. In his last letter to his daughter he had written, "Exposure always agrees with me."[3] The men of the Second Division tried to rest in preparation for another day of hard fighting. Their attempts to sleep were interrupted by the moans of wounded men and the rifle fire between the lines. In the morning, Grant's forces would attack and capture the works.

It was ironic that Smith should be fighting at the fort named in honor of his West Point classmate Daniel Donelson. Both men graduated in the class of 1825, but Smith had remained in the army while Donelson had quickly resigned his commission to become a Tennessee planter and politician. In another irony of war, Smith faced Buckner, Pillow, and Johnston, who he had fought along with in Mexico. The day's battle had earned him praise from his commander and former student, Ulysses S. Grant. Smith regarded the charge as simply doing his duty and performing the responsibilities he learned as a cadet at West Point. Later as commandant of cadets, he guided the future officers using the same principles that he had learned under Superintendent Thayer and Commandant Worth.

During his time at the Academy, he had earned the respect and friendship of faculty, classmates, and pupils. Smith had garnered additional honors as a line officer and his performance in battle demonstrated that he was both educator and practitioner. Now he fought against the men whom he once called brothers and now labeled Rebels.

General Smith could not recognize that the events of the afternoon of February 15, 1862, would earn him a place in history. The capture of the Confederate rifle pits would be the pinnacle of his military career that began nearly forty-two years earlier on the Plain at the United States Military Academy.

"Excellent talents and with advanced elementary intuition"

It must have been both frightening and exciting for thirteen-year-old Charles Ferguson Smith to arrive at West Point. His appointment, at such a young age, might have been surprising, but it was hardly unexpected. Smith was born on April 24, 1807, in Philadelphia with a military bloodline. He was the oldest of eight children born to Dr. Samuel B. Smith and Margaret Ferguson. His father, Samuel, was an Assistant Surgeon in the United States Army, and his grandfather, Ebenezer Ferguson, was a Colonel of the Continental Army. With his father stationed at Fort Mifflin and Fort Delaware on the Delaware River near Philadelphia, Charles was exposed to army life and discipline as a child. So it was only natural for the young boy to pursue a military career.[4] His paternal grandfather, John Blair Smith, was a prominent Presbyterian clergyman in Philadelphia and president of Hampden-Sidney and Union colleges. John Blair Smith was the son of Robert Smith, who was a well-known theologian and president of Princeton University.[5] These religious, academic, and military roots provided the foundation for Charles Smith to become one of the most admired officers of his time.

When Charles was twelve, his father asked Secretary of War John C. Calhoun to admit his son to the United States Military Academy at West Point:

> I am very anxious that my eldest son Charles F. Smith should receive a military education at West Point and would esteem it a very great indulgence if you would grant him a warrant as cadet this winter—He is fourteen years of age and of large size—strong constitution—excellent talents and with advanced elementary intuition.[6]

This misrepresentation of Smith's age is likely an attempt to circumvent recommendations made by the Academy's Board of Visitors that "no person should be admitted as a Cadet to the Military Academy except between the age of 14 and 18 years and should be well versed in Reading, Writing, English Grammar and Common Arithmetic, including Vulgar[7] and Decimal Fractions and the extraction of the Square & Cube Roots."[8] Dr. Smith was granted his request, and Charles was invited to be an applicant to compete for one of 250 appointments to West Point.[9]

In mid–June 1820, Charles made the journey from his home in Wilmington, Delaware, to West Point, New York. He took the steamer *Constitution* from the dock at Cortlandt Street in New York and arrived at West Point around 11:30 a.m. The passengers with their "West Point baggage" were put ashore in a small boat.[10] An orderly from the Superintendent's staff led Charles to the Adjutant's office to sign his articles of enlistment as a candidate for admission to the Military Academy.[11]

Like every candidate since 1818, he was required to pass an oral examination to demonstrate his ability in writing and arithmetic. The applicants were left on their own to prepare for these tests. However, the candidates had little time to study for their entrance tests. In addition to cramming for the oral exams, they had to spend much of their day drilling for the summer encampment.[12] The entrance exams were easy at this time, and every entrant with the equivalent of a high-school education passed with no trouble.[13] The exams were held in the second half of June. The faculty grilled each prospective student at the blackboard. The admission tests were designed to eliminate applicants who lacked the intelligence to graduate. Thirty to sixty percent of the candidates failed, and, of those that were accepted, less than half graduated.[14]

The Academy was run by Superintendent Sylvanus Thayer whose educational and administrative reforms created the preeminent school of engineering and earned him the title of "the father of the military academy."[15] The thirty-two-year-old engineering officer organized the cadets into a battalion of two companies and appointed Captain William C. Worth as commander. "Haughty Bill" looked and acted like a soldier, and the position was soon designated as Commandant of Cadets. Other tactical officers or "tacs" were added to assist Worth in training the cadets.[16]

Superintendent Thayer defined the format used to present instruction and the recitation method to assess the cadets' knowledge of a subject.[17] He authorized weekly class reports charting daily progress, formalized a grading system, and published the annual register. Thayer outlined, improved, and extended the curriculum of studies and held semi-annual cadet examinations to demonstrate the Corps of Cadets competency.[18]

Charles was thrust into this demanding academic and disciplinary structure. His days were filled with study and drill. He also had his first taste of Academy food, which was kindly described as bland. The daily diet was heavy on bread, potatoes, and meat, especially beef, veal, and mutton, but skimpy on green vegetables and sweets. The tasteless menu was a consequence of Thayer's desire to have the mess hall food be similar to army field rations.[19]

Charles' first few nights in the barracks were interrupted by upper class cadets pretending to be officers, bursting into their rooms, and issuing absurd orders to the terrified recruits. His indoctrination into the United States Army had begun.

"A time of trouble and fatigue"

After completing their exams and waiting several days to learn whether they were accepted, the candidates were summoned to drill in front of the barracks. The captain called the names of those who were admitted and ordered them to take three steps forward. Fortunately, Charles' prior academic training had prepared him, and on July 1, 1820, he was admitted as a "plebe"[20] in the Fourth Class.[21] At the age of thirteen years, three months, he was the youngest member of his class of seventy-four plebes that averaged sixteen to seventeen years old.[22] As a cadet, Charles became "part of the land forces of the United States," and as such was "constitutionally subjected to the Rules and Articles of War and to trials by courts-martial."[23]

The cadets were given their knapsacks and sent to their temporary quarters to pack their civilian clothing. Cadets received an annual pay and allowance of $388[24] from which he purchased textbooks, drawing material, clothing, and equipment.[25] His uniform consisted of a gray coatee[26] with standing collar, gilt bullet buttons, and a black silk cord. He wore a gray vest and pantaloons in winter and white in summer with white belts for the bayonet and cartridge box. The dress cap was black felt with a round crown, black pompon, brass front plate, and an eagle on the front of the cap. Cadets wore a forage cap when off duty.[27]

After the cadets had gathered their uniforms, they marshaled again in front of the barracks and prepared to join the upper classmen for the annual summer encampment on the West Point Plain. The cadets formed into companies in front of the barracks. Then, on Major Worth's order, the battalion, with the band and with colors unfurled, marched to its summer home. The cadets were expected to spend two months each year in summer camp where they would be taught "all of the duties of a private, a noncommissioned officer, and officer."[28]

Each summer camp was named in honor of a famous military or government leader. Charles' first camp was named Fort Clinton for American Revolutionary War hero James Clinton. The camp was located on the northeast portion of the Plain and consisted of four rows of tents opening on two parallel streets. The tents for the company officers and instructors of tactics were located opposite their respective companies. A wide road ran through the center of camp and terminated at the east end in front of Major Worth's tent.

Charles and the other newly admitted plebes were quickly assigned to their respective companies. Over the next two months, the plebes went through a daily schedule of rigorous military instruction under the direction of Worth and his assistant instructors. They lived in Camp Clinton under the rules, regulations, and discipline consistent with a war-time army.[29] During summer camp, upper class cadets expected the plebes to perform menial tasks such as carrying water, gathering firewood, policing the camp grounds, and other duties than might be done by ordinary soldier.[30]

The cadet battalion officers were selected from the First through Third Classes. The corporals were appointed from the cadets in the Third Class, the sergeants from the Second, and the captains and lieutenants from the First Class. The Fourth Class cadets and non-officers from the other classes completed the ranks as soldiers. The soldiers served as either artillery, infantry, or riflemen.

The camp day began at 4:00 a.m. with the morning gun. The cadets gathered for drill at 5:00. They marched to the mess hall for breakfast at 6:30 a.m. Morning parade, accompanied by the Academy band, was at 8:00. After their meal, they had infantry or artillery instruction until dinner at 1:00. They spent the afternoon practicing other military exercises. The regimen concluded with another parade at 6:00 p.m. followed by a light supper. The day mercifully ended at 10:00.[31]

The plebes spent the summer learning the School of the Soldier.[32] During their assignment as artillerymen, they were taught how to use the cannon, mortar, and howitzer. The plebes were instructed in the saber, rapier, broad, and small sword. They learned how to load, aim, and fire the 1816 model United States Flintlock Musket.[33] The student-soldiers were instructed in the construction of field works and the preparation of all kinds of munitions and matériels of war.[34]

Charles had day and night guard duty during the encampment. A chain of six or eight sentinels surrounded the camp. When he was assigned guard duty, he stood his post for four hours during the day and four hours at night. During daytime duty, he wilted in the summer heat in full uniform during daytime duty and the sun blistered his nose and burned his cheeks. At night, he suffered through the cold, dark, and rain. As if standing alone in the darkness was not enough, the older cadets taunted the plebes by crossing through the post and frightening them. However, the plebes were at greater risk from their own exhaustion and were sometimes found asleep on the ground when the guard was changed.[35]

The annual tour was the only relief from the monotony of drill. In order to publicize the Academy, Thayer introduced the cadets to the public through a series of summer marches. In 1820, the Corps went to Philadelphia, but did not enter the city because of the yellow fever outbreak in the area.[36]

Charles' survived his first summer encampment. Military instruction would continue, but he could spend his nights in the relative comfort of the overcrowded barracks. Soon academic studies would be added to the rigors of drill.

Class Begins

On September 1, after a grueling summer of military training, the cadets broke camp and marched to their barracks to begin classroom instruction. Like other Fourth Class cadets, Charles' curriculum included Algebra, Geometry, Plane and Spherical Trigonometry, Logarithms, and French.[37]

His day was long and full with the schedule announced by the sound of drums. Reveille was exactly at sunrise. Roll call was twenty minutes later, followed by room inspection by the officer of the day. Then the Corps assembled for two hours of drill. The cadets marched to breakfast, which was from 7:00 to 8:00 a.m. The drums summoned the cadets to French recitations which lasted from 8:00 until 11:00 a.m. Dinner was at 1:00 p.m. followed by mathematics recitations from 2:00 to 6:00 p.m. Evening drill was held from 6:00 to sunset. A light supper meal was served after drill. The evening was allocated to individual study and recreation. Lights out was at 10:00 p.m.[38]

The mess hall rules were set by Thayer's predecessor, Alden Partridge, and cadets had to march to and from the table and eat in silence. Breakfast consisted of "Good Coffee with a sufficient quantity of Milk and Sugar; Fresh Bread & Butter, Smoked beef or ham or cold meat." The dinner menu was "Fresh meat either Beef, Pork, Veal or Mutton well roasted, with good bread & Potatoes & two of the following kinds of vegetables: Beets, Onions, Turnips, Cabbage or Carrots ... in their season dried Beans may be given, but not to exceed once in every six days; there shall always be proper sauce or gravy for the meat." Supper was "Tea of good quality with Milk & Sugar; fresh bread and butter." Partridge said, "The steward should serve, once a week, pie for supper and a pudding for dinner."[39]

Superintendent Thayer introduced a classroom methodology where students were continually required to demonstrate their proficiency. Every day Charles received assignments from his textbooks. At the next class, he was quizzed on the material at a blackboard in front of his class, and graded on his performance. The teaching was extremely practical, and professors devoted little or no time to explain the theory behind the lessons.[40]

Under the cadet grading system, a perfect recitation received a mark of 3.0; good earned a 2.5, indifferent a 2.0, bad 1.5, very imperfect 1.0, and complete failure 0.0.[41] Thayer also devised a merit roll. This impartial system allowed him to rank the cadets in each class and eliminate subjective opinions of the professors and staff in making corps recommendations for the graduates.[42] In the classroom, each cadet was graded every day and ranked every week. He was also marked on his performance in the semi-annual examinations. The grade in each subject was weighted in compiling the final academic standing.[43]

Thayer built the curriculum on French and mathematics. French was important because many of the scientific, technical, and military textbooks were only available in that language. Similarly, mathematics was the language of engineering.[44] Charles studied algebra using a translation of Lacroix's *Elements of Algebra* and A. M. Legendre's text on *Elements Geometry and Trigonometry*. French language recitations were held daily under the direction of Claudius Berard, 1st Teacher of the French Language, and Joseph Du Commun, 2nd Teacher in French.[45] The one-hour recitations required an additional two hours of study for each class.[46] In January 1820, the Academic Board described the requirements as follows: "The course of French shall consist in teaching to pronounce that language tolerably, to read and translate French into English, and to convert English into French."[47] Charles used Masson's *French Grammar* and Masson's *French Reader* in this class. Wonostrocht's *French Grammar* and *Lecteur Francais* by Gil Bias, Vol. I, were used in the Spring Semester.[48]

Military practice was the one constant in Charles' education. The cadets were drilled daily from Monday to Friday during the year. Major Worth and his tactical assistants directed the instruction using *Rules and Regulations Prescribed for Infantry Drill Service*, Jonathan Williams' *The Elements of Fortification*, Louis Tousard's *American Artillerist's Companion, or Elements of Artillery*, and Guy Vernon's *A Treatise on the Science of War and Fortification*.[49]

Among Charles' fellow cadets in the class of 1824 were Dennis H. Mahan who served as head of the Department of Civil and Military Engineering at West Point for forty-one years and became a legendary military theorist in the areas of fixed fortifications, field fortifications, strategy, and tactics, and Robert P. Parrott, inventor of the Parrott guns and projectiles. Out of a class that began with seventy-four plebes in July 1820, only thirty-one graduated in 1824. Nineteen members of that graduating class died before the Civil War and only two saw active service.[50]

West Point life was rigorous and Charles' only escapes were swimming in the Hudson River, hiking through the nearby hills, and participating in sports. Christmas and New Year's Day were the only holidays of the academic year.[51]

Three to four cadets lived in a twelve-foot square room.[52] There were no beds and cadets slept on the floor on bedrolls or on cots. Each room had a fireplace, which meant that fire prevention was a serious concern. "Neglect of tender" was punishable by from three to five demerits. The cadets obtained water from springs or cisterns, and there were no indoor bathrooms.[53]

The annual June examinations were held before the Board of Visitors. The Board of Visitors was a select group of distinguished officers and civilians, which provided advice and suggestions to the Academy. Thayer designed the thorough examinations to impress the Board. The oral exams were conducted each day from 8:00 a.m. to 1:00 p.m. and 3:00 p.m. to 7:00 p.m.[54] Thayer and the instructors sat at one long table and the Board of Visitors sat at another. Three large blackboards on easels were set up in front of this imposing group of interrogators. Thayer called in six cadets at a time and assigned two students to each blackboard. While one cadet recited orally, the others prepared their answers. Each cadet went through the ordeal of at least five hours of rigorous testing on all their courses.[55]

Unfortunately, Charles' introduction to military life was not distinguished. He finished his first year ranked fifty-seventh out of seventy-three cadets.[56] His performance forced him to repeat his first year along with twenty-nine of his classmates.[57] Charles' performance undoubtedly displeased his parents and relatives because his failure was not in keeping with his family's strong academic credentials.

Starting Over

The following year Charles joined a new group of sixty-five cadets in the class of 1825. Among his fellow plebes were Robert Bache, Benjamin Huger, Robert Anderson, and Daniel S. Donelson. The summer encampment began in the usual fashion with the new plebes marching to the tents on the Plain. This summer, Charles joined the other cadets in erecting the camp. The highlight of this summer's activities occurred in mid–August when the corps of cadets marched to Boston and set up camp on the Common. While in Boston, the cadets ate at Harvard College and Faneuil Hall.[58] The ladies of the city presented a white silk embroidered flag to the corps bearing figures of Minerva, Mars, and the Goddess of Liberty and the inscription "Essayons." The citizens of Boston gave the corps a blue flag with an eagle, coat of arms, and the words "Presented by the Inhabitants of Boston." Former president John Adams addressed the corps at his home in Quincy, Massachusetts.[59] Then the cadets marched to Providence, Rhode Island, where they spent several days. They resumed their journey to New London, Connecticut, having marched more than 310 miles. They traveled by steamer from New London to New Haven. After staying there a few days, they embarked on the steamer for New York and reached West Point on September 25.[60]

Unfortunately, the second fall semester was as difficult for Charles as his first. On October 15, 1821, he was charged with unmilitary conduct and was ordered to appear before a court-martial. The demerit system had not yet been installed at West Point and cadets who had committed infractions of the Academy's strict rules were subject to courts-martial.

Charles' offense was that he "did insult and abuse a centinel [sic] whilst in the execution of his duty by abusive language and throwing stones at him." He pleaded not guilty and was acquitted.[61]

Cadet behavior problems should have been anticipated. Although the students were expected to act as men, the rules and regulations assumed the cadets were "wild youngsters who had to be watched and from whom temptation had to be removed." Thayer forbade the cadets "to drink; play cards or chess; gamble; use or posses [sic] tobacco; keep any cooking utensils in their rooms; participate in any games; read novels, romances, or plays; go off the post; bathe in the river; or play a musical instrument."[62] The young men regarded these restrictions as vices to be pursued not avoided. For many cadets, West Point provided their initiation to a lifetime of drinking, gambling, and smoking.

Fortunately, Charles' performance improved slightly during this second attempt, and he finished twenty-sixth out of sixty-five cadets.[63] In September 1822 Charles entered the Third Class or "yearling" year where he studied French, Descriptive Geometry, Application of Algebra to Geometry, Analytical Trigonometry, Integral and Differential Calculus, Chemistry, English Literature, and Drawing. Military instruction was presented in artillery and the school of the company.[64] The importance Thayer attached to each subject was determined by a weighting system the Academy applied to the cadet's performance. The Mathematics grade was multiplied by three, French by one, and Drawing by one-half.[65]

Charles' immaturity continued to cause problems. Perhaps his worst offense was being arrested for public intoxication in December 1822. During his five years, he would receive 195 demerits ranging from being late to morning call to visiting during study hours.[66]

A Light Dawns

Charles might not have graduated except that his grades finally improved after his third year at West Point. His Second Class or "cow" year curriculum included natural philosophy (physics mechanics, and astronomy), chemistry, and drawing.[67] In the January 1824 exams, Charles placed twentieth out of forty-seven cadets in philosophy,[68] twenty-ninth in chemistry,[69] and twentieth in drawing. Military training was in artillery, the school of the battalion, and the duties of sergeants.[70]

Cadets continued to test the limits of the Academy's strict regulations. On February 27, 1824, several cadets were dismissed after a court-martial found them guilty of intoxication. In response, many of the cadets signed a voluntary temperance pledge, and the Superintendent interceded with the president who canceled punishment for these students.[71]

During 1824, Smith received $28.30 in monthly pay and allowances. Out of that allotment, he was required to contribute to a fund for books and stationery, to pay for the Academy band, and to provide $10 a month for board.

At the General Examination on June 27, 1824, Charles earned a grade of 202 in Philosophy, 80 in Drawing, and 65 in Chemistry for a total General Merit Score of 347. This placed him nineteenth in his class of forty-four.[72]

In the 1824 summer encampment, Charles was appointed as 2nd Sergeant of the First Company.[73] By this time, the Corps of Cadets had grown to the extent that it was divided into four companies.[74] On August 21 Charles was promoted to the rank of 2nd 1st Lieutenant in the Second Company.[75]

In 1824, Charles entered the First Class. That fall Revolutionary War hero General

Lafayette visited West Point and reviewed the troops in front of the Superintendent's quarters. The General was received at the public dock by professors and officers. As he arrived, a national salute was fired from the battery at the artillery barracks.[76]

As was the procedure, Charles' class was divided into sections based on their academic abilities. According to Orders No. 175, the First Class was divided into five sections. Charles was placed in the third section with Cadets Donelson, Harrison, Harris, Robert Anderson, Brisbane, and Mackay.[77] Civil engineering was the principal course in the First Class curriculum. The class covered subjects such as topographical engineering, which included using geometry and trigonometry to draw plans, surveying, and leveling; and construction of roads, bridges, canals, and hydraulics; and map drawing. He also studied mineralogy and took a course in rhetoric and moral and political science.[78] In the January 1825 exams, Charles placed twenty first in engineering,[79] nineteenth in geography,[80] and sixteenth in mineralogy.[81] He was ranked nineteenth in his class of thirty-seven.[82]

Charles also studied military topics, including artillery construction and mechanics, permanent fortifications, attack and defense of places, tactics, and the art of war.[83] Although some subjects did not capture his interest, he excelled in the engineering and military subjects. Charles received 198 out of 200 on his tactics exam, placed eighteenth in artillery, and scored 200 in engineering at the June examinations.[84] His overall grades were mathematics 224, French 79, philosophy 202, drawing 80, engineering 200, chemistry and mineralogy 176, geography and national issues 64, tactics 198, and conduct 230½. The total of Charles' scores including conduct was 1,453½. This placed him eighteenth in his class of thirty-seven, which earned him a recommendation for promotion in the artillery.[85]

Along with his improvement in grades, Charles' rank in the Corps of Cadets rose as he progressed from a Fourth Class to First Class cadet. When the 1825 summer encampment began, Smith was "invested with the command" and "charged with the police of the newly appointed Cadets and will be obeyed and respected accordingly."[86] Among his sixty-six charges that summer were two Virginians, Robert E. Lee and Joseph E. Johnston.[87]

On June 25 Charles was appointed Adjutant of the Corps of Cadets.[88] In this capacity, he was the principal link between Commandant Worth and the Corps. His duties were primarily administrative. Each day the adjutant held formation, took reports of the companies, and delivered them to the Commandant. In the evenings, he received reports from the companies and transmitted any absentees to the officer of the day. At this time, he would also present the officer of the day with the list of cadets who were to serve punishment on that day. In addition to these standard duties, the adjutant supervised a staff of three fellow cadets, consisting of a sergeant major, quartermaster, and quartermaster sergeant. Their duties included the administrative and logistical requirements of the companies.[89]

Smith graduated on July 1, 1825, with the rank of brevet 2nd lieutenant and was immediately promoted to a 2nd lieutenant. Military instruction continued for the new officers after their graduation. The brevet lieutenants received additional training and served as officers in the summer encampment. Smith performed his duties as Adjutant through the summer. This assignment helped prepare him for his future responsibilities as Adjutant to Superintendent Thayer. Lieutenant Smith's position involved delivering orders prepared by the Commandant of Cadets to the Corps of Cadets and receiving reports from the cadet officers for the Commandant.[90]

As adjutant, he learned to deal with the volume of paperwork that was an integral part of military life. Smith issued orders from Major Worth on a variety of topics including duties of the officers of the guard, schedules for instruction and drill, and seating assignments at the cadet mess.[91] Adjutant Smith also transmitted directives that dealt with the most mundane aspects of military life including drying bedding, issuing passes, room assignments, schedules for bathing, and times to the report to the post surgeon.[92] Many of the Battalion Orders handled by Adjutant Smith dealt with the daily "Detail and Countersign." These orders designated the officer-in-charge, officer of the day, officer of the guard, and officer of police. The orders also stated what challenge password would be used on that day.[93]

Smith also developed a different perspective on punishment than he had as a cadet receiving demerits and courts-martial. By this point in his education, he realized the importance of discipline and studied how Thayer and Worth administered military justice. Smith conveyed several Battalion Orders that summer concerning arrests and courts-martial of cadets for offenses including abandoning their post, improperly permitting a cadet to pass a guard post, and disobeying orders. Continued violations and exceeding the maximum number of demerits could lead to cadets being "discharged from the service of the United States."[94]

There was no formal graduation ceremony at the Academy. The only official recognitions were a congratulatory sermon in honor of the cadets and the order announcing their promotion from cadet to brevet 2nd lieutenant.[95]

> The following promotions and appointments in the Army of the United States, have been made at the War Department, since the publication of the order of the 8th March, 1825.
> Cadet Charles Ferguson Smith, to be brevet 2nd Lt. 2nd Regiment Artillery 1st July 1825.[96]

On September 1 the newly commissioned officers were granted four months furlough before reporting to their post.[97]

"Transition from the highest state of mental tension"

Smith's brevet designation was quickly dropped, and the 2nd lieutenant was assigned to the 2nd Artillery Regiment to attend the two-year, post-graduate artillery school at Fort Monroe.[98] Beginning in 1824, ten companies of artillery (two each from the First and Third and three each from the Second and Fourth) were assembled at Fort Monroe and organized as a regiment designated "The Artillery Corps for Instruction."[99]

However, instead of serving at Fort Monroe, Smith's unit was sent to Fort Delaware on Pea Patch Island in the Delaware River. The posting was like coming home because Smith's father, Samuel Smith, served as the post's assistant surgeon. Construction of the fort had begun on December 8, 1817, but building was delayed due to uneven settling on the marshy terrain. When Smith arrived he found the structure deteriorating because of inadequate foundations and its walls suffering from "great and unequal subsidence."[100] Smith's time at the fort was unremarkable with his days spent leading artillery drill and directing construction.

Lieutenant Smith joined his father in the unfinished fort and lived with the officers in a large stone house inside the garrison. While Smith was at Fort Delaware, one of the senior lieutenants got drunk and tried to shoot a soldier. The officer was arrested and Smith was placed in command. During Smith's time at Fort Delaware, illness struck the garrison. When informed of the outbreak, Dr. Smith ordered the sick men to the icehouse. Lieutenant Smith was concerned about the health of his body servant, Moses Shipley, and sent him to his parents' home in Wilmington.[101]

After two years at Fort Delaware, Smith's regiment was ordered to the Augusta Arsenal in Georgia. He was posted at the arsenal from 1827 to 1829 as part of a new system of periodic military unit rotations. The army operated the arsenal as a manufacturing facility for the production, repair, storage, and distribution of weapons and ammunition.[102] Regrettably, the arsenal's proximity to the river was unhealthy for the soldiers and their families, and they suffered from frequent fevers and subsequent deaths. Therefore, in the late 1820s, the government decided to relocate the facility to Summerville, Georgia, and in November 1826, a seventy-acre tract on a hilltop site was purchased for the new arsenal.[103] Smith worked on construction of the new facility. With $49,000 and some building materials from the original arsenal, four buildings connected by a loop-holed wall were completed in 1828. The first occupants were Company C, Second Artillery. By the end of that year, the arsenal was supplying arms for the Georgia militia and for the Harpers Ferry Armory.[104]

Smith's duties at the arsenal allowed him time to visit nearby Augusta and experience the antebellum South. At this time, Augusta was a leader in the production of paper, textiles, and gunpowder.[105] Unfortunately, there were no members of the West Point class of 1825 from Georgia or its neighbor South Carolina posted at Summerville to provide the introductions necessary to enter Augusta society. At the time of Smith's posting, the relations between the federal government and the state authorities in South Carolina and Alabama were somewhat strained over import tariffs. This disagreement fostered a cold reception for the troops garrisoning the post.[106]

With the mundane duties required by officers at these posts, Smith might have criticized West Point for failing to prepare him for life in the military. As another graduate complained, "I think the sudden transition from the highest state of mental tension to one of perfect inactivity, which occurs in most cases on the graduation of a cadet, is exceedingly injurious." The void was either filled by "an undue gratification of the licentious passions, or else by the trashy literature with which our country is flooded." Not surprising, nearly a third of the cadets in Smith's class chose another option—resignation.[107]

2. "Thirteen years of service"

"Drilling our company of Cadets"

Because of the Congressional cut in the size of the army in 1821, the Military Academy was graduating more men than the army could use. Instead of an exciting military career, the brevet second lieutenants waited for removal of temporary rank. The officers existed in a state of hopefulness that an opening would occur through death or resignation that would transform them into second lieutenants.[1]

The army was held in low esteem by the people and the government, and there was nothing to compensate the officers for the country's lack of respect. In spite of the poor public opinion, West Point graduates were instrumental in developing America. They built roads, canals, and railroads to help grow the economy and advance the frontier.[2] This knowledge provided the young engineers with lucrative civilian opportunities instead of a stagnant army career.

The peacetime army had no significant enemy except the American Indian. While the Indians were a serious and continuing threat, fighting them made little use of the young officers' training in tactics or the art of war. The new officer was likely to be stationed on "the very edge of civilization with a few resentful privates to command and a few savages to fight." If the newly graduated, brevet 2nd lieutenant was lucky, he might get a post on the East Coast, where he probably would be assigned quartermaster's duties. In this position, for which he had received no training, he "would spend his days adding figures, proving to the auditors that he had not lost a single horseshoe and feeling much like a common clerk." His pay was $25 a month, which was too low to afford a wife and family, and the possibilities of advancement to a better-compensated rank were practically zero.

> Line officers received their promotions on a regimental basis. A second lieutenant could move up to first lieutenant or a lieutenant colonel to colonel only if a vacancy occurred in his own regiment. There was no compulsory retirement law, and most officers stayed in the army, and thus in theory in command of their outfits, until they died. Many lieutenants had to wait twenty-five or thirty years for their captains to die before they could be promoted. Excellence, devotion to duty, heroism—all counted for nothing. The result was that few men of talent stayed in the army.[3]

The young lieutenants wondered why anyone would want a commission. An army career was unappealing and morale was low.

This was Charles Ferguson Smith's world in the spring of 1829 when he had the opportunity to leave the doldrums of post life and return to the Military Academy. The call to West Point was the redeeming aspect of his young career. The army reserved positions at the Academy for its best and most promising young officers. Charles was twenty-two years old, handsome, and single. He was six feet two inches tall with light brown hair and blue eyes.[4]

Smith arrived at West Point on June 25, 1829, and was appointed an Assistant Instructor of Tactics. Smith served under Captain Ethan Allen Hitchcock who was Instructor of Tactics and Commandant of Cadets. In addition to Smith, Lieutenants Lucien J. Bibb and Joseph L. Locke also held positions as Assistant Instructors. The three "tacs" assisted in the instruction of military tactics using *Infantry Tactics* or *Rules for the Exercises and Maneuvers of the Infantry of the U.S. Army* written by Major General Winfield Scott.[5]

The "tacs" lived in the barracks where they served as instruments of the Academy's disciplinary process. Rooming and boarding with the cadets kept the instructors in twenty-four hour contact with the Corps and allowed them to immediately report any infractions and assign demerits.[6] The tactical officers inspected rooms frequently to ensure that cadets were in their quarters at the required times and respected the rules about entertainment, gambling, and drinking.[7]

Smith arrived at the Academy in time to direct a new group of plebes in the summer encampment. The camp was named Camp Worth in honor of the past Commandant. There was a significant improvement in the camp that summer with the addition of board floors in the four-person tents.[8] Military training continued throughout the academic year as Hitchcock's instructors drilled the Corps. Lieutenant Smith made an immediate impact. Cadet George W. Cullum recalled "the tall, graceful, and handsome Lieutenant drilling our company of Cadets in marches and the manual of arms."[9] Among those whom Smith taught in the Class of 1830 were William N. Pendleton, John B. Magruder, Lloyd J. Beal, and Robert C. Buchanan.

The following academic year (1830–1831), Captain Hitchcock's tactics instructors included Smith, Locke and, newly appointed assistants Lieutenants Nathaniel S. Harris and Simon H. Drum. Some of the notable members of the Class of 1831 were Roswell Park, Jacob Ammen, Andrew A. Humphreys, William H. Emory, Bradford R. Alden, Samuel R. Curtis, and Charles Whittlesey.

On March 22, 1831, Smith asked Secretary of War John H. Eaton to clarify fees levied on officers at the Academy for mess allowances which the West Point Quartermaster refused to dismiss. The Quartermaster would not commute Smith's allowances unless Smith presented a certificate. Smith argued, "If this certificate is insisted upon, your order granting the commutation of mess allowances of the officers on duty at this post, is virtually annulled, and they are deprived of allowances which the Regulations of the Army would give to them at any other military station in the country." The letter reveals Smith's willingness to contact the second highest military authority on such a trivial matter and the lieutenant's dedication to the strict interpretation of military rules and regulations. This correspondence reveals Smith's commitment to present ideas and argue aspects of military regulations that would become a trademark of his career. Smith said the Quartermaster "acts in this matter in accordance to instructions from the chief of his Department" and appealed to Secretary Eaton for a decision. The Secretary granted the commutation for officers.[10]

Perhaps the most intriguing and challenging assignment facing Smith and his fellow instructors was presented by Cadet Edgar Allan Poe. There are many stories, anecdotes, and fantasies about Poe's exploits at West Point. He became notorious for cutting mandatory drills, skipping classes, and making "nocturnal visits to Benny Havens." One night Poe stumbled back to his barracks and sprawled on his back on the steps of his tactical officer's quarters. When the tactical officer awoke and inquired as to who might be outside his door, Poe allegedly responded in verse: "On Linden when the sun was low/All bloodless lay the untrodden snow/And dark as winter was the flow/Of I SIR, rolling rapidly!" Cadet Poe was eventually court-martialed and dismissed from the Academy. Some attribute his discharge to his frequent trips to Benny Havens or his "uncontrollable urge to hurl baked potatoes across the Academy mess hall." Another story blamed his dismal on reporting to a parade naked except for his crossed white ammunition belts and hat. One account said that Poe, in a fit of rage, threw his tactical officer off a cliff into the Hudson River and was subsequently charged with murder.[11] Assistant Tactical Instructor Lieutenant Locke was one of the victims of Poe's humor: "John Locke was a very great name; Joe Locke was greater in short; The former was known to Fame, The latter well known to Report."[12] Poe's time at West Point was certainly trying for Smith and his fellow "tacs." As serious military men, they were happy to see him leave. As former cadets, they probably enjoyed his outrageous behavior and the legends that grew out of his time at the Academy.

"Position of exacting details"

On September 1, 1831, the twenty-four-year-old Smith was promoted to Adjutant of the Academy under Superintendent Thayer. From his desk in the basement of the Superintendent's office,[13] Smith served as Thayer's administrative assistant. The Adjutant was responsible for keeping all of the Academy's records and papers and acting as recording secretary for the Academic Board. He circulated "all orders, bulletins, circulars, memorandums, and regulations issued by the Superintendent's office" and "maintained official correspondence and policy files." Smith acted as the college registrar responsible for candidate records, cadet personnel files and grades, and other academic records. The Adjutant also served on numerous Academy boards and committees.[14]

The assignment came at a difficult time for the Academy and especially for Colonel Thayer. West Point's policies were under fire and its existence was threatened. In spite of its success, many citizens had a low opinion of the Academy. After Andrew Jackson was elected president in 1829, West Point and Thayer became targets of Jacksonian Democracy's "war on privilege" and "artificial or accidental advantage."[15] The Jacksonians wanted to abolish the existing socio-economic system that granted special privileges to the few and replace it with one in which political freedom provided social and economic opportunity. Their campaign attacked American colleges because the Jacksonians believed the "rich and well born" were receiving significant educational benefits. West Point was an easy target because it was totally dependent on federal funds. Jacksonians believed that the cadets were taking advantage of the free education. After graduation, they became snobbish officers in a "caste-ridden army" or resigned their commission to "cash in on the mathematical and engineering knowledge" provided by the government.[16]

In addition to this criticism, Jackson interfered with Thayer's disciplinary actions. The president frequently reinstated cadets who had been dismissed from the army following a West Point court-martial. Additionally, "when the cons of protégés of influential politicians failed in academics on the first attempt they were often given a second chance." During the first two years of Jackson's presidency, the Secretary of War overturned seven of sixteen courts-martial that recommended dismissal. The president's actions undermined Thayer's authority and weakened the disciplinary process. In 1831, Commandant Hitchcock bitterly said, "A cadet who was really a disgrace to the Academy would frequently be thus returned to the institution after dismissal, to scoff at the regulations he had defied and furnish an example by which great numbers of the thoughtless would also become reckless."[17]

Jackson's attitude became common knowledge among the students. Cadets threatened to report the Academy to the president unless they were treated favorably. Cadet William

Frazer believed the professors showed favoritism and started a rumor that Jackson was "going to clear every officer off the Point, professor and all." "The President," Frazer boasted, "is not agoing [sic] to have the cadets treated like a parcel of dogs, by these lazy, drunken officers, which has been the case too long."[18]

Smith's new position inserted him into this struggle between the Academy and the government. He assisted Thayer in preparing documents to defend the Superintendent and the Academy. In the midst of these hostilities, Smith was promoted to 1st Lieutenant on May 30, 1832. Because of this experience, Smith distanced himself from politics, refused to court political favors to advance his career, and viewed elected officials with condescension. He observed how compromising authority could affect a military unit, and he developed contempt for political interference in military affairs. The political struggles instilled in Smith a commitment to regulation and obedience that would become a hallmark of his steadfast character.

As West Point's Superintendent, Thayer was the logical target for complaints and became the first casualty in the conflict. Jackson's interference in the Military Academy reduced the Superintendent's power, created an unruly Corps of Cadets, and frustrated the staff and faculty. Jackson's attacks on West Point were also personal assaults on Thayer because of the Superintendent's friendships with the Secretary of War John C. Calhoun and Brigadier General Winfield Scott. The president hated both of these men and developed the "most extreme dislike of Colonel Thayer."[19] Jackson's private secretary, Andrew Jackson Donelson, believed that Thayer had mistreated him while he was a cadet and complained about conditions at the Academy.[20]

Although Thayer's program was under attack, the disciplinary system continued to evolve. In July 1831 Military Order Number 30 helped to codify the process by defining a set of rules for demerits and dividing the offenses into seven categories. A cadet with more than 200 demerits in a year was deficient in conduct and would be discharged.[21] As Adjutant, Smith communicated the new regulations and recorded demerits.

During the 1832 election, Jackson followers planted hickory trees as a sign of support for the president. Thayer awoke one morning to find a pro–Jackson tree planted in the middle of the Plain. An investigation revealed that Cadet Norris was the culprit. Thayer dismissed Norris, but Jackson overruled the decision. After his reinstatement, Norris thought that he was untouchable. He was finally expelled after he made a scattergun out of a candlestick and brass buttons and fired it at a tactical instructor.[22]

After another series of dismissals and reinstatements in 1832, Thayer requested clarification from Secretary of War, Lewis Cass. "I am led to believe that there is something at this institution which does not altogether meet with the President's approbation, but I am at a loss to conjecture whether the dissatisfaction ... relates to persons or things." Thayer asked if there were any specific incidents of corrupt or incompetent administration that had prejudiced Jackson against him and requested an investigation to determine if such events had occurred. The Superintendent added, "I am certain that the President is too just and generous to pass sentence of condemnation on any one without a hearing, or to have formed unfavorable opinions respecting the administration of the Academy from information derived from interested and prejudiced persons." Cass replied that Jackson has "not the slightest shade of unkindly feeling towards you." However, Cass added that the president was "not altogether happy with the regulations, but did not blame Thayer for them."[23]

The Superintendent was not satisfied. On January 19, 1833, Thayer resigned after working nearly fifteen years to build the nation's premier engineering school. The "Father of West Point" left the Academy on July 1, 1833, and never returned.[24] However, Thayer's departure did not stop the attacks on West Point. The Tennessee legislature in 1833 and the Ohio legislature in 1834 voted to abolish the Military Academy.[25] On January 14, 1836, Kentucky Congressman Albert Gallatin Hawes led a debate in the House of Representatives on whether "it might be expedient to abolish the United States Military Academy."[26] However, the Military Academy survived because its alumni were building the infrastructure needed to develop the country. West Point civil engineering graduates helped construct canals, harbors, roads, and railroads that increased commerce and opened the frontier to new settlers. Secretary of the Treasury Albert Gallatin said it best: "No single operation, within the power of Government, can more effectually tend to strengthen and perpetuate that Union which secures external independence, domestic peace, and internal liberty."[27] The new Superintendent Major René E. DeRussy retained Smith as Adjunct. The criticism of West Point subsided and finally ended in March 1837 when Jackson left office.

In April 1834 Charles commissioned an artist to paint his portrait for his mother, Margaret. He enclosed the following note with his gift.

> West Point, NY
> April 28, 1834
> My dear Mother,
> This painting was finished on the same day I attained my 27th year. I have had it taken by Miss Thibault, the most celebrated artist in her line in New York; and in the judgment of my City friends I ought to be satisfied with it. They say it is a good though not a flattering likeness; its only defect a want of liveliness in the eye. So be it: if you are well pleased I certainly am. I know of nothing I thought would please you better or I would have procured it. I hope you will get it safe—let me know.
> As ever, dear Mother your affectionate Son
> Charles F. Smith
> For Mrs. Margaret F. Smith
> Annapolis, Maryland
> Same to Father and the girls, and Thanks to all[28]

Smith's days passed slowly over the next two years with monotonous paperwork while life at the Academy evolved with new buildings, courses, and regulations. Candidates and cadets came and left some with commissions and others with dismissals. During Smith's tenure as Adjutant, he greeted many new applicants. Among the distinguished graduates he registered were George Meade, Henry Prince, and Herman Haupt in 1831; Montgomery C. Meigs, Robert Allen, and Lloyd Tilghman in 1832; Braxton Bragg, Alexander B. Dyer, Jubal A. Early, William H. French, John Sedgwick, John C. Pemberton, and Joseph Hooker in 1833; P. G. T. Beauregard, William F. Barry, Irvin McDowell, William J. Hardee, and Henry H. Sibley in 1834; Isaac I. Stevens, Henry W. Halleck, Edward C. Ord, Henry J. Hunt, Eleazer Paine, and Edward R. S. Canby in 1835; William T. Sherman, Stewart

Portrait of Charles Ferguson Smith at 27 years for his mother (courtesy C. F. Smith Collection at U.S. Military Academy Library, Special Collections).

Van Vliet, George H. Thomas, Richard S. Ewell, George W. Getty, and Bushrod R. Johnson in 1836; and Horatio G. Wright, Josiah Gorgas, Thomas Rodman, Nathaniel Lyon, John F. Reynolds, Richard B. Garnett, Don Carlos Buell, Alfred Sully, and Israel B. Richardson in 1837. Some of these men would learn from him as Instructor of Tactics, some would serve with him in the Union Army, and some would fight against him as Confederate generals.

Smith's cousin, John Blair Smith Todd,[29] was a cadet when Smith was Adjutant. Todd graduated in 1837 placing 39th in his class of 50.[30] Although he was Captain in the Corps of Cadets during his last year, he managed to accumulate 184 demerits and placed 187 out of 211 cadets at West Point.[31] Todd served as a brigadier general in the Civil War.

On February 19, 1838, the old two-story stone Academy building was destroyed by fire. The building housed the library and the departments of chemistry, natural philosophy, and engineering.[32] The books and records of the Adjutant's Office were lost. Most of the records that Smith had so diligently created were ash.

Smith's term as Adjutant ended on April 1, 1838, when he was appointed Commandant of Cadets. Five months later Colonel De Russy was relieved as Superintendent and succeeded by Major Richard Delafield.[33]

3. Commandant of Cadets

"Many responsible duties"

First Lieutenant Smith's career was on the rise with his appointment as Commandant of Cadets on April 1, 1838.[1] Only the most accomplished army officers received the highly desired position. The Commandant was considered by many as the most important person on the faculty because he directed the military program and administered discipline. As Commandant, Smith had three distinct but overlapping responsibilities. First, he was in charge of military training as Commander of the Corps of Cadets and Instructor of Infantry Tactics. Second, he was responsible for enforcing military regulations on cadets, faculty, regular army soldiers, and civilians. Third, he served as a communication link between the cadets and the Superintendent presenting their grievances and reporting their infractions. The Commandant was an unofficial role model for the cadets on how to conduct themselves as officers and gentlemen. As a former Commandant explained: "It is thus by constantly and unceasingly, patiently and earnestly placing before the Cadet his obligations to duty, and impressing upon him the qualities of mind and character that constitute the high-minded, truthful, and conscientious officer, that the Commandant of Cadets ... fulfills the most important part of his many responsible duties."[2] More than any other individual, he exercised an "important influence on the military character and opinions of the junior officers of the Army."[3]

Smith immediately made his presence known. On his first day, he placed Cadet Rankin under arrest and confined him to his room for neglect of his duties as a sentinel.[4] Several days later, he ordered a general policing of the barracks. Smith instructed the orderly of each room and his roommates to wash the floor, washstands, and mantelpiece and polish the candlesticks as required by paragraph 192 of the Academic Regulations.[5]

Cadets soon learned that Commandant Smith had high expectations and would not tolerate excuses. On April 18 he warned that cadets would no longer be allowed to plead ignorance of regulations or orders as a justification for neglecting their duty. The following month, he issued Battalion Orders No. 44, which noted that cadet officers were negligent in promptly correcting infractions. Smith explained, "The person in authority" should "not merely to report the offender, but ... give an order for correcting the evil, personally to the offending party, and see that such order is obeyed."[6] Smith recognized the importance for the future officers to understand regulations and faithfully carry out orders. He also valued the structure and guidance this system had brought to his own life and was determined to share the lessons learned with his cadets. Thus began Commandant Smith's term of instilling in his young charges the ideals of dedication to duty, strict integrity in word and deed, and gentlemanly conduct.

The Commander of the Corps of Cadets directed drill and military exercises for the four-company battalion. The battalion provided the cadets with practical experience in military training and tactics as both soldiers and officers and offered leadership opportunities for deserving cadets.[7] The Superintendent and Commandant selected the Corps officers based on their military bearing and qualifications. The adjutant, quartermaster, four company captains, and twelve lieutenants were selected from the First Class; the sergeants were chosen from the Second Class; and the corporals designated from the Third Class. With the small garrisons at most army posts, the battalion presented the only opportunity for the future officers to study and practice large unit tactics. The system also created a competitive environment that prepared the prospective officers for the limited positions in the peacetime army.

As Instructor of Tactics, Smith taught the First Class course on Army Infantry Tactics. Tactics was the capstone course of a cadet's military education that began with the first roll call. He presented lessons on military fundamentals and managed the practice of these principles.[8] The cadets applied Smith's lessons "on the drill field, in the barracks, and in summer encampments."[9] Smith used General Scott's three-volume textbook *Rules and Regulations for the Exercise and Maneuvers of the United States Infantry*.[10]

In terms of military proceedings, the Commandant was "God" and the manuals of Army and Academy Regulations were his "Bibles." Smith demonstrated the depth and breadth of his knowledge of rules and conventions through his many Battalion Orders. He quoted the pertinent sections from the handbooks to indicate that there was a guideline for every aspect of military life and to encourage his young charges to commit these rules to memory. Smith's attention to regulations was a characteristic ingrained at West Point and maintained throughout his career.

Typical of Instructor Smith's lessons was Battalion Orders No. 15 from February 1840.

> In being dismissed each squad leader will form his section quietly near the door of the section room, and conduct it from thence to where it is to be dismissed in an orderly and soldierlike manner, as explained by Para. 299 of the Academic Regulations.[11]

Smith cited Academy Regulations in explaining the proper way to give commands.

> 81 ... The voice of command will always be instructed and elevated in voice in proportion to the number of men under instruction.
> 82 ... Command will be of two kinds, command of caution, and those of execution.
> 83 ... The Command of caution will be pronounced and in an elevated tone of voice lengthening a little syllable.
> 84 ... The command of execution will be pronounced in a tone firm and brief.[12]

Smith not only dictated cadets' conduct during drill, but he also defined how they lived in the barracks, marched to classes and meals, and even when they bathed. Every aspect of a cadet's day was regulated from when they rose to when they retired. The Commandant was like some mythical deity who knew all things, saw all events, and controlled every activity. For example, Orders No. 54 charged "the days on which the cadets are permitted to bath [sic] in the river ... to Tuesdays, Thursdays, and Saturdays."[13] The cadets also had strict instructions about how to arrange the furniture in their rooms, and the Commandant had lithographs of the "arrangement of furniture" posted in their quarters.[14] Cadets were expected to act in the proper fashion at all times including marching from classes in a "soldierlike manner."[15]

While the Commandant was omnipresent at the Academy, his personal domain was the West Point parade ground. Smith was most particular in organizing drill as demonstrated in these instructions for training the Third and Fourth Classes in the School of the Soldier.

1. The distance between the guides in a Battalion deployed into close column should be 5 or 7 paces, depending on the formation being in 3 or 2 ranks. It is directed to be 6 or 5 paces throughout the Tactics, which is an error.
2. When an Officer renderers the marching salute with his sword, he will bring it to a recover after passing the individual saluted 6 paces, as prescribed in Tactics, and not 10 paces as laid down in the Regs.
3. When an Officer in uniform returns the salute of an armed body of men he will do so by touching his cap or hat, not by uncasing the head.[16]

Smith's orders were intended to educate not punish. In Battalion Order No. 36, he demanded the end of the practice of exchanging tours of guard duty. He was kindly in his instructions noting, "No particular blame is attached to the present incumbents," while insisting that the irregularity must be stopped.[17]

Drill was of particular importance to the Commandants because it was a reflection on their stewardship of the military program. The Commandants were proud of the Corps' reputation as a marching unit, and the cadets spent many hours each day working to maintain this proficiency. The Commandant usually introduced a new system during the academic year. He made the cadets work long and hard to learn and master the new procedure so he could demonstrate their skills to the Superintendent and the Board of Visitors[18] during the annual review.[19]

Smith also had to respond to questions posed by the Board of Visitors. In 1842, the Board asked about the time allocated for sleep and recreation. Smith's answers reveal the regimented nature of cadet life.

> First, that seven hours per diem are "allotted to the cadets for sleep" from the 1st of April to the 30th of Sept., and eight hours per diem for the remaining six months of the year. (See par 177, and Table "A" of the Regs. for the Mil. Acad.)
> Secondly, that "the hours allotted to the Cadets for recreation" vary according to the period of the year, but may be stated in general terms thus:
> During the Academic term—say from Sept. 1 to June 20.
> 1. Thirty minutes after each meal.
> 2. Saturday afternoon.
> 3. On Sunday, in addition to the half-hour after dinner, one hour is [illegible] from 2 to 3 p.m., also on the Sa day [Saturday], one hour before Sunset from March 21 to Sept. 21,
> 4. Except on Sunday, from 4 o'clock p.m. until Retreat, [deducting], one hour and 15 minutes for drill between Mch. [March] 15 and Sept. 30 (See par. 113 of Regs. for the Mil. Acad.)
> During the encampment—say from June 20 to Sept. 1st
> At the period no restraint is put upon the cadets movements, (except with reference to limits—for which see pars. 125, 286, and 287 of the Regs. for the Mil. Acad.) between Reveille and Retreat when they are not required for the duties then prescribed. (see par. 177 also Table "A" of Regs. for the Mil. Acad.)
> Thirdly, "the nature of the cadet recreation?"
> It consists principally of walking about within the prescribed limits on six days of the week, and in rambling over the public lands on Saturday afternoon—also the latter during the encampment much more frequently. In the Spring and Autumn—particularly during the latter season—foot ball is a general and favorite recreation.
> During the encampment they are permitted to bathe three times a week. At this same period they daily take a dancing lesson or practice what has been taught them of this accomplishment.[20]

The Commandant also dealt with a variety of administrative tasks such as nominating cadets for promotion in the Corps, ordering materials and munitions, conducting inventories on supplies, requesting leaves of absence, transmitting reports to the various military entities, and attending to the many dignitaries who visited the Academy. Smith's performance of these duties won him approval for his attention to details and criticism for being finicky and faultfinding.

The Cadet Mess Hall was the subject of numerous regulations and the source of many complaints. The food was bland and limited, and the cadet conduct was highly regimented. The fare had improved slightly since Smith's days as a cadet, but students were more likely to criticize the mess instead of praising it. The daily diet was heavy on bread, potatoes, and meat, especially beef, veal, and mutton, but skimpy on green vegetables and sweets.[21] For breakfast the cadets had the meat left from the previous night's dinner that was diced and served with potatoes and chunks of bread and covered with "considerable gravy," butter, and coffee. At dinner, the cadets were served roast beef, boiled potatoes, and bread without butter.[22] The roast beef was so tough that one cadet compared it to "India rubber boiled in *Aqua forte*." Bread was served cold except, as the joke went, when a cat had slept on a loaf. Fish from the Hudson River was served on Friday.[23] Thayer requested the mess hall food be similar to Army field rations which is why the food was tasteless. He wanted cadets accustomed to Army rations so when they graduated, they knew what to expect upon joining their first unit.[24]

On March 24, 1841, Smith criticized the performance of the Cadet Superintendent of the Mess Hall because "certain usages formally practiced" had been "lost sight of." The Commandant was particularly concerned about cadets "entering or leaving the hall in a rude manner; helping themselves before taking their seats; [and] rising from their seats to help themselves instead of asking each other courteously for what might be wanted." Smith referred to paragraph 90 of the General Regulations on the proper behavior in the dining hall.

> Department of the Mess should be marked with all that propriety which characterizes the Society gentleman. Undue familiarity should be discountenanced as it tends to disturb the harmony of the mess and may be productive of the most unhappy consequences. The rules of good breeding must therefore, be punctiliously observed, and the infringement of them at the mess will be considered military offence [sic], calling for the interposition of the authority of the senior officer present to check the same and other irregularity.[25]

Cadets were required to wear the proper uniform while dining, and they could only sit or rise from the table on the command of the Cadet Mess Hall Superintendent. Food and table wear could not be removed from the Hall, and broken dishes were recorded against a cadet's account.[26]

Occasionally, disturbances occurred in the Hall, such as Cadet Don Carlos Buell had with a servant, John Southern. Buell was angry because Southern refused to shut the door from the kitchen to the lower hall. Buell had asked the man several times that day and on other occasions to close the door. Finally, Buell got up and told Southern to shut the door. "With his usual insolent air he passed on without doing so," declared Buell. The cadet became so enraged that he followed Southern up the stairs to the second floor dining area and "caught him by the collar, struck him in the heart, and dragged him down stairs breaking 2 of the plates and seating the victuals on the floor." Cadet Buell was confined to quarters for three days for mistreating a servant in the Mess Hall, and Southern was fined for refusing to comply with Buell's order.[27]

However, most of the disputes in the dining room were over the food. The grievances raised by the Cadet Superintendents were treated seriously by Smith. The cadets were most critical of the butter and often complained that it was "unfit for use, being very strong."[28] On November 9, 1838, Smith sent a note and sample to Superintendent Delafield indicating that "the accompanying butter is ... too strong for use."[29] Major Delafield disagreed with Smith's determination: "On examination I did not find the butter to strong for use. It was not as sweet as some the Cadets have placed on their table most generally. On my own table often times do I see butter that is not even as good as that complained of by the present instance and it's far better than most tub butter that can be purchased."[30] Smith forwarded a protest from Cadet Gilmer who reported that the meat was "unfit for use." Gilmer said, "To attempt a description of it; would be a vain undertaking; I would simply say, that it was a difficult matter to decide whether it was the flesh of a horse, hog, or canine."[31] On December 23, 1838, Smith told Delafield that Cadet Barry judged that the coffee furnished this morning was muddy and "unfit for use."[32]

Many changes occurred at the Military Academy during Smith's time as Commandant. The service requirements for graduates were increased in July 1838 from five to eight years.[33] Cadet rooms were outfitted with bedsteads for the mattresses.[34] In April 1839 cadets were allowed to receive dancing lessons. A sergeant and five troopers of dragoons were sent to West Point in June to provide riding lessons, and a riding master, James McAuley, was appointed in September.[35] Robert Anderson's *Instruction for field artillery, horse and foot, translated from the French and arranged for the service of United States* was approved for use at the Academy in 1841.[36] A separate department of practical military engineering was formed in 1842. Before this time, instruction was provided in the department of civil and military engineering.[37]

Benny Havens was the preferred cadet off-campus hangout. In the winter of 1839–40, an assistant surgeon named Lucius O'Brien visited some friends at West Point. The officers took O'Brien to Benny's to show him where they had spent time during their days as cadets. O'Brien was so impressed by the tavern that he wrote a drinking song to the tune of the Irish standard "The Wearing of the Green." "Benny Havens' Oh!" became an instant favorite among the cadets.

> Come fill your glasses, fellows, and stand up in a row,
> To sing sentimentally, we're going for to go;
> In the Army there's sobriety, promotion very slow,
> So we'll sing our reminiscences of Benny Havens, oh!
> Oh! Benny Havens, oh! Oh! Benny Havens, oh!
> We'll sing our reminiscences of Benny Havens, oh![38]

However, the most significant change in Charles' life was his marriage on March 24, 1840, in Baltimore to Miss Francis[39] Mactier of Philadelphia. Charles was thirty-two and Francis seventeen. Francis was the daughter of Henry and Elizabeth Mactier. He took his young wife to West Point and set up residence in the Commandant's Quarters.[40] Francis soon became pregnant with their first child Henry Mactier Smith. The boy was born on March 18, 1841, but lived less than seven months and died on October 5, 1841.

In spite of this personal tragedy, the couple enjoyed the social life of the Academy. They entertained officers, faculty, and cadets in their home and attended social engagements on both sides of the Hudson River. The annual review brought senior army officers to the Academy and expanded the Smiths' social circle. Activities around West Point increased in the summer as wealthy families left New York City for their summer homes on the Hudson. The summer dances added to the social calendar, and young women and their families attended parties at the Academy. With Smith in charge of the summer encampment, the newlyweds mingled with a number of prominent military, business, and political figures.

During Smith's four-year tenure as Commandant, April 1, 1838, to September 1, 1842, he introduced many of the most prominent generals in the Civil War to the School of the

Soldier. Among those ranks were Henry W. Halleck, Isaac I. Stevens, Edward O. C. Ord, Henry J. Hunt, and Edward R. S. Canby in the Class of 1839; William Tecumseh Sherman, George Henry Thomas, Richard E. Ewell, and Bushrod Rust Johnson in the Class of 1840; Josiah Gorgas, Thomas Rodman, Nathaniel Lyon, John Fulton Reynolds, Don Carlos Buell, and Israel Richardson in the Class of 1841; James Longstreet, Lafayette McLaws, John Pope, William Starke Rosecrans, Gustavus Woodson Smith, George Sykes, and Earl Van Dorn in the Class of 1842; Ulysses Simpson Grant in the Class of 1843; Alfred Pleasanton, Simon B. Buckner, Winfield Scott Hancock, and William F. Smith in the Class of 1844; and Barnard B. Bee, Fitz John Porter, and Edmund Kirby Smith, in the Class of 1845.

Although Smith was posted at West Point, he was still a member of the Second Artillery Regiment. When Company K was added to the regiment, Smith was promoted to be its first captain on July 7, 1838. While Smith was at the Academy, his regiment was stationed in Buffalo, New York, where the officers focused on bringing the troops up to as high a standard as possible. There was keen rivalry between the companies, and the presence of some crack British regiments in Canada added to the competition. In August 1841 Company K left Buffalo and went to Fort Monroe.[41]

"Schools of the Soldier and Company"

An important part of Smith's duties was directing the annual summer encampment. The camp was dedicated to teaching the cadets as much as possible about practical soldiering and to indoctrinate the candidates into military life and help them become plebes. The encampment focused on the fundamentals: the manual of arms, marching in various formations, and maneuvering on the field. The summer program began in June after the yearly exams when cadets erected the camp and got into full swing when the new candidates for admission arrived. The encampment lasted until the end of August when the battalion marched into the barracks. The summer programs were named in honor of various military and political figures: Camp Fowle (Summer 1838), Camp Fenwick (1839), Camp Biddle (1840), Camp Tyler (1841), and Camp Spencer (1842). Smith supervised the training program through a series of battalion orders that outlined the organization of the Corps, scheduled drill for each class, and described other operational details.

Captain Smith had the candidates quartered on the south side of the South Barracks and assigned regular army and cadet officers to oversee their "military instruction and police."[42] The upper class cadets drilled the prospective plebes and tutored the new boys to prepare them for the entrance exams.

Commandant Smith used Scott's *Rules and Regulations for the Exercise and Maneuvers of the United States Infantry* for infantry drill. Lieutenant Miner Knowlton presented artillery instruction using Robert Anderson's *U.S. Artillery Tactics*, Kinsley's *Pyrotechny*, Thiroux's *Instruction Theorique et Pratique d'Artillerie*, and Knowlton's *Notes on Gunpowder, Percussion Powder, Cannon and Projectiles*.[43]

Smith outlined the duties for the four classes of cadets in orders issued in early July.

> During the encampment the duties of the 4 classes of Cadets will be in addition to those prescribed by the Army and academic Regs. as follows.
> First Class
> 5 to 7 o'clock A.M.—Infantry drill and riding exercises, detail to be made by the Comdt [Commandant] of Cadets and instructor of artillery.
> 9 to 10 a.m.—Artillery drills, details for this duty to be made by the Instructor of Artillery

> 11 to 12 p.m.—Artillery drill, broadsword, fencing & laboratory exercises, details to be made by the Instructor of Artillery
> 2 to 5 p.m.—Recitations in artillery, riding & fencing, details to be made by the Instructor of Artillery
> 5 to 6 20' P.M.—Infantry drills & dancing
> Second Class
> 5 to 7 a.m.—Infantry drill
> 9 to 10 a.m.—Artillery drill, detail to be made by the Instructor Arty.
> 11 to 12 p.m.—Attendance on Squad drills, as long as the Comdt. of Cadets may direct.
> 2 to 4¾ p.m.—Riding & dancing lessons, riding detail to be made by the Instructor Arty. [Artillery]
> 5 to 6 20'—Infantry drill
> Third Class
> 5 to 7 a.m.—Infantry drill
> 9 to 10 a.m.—Artillery drill, detail to be made by the Instructor Arty.
> 11 to 12 Nn. [Noon]—Squad drills, as long as the Comdt. of Cadets may direct.
> 11½ to 1 p.m.—Dancing lessons after the discontinuance of drills.
> 3 to 4 p.m.—Riding, detail to be made by the Instructor Arty.
> 5 to 6 20' P.M.—Infantry drill
> Fourth Class
> 5 to 7 a.m.—Infantry drill
> 9 to 10 a.m.—Artillery drill, detail to be made by the Instructor Arty.
> 11 to 12 Nn.—Squad drills, as long as the Comdt. of Cadets may direct.
> 11½ to 1 p.m.—Dancing lessons after the discontinuance of drills.
> 3 to 4 p.m.—Riding, detail to be made by the Instructor Arty.
> 5 to 6 20' P.M.—Infantry drill.[44]

Instruction progressed from the School of the Squad to the School of the Company and concluded with the School of the Battalion.

The camp was organized like any Regular Army battalion in the field. Cadets were prohibited from using the privy in the North Barracks and were required to use the sinks in the Encampment.[45] A picket guard was posted near a point on the Hudson River to prevent all boats from landing, cadets from bathing at improper times and to arrest all cadets who were "beyond limits in that direction without authority."[46] Cadets were restricted in where and when they could walk on public lands."[47]

In addition to military drill, the cadets also received dancing lessons as part of their training to be gentlemen. This prepared them for the weekly dances hosted by the Academy in the Mess Hall. The dances were a pleasant interruption to the routine of the encampment. The presence of many young women who were spending the summer on the Hudson with their families added to the festivities. If Cadets were to dance, they would do it in the proper fashion, and dancing lessons began in April 1839.[48] The young men were drilled in both the School of Soldier and the School of the Dancer. As Cadet Cullum observed in 1832, "It is rather dry business dancing without ladies, however we cannot complain for the want of them in the evening."[49] The summer concluded with a grand formal ball, which was attended by people from around the country.[50] Cadet Jacob Bailey expressed his delight on the occasion in a letter to his brother.

> We shall go into Barracks next week, The day before we move we are to have a Grand Fancy Ball, all Cadets who will wear fancy dresses will be allowed to attend, the others will see the fun. The objections which exist against Fancy Balls in cities, do not exist here. In the city any ragamuffin can obtain admittance, here all the actors are Cadets. It really seems like "old times" to get into a room with men, women, girls and boys, dressed as they used to when we were in the world.[51]

"An excellent disciplinarian"

Superintendent Thayer developed the West Point disciplinary system, and he considered "the maintenance of Discipline as a first principle in Military Economy." Thayer believed "the observance of its rules is at least as essential to the prosperity of the Military Academy as to the well being of the Army." Therefore, Thayer said the Academy must instill the "habits of obedience" in the candidates for the army before the officers enter upon the "Theater of Military Life."[52]

As Commandant of Cadets, Smith was in charge of maintaining obedience, discipline, and self-control. Under the Thayer system, the Commandant "would watch over and inflict the punishments for all minor delinquencies."[53] The lessons Smith learned as a cadet, tactical assistant, and adjutant provided the foundation upon which he administered military law and order. He believed that it was his own rocky beginnings at West Point that made his form of justice respected and even loved by the cadets.[54] Henry Coppee wrote, "We all feared him, but thoroughly respected him, and we believed no commandant ever accomplished as much for the discipline of the corps as he did."[55] In supervising the demerit and courts-martial system, Smith would make friends and create enemies. Some of the strained relationships were his own choosing and others were from cadets who disliked Smith's enforcement of the Academy's code of conduct and maintained a life-long hatred of their former Commandant. However, whatever favorites he had, he showed no preference in citing and punishing those who violated regulations.

Perhaps Smith was modeling his behavior on the authoritarian style of his mentor Sylvanus Thayer. Thayer tried to set an example for the cadets by maintaining an orderly life and impeccable behavior. Although he was warm and engaging, he was exacting, stern, and impartial towards the cadets.[56] Thayer prohibited the cadets from using alcohol, tobacco, or visiting taverns. Card-playing, fighting, and growing mustaches were also forbidden. Cadets were also required to attend chapel services on Sundays.[57] Unfortunately, these restrictions were temptations that few boys could resist. In the rigidly controlled environment, these banned pastimes were sought out by many cadets as a way to experiment with new pleasures and rebel against authority. However, these revolts came with a price that might result in dismissal and disgrace.

To instill the importance of discipline, the final ranking for cadets included a conduct grade determined by the total number of demerits. Additionally, the weight of conduct increased as cadets advanced into the next class. The offenses counted more by adding one sixth of the cadet's total to the number of demerits for his second year, one third for his third, and one half for his fourth.[58] If a cadet received more than 200 demerits in a year, the Academy considered "the cadet deficient in conduct" and recommended he be discharged.[59]

Academy authorities controlled cadet conduct with a system of demerits. Demerits were issued for various offensives that regulated every aspect of their behavior. The fledgling officers earned demerits for tardiness or absence at roll calls for meals, chapel, drill, and inspections; for dirty quarters or equipment; for visiting after taps; for disturbances during study hours; for unshaven faces and uncut hair; for smoking; for improper behavior toward cadet officers and academy officers; and for altercations or fights. A cadet who earned two hundred demerits in a year faced expulsion from the academy.[60] Thayer devised the concept of additional tours, which were walked during a cadet's free time, which could reduce a cadet's number of demerits. Cadets who exceeded two hundred demerits in a year were subject to dismissal.[61] Punishments for more serious violations included extra tours of duty, confinement to quarters, imprisonment, and dismissal. Courts-martial were held for cadets guilty of disobeying orders, disrespecting officers, and violating the code of honor.[62] Smith was meticulous in documenting the infractions of his students and made sure that all the professors and officers had copies of army regulations so they could properly enforce the rules.[63] During his term as Commandant, Smith wrote 146 letters concerning disciplinary actions. The charges included being absent without leave, desertion, difficulties between cadets, using intoxicating liquor, smoking, going beyond the limits of the post, and neglect of duty. Most of the demerits were awarded by the tactical officers. Unfortunately, the "tacs" were inconsistent in their administration which meant that cadets might receive a different number of demerits for the same offense. Some cadet officers took pleasure in reporting their fellow cadets and were universally despised by the Corps.[64] However, it was often difficult to punish cadets because witnesses refused to testify before courts of inquiry to avoid incriminating themselves.[65]

Other penalties were added to confinement in quarters. In Order No. 57, Smith informed the Corps that although cadets under arrest are allowed to receive dancing lessons, they were not permitted "to attend the cotillion parties in the evening." The order also stipulated, "An officer under arrest will not wear a sword, or make a visit of etiquette" to the Commanding Officer, or other superior officer, or "call on them, unless sent for; and in case of business he will make known his object in writing."[66]

It did not take long for Smith to begin punishing the cadets under his supervision. On April 2 he reported the arrest of Cadet Caldwell for smoking. Two days later, the Commandant ordered the arrests and confinement to quarters of Cadet Higgins for disobeying orders of the commander of his squad and Cadet Sherman for going beyond the cadet's limits the prior evening.[67] Soon other cadets joined the ranks of the chastised. On May 30 Cadet Hughes was noted for disobeying a Special Order, Cadet Edmunstan for presiding over an unauthorized meeting, and Cadet Totten for neglect of duty as an orderly.[68] On July 23 Cadet Baldwin was charged for using tobacco,[69] and the next day, Cadet Sykes for letting a cadet pass his post after retreat.[70]

However, these infractions were minor compared to the outrage Smith reported on July 31, 1838.

> It is with pain the Commandant is obliged to announce to the Cadets, that certain members of their body, having been reported for an offense which is a reflection upon the gentlemanly behavior of the Corps. It is stated, that on Saturday afternoon last, about 6 o'clock, three Cadets swam across the river from Gee's Point to the rock opposite Mr. Marner's house on Constitution Island, and there for a length of time, exposed their naked persons directly before his house and in full view of its inmates (some of whom were ladies) from the porch and windows; at the same time, directing attention to themselves by hallowing to their companions on the opposite shore. The individuals alluded to cannot now plead youthful indiscretion for their misconduct, or, when spoken to as was the case, they would have apologized; which they failed to do. The Cadets owe it to their reputation as gentlemen, to discover the authors of such a gross outrage against decency.[71]

Cadets were expected to conduct themselves as gentlemen and many citations were awarded for "inappropriate behavior" or "unsoldierlike conduct." Smith arrested Cadet McCown and confined him to his room because of "highly individualist conduct at Light Infantry drill."[72] Cadet Gareschi was reported for making an improper use of the company parade ground by urinating at reveille and was given extra guard duty for the infraction.[73] In January 1839 Smith reported disorderly behavior during a concert in the chapel when the cadets expressed disapproval over the playing of "Capt. Smith's quick step" by "stamping, hallooing, whistling &c." The noise was "so great and so disagreeable to the ladies and officers present" that the officer in charge ordered the cadets to their quarters.[74]

Smoking and using tobacco had been forbidden at the Academy since 1823. However, banning smoking only increased the cadets' temptation. In July and August of 1838, six cadets were arrested for using tobacco, confined to their rooms for five to seven days, and given two or three extra tours of guard duty.[75] In June 1839 Smith reported Cadets Hamilton, Lay, and Van Dorn for smoking "in one of the vacant rooms in the south barracks."[76]

The use of alcohol was a more serious offense. Cadets Crittenden and Disbrow were arrested in September 1840 for "using intoxicating liquor."[77] The following month Smith reported that a room in the barracks "smelled of ardent spirits."[78] These offenses were often related to nocturnal visits to Benny Haven's tavern. Alcohol-related offenses had reached such a level of concern that on May 13, 1840, 168 cadets from the First, Second, and Third classes signed a pledge to "abstain from all intoxicating liquors" and "aid the Superintendent in preventing such an act."[79] The cadets noted that they would not be expected to report on each other, but they "were left to the full liberty of following their own judgment as to what means they should take to fulfill this pledge."[80]

Infractions that civilians might regard as trivial were taken seriously by Smith and Superintendent Delafield. In one case, a cadet left his room and returned to it "without being spoken to by the sentinel on the subject."[81] Major Delafield cited paragraph 178 of the Academic Regulations that required a cadet when he left his room to "report his departure and return to the sentinel of his division."[82] Other cadets were punished for unexcused absences, such as Cadets Wells and Thurston who were reported for being absent during study hours and taking an axe from the lumberyard.[83] Another common cadet transgression was being "beyond their limits" which meant that a cadet was at a place or at a time where they were not allowed or permitted.[84] Even the Dialectic Society could not escape the Commandant's scrutiny. On February 16, 1840, Smith reported that the cadet debating club was in session after taps. He believed that this was "contrary to the intention of the Superintendent" and felt he should mention it to him "for his information."[85]

Some notable cadets experienced disciplinary problems at the Academy. During his first year at the Academy, Gustavus Woodson Smith along with cadets Napoleon Buford, John Newton, and Theodore S. Laidley were arrested for going to Meeds Landing without authorization. They received extra guard duty as punishment for their offense.[86] Henry Jackson Hunt compiled an impressive list of offenses in a "studied attempt to circumvent or flout the rigid moral code" of the Academy. During Hunt's Second Class year, he was "continually on report for tardiness in answering roll calls, for loitering in areas off limits to cadets, for sleeping through reveille, and for similar infractions." He earned many demerits for having his coat and shoes "out of order" at drill and guard mounting, for not wearing a vest at inspections, and for allowing his hair to grow long and unkempt. Inspecting officers noted that he was habitually neglectful of hanging up his uniform and keeping his quarters neat. He also earned black marks for pranks, such as "tossing bucketfulls of water down the halls of the cadet dorms and bursting into laughter while in the ranks on the drill plain." Hunt also received demerits for "smoking cigars and chewing tobacco after hours in his room" and was frequently reprimanded "for using profane language at cadet gatherings."[87] Some future generals managed to accumulate an impressive number of demerits: Don Carlos Buell (193), E. O. C. Ord (192), Irvin McDowell (190), Eleazer Paine (187), Earl Van Dorn (183), Henry H. Sibley (163), Henry J. Hunt (159), William T. Sherman (148), Lafayette McLaws (147), Winfield S. Hancock (140), and E. R. S. Canby (139). In contrast, James Longstreet received 102, Fred Dent 94, and Ulysses S. Grant 66.

Cadet Hunt was not the only cadet to be punished for insubordination and reckless behavior. In May 1840 Smith reported, "Cadet Totten was at Muster yesterday but declined answering to 'James G. Totten' when called saying that is not his name, it being James Totten."[88] On New Year's morning a group of cadets discharged a musket in the direction of the Mess Hall.[89] Smith was furious when a piece of coal was intentionally thrown at Lieutenants Allen and McDowell from a window in the North Barracks Hall.[90] Disrespectful remarks could also result in charges. When Smith and another officer were leaving the campgrounds, Smith overheard a comment by Cadet Johnstone. According to the Commandant, Johnstone said, in what Smith thought was a contemptuous tone, "that's a fine reviewing officer." The remark "was loud enough to be heard throughout the campground" and resulted in Johnstone's arrest.[91] In April 1842 Smith preferred charges against Cadet Wharton for "writing and presenting to his commanding officer an undecorous [sic] and improper excuse, and making an erroneous statement therein, denying a report which was Correct."[92] In Orders No. 26, Smith placed Cadet Barclay "in arrest, charged with disobeying the order of his Instructor at drill" and had him confined to his quarters.[93]

Even with Smith's strict enforcement of the Academy's code of conduct, he was willing to listen to the cadets as in the case of Cadet Barklay who was arrested by a tactical instructor for refusing to scrub out his room. Captain Smith sent for the cadet and carefully explained the situation. Barklay thought he was no longer a cadet or required to attend to duty after he was reported as deficient. Smith released him from arrest after Barklay promised to scrub out his room and regularly attend to duty.[94]

Some cadets refused to obey orders from the student officers. Cadet Captain Darne ordered Cadet Williams to put his uniform "in order," but at the next inspection he appeared even more unkempt and was sent to his tent. Darne went to Williams' tent, again ordered him to get his accoutrements in better shape, and threatened to report him for "disobedience of orders." Williams angrily replied, "I do not care a damn whether you do or not." Darne ordered him to the guard tent, but Williams refused to go.[95] Subsequently, Williams was confined to the light prison.[96] When Williams met with Smith before being confined, the Commandant asked him what he had to say about his conduct and punishment. Williams said he did not think Captain Darne had the right to give him the orders but was unable to offer any "extenuations of his behavior" to Captain Smith. When Smith ordered Williams to obey the orders for confinement, the cadet turned away, muttered to himself, and swore "I'll be damned if he…" Smith cautioned Williams to be careful of his language. The cadet "turned to me [Smith] suddenly & saw in an abrupt turn of voice knitting his eyebrows &c. 'I won't be careful' or 'I'll say what I please' or something implying contempt for the administration of his comdg. officer."[97]

At times cadets recognized that they were unable or unwilling to meet the Academy's rigorous standards as was the case with Cadet Gage who was arrested for being absent from his quarters. In response to his confinement, Gage decided to resign.[98] In other situations, it became clear to the cadet that he could not master the academics. Cadet Brady resigned because he and his professor did not believe Brady could pass the coming examination in Mathematics.[99]

Infractions of rules and decorum were not limited to the Corps of Cadets, and Smith ordered arrests of faculty, military staff, and visitors for infractions. On October 24, 1839, the Commandant complained to Major Delafield about the "informality" by the Adjutant of the Military Academy and protested that he had assumed unwarranted authority in regard to a note the Adjutant sent to Smith calling his attention to a paragraph of Post Orders No. 21.[100] On November 1, 1841, Smith reported Professor Mahan for leaving the post without his authority.¹⁰¹ Other West Point faculty were also cited for transgressions. Lieutenant Gogdes, Assistant Professor of Mathematics, was cited for being in the Cadets Guard Room "about 25 minutes after the call to quarters in conversation with the Corporal of the Guard."¹⁰² Not all professors responded favorably to Smith's rule. Mr. Berard, the First Teacher of French, said Academy professors only needed permission from the Superintendent to be absent from duty. Professor Berard said he considered the Commandant as "an officer of inferior Rank to himself."¹⁰³

Smith's disciplinary measures were also imposed on the regular army troops stationed at West Point. He requested "a garrison court-martial" for Lyman F. Butler and other privates of the dragoon detachment. Butler was accused of stealing and the others of drunkenness and absence from post without permission.¹⁰⁴

The Academy Band also was the subject of a Smith scolding.

> I have to bring to your notice for correction, unless it is by order of the Comdg. [Commanding] offr. [officer], that on marching to parade yesterday morning, and marching to and from parade yesterday evening, the Band played a quick step, but in common time. I timed it in the evening & found it to be 90 & 91. From this taking place thrice in succession I supposed it to be from design. A quick step ought to be played on at the rate of 110 beats per minute.¹⁰⁵

Smith's application of military regulations was not limited to those stationed at West Point. On September 22, 1840, he arrested recent graduate Lieutenant William T. Sherman, who was visiting the Academy. Sherman was confined to the hotel "for unfavorable conduct in violating the Regulations of the Military Academy."¹⁰⁶

> Lieut. Sherman, a visitor at the post, was seen visiting in the Cadet Barracks a short time since (10 o'clock) by Lieut. Freeman, officer in charge, by whom he was required to leave them. Lt. Sherman graduate [sic] in June last and is therefore of necessity perfectly familiar with para. 205 of the Ac. [Academy's] Regulations, which he thus boldly violates. I report his case in the hope that such steps may be taken or [that] will deter others from similar unsoldierlike conduct.¹⁰⁷

While the logic of the disciplinary system may have escaped the cadets, its importance was understood by their parents. Cadet Edmund Kirby Smith complained to his father about life at the Academy and doubted its value. His father urged him to "strive honorably virtuously and ardently to be distinguished—and God will give you distinction." While it seemed neither "remarkably sensible nor philosophical" to award demerits "for a button off his coat, or for one unbuttoned or because his clothes, bed, windows, room, mantle, shelves, books, face, hair, hands, or nails were out of order," Judge Smith recognized the "importance of these things in the aggregate." "They go far to make the man; much farther to make the officer and gentleman." Many years of army life had clearly demonstrated to him that strict attention to these seemingly small matters improved the health, efficiency, courage, and morality of both officers and soldiers. If such rules were not enforced at the Academy, "the filth, the irregularity, the vermin even, would become intolerable."¹⁰⁸

4. "At West Point always"

"My object is to enter the Academy"

Neither man realized the significance of the event. However, when Hiram Ulysses Grant arrived at West Point on May 30, 1839, it began a twenty-three year association with Charles Ferguson Smith. Grant regarded Smith as one of "the two men most to be envied in the nation."[1]

During his journey to West Point, Grant met Frederick Dent while staying at the same hotel in New York City. The two westerners became friends, but they never talked about going to West Point. Therefore, it was a delightful surprise when they were reunited aboard the steamer *Cornelius Vanderbilt* en route to appointments at the Military Academy.[2]

Grant's initial reluctance to his candidacy at West Point yielded to perseverance. He viewed the trip east as an opportunity to visit Philadelphia and New York. After touring these two grand cities, he hoped that a temporary injury would postpone his enrollment. Unfortunately, no such accident or illness occurred, and he arrived safely at the Academy.

After checking in at Roe's Hotel next to the military post, Grant and Dent reported to the Adjutant's office. Grant signed the register "Ulysses H. Grant." First Lieutenant George G. Waggaman examined the signature and compared it to the official list supplied by the War Department. The Adjutant looked at Grant and informed him that there was no "Ulysses H. Grant" on the register. Waggaman said the list contained two Grants: Ulysses S. Grant from Ohio and Elihu Grant from New York. Grant said that he was the candidate from Ohio, and his Congressman had simply entered the wrong middle initial on the appointment papers. Grant thought it would be a simple matter to correct the error. Waggaman informed him that the name could not be changed and any alteration had to come from the War Department.

Even though his proper name was actually Hiram Ulysses Grant, Congressman Thomas L. Hamer had forgotten the correct first and middle names, used the maiden name of Grant's mother, and nominated him as Ulysses Simpson Grant. Grant was a candidate due to his father's persistence in obtaining the appointment. Therefore, any difficulties or protests might be considered as an insult to Congressman Hamer. After a brief consideration, he announced to the Adjutant, "The change of an initial makes no particular difference to me; my object is to enter the Academy as a Cadet." When the last names and initials of candidates were posted on the bulletin board in the North Barracks, Grant soon had new nicknames. He was no longer "Lyss" but had become "United States Grant," "Uncle Sam Grant," "Uncle Sam," and "Sam."[3]

For the next few weeks, Grant and his fellow candidates lived in the barracks. They spent their days studying for the entrance exams under the guidance of Third Class cadets.[4] Grant's first task was passing the medical and academic examinations. The Medical Board inspected him to make sure that he was free of health problems that would "impair his efficiency." The list seemed endless and forced several candidates to return home. Conditions that would result in rejection included feeble constitution, deafness, bad teeth, speech impediments, curvature of the spine, hernia, and varicose veins.[5]

After meeting the medical requirements, Grant's next hurdle was the academic admission test. The exam was more rigorous than the simple quiz that Captain Smith had faced nineteen years before. Candidates had to read "with facility" from any book, using the proper intonation and pauses, and to write parts of a book aloud, with the proper spelling and punctuation. They also had to demonstrate proficiency in arithmetic, English grammar, descriptive geometry, and history.[6]

Brevet 2nd Lieutenant U. S. Grant (from Albert D. Richardson, *A Personal History of Ulysses S. Grant* [Hartford: The American Publishing Company, 1868]).

The prospective cadets were assessed on a Saturday, around two weeks after they arrived, and learned the results the following morning at drill. On Sunday, the candidates lined up in front of the barracks to learn their fate. Captain Smith walked to the front and made a powerful first impression. "Tall, straight as a pine, grandly mustachioed, the portrait of Mars, scion of a long line of Presbyterian clergymen and college presidents, famed for the exact justice of his administration."[7] He announced the names of those who were admitted,[8] and much to his own surprise, Grant heard Smith call his name. He was a plebe in the Fourth Class of cadets. The cadets took the oath of allegiance and joined the Regular Army.[9]

The new plebes marched to the stores building to pick up their knapsacks and their uniforms and paraded to the camp on the West Point Plain that they would call home for the next two months. Grant believed "military life had no charms" for him. He also professed "not the faintest idea of staying in the army" even if he graduated, which he did not believe he would accomplish.[10]

The plebes were drilled by cadet officers under the watchful eyes of Smith and his assistant tactical instructors. The student officers embraced the task of applying their military training and delighted in teasing the new plebes. Living on the West Point Plain was far from boyish adventures in the outdoors. Grant rose at 5:00 a.m., policed the grounds[11] until 5:30, drilled until 6:30, prepared for inspection, ate breakfast at 7:00, went to parade at 8:00, attended artillery drill at 9:00, policed again, ate dinner at 1:00 p.m., attended dancing class from 3:00 to 4:00, went to infantry drill at 5:30, had evening parade and inspection at 7:00, ate supper at 8:00, and went to bed at 9:30.[12] The monotony of his week was only interrupted by the required attendance at Sunday chapel and the weekly dances. Grant remembered the encampment as "very wearisome and uninteresting."[13]

Summer camp ended with two rituals. The first was the grand ball where cadets and plebes had the opportunity to demonstrate the skills they learned dancing with each other. The second event was the striking of tents the following morning. The cadets gathered around the floors of their tents with clubs and brooms. Two cadets grabbed each corner of the floor. On a signal, they picked up the floor and released thousands of rats. Then, the screaming and cheering cadets attacked the scurrying rodents and slaughtered as many of them as possible.[14]

Grant soon grew to love the Academy and said, "When the 28th of August came—the date for breaking up camp and going into barracks—I felt as though I had been at West Point always, and that if I staid [sic] to graduation, I would have to remain always."[15] As the Corps of Cadets traded their tents for barracks, Grant looked forward to sleeping in a bed. Unfortunately, overcrowding, poor ventilation, and unregulated temperature made the barracks uncomfortable.[16] The rooms were heated using firewood or coal and illuminated with whale-oil lamps. There was no running water, and the cadets had to carry water from an old wooden pump to their rooms. The cadet latrine, located outside the barracks, was described as "a place of barbaric filthiness, whose odors, but not those of Araby,[17] pervaded the whole neighborhood around."[18]

Grant met James Longstreet during his first year. Longstreet recalled the young cadet as a "fragile form" whose "distinguishing trait as a cadet was a girlish modesty; a hesitancy in presenting his own claims; a taciturnity born of his modesty; but thoroughness in the accomplishment of whatever task was assigned him." Longstreet said Grant never joined the usual cadet "larks and games" because of his delicate frame.[19] Cadet William Sherman said of Grant, "A more unpromising boy never entered the Military Academy."[20]

The rigors of studies accompanied the change of quarters. Grant and his fellow plebes studied French, algebra and applications, geometry, trigonometry, and measurement of planes and solids.[21] Fortunately, Grant's natural intelligence compensated for his lack of scholarship, and he completed his first year ranked twenty-seventh out of sixty plebes. Grant's roommate Rufus Ingalls described Cadet Grant as "lazy and careless."

> Instead of studying a lesson, he would merely read it over once or twice; but he was so quick in his perceptions that he usually made very fair recitations even with so little preparation. His memory was not at all good in an attempt to learn anything by heart accurately, and this made his grade low in those branches of study which required a special effort of the memory. In scientific subjects he was very bright, and if he had labored hard he would have stood very high in them.[22]

Grant confirmed Ingalls' assessment and wrote, "I did not take hold of my studies with avidity, in fact, I rarely ever read over a lesson the second time during my entire cadetship."[23] Ulysses' attitude was markedly different from the common cadet pledge, "I intend to bone it with all my might." To bone it, or to study hard, was the spirit that ran through the entire class.[24]

In addition to his classes and military drill, Grant was also confronted with a rigorous set of rules and regulations. Infractions were awarded for an incredible variety of sins including "visiting after taps, absences from roll calls, dirty room, long hair, making a disturbance during study hours, and disobeying orders."[25] Grant explained the demerit system in a letter to his cousin McKinstry Griffith.

> I came near forgetting to tell you about our demerit or "black marks" They give a man one of these "black marks" for almost nothing and if he gets 200 a year they dismiss him. To show how easy one can get these a man by the name of Grant of this state got eight of these "marks" fer not going to Church today. He was also put under arrest so he cannot leave his room perhaps

fer a month, all this fer not going to Church. We are not only obliged to go to church but must march there by companys. This is not exactly republican. It is an Episcopal Church.[26]

Attending Episcopal Church was punishment enough. Marching to sit through two hours of a boring sermon while squeezed together on a backless bench was torture. The only pleasure the cadets had was from chewing tobacco hidden from the prying eyes of the Academy's staff and faculty. Grant received fifty-nine demerits and ranked 147th out of 233 cadets.[27] Ingalls noted that his roommate's demerits came from slouchiness rather than disobedience.[28]

Sam Grant soon discovered the West Point library, which had grown in variety and size to between 8,000 and 10,000 volumes.[29]

> There is a fine library connected with the Academy from which cadets can get books to read in their quarters. I devoted more time to these, than to books relating to the course of studies. Much of the time, I am sorry to say, was devoted to novels, but not those of a trashy sort.[30]

Grant joined the Dialectic Society, which debated some of the most difficult issues facing the country and the military. On September 19, 1840, the Dialectic Society argued, "Whether it would be beneficial to the service to prohibit officers of the Army under the rank of captain from being married." It was decided in the negative by a vote of 11 to 4.[31] On March 15, 1841, the subject for debate was "Has a State a right to secede from the Union?" The *Journal of the Dialectic Society* reported the question was decided in the affirmative.[32]

The one constant during Grant's first year was Captain Smith, whose presence pervaded the whole Academy. Grant's initial fear of Smith grew to respect, admiration, and genuine affection. Smith took special interest in Grant and often had pleasant chats with the cadet.[33]

Although it was forbidden, Grant tried smoking, became sick, and gave it up. Cadet Grant noted, "The fact that tobacco in every form was prohibited, and the mere possession of the weed was punished, made the majority of the cadets … try to acquire the habit of using it."[34] Grant drank with his fellow cadets, but when several members of the class swore off in an attempt to remove temptation from a weak member of the class, he joined the temperance movement.[35]

Grant completed his Third Class studies ranked twenty-fourth out of fifty-three and received sixty-seven demerits, which placed him 144th out of 219 cadets.[36] At the summer encampment, President Martin Van Buren visited West Point and reviewed the cadets. Grant was not impressed and said, "In fact I regarded General Scott and Captain C. F. Smith, the Commandant of cadets, as the two men most to be envied in the nation."[37]

After two years at the Academy, Grant received the usual two-month summer furlough and traveled to Ohio to visit his family. When he returned to West Point for his third year, Grant learned he was promoted to sergeant in the Corps of Cadets. He was the lowest rated of the eighteen sergeants and the promotion proved to be too much for him. His performance was unsatisfactory and the future general was reduced in grade and served his fourth year as a private.[38] Although he failed as a sergeant, Grant did well in his academic studies and his position improved to twentieth out of forty-one. Under the tougher standards as a Third Class cadet, Grant received ninety-eight demerits and dropped thirteen places in the Academy rankings.[39]

During Grant's first three years at the academy, he received 224 demerits, which meant that he had occasion to encounter Smith on disciplinary matters. However, Grant found it more distressing to report to the commandant on infractions by fellow cadets. One such instance was in the case of Cadets Taylor and Hammond. Captain Smith ordered Grant to make a written report describing what he witnessed. The report said,

… during maneuvers Hammond had ordered Taylor to "dress up" and when Taylor "did not appear to obey," had repeated the command "in a very loud and harsh manner," provoking Taylor to call Hammond "by several bad names such as d—d little b—d and other names quite as vulgar and said that he caught Cadet Hammond out of ranks and if Cadet Hammond spoke to him in such a manner out of ranks—I do not remember which—he would kick him.

Grant concluded by weakly indicating: "These are the principal circumstances that I remember not expecting to have been called upon to make a statement of them."[40]

The Last Encampment

In the spring of 1842, Smith received an inquiry from Lieutenant Allen about Smith's interest in joining Colonel James M. Bankhead's Second Artillery Regiment on Governor's Island in New York Harbor. Bankhead explained that the message expressed his wish to have Smith's "efficient services with the Regiment" rather than any serious intention on his part to formally request Smith's reassignment. Bankhead was aware that Smith's "present situation is highly eligible and very honorable to the individual selected to fill it." The Colonel did not want to "cause your removal from that to another [position] less important or less agreeable to you." Bankhead hoped to induce Smith to replace the current captain of Company A. Bankhead concluded by begging Smith to consider it as "evidence of the high estimation I place on your qualifications for the command of the most important Company of the Regiment and of the gratification it would afford to me to have you with the Regiment whenever that can be done agreeably & beneficially to yourself."[41]

Smith was unwilling to leave West Point for what he considered a less desirable position and did not pursue the opportunity. General Stewart, a member of the Board of Visitors, seemed to validate Smith's decision, when he expressed "the gratification I enjoyed today and yesterday in the examination of the First Class in Infantry Tactics." Stewart declined to compliment Smith and his assistants because he knew "they have in the consciousness of doing their duty, a more [illegible] reward than in any commendation from me."[42] However within two months, Smith's time at West Point was abruptly terminated. He was thirty-five years old and had spent over half of his life at the Military Academy.

It must have been with some degree of sadness that Smith's last responsibility as Commandant was directing the 1842 summer encampment. As he looked upon the new group of Fourth Class cadets, he could not have anticipated that these young men of the class of 1846 would produce some of the leading generals of the Civil War. From their ranks came four brigadier generals, fourteen major generals, and two lieutenant generals. The list included nine who served in the Confederate Army, including A. P. Hill, Thomas Jackson, and George Pickett. Those who remained loyal to the United States were John Gibbon, George B. McClellan, and George Stoneman.

On July 7, 1842, Captain Smith received a letter from Joseph Totten, Chief Engineer of the Army and Inspector of the Military Academy. He explained to Smith that he was being relieved because the Secretary of War decided that the "position of Instructor of Tactics & Commandant of Cadets" would be filled by "an officer of lower rank than enjoyed by you and, accordingly, you will be relieved, on the 1st of September next, from your duties at that Institution by a Lieutenant." Totten added that the Secretary of War "is fully aware of, and duly appreciates, the talent and fidelity with which your [Smith's] several duties have been performed, during the long period of 13 years in which your zealous services have connected you with the Academy."[43]

Two days later Special Orders No. 56 made it official. General Scott said, "1st Lieutenant J. A. Thomas, Third Regiment of Artillery will relieve Captain C. F. Smith, Second Artillery, as Commander of the Corps of Cadets and Instructor of Tactics at the Military Academy, and will report himself for duty to the Superintendent at West Point, on or before the 1st of September. Captain Smith on being relieved will proceed to join his company."[44] Scott granted Smith a six-month leave of absence.[45] Smith said his farewells to the Corps of Cadets after the encampment and promised to return occasionally to check on their progress while he was nearby in New York City.

Totten's letter seems a poor excuse for removing Smith. It is more likely that Smith's transfer was the result of several factors. His memorandum in 1838 requesting that line officers be placed on the same footing with staff officers certainly ruffled some feathers in the War Department. As chief disciplinarian at the Academy, Smith was the target of cadet complaints about punishments. These objections probably reached the Congressmen who nominated the candidates. Smith's knowledge and enforcement of military regulations placed him in juxtaposition with visiting field officers who had a more pragmatic view of discipline. It is also possible that there were some residual effects from Smith's service as Adjutant to Superintendent Thayer. Another consideration is that Colonel Bankhead, whose advances were spurned by Smith, might have initiated the action in order to have Smith transferred to his command. These reasons seem more likely than Totten's explanation because Smith's replacement, Lieutenant Thomas, was promoted to captain on November 19, 1843, around sixteen months after his arrival.

Charles and Francis spent his leave with his family in Philadelphia. Tragedy struck Smith's family again on August 29, 1842, when his sister, Elizabeth Smith Burton, died at Fort Moultrie, South Carolina.[46]

5. "Riot raging in Kensington"

On March 1, 1843, Smith reported at Fort Columbus, New York Harbor as commander of Company K of the Second Artillery Regiment.[1] He quickly discovered that there was a big difference between giving orders to enlisted men compared to instructing student-officers-in-training. Discipline at the Military Academy was more strictly enforced than in the Regular Army.

> In the Regular Army, officers and men belonged to different castes, and a practically impassable barrier was between them. Most of the men who had enlisted in the long years of domestic peace were, for one cause or another, outcasts to whom life had been a failure and who followed the recruiting sergeant as a last desperate resource when every other door to a livelihood was shut.[2]

This difference in the character of the men that Smith commanded soon became evident in his expectations and application of discipline. The soldiers had to adjust to Smith's strict authority, and Smith had to reconcile dealing with a rougher group of men. He quickly started to whip them into shape, and his troops had to make most of the concessions.

Although the Smiths were still mourning the loss of their first child, their grief was softened by Francis' pregnancy. Edward DeRussy Smith, named after Charles' Superintendent at West Point, was born on July 5, 1843. Captain and Mrs. Smith remained at Fort Columbus until July 1844. However, events at Frankford Arsenal would result in their relocation to Philadelphia.

From its opening in 1816, Frankford Arsenal in northern Philadelphia was the center of small-arms ammunition design and manufacturing for the United States military.[3] Life at the arsenal was uneventful until troubles with Pennsylvania citizens began in 1838. When Captain George Douglas Ramsay, commander of the Arsenal, learned that a mob had ransacked the state arsenal at Harrisburg, he became concerned that the unrest in Harrisburg might affect the security at Frankford. The Ordnance Department refused Ramsay's request to increase the size of the garrison at the post but allowed him to hire private guards.

Public unrest broadened and reached the growing industrial community of Kensington where the arsenal was located. On May 8, 1844, Captain Ramsay warned Colonel George H. Talcott, the Acting Chief of Ordnance, about the "riot raging in Kensington." Ramsay said fires were raging in the district, rioters destroyed St. Augustine Church and the surrounding buildings, and General Robert Patterson, commanding the Pennsylvania militia, was holding a "large body of Irish" in check.[4] Ramsay sent arms and ammunition from the arsenal to the Philadelphia sheriff. Then he made a desperate appeal for help when he heard rumors that "rioters intend to attack the Arsenal and the Catholic Church at Frankford." After Ramsay's many requests, the War Department sent Captain Smith's company to defend the apparently threatened arsenal.[5]

Lieutenant Townsend, a fellow officer from Fort Columbus, informed Smith that Captain Ramsay would "furnish you with everything in the way of arms, accoutrements, &c."

Townsend said that Company K and the rest of the regiment would be receiving new muskets with percussion locks. At the time of the letter, Francis Smith was still at Fort Columbus, and Townsend sent the anxious father an update on her condition.

> Mrs. Smith seems to be pretty well. She has taken the liberty of differing from our [illegible] Doctor, and sleeps when she can, instead of keeping awake all day that she may rest at night. Last evening, the young ladies from the Colonel's house paid her a visit and the head of the house met them. You may be sure there was a running of the unruly members.[6]

Several days after his arrival, Smith received a letter from his friend Irvin McDowell. McDowell noted that Congress had "cut us down" (reduced the size of the army). West Point continued to be under scrutiny, and a Grand Jury was ordered to investigate "the affairs of the Point." McDowell hoped "the place may be purified under their united influence to the peoples full content and satisfaction." He concluded by extending his "warmest regards to Mrs. Smith" and hoped that she was "well after the painful and affecting trial she has passed through."[7]

Charles was soon joined in Philadelphia by his pregnant wife and infant son. The Smiths had hardly arrived when thirteen-month-old Edward died. Charles and Francis did not have long to grieve his loss. Francis gave birth to a daughter, Fanny Mactier Smith, on September 25, 1844, a little more than a month after their son's death.

The presence of the additional forces had the desired effect. There were no attacks or rumors of aggression while Company K was at the post. Captain Smith settled into the usual mundane clerical work filing the monthly return reports.[8] He complained about the size of the sick list and instructed the post surgeon to limit men on the roll "to those who really need his care."[9] He ordered equipment and clothing for his men and submitted accounts of property, clothing, and ordinance.

The remainder of Smith's time seemed to be devoted to arresting and punishing the men in his command. The records of the Frankford Arsenal report about five courts-martial prior to Smith's arrival. He nearly equaled that number in one year. His commitment to rules and regulations was unleashed upon the troops of Company K. He disciplined, court-martialed, and discharged seven or eight soldiers.[10] On November 18, 1844, Smith requested a court-martial for Privates Hammer, Hawkins, McGuire, and Devenport.[11] Captain Smith ordered a general court-martial for Devenport, who was sentenced to hard labor for one month with a ball and chain. After his release, Devenport disappeared for three days. When he was captured, he escaped again and went to Philadelphia. Consequently, Smith requested a "more severe sentence than a Minor Court could pronounce."[12] A soldier who was drunk at drill received five days' of hard labor and a pay suspension of $3.[13] Some soldiers ran away rather than face punishment. Private Edward Ellis deserted after being arrested. Smith asked for help in apprehending Ellis and described the private as a shoemaker whose speech was "thick."[14]

Especially noteworthy was the case of Private Glass who spent 102 of his 239 days in the service under "the restraint of the guard." In one court-martial, "he was charged with drunkenness ... altho' the evidence shewed him to be quite crazy it failed to satisfy the Crt. [Court] his craziness proceeded from drink, still there is little doubt of the fact." Smith concluded from Glass' "intemperate habits," he "is of evil example to the Co."[15] Twelve days later Private Glass was dishonorably discharged for drunkenness.[16]

In a letter to Colonel Bankhead, commander of the Second Artillery Regiment, Smith explained why he had held so many courts-martial since his company's arrival at the Arsenal. He attributed the problems to the ease with which men could leave the post and the lack of a means for adequate punishment. He believed that a proper guardhouse, a place to confine soldiers, and repeated imprisonment would "effect a cure in most cases."[17] He followed this explanation with a request to build "a place of confinement" for the men of any company "who are irregular in their conduct." Smith asked for permission to obtain material to erect rough cells adjacent to the guardroom, which he estimated would cost about $30 to build. He also requested four pairs of handcuffs.[18]

In spite of his insistence on proper military behavior, Smith was not a tyrant and treated his men kindly. He asked Ramsay to furnish, "Two coal stoves to warm the company quarters and guard room, materials to build an exterior-covered stairway to allow the men to go from the second story without passing through the guard house and shed or piazza in front of the company quarters for roll call, a new guard house as previously requested and discussed with General Scott for 'comfort and discipline.'"[19] Smith helped Private Lynch obtain an early release from the service so Lynch could take advantage of "a desirable opening" that might not be available when his term of enlistment was completed.[20] Smith approved a request from Private Conner to allow his son James to earn "a living in any way he may see fit."[21] Captain Smith nominated soldiers for promotion,[22] but refused to transfer Private Gardner because he was "a good soldier & one I have no desire to lose."[23] Smith wrote a soldier's father about the son's debt to the father and suggested that the son send his father $5 from every payday. Captain Smith said the soldier's behavior had been "perfectly correct" except for one incident which Smith attributed to drink.[24] The captain recommended remission of Private Peterson's sentence because of good conduct.[25] He sent a letter to the paymaster about the method and inconsistency of stopping pay for soldiers in Company K who owed money to the army.[26] Captain Smith disputed the amount owed by his men to the Post Sutler at Fort Columbus and requested details of the debts claimed by sutler, William Kendall. He refused to authorize payment until Kendall provided a reconciliation and additional evidence on the amounts due. Eventually, Smith decided to prefer charges against Kendall.[27]

Smith saw a number soldiers leave the army during his command of Company K. Some of them went after completing their service while others were separated for unacceptable behavior. Smith asked Corporal Timothy B. Hicks to be discharged because, although Hicks was "of excellent character and neat, soldierly appearance," Smith believed Hicks lacked the energy to be a non-commissioned officer and could "neither set him aside nor fail to present him for promotion in the event of a vacancy."[28] Private David Shelly was dishonorably dismissed from the Company following the sentence of a general court-martial.[29] After Francis Sheerom had completed his term of service, Smith drafted a reference describing him as "honest & sober, & a good soldier" and provided a description of him "to prevent an improper use of this certificate by any person."[30] Captain Smith described one soldier, whose enlistment had expired, as "inefficient as a soldier" but whose "general conduct was good and he was sober."[31]

The procedure for these separations concerned Smith, and on January 12, 1845, he suggested to Brigadier General R. Jones, Adjutant General of the Army, that the military use a discharge form similar to that used by the British Army.

> It has often occurred to me that the service would be benefited if a discharge somewhat similar to that granted in the British Army was given in ours. I mean to make it obligatory on the Comp. Commander to state that the man's genl. conduct has been good when such is the case and to cut off the space for character whenever it has been such as ought to prevent a re-enlistment.

Smith believed that because of the lack of information on a man's character, "many worthless men have been re-enlisted who were discharged under the late law for reducing the army." For example, a captain of artillery who was refused re-enlistment in the East could go to the West and get into an infantry regiment or a soldier in the infantry in the West who was refused re-enlistment in the infantry who could come to the seaboard and join the artillery. Smith had two or three men, who came from the infantry, whom he believed would "never have been re-enlisted by their former company commander based on their qualifications & conduct since joining his Company." He enclosed a copy of the discharge form used in the British Service and proposed a form based on the British document that "might be used advantageously in our Service."

> The soldier's character would be inserted only when recommendatory. If the general conduct of the soldier, while in the service, has been such as to give him no claim to having anything said in his favor, the space for character in the above certificate is to be cut off under the black line following the confirmation of the discharge, thereby leaving no opportunity for an addition to be made after the certificate is given to the man.
>
> When a soldier is discharged on account of disgraceful conduct that will appear in the body of the certificate.[32]

Ultimately, Colonel Bankhead became annoyed with Smith's disciplinary requests and started routinely to deny them. Bankhead might have had a more lenient attitude towards the soldiers than Smith who was determined to instill order to his undisciplined troops. This desire was heightened by the competition among fellow company commanders in the regiment.[33] Finally, because of either reduced public unrest or Bankhead's weariness of Smith's courts-martial requests, Company K was ordered to return to Fort Columbus on August 26, 1845. Their stay at Fort Columbus was brief and they were soon deployed to Texas with the rest of the regiment.

Part Two

Corpus Christi to Mexico City: 1845–1848

"An accomplished general; a superb soldier, a dignified and punctiliously honorable gentleman." —Henry Coppee[1]

Charles Ferguson Smith during the Mexican War (courtesy Dr. William J. Schultz).

6. "A tussle with the Mexicans"

"So close to the United States"

The road to Texas statehood began in May 1821 with Moses Austin's contract with the Spanish authorities to establish a colony in Texas.[1] Nearly fifteen years later, delegates met at Washington-on-the-Brazos to write the Texas Declaration of Independence. The convention proclaimed, "our political connection with the Mexican nation has forever ended; and that the people of Texas do now constitute a free, sovereign, and independent republic."[2] While the delegates met to sever Texas' ties to Mexico, Mexican forces under Santa Anna captured the Alamo in San Antonio.[3] At Goliad another Mexican Army defeated and executed the 300 Texans who surrendered. "Remember the Alamo" and "Remember Goliad" became rallying cries of the revolution.[4]

The Texans had their revenge when they destroyed the Mexican Army at San Jacinto on April 21, 1836. Santa Anna was captured and forced to agree to the terms of the Treaty of Velasco. The Mexican ruler promised never to fight against the Texans, to order all Mexican forces out of Texas, and to bring about Mexican recognition of Texas independence.[5]

Following its independence, Texas worked to pay off its debts from the war with Mexico, defend itself from hostile Indians and Mexican bandits, and seek admittance to the United States. However, problems soon developed concerning the annexation. Mexico refused to recognize the new republic and abolitionist groups opposed Texas statehood because it would add another slave state to the Union.[6] In November 1844 Democrat James K. Polk was elected president on a platform of territorial expansion and acquisition of the Republic of Texas and the Oregon Country. The Tyler administration viewed Polk's election as a referendum approving Texas statehood. The outgoing president pushed the fight in Congress to obtain Texas. On February 26, 1845, six days before Polk took office, Congress passed a joint resolution declaring that Texas would be admitted as a state provided it approved annexation by January 1, 1846. In July 1845 the Texas Congress endorsed the American annexation offer and began composing a state constitution. The citizens of Texas approved the new constitution and the annexation ordinance in October 1845. In spite of the Treaty of Velasco, the Mexican government refused to recognize Texan independence and regarded the Republic as a rebellious territory that soon would be returned to their control. Mexican authorities viewed plans to add Texas to the United States as a deliberate attempt to prevent Mexican reunification and threatened to declare war on the United States if they took control of Texas.[7]

In addition to the issue of independence, there was also the disagreement about Mexico's boundary with the Texas Republic. Texas claimed that the Rio Grande River was the southern border, while Mexican authorities maintained it was the Nueces River.[8] This border dispute was omitted from the annexation resolution passed in Congress.

As the annexation process continued in Texas, the Mexicans started assembling troops near Matamoros. In response, President Polk ordered "an efficient military force to take a position between the Nueces and the Rio Grande rivers." The president said this measure was necessary "to meet a threatened invasion of Texas by the Mexican forces." He concluded that because the "invasion was threatened solely because Texas had determined ... to annex herself to our Union ... and ... it was plainly our duty to extend our protection over her citizens and soil."[9] Even before Texans approved annexation, President Polk began measures to seize the region. At Fort Jessup, General Zachary Taylor was instructed to prepare troops composing an "Army of Observation" to defend Texas. Taylor selected Corpus Christi as the base for his operations and began sending troops into Texas. In August 1845 companies from the Second Artillery Regiment started to leave Fort Columbus for Texas. Lieutenant James Duncan's Company A left in August and Captain Charles Smith's Company K left in late September on the USS *Lexington* for Corpus Christi.[10]

Before the "Army of Observation" arrived in Corpus Christi, the place was a village of less than 100 people centered on a small American trading post where goods were sold to Mexican smugglers. After annexation, Taylor's "Army of Observation" was renamed the "Army of Occupation." The soldiers began clearing the campsite of snake-infested thickets, and the small town was gradually transformed into a major military post with more than 3,000 men. Taylor's command consisted of seven companies of the Second Regiment of Dragoons; four companies from the Second Artillery Regiment; five regiments of infantry, the Third, Fourth, Fifth, Seventh, and Eighth; and one regiment of artillery acting as infantry.

Polk and some Mexican officials still hoped to avoid war. On November 10, 1845, Polk sent John Slidell to Mexico City to negotiate acquisition of the Rio Grande border in Texas and Mexico's provinces of Alta California and Santa Fe de Nuevo México. Unfortunately, Mexico was not interested in selling land to the United States and political turmoil in the Mexican government frustrated any possible negotiations. Mexican citizens and politicians agreed that selling the territories to the United States would tarnish the national honor. They declared, "The annexation of Texas is an act of aggression, the most unjust which can be found in history" and claimed that Mexico had the right to recover her lost property. Slidell returned to the United States convinced that Mexico should be "chastised."

Texans waited for Congressional approval of their bid for statehood and the expected Mexican invasion. On December 29, 1845, Polk signed the documents integrating Texas into the United States, and, in response, the Mexican government broke diplomatic relations.[11]

"We were sent to provoke a fight"

With the threat of a Mexican invasion, the War Department rushed reinforcements to Corpus Christi. By the middle of October 1845, the Army of Occupation consisted of 3,922 officers and men.[12] The size and complexity of this army created problems that the military was ill equipped to handle. Before the Mexican War, the army's main responsibility was guarding the frontier from hostile Indians. The forces were distributed in small posts along trails and near settlements. Most of the troops were organized in companies or battalions. This provided good training for the lower rank officers, but afforded no opportunity for developing regimental, brigade, and staff officers. The lack of officers with large unit experience created problems in finding middle grade positions. The former West Point

Commandants of Cadets, Worth, Hitchcock, and Smith, were among the few officers with battalion leadership experience.

Congress had limited the U.S. Army's size to 8,613 officers and men. The number of senior officers was restricted to three generals and one colonel, one lieutenant colonel, and one major for each regiment. Promotion was based on the vacancies occurring in each regiment and seniority within the regiment. There was no provision for retirement so that old officers who were physically unable to hold field command blocked middle grade officers. To address the problem, the Army created brevet rank. A major might be promoted to brevet lieutenant colonel and required to perform the duties of his brevet rank without more authority or pay.[13]

From the Revolutionary War through the end of the 19th century, the standard method of recognizing the performance of U.S. Army and U.S. Marine Corps officers was through the conferral of brevet promotions. The brevet promotion was an advancement in rank without an accompanying advancement in pay or assigned position. During the first half of the nineteenth century, brevet promotions were awarded to officers for ten years of faithful service at the same rank if no regular vacancies were available at the next higher rank. Although normally the brevet rank carried no greater authority, an officer might be required to perform the duties of his brevet rank. However, more significantly, brevet promotions were presented to officers for gallantry in the presence of the enemy or for other distinguished service. The brevet promotion was recorded in an officer's permanent record and was a mark of honor and high distinction in the small professional army.[14]

With the expansion of the Army and assignment of new commands, the officers debated the subject of brevet vs. ordinary or lineal rank. In October Taylor raised the issue in respect to the seniority to Colonels David E. Twiggs and Worth. Twiggs was senior to Worth as a colonel according to lineal rank, but Worth's brevet rank as a brigadier general made him superior under that system. In this situation whoever was senior would be the second-in-command of the army. General Winfield Scott said that Worth's brevet rank was superior to Twigg's lineal rank.[15]

The debate among the officer corps continued, fueled by a circular issued on December 12, 1845, by General Scott to the army. An officer characterized this circular as "an impertinent interposition between General Taylor and the President" and criticized Scott for giving "precedence to brevet rank." Annoyed by Scott's circular, Lieutenant Colonel Hitchcock studied the topic and prepared the paper "Brevet and Staff Rank and Command." The paper became the subject of a memorial signed by 130 officers asking the Senate to pass legislation to settle the question.[16]

President Polk used his position as commander-in-chief to declare brevet rank inferior to lineal rank. Outraged by the ruling that Twiggs outranked him, Worth resigned from the army before the battles of Palo Alto and Resaca de la Palma. Following these engagements, Worth withdrew his resignation and returned to duty vowing to earn either a grade or a grave.[17]

In the Corpus Christi camp, the reorganized brigades began extensive training programs. The former West Point commandants and tactical instructors quickly resumed their former duties. The new army provided Captain Smith with another opportunity to exercise his training skills on the young West Point officers and their soldiers. Instruction took place on a 150-to-200-acre field about a quarter of a mile from the camp. The training was so relentless that one soldier complained that life became "nothing but drill and parades and your ears are filled all day with drumming and fifing." The work produced the desired results and the companies and regiments were soon forged into an army.

Drill stopped when the pleasant conditions of the fall changed to the cold, wet, and dismal winter weather. With the change of the season, illness increased and discipline decreased. Lieutenant D. H. Hill described the conditions at Corpus Christi where the men used worn out, rotten, gauze tents. "The tents provided no protection against the intense heat of summer, or the drenching rains and severe cold of winter." Hill said as a result of the unhealthy conditions, "Dysentery and catarrhal fevers raged like a pestilence." The encampment soon resembled a marsh with water as high as three of four feet in some areas.[18] The camp also contained "the numerous employés of the quartermaster and commissary departments,—the artisans, the teamsters and mule-drivers; the clerks, factorums, and servants; the contractors, speculators, and letter-writers; as well as the blacklegs, whiskey-sellers and pickpockets, with their coadjutors, the courtezans of the camp."[19] Crimes committed against Mexicans and fellow Americans marred the role of the volunteers in the Mexican War. The *Niles' National Register* cited criminal acts committed by volunteers as "innumerable proofs of the lack of discipline and the prevalence not only of insubordination, but also of disgraceful rowdyism amongst the volunteers."[20]

On January 13, 1846, President Polk ordered General Zachary Taylor to move his force of 3,550 men to "a position on or near the Rio Grande River well suited to repel any invasion." Polk said that Taylor should not treat Mexico as an enemy; but should she assume that character by a declaration of war, or any open act of hostility towards us, you will not act merely on the defensive, if your relative means enable you to do otherwise."[21] When Polk's order reached Taylor on February 4, the general made plans to march his troops to Point Isabel or Brazos Santiago and use either one as a supply depot. He wrote the Adjutant General, "That point and a position on or near the river opposite Matamoras [sic] will I think answer all present purposes." Taylor replied that he would lose no time in making the necessary preparations for carrying out those instructions."[22]

Taylor alerted the army and sent a party to reconnoiter the road to Matamoros. The men found the road "muddy but passable."[23] "It is possible," Lieutenant Colonel William G. Belknap informed his wife, "but barely so, that we may have a tussle with the Mexicans."[24] "But fight or no fight," Lieutenant Grant told his fiancé, "evry one rejoices at the idea of leaving Corpus Christi."[25]

On March 8 General Taylor's Army of Occupation of Texas started to leave Corpus Christi on the Matamoros Road. Taylor left about 1,000 men in Corpus Christi and sent the remaining 2,300 in four columns with a day between their departures. Colonel Twiggs, with seven companies of dragoons and a battery of light artillery left first. They were followed by the First Brigade under General Worth on the ninth, the Second Brigade led by Colonel James S. McIntosh on the tenth, and Third Brigade on the eleventh. Smith departed with the Second Artillery at the rear of the First Brigade.

The road from Corpus Christi to Matamoros was about 150 miles long over uninhabited flat prairie with few waterholes. The "ponds of drinkable water were separated by a whole day's march" which governed the distance covered.

> Besides the streams, there were occasional pools, filled during the rainy season, some probably made by the traders, who traveled constantly between Corpus Christi and the Rio Grande, and some by the buffalo. There was not at that time a single habitation, cultivated field, or herd of domestic animals, between Corpus Christi and Matamoras [sic].[26]

Although the weather was dry and relatively cool during most of the journey, the march was not entirely agreeable. The road ran through deep, sandy plains, glistening with specks of salt. In some places the men crossed briny marshes or sticky black dirt. The Mexicans

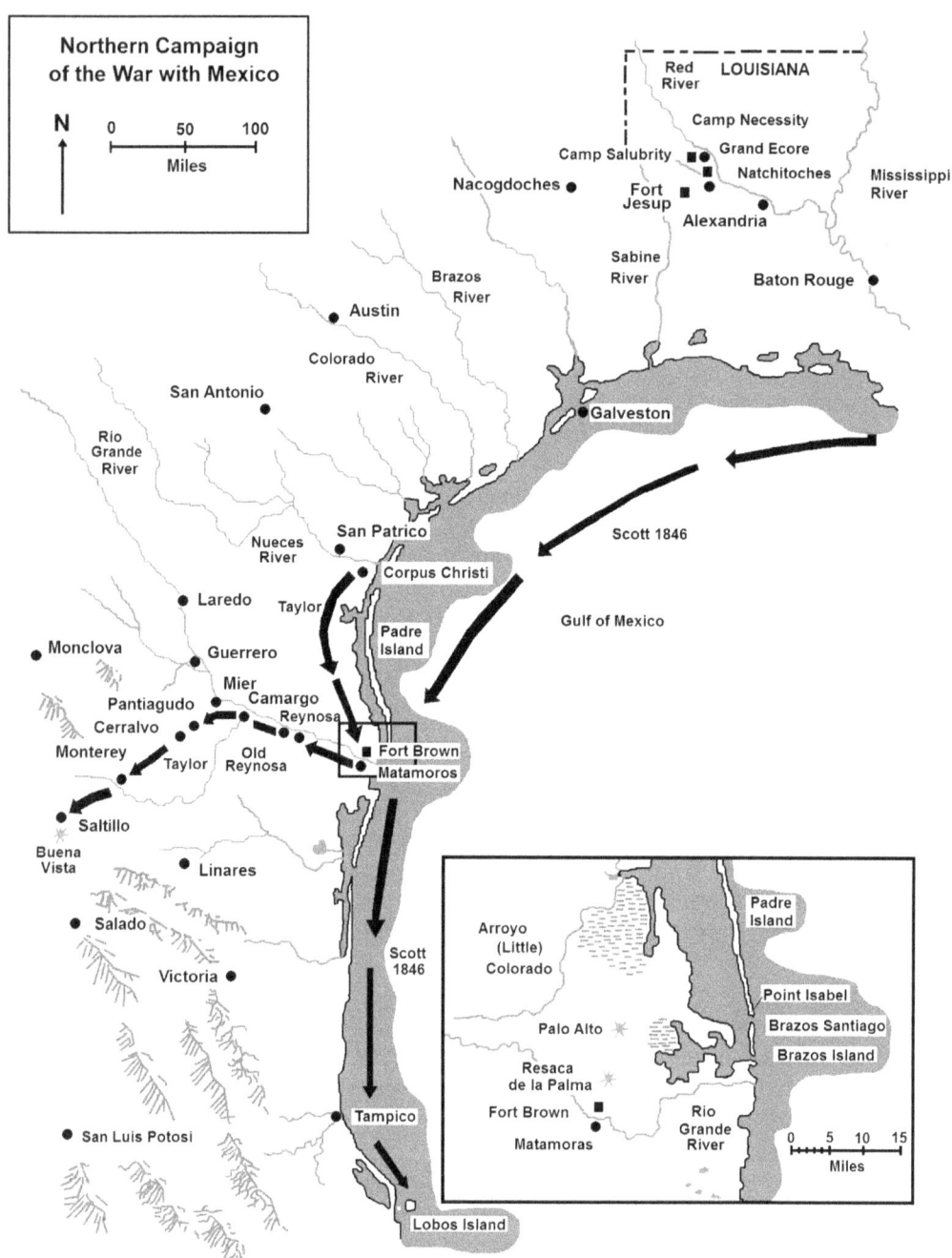

Northern Campaign of War with Mexico (author's drawing based on map from *Papers of Ulysses S. Grant* and Ulysses S. Grant Association).

had burned the vegetation along the route and the ashes turned the American's faces black. The men suffered from thirst and what little water they found was brackish. In some places the men greeted wild horses, ducks, and geese, but centipedes, tarantulas, and rattlesnakes were unwelcome guests.[27]

On March 14 Colonel Twiggs' advance guard met a small group of Mexicans, who fled after they set fire to the prairie. The following day, Lieutenant Fowler Hamilton's six-man advance party met Lieutenant Ramon Falcon and a Mexican detachment. Lieutenant Falcon demanded to know what the soldiers were doing on Mexican land. Hamilton informed him that the American troops were en route to occupy the left bank of the Rio Grande River. Falcon said that he would report these plans to his superiors and warned that Mexico would oppose any further advance.[28] Mexico responded to the troop movement by sending additional forces to Matamoros.

The opposing armies were gathering at the Rio Grande and it was only a matter of time when a misstep by either party would lead to war.

"On the verge of a fierce and bloody conflict"

General Taylor expected that his force could travel the first 100 miles without being challenged by the Mexicans. He thought he might be attacked after crossing the Arroyo Colorado (Colorado River) that was about thirty miles from Matamoros. Taylor ordered the brigades to continue the advance closer to each other so they could gather quickly to meet any opposition. The advance units camped about three miles from the Colorado River on March 19, and Taylor decided to concentrate the entire force before crossing the river.

It soon became obvious that General Francisco Mejia, the commander at Matamoros, planned to prevent the Americans from fording the river. A reconnaissance force of American dragoons met Mexican cavalry who declared that crossing the river would be considered "an act of hostility." The enemy resistance appeared to be confirmed by the number of bugle calls coming from the Mexican camps hidden in the chaparral.[29] The Mexican opposition was confirmed when Captain José Barragan delivered a copy of General Mejia's March 18 proclamation that called on the citizens to oppose the "degenerate sons of Washington." Barragan repeated Mexico's intention to oppose crossing the Colorado River.

In response to this challenge, Taylor decided to cross the Arroyo Colorado immediately. The brackish slough was a little more than a hundred yards wide. However, its timber-lined banks dropped too steeply for horse teams to cross.[30] Taylor selected Captain Smith to lead four light infantry companies across the river and seize the opposite bank. On the morning of March 20, working parties cut down trees on the American side.[31] Taylor placed his dragoons and Worth's First Brigade in position at the river and had Captain James Duncan's and Major Samuel Ringgold's artillery batteries prepare to support the crossing. The Second Brigade arrived and took up position to the right of Worth's First Brigade.

At 10:30 a.m. C. F. Smith led his force "in perfect order" into the stream. The situation was tense and Kirby Smith called it "one of the most exciting moments of my life." Everyone in the army, Smith recalled, "from the General-in-Chief to the smallest drummer boy, felt morally certain that we were on the verge of a fierce and bloody conflict, yet I saw no one who was not cheerful and apparently eager for the game to begin."[32]

Smith's men were in the open, wading in water up to their armpits and vulnerable to rifle and cannon fire from the opposite bank. The men heard the sound of the Mexican buglers and prepared for an attack. "We watched them in breathless silence as they deepened in the water, expecting that at every step they would receive a withering fire." In the midst of this tense situation, General Worth charged into the water to take command and glory. The assault reached the midpoint of the stream, but the Mexicans still had not attacked. The soldiers expected stiff resistance and were eager for an intense fight, but nothing happened, and "the disappointment of the men was shown from right to left in muttered curses." When Captain C. F. Smith's troops reached the other side, Taylor's forces on the opposite bank cheered and the bands struck up "Yankee Doodle" and "Garry Owen." Smith urged his men to the top of the bank. As they reached the crest, they saw the Mexican cavalry riding away. The ruse of the Mexican dragoons and their bugles was the extent of resistance with which Mejia hoped to stop the American advance. Taylor succinctly reported, the "crossing was then commenced and executed in the order prescribed" without a shot being fired. The anticipated "great battle of Arroyo Colorado was terminated."[33]

Although the Mexican ploy had failed, the advance forces were still vulnerable and General Worth warned the men to be alert for a possible attack. None came and the most serious assault the Army of Occupation had to endure was from the Texas-sized mosquitoes who were proving to be more of an annoyance than Mejia's troops.

While Taylor was pleased with the effortless seizure of the opposite bank and Worth basked in his moment of glory, Captain Smith was outraged. From the camp near the Colorado River, Smith complained that Worth had interfered with his command.

> Having been assigned to the command of the four advanced companies at the passage of the Colorado yesterday (a detached service as expressed in the order of the Commanding General of the Army of Occupation) it seems to me that my right of command should not have been interfered with without reasons of the strongest kind. I think it unquestionable that in case of defeat or disaster the censure would have fallen upon me.
>
> At the instant of crossing the river I was virtually, and at the critical moment, superseded in that command by the Brigadier General commanding the First Brigade personally giving orders for the conduct of the Battalion. I fear I should fail in the respect due to the Brigadier General did I use the language that would best express the feelings I experienced at the moment: Mortification was then as now predominant.
>
> The deliberation of twenty-four hours has brought me to the conclusion that an officer of the Brigadier's reputation as a soldier would not thus have acted without some grave reason; and hence that his action must be regarded as a reflection on my courage, capacity, or conduct, either or all. If such is the case I request that a Court of some kind of Inquiry or otherwise may be asked of the commanding General to pass upon my conduct under the circumstances.[34]

General Worth dismissed the complaint saying that Smith could infer whatever he wanted from the actions. Smith took no further steps and the incident was forgotten.

Taylor resumed the march on the morning of March 23, and the army reached the junction of the roads from Point Isabel and Matamoros the next day. General Taylor divided his forces and sent General Worth towards Matamoros with the light infantry brigades. Taylor took the cavalry and supply train to Point Isabel. Worth led the main body of the army to Palo Alto, ten miles from the Rio Grande, and made camp. After establishing his supply base at Point Isabel, Taylor rejoined the army on March 28 at Palo Alto.

The Army of Occupation continued their advance to the Rio Grande River opposite Matamoros, and the soldiers had their first view of Mexico and their army. Taylor made a great spectacle of his arrival and paraded his troops upstream along the bank of the river with flags flying and bands playing. Taylor established his camp in a plowed cornfield opposite Matamoros.[35]

The opposing forces stared angrily at each other across the Rio Grande. Each side seemed to be challenging the other to battle. The Mexicans would draw first blood.

"American blood on American soil"

Following the arrival of the American forces, the Mexicans started building breastworks and placed a cannon where it could fire on the American camp. In response, Taylor placed an artillery battery in position to fire on General Mejia's headquarters. The Americans constructed an elaborate redoubt for the battery that Taylor named Fort Texas.

The situation along the Rio Grande increased with the Mexicans regarding the U.S. troops as invaders and Taylor defending American rights to be across from Matamoros. The Americans feared that the Mexicans might slip cross the river at night and attack the sleeping Americans. On March 26, the Army of Occupation spent a restless night sleeping with their weapons.[36]

Taylor's biggest problem was from desertion. Opportunistic soldiers swam the river to the Mexican side to escape the rigors of military life. Mexico, with its beautiful senoritas and freedom, was a difficult place to resist. The Mexicans encouraged desertion by appealing to the Irish soldiers as fellow Catholics and offering 320 acres of "good Mexican land" as an added inducement. During the initial period of occupation, over 200 men swam the Rio Grande to pursue what they hoped was a better life. After fourteen men crossed the river one night, Taylor ordered the guards to shoot the deserters. The mass desertions began to decrease after two men were killed.[37]

The Mexicans soon ended the uneasy peace. On April 9 the army was upset when Colonel Truman Cross, Taylor's quartermaster, failed to return from a routine horseback ride. Concern grew when it was learned that a band of guerrillas was seen in the area. On April 11 General Pedro de Ampudia arrived in Matamoros with 3,000 men. Ampudia began plans to attack Taylor's army and sent Taylor an ultimatum threatening war unless the Americans withdrew to the Nueces River within twenty-four hours. As Ampudia prepared to attack, he learned that he was being replaced by General Mariano Arista. On April 15 General Taylor considered the two nations at war by force of Ampudia's ultimatum.

The Americans still had not learned what had happened to the missing Colonel Cross, and Taylor sent Lieutenant David Porter with ten men to investigate. The soldiers were ambushed, and Porter was murdered. Cross' body was found shortly after the attack.[38] Ampudia's ultimatum and the deaths of Cross and Porter escalated the tensions. An uneasy peace prevailed until the morning of April 24, when General Arista sent a force of 1,600 cavalry across the Rio Grande above Matamoros. That evening Taylor sent out a sixty-three-man reconnaissance party, which was attacked by Mexicans. Eleven American soldiers were killed and the rest were wounded or captured. If the other attacks were not enough to provoke Taylor, the latest incident was all he needed.

On April 26 General Taylor notified Washington that hostilities were now "considered as commenced."[39] Taylor's dispatch to President Polk was delivered on May 9. President Polk's message to Congress proclaimed, "American blood has been shed on American soil!"[40] The war of words was over. The battle for manifest destiny had begun.

7. "War at last sure enough!"

"The battle opened on both sides"

On May 11 the House of Representatives approved the declaration of war. The bill was quickly passed by the Senate and signed by President Polk on May 13. When the United States declared war on Mexico, Cadet George McClellan exclaimed, "War at last sure enough! Aint it glorious! 15,000 regulars and 50,000 volunteers." For McClellan and other young Regular army officers, the war offered an opportunity to distinguish themselves and earn a brevet or regular promotion. Even if they did not participate directly in the hostilities, the expansion of the army meant that graduates in the West Point class of 1846 could expect a commission as a second lieutenant without the brevet designation.[1]

Neither side waited for Polk's declaration. The Mexicans sent approximately 4,000 troops across the Rio Grande about thirteen miles below Fort Texas across from Matamoros to cut the Taylor's army off from its supply base at Point Isabel. When Taylor learned about the Mexican activity, he was worried about the security at Point Isabel. He left a small force at Fort Texas and led a forced march to the supply depot.[2]

The wagon train arrived at Point Isabel at noon on May 2, and Taylor's men started loading supplies and improving the defenses. The work was interrupted when the men heard the sounds of cannon fire from the south. Lieutenant Grant, "who had never heard a hostile gun before," said he "felt sorry that I had enlisted."[3] Several days after Taylor arrived; he found out that the Mexicans were bombarding Fort Texas. He decided to finish loading the wagons and strengthening the depot's defenses before returning to Fort Texas. On May 7 the army and supply wagons finally set off to relieve Fort Texas. Taylor expected a battle and warned "the battalions of Infantry that their main dependence must be in the bayonet." The next day Taylor's scouts reported that the Mexican army was drawn up in a mile-long double line on the plain at Palo Alto.[4]

General Arista had taken advantage of Taylor's absence from Fort Texas, moved 4,000 troops across the Rio Grande, and attacked the fort. When Arista learned that Taylor was returning to break the siege, he left around 600 men to maintain the investment and led 3,400 troops north to intercept Taylor near where the Rio Grande had once flowed. The meandering path of the Rio Grande had changed over time and now traveled four or five miles west of its former route. At Resaca de la Palma, The old riverbed was filled in some places creating a number of lakes or ponds. North of this area, tall trees had grown around the banks of the river and had given the area its name, Palo Alto or "Tall Trees." On May 8 General Arista's forces moved into position beyond the edge of the woods that ran along the plain of Palo Alto.[5]

After locating the Mexican Army, Taylor's troops advanced slowly until three o'clock when the opposing armies were about two miles apart. Grant described the forces blocking their passage: "Early in the forenoon of May 8 as Palo Alto was approached, an army, certainly outnumbering our little force, was seen, drawn up in line of battle just in front of the timber. Their bayonets and spearheads glistened in the sunlight formidably. The force was composed largely of cavalry armed with lances."[6]

Taylor formed a line of battle, with artillery placed at intervals along the line, and ordered his troops to advance. The Mexican artillery and infantry opened fire on the Americans.

> At first their shots did not reach us, and the advance was continued. As we got nearer, the cannon balls commenced going through the ranks. They hurt no one, however, during this advance, because they would strike the ground long before they reached our line, and ricocheted through the tall grass so slowly that the men would see them and open ranks and let them pass. When we got to a point where the artillery could be used with effect, a halt was called, and the battle opened on both sides.[7]

The American artillery began to fire on the enemy positions. Shells from the 18-pound gun battery and Major Ringgold's light artillery quickly scattered the cavalry on the enemy's left side. The Mexican cavalry and artillery attacked the American right flank, but the assault was repulsed with the Fifth Infantry "repelling a charge of lancers, and the artillery doing great execution in their flanks." The Third Infantry was sent to help defend the right flank, which was still threatened by the enemy. Another section of artillery, directed by Major Ringgold and supported by Grant's company, fired from a forward position.[8]

The battle evolved into a three-hour artillery duel. The American artillerists used the "Flying Artillery" tactic developed by Ringgold and Anderson. The strategy employed highly mobile, light artillery that fired at the enemy, quickly moved to another location, and fired again. The light artillery was especially effective in repelling Arista's cavalry charges. The American artillery was winning the battle against the heavy and slow Mexican artillery.

During the engagement the prairie grass caught fire and the smoke partially obscured the armies from each other. During the lull in battle, Taylor moved his heavy artillery on the road toward the position initially held by the Mexican guns and placed the Fifth Infantry to the extreme right of the new line. The enemy adjusted their position and the action resumed an hour later after the smoke cleared.

The American artillery fire was destructive and ripped openings in the enemy's ranks. The Fourth Infantry, which supported the 18-pounder battery, was exposed to destructive fire from the Mexican artillery and several men were killed.[9] Grant said: "[O]ne cannonball passed through our ranks, not far from me. It took off the head of an enlisted man, and the under jaw of Captain Page of my regiment, while the splinters from the musket of the killed soldier, and his brains and bones, knocked down two or three others, including one officer, Lieutenant Wallen,—hurting them more or less."[10]

The Mexican batteries concentrated their fire on the 18-pounder battery and Ringgold's guns. Ringgold was hit by a cannon ball and mortally wounded. In the meantime, Taylor ordered another battalion of artillery brought up to support the artillery on the right. The Mexican cavalry attacked this part of the line, but a "well-directed volley ... silenced all further firing from the enemy in this quarter." Taylor reported that it was "nearly dark, and the action was closed on the right of our line—the enemy having been completely driven back from his position, and foiled in every attempt against our line."[11]

Smith experienced his first taste of large-scale combat at Palo Alto watching the damage American artillery fire did on the enemy and avoiding the Mexican cannon balls sweeping through the high grass. Taylor's forces had won the first major encounter between the armies and held the ground previously occupied by the enemy. The victory was a tribute to the operational skills of Smith's fellow officers in the Second Artillery. The Americans suffered fifty-five casualties, including Ringgold whose light artillery tactics were used so successfully in the victory, and Arista's army lost over 600 dead and wounded. Taylor praised his troops: "The conduct of our officers and men was everything that could be desired. Exposed for hours to the severest trial, a cannonade of artillery, our troops displayed a coolness and constancy which gave me, throughout, the assurance of victory."[12]

"The superior quality of our officers and men"

About a half mile south of the Palo Alto battlefield the terrain changed from a flat prairie to a dense maze of chaparral and trees that extended nearly seven miles to the Rio Grande River. The gently rolling landscape was marked by a number of long depressions indicating the former courses of the meandering river. Some of the eroded areas were filled with stagnant water forming pools while the others were dry channels or resacas.[13]

In spite of the defeat at Palo Alto, General Arista sent a dispatch to the minister of war and marine with an "eloquent account of what he claimed as his victory."[14] The next morning, the Mexican general selected a point across the Matamoros road, which would limit the use of the American artillery.

> At this place the road crosses a ravine sixty yards wide and nearly breast high, the bottom being wet, forming long and serpentine ponds through the prairie. Along the banks of this dry river, and more particularly on the side then occupied by the Mexicans, the chaparral grows most densely, and at this time, save where it was broken in by the passage of the road, formed almost a solid wall. The enemy occupied this ravine in double line; one behind and under the front bank, and the other entrenched behind the wall of the chaparral on the top of the rear ridge. A battery was placed in the center of each line on the right and left of the road, and a third battery was on the right of the first line. Six or seven thousand troops were thus strongly fortified in a form resembling a crescent, between the horns of which the army had to pass, while the Mexican batteries were enfilading and cross firing the narrow road which formed the only unobstructed approach to their position.[15]

The Mexicans called the place Resaca de la Guerrero while the Americans named it Resaca de la Palma.

At daybreak on May 9, Taylor's army was ready to renew the battle at Palo Alto. However, scouts reported that the enemy had left the field during the night. Lieutenant Grant described the conditions facing the Americans.

> The chaparral before us was impenetrable except where there were roads or trails, with occasionally clear or bare spots of small dimensions. A body of men penetrating it might easily be ambushed. It was better to have a few men caught in this way than the whole army, yet it was necessary that the garrison at the river should be relieved. To get to them the chaparral had to be passed. Thus I assume General Taylor reasoned. He halted the army not far in advance of the ground occupied by the Mexicans the day before, and selected Captain C. F. Smith, of the artillery, and Captain McCall, of my company, to take one hundred and fifty picked men each and find where the enemy had gone.[16]

Captain George McCall of the Fourth Infantry was in command of the 220-man "advance" with orders "to follow and observe the movements of the enemy on the route to Matamoras [sic]." Smith's light battalion consisted of Company K of the Second Artillery Regiment under Brevet 2nd Lieutenant H. F. Clarke, Company I of the Fourth Artillery

7. "War at last sure enough!" 57

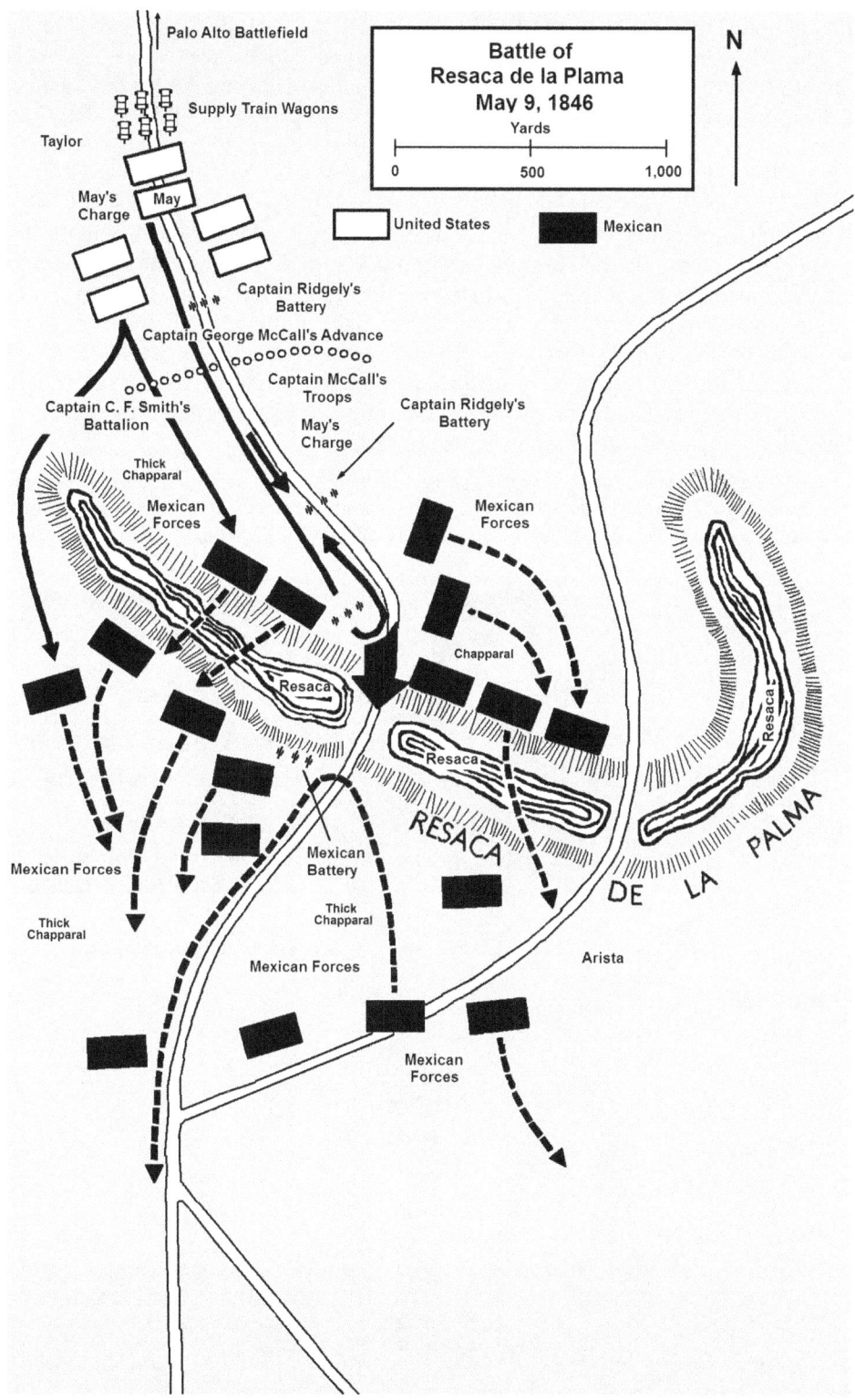

Battle of Resaca de la Palma (author's drawing based on numerous sources).

Regiment under 1st Lieutenant J.C. Pemberton, Company A of the Eighth Artillery Regiment under 1st Lieutenant A. T. Lee and 2nd Lieutenant J. Longstreet, and F Company of the Eighth Artillery Regiment under 2nd Lieutenant J. Beardsley and Brevet 2nd Lieutenant T. T. Montgomery. McCall's troops were composed of Captain Sam Walker's detachment of Texas Rangers, Lieutenant Alfred Pleasanton with the Second Dragoons, and Captain Randolph Ridgely in charge of Ringgold's artillery battery.

McCall sent Walker's mounted Rangers south on the Matamoros Road. Walker reported that the way was clear and the rest of the column advanced on the road. When the head of the column reached the open ground at Resaca de la Palma, they received three rounds of canister shot from a hidden battery, which forced the men to take cover.

Captain Smith's detachment advanced to the right of the road to attack the flank of what McCall believed was the rear-guard of the retreating Mexican Army. Captain McCall's detachment of artillery and infantry advanced on the left. Smith moved his battalion forward into the chaparral about fifty yards on the right side of the Matamoros road.[17]

Smith described the attack in his report to McCall.

> Agreeably to your desire to-day I have the honor to report, that, pursuant to your orders on the 9th instant my command (consisting of the 4 light comps. [companies] of the Brigade) advanced on the right of the road, flanking our Artillery, and about 80 yards from it. The moment the fire

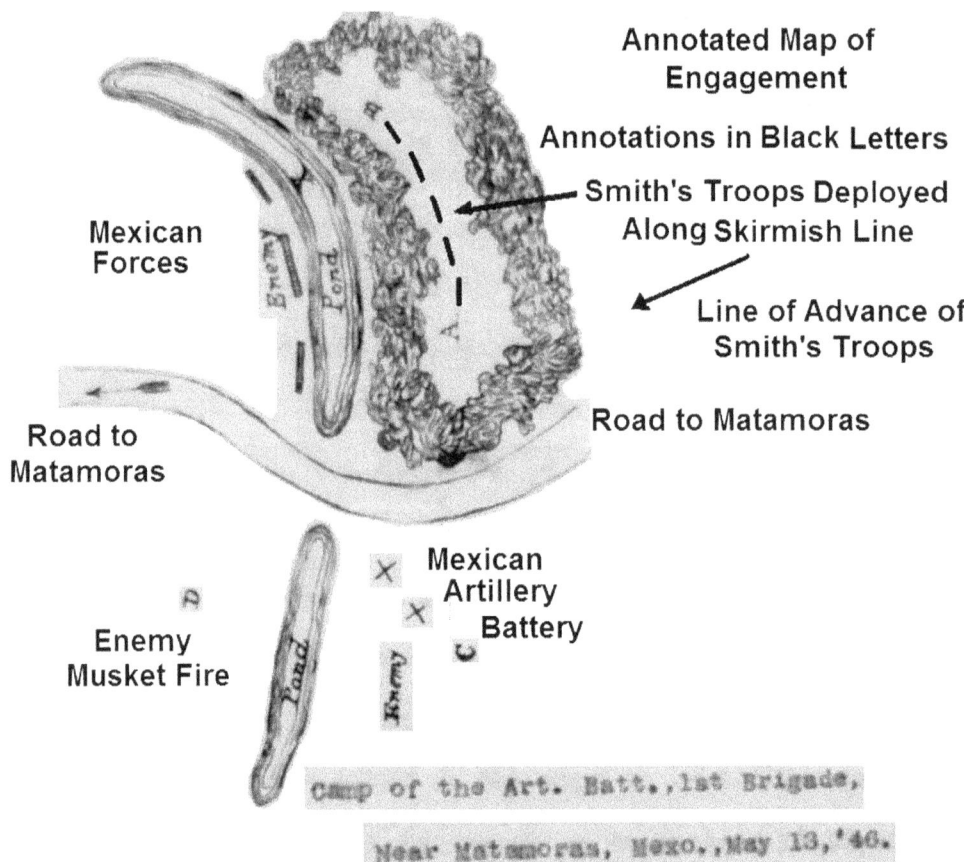

Map from Smith's Report to McCall (courtesy C. F. Smith Collection at U.S. Military Academy Library, Special Collections).

of the enemy was heard, I hastened the Battalion, marching it by the right flank, in the direction of the pond x until stopped by the thick chappuall [sic]; when it was faced to the front and advanced in the direction of the enemy's battery C. It being impossible to get through the chapperall advancing in line of battle I ordered an advance by the heads of comps. and to have the line reformed as soon as we could get through—a matter that seemed difficult if not impossible. We had advanced but a few paces when a discharge of musketry was given by the enemy towards the Battery and from our right to rear. This rendered a corresponding change on my part necessary. Accordingly I ordered the Battalion to deploy as skirmishers facing the pond (from A towards B) and to advance through the Chapperall as far as possible. The moment this deployment was attempted a heavy and well sustained fire of musketry was opened upon us from the opposite edge of the pond, and kept up until the enemy retired. The chapperall was too dense for the men to charge through; but they maintained a steady fire, and with considerable effect until a short time before the close of the section; when, my own observation confirming the report of the officers and men that a severe cross-fire of musketry, which had been opened upon us from the left (D), came from our friends I withdrew the battalion about 200 yards, an[d] then moved up the road to report for orders. Genl. Taylor (by his Adjt. Genl.) directed me to sustain Lt. Duncan's battery, just about to pursue the enemy, which I did until it halted here.[18]

The light battalion lost four men killed and nine men wounded. Smith reported, "The behavior of the company officers and men was all that could be desired," and commended Captain J. B. Scott for his assistance as an acting field officer.[19]

While Smith probed the right side of the Mexican defenses, McCall's men entered the chaparral on the left, with orders "to bring on the action, and then flank the enemy." After moving forward about 300 yards, they engaged the enemy's infantry. The Mexican Army was in a well-defended position in the ravine on the near side of the pond and was supported by another line across the resaca. McCall's men faced musket fire from both lines and canister rounds from two field pieces located at the rear of the Mexican center. The Americans advanced and drove the Mexican defenders towards the road. As McCall's troops pursued the enemy across the Matamoros Road, the Americans were exposed to fire from their own battery, which forced them to abandon their attack and withdraw to their former position.[20]

About three o'clock, Taylor learned that the enemy had placed an artillery battery on the Matamoros Road. He called up his remaining force of 1,400–1,500 men from camp. McCall told Taylor that the enemy was "in force in our front occupying a ravine which intersects the road, and is skirted by thickets of dense chapparal." The enemy had at "least eight pieces of artillery" which "maintained an incessant fire upon our advance." Taylor sent Captain Ridgely's battery on the road and deployed McCall's and Smith's units as skirmishers to cover the battery and engage the Mexican infantry.

The Americans had difficulty advancing under heavy fire through the dense chaparral. The units became disorganized and fragmented, and the attack dispersed into a series of uncoordinated actions by groups of soldiers. Ridgely's artillery was harassed by Mexican cavalry and artillery fire as they moved on the road. The Americans gradually pushed the Mexican skirmishers back to the resaca until they were stopped by enemy artillery. The enemy battery was eventually captured which forced the Mexicans to abandon their positions on the east side of the road. American forces west of the road discovered a trail around the left of the Mexican position. Although Arista sent reinforcements to defend the path, the Americans crossed the resaca, captured the gun emplacement on the Mexican left, and repulsed enemy counterattacks. The attack turned the Mexican flank and, combined with the loss of the positions on the east side, panicked the Mexican Army.

The troops ran from the field in disorder leaving behind "baggage of every description." The Battle of Resaca de la Palma now degenerated into a rout and the Mexicans ran to the

Rio Grande River. The American troops not engaged on the sides of the road pursued the Mexicans and captured many prisoners. Taylor said the "victory has been decisive." He boasted that his small force had overcome immense odds against "veteran regiments, perfectly equipped and appointed" representing "the best troops that Mexico can furnish." He attributed the victory to "the superior quality of our officers and men."[21] Captain Smith's performances at Arroyo Colorado and now at Resaca de la Palm established him as a skilled and gallant officer among his peers and superiors in Taylor's army. He was rewarded for his efforts with a brevet promotion to major for "gallant and distinguished conduct" in the battles of Palo Alto and Resaca de la Palma.[22]

The American public was thrilled by "the glorious and spirit stirring news of the victory of the 7th and 8th." The people were enthusiastic in their praises for "our gallant little army." M. H. Deltast, an officer of the Second Regiment stationed in New Jersey, asked Smith to "tell all friends around you, particularly of our regiment, which did nobly, that we salute you all, officers and privates, with our best love and admiration." His only concern was "that you will so whip the Dons, as not to leave any thing for us to do." Deltast reported that Charles' wife and child were both well and were visiting friends in Baltimore. He praised the regiment's officers and teased: "consideration for your modesty, only restrains me from saying a great deal of Captain Smith."

> I can well picture to myself, the gallant soldiery, pressing down upon the enemy at "every port"—and then as they approached with a rapid step leveling the bayonet and dashing upon, and [illegible] all before them—the enemy's artillery is carried, his line broken, and the shout of the men proclaim that 1600 are victorious over 6000. Thank God! for that—and again the whole nation is indebted to you.[23]

Lieutenant Grant was equally impressed by the quality of Taylor's army.

> The men engaged in the Mexican war were brave, and the officers of the regular army, from highest to lowest, were educated in their profession. A more efficient army for its number and armament, I do not believe ever fought a battle than the one commanded by General Taylor in his first two engagements on Mexican—or Texan soil.[24]

"No lack of generals"

After Resaca de la Palma, Zachary Taylor's army returned to its camp at Fort Texas and "Old Rough and Ready" considered his next move. When General Taylor heard rumors that the Mexicans were gathering troops in Matamoros, he crossed the Rio Grande, captured the town of Barita on May 17, and established a base for the Army of Occupation in Mexico. Several days later, the Mexican forces evacuated Matamoros and Taylor ferried the rest of his army across the river and established a camp just outside the town.[25]

While the American Army was winning battles in Texas, officials in Washington were working to increase the size of the army by recruiting volunteer units. Although Taylor requested Secretary of War Marcy to send only eight volunteer regiments or 5,000 men, Washington wanted to raise an army of 20,000. Based on his experience with the Texas and Louisiana volunteers, Taylor realized that these new regiments would overwhelm his army with untrained and undisciplined officers and soldiers.[26]

The Polk administration believed that volunteers would be needed to supplement the Regular Army in order to defeat Mexico. Congress approved recruiting quotas for each state, and the new soldiers were sent to New Orleans and then either overland or by sea to the mouth of the Rio Grande. The officers were chosen by an election among the men and had the same status as their Regular Army counterparts.

Meanwhile, Smith waited at Matamoros with the Regular Army units. His time was spent on administrative duties—monthly reports, promotions, discharges, and clothing requests. Grant described their stay in the Mexican town across the Rio Grande from the newly named Fort Brown.

> The time was whiled away pleasantly enough at Matamoras [sic], while we were waiting for volunteers. It is probable that the most important people of the territory occupied by our army left their homes before we got there, but with those remaining the best of relations apparently existed. It was the policy of the Commanding General to allow no pillaging, no taking of private property for public or individual use without satisfactory compensation, so that a better market was afforded than the people had ever known before.[27]

In May, the first volunteers arrived at Point Isabel and were lodged in overcrowded tent cities. The volunteers were unruly and immediately began to steal and vandalize property. Their bad behavior continued when they reached Matamoros.[28] General Taylor reported that many of the volunteers "have committed extensive depradation and outrages upon the peaceful inhabitants.... Were it possible to rouse the Mexican people to resistance, no more effectual plan could be devised than the one pursued by some of our volunteer regiments."[29] An article in the *Niles Register* explained the disruptive behavior: "The graceless and lawless spirits, being the most difficult to control, join the ranks and carry with them their lawless propensities."[30] The Texans were the worst of the volunteers.[31] Many of these men had been fighting the Mexicans since 1836. When they joined Taylor's army, they "brought their old sets of enemies with them" and ruthless rules of engagement that took few prisoners. Their "contempt for all things Mexican" conflicted with Taylor's efforts to promote friendly relations with the Mexican civilians.[32]

Crowded camps promoted the spread of disease, causing outbreaks to reach epidemic proportions in some regiments. Influenza, smallpox, and measles wreaked havoc among the army's ranks.[33] Inadequate sanitation, limited medical supplies, and lack of knowledge added to the unhealthy conditions. One professional soldier concluded that a third of the volunteers were sick and the remaining two thirds "not worth a straw."[34]

In addition to their lack of discipline, the army reflected the prejudices of the society from which it is drawn. Protestant volunteers brought their bigotry and disrespect for people of other faiths, especially Roman Catholics and Mormons. This caused problems with the Mexican Catholic Church and the Catholic enlisted men in the Regular Army.[35] United States Catholic soldiers acted respectfully toward the church and clergy and regularly attended mass. Others, especially some of the Texas volunteers, desecrated and burned church property and harassed religious processions and ceremonies.[36] The disrespect of the national religion angered citizens and intensified opposition to the American invaders. Washington officials were concerned that the Mexican government might turn the conflict into a holy war and initiated a program to repair damages done by the volunteers. President Polk recruited the American Catholic church to send priests to Mexico to serve as civilian chaplains. Government officials prepared a proclamation for Taylor which promised the Mexicans: "Your religion, your altars, and churches, the property of your churches and citizens, the emblems of your faith and its ministers, shall be protected and remain inviolate."[37] The volunteers' behavior made a lasting impression on the Regular Army officers. They concluded that the men were undisciplined soldiers who could not be relied upon to engage the enemy in battle or maintain peaceful relations with civilians.

After the first contingent of volunteer officers arrived, Taylor commented that there would be no shortage of generals and instead wished that there had not been so many.[38] The presence of the politically appointed "immediate commanders" was discouraging to the professional military officers whose upward progression was painfully slow. It infuriated the Regulars that they had "to salute a group of well-connected, undisciplined civilians who didn't know rank and file from a fighting square and who had never heard a shot fired in anger."[39] Career army officers became disenchanted with a military that rewarded political connections and seniority rather than ability. The situation was so unsettling that many young officers resigned their commissions after the war to pursue more lucrative civilian opportunities.

8. "The brilliant *coup de main*"

"How enviable has been your lot"

After fighting broke out, William Worth decided to rescind his resignation and rejoin Taylor's army.[1] Companies A, C, G and K of the Second Artillery were assigned to Worth's Second Division which placed Captain Smith again under the command of his former Commandant of Cadets.[2]

In May, Charles wrote his brother-in-law, William Mactier, under the heading "Reporting for Peace from Mex." Although General Scott thought that U.S. troops would be out of Mexico in three months, Charles had "no faith" in that prediction and believed the entire country would have to be occupied.[3]

In the midst of the buildup of forces in Matamoros, Smith took the time to send a letter to the Adjutant of the Second Regiment Artillery at Fort Columbus.

> It has frequently occurred to me that any change in the dress clothing of our soldiers that ought to appeal to their pride, wld [would] have a happy effect; especially such a change as wld, at a glance, enable the non-comd [commissioned] officers to be distinguished from the private soldiers.
>
> Such a change has been adopted in the 3rd Regt. of Inf.—by what authority I do not know; and involves the U.S. in no expense. It consists simply in a chevron on each arm above the elbow, made of white cotton binding, similar to the trimming on the collar of the jacket, but wider, say ½ inch in width. The mode of distinguishing ranks is similar to that used by the Corps of Cadets. On the next sheet I have represented the chevrons used by the 3d Inf.
>
> In the 3d Inf. they have dispensed with the Service Chevron; which I think objectionable; nor does the chevron above the elbow, designating rank, prevent it being worn.
>
> I would suggest that the service chevron be simply a bar (on each arm) for each 5 yrs. of service, worn below the elbow, & crossing the arm diagonally from the bend of the elbow outward; when 2 or more bars are worn the space between them to be equal to the width of the bar or ½ of the width…
>
> Shld [Should] the above suggestion or something similar, having the same object, in view, merit the approval of Col. Bankhead, I hope he will endeavor to procure the Sanction of the War Dept. for its adoption by our regt. if not for the army generally.[4]

In June, Charles received a teasing letter from Major John L. Smith. "How enviable has been your lot since you left us!" John praised Charles' efforts which made "the crossing of the Colorado a mere break a light affair which some of your neighbors were on the tip toes of solitude for the resulting each necessary step." John added, "But all that way nothing in comparison with the luck of being in those two battles [on May] 8 & 9 and the further luck (secondary) of escaping without injury and especially as you must have been greatly exposed if the reports that have come to us be true that you were in command of a battalion of light infantry which was further back still. These Smiths after all are not much very unlucky fellows."[5]

General Taylor formulated plans to attack Monterrey. He decided to transport the army by steamboat up the Rio Grande River and establish a depot at Camargo, Mexico. From the supply base, the army would advance to Monterrey.[6] The Army of Occupation's move to Camargo began on July 6. General Worth's command, including Grant's Fifth Infantry and Smith's Second Artillery regiments left Matamoros later that month.[7] Smith arrived at Camargo around July 29[8] and Taylor and his staff reached the depot in early August. Colonel Ethan Allen Hitchcock described the village as "one of the most miserable places I ever saw, dirty and dilapidated." The place was breeding grounds for diseases, and the soldiers suffered and died from dysentery, pneumonia, yellow fever, and malaria.[9] The conditions at Camargo resulted in the deaths of approximately 1,500 men.[10] The situation forced Taylor to establish a new supply depot at Cerralvo. General Worth's division was ordered to lead the advance to Cerralvo. Colonel Smith was assigned the duty of protecting the wagon train of provisions that accompanied the division. A company of dragoons was assigned to Smith "to accompany his march, guard the wagon train to Cerralvo, and return with it to head-quarters."[11] General Worth's Second Division left Camargo on August 19 and completed its difficult sixty-mile march to the picturesque town on August 25. The rest of the army arrived on September 13 bringing Taylor's force to 6,640 officers and men.

While Taylor's army moved closer to Monterrey, there was a change in the Mexican political landscape. With the help of the Polk administration, Antonio López de Santa Anna had returned to Mexico from exile in Cuba. The former Mexican leader had gained favor in Washington by promising to arrange a negotiated settlement to the war.[12] Following the previous military setbacks, the people were ready to allow Santa Anna to take command of the army and dedicate himself "to the defence [sic] of the liberty and independence of the Republic."[13] He quickly abandoned ideas of a negotiated peace in which "territorial concessions would be granted in exchange for Yankee dollars." Santa Anna had changed from a "negotiator" to a "savior," who was committed to driving the gringos out of Mexico.[14]

William J. Worth (Library of Congress).

Initial reports indicated that Santa Anna, now in charge of the Mexican Army, intended to withdraw troops from Monterrey and abandon the city. In spite of Santa Anna's orders to move the garrison to Saltillo, General Ampudia and General Mejia refused to give up Monterrey to Taylor without a fight. General Ampudia reinforced the garrison with three brigades when he assumed command at the end of August. Mejia had constructed new breastworks on Federation and Independence hills and fortified the ruined Bishop's Palace. The generals believed that it would be dishonorable and shortsighted to surrender the city.[15] Therefore, the generals determined to stop the American invasion at the gates of Monterrey.

On September 11 Taylor ordered the resumption of the march to Monterrey.[16] Worth's division woke early September 14

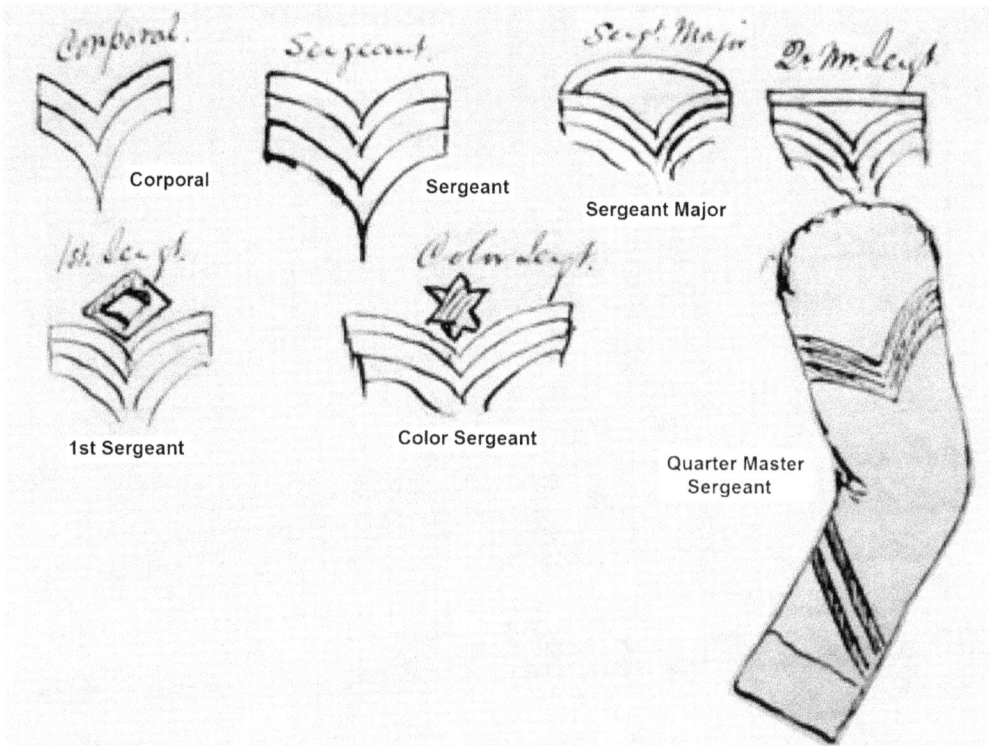

Diagram of shoulder patches (courtesy C. F. Smith Collection at U.S. Military Academy Library, Special Collections).

and marched 10½ miles before bivouacking next to a beautiful stream. The next day the division advanced two miles to Papagalia, a "miserable ranch of ½ dozen houses from which the people had been driven."[17] Two days later, Smith's company was assigned to the rear guard as the division marched thirteen miles and made camp two miles beyond the deserted town of Marin. Smith said the nearby mountains were high and "the sunset grand."[18] The American forces rested at Marin to allow the army to gather and advance together.[19] The evening of September 17 Charles sent a four-page letter to Francis while admiring another beautiful sunset. The column left Marin on September 18 and traveled nine miles to a small ranch at San Francisco. The next day the army awoke at four o'clock and was on the march by seven o'clock. Shortly after nine o'clock, Taylor's advance units were fired on by Mexican skirmishers. An hour later, the batteries in Monterrey shelled Taylor and his staff. The column proceeded seven miles and stopped within 2½ miles of Monterey. Smith's company spent the night in the rain with "no coat; no fires" as guards in front of the artillery battalion.[20]

"Mucho fandango at Monterrey"

The city of Monterrey was an absolute fortress. Its stone buildings with flat-topped roofs were connected by straight streets that turned each house into a strong defensive position.[21] On the west side of the city, rugged Independence Hill on the north and Federation Hill on the south overlooked the road to Saltillo. There were fortifications on both

Storming of Palace Hill at the Battle of Monterrey (Library of Congress, LC-DIG-ds-05570).

hills that protected the road. The Bishop's Place was located on the portion of Independence Hill that sloped toward the city. The building was rebuilt as a fort and reinforced by a redoubt. On Federation Hill, which was half as tall as the 1,800-foot Independence, the Mexicans had placed a redoubt to the west and Fort Soldado to the east. The Santa Catarina River provided a natural barrier on the south and east. The Federation Hill works guarded the river and the road.[22]

The east side of Monterrey was protected by two forts, the Teneria or Tannery and Fort Diablo or Devil's Fort. The massive Citadel fortification controlled the northern approaches to the city. The bastion had thirty-foot-high walls and was enclosed by a quadrangle earthwork. The Citadel had eight guns, which could reach most places north and east of the city, and a 400-troop garrison. The Citadel had a dark, menacing look and the Americans named it the Black Fort.[23]

Although the defenses were formidable, they were too far apart to support each other. General Ampudia did not designate a mobile reserve to reinforce a position that was under heavy attack. Taylor recognized this vulnerability and decided to take the city by capturing its defenses one at time.[24]

Taylor believed that control of the Bishop's Palace on Independence Hill was the key to taking Monterrey. His engineers found a route north of the city out of range of the Black Fort's guns. The general decided to send the Worth's division around the north side of the city and attack Independence Hill from the southwest while the rest of the army demonstrated and probed the eastern defenses.[25]

At one o'clock on September 20, the Second Division left camp to perform the required turning movement. The force consisted of Lieutenant Colonel Thomas Staniford's First Brigade and Colonel Persifor F. Smith's Second Brigade. Captain Smith's company was with

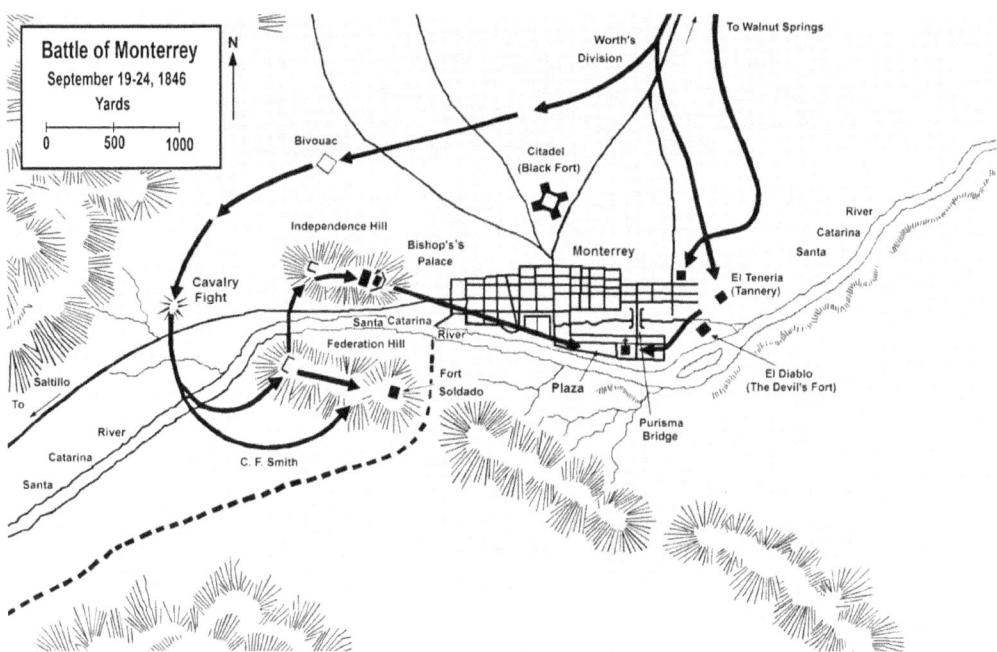

Battle of Monterrey (author's drawing based on numerous sources).

the First Brigade that included the Eighth Infantry, Colonel Thomas Child's dismounted artillery battalion, and Lieutenant Colonel Duncan's battery. Colonel Persifor Smith's Second Brigade was composed of the Fifth and Seventh Infantries, Colonel Albert G. Blanchard's Louisiana Volunteer Company, and Captain William Mackall's artillery battery. Colonel Jack Hay's regiment of Texas Rangers led the division as it marched from camp in a "thoroughly military and soldier-like" fashion. Unfortunately, Ampudia detected Worth's movements and rushed reinforcements to Independence Hill. It took most of the afternoon for Worth's forces to reach a position north of Independence Hill where they bivouacked for the night.[26]

At sunrise, the division continued its march southwest toward the Saltillo Road. Worth sent Captain Smith's Company K and Major John Scott's Company J ahead with Colonel Hay's Rangers in the lead as skirmishers. Around 8:30 a.m., the advance party had almost reached the road when they were attacked by about 200 Mexican cavalry and a brigade of infantry. The assault was "handsomely repelled" by the Rangers and Smith's and Scott's light artillerymen.[27] The fight was over in about twenty minutes with a few American casualties and around 100 Mexican casualties. The skirmishers "pressed on handsomely" and, as they approached the crest, they saw "quite a large force of cavalry" in full retreat towards their redoubt. Smith said his men "behaved with their accustomed gallantry" during the advance. The troops spent the next one to two hours "scouring the fields in front in search of enemy."[28] The action had opened the road to Saltillo.[29] Worth had accomplished part of his assignment, "to turn the hill of the Bishop's Palace" and "to occupy a position on the Saltillo Road."[30]

Around 11:00 a.m., Worth ordered Smith "to storm the battery of two guns on the hill which was worrying his command very much." After Smith captured the guns, he was instructed to move down the spine of the hill and attack Fort Soldado. The *New Orleans Daily Picayune* reported:

> This gallant officer (Smith) cheerfully undertook and was followed with enthusiasm by the officers and men of his command. It was considered on all sides to be a most dangerous undertaking, and this party was considered most emphatically a forlorn hope.[31] The distance to be climbed after reaching the foot of the hill was about a quarter of a mile; a part of the way was almost perpendicular and through thorn bushes and over sharp pointed rocks and loose sliding stones.[32]

General Worth placed a 400-man force under Smith to take the battery. The troops consisted of four companies of light artillery from the Second, Third, and Fourth Regiments, and five companies of Texas Rangers.

Smith's troops had to cross the Santa Catarina River and move along its south bank to reach Federation Hill. It was difficult to find places to ford the river, and Smith was forced to move upstream under the cover of some cornfields before he located a suitable place to cross. Unfortunately, the movements were observed by the batteries on top of the hill. As his men entered the swift, cold river, the enemy guns erupted in a "terrific storm of shot and grape." The men waded through the deep water and hail of bullets and arrived safely on the opposite bank.[33]

Smith hurried his men along the south bank through the hail of ineffectual fire from the hill. They advanced a short distance and found cover in the thickets. "This command crossed the plain to the base of the hill under a very annoying fire of Musketry, & of round shot & canister from the battery; and from musketry in ascending the hill."[34]

While the men rested, Smith went to find the best route to the top.

> Pushing on then, after pausing for breath under the cover of thickets, they came at length to a low eminence, and concealed themselves behind a hedge while the captain reconnoitered. The main hill, which appeared to be nearly four hundred feet high, was rough, steep and covered with chaparral. The garrison seemed to be strong and resolute. The two guns made heavy odds. For quite a while Smith studied the hard problem, doubting whether it was practicable to assault the position, but finally he ordered the men forward; and soon lines of dark blue Mexican skirmishers, descending from the redoubt stationed themselves at favorable points to meet him.[35]

During Smith's reconnaissance, General Worth noticed that additional Mexican infantry had arrived on the hill. He was out of contact with Smith and decided to send Colonel Dixon S. Miles with Jack Hays' Texas Cavalry to support Smith. Miles found a shorter route to the base of the hill and arrived before Smith had returned. After sending Miles' troops, Worth ordered Persifor Smith's Second Brigade to join the attack.[36]

Then C. F. Smith led the charge and his men climbed over the walls and into the redoubt. They drove the enemy from the works "like chaff before a whirl wind."[37] The Texans joined the attack and the remaining Mexicans were quickly subdued. After the battery was taken, Smith ordered Lieutenant George Deas to turn a captured gun and fire on Fort Soldado. Smith summarized the action: "The height was gained, the battery carried, and the enemy was driven off."[38] Lieutenant Edmund Hamilton described the action.

> We saw firing from the hill and the Mexicans advancing down it. From this we thought our men were being repulsed and another regiment was sent forward. The enemy kept firing for half an hour without a gun being fired by our own men. Eventually we saw the firing commencing by our troops and the Mexicans running up the hill. We then raised such a shout as I have hardly ever heard. In a few minutes Captain Smith was on the top. He had followed them so fast that they had not had time to carry off one of their guns. This gun was immediately captured and turned on them.[39]

While Smith's and Mile's men seized the redoubt, Colonel Persifor Smith's troops began advancing on Fort Soldado. Deas and several men moved the gun into position, and part of Smith's command advanced toward the fort. The gun crew made "a capital shot" that knocked the enemy's gun "out of position" and forced their cannoneers and riflemen to retreat. The shot "doubtless aided in some degree the splendid" attack made by Persifor Smith's Second Brigade. After the fort's gun was destroyed, Smith ordered his men to charge. Smith's and Hays' troops raced ahead to see who would be the first to reach the works. The Mexicans abandoned the fort and fled into the city. The fort was carried "in beautiful style" after about thirty minutes of artillery and musketry fire from Smith's force and Colonel P. Smith's Fifth & Seventh Infantry Regiments.[40] Worth's men held Federation Hill and the American flag flew over Fort Soldado. Captain Smith's men returned to the redoubt where they spent the night in the rain without food or fires.[41]

Smith praised "all under my command for their soldierly conduct throughout this affair."[42] Meanwhile, the *New Orleans Daily Picayune* applauded Smith for leading "the brilliant *coup de main* made almost without bloodshed."[43] A month after the battle, Captain John Grayson of the Second Artillery wrote, "I am rejoiced to see that you are spoken of in terms of admiration for gallant conduct in the late campaign and that you have placed yourself aside of those who had the happiness to distinguish themselves. You have been successful and your success will give greater pleasure to yourself and your wife in meeting."[44]

The following morning, General Worth complimented Smith on the previous day's work.[45] Smith was later awarded his second brevet promotion to lieutenant colonel for "gallant conduct in the several conflicts at Monterey."[46] Other units from Worth's command attacked the Mexican positions on Independence Hill and captured the Bishop's Palace. By the afternoon, the Americans controlled the western defenses of Monterrey, and Worth's forces prepared to descend the slopes into the city.

At one o'clock September 23, Worth sent the Second Division into town. Smith led Company K and Lieutenant Stewart Van Vliet's command during the assault. Rather than moving through the well-defended streets, Worth's forces advanced through the houses by cutting passageways from one to another. They reached the market plaza and prepared to bring up artillery. The fighting in the square continued the rest of the afternoon and into the night.[47]

The fighting began again on the morning of the 24th but stopped at eight o'clock under a Mexican flag of truce. General Ampudia asked for terms and meetings were held that afternoon between the commanding generals. While Smith's command remained in the captured house, he "wrote a hasty lead pencil note to Fanny ... to apprise her of my safety."[48]

On September 25 the Mexican and American troops passed each other as the victor entered the city and the vanquished left. Lieutenant Grant said he was filled with pity "by the sight of the Mexican garrison of Monterrey marching out of town as prisoners, and no doubt the same feeling was experienced by most of our army who witnessed it."[49] Smith paused to remember a more significant event: "My daughter's birthday—2 years old! God bless her."[50]

Taylor appointed Worth as governor of Monterrey and his division occupied the city.[51] The army settled into a "quiet camp life" until midwinter. The educated and wealthy people abandoned their homes and left the city. The remaining residents conducted business and fraternized with the "Yankees." Merchants enjoyed favorable terms trading with the Americans, and Taylor made sure that citizens and their property were thoroughly protected.[52]

Despite his gallantry and successes in the campaign, Smith was still only a captain. Robert Anderson complained about the injustice in a letter to his wife.

> Look at the case of my friend, Charles F. Smith. He has been foremost in every battle in which he has been engaged, and he has been in all save Genl. Taylor's last, and he has not even received the notice of an empty brevet. A man known and admired by all the Army for his well-tried

courage, his cool self-possession in danger, and his high military attainments, and over this man's head are placed a score of men whose sole recommendation is that they or their friends have proved faithful in their worship of the President's party. Enough. enough.[53]

Rather than worry about such matters, Smith focused on being the best possible soldier. "His life was that of a true soldier. The honor of his country and his profession were the objects of his devotion. The arts of money-getting and creation of court favor or influence were unknown to him, or if known, were only despised."[54] General Worth recognized Smith's contributions and recommended him for "consideration by the general-in-chief and government" for a brevet promotion.[55]

9. "A political war"

"My proposed theatre is different"

As Grant described it, "The Mexican War was a political war, and the administration conducting it desired to make party capital out of it."[1] President Polk's Democratic regime faced the difficult balancing act of winning the war while neutralizing the political positions of the Whig generals Scott and Taylor. Taylor's victories had made him the leading presidential candidate. To reduce Taylor's popularity, the administration decided to send General Scott to Mexico to replace Taylor, end the northern campaign, and implement a new strategy.

Scott was opposed to the conquest of Mexico by way of the Rio Grande, Matamoros, and Saltillo. In spring 1846 Scott proposed a plan to land the army at Veracruz, march west, and capture the Mexican capital. The administration hoped "Scott's ambition would lead him to slaughter Taylor or destroy his chances for the Presidency."[2] After Scott was placed in command of forces in Mexico, he informed Taylor.

> I am not coming, my dear general, to supersede you in the immediate command on the line of operations rendered illustrious by you and your gallant army. My proposed theatre is different.... But, my dear general, I shall be obliged to take from most of the gallant officers and men (*regulars and volunteers) whom you have so long and nobly commanded.... But I rely upon your patriotism to submit to the temporary sacrifice with cheerfulness. No man can better afford to do so...[3]

The rank-and-file of the Army of Occupation were unaware of these political machinations and spent the rest of the fall engaged in routine camp duty. Smith conscientiously filled out his reports and drilled his troops that were garrisoned in the same house that they had occupied when advancing on the plaza in Monterrey. The confident officers predicted that the war would end soon because the Mexicans had enough of the fighting.

On November 9 Taylor sent General Worth's command to Saltillo. The seventy-mile journey transported them from a tropical to a temperate climate and from citrus groves to cornfields and cattle.[4] When General Santa Anna heard that Taylor was moving most of his army to Victoria, the Mexican general decided to attack Worth's force at Saltillo. In response to the threat, Taylor ordered all the units in northern Mexico to converge on Saltillo. When Santa Anna learned about Taylor's moves, the Mexican general decided to postpone his northern campaign until his forces were better prepared.[5]

An unpleasant, yet necessary, aspect of Smith's duties was corresponding with the families of soldiers in his command who died while in service. Private James Cashman's uncle requested the soldier's effects. Although Cashman left no effects, Smith said his heirs were due $78. Smith told the family how to collect the sum. He was pleased "to state that your late nephew's conduct whilst under my command was exemplary."[6]

The new year arrived without much fanfare, marked only by Smith's routine monthly reports to Second Artillery Regiment headquarters at Fort Columbus. Later that month, he communicated with Mrs. Ellen McGwin about her husband. He informed her that the man had deserted from the company near Matamoros around April 8, 1846. Smith noted, "As a deserter he, of course, forfeits all pay & allowances from that date." He reported that Lieutenant Deas had seen her husband around 100 miles from Matamoros in April or May. Smith closed by advising, "You had better turn your attention to getting your living without reference to your husband. I feel sorrow that his bad conduct should have placed you in this unpleasant situation."[7]

After he arrived in Mexico, Scott moved quickly to strip Taylor's command and prohibit his forces from conducting new campaigns. Scott's army was composed of three divisions: First Regular Division under General Worth, Second Regular Division lead by General David Twiggs, and Third Volunteer Division commanded by General Robert Patterson.[8] As part of this reorganization, Grant's Fourth Infantry Regiment was placed under General Worth.[9] Scott began to move these troops from northern Mexico to the mouth of the Rio Grande to prepare for his invasion of the Mexican heartland. The Second Artillery Regiment was re-formed for the assault on Veracruz. The regiment's companies in Mexico were moved to the Gulf Coast and the rest of the regiment was transported from New York to Mexico.[10]

On January 8 General Scott issued General Orders No. 170 that declared that Brevet Lieutenant Colonel Smith of the Second Artillery and two other officers would be "assigned to duty according to their brevet rank."[11] Less than two weeks later, Smith was with Worth's command on board the steamer *Whiteville* on the Rio Grande River en route to the American camp at Palo Alto, Texas.[12] He remained at camp "upon the sand-beach in the neighborhood of the mouth of the Rio Grande for several weeks" waiting for transportation to the new theater of operations.[13] Finally in late February, Smith boarded the steamship *Massachusetts* for the voyage to Veracruz. The "passage was a tedious one" and "many of the troops were shipboard over thirty days." The uncomfortable accommodations and tropical climate made it a difficult journey for Scott's new army. The *Massachusetts* arrived near Lobos, Mexico around March 1,[14] and by March 7 Scott's Army of Invasion was ready to attempt the largest amphibious landing in American military history.

"The flag floats triumphantly"

Veracruz was surrounded by massive walls that "extended from the water's edge south of the town to water again on the north." The Mexicans had "fortifications at intervals along the line and at the angles." The fortress San Juan de Ulloa, "an enclosed fortification of large dimensions and great strength for that period," was located in front of the city on an island half a mile out in the Gulf of Mexico.[15] After a reconnaissance by Scott, he selected the beach near the island of Sacrificos, three miles south of Vera Cruz, for the landing. General Worth's First Division was chosen to make the initial landing on March 9, and, in mid-afternoon, the division was rowed ashore.[16] Just before the main force reached the beach a gig boat[17] with General Worth aboard raced ahead. Worth jumped out into shoulder deep water and waded ashore to be the first man on Collado Beach.[18] The rest of his division followed him onto the sand, and Worth had the satisfaction of forming his command on the beach and neighboring heights just before sunset. The rest of Scott's army came ashore that day without being challenged by the Mexican Army.[19]

Because of the rough seas and high waves, it took several days to land the army's equipment, provisions, and ammunition. As Lieutenant Grant recalled, "The Mexicans were very kind to us, however, and threw no obstacles in the way of our landing except an occasional shot from their nearest fort."[20] The Army of Invasion marched northward from Collado Beach to invest the city. General Twiggs' forces moved north and seized the road from Veracruz to Jalapa, Patterson's volunteers occupied the Sand Hills to the southwest of the city, and Worth's First Regular Division controlled the road from Veracruz to Oriziba and the southern perimeter to the Gulf of Mexico. A squadron of gunships blockaded Veracruz and prevented the city from being reinforced by sea.[21] By March 9 the "investment of Veracruz, from the Gulf of Mexico south of the city to the Gulf again on the north, was soon and easily affected."[22]

Scott placed mortar and howitzer entrenchments east and south of the city, and Captain Robert E. Lee positioned heavy naval guns on the west side.[23] Scott issued an ultimatum to General Juan Morales, commander of the Mexican forces, to surrender the city and its defenses. Morales refused the offer, and Scott opened fire on the evening of March 22. The artillery attack had its desired effect. After several days of shelling, the Mexican general asked for terms, and Scott ordered a cease-fire. After several days of negotiations, the Mexicans agreed to surrender the city. The U.S. soldiers saw the effects of 463,000 pounds of shot and shell as they marched into the city.[24] On March 29, Scott announced the capitulation of Veracruz to Secretary Marcy. "The flag of the United States of America floats triumphantly over the walls of this city and the castle of San Juan d'Ulloa." Scott appointed Worth to command the city and its defenses.[25] The commanding general also announced that he had "commenced organizing an advance into the interior."[26]

The siege of Veracruz was over. The Army of Invasion captured about 5,000 prisoners and 400 artillery pieces while suffering sixty-four casualties. Now the Americans faced a more dangerous enemy than the Mexican Army. The seasonal outbreak of yellow fever or *vomito* was beginning along the coast. Scott decided to move his forces inland as soon as possible to protect his men from the tropical disease. He began to assemble transportation and supplies for the sixty-five-mile march on the National Road to Jalapa. Twiggs' division was closest to the Jalapa road and left Veracruz on April 8. He was followed several days later by Patterson's volunteer forces. Worth's division, in control of the city and furthest away from the route to Jalapa, was the last to leave.[27]

Santa Anna decided to stop the Americans at a mountain pass near Cerro Gordo about twenty-one miles southeast of Jalapa. The Mexican commander selected a point where the National Road went through a narrow, four-mile pass between almost perpendicular hills. The Mexican defenses were strongest where the road passed through Cerro Gordo or Fat Mountain and La Atalaya on the northwest side and the sheer cliffs of the Rio de La Plan.[28]

When General Twiggs learned that Santa Anna was assembling a strong force at a pass on the National Highway, he stopped his march at Rio del Plan. Patterson's Third Division arrived the next day, and the generals decided to postpone the attack until Scott arrived.[29]

In the first week of April 1847, the president finally approved Worth's brevet promotions.[30] Smith was awarded two brevets for "gallant and distinguished conduct" at Palo Alto and Resaca de la Palma and for "gallant conduct" in several engagements at Monterrey. Anderson rejoiced in Charles' recognition and he told a friend: "Reasonably good news from Washington as the President has, in his benevolence, condescended to give a friend Charles F. Smith, two brevets. He is now a Brevet Lt. Colonel, a very slight reward for his many gallant acts."[31]

On April 11 Worth issued Orders No. 8, which recognized Smith's promotion and announced the departure from Veracruz at noon the following day. Worth directed "the

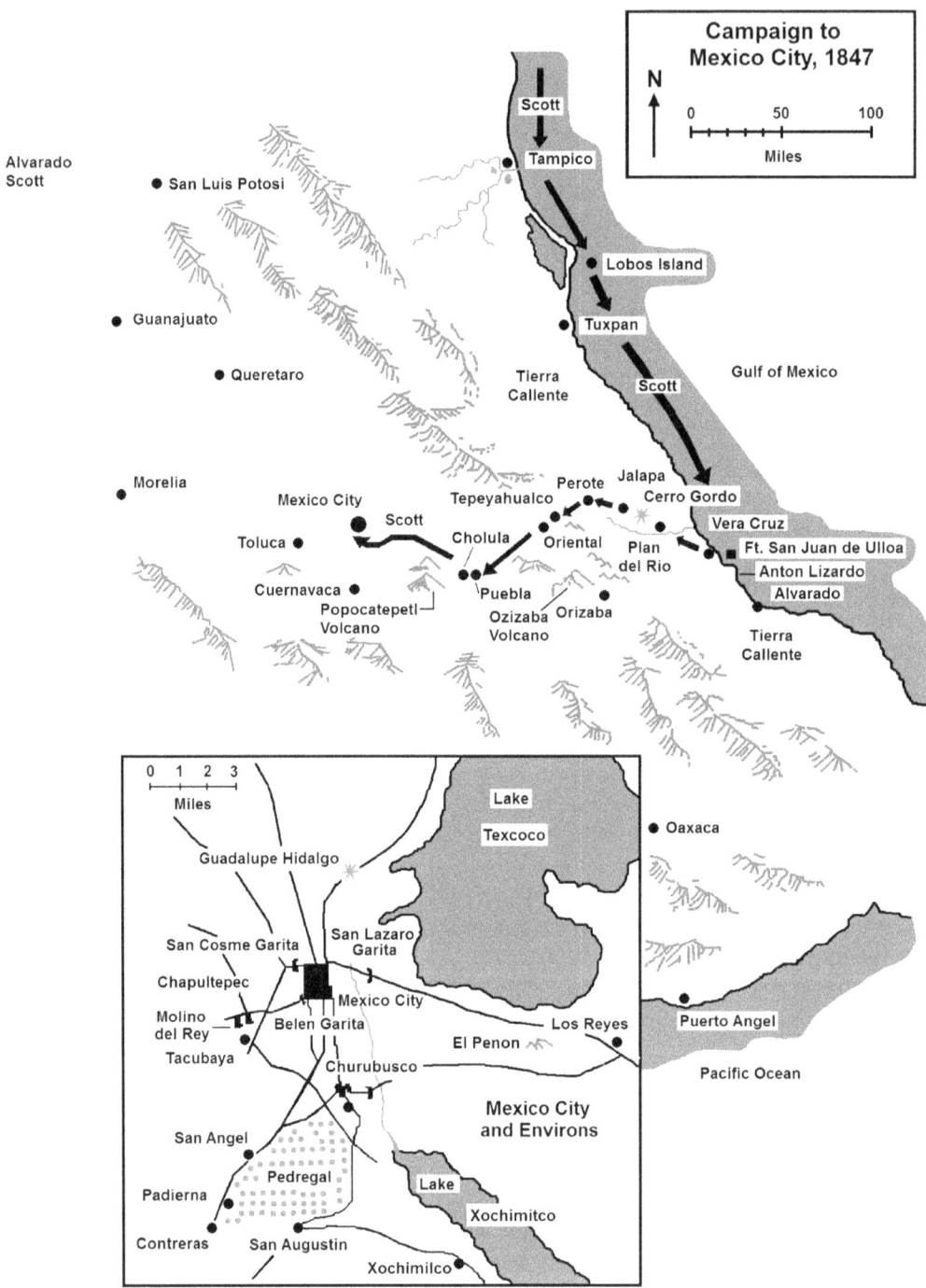

Campaign to Mexico City (author's drawing based on map from *Papers of Ulysses S. Grant* and Ulysses S. Grant Association).

light comps. [companies] of the 5th & 8th—viz., Capt. E. K. Smith's & Capt. Reeve's will rejoin the light Battalion under command of Bvt. Lt. Col. C. F. Smith, 2nd Arty."[32] The light battalion now consisted of Smith's Company K and Company I from the Second Artillery Regiment and one company each from the Fifth and Eighth Infantry.[33]

"Quite embarrassed with the results"

When Scott reached Twiggs and Patterson's camp at Plan del Rio east of Cerro Gordo, he assigned Captain Lee to examine a northern route around the Mexican position discovered by 1st Lieutenant P. G. T. Beauregard. Lee investigated further to the rear of the enemy position, and Scott ordered a road constructed on this trail. The road through dense woods was completed by the time Worth's division arrived on April 17.

The following day Scott launched a multi-pronged attack on the flanks and rear of the Mexican position. Scott was confident of success and allowed his forces to pursue the Mexicans "until stopped by darkness or enemy fortifications." Twiggs' Second Division marched to the base of La Atalaya, a flat-topped hill about a half-mile east of Cerro Gordo. Twiggs expected the hill to be lightly protected, but the Mexicans sent reinforcements from Cerro Gordo. The Mexican infantry and artillery repulsed the American assault and the troops were forced to withdraw.[34]

Scott issued General Order No. 111 that outlined a new attack on April 18. Twiggs was to continue along the road on the enemy's left flank and seize the ground overlooking the National Highway. General James Shields' brigade was assigned to Twiggs' division and would lead Worth's division on the newly constructed road. Gideon F. Pillow's troops were to march south from the National Highway and attack the Mexican batteries between the National Highway and the Rio del Plan.

The attack of April 18 began with an assault from La Atalaya under the command of Colonel W. Harney. Harney's brigade consisted of the Third and Seventh Infantry Regiments, Colonel C. F. Smith's infantry battalion, and the First Dragoons. The attack was fierce and decisive as Scott stated in his report.

> The plan of attack sketched, in general orders, No. 111, herewith, was finely executed by this gallant army before two o'clock, p.m. yesterday. We are quite embarrassed with the results of victory—prisoners of war, heavy ordinance, field batteries, small arms, and accoutrements. About 3,000 men laid down their arms, with the usual portion of field and company officers, besides five generals, several of them of great distinction—Pinson, Jarrero, La Vega, Noriega, and Obando. A sixth general, Vasquez, was killed in defending the battery (tower) in the rear of the whole Mexican army, the capture of which gave us those glorious results.[35]

The American troops chased the fleeing Mexicans and "added much to the enemy's loss in prisoners, killed, and wounded." General Scott supposed the "retreating army to be nearly disorganized; and hence my haste to follow, in an hour or so to profit by events." He intended to reach Jalapa early the next day. "We shall not probably again meet with serious opposition this side of Perote—certainly not, unless delayed by the want of means of transportation." When Worth's First Division reached the battlefield, he detached Colonel Smith's light brigade to support the assault, but it was too late because the Mexicans had raised the white flag.[36]

Following the victory over the Mexican forces, the Army of Invasion camped near Jalapa where they remained until May 6 when they advanced to Puebla. While most of the army traveled to Jalapa, Scott sent Worth's First Division as the advance column to Puebla.

Worth alerted his command "to be at all times, on the march or in camp in the strictest attitude of defence [sic] and always prepared to receive or give battle."[37]

On May 7 Captain J. B. Scott of the Fourth Artillery wrote Smith about "the shining events of Vera Cruz and Cerro Gordo" and congratulated Charles on "the beautiful Brevet."

> The later I am not sorry to know, was done without the very active cooperation of Gn. Worth's forces (now don't imagine you are included). You know how much satisfaction it would have afforded me to have heard that your light atly. [artillery] were as usual just there.[38]

Worth's First Division reached Puebla on May 15 and waited for the rest of the army to join them. The army stayed in the mountain village for around three months while the veterans rested and the newly arrived volunteers adjusted to conditions.[39] Scott had fewer than 8,000 men of which 3,000 were sick and unfit for duty. The arrival of the new volunteers increased his army to 14,000 men for the attack on Santa Anna's 25,000 defenders of the Mexican capital.[40] Scott reorganized his larger force into four divisions under Worth (First), Twiggs (Second), Pillow (Pillow's), and John A. Quitman (Quitman's).[41] Colonel Smith remained in Worth's division where he prepared requisitions, completed returns, and drilled troops. In his leisure time, Charles composed letters to Francis.

The march to Mexico City finally got underway when General Twiggs led the Second Division out of Puebla on August 7.

10. "Off for the far famed City of Mexico"

"Cutting off his retreat"

"We are, at last, off for the far famed City of Mexico," declared an American officer.[1] The army's seventy-six-mile march took them along sun-scorched, dusty roads; between cultivated rich fields; and into cool mountain-air forests of oak, cedar, and pine. Finally, after a stiff five-mile climb, the troops reached the narrow plateau 10,500 foot-summit.[2] The beautiful valley about 120 miles around came into view below them.[3] A few miles down the steep descent lay the valley of Mexico. The men saw ten small dormant volcanoes, six broad lakes, and numerous ash colored roads, gleaming canals, straight lines of poplars, villages, fields and groves, and every hue of green.[4] It was the same view that Hernán Cortés witnessed more than three hundred years ago.[5] As the army gazed upon Mexico City, the men exclaimed, "That splendid city shall soon be ours!"[6]

On August 17 Worth's forces reached San Agustin, about three to four miles from Mexico City, and began reconnaissance of the enemy defenses around the capital. From San Agustin, the First Division marched towards San Antonio where Santa Anna had placed his main force. The First Division advanced the causeway leading to San Antonio, which was defended by a "well-fortified front" with heavy guns that "commanded the approach through the whole length and at various angles of the direct route." Worth decided to seize the Mexican position and ordered an attack 11:00 a.m. on August 19. He selected Colonel Clarke's Second Brigade and Colonel Smith's light battalion to initiate the assault. The force, guided by topographical engineer Captain J. L. Mason, "moved to the left and divergent from the causeway, taking such a direction as to strike the high road from San Antonio, with the double object of enveloping the right of the enemy's position, and at [the] same time of cutting off his retreat towards the capital." Colonel Duncan's artillery and the First Brigade "advanced to an angle in the causeway which partially masked it from the enemy's direct fire" and prepared for action when the Second Brigade "attracted attention" and engaged the enemy.[7]

Mason began his investigation of San Antonio's defenses by probing the right side of the causeway. The Mexicans fired on the engineering officer and his dragoon escort "forcing us to retire and resume our examination with greater caution." Mason decided that the route "presented great difficulties and a powerful front." Next Captain Mason examined the left side of the road, supported by Colonel Smith's battalion, to find a path over "which the enemy's batteries could be turned and the road to Mexico in rear of them could be gained." Mason continued the reconnaissance the next day, again escorted by Smith's light battalion, to gain additional information and to focus the enemy's attention on a possible attack on San Antonio. This reconnaissance prevented Santa Anna from sending assistance to his forces fighting the Americans near Contreras.

During Mason's reconnaissance, Mexican forces were defeated by other elements of Scott's army at the battle of Contreras. Mason returned with a route to the rear of the Mexican position and Worth ordered him to guide Clarke's brigade and Smith's battalion along the path to the rear of the San Antonio works. Mason reported, "The path to the rear was three miles in length, the first and last half miles being through cornfields and chaparral and the middle portion (two miles long) over a perfect honey-comb of lava full of elevations and depressions." The Mexicans evacuated the works when they saw Clarke's and Smith's soldiers behind their position. Then the entire First Division attacked the 3,000-man force from the front and rear and dispersed the enemy in all directions.[8]

Smith described the role his light infantry battalion played in the battle.

> Having been detached on the morning of that day with the 2d Brigade to cut off the retreat of the Mexican forces from San Antonio, after a hard march of two hours over the rough ground in rear of the position occupied by the Divn. [Division], the Battn. [Battalion] came up to the road leading from San Antonio to Churubusco just as the head of the 1st Brigade was passing out of the former; a part of the 2d Brigade having a few minutes before this cut the enemy's line & compelled the rear portion of his force to retreat in the direction of Mexicalrinco.[9]

Smith's efforts did not go unnoticed and Worth concluded his report to Scott by noting, "Brevet Lieutenant Colonel Smith commanded and directed his light battalion with characteristic gallantry and ability."[10]

After the Mexicans abandoned their defenses at San Antonio, they retreated along the road to Churubusco. Clarke's Brigade attacked the enemy flank and chased them along the National Highway. Smith's light battalion joined the pursuit of the Mexicans fleeing from San Antonio. Clarke's and Smith's men continued their pursuit until they were in range of the enemy batteries at Churubusco. Then the battalion followed the Second Artillery Regiment into a field on the right of the road. Smith's battalion continued their advance on the right of the regiment and marched in columns of companies as well as possible through a cornfield intersected by irrigation ditches.

"The assault of the tete-de-pont"

Following their defeats at Contreras and San Antonio, the Mexicans withdrew to the village of Churubusco. Worth's troops advanced north along the road from San Antonio while Scott's other divisions marched north from Contreras. The American forces regrouped near Churubusco to continue their pursuit of Santa Anna's army.

The best available attack route to Mexico City was across the Churubusco River north of the town of Churubusco. Unfortunately, two Mexican strongpoints defended the bridge and prohibited Scott's forces from crossing.[11] The bridge was defended by the fortified Convent of San Mateo (Pablo) and a strong fieldwork or *tete-de-pont*.[12]

During the advance, Smith's battalion lost contact with the Second Regiment. When Smith saw a long line of several thousand Mexican infantry extending far to his right, he formed his battalion into line of battle and moved by the left flank to get within supporting distance of the Second. This movement put his command at the rear of the regiment. The battalion began to receive enemy musket fire and prepared to attack. When two companies of the battalion were formed into a line, an officer from Worth's staff reached the line and

The Battle of Churubusco (Library of Congress, LC-USZC4-6128).

ordered the men "forward." The men rushed across a ditch and through the cornfield towards the enemy without waiting to receive orders from Smith. Smith quickly followed the two units. The officers of the remaining companies were unable to locate Colonel Smith, and, on their own initiative, they led their men towards the *tete-de-pont*.

The disjointed attack and terrain quickly scattered Smith's battalion. After Smith passed through an open field, he became separated from the rest of his command with less than twenty men from his unit. He assembled half of his force by using signals. This force was joined by several officers and about 100 men from the Fifth, Sixth, and Eighth Infantry Regiments. Smith quickly assumed command of these mixed troops and advanced on the *tete-de-pont*.[13]

The first assault by Worth's and Twiggs' divisions was successfully repulsed.

> A dreadful cry came from the left and rear that we were repulsed. A rush of men and officers in panic followed. I shouted that we were not repulsed—to charge—and the day would be ours. Our Colonel, Charles F. Smith, now joined us, and the cry throughout was "Forward!"[14]

The Mexican defenders fought valiantly and resisted many attacks on the bridge. As the bridge was on the verge of being taken, three small groups of Mexican militia arrived and reinforced the position. An intense exchange of fire continued for three or four hours until the Mexicans ran out of ammunition. During the battle two of the Mexican cannon had melted and a third had fallen from its mount.

The officers nearest the fort noticed that the Mexican firing had slightly diminished, and the Americans launched an attack. Captain James V. Bomford, with the Eighth Infantry, saw an opportunity and ordered his men to charge the Mexican fortification. The combined forces from the Eighth and Fifth Infantry Regiments and Smith's light battalion charged over the bridge and, within minutes, the Americans overran the *tete-de-pont*.[15]

The Convent of San Mateo was the last stronghold of the Mexico City defenses leading to the western causeways. The Americans pressed the attack. Lieutenant Edmund Hardcastle

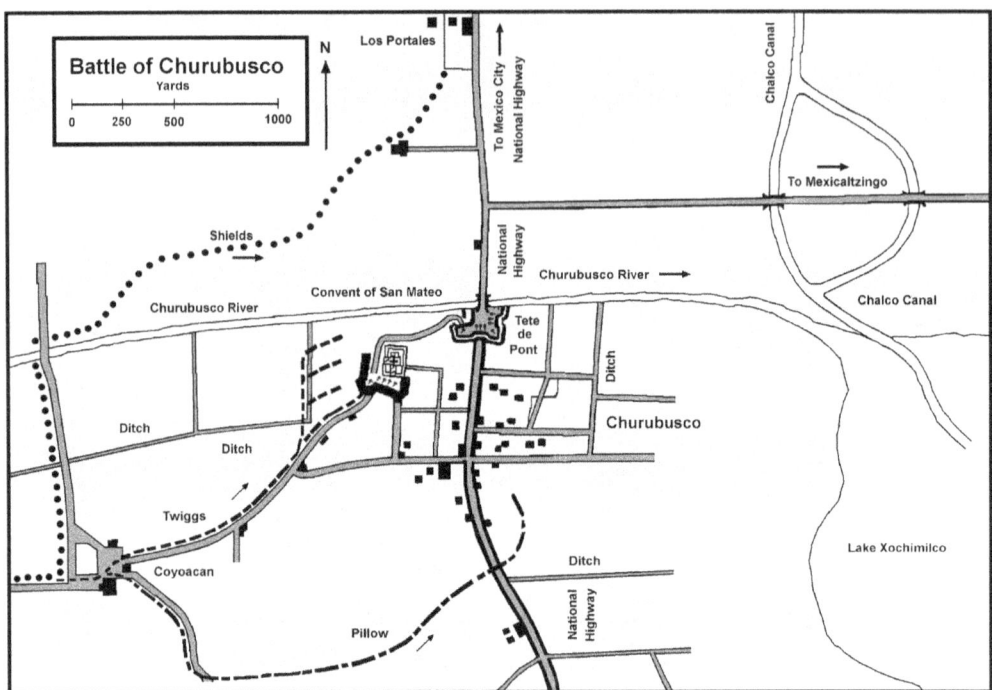

The Battle Churubusco (author's drawing based on numerous sources).

wrote, "Men were shot down on all sides of us and the messengers of death flew about us in all directions." As severe as the attackers' dangers, the troubles of the defenders of the fortified walled convent of San Mateo were much worse. The fall of the tete-de-pont defensive works at the Churubusco River cut off the retreat from the convent. When the Americans turned a captured four pounder cannon on the convent, the Mexican officers tried to surrender. Their attempts to raise white flags were repeatedly defeated by the San Patricios who tore the surrender flags out of their hands. Many of the San Patricios fought to the death in hand-to-hand combat. Finally, with the remaining San Patricios almost out of ammunition, the Mexicans surrendered and the bloody Battle of Churubusco was over.[16]

Although the battalion was scattered, Smith learned the companies were "far in the advance and did gallant service." He commended the command for its work and cited several men for their conduct in the battle.

> After the fatiguing service of the morning, the rapid advance of the Battn. under a severe fire of grape and musketry entitles the officers and men to the highest praise. The return of casualties already rendered shows that very nearly one fifth of the number who went into action were put out of condition; and thus justifying my language.

He had particular tribute for his second in command, Captain E. Kirby Smith,[17] and others who seized the *tete-de-pont*. Smith reported that Captain Smith "exerted himself throughout in the most energetic manner." The colonel also praised Lieutenant Pitcher, who "got well in advance and was engaged in serving one of the enemy's guns against upon him" and complimented his other officers who, although weak from "indisposition and exhaustion," "struggled manfully forward." Smith's report also mentions several non-commissioned officers "who by gallant bearing and good conduct attracted the observation of their officers."[18]

The battles at Contreras and Churubusco were resounding victories for Scott's Army of Invasion. The Americans defeated, dispersed, and dissolved an enemy force of 32,000. They killed or wounded 4,000, captured about 3,000 including eight generals and 265 other officers, captured thirty-seven cannons, a large number of small arms, and a "full supply of ammunition of every kind."[19] Smith's contributions to the victories were recognized by General Worth who awarded him a brevet promotion to colonel for "gallant and meritorious conduct in the battles of Contreras and Churubusco on August 20, 1847.[20]

"Tomorrow will be a day of slaughter"

Scott stopped a few miles from Mexico City and formulated plans to capture the city. On August 21 the Mexicans proposed a truce, which was accepted on August 24. Both sides agreed to an armistice to conduct peace negotiations.[21] Kirby Smith described the circumstances, "We are in a strange situation—a conquering army on a hill overlooking an enemy's capital, which is perfectly at our mercy, yet not permitted to enter it, and compelled to submit to all manner of insults from its corrupt inhabitants."[22] While negotiations were going on, General Santa Anna violated the armistice by continuing to fortify the city. Scott responded to the Mexican actions on September 6 by ending the ceasefire and preparing to attack the city.[23]

General Scott considered a southern approach to avoid the Castle of Chapultepec that guarded Mexico City's west side. The southern gates were covered by Pillow's division and one of Twigg's brigades. Scott surveyed the defenses and found that the Mexicans had "four times our numbers, concentrated in our immediate front." This forced Scott to reconsider an attack on the formidable western defenses.[24]

Several Mexican fortifications guarded the entrances to the western causeways leading

The Battle of Molina del Rey (Library of Congress).

into Mexico City. The first was Casa de la Mata, a very solid, stone structure that was formerly used as a powder magazine. About a half a mile to the east was the Molina del Rey, a flourmill composed of a long complex of stone buildings. Castle of Chapultepec was on a hill about 1,000 yards east of the mill at the junction of the Belen and La Veronica causeways into the city. Reports indicated that the Mexicans were no longer preparing flour in the mill but were casting cannon needed for the defense of the capital. Scott decided to destroy the suspected armory and Casa de la Mata. On September 8 the commander selected Worth's division for what Scott assumed would be an easy task.[25]

Unfortunately for Worth's soldiers, Scott had grossly underestimated the strength of the Mexican position. Molino del Rey and Casa de la Mata were linked by earthworks with a four-gun battery and garrisoned by 8,000 or 9,000 troops. In addition, Santa Anna had placed 4,000 Mexican cavalry to the west to charge the flank of American forces attacking either stronghold. General Pillow had learned that Santa Anna had moved the machinery for casting and boring cannon into the city and tried to get Scott to reconsider the attack. However, Scott had decided to attack the mill and refused alter his plans.[26] The night before the battle, Captain Kirby Smith composed a letter to his wife. "Tomorrow will be a day of slaughter," Smith wrote, "I firmly trust and pray that victory may crown our efforts though the odds are immense. I am thankful that you do not know the peril we are in. Good night."[27]

Early the next morning, Worth deployed his 3,450-man division for the attack. He placed Duncan's battery in the center to shell the enemy guns and fire on the Molino del Rey. He sent Garland's brigade with Captain Benjamin Huger's battery to cut off reinforcements from Chapultepec and to attack the Molino from the east. Worth ordered Clarke's brigade to assault Casa de la Mata and Sumner's dragoons to defend against cavalry raids on the American flank. Worth formed a 500-man force commanded by Major George Wright to

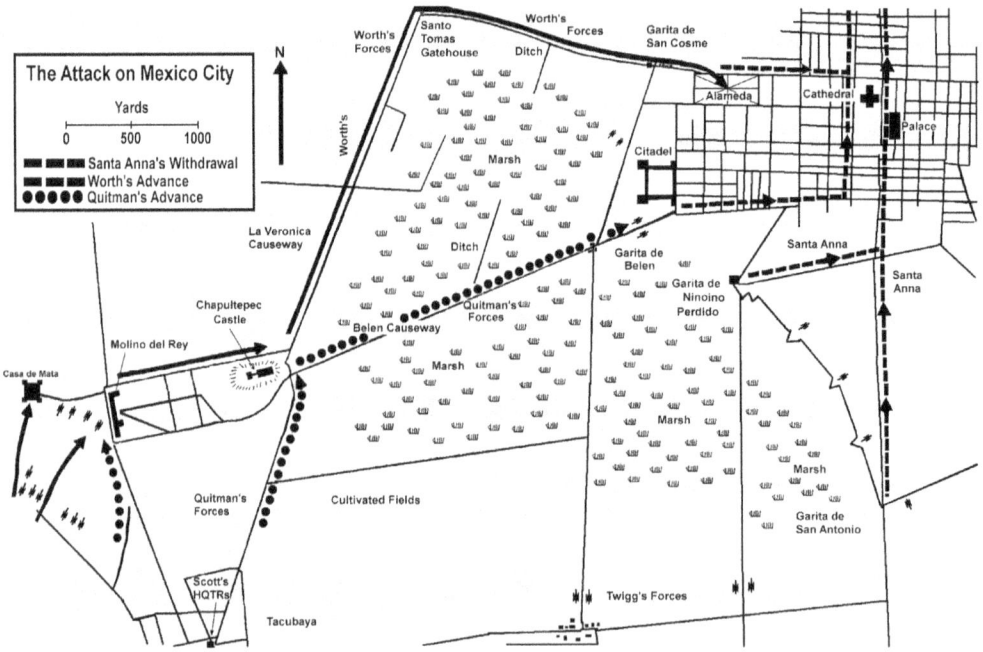

The Outer Fortifications of Mexico City (author's drawing based on numerous sources).

storm the Molino.²⁸ Colonel Smith's light battalion was assigned to support Huger's artillery. Colonel Smith was ill that morning and command was assigned to Captain Kirby Smith.

About six o'clock the American artillery began shelling the Mexican positions. The enemy guns did not respond to the barrage. The American officers believed that the Mexicans had abandoned the complex and recommended an immediate infantry attack. Actually, the Mexicans were still in the buildings and entrenchments waiting for the American assault. As Major Wright's column charged the Molino, the Mexicans opened up with artillery and musketry and cut down the men of the "forlorn hope." Initially, Wright's storming party overran the Mexican infantry, captured their batteries, and turned the guns on them. Then the Mexican defenders and additional troops from Chapultepec counterattacked Wright's small force and directed "a terrific fire of musketry, which struck down eleven of the fourteen officers that composed the command, and non-commissioned officers in proportion." At this point in the battle, Worth's forces attacked from the west.

> The light battalion, held to cover Captain Huger's battery, under Captain E. Kirby Smith, (Lieutenant Colonel Smith being sick,) and the right wing of [General George] Cadwalder's brigade, were promptly ordered forward to support, which was executed in the most gallant style; the enemy was again routed, and this point of his line was carried, and fully possessed by our troops.²⁹

During the American attack, Captain Smith led the light battalion to the foot of Chapultepec Castle and fell "in the moment of victory."³⁰ The death of his second-in-command was difficult for Colonel Smith. Kirby was killed leading the battalion in Charles' place against what was supposed to be a lightly defended position. Charles was confident that Kirby was capable of leading the battalion in support of Huger's guns. It seems that only the valiant Kirby saw the danger they faced.

The Americans suffered 116 killed, 665 wounded, and eighteen missing at the battle of Molino del Rey.³¹ No American could find satisfaction in a "barren victory gained with such difficulty and at such a cost." The men were upset with Scott over his evaluation of the strength of the Mexican position and his determination to attack the place. The officers and men lost confidence in Scott and Worth because of these mistakes.³²

Several months after the battle, Smith received a note from fellow officer J. B. Scott.

> I am but too thankful that you were not well enough to engage in the bloody conflict of the Molino for as your successor in command has died of his wounds. I can but feel that you have had a happy escape. I read with the painful anxiety the long and melancholy lists of the killed and wounded and breathed the more freely when I found that you and [illegible] had escaped. How many of our good friends have fallen victims to the unfortunate war—and as your say cur lions [coeur de lion, courage of a lion]?³³

Smith might have escaped, but he was certainly dejected that Kirby Smith had died in his place. While the men were bitter toward Scott, they saved most of their animosity for the Mexicans and were eager for revenge.³⁴ The opportunity would come in several days.

"Press on, carry the Garita"

During the Battle of Molino del Rey, the Americans had driven the Mexicans into Chapultepec Castle. General Scott decided to seize Chapultepec and attack the capital from the west. Chapultepec Castle, located on top of a rocky 200-foot hill, was the home for the Mexican military academy. The southern and western approaches to the fort were steep and the northern and eastern accesses were sheer cliffs. The fortress was enclosed by walls

The Attack on Chapultepec Castle (Library of Congress).

and garrisoned by 6,000 Mexican troops and several dozen cadets from the military academy.[35]

On September 12 the Army of Invasion began a heavy artillery bombardment and an infantry feint toward the southern gates.[36] The American guns fired solid shot into the castle walls and occasionally directed rounds of canister across the causeways to prevent troops from the city reinforcing Chapultepec. The artillery fire was ineffective and the Mexican engineers quickly repaired the minor damage to the walls. This left the infantry with the difficult task of seizing the fortress the following morning.

Scott's plans called for a multi-pronged attack on the Mexican stronghold. Pillow would attack up the western slope from Molino del Rey supported by Worth's division. Quitman would march up the Tacubaya Road and assault the castle from south. Two special 250-man storming parties from Worth's and Twigg's commands would lead the attacks by Pillow and Quitman respectively.[37]

The infantry attack began at eight o'clock on September 13. Both storming parties made good progress until they were forced to wait for ladders to scale the walls. Worth's troops moved into position to follow Pillow's soldiers, and Worth sent a messenger to Pillow that he was ready to support his attack. Pillow had been wounded after the assault began, and he requested Worth "to bring up my whole division, and make great haste, or, he [Pillow] feared, I would be too late." Worth immediately ordered Colonel Clarke's Second Brigade to advance. The brigade "passed on, mingled with the advancing forces, and entered, with them pell-mell into the assaulted work." At the same time Colonel Garland's First Brigade, Colonel Smith's light battalion, and Colonel Duncan's battery "were put in motion, around [the] north-eastern base of [the] hill of Chapultepec, and moved in operation, upon the San Cosme route and aqueduct."[38]

Scaling ladders finally arrived and the first wave climbed the walls. The strong attacks forced the Mexican commander to abandon the fortress and the soldiers fled into the city. The American flag was soon raised over the castle.[39] Six Mexican military cadets, Los Niños Héroes, the "Boy Heroes," refused to leave the castle and fought to the death against the superior American forces. The valiant cadets leaped to their death and the last "heroic child" grabbed the Mexican flag, wrapped it around his body, and leaped to his death.[40] Thirty men from the Saint Patrick's Battalion, of the seventy-two captured at the Battle of Churubusco, were executed after the battle. General Scott specified that they were to be hanged at the moment when the American flag was raised on Chapultepec Castle.[41]

After Scott reached Chapultepec, his troops continued their advance into the capital. There were two routes from Chapultepec into the city: the San Cosme and the Belen elevated causeways. Each of these routes had "a double roadway on the sides of an aqueduct of strong masonry, and great height, resting on open arches and massive pillars." Strong gates or *garitas* defended the entrances into the city. Scott sent Worth's forces along San Cosme Causeway and Quitman on the Belen Causeway.[42]

The enthusiastic Americans chased the Mexicans on the causeways leading into the capital. The U.S. troops continued their advance in spite of the fire from enemy batteries along the causeways. General Worth's troops rushed along the San Cosme Causeway, and General Quitman's division attacked the Mexican left. Worth's men "discovered an arched passage through the aqueduct, and a cross route practicable for artillery, for a considerable distance, over the meadows, in the direction of the battery, and left of the enemy's line, which was galling, and endeavoring to check Quitman's advance." Colonel Duncan, with a section of his battery, protected by Smith's light battalion, advanced along this route until they were about 400 yards from the enemy's line. Duncan's guns fired on the Mexican battery and then on the retreating troops "great numbers of whom were cut down." After clearing the way for Quitman's command, Worth withdrew his forces and continued their advance on the San Cosme Causeway.[43]

Meanwhile to the south of the city, General Persifor Smith's brigade from Quitman's division advanced on the Belén Causeway and drove the retreating Mexicans into the city. Scott tried to get Quitman to stop and transform his attack into a feint so that Scott's old friend Worth could have the honor of taking the city, but Quitman ignored the orders.[44] In response, Scott instructed Worth "to press on, carry the Garita San Cosme, and, if possible, penetrate to the Alameda."[45] During the afternoon, the Mexican resistance stiffened, American casualties increased, and Worth's and Quitman's progress slowed.[46]

11. "This glorious army hoisted the colors"

"Already in the City of Mexico"

Scott's forces continued to advance along the causeway in spite of strong resistance by the Mexican defenders and high casualties by the Americans attackers. Around 1:30 p.m. General Quitman's troops captured the Belén Gate. Later that afternoon, Worth's division reached the intersection of the La Verónica and San Cosme Causeways. Their progress was stopped by a "single piece of artillery at the angle of the roads and the infantry occupying house-tops back from it." Lieutenant Grant and several men advanced toward the flank of the enemy gun and forced the Mexican gun crews and soldiers firing from the housetops to abandon their positions. With the road cleared, Worth's troops turned onto the San Cosme Causeway.[1] They defeated a counter attack by 1,500 enemy cavalry and pressed on along the causeway towards the San Cosme Gate. Enemy fire from buildings on both sides of the road slowed the advance and increased casualties.

Worth's men reached another Mexican battery about 250 yards in front of the San Cosme Gate. The approach to the gate was swept by grape, canister, and shells from a heavy gun and howitzer supported by musketry fire from the tops of the adjacent houses and churches. Worth sent Colonel Garland's First Brigade and Colonel Clarke's Second Brigade armed with pickaxes and crowbars into the buildings "to force windows and doors, or to burrow through walls." In this fashion, the Americans advanced house-to-house and drove the Mexicans toward the city gate.[2]

Lieutenant Grant saw the San Cosmé Church south of the causeway and decided that the belfry might "command the ground back of the garita San Cosme." He commandeered a mountain howitzer and its crew, waded through ditches of breast-high water, and carried the gun to the belfry. Grant's crew reassembled the howitzer and "the shots from our little gun dropped in upon the enemy and created great confusion."[3] By 5:00 p.m., Worth's men were in position for the final assault on the gate. Lieutenant Henry Jackson Hunt moved a gun to the spot formerly occupied by the Mexican battery and fired on the gate.

> The ... combined attack ... was made, by our men springing, as by magic, to the tops of the houses into which they had patiently and quietly made their way with the bar and pick, and to the utter surprise and consternation of the enemy opening upon him, within easy range, a destructive fire of musketry. A single discharge, in which many of his gunners were killed at their pieces, was sufficient to drive him in confusion from the breastworks; when a prolonged shout from our brave fellows announced that we were in possession of the garita of San Cosme, and already in the city of Mexico.[4]

As evening approached, the fighting subsided on all fronts. The Mexicans withdrew further into the city, and the remainder of Worth's division marched inside the San Cosme gate. Worth placed a 24-pounder and 10-inch mortar near the gate, and the guns began shelling the capital at 9:00 p.m. Worth reported, "They told with admirable effect, as at 1 o'clock at night a commission from the municipality came to my advanced post with a flag, announcing that immediately after the heavy guns opened, the government and the army commenced evacuating the city, and that the commission was deputed to confer with the general-in-chief."[5] Worth's troops spent the night in houses near the captured gate. The Army of Invasion s had taken the western and southern gates to the city and prepared to march triumphantly into the capital.

In his report to Scott, Worth wrote, "Officers and men of every corps carried themselves with wanted [desired] gallantry and conduct." The general's "acknowledgements" included many junior officers who would play significant roles in the Civil War: Armistead, Grant, Hunt, Jackson, Lee, Magruder, McClellan, Pemberton, Pickett, Ruggles, Semmes, Smith, and Sumner.[6] In Scott's account of the campaign, he noted the contributions of "Lieutenant Colonel C. F. Smith's light battalion" and "Lieutenant Jackson's section of Captain Magruder's field battery" in the battles of Molina del Rey and Chapultepec.[7]

"The pick of the whole command"

The morning of September 14, Worth's and Quitman's forces marched cautiously into the undefended capital. Quitman's Division had the honor of being the first American force to enter the city. Quitman proceeded to the plaza in the center of the city and accepted the formal surrender in front of the National Palace. When Worth's division entered Mexico City, stragglers from the Mexican Army began shooting at the American soldiers from the roofs of houses. This "assassin-like fire" from the housetops continued in various parts of the city throughout the day. Colonel Garland was mortally wounded and later that day Lieutenant Sidney Smith was fatally shot.[8]

To add to the army's problem, Santa Anna had released 30,000 prisoners, and the convicts joined the Mexican stragglers in attacking the occupying army. In response to this outrage, Worth used "heavy battering guns upon every building from which fire proceeded" and musket fire "from some of our men thrown out as skirmishers" to get the sniping under control. Worth reported, "This was no time for half-way measures; and if many innocent persons suffered incidentally, under the just infliction of punishment we found it necessary to bestow on these miscreants from the jails, the responsibility should rest upon the barbarous and vindictive chief who imposed upon us the necessity."[9]

Typical of Worth, he personally took down the flag flying over the National Palace, and a Marine hoisted the American flag in its place.[10] Scott established his headquarters in the National Palace and appointed General Quitman as military governor.[11] Scott sent news of the capture of the Mexican capital to Secretary Marcy. "At the end of another series of arduous and brilliant operations, of more than forty-eight hours continuance, this glorious army hoisted, on the morning of the 14th, the colors of the United States on the walls of this palace."[12]

Several days after the capital was captured, General Worth issued Orders No. 101, which disbanded the light battalion and reassigned Colonel Smith to "act as Field Officer to the 2d Artillery." Worth reasoned, "The reduced numbers of the several corps of the 1st Division and the present state of operations requiring re-organization, it becomes a necessity, to which, the General yields with regret, to throw back the gallant Light Battalion upon the Regiment, from which the companies have been drawn; and in doing so, the General tenders to Lt. Col. Smith, his officers and men, his cordial and grateful thanks for the distinguished, most ready and gallant service which that corps has always promptly rendered on various battle fields under its accomplished Commander."[13]

Once Scott's men had seized Mexico City, they faced the difficult task of governing the capital and other captured territory with the goal of winning the most friends and creating the fewest enemies. General Quitman retained the principal local officials to reduce irritation to the citizens and minimize the friction between the residents and the occupying soldiers.[14] Scott republished General Order 20 with several additions. He authorized military commissions to try Americans charged with civil crimes such as murder, rape, robbery, theft, desecration of churches, and destruction of private property. The military authorities had jurisdiction over cases involving both Americans and Mexicans.[15] Scott declared: "This splendid capital—its churches and religious worship; its convents and monasteries; its inhabitants and property, are, moreover, placed under the special safeguard of faith and honor of the American army."[16] The orders also imposed a $150,000 fine on the city. Twenty thousand dollars was for "easing the suffering of the sick and wounded," $90,000 for blankets and shoes for the American troops and $40,000 for other "military purposes." Scott also issued General Orders 296 warning his troops about "an extensive conspiracy" to "murder our officers and men" and cautioned the men "to be constantly on the alert" and "to avoid all obscure places—particularly treacherous dram and liquor stores."[17]

To help maintain the peace, a battalion, designated the City Guards, was organized to police the capital. The battalion was composed of five companies with eighty men and two officers in each company. Colonel Smith was appointed to lead the unit and he personally selected the battalion's officers. Smith set up the City Guards headquarters at the National Palace and divided the city into five wards with one company assigned to each. There was a Spanish interpreter stationed at each company's quarters and one officer was always present in the building. Each company provided a force of twenty-one men with three non-commissioned officers to patrol the streets day and night, arrest disorderly persons, and preserve order. This duty was performed so well "the best class of Mexicans were profuse in praise of the Guards."[18]

The men who served in the Guard drew double pay with their army pay supplemented by an equal amount from the City Treasury. Smith worked hard to achieve the highest possible proficiency for the Guards. If a man was not up to Smith's "high soldiery standards," or the company officer had any problems with him, the soldier was returned to his regiment and another assigned in his place. These measures made the City Guard "the pick of the whole command." The officers and men had such a high esteem for Colonel Smith that they tried hard to please him "down to the smallest details of duty, drills and dress." Smith was equally proud of the Guard and showed them off in the daily dress parade held at the Palace. Lieutenant Henry Crosby said he never saw "a Regiment or Battalion in the Army, other than the Corps of Cadets, anywhere approach it in personal appearance or marching."[19]

Reminiscent of his time at West Point, Smith was cordial with his junior officers and visited with them when they delivered the morning reports. The colonel often invited them for breakfast where he discussed their personal welfare and the proper discharge of their military duties. Lieutenant Crosby regarded Smith as "the highest embodiment of a great soldier and the best specimen of an elegant and accomplished gentleman" that he had ever seen.[20]

During the two months after the defeat of the Mexican Army and with no one to fight, the generals began to quarrel among themselves over the wording of battle reports. Pillow had filed improper reports understating Scott's role at Contreras and omitting the commanding general involvement at Chapultepec. Then two weeks later, Scott accused Pillow of taking two small field pieces as souvenirs. The situation quickly got out of hand because of newspaper articles published in the New Orleans *Picayune* on September 16 written by "Leonidas" that claimed that Pillow was "in command of all the forces engaged" at the Battle of Contreras. Another letter that appeared in the Pittsburgh *Post* that declared that the march southward around Lake Chalco had been the sole idea of General Worth and not Scott. Scott issued an angry order calling attention to the army regulation that prohibited writing letters for publication. Colonel James Duncan admitted writing the letter about Worth. Scott ordered all three officers, Duncan, Pillow, and Worth, placed under arrest for insubordination.[21]

The Polk Administration was now as worried about Scott as a presidential candidate as they once were about Taylor. In the middle of February, a court of inquiry was convened "to inquire into the conduct of the accused and the accuser." Soon afterwards Scott was relieved from "command of the army in the field" and Pillow, Worth, and Duncan were released from arrest.[22]

"The more glorious institution"

The capture of Mexico City and the end of fighting allowed the officers to consider several problems in the military that were revealed during the war. The conversations among the officer corps resulted in two petitions that were sent to Congress in September and October of 1847. The September 24 petition asked for the "passage of a law providing for the retirement of old and disabled officers" and was "signed by almost every member of the old regiments serving" in Mexico. The petitioners argued that because of "age, infirmity, and other causes" many officers are "permanently unfitted for active duty in the field" and their duties are performed by junior officers "to the great injury of the service, and to the prejudice of the younger officers." The signers requested that the retiring officers be "entitled to an honorable competence." The petition contained four clauses: (1) the army can force an officer to retire when he became "permanently unfitted for duty in the field," (2) an officer could retire after thirty years of service, (3) retired officers would be compensated according to their rank when they retired, and (4) the openings created by retiring officers will be filled by "regular promotion of the officer next in rank." The officers believed that a law would be beneficial to individual officers and improve "the usefulness and efficiency of the army."[23] The document addressed the problem of promotion that infested the peacetime army and would lead to the resignation of many young officers following the Mexican War.

The second petition, drafted in October, requested "an amendment of the pension law for widows and orphans of officers and soldiers of the army." The officers were concerned that if they died during service in the army, their wives and children would "be helplessly thrown on the cold charities of the world." The men asked for assurance in the event of their death, that the government would "provide for our destitute widows and orphans" by passing a law that will provide pensions to their wives and children "during the natural life or widowhood of the wife, and during the minority of the children."[24]

On a more pleasant note, an officers' club, the Aztec Club of 1847, was opened on October 13. General Quitman was selected as the first president and Colonel C. F. Smith and Captain John B. Grayson were chosen as First Vice Presidents. The organization included men who would rise to prominence and position in the Civil War: Beauregard, Bee, Buckner, Ewell, Grant, Hancock, Hardee, Hunt, Lee, Longstreet, Porter, Pierce, Sherman, Sibley, Sykes, and van Dorn. The Club added Generals Scott and Taylor as honorary members.[25]

The club was "organized for the purpose of forming a resort for officers, as a promoter of good fellowship, and of furnishing a home where they could pass their leisure hours in social intercourse, and where more palatable and healthful viands [foods] could be procured at a reduced price than at the best Fandas [establishments] of the city." The club's first officers were president: General John A. Quitman, first vice presidents: Captain John A. Grayson and Colonel Charles F. Smith, second vice president: Captain John A. Magruder, Treasurer: Lieutenant Richard B. Hammond, and secretaries: Captain George B. Deas and Lieutenant Henry Coppeé.[26]

The formal constitution, adopted on January 13, 1848, limited membership to officers from Regular, Volunteer units of the army and navy, and required a $20 initiation fee. The club allowed the officers to pool their resources to provide members a place to live together, dine together, and entertain their guests. The Aztec Club was destined for higher honors than first envisioned by its founders. Instead of fading away after the troops left Mexico, the club grew in stature because of its esteemed membership.[27] In November 1849 G. D. Ramsay wrote Smith "that the glory [illegible] in the valley of Mexico had been [illegible] by the more glorious institution of the Aztec Club. Of this, he [Lieutenant Thomas] speaks as an institution to live hereafter—one which I should become a member if I aspire to the red ribbon of the Legion of Honor. In short The Aztec Club is great! I should forthwith apply for honorary admission—nothing else."[28]

On November 3 Smith received orders to assume command of the Second Regiment of Artillery[29] in place of Major P. H. Galt who was placed in command of the First Brigade in Worth's division.[30] Smith's friend, Lieutenant Anderson, was assigned the duties of Assistant Adjutant General under Galt. In May, Smith met with General Worth and the officers of his division to "adopt some memorial of association among the officers." At that meeting, Worth invited Smith to join his staff as Inspector General.

American diplomat Nicholas Trist and Mexican representatives signed the Treaty of Guadalupe Hidalgo on February 2, 1848. The United States Senate approved the peace treaty on March 14, and the Mexican Senate ratified the agreement on May 19. Peace was finally here and the United States military would soon be headed home.

As the American forces prepared to leave Mexico, the members of the Aztec Club met on May 26 to determine the organization's future. The club had grown to 160 regular and three honorary members by the May meeting. They elected officers for a term ending September 14, 1852, and made plans to hold a reunion on or before that date at the Military Academy. General Persifor F. Smith was elected as club president and Captain John Grayson was chosen as "substitute president" and "acting treasurer." The treasury contained $1,669 when the club left Mexico and "various modes [were] presented for the final disposition of the funds." There were several proposals on how to allocate these funds: hold a dinner, purchase a present for the Military Academy, distribute the money among the widows of officers killed in battle, or invest the funds in an interest-bearing account. According to Captain Grayson, none of the plans was adopted.[31] The Aztec Club closed its doors in June as the Army of Occupation began leaving Mexico City.[32]

Colonel Smith's Company K and the rest of the Second Artillery Regiment had conducted themselves admirably during the war. Unfortunately, the regiment had lost so many men that Companies C, G, K, and L were temporarily disbanded and the personnel distributed among the other companies.[33] Company K had fought in eight major battles and suffered thirty-three casualties equal to about half of the company. The most costly engagements were Churubusco (10) and Molina del Rey (15).[34]

Smith's time in Mexico was ending. On June 3, 1848, he was formally "relieved from duty as the Chief of Police of the City of Mexico" by Orders No. 25 issued by General Phil Kearney.[35] The following day Smith reported to General Worth to "enter upon the duties of Inspector General to the 1st Division."[36] That night, Charles sent his 142nd letter to his wife. After the treaty was ratified on May 30, 1848, the Stars and Stripes was taken down and replaced by the flag of the Mexican republic as the U.S. troops left Mexico City on June 12.[37] Worth's division left its camp and began the long march to Veracruz. The First Division reached the seacoast on July 14 and left the next afternoon on the steamer *Alabama*.[38]

The war with Mexico was over. The officers and enlisted men of the Regular Army returned to their posts and the volunteers returned to their homes. General Scott praised the contributions of West Point officers. The junior officers left Mexico with mixed feelings. They had triumphed over a numerically superior enemy fighting in his own country, but they had lost many friends in battle and from disease in the victory. The military establishment had betrayed them over the brevet policy and the favorable treatment accorded to the volunteers and their officers. The officers entered the post-war period with a dismal outlook. As they boarded the steamers bound for America, the West Point officers recalled the words of their famous drinking song.

> 'Tis a proverb that "Republics to their veterans thankless grow,"
> And to a youth of service oft awards an age of woe;
> But if a lowly station most honor doth bestow
> Give me the one now occupied by Benny Havens, oh!
> May the Army be augmented, promotion be less slow;
> May our country in the hour of need be ready for the foe;
> May we find a soldier's resting-place beneath a soldier's blow,
> With space enough beside our graves for Benny Havens, oh![39]

Part Three

Between Wars: 1848–1861

"The more perfect beau ideal of a soldier never existed in any army than was General Smith."—William T. Sherman[1]

Colonel Charles F. Smith (courtesy C. F. Smith Collection at U.S. Military Academy Library, Special Collections).

12. "The most perfect soldier in the Army"

"Affording protection to the inhabitants"

Colonel Smith arrived in New Orleans on July 17 and reached Washington on July 29. The following day, Smith met with Secretary of War Marcy and President Polk. He spent several days in Annapolis visiting his family before leaving for Philadelphia and New York. On August 3 he "arrived at Fort Hamilton at 11½ [11:30 a.m.] & have the pleasure—the happiness—of once again meeting my wife & child—absent from 3 years wanting 23 days and thru the Mex. Campaign."[1]

Smith reported to Colonel Crane in New York on Saturday August 5, and on Sunday, Charles attended church for "the first time in 3 years!" Charles enjoyed his reunion with "the Fannys" until August 25 when he went to West Point to serve on a general court-martial for nine days.[2] Later that month, General Scott granted him a four-month leave of absence.[3]

During Smith's leave, Professor Mahan asked him for help in preparing comments on field fortifications. Mahan was interested in Smith's observations from his Mexican War experiences and encouraged him to "criticize and recommend freely." The West Point scholar said Smith's opinion "will carry more weight with it than any one else in service."[4]

Smith considered new opportunities while on leave. He was interested in returning to West Point in his former capacity as Commandant. Regrettably, his friend Captain Irvin McDowell, citing "local politics," reported, "Lee and Johnston had their own candidates."[5] Smith was also considered for the position of Inspector General of the Army. Colonel Duncan received the assignment in spite of his troubles with General Scott in Mexico. Captain W. N. Chapman, from his post at Brazos Santiago, Texas, thought Smith was better qualified.

> Duncan is a gallant, noble fellow, but the Army pointed to you as better qualified for the office of Inspector General. I say without any desire to flatter that you were my choice, as well as that of all the officers on the Rio Grande. Dr. Jarvis, Major Brice and Major Surmotti particularly spoke of you, and was disappointed when they heard of Duncan's confirmation. I will tell your wife, though I dare not tell you, that you are considered by the officers serving on both lines as the most perfect soldier in the Army. You are known, my dear Colonel, and your merits will ensure your preferment, though in these degenerate days of political influence you may have to "learn to labor and wait."[6]

After they returned from Mexico, companies from the Second Artillery Regiment were sent to Fort Columbus for reassignment.[7] In January 1849, Colonel Smith's K Company was transferred to Fort Marion at St. Augustine, Florida. At this time, the army was still dealing with the Seminole Indians with whom they had fought two wars. Following their victories, the government sent most of the Seminoles west to Indian Territory and only 600 remained on a reservation in Florida. The peaceful conditions and Federal Armed Occupation Act encouraged settlers to move to Florida. President Polk's act awarded 160 acres to single or head-of-household adult males. During the act's existence, 1,184 permits were issued for 189,440 acres between Gainesville and the Peace River. The settlements spread south toward the Seminole reservation and led to conflicts between the two groups. To deal with the problem, Polk designated a twenty-mile-wide buffer zone between the reservation and the permit communities.

The Seminoles were allowed to leave the reservation to trade with merchants in the white settlements. These exchanges sometimes led to disagreements, and the Indians accused the trading post operators of cheating them. The Indians already mistrusted the government because of past treaty violations, and this distrust added to the tension between the parties. The settlers wanted the Indian lands, and they pressured the Florida governor and legislature to restrict the Seminoles to the reserve until they could be relocated to Indian Territory. In 1848, Governor William D. Moseley asked Polk to remove the Indians "peacefully if they can, forcibly, if they must." On January 13, 1849, the governor confined the Seminoles to the reservation.[8]

By the time Smith and his family left for St. Augustine, relations between the Seminoles and the government were in a contentious peace. Family friend Hugh Campbell was happy to learn of their trip and safe arrival in Florida. "It gives so grafic and vivid a detail of your journey and your new home, that I feel as if I had travelled with you and could walk around the veranda of your 'Cottage Orose'[9] (is that good French?) if blindfolded." Francis was several months pregnant, and little Fanny was only five years old when they reached St. Augustine.[10]

Smith, like some Mexican War veterans, still suffered from the effects of the intestinal illnesses they had contracted during the campaign. The St. Augustine climate aggravated his condition, and he aggressively sought healthier posts in the northeast. His physician prepared letters explaining how the coastal climate was affecting Charles' health, and his friend Irvin McDowell, who was on General Scott's staff, tried to get Charles transferred. "You may be assured that anything I can do to effect your wishes will not be left undone. There is now in progress a matter which I hope may be to your interests."[11] The "matter" continued to evolve and it appeared that his friends might be able to get Smith relocated. One attempt was a transfer to Fort McHenry in Baltimore. The post was very appealing to Charles and Francis because it was near to the Mactier and Smith families. In early April, Major George Ramsay said the prospect of the Smiths coming to Baltimore was "very agreeable to us."[12] Ramsay hoped "the genial climate of Washington would at once restore you to health."[13]

On April 20, Colonel and Mrs. Smith were proud parents of a son, Allen. Major John Scott[14] sent his good wishes: "May he have a long & happy life, and be worthy of his sire."[15] Major Ramsay added his "congratulations to Mrs. Smith and yourself on the birth of the young Colonel! [A]nd sincerely hope that mother and boy continue to do well." Ramsay hoped that "the young gentleman will grow up to be the prototype of his worthy Papa."[16]

Charles' brother-in-law Richard Swann met with Secretary of War George W. Crawford on May 13 to discuss the possible transfer to Baltimore. The Secretary promised that Charles would be moved "provided it was in accordance with the practice of Department." Shortly after the meeting, Adjutant General Lorenzo Thomas informed Swann that it was neither "just or proper" to transfer Smith.[17] Swann also received a letter from Secretary Crawford indicating that General Bankhead, commander of the Second Regiment, refused to make an exception to the rules. Richard was disappointed that his efforts had failed and wrote to Bankhead about his meeting with the War Department. Richard hoped he "might be of great service" by advocating on Charles' behalf. Upon reflection, Richard thought he did the wrong thing. He suspected "some double dealing" with Adjutant General Thomas and sent Crawford's and Thomas' letters to General Bankhead.[18] Swann explained that he, and not Charles, had lobbied for the transfer. Swann acted on Smith's desire to relocate to a healthier climate. "Knowing the Col's strict ideas of military matters," Swann sent Bankhead a copy of Secretary Crawford's letter blaming the failed transfer on the general. "I have thought it was due to him and you as his commander to send the Secty's [Secretary's] letter asking you the favor to read it and return it to me."[19]

In the middle of June, Major Samuel S. Anderson replied to Smith's letter on the affair. Anderson agreed "perfectly" with Smith that his name was only used to "cut-out" Brooks.[20] Anderson was convinced that there was "double shuffling" and hoped that the "found & lofty tumbling" would be exposed soon.[21]

Bankhead blamed the refusal on Smith. The general said although he was inclined to offer it to Colonel Smith, Banks believed Smith would be unwilling to make the exchange from his current company and post to a company at Fort McHenry where he would be only second in command.[22] Two months later, Bankhead changed his story and blamed army regulations for the refusal.[23] It is difficult to know whether there was some "double dealing at Washington," issues with General Bankhead, or both. The events seem to point to some political backstabbing on the part of Thomas and Bankhead.

Smith continued to perform his duties in spite of suffering from poor health. His friend Major Anderson hoped it had improved and "if it is not I beg that you will leave St. Augustine soon" and go to the mountains of Virginia or South Carolina.[24]

Following the death of Colonel Duncan in July, Smith received a letter from Major William A. Nichols, stationed at Fort Monroe, requesting Smith's permission to nominate him for the post of Inspector General. Nichols informed Smith that General Bankhead had written a letter to the Secretary of War recommending Smith for the position. Bankhead presented Smith's "high claims" and "favorable notice" and expressed confidence "that his superior cannot be found."

> He unites in himself, in eminent degree; every quality for this particular office. He is of unimpeachable habits, intelligent, an accomplished soldier, deeply skilled in all the duties that devolve on an Inspector General, active, industrious, and devoted to his profession.[25]

Nichols urged Smith to "cast about, write your friends in the north, and use whatever political influences you can command to secure this position."[26] In August, Nichols said reports from Washington indicated that Smith's "chance is very fair, and much talked of for the vacant Inspec. Genl., but that McCall's[27] political friends are worrisome."[28]

The peaceful winter and spring in Florida ended on July 12 when members of a renegade band of Seminoles, who lived off the reserve and were banished from the tribe, attacked a small town north of Fort Pierce. The four Indian "outsiders" were given food, but returned the hospitality by killing one man, wounding another, burning one house, and robbing and vandalizing two other homes. A second attack occurred on July 17 at a trading post where one man was killed and several other people were wounded. The raids panicked the settlers who fled to St. Augustine for protection by Smith's troops at Fort Marion.[29]

In spite of the past wars with the Seminoles, the army outposts in Florida were ill prepared for a renewal of hostilities. State authorities only allocated two companies of mounted volunteers to guard the settlements near the reservation. The forts had small garrisons that had few arms and little ammunition. Colonel Smith was unable to respond to requests for help because he lacked the capability to move quickly troops to the danger spots. "If I had the means of transportation by water at my instant disposal I would at once send an officer and some men to Indian river [sic] to procure intelligence but the only boat we have at all fit for such purpose is one of the Vera Cruz surf boats without mast or sail."[30]

When Secretary Crawford learned about the attacks, he assigned Major General David E. Twiggs to command a 1,400-man force that could be sent to Florida if the events at Indian River escalated into hostilities with the Seminoles. Crawford instructed Twiggs to try to arrange a peaceful relocation and to use force if the negotiations failed.[31]

On August 2, the War Department notified Smith that they were unhappy about the conduct of his troops. The Department was upset because Major Ripley's detachment returned to St. Augustine "instead of remaining near the scene of the apprehended hostilities so as to quiet the fear the frontier settlers." They were also angry that part of Ripley's force "had delegated responsibility to volunteers." Adjutant General Jones reminded Smith that the government was trying to convince state officials that the Regular Army forces were "adequate to all the emergencies which may probably arise from the outbreak of the Indians." Jones emphasized that Smith's mission was "to employ your command to the best advantage in affording protection to the inhabitants of Florida south of St. Augustine; and in sending reinforcements to that state it was by no means expected that they would be kept in garrison, but be pushed forward to the parts of the country most liable to have Indian depredations in order to protect the border settlers and allay the fears of the people." The Adjutant General ordered Smith to send troops "to the frontier, there to give protection, and if possible, that assurance of safety, which their presence only is likely to effect."[32] Smith was outraged by the criticism and complained to Secretary Crawford. The Secretary attached two comments and returned Smith's letter. "Let it be stated to Bvt. Col. Smith (what I have heretofore said to him) that the language used, and of which he complains, was not intended to censure him, and that when such was my purpose, it would not be misunderstood." The Secretary added, "I will not aid by further explanation on this subject, the judgment of those to whom he refers, in their discrimination between the explanation of my feelings at an occurrence which was unexpected, and a purpose to rebuke or censure."[33]

Secretary Crawford's testy response was prompted by the urgent situation in Florida. The Indian River murderers had to be captured before events got out of control. On September 4 the Seminole emigration agent, Captain John Casey, obtained the names of five of the men who were involved in the attacks and learned that the "killings had been committed without knowledge or consent of most of the tribe." Subsequently, Seminole leader Billy Bowlegs met with General Twigs and promised to deliver the renegades.[34]

On August 6, Smith received orders to join a board "to prepare a complete system of Artillery instruction for Siege, Sea-Coast, and Mountain Service." The members were directed to assemble at West Point on August 20.[35] The problem with the Seminoles interfered with Smith's attendance. "In consequences of the unsettled state of Indian Affairs in Florida, the Secretary of War directs that you defer proceeding to join the Board of Officers ordered to convene at West Point the 20th instant, until further orders."[36]

Thanks to Captain Casey, the tension between the Seminoles and the federal government decreased and the Indians committed no new outrages. On August 24, Adjutant General Jones said "the occasion that detained Smith at St. Augustine is no longer apparent" and gave him permission to go to West Point to assume his responsibilities on the Artillery Board. The Adjutant General added that the "state of your health is not such as would enable you to perform active field service at this time."[37]

"Keep those youngsters straight"

On July 27, 1849, Winfield Scott issued General Orders No. 12 directing that a board of officers be convened to develop a complete system of instruction for siege, garrison, seacoast, and mountain artillery. The board was composed of Benjamin Huger, Captain of Ordinance and Brevet Colonel; C. F. Smith, Captain Second Artillery and Brevet Colonel; F. Taylor, Captain First Artillery and Brevet Lieutenant Colonel; R. Anderson, Captain Third Artillery and Brevet Major; and J. W. Phelps, Captain Fourth Artillery.[38] It was a West Point reunion for the class of 1825 with Huger, Smith, Taylor, and Anderson among the graduates. John Phelps was a member of the class of 1836.[39]

Assistant Adjutant General Freeman was pleased with Smith's appointment and wrote, "You will soon be able to report to the War Dept. that your services in Florida can be dispensed with and receive orders to join the Board." Captain Irvin McDowell, on the United States Army staff in New York City, hoped that Smith would accept the duty, but if he did not, they would find some other position. McDowell thought, "you, and of course Mrs. Smith would be here on the 20th inst. But I did not count on another Florida War."[40] Brevet Major William A. Nichols congratulated Smith on his appointment and hoped he would "keep those youngsters straight." Nichols supposed that Smith, being a "traveled 'hombre,'" would introduce some "European styles."[41]

On September 17, 1849, Brevet Captain Jesse L. Reno, acting under Colonel Huger's direction, sent Colonel Smith an outline of the plan adopted by the current members of the Artillery Board. The Instruction for Heavy Artillery was to be composed of three parts: Siege Artillery, Garrison and Sea Coast Artillery, and Mortars. Reno indicated that each section would include the following elements: general instructions; maneuvers with the gun; mechanical maneuvers, general instructions on embarkation, debarkation, construction of platforms, ranges, etc.; and instruction for mountain howitzers. Captain Reno then listed the assignments for the various board members. Lieutenant Colonel Taylor was assigned the mountain howitzer, Major Anderson was tasked with Instruction for Barbette Artillery, Colonel Huger and Lieutenant Phelps were delegated Siege Artillery. Reno explained, "The members will, at their respective posts, revise and test every part of the work or exercises referred to them and submit their report at a future meeting of the Board." Smith had not been given a specific task because of his delay in leaving St. Augustine and his poor health. However, Reno concluded, "Should Colonel Smith report as a member of the Board, a portion of the exercises now proposed to be made at Fort Monroe, will be assigned to him."[42]

In early October, Colonel Huger asked about Smith's health. "I heard from others that you are still unwell at the end of the month of Sept., and if West Point suits you, you had better stay there until you feel strong enough to keep [remain] well." Huger planned to assign Smith "the Casemate drill & handling of the Casemate guns—mounting, dismounting &tc." and thought the work could be done at the Second Regiment's post at New York harbor. Colonel Huger cautioned Smith to "just take care of yourself" and "let me hear how you get on, & when you want work I will send you an official letter."[43] Charles' health continued to be a problem over the next year, and Dr. Henry A. Stinnecke said Smith's condition precluded the "ability of his returning to duty in a Southern atmosphere" without injuring his health.[44]

After nearly a year of work, the board submitted the completed manual to Army Headquarters on August 23, 1850.[45] Smith was assigned "the duty of preparing the manuscripts; and, should it be authorized, of superintending the publishing of the system of instruction for Siege, Garrison, Sea-Coast and Mountain Artillery."[46] In December 1850 Smith was given permission by the Adjutant General's office to provide a copy of the Instructions for the Service Mortar to Professor H. H. Lockwood, provided he only used the material "to import instruction at the U.S. Naval School at Annapolis" until the work was printed by the War Department.[47] The manual was approved by the president, adopted, and published for use by the army and militia on May 10, 1851.[48]

The manual contains forty-four lessons on artillery operations. The first part deals with servicing heavy artillery. Article One contains sixteen lessons on various pieces, including Columbiads, howitzers, and mortars. Article Two describes the formation of a company into detachments to service a battery of several pieces and instructions to operate and maintain the battery. The third article presents instruction on pointing guns, howitzers, and mortars and hot shot, ricochet, and night firing. The second part of the guide covers mechanical maneuvers. The first article contains general information. Article Two describes primary maneuvers with seven lessons. Article Three presents maneuvers with the hand pike, which are illustrated with ten lessons. Article Four contains instructions for maneuvers with machines and the lifting jack that are demonstrated with ten lessons.[49] The request to print 2,000 copies was approved the following month.[50]

As 1850 concluded, the War Department ordered Smith to Washington to serve on a board "to revise the uniform dress of the Army of the United States." Adjutant General Jones said, "The subject will be carefully examined; and the uniform agreed upon by the Board will be described and illustrated by drawings." According to General Orders No. 48, Smith was the sole officer on the Board.[51]

Smith received a letter from Major Ramsay, who like Charles and many other Mexican War veterans, still suffered from bouts of diarrhea. Ramsay had just recovered from a "four-week occurrence of the affliction." He thanked Charles for his "experience and prescriptions" and gave Charles his own cure based on fat or suet from the kidney combined with "new milk." Ramsay said he took it every two hours until "appearances are favorable," and added, "It is quite palatable, nutritious, and did [illegible], I think work [illegible]."[52]

After the artillery manual was approved, Smith began distributing copies. Brevet Major Fitz John Porter, Assistant Instructor of Artillery at West Point, thanked Smith for sending him two copies of the section on Mountain Artillery. Porter praised "the simplicity and ease of the maneuvers" that the cadets easily grasped. Porter hoped that the warm weather had restored Smith's health and invited him to visit the Academy. "If you pass this way this summer you will find many here glad to see you and something to comfort the inward man, and a warm welcome in the room of the subscribers."[53] A month later, Porter asked Smith whether there were enough copies of the Heavy Artillery and Mountain Artillery Manuals to purchase copies for each member of the graduating class. Porter wrote, "there is much of the former [Heavy Artillery Manual], useful in the course of artillery." He added an interesting point: "Bob Lee's son & Gen Wood's son are in trouble for having liquor in their room. They are to be tried. If you wish to come north could you get on the court?"[54]

In the fall, Major Porter told Smith how he was using the artillery manuals at West Point. "Be pleased to accept my thanks. The manuscript was of much value to me. I drilled at everything in it this year, and I think, by [sic] it's given a good foundation to the first class for their studies in artillery this winter."[55] Colonel Francis Taylor was "very much pleased with the execution of the book and do not doubt for a moment that it will give general rules for service." He had not discovered any errors and said that if he found any he would not "mention them to you for they could only give annoyance now."[56]

Perhaps the most gratifying response that Smith received was from his former Superintendent at West Point, Colonel Sylvanus Thayer. Smith sent copies of two artillery manuals to Colonel Thayer who thanked him for the guides and his "thoughtful letter." Thayer said, "You cannot doubt that the kind sentiments therein imported are fully & warmly reciprocated." He recalled Smith's time at West Point when the two men were "closely & intimately connected by official & friendly relations—a connection of which I have abundant reasons to be proud." Thayer concluded by observing that Smith had a "brilliant past" and was destined to have a "yet more brilliant" future.[57]

Board of Inquiry

Smith continued to suffer his "affliction of the bowels" and early in November 1851, he was granted a two-month leave of absence "for the benefit of his health."[58] This brief furlough was extended until April 2, 1852, when he was placed on sick leave until September 1852.[59]

On September 7, 1852, Secretary of War C. M. Conrad appointed Colonel Smith, Lieutenant Colonel Charles Thomas, and Major Richard B. Lee to serve on a "Board" to "examine and report to Congress upon all such claims as may be presented for funds advanced, and subsistence or supplies furnished or taken for the use of the volunteers serving under the command of Captain John C. Frémont in California, in the year 1846."[60] Because of his brevet rank, Smith was appointed president of the Board and assigned to detached service in Washington, D.C., from September 1852 to April 1855.[61] The Board met south of the city at Fort Washington, Maryland. Washington was an expensive billet, and he and his family had to subsist on his annual captain's pay including rations of $1,324.[62] Charles and Francis welcomed a daughter, Henrietta Laurens Smith, to their home on October 15, 1853.[63]

The claims were from citizens for goods and services that Colonel Frémont had authorized for the use of his battalion during the Mexican War. In most cases, the justifications for the expenditures were Frémont's "certificate" stating they were "correct and just and had been applied to the public service." However, there was nothing to prove that the supplies were actually used by his battalion.[64] Although a number of these claims were recorded by the Treasury Department, they were not settled because there was no legal authority for their payment. This problem was corrected by the sixth section of the army appropriation act that was approved on August 31, 1852. The provision stated, "That for the pay and equipment as mounted riflemen, finding their own horses and forage, of the volunteers serving under the command of Captain John C. Frémont, in California during the year 1846, as appears by the muster rolls on file in the War Department, and for the subsistence and supplies consumed by said volunteers in said service, one hundred and sixty-eight thousand dollars is hereby appropriated out of any money in the Treasury not otherwise appropriated; and the Secretary of War is authorized and empowered to appoint three competent and disinterested officers of the army to examine and report to Congress upon all such claims as may be presented for funds advanced, and subsistence and supplies of all kinds furnished or taken for the use of said command, whilst thus engaged in the public service." This provision created the Board and granted it the authority to evaluate claims and authorize payment.[65] The allowed claims were later expanded to include destruction of property. After the Board was formed, the Treasury Department transmitted the filed claims to the Board for detailed examination.

During the proceedings, the Board of Claims voted on the payment of the various claims and awarded amounts to the claimants. The following is typical of the liabilities and the awards granted.

> Board for the examination of claims contracted in California under
> Lieutenant Colonel John C. Frémont.
> Opinion on the claim of Julio Carrillo. Horses, &c., $17,500. No. 11.
> On the additional testimony produced the board is of opinion that a part of this claim, amounting to two thousand six hundred and seventy dollars, ($2,670,) is just, and accordingly recommends so much of it in amount to the favorable consideration of Congress; the balance, fourteen thousand eight hundred and thirty dollars, ($14,830,) being disallowed. This amount is arrived at by allowing the undermentioned rates, viz:
>
> | | |
> |---|---:|
> | Forty horses, second quality, at $20 | $800 00 |
> | Eighty horses, third quality, at $10 | 800 00 |
> | Eighty mares, at $10 | 800 00 |
> | Four saddles, at $30 | 120 00 |
> | Three rifles, at $50 | 150 00 |
> | | $2.670 00 |
>
> Vote unanimous.—(See journal, page 226.)
> C. F. SMITH,
> Colonel United States Army, President of the Board.
> JANUARY 17, 1854.[66]

The Board transmitted its findings to the Secretary of War who sent the approved list of the recommended claims to the Treasury "for final settlement and payment." With its work essentially completed, the Secretary of War abolished the Board on April 3, 1855. Any "unfinished business before the board at the time of its dissolution" was turned over to Colonel Thomas. However, the government was not finished with Frémont, and he was eventually convicted of misappropriation of government funds.[67]

While at Fort Washington, Smith interceded on behalf of his nephew, who was a cadet at West Point. Smith asked Superintendent Robert E. Lee why he denied a leave of absence for the boy. In October, Lee explained the Cadet's situation. Lee described the young man's case as a painful one. The Academy doctor refused to recommend a sick leave and described his disease as "an insuperable objection to his remaining at the Academy." The Superintendent thought the best course was to let the boy "try what he can do, if you do not think it injurious." Lee reported that his professors did not have favorable reports on his progress. However, Lee assured Smith "that he shall receive every attention while here that his situation calls for."[68]

While Smith was concluding his work on the Board of Claims, an opening occurred in the First Artillery Regiment. Smith was selected to fill the post and he was promoted to major on November 25, 1854.[69]

13. "Courage and Fidelity"

"Courage and Fidelity"

On March 3, 1855, the creation of the Tenth Infantry Regiment at Carlisle Barracks, Pennsylvania, provided a new opportunity for Smith. Colonel E. B. Alexander was appointed commander of the regiment and Major Smith was promoted to lieutenant colonel and second-in-command. Smith was transferred from Washington to Pennsylvania to begin training the new unit. Among the regiment's other officers were Major Edward R. S. Canby, Captains Barnard E. Bee and Jesse A. Gove, and First Lieutenant Henry Heth. It was a reunion for Smith and many of the officers who had attended the Academy during Smith's terms as Adjutant and Commandant.[1]

Smith was in charge of the regiment until Colonel Alexander assumed command on August 25, 1855. Smith's promotion provided an escape from clerical administrative duties and a return to teaching and training soldiers. The regiment was divided to facilitate military instruction with Companies A, B, D, G, and K under the supervision of Lieutenant Colonel Smith, and C, F, H, and I, under Major Canby. Fifty-seven percent of the initial 500 recruits were immigrants. Over half of the men deserted before completing their term of service. The Tenth Regiment's uniforms were the same as other infantry regiments, with the exception of the knapsack straps and waist belts, which were like those of the French *Chasseurs-a-pied*.[2] The regiment was also furnished with bugles instead of drums.[3]

Colonel Alexander coined the regimental motto "Courage and Fidelity!" from his "Order of the Day" speech that was made when the colors were presented to the regiment at Carlisle Barracks on September 25, 1855:

> Officers and men of the Tenth; you are formed this morning in line of battle in order that I may present to you the National and Regimental colors. In your hands and to your Courage and Fidelity are now entrusted the honor of your country and the reputation of your Corps. In time of peace conduct yourselves that neither shall be sullied. In time of war and in the presence of the enemy, remember, that these colors which I present to you now are more precious than life itself. Follow wherever they may lead. Gather round them in moments of peril and rather than see yourself deprived of them, die like faithful Soldiers beneath their cherished folds.[4]

The training proceeded well and in October, the regiment traveled to its first posts. The troops left Carlisle Barracks on October 13 and arrived at Galena, Illinois, on October 17. From Galena, Headquarters and A, C, D, I, and K companies travelled by steamboat to Fort Snelling in the Minnesota Territory and arrived on October 20. Companies B, F, G, and H, under Major Canby, left Galena on October 18 and arrived at Fort Crawford, Wisconsin, on October 19. Company C reached Fort Ripley in the Minnesota Territory on October 31. During the movement to these posts, Smith served on court-martial duty at Fort Leavenworth.

Smith reached Fort Crawford in December 1855 and began corresponding with his eleven-year-old daughter Fanny. Francis was in New York City with six-year-old Allen and one-year-old Henrietta. Fanny was living with Charles' mother Margaret in Annapolis. Other nearby relatives included Fanny's Aunt Ann ("Anna") Swann, Charles' sister; Aunt Lucy LeGrand Smith, Charles' sister who was married to Commodore William Nicholson Jeffers III; and Uncle Richard Swann, Charles' brother-in-law and Ann's husband. Fanny's cousins included fourteen-year-old Tom and five-year-old Carry Swann; four-year-old Ann ("Annie") Burton Jeffers; and Elizabeth ("Lizzie") Ferguson Burton. Richard was Commissary at the United States Naval Academy from 1851 to 1877 and mayor of Annapolis during the time Fanny lived in Annapolis. Tom was to become Commander Thomas Laurens Swann of the United States Navy. Lizzie was named after Charles' deceased sister Elizabeth Ferguson Burton. Carry was Carolina Laurens Swann.[5]

On December 18, Charles sent Fanny Christmas greetings and instructions to "tell Grandma, and Ma, and your Aunts & uncle, brother & sister, and cousins, each and all a merry Christmas for me. I hope you may enjoy yourself very much on that day." His letters described occurrences at Fort Crawford, the weather and river conditions, family news, and fatherly advice.[6] Early in 1856 Charles expressed delight with Fanny's most recent letter, encouraged her to write "once a week or ten days," and correspond "just as you would talk to me if I were near you."[7] He was happy with Fanny's academic progress and wanted her to begin French lessons.[8]

Charles wrote his mother about the frigid weather at Fort Crawford. He said the "thermometer shews [sic] intense cold, say from 15° to 23° below zero almost habitually, & yet to our senses it is not to unpleasant as when with you it is but little below the freezing point." In spite of the subzero temperatures, Charles said, "I am quite well & getting so stout that my coat & trousers are now a tighter fit."[9]

In February 1856, Alexander, Canby, and Smith examined the junior officers at Fort Crawford to determine whether the men would be reappointed when their commissions expired on May 1. After they had reviewed the officers at Fort Crawford, the commanders went to Fort Snelling and evaluated the officers at that post. Smith made the 300-mile trip to Fort Snelling in a covered sleigh on the frozen river and did not return to Fort Crawford until the middle of March.

Smith learned from Washington authorities that six companies from his regiment would be sent north on an expedition to Pembina.[10] He suspected that Colonel Alexander would be stationed there because the garrison would contain most of the regiment. The remaining companies would be divided between Fort Ridgely, about 200 miles west of Fort Snelling on the St. Peters or Minnesota River, and Fort Ripley, about 200 miles north of Fort Snelling on the Mississippi. Smith believed he would be located at Fort Ridgely.[11]

In March, the officers established a program of regimental instruction. The men were "zealously" exercised in drill, target practice, and marching. The training emphasized that their duties as "Light Infantrymen" required "a complete knowledge of the use of the rifle, and especially deliberation and calmness in firing, that each shot might be effective."[12] Charles learned in April that establishing a post at Pembina would probably have to be postponed until next year because the Senate refused to appropriate $50,000 to build the fort.

> This will in all probability prevent troops from being sent there until next year; but it will not prevent our leaving here in a few weeks—4 to 6. The companies of the 2 regt. of Infantry now at Forts Ridgely and Ripley will be relieved by the 4 cos. here. This is guess work, but I imagine it will be near the truth, it will not be long before our "orders" will tell us where we are to go.[13]

Two weeks later, Charles told Fanny: "I have nothing of special interest to tell you, and only write now to show that I always think of you." He noted that today (April 20) was Allen's birthday, and he had "sent the dear little fellow some money to have it duly celebrated by a party." With the warmer weather at Fort Crawford, the river was free of ice and steamers were traveling up and down the Mississippi.

> We have fine spring weather now. When the leaves are out the view from my window will be beautiful. The river resembles a mountain lake with islands in it. I should like to remain at this post if but to have the pleasure of rowing about on it. I walk a great deal every day; in part for exercise, & then too in looking at the soldiers drill & fire at the target. The target is at the foot of the high hill back of us, & is a mile off, so I get exercise enough.[14]

Charles remained at Fort Crawford until June 10, 1856, when he was transferred to Fort Snelling. He was in command of the post until he left on July 23, 1856, to lead the expedition to the Red River of the North.[15]

"An expedition to the Red River of the North"

The westward expansion following the Mexican War increased settlement of the Minnesota and Mississippi valleys and forced the Indian tribes from their hunting grounds. This encroachment promoted conflicts between the settlers and the Indians. Many of the disagreements occurred along the United States–Canadian border between the American settlers and the Canadian Indians and half-breeds who entered the United States to hunt, trap, and fish. On June 9, 1856, Lieutenant Colonel Smith was ordered to lead an expedition through that section of the country, warn the foreign hunters, and select a site for a post to maintain peace between the settlers and Indians.[16] Smith chose nearly the same route that Major Samuel Woods charted in 1849. However, instead of traveling by the usual road to Pembina, the expedition planned to detour to Lake Mini-Waken or Devil's Lake. Smith's formal orders outlined the following objectives:

> I. To note the features of the country with reference to the selection of sites for the establishment of military posts.
> II. To hold interviews with the Indians occupying the opposite sides of the Red River, with the view to require them to keep within their own districts of country; to keep at peace with the United States, and to discontinue hostilities with each other; and to commit no depredations on the whites or on each other; and
> III. To notify all British subjects who are in the habit of entering the territory of the United States for the purpose of hunting and trapping, &c., that such depredations will no longer be permitted.
> In addition to these general directions, the same orders contained specific instructions to visit Lake Mini-waken in going or returning, for the object indicated in No. 3; to examine the mouth of the Shayenne[17] with reference to its fitness as a site for a military post; and to return on the east side of the Red River.[18]

The march to Pembina and the return to Fort Snelling was around 1,000 miles. Smith was concerned that the expedition was starting very late in the year "to accomplish the objects set forth and return to this post before the winter had fairly commenced." Therefore, time was critical in planning the expedition, and Smith chose his route carefully to avoid retracing his steps.[19] He thought that the trip would be pleasant "except on account of the Mosheto's [mosquitoes]—which are represented as perfectly insufferable—in such numbers & so vigorous as to prevent horses from eating to an extent."[20]

The expeditionary battalion was composed of the six officers and 116 enlisted men of Companies B and F.[21] The thirty-four wagon supply train carried supplies for four months. Four of the wagons were built of corrugated iron and could be used as pontoon wagons.[22] Each of the wagons was drawn by five or six mules. Most of the 180 mules were young and unbroken and the teamsters had little or no experience with mules.[23]

The battalion left Fort Snelling on July 23 and made slow progress because of the "unbroken mules & men for teamsters who certainly never saw a mule before & probably not a horse—judging by the ignorance displayed." The mule teams started to perform better after the sixth day. The expedition moved gradually because of delays in crossing numerous rivers, streams, and marshes. The weather was hot during the day with heavy rains at night.[24] In spite of their rough start, Charles described the landscape as "a beautiful country all together [sic]." He said, "We lunched yesterday at the Min-e-ha-ha falls, (about 1 mile from Ft. Snelling,) which name Mr. Longfellow has introduced into his ridiculous poem of Hi-a-wa-tha."[25]

The area was "dotted with a countless variety of small lakes" and "many extensive marshes (*terres tremblantes*[26]) of formidable character."[27] The marshy soil caused problems and the wagons were only able to cross them because the season was unusually dry and the expedition started late, which "allowed the prairie to become measurably dry."[28]

Smith's daily record described how the battalion dealt with the many obstacles it encountered. When possible they crossed rivers using existing ferries and bridges. Some bridges were fortified to support the heavier loads, but new bridges had to be constructed at other crossings. The battalion forded shallow rivers using guidelines, but difficulties were often encountered in moving the wagons down and up the steep banks. Sometimes the pontoon wagons were converted into boats to form floating bridges or to ferry supplies. The men constructed corduroy roads or grass bridges to cross the marshes. In some places, the soldiers cleared the woods and built new roads. The battalion dealt with sand on the hills and in the river and streambeds.[29] The mules were a concern throughout the march. Initially, the train was slowed by the untrained animals and drivers. On the return, the animals suffered and died from the lack of proper food and freezing weather. En route to Pembina, the days were hot and the nights were rainy. The rains turned the roads into mud and caused delays in freeing animals and wagons. On the return trip, the expedition suffered from snow during the day and freezing temperatures and ice at night.[30]

On August 19, the battalion expedition crossed the trail of the annual summer hunting party of the Red River people and came to the camp where they had slaughtered the buffalo. "It was filled with the remains of the buffalo, on which numbers of wolves were feasting; the stench intolerable." A week later, the expeditionary force encamped on a small branch of the Shayenne River near Lake Chicot where they saw a herd of buffalo cows. Their guide killed two buffalo, and the men came down with diarrhea "from eating so much buffalo meat."[31]

The battalion finally encountered Indians at St. Joseph where Smith met with La-kik-wa-nel (Green Feather), the head chief of the Pembina band of the Chippewas. At this conference, Smith told them that their Great Father, the president, wanted them to remain at peace with the United States and to end hostilities with the Sioux. Colonel Smith warned that if they failed to comply with the president's request, the United States would post soldiers among them to enforce the peace. The soldiers "would deliver up to the opposite party the perpetrators of any murder or other outrage, to be dealt with as the outraged party or the relatives and friends of the same might see fit." Smith explained that the president desired the tribes to remain within their own districts of the country to avoid possible confrontation over the decreasing number of buffalo and game. The president wanted the

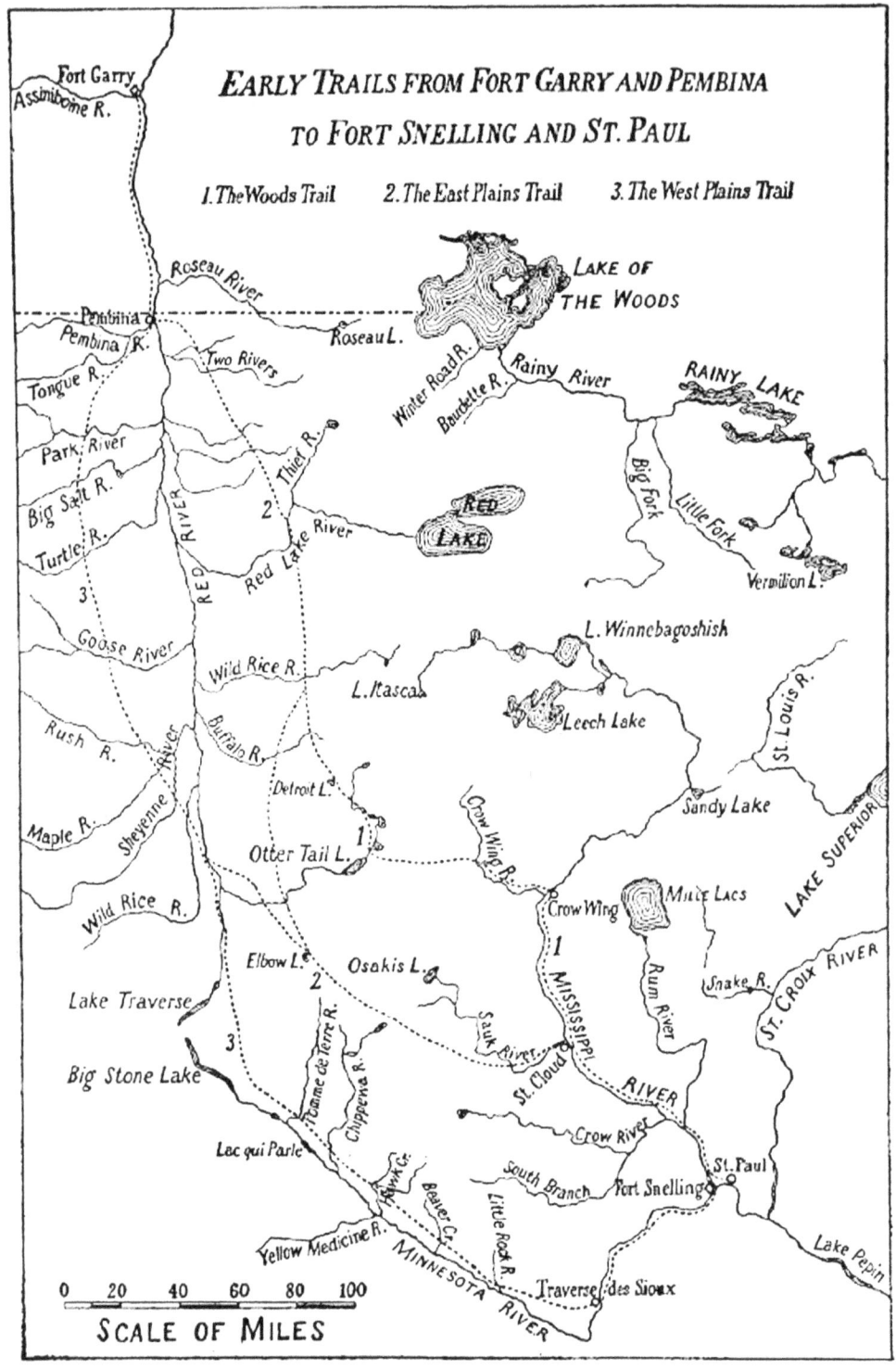

Early trails from Fort Garry and Pembina to Fort Snelling and St. Paul, drawn by Dr. Warren Upham (courtesy Minnesota Historical Society).

tribes to start cultivating the soil so that they had enough food, and offered to help them, if they wished, after signing a treaty with the United States.³² Green Feather indicated that his people would like to get farming implements and other assistance. However, he would have to consult his tribe about the treaty. Under his time constraints, Smith was only able to meet with other Chippewas at the Indian agency near Crow Wing. Smith learned that the Chippewas in northern Minnesota would be happy to sign a treaty.

Smith's next task was to warn Canadian hunters and trappers against trespassing into the United States. Time limitations prevented him from giving notice to the parties in person so he issued a proclamation in French and English and had it circulated in St. Joseph, Pembina, and Selkirk.³³

> Notice to all whom it may concern.
> HEADQUARTERS BATTALION 10TH INFANTRY, PEMBINA EXPEDITION
> Camp at St. Joseph's, Minnesota, September 3, 1856.
> The undersigned, the commanding officer of a military expedition which arrived here to-day from Fort Snelling, via Lake Mini-waken, has the instructions of the President of the United States to notify such of the inhabitants of the British Possessions as are in the habit of crossing the boundary line between the United States and Great Britain (49th parallel of north latitude) for the purpose of hunting and trapping, &c., on American soil, that such depredations will no longer be permitted. The undersigned, accordingly, hereby warns all such persons not to enter the territory of the United States for the above mentioned purposes.
> C. F. SMITH,
> Lt. Col. 10th Inf. and Bvt. Col. Commanding.³⁴

The British response to Smith's proclamation ranged from concern to amusement. Sir George Simpson, Canadian governor of the Hudson's Bay Company, requested soldiers at Red River to "serve as a counterpoise to the growing influence of the United States in the Northwest Territory."³⁵ Some of the Red River settlers believed that annexation by the United States was their only hope of escaping the rule of the Hudson's Bay Company.³⁶ The British feared that Smith's proclamation was an attempt by the United States to seize the Hudson's Bay Territories by encouraging the people of the settlement to "agitate for annexation" if they were cut off from access to buffalo.³⁷ Simpson explained, "It would be difficult to make those semi-savage people comprehend that hunting on one side of an imaginary line was perfectly legal, whereas the same pursuit on the opposite was a grave offence."³⁸

On September 9 the expedition arrived in Pembina after traveling 504¼ miles. Smith portrayed Pembina as "a decaying town of around two dozen wooden buildings." He said it was a "town of about 1000 inhabitants, who are almost, if not altogether half-breeds, the descendents [sic] of Canadian French and Chippewa Indians, where the French language is generally spoken—sometimes the Chippewa, but no English."³⁹

With their assignments at the border completed, the expedition began the trip home. By September 20, the battalion was forty-eight miles from Pembina and encamped on the Middle River.⁴⁰ The journey continued to the Red Lake River, which Smith described as "the best looking river" on the march.⁴¹ Smith said the weather turned very cold at night and from an eighth to a fourth of an inch of ice froze on his tent. The road was more difficult than the route to Pembina and required more labor and greater attention. Four days after their departure, the expedition was eighty-three miles from Pembina and the battalion had already bridged two rivers and built several hundred yards of corduroy roads. That night Charles wrote Fanny and wished her a happy birthday. "Many, many happy returns of the day to you my dear daughter. I wish I were able to say so personally. I want to see you very much. Twelve years old. Why you are quite a young woman Fan."⁴²

As October began, the men continued their march south by starting a bridge over the Sand Hill River. They finished the bridge, marched ten miles, and encamped on the *Riviere aux Marais*. Two days later the battalion built another over the Wild Rice River. When the force reached the Buffalo River, Smith crossed the river and rode to the Red River to examine the mouth of the Shayenne River.[43]

On October 14, the guide estimated that the middle or "wood" road was about 2½ miles east of their position.[44] They traveled eastward to reach the road and find grass for the animals. However, three days later, they had still not found the road, and Smith sent the guide to find it. The guide returned and reported that the Wood Road was far to the north and east of their current location. The camp was struck and the men retraced their steps to where they camped four days ago. They had lost eighteen miles in searching for the road.[45]

On October 24, 1856, Smith sent Lieutenant Clinton to Fort Ripley, about eighty miles away, to purchase grain for the animals and obtain oxen to replace the sickly mules. The battalion marched northeasterly and finally reached the Wood Road. The men made several roads through the woods and over "villainous" marshes as the battalion marched south. The men faced alternating rain and snow during the day and snowstorms at night.[46] Thirty mules died from October 20 to November 1.[47] On November 5 Lieutenant Clinton returned from Fort Ripley with seven yoke of oxen, a pair of horses, and a supply of oats and hay. Clinton also brought shoes for the now barefooted soldiers. However, in spite of the new supply of feed, horses and mules continued to die.

The journey settled into a daily routine of small marches, river crossings, and dying animals. As the expedition dragged into November, the weather turned "excessively cold" with the temperature "several degrees below zero." On the 110th day of the march, Smith was forced to leave six wagons because he had no animals to haul them. The cold weather provided one benefit because the marshes froze and eliminated the need to corduroy them.[48] On November 18 the expedition finally reached Fort Ripley, where they turned over the surplus wagons, stores, and weak mules to the quartermaster and received grain and subsistence stores for the march to Fort Snelling.[49] They made good time after leaving Ripley and reached Fort Snelling on November 27, after an absence of 128 days and a journey of 952½ miles.

One of Smith's assignments was to evaluate possible sites for military posts. He recommended a post near St. Joseph and cited its advantages: "It has the requisite timber for building; good clay for bricks; sand; a sufficiency of stone, boulders of granite, for foundations; is perfectly healthy; has plenty of wood for fuel, with an abundance of excellent grass, and a good soil for barley and oats, both of which are already cultivated to some extent; can be readily supplied with subsistence and other stores by the Red and Pembina rivers; would be at the precise point to intercept or pursue trespassers upon our soil; and from whence detachments could be readily sent to Lake Mini-waken and elsewhere to overawe [intimidate] the Indians and coerce them into proper behavior."[50]

Smith recommended the small French cart, used by the Red River people, as the best means of transportation. The wooden wagons, which were drawn by a single ox, could carry 1,000 pounds. Smith was so enamored with these carts that he had his quartermaster purchase one as a model. He said the heavy government wagons used for the expedition were not suitable for the terrain. Smith approved the corrugated iron-body pontoon wagons that were invaluable as boats or floats in ferrying or bridging streams.[51]

Colonel Smith noted that labor of some form was almost a daily occurrence during the march, and the men were as familiar with the axe, the spade, and the pick as they were with the rifle. Smith praised the officers and men of the expedition and said it gave him "much pleasure to bear testimony to the cheerfulness, zeal, and activity with which the battalion met the constant labor imposed upon it from necessity in bridging numerous streams, cutting roads, corduroying marshes, &c., &c., in the worst possible weather."[52]

"Our doings are so very monotonous"

After completing the expedition to Pembina, Colonel Smith relieved Colonel Canby from command of Fort Snelling. The garrison was composed of four companies from the Tenth Regiment and Lieutenant Thomas W. Sherman's light artillery company.[53] In this position, Smith was "obliged to keep house" so he could "exercise the rights of hospitality to officers and others coming to the post." He had "a fine house; four rooms on the same floor with a bath as nice as the rooms, attic, kitchen & cellars." He purchased the necessary furniture from Colonel Canby and hired Canby's housekeeper who was "an excellent cook & laundress, and good manager." Smith was getting adjusted to living "under a roof" after spending most of the last six months living in the open air. "I don't sleep so well & feel oppressed by the heat—altho' the thermometer shews usually zero & below it." He complained that the post was "rather an expensive place" with daily living costs of 75 cents. Charles did not expect to stay long at the fort and thought his five-company garrison would "all be pushed off to establish one or more posts in the Red river [sic] country" in the spring.[54]

On New Year's Day, Charles sent his family holiday greetings. He wrote, "The great amusement is sleighing, for which the climate is well adapted, being clear, cold & dry with just snow enough to make the sleighing good. Our ordinary temperature is about 6° below zero & yet I walk about the garrison without an overcoat, but it is necessary to keep the ears covered & to look out for the nose else Jack-Frost will have of them before you know it." The monotony of garrison life was interrupted on New Year's Eve by a small fire in the blacksmith's shop. Although the blaze was well under way, the soldiers "literally snowballed it out." A more serious accident occurred the night before when a soldier left the guardhouse without permission and crossed the river to Mendora to get some whiskey. He was drunk and drowned in the river on his return to the camp. The sentinels heard his desperate cries for help, but it was too late to save him. "His body was fished up this morning. And thus paid the penalty for his folly by an untimely death."[55]

Charles complained to Fanny in early February: "I have literally no news to give you. Our doings are so very monotonous that it could not interest you to describe them. During the day, the ladies and gentlemen go to St. Paul, and in the evening, they have small parties in each other's rooms." Every week, he invited some of the officers to his quarters "for a little card party and a glass of wine and piece of cake."[56] When Fanny complained about a snowstorm in Annapolis, he found it amusing and replied, "You ought to be here to know what cold is."

> My breath froze on my mustache this morning the moment I put my face out of the door—the thermometer being -37°. You don't know exactly how cold that is but the mercurial thermometer can only mark two more degrees when the mercury freezes. We have a good many cases of frost bitten fingers &c. among the soldiers who will not take care of themselves. And there is one case among others in the hospital where the Doctor with difficulty saved the man's legs; the poor wretch being drunk took no care of himself after he was bitten by the frost. As it is he will lose all the toes of both feet & one heel & several fingers from each hand. So much for whiskey.[57]

In March, Smith learned that a proposed amendment to the Army Appropriation Bill would give him extra compensation for his service on the California Claims Board. He hoped the additional funds would make him "richer by a few thousands of dollars than I was on the 14 of Feb., the date of the last proceeding of Congress."[58]

The Tenth Regiment's headquarters was temporarily established at Fort Snelling in April because of problems with the Indians and the post's advantages in receiving "daily mail in summer, and a tri-weekly mail in winter."[59] In May, one of the white women, who was at the Spirit Lake massacre,[60] was surrendered to an Indian agent and taken to Fort Ridgeley. While negotiating the return of two others held by the Indians, the army decided to suspend its planned military operations. Most of these exercises were to be conducted by the Tenth Infantry, under the command of Smith and Canby. Therefore, as the summer began, Smith waited restlessly at Fort Snelling for hostage negotiations to conclude or some other event that required his presence. He would not have to wait too long.

On June 2, 1856, Smith received a telegram from the War Department ordering eight companies from the Tenth to "proceed without delay by water to Fort Leavenworth." Smith forwarded the order to Colonel Alexander at Fort Ridgeley. Smith thought Alexander's troops would reach Fort Snelling in eight days, which would permit the combined force leave for Fort Leavenworth by the middle of the month. In the midst of the reassignment instructions, his plans were "knocked in the head" when he had to send troops from Fort Snelling to capture the Indian who committed the murder near Spirit Lake. He also had to wait for four companies from the Second Infantry at Fort Randall to march across the country and garrison Fort Snelling and Fort Ridgley. Smith grumbled, "This constant change of orders is absurd, but there is no use in saying anything about it. New Secretaries [Secretary of War]—new ideas."[61]

As Charles was waiting to leave Fort Snelling, his wife decided to purchase a permanent home for her family. She selected Fishkill Landing on the highlands of the Hudson River. She told Charles that there was a good school nearby for Fanny to attend. On June 12, 1857, Charles explained her mother's decision and how Fanny would enjoy joining her mother and siblings in their new home.

> I know you will like your new home. It is in the finest part of the country for health scenery &c. I mean that about West Point. Of course you will go to West Point and see the Cadets &c. When you see them on parade you must try and fancy me standing among them a boy of 13 years old, which I was when I first shouldered a musket just 37 years ago. It makes an old man of me Fan to look back in this way. I hope that Allie [Allen] won't be made a soldier of by seeing the gray-coated lads, for I am opposed to it out-and-out.[62]

14. "A war must be waged"

"Organized and open rebellion"

On July 18, 1857, the Tenth Infantry Regiment was ordered to restore federal control in the Utah territory. The movement of troops to the territory began what was called the Utah War, Mormon War, or Mormon Rebellion. This enforcement of jurisdiction was among other national calamities that year: Kansas was a bloody battleground, Dred Scott was returned to bondage, and a financial panic damaged the economy.

The problems that led to the Mormon War began when the Church of Latter Day Saints or Mormons arrived in the basin of the Great Salt Lake in 1846. After years of religious persecution, the Saints reached what they prayed would become their New Zion. When they established their colony, the region was under the disinterested rule of the Mexican government. This governance changed after the Mexican War when the United States gained control of the area. As the West was opened to settlers from the East, non–Mormons began to travel through the new Utah territory. The Saints resented the intrusion of these non–Mormons or Gentiles in their sanctuary. The Gentiles had treated the Mormons badly in Missouri and Illinois. Now the Saints returned the favor by dealing harshly with travelers crossing their lands. After living under Mexican rule, the Mormons were reluctant to comply with the newly installed federal officials and to obey laws they disliked or conflicted with their religious beliefs. The U.S. government compounded the problem by appointing unqualified men with antagonistic attitudes to administer the territory. When gold was discovered at Sutter's Mill in 1848, thousands of people traveled through the Salt Lake City area on their way to the California Gold Rush. These would-be prospectors brought opportunities for trade, but ended the Mormons' isolation.[1]

By 1857 disregard for federal authorities and crimes against Gentiles had reached the point that President James Buchanan decided to send troops to install a new territorial government. The Buchanan Administration concluded that Utah was "in a state of organized and open rebellion against the laws" and this defiance demanded stern measures. Buchannan said the Mormons' ecclesiastical despotism, fanaticism, and illegal Indian policy indicated that the people of Utah were in revolt against federal authority. The president later added the expulsion of federal officers, disruption of the courts, and other forms of misbehavior as further evidence of "insubordination" in the territory.[2]

However, for many Americans the real purpose of the government's intervention was to eradicate polygamy. The public did not know that polygamy was not widely accepted by Mormon men and only five percent of the people were involved in plural marriage. Instead, they focused on Brigham Young's relations with his "concubines" and compared it with the harems of the Moslem world. Americans were convinced that polygamy "produced not only sensuality but bestial behavior with men and their daughters at the same time, sleeping with several wives in the same bed, and committing other dark acts akin to 'oriental' degeneracy."[3] Newspapers added to anti-Mormon attitudes. The editor of *The New York Times* wrote, "A new Governor should be sent at once to Great Salt Lake City—backed by an imposing military force to render the Constitution with one hand while a drawn sword is held in the other."[4]

However, instead of quickly suppressing the insubordination, the Buchanan Administration waited weeks before taking action. During this time, the president's initial enthusiasm for action was diminished by opposition from important military officers. The Commander-in-Chief of the Army, General Winfield Scott, was concerned about terrain and logistical problems facing the military expedition. Scott believed it was too late in the year to send troops west and asked to postpone the movement until 1858. General William S. Harney, who was appointed commander of the expedition, was reluctant to accept the position, preferred to wait another year, and hoped to escape the assignment altogether.[5] Unfortunately, Scott's cautions were disregarded.

According to General Order No. 8, issued on May 28, 1857, the force was to be composed of the Fifth Infantry, eight companies of the Tenth Infantry, and the Second Dragoons. In June, two artillery batteries under Captain John W. Phelps and Lieutenant Jesse Reno were added to the command. It was difficult to assemble quickly these troops. The Second Dragoons were near Fort Leavenworth, the Tenth Regiment was in Minnesota, and the Fifth Regiment was chasing the Seminoles through the Florida swamps.[6]

The Tenth Infantry left Fort Snelling in June and traveled down the Missouri River to Fort Leavenworth. The Tenth established Camp Walbach along the banks of the river about one mile from the fort.[7] By June 30 all of the regiment was in camp except for Company A and Company D.[8]

On June 29 Scott sent instructions to General Harney that declared "the community and, in part, the civil government of Utah Territory" were "in a state of substantial rebellion." In spite of the situation, Scott limited the military's role to that of a *posse comitatus*.[9] He left the power to utilize the army to preserve the peace and execute the laws in the hands of the territorial governor, judges, and marshals. The army was authorized to obey promptly requests for help with the necessary number of troops. The army could employ force in serving as a *posse comitatus* or in self-defense. General Harney was "responsible for a zealous, harmonious, and thorough cooperation" with the governor through "frequent and full consultation."[10] The following day Scott ordered the task force to establish a post at, or near, Salt Lake City. The military expedition was designated as the Army of Utah, and its official purpose was to establish a new military department in Utah, not to suppress a Mormon rebellion.[11] The hidden agenda was to establish federal authority in Utah.

The Tenth Infantry was designated as the advance for the march. While the health of the soldiers in the regiment was excellent, the capabilities of their commander remained highly suspect. Captain Jesse Gove of Company I was impressed by the large gathering of troops but considered Colonel Alexander to be "in his dotage."[12] At six o'clock on July 18, the Tenth Infantry began the march to Utah. Gove said, "It was a splendid sight as Colonel Smith led the 600 men with the band playing past General Harney's quarters in Fort Leavenworth."[13] The expedition was immediately in trouble. The army was "much diminished by sickness and desertion" and had only half of the 2,500 men Scott wanted in the command. No cavalry was assigned to the advance force to protect the supply trains. The expedition also lost its commander when Kansas Governor Walker complained to President Buchanan about Harney's reassignment, and the president assured Walker that General Harney would remain in Kansas.[14]

14. "A war must be waged" 113

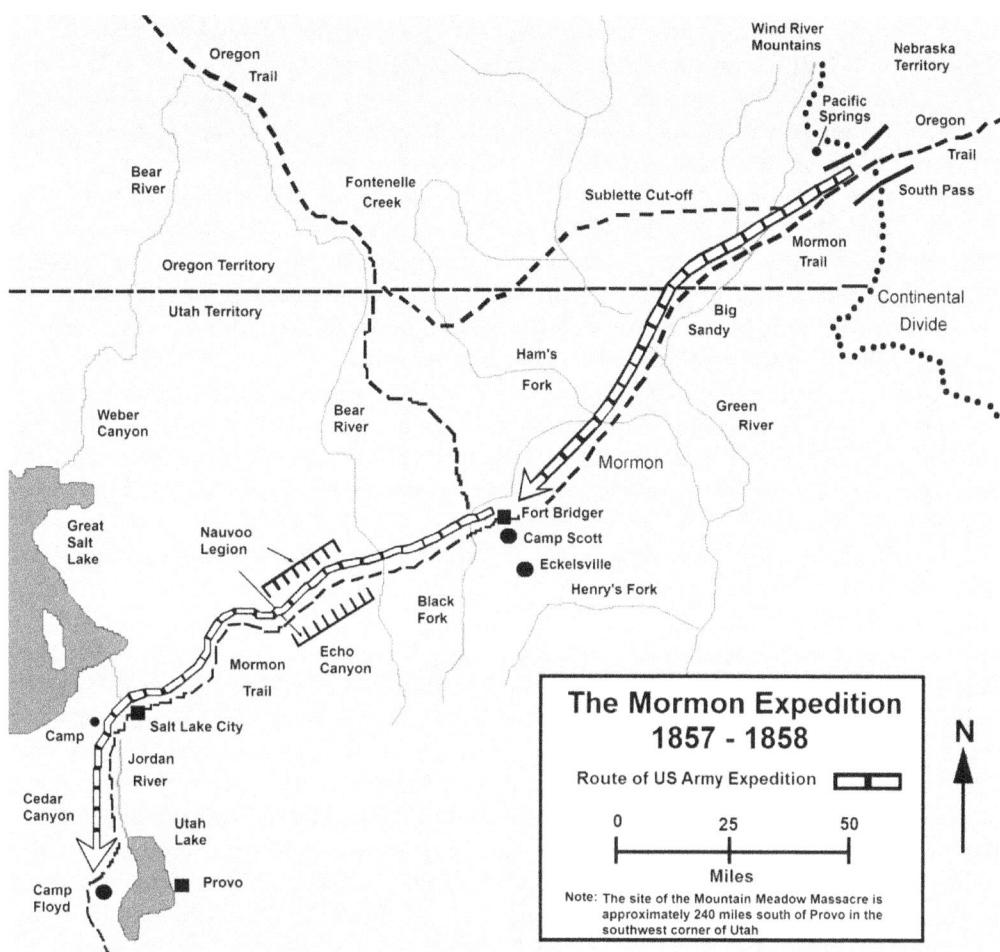

The Mormon Expedition (author's map based on map of the Mormon Expedition from Robert W. Coakley, *The Role of Federal Military Forces in Domestic Disorders 1789–1878*).

In the spring, rumors reached Utah that an army was invading the territory and the federal government was replacing Brigham Young as governor. The lack of information on the army's mission created fear among the Saints and encouraged them to prepare to defend their community.[15] In response to the military intervention, Governor Young activated the Nauvoo Legion in early August. The Nauvoo Legion or Utah militia was composed of all able-bodied men between fifteen and sixty. Young ordered the Legion to monitor the movements of the invading army and to harass the troops if they entered the territory. The governor needed to gain time for the settlements to prepare for battle or evacuation and for his representatives to initiate negotiations with the Buchanan Administration.[16] In pursuit of an agreement, Young enlisted the help of Colonel Thomas J. Kane, a Mormon ally who had influence in the Buchanan administration.[17]

The Army of Utah was divided into four components. Colonel Alexander and Captain Phelps were in the lead with eight companies of the Tenth Infantry Regiment and the artillery at Ham's Fork. Colonel Gilbert Waite and the Fifth Infantry were about twenty-five miles back on the Green River. Colonel Smith was camped on the Sweet Water River with two companies from the Tenth Infantry and Lieutenant Smith's company from the

Second Dragoons. The remainder of the Second Dragoons under Colonel Philip St. George Cooke were at Fort Laramie to escort the group of federal officials.

Colonel C. F. Smith reported that his group was making good progress and were about 124 miles from Fort Leavenworth. The men were in good shape and they were averaging seventeen miles per day marching over the "boundless sea of grass." Smith learned from a man returning to the East that "the Mormon Prophet and his Elders preached war to the knife[18] against the Gentiles." The Mormons threatened to attack the army as it passed through Echo Canyon en route to Salt Lake City. Governor Young's threats did not frighten Smith, and he declared, "I fear this is too good to be true. Should they act when the onus would be thrown upon them and we could act without hesitation and with a clear conscience in razing the city of the Saints and sowing Salt on its Surface."[19]

The army finally appointed Colonel Albert Sydney Johnston in late August to replace Harney. Johnston, commander of the Second Cavalry in Texas, was on leave in Washington and did not reach Fort Leavenworth until the second week of September. He joined the Second Dragoons and the new governor and other officials at Leavenworth and the group left for Fort Laramie.[20]

On July 18, 1857, General Harney ordered Captain Stewart Van Vliet, an assistant quartermaster, and a small escort to travel from Kansas to Salt Lake City, ahead of the main body of troops. Van Vliet carried a letter to Young from Harney ordering Young to make arrangements to accommodate and supply the troops entering the territory.[21] In early September, Governor Young met Van Vliet. Captain Van Vliet delivered General Harney's letter to Young announcing the formation of the Military Department of Utah, explaining that troops were on the way, and requesting Young's help in obtaining supplies. Van Vliet tried to lessen Young's concerns. "I do not think it is the intention of the government to arrest you," he said, "but to install a new governor of the territory." The captain explained that the troops would only be used as a *posse comitatus* when the federal authorities requested their help to enforce the laws. When Van Vliet asked for assistance in purchasing provisions, Young replied that the Mormons were unanimous in their intention "to guard against any invader." Van Vliet was unable to persuade the church leaders that the army's mission was peaceful, and he realized that the Mormons would not provide supplies or quarters for the soldiers. Young told Van Vliet that the Mormons did not want war, but they would prohibit the new governor and federal officers from entering Utah.[22] On September 21 Van Vliet met Colonel Alexander on the road from Fort Laramie. Van Vliet reported that the Saints planned to delay the troops without engaging in hostilities, were ready to destroy their crops and homes to deny food and shelter to the army, and were fortifying the route through Echo Canyon to Salt Lake City and it would be a "death trap for a large body of troops."[23]

After Van Vliet's departure, Young declared martial law in Utah and prohibited "all armed forces of every description from coming into this Territory, under any pretense whatsoever." He ordered, "All the forces in said Territory [to] hold themselves in readiness to march at a moment's notice to repel any and all such invasion." His proclamation also prohibited settlers traveling to California and Oregon "to pass or repass into, through or from this territory without a permit from the proper officer."[24]

Young's Nauvoo Legion made initial contact with the leading elements of the federal expedition in late September just west of South Pass. The militia began their harassment tactics by burning grass along the trail and stampeding the army's cattle. The absence of a cavalry escort left the advance forces vulnerable to the militia's tactics.[25] During October and November, between 1,200 and 2,000 Nauvoo Legion militiamen were sent to defend the passes in Echo Canyon and Weber Canyon. The Legion built fortifications, dug rifle pits, and dammed streams and rivers to prepare for a possible battle that fall or the following spring. Several thousand more militiamen received military training and prepared to evacuate their families.

On September 5 Colonel Smith arrived at Fort Kearney in the Nebraska Territory. He wrote, "the weather proved propitious for the march until within the past ten days when first we suffered from great heat and myriads of sand—this or buffalo gnats, and yesterday with a drenching rain all day, with an accompaniment of mosquitoes." The nights were becoming "sufficiently cold [enough] to make the driver's blankets comfortable giving reason to know that we are approaching the Rocky mountains." He thought the fort was "by some degree worse than any military post it has yet been my fate to dwell in."[26]

The Tenth Infantry continued their march from Fort Kearney into the Utah Territory. On September 23 Smith's command made camp on the North Fork of the Platte River approximately sixty-six miles from Fort Laramie and nearly halfway to the Utah Territory.[27] Three days later the vanguard reached Fort Laramie.[28] At Fort Laramie, the soldiers learned that the Mormons had "virtually declared war." Local mountain men said that a large force was in the mountains with plans to attack the army and urged the officers to "keep a sharp lookout for them."[29] Captain Gove was impressed by "how wonderfully the Mormons have their express and spy system perfected." Gove correctly concluded that the Saints' objective "appeared to delay progress to Salt Lake City by stampeding the army's animals rather than forcing a fight." He was relieved that "our supplies are now with us, at least there is no train ahead of us, so we shall give ample protection to them."[30]

As the invading army encountered the Saints, the men began to form their own opinions of Young's followers. Captain Gove said the first Mormon who "shows his head will get it cracked to a dead certainty." The captain wrote that the oppression in Utah was "heart rending in the extreme." Those people "who do not bow to Mormondom" or try to leave the territory are murdered. The Saints tried to induce the soldiers to desert. They also attempted to forge alliances with the Indians by requiring Mormons living in Indian Territory to marry squaws and giving white women to Indians. Gove remarked that the efforts have not been successful and no important tribes have allied with them. Instead, the Indians "want to go with us to fight them."[31]

The Army of Utah entered the territory in late September. The eight companies of the Tenth Infantry camped at Ham's Fork on September 28, and Captain Phelps' artillery battery joined them the next day. The Fifth Infantry, following the vanguard, advanced to a place about twenty-five miles back on Green River. The separation of forces exposed Colonel Alexander's supply trains, and he wanted to consolidate the units in a defensible location. However, the colonel was reluctant to assume command of the entire advance force. Shortly after arriving at Ham's Fork, Alexander received a message from Brigham Young demanding that the troops "retire forthwith from the territory" by the same route they had entered. "If this was impractical immediately because of approaching winter," he conceded, "they could remain until spring on condition they turn over their arms to the territorial quartermaster."[32]

On October 2 Alexander acknowledged receipt of the letter with its "absurd" claims and promised to pass it on to the "general commanding" as soon as he arrived. The colonel responded, "I have only to say that these troops are here on orders of the President of the United States, and their future movements and operations will depend entirely on orders issued by competent military authority."[33]

While the Fifth Infantry Regiment was marching toward Alexander's forces, a Mormon detachment attacked the supply trains following Alexander's infantry. The Mormons burned three unprotected wagon trains. The army lost seventy-two wagons containing 300,000 pounds of food. The attacks forced Alexander into action, and he assumed command of the advance force. He learned that Johnston had replaced Harney, but he would not reach Ham's Fork before the end of the month. Alexander realized that he needed to move his command and decided to advance through the Bear River valley into the Mormon settlements. This route was 100 miles longer than the direct approach through Echo Canyon, but avoided fighting the Mormons in the narrow mountain passes. He assumed that Colonel Smith's two companies and Lieutenant Smith's units from the Second Dragoons were advancing toward a point on this route and could easily join with the main force.[34]

Under the watchful eyes of the militia, Alexander started to march northward on October 11. The expedition captured a Mormon detachment and learned about their plans and tactics. Alexander's forces had only advanced eleven miles in eight days when the column was hit by a snowstorm. About the same time, Alexander learned that he had been misinformed about Colonel Smith's position and movements. The situation forced the advance column to return to Ham's Fork.[35]

On October 13 Colonel Smith's troops were camped on the Sweet Water River 257 miles from Fort Laramie in the Nebraska Territory. Smith was surprised to learn about the attacks on the supply trains.

> The Mormons are in front of me about Green River & swear no supplies shall pass for the Army. They are mounted & various estimates at [are] from 80 to several hundreds. They say they will not shed blood but if one of the Saints' blood is shed, they will exterminate the Gentile Army. I intend to give them a chance to execute their threat, for if the miscreants come within range of my rifles I mean to fire into them. They justify me in so doing by their destruction of Govt trains—in itself an act of war—coupled with their threats to Captain Van Vliet. They are at least high way [sic] robbers, if not traitors—let them therefore keep clear of me.[36]

Colonel Johnston finally reached the Sweetwater River in mid-October. The Mormon raids astonished Johnston and ruined his plans to enter Utah before the winter. He decided to gather his scattered troops, protect the supply trains, and locate a suitable place to spend the winter. Johnston ordered Alexander to retire and join Johnston's forces at Pacific Springs. Johnston told General Scott that he could not advance against the Mormons until spring. After the events over the past month, Johnston was convinced that "a war must be waged."[37]

"The Mormons will not fight"

By October 26 Colonel Johnston had gathered all of the army's rear elements at South Pass, and on November 4 he collected Colonel Alexander's command at Ham's Fork. Johnston's Army of Utah was now together except for Colonel Cooke's dragoons that were escorting the new governor and federal officials from Fort Laramie.

Johnston decided to spend the winter at Fort Bridger. En route to the fort, Smith's command waited by the Sweet Water River, near the "South Pass," for eight days to allow the supply trains and troops in the rear to catch-up. Then Smith's 320 men and the 343 wagons they guarded marched to link up with the rest of the army. The supply trains started traveling together in a five or six-mile line. The Mormons stopped harassing the wagons thanks to "the presence of the cavalry and the judicious dispositions and vigilance of Colonel Smith."[38] After the wagons joined the main body, the army traveled to Fort Bridger from Black's Fork on the Green River. Smith characterized the march as "more like the retreat of a routed army than the advance of troops animated with the expectation of success." He attributed the low morale to "the enfeebled condition of horse, mules & men, want of grain or grass for them, the severity of the weather, the thermometer & ongoing for many days from the middle of Oct. in fact—from zero to minus 16° and snow."[39]

Johnston prepared his army for battle in case they would have to fight to capture Fort Bridger from the Mormons. The column ran into a severe blizzard when they started the thirty-five-mile march, and it took them two weeks in the cold and snow to reach the fort. The sub-zero temperature and lack of shelter along the route took a disastrous toll on horses, mules, and oxen.[40] The Tenth and Fifth Regiments reached Fort Bridger on November 20 and camped nearby. Cooke's dragoons, escorting the civil officials, reached the fort a few days later, after suffering even more severely from the storm.

By the end of November, the Army of Utah and the federal officials were together in winter quarters at Fort Bridger. Unfortunately, Bridger was more a ruins than a fort as the Mormon militia had burned the fort to deny shelter to the army. All that remained of the burned fort was a "high, well built, strong stone wall, enclosing a square of one hundred feet." The Saints also destroyed houses, crops, and stores of grain in the area. Johnston's troops placed their supplies in the stone enclosure and erected a tent city that they named Camp Scott.[41]

Captain Gove said, "The health of the regiment was remarkably good, but many cases of frost-bite occurred during the month." Smith and the other officers conducted theoretical and practical military instruction as regularly as permitted by bad weather, the absence of men assigned to guard and outpost duty, and the delegation of soldiers to carry fuel four or five miles. These difficult duties were performed in spite of "a restricted and indifferent allowance of food." There were enough rations to last through the winter, although the flour allowance was cut, much of the food was unpalatable, and there was a shortage of salt.[42]

Johnston sent an emergency request to Fort Laramie for salt and asked that other supplies be delivered as early in the spring as possible. Johnston sent Captain R. B. Marcy to Taos, New Mexico, to obtain animals to replace those lost during the march. Johnston planned to resume the march in the spring "as soon as the supply of horses and mules arrive, and the grass on the mountains shall be found sufficient to sustain them."[43]

Charles told his family that Camp Scott would "be our abiding place for the winter." The camp was two miles from Fort Bridger, which was "nothing but a square wall 15 ft. high and 100 feet on a side built of rubble stone" that "a six pounder could have breached in a few minutes." The men improved the fort by building two lunettes[44] and erecting storage shelters to hold their supplies.

Charles said he was quite comfortable in Camp Scott's tent city.

> I am quite so, nay, rather elegant for my spacious apartment 18 ft. by 9 ft.—2 small tents sewed together—is covered by a Brussels carpet—the floor on which it rests consisting of willow twigs. My small sheet iron stove is the greatest treasure—it is invaluable. The winter commenced more than six weeks since; but we are as comfortable under our canvass in the middle of snow & ice, at an altitude of between 6 & 7,000 feet, as you are in your cottage.

His hardest duty was every five days when he was field officer of the day and required to spend twenty-four hours on horseback inspecting the camps, guards, sentinels, and pickets.[45]

Johnston recruited volunteers from the discharged wagon drivers and other "unemployed" Americans and organized the men into companies he thought would make excellent light troops. Three companies were already on duty and a fourth company was being organized. Johnston asked Smith to lead the new volunteer battalion. Smith regarded this assignment as "most disagreeable duty possible" and pleaded that "some person who valued such a command might be selected."[46] Johnston finally gave in to Smith's "earnest & repeated requests not to have any bit to do with these men" and assigned the duty of organizing the battalion to Captain Barnard E. Bee. Bee was brevetted to a lieutenant colonel and appointed an aide-de-camp to Governor Cummings. Colonel Bee worked hard trying to get his volunteers, or as his fellow officers teased him, "Bee's Vagabonds," into shape.[47]

The Mormons' actions during the fall increased the army's animosity toward them. Johnston condemned the Saints' rebellion and criticized their "repugnant" social and political system. He asserted, "The time for any further argument is past, and in my opinion, the people of the United States must now act or submit to an usurpation of their territory and the ingrafting upon our institutions, a social organization and political principle totally incompatible with their own."[48] The officers and men agreed with their commander and looked forward to crushing this devious enemy. Johnston established a tight security system that prevented Mormon spies from entering the camp, prohibited wagon trains to or from Mormon settlements from passing through camp, and declared that Mormons carrying guns would be treated as enemies.

The civil officials were quartered near Camp Scott in a tent city called Eckelsville in honor of the chief judge, Delana Eckels.[49] Cummings issued a proclamation from Eckelsville to the people of Utah announcing his appointment as governor and his intention to organize the territorial government. He labeled the attacks on the army as "treasonable acts of violence committed by lawless individuals" and said they would be brought to trial in Judge Eckels' court. In his capacity as commander-in-chief of the territory's militia, Cummings ordered "all armed bodies of individuals, by whomsoever organized, to disband and return to their respective homes." The penalty for disobedience would be "the punishment due to traitors." Cummings sent the proclamation to the "Ex-governor of Utah" Brigham Young.[50] Young refused to recognize Cummings' authority, and when Young offered "the military commander" 800 pounds of salt to meet the troops' extreme need, he signed the letter as "Governor of Utah." Johnston quickly rejected the offer from "enemies of the government."[51]

In his first annual message to Congress on December 8, 1857, President Buchanan seemed determined to meet the Mormon challenge. "This is the first rebellion which has existed in our Territories," he stated, "and humanity itself requires that we should put it down in a manner that it shall be the last." The president asked Congress to authorize four new regiments for the army and appropriate funds for the expedition. While Congress debated the military and financial options, the War Department formulated plans to increase the Army of Utah to the size required to defeat the Mormons. In early January 1858, the army ordered reinforcements sent to Utah "as soon as possible." The nearly 4,000 additional troops would bring the army's strength in Utah to nearly 6,000.[52]

For the men at Camp Scott, the monotony was interrupted by the mail delivering information from their families and news from the outside world. Smith claimed that the soldiers were very healthy and quite cheerful when they had light duty. The weather was cold, especially at night when the thermometer dropped to zero or below, but they only had occasional storms with small amounts of snow.[53] Smith spent his evenings reading or playing a game of Boston Whist[54] for a "nominal stake." The card parties were "usually followed by a supper at which there is wanting most of the delicacies of the season."[55]

Smith attributed the excellent health of the troops to "pure air and plenty of exercise," and he thought that the men were "all contented and cheerful." Ever the teacher, Smith took the opportunity to provide instruction to junior officers in the Tenth Infantry. "I have been playing the schoolmaster for some time past in hearing the offs [officers] of the regiment recite in Infantry Tactics—to me a great bore. But our Colonel, altho' recognizing the subject, has not all the confidence in the world in his ability to play the part of an instructor, & thus the duty devolves upon me."[56]

The winter had done little to dampen Smith's desires to fight the Mormons. The colonel concluded regrettably "the Mormons will not fight." Smith's "earnest wish" was to "have an opportunity to give these rebels a sound drubbing" before the new volunteers joined the army.[57]

The Army of Utah impatiently waited for spring and the arrival of supplies and additional troops. As Johnston's army prepared for battle, President Buchanan was engaged in his own conflict with Congress over the cost and mismanagement of the expedition. Buchanan needed to resolve the situation, and he thought that Mormon advocate, Thomas L. Kane, might provide the solution. In December 1857 Kane met with the president and offered to mediate between the parties. The president offered to pardon the Mormons for their rebellious acts if they would agree to obey federal authority. Buchanan granted Kane unofficial permission to present these terms to the Mormons.[58]

Kane arrived in Salt Lake City in February 1858 and convinced Young to accept Cumming as territorial governor. Then Kane traveled to Fort Bridger and met with Governor Cummings and Brevet Brigadier General Johnston on March 12.[59] Although Kane failed to persuade Johnston, he convinced Cummings to accompany him unescorted to Salt Lake City to meet with Young.

While Kane was trying to broker a settlement, the Mormons started leaving their homes and moving south. Their strategy was to evacuate all the settlements north of Provo, leave a few guards behind in each town, and avoid contact between the settlers and the army. Young decided to abandon the territory and leave it in ruins instead of fighting the army. The Church moved its headquarters to Provo where its leaders evaluated the army's intentions. Therefore, when Cummings entered Salt Lake City, most of the Mormons living in the city and in northern settlements were on the road south.

Charles told Fanny that "Mr. Col. K" went to Salt Lake City as "*compagnon de voyage*"[60] to Governor Cummings. He labeled the visit as improper and "inconsistent with the dignity and propriety of his position."

> If the Governor's mission is to assert his lawful authority as the chief ruler of the people, to demand the seals of office, and to require the ring-leaders of the outrageous acts perpetuated within the last 5 or 6 months to be delivered over to him for trial, it would be one to command respect, altho' knowing the people with whom he is to deal, it would be an act of consummate folly; for it's certain that in such a case they would treat him with official indignity—laugh at him, deride him, and very likely set him on a mule with his face to the tail of the animal and turn him out—possibly in this direction probably towards the Pacific.

The colonel declared: "There can be no terms made with mutineers or rebels with arms in their hands, such people must lay down their arms and submit to the laws unconditionally before lawful authority can hold intercourse with them; failing to do this they must be coerced. But as I said in the beginning under no circumstances should he have gone in accept under the flag of his country—this he has not done."[61]

Governor Cummings arrived in Salt Lake City on April 12 and was cordially received by the church leaders, who returned from Provo. After meeting with Young and other leaders, Cummings sent a triumphant message to Johnston: "I have been everywhere recognized as the governor of Utah, and so far from having encountered insults and indignities, I am gratified in being able to state to you that, in passing through the settlements, I have been universally greeted with such respectful intentions as are due to the representative of the executive authority of the United States in the territory."[62]

On April 15, 1858, Major General Persifor F. Smith was appointed to command the Military Department of Utah and Generals Harney and Johnston were placed in charge of brigades under him. Smith and Harney were ordered to supervise the movement of troops to Utah as soon as possible. After General Smith died in May, Harney was appointed to lead the command. Harney expected the reinforcements and supplies to arrive in August and planned to travel to Camp Scott to take personal command.[63]

Johnston had no intention of waiting for Harney and decided to march to Salt Lake City with the forces he had at Camp Scott. He planned to enter the territory as soon as supplies arrived from Fort Leavenworth and Fort Laramie and Captain Marcy returned from New Mexico with horses and mules. Johnston was confident that he had enough men to travel through the passes to Salt Lake City, and he was positive the action was necessary.[64]

The optimistic Cummings exaggerated the extent of Mormon submission. The Saints continued to leave their northern settlements, the Nauvoo Legion remained stationed in the passes leading to Salt Lake City, and Mormon leaders continued to believe that peace was impossible as long as the army remained near their settlements.[65] The agreement between Cummings and Young allowed the new governor to exercise his powers as long as he took "no action detrimental to the Mormon hierarchy." This concession created a shadow government under which the Mormons maintained control of the territory.[66] Cummings tried to convince Johnston that there was no urgent need for the military in Salt Lake City, but Johnston could not be persuaded. "To compromise with these people on any other terms than an unconditional surrender would in my opinion be unsafe, unwise, and impolitic."[67]

The disagreement between Cummings and Johnston convinced Buchanan to take the situation out of their hands. In April, the president decided to send a commission to investigate conditions before allowing military intervention. He chose Lazarus W. Powell, former governor and current senator-elect from Kentucky, and Ben McCulloch, hero of the Texas revolution and the Mexican War and now a U.S. Marshal in Texas, to serve as commissioners. Their evaluation would allow Buchanan to form his own opinion of the situation. Buchanan repeated his threat to punish those who resisted federal authority but offered a "free and full pardon" for those who agreed to federal jurisdiction. Buchanan said the military would remain in Utah "until the inhabitants of that Territory shall manifest a proper sense of duty which they owe to this Government."[68] President Buchanan made his terms official when he issued a proclamation "offering the inhabitants of Utah, who shall submit to the laws, a free pardon for seditions and treasons heretofore by them committed; warning those who shall persist, after notice of this proclamation, in the present rebellion against the United States, that they must expect no further leniency, but look to be rigorously dealt with according to their desserts; and declaring that the military forces now in Utah, and hereafter to be sent there, will not be withdrawn until the inhabitants of that Territory shall manifest a proper sense of the duty which they owe to this government."[69]

Powell and McCulloch hoped that the president's pardon would be sufficient inducement to persuade the Mormons to accept the federal officials. By agreeing to Buchanan's terms, the Saints could remove the indictments and eliminate the possibility of being tried for treason. The Secretary of War's directions to the commissioners were slightly different from the president's instructions. They were told not to make a treaty with the Mormons and to try to "bring these misguided people to their senses ... and spare the effusion of human blood." After the federal officials were installed and the Mormons agreed to obey the laws, the army troops in the territory would focus on "the normal functions of keeping the Indians in check and protecting the emigrants."[70]

The commissioners met with Cummings and Johnston at Camp Scott in late May and agreed with Johnston's assessment of the situation. The commissioners said the "leaders of the Mormon people have not given the governor correct information as to the condition of affairs in the valley" and concluded that the Mormons were still guarding the approaches to Salt Lake City. The commissioners decided the continued threat of the army was the best guarantee to force the Mormons to agree to terms. "We deem it a matter of first importance that the army advance into the valley of Salt Lake before the Mormons can burn the grass or harvest or burn the growing crops."[71]

Smith was pleased with the commissioner's judgment. "They breathe the right spirit, that these people must submit to the law unconditionally." He said that although the people "are in a state of rebellion," he thought "the mass of people have been beguiled by designing men." However, Smith disliked offering "a full pardon to all without distinction who will at once submit to the law and promise to be good boys for the future." He was in favor of "a sound drubbing" that would lead "more effectually to a proper state of subordination on their part than if that ceremony should be omitted," and he considered that such action was "a good rule" in regard to nations that was "especially applicable here."[72]

Eventually, Powell and McCulloch obtained most of the required pledges from the Mormon leaders and the Saints accepted the presidential pardon. The Mormons agreed to allow civil and military authorities to enter the Territory of Utah and perform their official duties. The army would establish military posts in the territory necessary to police the Indians, protect emigrants, and, if necessary, act as *posse comitatus*.[73]

While the Mormons were satisfied with the negotiations, Captain Gove said, "The Mormons have accepted the pardon, but it is no more in earnest than the wind: they are as impudent and villainous as ever. They have accepted only to gain time. The President has damned himself and the country."[74] The commissioners notified Secretary of War John B. Floyd that they had settled "the unfortunate difficulties existing between the government of the United States and the people of Utah." President Buchanan had already decided the troubles were over and had cancelled the plans to send additional regiments to Utah.[75] Powell and McCulloch reported to Secretary Floyd, "We are firmly impressed with the belief that the presence of the army here, and the large additional force that had been ordered to this Territory, were the chief inducements that caused the Mormons to abandon the idea of resisting the authority of the United States. A less decisive policy probably would have resulted in a long, bloody and expensive war."[76]

The successful negotiations failed to reduce the hostility, and the tense situation continued through the spring of 1858. While Young was willing to support Cumming as governor, the Mormon leaders remained concerned about possible persecution and violence if the army entered Utah. The opposing forces increased the size of their commands. Approximately 3,000 reinforcements headed west to strengthen Johnston's forces, and an additional thousand volunteers were added to the Nauvoo Legion.[77]

On June 11 provisions, new uniforms, and additional troops arrived at Camp Scott, and the army left for Salt Lake City. The Tenth Infantry was deployed as the rear guard. Smith said, "The Young Men of 'ours' are grumbling at this arrangement forgetting the scriptural rule that the 'last shall be first.' I know when we reach Bear River—distant about 40 miles—the order of march will be changed, & the 10th take the lead, as it ought."[78]

Johnston did not intend to invite an ambush by going through the canyons. After reaching Bear River, he planned to deflect the column to the right and flank the enemy's position. Smith believed this could be easily accomplished by building a road through the mountains and advancing to Salt Lake City through the Weber River Valley.

> Genl J told me long since of his plan concealed even yet from prudential considerations wishing the Mormons to think he intended to free the passes, and thus let them exhaust their energies in fortifying them, when he never intended to attack them. They must have thought us babes in the art of war to suppose so.
>
> Whether these rascally "Saints" intend to make fight is not known; I think not; but if they do they will get a lesson they little dream of.[79]

Johnston's force left Camp Scott on June 13, 1858. The army camped at Bear River, and Johnston issued a proclamation assuring the people that they had nothing to fear from the army, which would protect them and their property as long as they obeyed federal laws.

In spite of the agreement with the Mormons, the split between Cummings and Johnston continued to widen. Cummings wanted to move forward and permit the Mormons to govern themselves under a minimum federal oversight. Johnston wanted to impose strong federal authority and punish Mormon leaders for their past crimes. On June 19 a *New York Herald* reporter wrote, "Thus was peace made—thus was ended the 'Mormon war', which ... may be thus historisized:—Killed, none; wounded, none; fooled, everybody."[80]

As Smith had predicted, the Tenth Infantry led the column into Salt Lake City.[81] The army marched through the city on June 26 and made camp outside town across the Little Jordan River. Smith said the march was like "treading the deserted streets of a city of the dead." There were only around 100 to 150 people and one-third were Gentiles. As he rode through the empty streets, a disappointed Johnston said that he would have given "his plantation for a chance to bombard the city for fifteen minutes."[82]

The army remained at the camp on the Jordan River for several days until they moved about eighteen miles southwest to obtain grass for the livestock. Smith was selected to be a member of a board to examine several of the valleys to choose a site for a permanent post. After traveling 100 miles over several days, the board selected Cedar Valley.[83] On their way to Cedar Valley, the army met Mormon families returning to Salt Lake City. The encounters were peaceful because each group was careful to avoid offending the other. "The road was literally covered with wagons and families and animals of the people, as it had been for two days before & will be 2 days to come." Smith was impressed by the people but shocked by their poverty.

> I never witnessed such a sight—such poverty as the dress indicated in both sexes. I saw many women and half grown girls wearing a simple calico garment and that in tatters. They had a straw hat or calico sun bonnet but no stockings or shoes. All were trudging on foot in the hot sun and excessive dust as if it were the most natural thing possible. They were mostly foreigners—English, Scotch Welsh & Danes. They greeted us politely and when talked to answered in the most civil manner.[84]

While he thought kindly of the emigrants, he had no good wishes for their leaders "who are low, vulgar, American rascals, [and] are quite surly."[85]

The proposed Cedar Valley campsite was about midway between Salt Lake City and Provo with good grazing land and few inhabitants. After a short time, the camp was moved to the north end of Cedar Valley where Johnston claimed the land as a military reserve and designated it Camp Floyd.[86] Although the campsite was the best place for the troops, it was unbearably dusty. "With the high winds that prevail the almost unpalatable powder into which the light soil is ground by man & beast is whirled about us to a distressing degree. I have never suffered such annoyances in a permanent camp within my remembrance; the worse is there is no end of it."[87]

On July 27 the U.S. Attorney for Utah, Seth M. Blair, visited Johnston at Camp Floyd. During the meeting, Smith made some disrespectful remarks about the Mormons. Someone present said, "Sir, you had better beware how you talk about Mormons as they might hear you." Smith said he "did not care a damn who heard him" and he "would like to see every damned Mormon hung by the neck."[88] Smith's angry outburst was widely circulated. The remark was certainly not directed toward all Mormons, many of whom he looked on with pity, but toward their leaders whom he regarded with contempt. Smith's comment was characteristic of his direct language that was uncompromised by political niceties.

It was soon apparent that the Saints' conciliations were superficial and "more nominal than real." Although the federal officials had taken their positions in the territorial government, the Mormon leaders' continued their tight control over the people, and the shadow government of the Mormon Church still governed Utah. Governor Cummings cooperated with the Mormons to maintain peace. On the other hand, the federal judges, supported by General Johnston, thought that federal authority should be more strongly asserted and trials should be held to convict Mormons of their crimes.[89]

A sort of malaise settled over Camp Floyd. The soldiers, who were once eager for a fight, became depressed by the government's actions. Smith said that without "the stimulation of active service" boredom soon pervaded the camp. The soldiers became weary and deserted and the officers asked for leave. However, Smith believed that the Mormons were in far worse condition than the men at Camp Floyd were. He berated the Saint's leaders for keeping their followers destitute prisoners. The colonel characterized the Mormon officials as "vulgar rascals" and described the "only other class" as composed of "ignorant and deluded foreigners with a fanaticism as unbounded as their ignorance."[90]

Colonel Smith assumed command of the regiment August 6 when Colonel Alexander went on leave. The regiment moved Camp Floyd from its temporary location to a permanent site on September 7.[91] Construction of the permanent post continued during the fall, and the men were "as busy as bees in erecting their adobe quarters." Charles complained to Fanny, "We are infinitely more distressed now and have been on account of dust & heat during the day than we were all last winter from cold & snow."[92]

> The high wind seemed to encase the surface of the earth in a thick cloud, everything was thickly overlaid with it, and when after many hours of endurance of this annoyance, there occurred a cold rain—the wind a little high in trying to take care of one of my tents which was thrown down & torn in every direction. I became a walking adobe—each drop of rain converting the dust on my person into mud.

Smith had his "nose out of joint" when Lieutenant Colonel Morrison from the Seventh Infantry arrived in camp, and, as the senior officer, assumed command of the post.[93] The regiment moved into their permanent quarters on October 16.[94]

> Our labor is now done and we present the appearance of a town of respectable size. The buildings occupy a space of about ¾ of a mile square with a population of say 3500 people, officers, soldiers & camp followers.
> We are all living in our new houses now and are quite comfortable. If you were to walk into my room at this moment you would be surprised to see how nicely it looks. Curtains to the windows of a most pastoral cherubs pattern, and a handsome Brussels carpet on the mud floor.[95]

In early January 1859, Smith wrote his daughter and apologized for not corresponding. He blamed it on snow storms for stopping mail delivery and "the presence of business commanding the post."

> A Major General's command without the staff of such a grade—having not a single assistant who discharges the duty of Adj of the post as well as that of the regiment. It may not be known to you that I have been placed on duty in Utah ascending to my brevet rank of Col.—but such is the melancholy fact. On the 19th of Dec. I assumed command of the post in virtue of that rank relieving Lt. Col. Morrison of the 7th Inf.
>
> As soon as it was known in camp that I was in command, I had a deluge of visits of congratulation, even from those, who will be delinquents and have the thumb screws applied to them if they err in a military way. The fable of King Log and King Stork[96] may apply in this instance, as some already know to their cost. However, if not altogether liked I am at least respected, and time will show to those who depart from military propriety that the fault is with them not me—the usual rule one is apt to find fault with every other person except the proper one—himself or herself as the case may be. Since assuming command of the post my entire day is, as a general rule consumed in office work with the pen, or riding about to look after the police and discipline of the camp.[97]

Another factor affecting his communications was the lack of reading glasses. He had broken his glasses and was unable to get them fixed in Salt Lake City. He could not read at night, but he managed during the day to read the small print with a borrowed pair. Off duty, Smith passed time visiting his friends, playing cards, and reading. He frequently spent his evenings with General Johnston. He told Fanny, "You do perhaps not know that we were well acquainted as students in the milty. [military] academy. I was his senior in rank there by one year, tho' he is several years my senior in age."

Smith complained that, "The weather was worse than last winter. It was much colder although the altitude was 2,000 feet lower." The harsh weather did not interfere with drills and military services. Smith said, "this is the best period for military instruction" because in the "summer the nature of the soil, producing clouds of dust" will make it impossible to march.[98]

Although Smith enjoyed courteous relations with his Mormon neighbors, he had a very low opinion of them and felt they should be punished for their wrongdoings.

> Justice cannot be administered in letter or spirit here according to the system in the States. There is but one mode of ever getting rid of this Mormon question, and that is for Congress to declare this people in a state of insurrection, which they are virtually, and suspend the writ of *habeas corpus*,[99] thus placing the country under martial law, when all offenders would come under the jurisdiction of military courts. Justice would then be rendered, and these rascals punished or driven from the country—the latter a consummation most devoutly prayed for.[100]

"Assist as a posse comitatus"

Smith was now in charge of both the regiment and the camp. He complained that he did not have "a single assistant" to help him with the required administrative duties. Smith spent his entire day "consumed in office work with the pen, or riding about to look after the police and discipline of the camp."[101]

With their limited mission, life at Camp Floyd settled into a dull routine of drill, guard duties, and maintenance of the grounds and equipment. The soldiers sought refuge from the boredom by attending a theater that offered dramas and minstrel shows. The officers had two billiard rooms, and Smith had allowed "certain citizens to erect ... two bowling salons with four way[s] each principally for the soldiers."[102]

The weather was worse than the previous winter with below zero temperatures at night. Thankfully, the snowfall and high winds were less than expected. However, the harsh weather did not interfere with drills and military services. Colonel Smith said, "This is the best period for military instruction" because in the "summer the nature of the soil, producing clouds of dust" make it impossible to march.[103]

Although Smith enjoyed courteous relations with his Mormon neighbors, he was frustrated with the failure of the federal courts to indict Mormons. He protested, "Justice cannot be administered in letter or spirit here according to the system in the States." Smith concluded, "There is but one mode of ever getting rid of this Mormon question, and that is for Congress to declare this people in a state of insurrection, which they are virtually, and suspend the writ of *habeas corpus*, thus placing the country under martial law, when all offenders would come under the jurisdiction of military courts. Justice would then be rendered, and these rascals punished or driven from the country—the latter a consummation most devoutly prayed for."[104]

While the activities at Camp Floyd were usually dictated by the winter weather, Captain Albert Tracy, commander of Company H of the Fifth Infantry Regiment, described an event that occurred during a snowstorm on February 28. Despite the threatening clouds over the mountains north and west of camp, Colonel Smith ordered a grand review. Tracy thought most other officers would have settled for "muster and inspection in quarters." However, Smith refused to be deterred by the weather and decided to hold a formal inspection. The men formed into battalions, marched across a stream, and past the town of Fairfield to a large area for the review. It took time for the formation to move into position because the sagebrush-studded ground "never yields upon mere occasions of military display." Meanwhile, the storm hit, sweeping "down so bitterly upon us ... that it was with difficulty the most resolute could refrain from turning in his place, to avoid its cutting cold. Some suffered slight freezing at the ear-tips, or extremity of nose, and many were so chilled as for the time almost to lose the use of hands and arms."

By the time Smith and his aides were in position to review the troops, the snow was advancing toward them like "a thick white wall ... and word of command, sound of bugle, or bray of band were, with the uproar of the storm soon muffled well nigh from hearing ... only the habit of the men kept them in line or step." The companies' flags and the line of march ahead could hardly be seen, and the men "only guessed at the points of wheeling, following ... in the track" of those before. "Coming round at the point of the reviewing officer—we distinguished through the cloud, dim objects, gray and ghost-like, believed to be Smith and his staff, and at these we saluted, agreeable to the regulation, with our sabers—doing the best we might." As the storm diminished, Tracy saw snow piled up on band instruments and epaulets. The men's broad-brimmed felt hats with ostrich plumes "were simply a mess, and shocking to behold." Finally, the dejected troops filed off the field toward their company grounds. After the review, Smith relented and ordered one gill[105] of whiskey per man, which "did much to salve over the wounded dignity and morale of the morning." Tracy concluded, "There is no other man in the army who could have done all this with impunity. Yet knowing the brave record, and the generally just character of Smith—it is likely he will be forgiven even the vagary of this review in a February snowstorm."[106]

The uneasy peace was disrupted in March 1859 when two federal judges arrived in Utah and decided to prosecute the Mormons. Judge Charles Sinclair tried to arrest the men who had disrupted the federal court and limited the authority of the probate courts. However, Judge John Cradlebaugh created the real crisis when he requested the army's help arraign prominent Mormons charged with murders and other crimes. On March 6, 1859, Cradlebaugh asked Johnston to send troops to guard prisoners to be tried in his court in Provo. Cradlebaugh planned to arraign Mormons accused of killing apostates and those involved in the Mountain Meadows massacre of September 1857.[107]

Johnston sent a company commanded by Captain Henry Heth to Provo to guard prisoners and deliver them to the marshal or district judge.[108] The presence of troops in Provo alarmed the residents, and city officials complained to the federal authorities. Cradlebaugh issued warrants for several leading Mormons, who left town to avoid being served.[109] It was soon obvious that the juries ignored the evidence and judge's instructions and made their decisions according to directives received from church officials in Salt Lake City. The residents of Provo grew angrier at the presence of federal troops and several incidents occurred that nearly injured Heth's men.[110]

Finally, on April 2 a frustrated and disgusted Judge Cradlebaugh adjourned his court, and Heth's company escorted the five remaining prisoners to Camp Floyd. The troops left Provo to the jeers and catcalls of the inhabitants and arrived at Floyd to the cheers and praise of their comrades. Afterwards, an angry Heth said, "Holding United States courts in Utah was a travesty of justice. President Buchanan said no blood would be shed during his administration. Brigham Young, who was kept well posted, knew this and acted accordingly."[111]

After Cradlebaugh closed his court, he traveled south to investigate the Mountain Meadows massacre. He suspected that Mormons, and not Indians, were responsible for the murders. Johnston sent a detachment of dragoons under Captain Reuben P. Campbell to the area to protect travelers on the road to California, provide an escort for the paymaster returning from California, and assist Cradlebaugh with his investigation.[112]

The Mountain Meadows massacre occurred September 7–11, 1857, near Cedar City, Utah. In 1857, the Baker-Fancher wagon train decided to go to California via Utah. The group was composed of wealthy travelers from Arkansas and Missouri. When the wagon train reached Utah, they wanted to purchase food from the Saints, but the Mormons had been ordered not to trade with the Gentiles. In addition to this difficulty, Indians started harassing the train. The Indians believed the travelers had poisoned a well that led to the deaths of several Indians. The Baker-Fancher train was also doing its best to antagonize the Mormons. Some of the Missourians bragged that they had participated in the 1838 massacre of seventeen Mormons in Missouri, and one claimed to have been part of a mob that killed Joseph Smith. The emigrants also boasted that after they reached California, they were going to return with an army. When the wagon train paused in Mountain Meadows to prepare for the final leg of their trip to California, the Mormons in the surrounding communities considered what to do. The Mormons regarded the wagon train as the vanguard of the military expedition. The local group sent a messenger to Brigham Young for instructions. Unfortunately, Young's orders to leave the group alone and let them pass did not arrive until after the massacre.[113]

While the Mormons waited for Young's instructions, the Indians increased their attacks. The Indians issued an ultimatum to the Mormons saying that unless they could kill all the Baker-Fancher party, "they would declare war against the Mormons and kill everyone in the settlements." Under the escalating situation, the Mormons decided to kill all of the emigrants, except for children too young to understand what had happened.[114]

On September 11, 1857, Major John D. Lee offered the emigrants safe passage to Cedar City, if they left their livestock, weapons, and wagons behind. The Baker-Fancher party had little choice and accepted Lee's terms. After they left camp, the Mormons and Indians murdered the entire party except for seventeen young children and infants. Between 120 and 150 men, women, and children were killed. When they received Young's instructions to leave the group alone, Lee's men blamed the Indians.[115]

Judge Cradlebaugh and Captain Campbell and his men visited the massacre site. Campbell found half-buried corpses and "human skulls, bones, and hair scattered about, and scraps of clothing of men, women and children." The bodies had been hastily buried by the Mormons and were eaten by predators. Long tufts of women's hair were found hanging among the sagebrush and bones.[116] Campbell's medical officer buried the remains. The Superintendent of Indian Affairs gathered the small children whom the Mormons had spared. The Saints thought the children were too young to remember. However, some of the older children were able to describe the attack. Based on information from the children and informants from Cedar City, Cradlebaugh was able to obtain the names of the Mormon suspects. With this evidence, the judge issued thirty-nine warrants; however, as usual, the suspects disappeared when the deputy marshal tried to serve the warrants. In pursuing these criminals, Cradlebaugh needed the military's help to guard prisoners, protect witnesses, and provide security for the court. Unfortunately, this support was scheduled to be withdrawn in mid–May. Without the military's help, Cradlebaugh could not proceed and he was forced to end the investigation. During the summer of 1859, Johnston and Smith supervised the eighteen young children. They arranged for matrons to care for the children and provided the children with transportation back to the East with an escort of dragoons for their protection. This event added to Smith's hatred of the Mormons.[117]

In Washington, Cummings' views prevailed over those of Johnston and the judges. On May 6 Secretary Floyd restricted the army's role only to "assist as a *posse comitatus* ... upon the written application of the governor of the territory and not otherwise."[118] This order effectively ended the army's law enforcement duties in Utah because Governor Cummings never asked a military posse to help enforce civil law. Johnston informed Judge Cradlebaugh that the military could not help arrest Mormon fugitives or guard prisoners and witnesses. Frustrated in his attempts to bring justice to Utah by Mormon leaders and federal officials, Judge Cradlebaugh gave up and retired. Johnston's Army of Utah focused their efforts on protecting emigrants, punishing plundering by Indians, and exploring the area.[119]

The Utah Expedition was an exasperating experience for the officers and men. In spite of their sentiments towards the Mormons, Johnston rigorously enforced his new orders and his men obeyed the instructions of the civil authorities.[120] In spite of their success in frustrating the army's mission in Utah, the Mormon leaders were forced to concede, if only superficially, to the federal government's demands because of the military's presence.[121]

General Johnston asked to be relieved from command of the Department of Utah, and on February 29, 1860, he turned over his duties to Colonel Smith. Captain Heth described Johnston's departure:

> General Johnston left Camp Floyd in the early spring of 1860, carrying with him the love and affections of every officer and soldier. On the day he left the troops were drawn up in the road he passed, and I do not believe there was a dry eye in that line. The command of the Department of Utah could not have fallen to a better soldier than C. F. Smith; everything moved on smoothly and well.[122]

Smith was pleased to be "rid of the drudgery" of directing Camp Floyd. Johnston went to Washington to present his perspective on the situation in Utah. Smith was pessimistic that Congress would maintain the whole force in Utah and "give it proper occupation and that is the hanging of Brigham Young & driving this leprous scum from our boundaries."

> We have never had troops in better condition for action both tactically and morally than those in Utah—they are in fine drill, contented & happy, no desertions; and with a latent hatred and contempt for Mormondom that now shows the happiest results in a collision. If the Mormon rulers give me ½ a chance I will leave my mark upon them in unmistakable characters—and glad of the occasion to do so.[123]

The new department commander maintained firm control and precisely followed Johnston's conduct. Smith ruled with strict discipline and kept disturbances to a minimum. After Smith's promotion, Major Canby was placed in charge of the Tenth Regiment. Captain Heth praised his new commander: "Major Canby was, I think the most accomplished and best informed officer I ever met, only excelled by that prince of soldiers, Lieutenant Colonel C. F. Smith."[124]

In 1860 Smith's friend, Henry Crosby, was appointed one of the federal judges for the Utah Territory and was assigned to "the district that is now Nevada." Judge Crosby believed Smith "had by far the best conception of the Mormon question of any of the leading military or civil officials and if he had been in command and permitted to carry out his views, would have for good and all settled that trouble."[125]

Although their initial assignments were completed, the command continued to be concerned about the possibility of renewed Indian troubles during 1860. Smith was in a difficult position commanding forces in a territory with both hostile Indians and Mormons. He informed Washington, "Should any outrage be committed on emigrants or on settlements by Indians, or the attempt be made by them to do so, let them be summarily punished or pursued to the bitter end, always making it an indispensable condition of peace for them to deliver up the defenders." Smith provided protection to the travelers on the Northern or Humboldt route to the Pacific against Indian attacks and was successful in preventing any major problems.[126]

In the spring of 1860, the War Department announced that Camp Floyd would be closed and the garrison reassigned to posts in New Mexico and Arizona. Smith was "to remain in command of the Department; but if we have nothing more to do than merely keep the Northern Road in this territory free from Indians, or supposed Indians, depredations I shall certainly request leave to visit my family, from which & from civilization, I have been separated for more than 4 years."[127]

With a degree of stability in the area, Smith managed the reassignment of troops from Camp Floyd. He directed the troop deployments to Fort Laramie, Fort Garland, and Fort Bridger in General Orders No. 10 issued on April 16, 1860. His instructions were very detailed, including the loads for wagons pulled by mule and ox teams, rations including bacon allowances, and the allocation of ordinance for the soldiers. The movements were scheduled to begin the following month.[128]

By June 8, 1860, the force at Camp Floyd was down to two infantry companies and two artillery companies. Smith believed the garrison was "entirely inadequate to guard the very large quantities of public stores on deposit and to protect the Camp from insult should this stiff-necked and rebellious people, (the Mormons) take it into their heads to play the fool." While the Mormons were pleased that the army no longer posed a threat to their management of the territory, they were unhappy with the loss of revenue from the departing troops. Smith suggested that the Mormon's were promoting disturbances by the Indians to have the troops recalled. He said that the loss of income was a strong motive for inciting the outrages in Carson Valley in April.[129] The attacks occurred in the valley and on the train route from Camp Floyd to valley. The Indians murdered Pony Express riders, burnt the stations, and took the stock. When the colonel heard about these attacks, he sent a company of cavalry to "chastise the Indians & endeavor to keep the road open." Eyewitnesses reported that white men were among the Indians involved in these attacks. Smith accused the Mormons of leading the attack and forwarded the evidence to Washington.[130]

On August 20 Special Orders No. 107 relieved Colonel Smith from command of the Department of Utah and placed him in charge of Camp Floyd.[131] After Secretary of War Floyd resigned on December 29, 1860, the post was renamed Fort Crittenden.

Smith had applied for a leave of absence in early 1860, but he was turned down because his "services cannot be dispensed with in Utah."[132] In January 1861, he renewed his request to visit his family. "Should I get the leave of which I entertain no doubt, I will not leave here before the beginning of April, perhaps not before the beginning of June, depending on the season and the means of traveling with comfort."[133]

Part Four

Disunion and Reunion: 1861–1862

"By reputation he was the best all-around officer in the regular army—a disciplinarian, stern, unsympathetic, an ogre to volunteers, but withal a magnificent soldier of the old school of Winfield Scott."—Lew Wallace[1]

Images of Paducah ("The War in Kentucky in and about Paducah," sketched by J. C. Beard and Bill Travis, *Harpers Weekly*, October 26, 1861).

15. "The storm will blow over"

"Free labor, free land, free men"

While the Buchanan Administration was settling the troubles in Utah, another more serious conflict was unfolding in the rest of the nation. While the seeds of disunion could be traced to colonial times, the catalyzing events may have started in Ripon, Wisconsin.

On February 28, 1854, in a schoolhouse in Ripon, opponents of the Kansas-Nebraska Act founded a new political party. The "anti-slavery expansion activists and modernizers" called themselves Republicans. With supporters in the Northeast and Midwest, the new organization quickly succeeded the Whig Party as the main opposition to the Democratic Party. Republican ideology was summarized in their campaign slogan: "free labor, free land, free men."

In the 1856 presidential election, the Democrats selected James Buchanan of Pennsylvania as their candidate and the Republican Party nominated John C. Frémont of California. Frémont condemned the Kansas-Nebraska Act and campaigned against the expansion of slavery. Buchanan supported the Act and said that expansion of slavery should be determined by popular sovereignty. Buchanan warned that a Republican victory would lead to civil war. Although Buchanan won, the Democrats realized that their regionally fractured party could lose the 1860 presidential election. All the Republicans needed was to capture Pennsylvania and Illinois.

Smith did not write about the candidates or slavery. On assignment in Minnesota, he was unable to vote in the 1856 election. He seemed to have a good opinion of Frémont, but many military officers were Democrats. Smith kept his views to himself, remained apolitical, and avoided self-serving alliances with politicians.

Frémont's campaign and the Lincoln-Douglas senatorial debates in 1858 clearly established the Republican Party as the anti-slavery, abolition party heading into the 1860 election. Abraham Lincoln became the Republican presidential candidate based on his strong support in the West and national reputation as the most articulate moderate. Lincoln won the election without a majority of the popular votes and became an instantly divisive figure. His victory catapulted the nation into disunion, and secession was underway before he arrived in Washington for his inauguration.[1]

While most of the country was focused on the election and its consequences, the soldiers returning East from the Mormon Expedition had a different priority. Captain Heth explained:

> To show the great interest the American people take in a prize fight I must relate what occurred on the route between Independence and Camp Floyd, when Mr. Lincoln was elected President. The pony express bringing the news of the election brought also the result of the celebrated prize fight in England between Heenan and Sayers. The first question put to the rider of the pony when en route was. "Who won the fight?" The next was, "who is elected President?"[2]

In December, South Carolina seceded from the Union. The following month, Southern states began to seize federal arsenals, forts, and other installations. In mid–January, the dominos began to fall. Alabama seceded on January 11, Georgia on January 19, and Louisiana on January 26. Washington authorities seemed unable or unwilling to interfere with states leaving the Union and confiscating federal property. As the wave of secession increased, military officers with ties to the departing states resigned their commissions.[3]

Newspapers from Washington and other cities kept the men at Camp Floyd (Fort Crittenden) "current of the treasonable doings of the South." Colonel Smith believed the national crisis would pass.

> However disheartening the aspect of the political horizon may be at the present moment, I do not despair but the storm will blow over with but little damage. The whole proceeds from a failure to retain power by an arrogant oligarchy. If I were an M.C. [Member of Congress] I should move that South Carolina be expelled [from] the Union as a nuisance, and not be permitted to return for five years. That length of absence from the family would more than suffice to punish the people of that state for their folly then madness. Should the other states join in their suicidal course it would I think, leave the Government of United States stronger than ever. The Army has, thank God! got rid of the roguish administration of Mr. Floyd; would to God the country could only have, months ago, got rid of that of the miserable imbecile that rejoices in the initials of J.B. [President James Buchanan]. If he could but hear the curses both loud & deep that are (here) showered on his head for his unreasonable course in permitting matters to go on as they have in Charleston harbor, especially in regard to Anderson, his old bones would rattle in his skin.[4]

On February 24, 1861, Smith received his transfer orders.

> Congratulate me! for I leave here under orders for the Hqts [Headquarters] of the Army in 4 days, going in by the mail that carries this. On the very day that rogue Floyd tenders his resignation Genl Scott issues the order for me to go in. I shall be in New York about the 25th of March. I shall stage it from here to St. Jo. and thence by rail straight to New York.[5]

In Special Orders No. 80, Colonel Smith was appointed to serve as Superintendent of the Eastern Department of the General Services at Fort Columbus, New York, in charge of recruiting duties "for the two years ensuing after the 20th June."[6] After a six-year absence, Smith was going home. Charles reached Fishkill, New York, on March 28 and was reunited with his wife and children.

The Republican majority in Congress passed the Morrill Anti-Bigamy Act of 1862 designed to end the Mormon practice of polygamy. However, President Lincoln decided not to enforce these laws and gave Brigham Young permission to ignore the Act in exchange for not becoming involved in the rebellion.[7]

"Fort Sumter is ours"

By April 1861, the United States had gone from the crisis of secession to the calamity of civil war. It became apparent that the disagreement between the north and south was not going to be resolved peacefully. The citizens of the Union and Confederacy were infected, and the war fever clouded their minds and inflamed their passions. If the Union would not grant them their freedom, the South was prepared to fight for their liberty. The northern and southern states eagerly began to organize their armies in preparation for the anticipated conflict.

In early April, Smith's leave was terminated and he was sent to Washington where he was given command of the Department of Washington.[8] While Smith's immediate concern was the defense of the capital, his thoughts were also with his good friend, Major Anderson, who was locked in an untenable and deteriorating situation in Charleston Harbor.

When South Carolina left the Union, Anderson, who commanded the federal forts in Charleston Harbor, decided to consolidate his forces at Fort Sumter. He withdrew the garrison from Fort Moultrie, spiked the guns, and destroyed any ammunition that could not be transported to Fort Sumter. Anderson informed Washington that the unauthorized move was "necessary to prevent the effusion of blood."[9] Within several days, the Confederate forces seized Fort Moultrie, Castle Pinckney, and the Charleston Arsenal.

In early January, the first attempt to relieve Fort Sumter failed when shore batteries fired on *The Star of the West*, and the ship was forced to return to New York.[10] Anderson appealed to Washington for help, but the outgoing Buchanan Administration was reluctant to take action that might escalate the stalemate, and General Winfield Scott said it was impractical to relieve the garrison. In early March, Anderson notified Washington that the fort could not be held without replacements and reinforcements. General Scott informed President Lincoln that the situation was reaching a crisis and the army could not reinforce the fort. Secretary of State William Seward opposed supporting Sumter because he believed it would escalate the conflict, and on April 1 he advised Lincoln to abandon the fort.

Finally, on April 5 the Secretary of the Navy ordered a rescue expedition and assigned four ships to transport provisions. Lincoln informed South Carolina authorities that, if the vessels were not interfered with, the expedition would resupply and not reinforce the fort. The Confederacy responded to Lincoln's request by increasing their state of readiness. Confederate Secretary of War Leroy Pope Walker ordered militia commander General P. T. Beauregard to demand the fort's surrender. On April 11 Beauregard, who was Anderson's student at West Point, demanded "the evacuation of Fort Sumter." Beauregard informed Anderson: "All proper facilities will be afforded for the removal of yourself and command, together with company arms and property, and all private property, to any post in the United States which you may select. The flag which you have upheld so long and with so much fortitude, under the most trying circumstances, may be saluted by you on taking it down."[11] Anderson understood his duty and politely replied "that my sense of honor, and of my obligations to my Government, prevent my compliance."[12]

Further discussions were unproductive, and at 3:20 a.m. on April 12, the Confederates notified Anderson that they would open fire in one hour.[13] At 4:30 a.m., a mortar round exploded over Fort Sumter and signaled the start of the bombardment from forty-three guns and mortars at Confederate batteries in the harbor. Anderson could not do much with his sixty guns. The fort was built to defend against a naval attack. The best cannons were mounted on the uppermost of its three tiers where his troops were most exposed to enemy fire. The fort was low on ammunition and had nearly run out by the end of the thirty-four-hour bombardment. The artillery attack lasted through the night until the next morning, when a shell hit the officers' quarters and started a fire that threatened the main magazine.

Anderson agreed to a truce at 2:00 p.m. on April 13, 1861. Terms for the garrison's withdrawal were concluded that evening, and the fort was turned over to Confederate officers at 2:30 p.m. April 14. Anderson defended his decision to surrender. The major said he had little choice because "the quarters were entirely burned, the main gates destroyed by fire, the gorge walls seriously injured, the magazine surrounded by flames, and its door closed from the effects of heat, four barrels and three cartridges of powder only being available, and no provisions remaining but pork."[14]

Fort Sumter became the spark that started the war, and the fort's flag became a Union symbol and rallying point. The Confederates were energized after their easy victory, and their leaders eagerly considered the next step. The undefended Union capital at Washington was only 536 miles away.

"A real state of siege exists"

After the surrender of Fort Sumter, many Americans expected that the first real battle of the war would be fought over Washington. The Union capital was surrounded by the slave states of Maryland and Virginia and lacked troops and fortifications. When General Scott insisted that the city could not be captured, Lincoln replied, "It does seem to me general, that if I were Beauregard that I would take Washington."[15]

The Lincoln Administration was also concerned about the many disloyal government employees and private citizens who supported the South. Hundreds of government workers had already resigned and left Washington following the inauguration. Others remained in their jobs and became Confederate agents.[16] It was estimated that at least one-third of the residents were southern sympathizers who were prepared to spy on the Union government and help Confederate soldiers capture the city.[17]

Washington was in a very dangerous situation. The capital was located sixty miles south of the Mason-Dixon Line between Maryland and Virginia. Its main transportation and communication links to the North were the single-track railroad line of the Baltimore & Ohio Railroad and the telegraph lines along the track. Both of these connections could easily be severed to isolate the capital. Washington had no natural defenses, and its main fortification was Fort Washington, which was located seven miles down the Potomac River in Maryland with a one-man garrison. The city was guarded by 1,500 soldiers, marines, and militia. Reinforcing the capital with additional Regular Army troops was unrealistic because nearly all of its forces were on the frontier west of the Mississippi River.[18]

Following the surrender of Fort Sumter, Lincoln issued a proclamation on April 15 calling for 75,000 volunteers to serve for three months to put down the rebellion. Lincoln wanted a number large enough to sound impressive but not so high that the goal could not be achieved. He knew that northern arsenals contained few weapons and little equipment, and the treasury was virtually empty.[19] This meant that it would be difficult to arm and outfit even that number of men. New York's goal was seventeen regiments (13,280 men), Pennsylvania's sixteen regiments (12,500 men), and Ohio's thirteen regiments (10,153 men). The requirements for other states ranged from one (780 men) to six (4,680 men) regiments. Fortunately, the governors of New York, Massachusetts, and Pennsylvania had anticipated the possibility of an attack on the capital following the November election. They designated regiments for possible service in Washington, ordered them to begin daily training, and instructed the officers to prepare their men for rapid deployment to the capital.[20]

Colonel Smith reached the capital at eleven o'clock on April 6. Later that day, General Scott issued Special Orders No. 58 assigning Smith "to the command of all troops stationed in this city and at Fort Washington.[21] From his room in The Willard Hotel, Charles described the day's events.

> As soon as I could wash & put on my uniform, I called upon General Scott, who expressed himself most delighted to see me & have the benefit of my services; and immediately entered into most confidential conversation with me, & finished by placing me at once in command of all the troops in the city & at Fort Washington.

WILLARDS' HOTEL,
Washington, D. C.

BILL OF FARE.—Wednesday, February 20, 1861.

SOUP.
Puree of Fowl, a la Royal.

FISH.
Boiled Rock, Caper sauce.

BOILED.
Corned Beef, with Turnips.   Smoked Beef Tongue.   Turkey, Parsley sauce.
Chicken, Butter sauce.   Leg of Mutton, Egg sauce.   Ham and Cabbage.
Roulade of Beef, braized with Vegetables.

COLD DISHES.
Pressed Brisket of Corned Beef, with Slaw.   Roast Mutton.   Roast Beef.
Turkey.   Chicken.   Hog's Head Cheese in form.

SIDE DISHES.
Small Tender Young Chicken, broiled, with rashers of Pork, Parsley sauce.
Veal Sweetbreads, larded and braized, with Olives, a la Financiere.
Small Tenderloin of Beefsteak, broiled and glace, aux rich gravy.
Galetiene of Chicken's Leg, braized and glace, with Tomato sauce.
Lamb Cotelettes, broiled, with Croustons, a la Tartan.
Calf's Head and Feet, smothered aux Fine Herbs, Country style.
Ragout of Lamb, with Vegetables, German style.
Macaroni with English Cheese, a la Italian.
Baked Pork with Beans, Farmer's style.
Fricasse of Turkey Wings, Oyster sauce.

ROAST.
Beef.   Turkey.   Chicken.   Pork, Apple sauce.
Ham, Madeira sauce.   Goose, Cranberry sauce.

VEGETABLES.
Mashed Potatoes.   Plain Potatoes.   Homony.   Rice.   Beets.
Onions.   Turnips.   Cabbage.   Oyster Plants.   Fried Parsnips.

RELISHES.
Pickles.   Horse Radish.   Chow-chow.

PASTRY AND DESSERT.
Apple Pie.   Prune Pie.   Bread and Butter Pudding.   Frozen Custard.   Ribbon Cake.

FRUITS.
Apples.   Raisins.   Almonds, &c.

NOTICE.—Gentlemen having friends to dine will please give notice at the office. Meals, Lunches, or Fruit, sent to room, or carried from the table by guests, will be charged extra.   Waiters are furnished with wine cards and pencils.

THE GONG will be rung for the early dinner only.

Bill of Fare for The Willard Hotel, 1861 (courtesy University of Houston Digital Library).

> After talking with the General for some time he took me to see the Secretary of War to whom he presented me with a glowing eulogium of my services & character as a soldier that made my flesh creep. He always does this. However, he told the Secretary that I was worthy of all trust & at once they began to talk of matters connected with the military service entirely unknown even to officials in the War Office Cabinet in fact. Of course I can only speak of this thing in this way for your information, not for that of others.
>
> My command at present consists of six companies; are at Ft. Washington (some 14 miles below this on the Potomac); 2 field batteries; a troop of dragoons & 2 companies of Artillery, serving as Infantry; which will soon be increased by several companies of horse & foot.
>
> I am to accompany John Todd this evening to call on his cousin Mrs. President Abe Lincoln & his sister Mrs. Grimsley[22] who is part of the Presidential family.[23]

Smith's status was clarified on April 11 in Special Orders No. 102, which stated, "The ten companies of militia called out and mustered into the service of the United States in obedience to orders from the President, dated War Department, April 9, 1861, will be placed under the command of Bvt. Col. C. F. Smith, commanding Department of Washington."[24] Smith selected Captain Theodore Talbot as his Adjutant to aid him with the mountain of paperwork.[25]

On April 15, *The New York Times* reported: "The Administration has satisfactory information that the Confederate States have proposed, immediately after reducing Fort Sumpter [sic], to march on Washington with their army of twenty thousand men."[26] In a note on April 15, Scott told President Lincoln that "Col. Smith, the commander of the Department of Washington, like myself, thinks our means of defence, with vigilance, are sufficient to hold this till reinforcements arrive." Scott assured Lincoln that Washington would be reinforced before Southerners could launch an attack.[27]

Smith quickly put a plan of action into effect. He ordered Captain King's Company I, First Infantry to "take post at the Arsenal" and Brevet Major J. A. Haskin's First Artillery to "proceed with his company as soon as practicable to Fort Washington."[28] In General Orders No. 4 on April 16, he designated "Col. Charles P. Stone, Inspector-General of the Militia of the District of Columbia" to command the "companies of volunteers from the District of Columbia now being mustered."[29]

On April 16 Scott estimated that 9,000 men were poised to attack the capital. To oppose this Rebel army, Scott had only 1,500 trained and experienced men consisting of 900 Regular Army troops and 600 District of Columbia volunteers.[30] The general was raising new volunteer companies from the district and believed these additional troops put "the Capital a little ahead of impending dangers." He anticipated that the city's forces would be doubled when the volunteers from northern states arrived in a week.[31]

The military leaders focused the city's defense on three key sites: The Capitol; the Old City Hall area, which included the White House, Patent Office, and buildings containing the War, Navy, State, and Treasury departments; and Treasury Building. The places were strengthened to withstand a ten-day siege and soldiers were stationed inside the buildings at night.[32]

On April 16, Charles wrote Francis about his meeting with President Lincoln and dinner with General Scott and Secretary of War Cameron.

> I have seen my connections at the White House (Todds & Grimsleys) who were very gracious to me. I have also seen the President by invitation partly to make my acquaintance as he said & partly to talk with me on military matters.
>
> I have dined with General Scott & the Secretary of War to enable us to talk over some matters of business.
>
> Every disposition has been made by me constantly for defense.

> This government has been so tardy in its operations that we are now virtually surrounded by thousands of armed men, whilst I with a small force of volunteers (comparatively) are standing on the defensive. I hate this being cooped up. Oh! If I only had my old Utah force. But regrets are vain. I expect an attack tonight; the first occasion I have thought such a thing might occur although the military precautions I have taken many nights [and] have been of such a character to frighten timid people. I have sat in my office for the last three nights getting about two hours sleep in a chair, and this with exercise of brain and body has much wearied me—tho' all say I never looked better.[33]

By April 18, the forces in Washington had increased to 2,800–3,200 men composed of 1,000 men from the army and marines, 1,200–1,500 men of the District of Columbia militia, and 600 to 700 Pennsylvania volunteers "in poor order."[34]

Then, after only thirteen days in command, Smith was removed from his duties and replaced by Major General Robert Patterson commander of the Pennsylvania militia. Patterson was placed in charge of an enlarged Military Department of Washington, which now included the District of Columbia, Maryland, Delaware, and Pennsylvania.[35] Scott telegraphed Patterson to see how quickly he could send men to the capital. Patterson replied that although he was "intensely anxious to be with and support you," a "very large proportion" of his men were "without muskets, all are without ammunition, service clothing, greatcoats, blankets, knapsacks, haversacks, canteens, &c." As soon as his soldiers were properly equipped, Patterson declared he could "have 5,000 men in Washington in five days."[36]

Meanwhile, the capital became more isolated from the North. On April 20, Maryland officials ordered the destruction of railroad bridges on lines connecting the capital with Baltimore. Telegraph wires were cut, and mail service to the District stopped.[37] Lincoln wrote, the "capital was put into the condition of a siege."[38] William Gulick agreed with Lincoln's assessment and noted that "a real state of siege exists."[39]

On Monday, April 22 Washington looked like an abandoned city with empty houses, closed businesses, and deserted streets.[40] There were rumors that 1,500–2,000 Rebels were preparing to seize Fort Washington, and 2,000 troops were coming on the Baltimore and Ohio Railroad from Harpers Ferry to join an attack on Washington. In spite of these threats, the general-in-chief remained optimistic that the city could be protected from attacks.[41] Fortunately, the volunteer units were slowly reaching the city. Although removed from command, Smith continued to perform his duties and issued numerous orders distributing the arriving troops to defend the city.[42]

Panic seized the city on April 23 when *The Philadelphia Inquirer* reported that General Beauregard had sent a note to President Lincoln, recommending that women and children be removed from Washington if Lincoln "wished to avoid the effusion of blood."[43] Once again, the main roads out of Washington were crowded with people trying to leave in carriages, wagons, and on foot in a "great caravan of flight."[44]

By April 23 secessionist forces were spread across the Maryland countryside outside Annapolis and Baltimore, waiting to attack the Seventh New York and Eighth Massachusetts regiments en route to Washington.[45] Colonel Smith advised Major McDowell, commander of the newly created Department of Northeastern Virginia, about troop dispositions. Smith wrote, "Should an attack be made tonight in the direction of the President's mansion, the Massachusetts troops will promptly move to its defense, leaving the District of Columbia volunteers and the Pennsylvania troops for the defense of the capital."[46]

By Easter Sunday, the Rebel siege was beginning to have its effect. A deathly quiet engulfed the city; interrupted occasionally by the sounds of marching infantry soldiers and galloping cavalry horses. Food supplies were getting low, and prices had risen more than fifty percent over the past few days.[47] There were also shortages of cloth, patent medicines, and candles. Rebel forces were starving the capital, and unless the siege was broken, the city's food supply would be gone by May 1.[48]

Finally, after a week of mounting uneasiness, the Seventh Regiment of New York arrived in Washington. *The New York Times* reported that the "steps and balconies of the hotels, the windows of the private houses, the doorways of the stores, and even the roofs of many houses were crowded with men, women and child, shouting, and waving handkerchiefs and flags."[49]

Although the threat of an investment was reduced, General Scott reminded his forces that "hostile bodies of troops" were near the city and "that an attack upon it may be expected at any moment."[50] On April 27, 1861, *The New York Times* reported that General Scott "assured a gentleman yesterday that Washington was safe against all present attacks."[51]

Charles described a different situation in his April 26 letter to Francis. He characterized the travel between Washington and Baltimore as "extremely interrupted." The military had seized railroad cars to transport the volunteer troops from Annapolis to the capital and the tracks between Annapolis and Washington were lined with troops to "prevent the destruction of the bridges, rails, etc." There were "now between 6 & 7000 men under arms in this city" and the number was increasing daily. Charles complained, "I have been worked very hard & got so little sleep that I am at times nearest to death. For the past sum days I have slept at night in my office—sitting in a chair."[52]

On April 27 Scott issued General Orders No. 12 that reorganized the Military Department of Washington and created two new departments. The Military Department of Washington was revised to include the District of Columbia, Fort Washington and the adjacent country, and the State of Maryland as far as Bladensburg. Colonel J. K. F. Mansfield was assigned to command the department in relief of Colonel Smith who was ordered to Fort Columbus to "assume the duties of superintendent of the recruiting service." Smith's replacement, Colonel Mansfield had a slightly different role than Charles. As reported in the *New York Herald*, Mansfield was tasked with exercising "a general supervision over the arrangements for quartering and feeding the troops." The newspaper said Mansfield's appointment ensured "greater efficiency in these departments, which are as important as any in the services."[53] Brigadier General B. F. Butler was assigned to lead the new Department of Annapolis that included "the country for twenty miles on each side of the railroad from Annapolis to the city of Washington, as far as Bladensburg, Md." A third department, called the Department of Pennsylvania, under the command of General Patterson was created to include Pennsylvania, Delaware, and all of Maryland not part of the other departments.[54] Colonel Mansfield arrived a day later, and Smith formally relinquished command of the department.[55]

Smith's brief tenure as commander of the Department of Washington was officially over. There are many reasons why he was transferred. His initial replacement by General Patterson was influenced by the number of troops (12,500 men) that Pennsylvania was required to contribute to the war effort and Scott's desire to rush these troops to the capital. Patterson's duties lasted only eight days until the crisis was over, and he was placed in charge of the new Department of Pennsylvania. Colonel J. F. K. Mansfield, who was selected to command the reorganized Department of Washington, outranked Smith and was a member of Scott's staff. Smith was already assigned to serve at Fort Columbus and his deployment to Washington was only an emergency posting. However, other issues may have factored into Smith's transfer.

It is probable that Smith was pestered by reporters hanging around The Willard Hotel who wanted to know the true status of military readiness in the capital. Smith was certainly unwilling to provide confidential information about Washington's defenses, especially with the number of Confederate spies and Southern sympathizers in the capital. The reporters decided to sabotage Smith and have him replaced with a more cooperative officer. A New York City newspaper reporter, possibly from the *New York Times*, circulated a rumor that Smith was drunk while on duty. The story was either a complete fabrication or a case of exhaustion being mistaken for drunkenness. Newspaper correspondents were quite willing to slander officers who prevented or limited their access to information. Smith's experience was similar to General Jacob Cox's encounter in West Virginia. When Cox refused to appoint two newspapermen as "volunteer aides with military rank," the reporters decided to "show" Cox that he needed their help and to "write him down." The correspondents sent reports to their papers that described the army as "demoralized, drunken, and without discipline, in a state of insubordination, and the commander as totally incompetent." Cox complained, "the printing of such communications in widely read journals was likely to be as damaging as if it all were true."[56] One of these devious correspondents was Mr. William Swinton of *The New York Times*,[57] who may have been the source of Smith's problems. Cox declared, "The relations of newspaper correspondents to general officers of the army became one of the crying scandals and notorious causes of intrigue and demoralization. It was a subject almost impossible to settle satisfactorily: but whoever gained or lost by cultivating this means of reputation, it is a satisfaction to have adhered throughout the war to the rule I first adopted and announced."[58]

Smith had formed friendships with Southerners during his military career and previous posting in Washington. With the large population of Southerners or Southern sympathizers in the Capital, it is not surprising that Smith had many friends who publicly or privately supported the Confederate cause. These associations could raise suspicions of being a southern sympathizer. The direct and undiplomatic Smith had little time to court government officials or make pro–Union speeches. He understood his duties as a professional soldier and was determined to carry them out without interference from civilians, reporters, or politicians. In the politically charged atmosphere of Washington, some government officials considered Smith a person of questionable loyalty. "He is strictly business and never bothered to utter fine phrases about the sanctity of the federal union."[59]

Both Charles' and Francis' had relatives who lived in Maryland. Charles' mother Margaret and sister resided in Annapolis where local militia had threatened to attack the volunteer regiments en route to relieve the Capital. Francis had family and friends in Baltimore, which was essentially in rebellion against the United States. Its citizens attacked federal troops passing through the city on their way to Washington in the infamous riot of April 19, 1861. One of the instigators, Samuel Mactier, who might have been related to Francis' family, was later indicted for his role in the uprising.[60] These connections added to suspicions about Smith's loyalty.

Whether it was the rumor of his public drunkenness, family connections, or political maneuvering, Smith left the city under a cloud of suspicion. While the volunteers were celebrated and honored, Smith quietly left the city. He informed Francis, "I have just been relieved by my senior officer Col. Mansfield & directed to go to Ft. Columbus as originally ordered."[61] His efforts in Washington were ignored, unappreciated, and minimized. He felt "a strong sense of injury" over his treatment.[62] Later that year, he complained to Francis, "I get with [in] a totally bad humor at times when I reflect on my displacement in Washington and by a man [Patterson] (however worthy as a gentleman) who could do nothing as a General and whom they rewarded and put on the shelf."[63]

"Where are the older officers of the army?"

Colonel Smith was in military purgatory. He left Washington under a cloud of rumors and suspicion. Charles wondered if he would be sentenced to spend the war chained to a desk overseeing mundane recruiting operations. This was not the way he wanted to end his career.

The war was on, the army was expanding, and politics was front and center. The frustrations of many military professionals were expressed by Captain Jesse Gove who wrote, "God help them, lawyers, merchants, loafers, etc., made to command masses of men, when they do not understand the first rudiments of a squad drill. How should they know? Do you suppose it possible for any man to be taken inexperienced from the desk and given a brigade or regiment of men and understand how to use them?" He warned that the Government's use of "party preferment" would lead to the Union's defeat even "though our men are as numerous as the sands of the sea." Gove asked, "Is political locality paramount to merit wherever found? Must soldiers' lives be raffled away on the 'sweat cloth' of political dice throwers? When will the people demand justice?" He angrily said that many of the men promoted to generals had resigned from the army and were rewarded, while those who were loyal were still captains and lieutenants. "Where are the older officers of the army, Col. Smith, Wright, Wool, etc., I have no heart to write."[64]

The New York Times announced Smith's appointment as General Superintendent of the New York Recruiting Stations and Commandant at Fort Columbus. The newspaper added: "Colonel Smith takes post agreeably to the regular orders of the War Department."[65] While the duties might not be "agreeable" or what Smith wanted, the responsibilities were important, and the post was near his home. He thought his family would probably join him in a few days, however, he believed that his "stay will [be] so short that it would scarcely be advisable to furnish a house."[66] Shortly after his arrival, Charles wrote Francis, "I may be a 'temporary or a 'permanancy' [sic]. When Congress meets, I must be promoted, when of course I quit here. A war of large proportions is upon us—there is no mistake about that now."[67] Although he would be focused on organizing, enlisting, and training men for the Regular Army, Smith would also oversee the processing and training of many volunteer troops. He was also in charge of several companies of regular army troops stationed at the fort.

Secretary of War Cameron's April 15 letter to the governor of New York asked for 13,280 troops, which was the highest requirement for any state.[68] New Yorkers responded well to the request for volunteers. They joined the army, raised funds for the troops, and provided assistance for the new regiments. Over a three-month period, New York City collected $150 million for the war effort. By the end of May, the state had recruited 30,000 men for the army.[69]

When Smith assumed command on May 2, the rush of applicants from "the mania for joining the volunteers" had reduced Regular Army enlistments from New York City to twenty-two men during the previous week.[70] When a detachment from Rochester arrived at Governor's Island, Smith formed them into companies and began their training. He supervised the drills and increased the time allocated to practice.[71] By May 22 Smith had nearly 600 troops at Fort Columbus with 400 "sufficiently prepared" for active service.

On June 6 *The New York Times* reported, "A small squad of men from Boston reached town last evening, and were immediately transferred to the charge of Col. Smith. Col. Smith has inaugurated pretty strict discipline among the officers, as well as the men, at Port [Fort] Columbus."[72] The following day the paper announced that the garrison on Bedloe's Island was moved to Governor's Island so Colonel Smith could use Bedloe's as a recruiting headquarters to instruct newly enlisted soldiers.[73]

June passed without contact from General Scott or Secretary of War Cameron. Smith continued drilling the new men in the same manner as he had done during the summer encampments on the West Point Plain nearly twenty years before. In early July, *The New York Times* announced, "Yesterday there was a general muster of all the troops on Governor's Island, when, in compliance with the usual bi monthly custom, the entire garrison was reviewed and inspected by the commanding officer of the chief recruiting station of the Eastern and Western Departments. Col. Smith inspected over 600 men, who appeared to great advantage; and, to day, makes a report of the circumstance to the War Department."[74] Although Smith was busy organizing and drilling the new recruits, he thought that he was "put out to graze on Governor's Island" and "he chafed under it like a caged lion."[75]

The reprieve came on July 1, 1861, in the form of President Lincoln's call for an additional force of 300,000 men.[76] The new volunteers required officers to lead them, and Smith and others were eager to receive the appointments. The onset of war was greeted with a mixture of concern and excitement by current and former officers. Those West Pointers who had left the military, like Grant and Sherman, saw it as a chance to return to their chosen profession. Current officers viewed the war as an opportunity to advance their careers after years of stagnation in the peacetime military. Perhaps their thoughts were best captured by Union soldier Cyrus F. Boyd: "War is hell broke loose and benumbs all the tender feelings of men and makes of them brutes. I do not want to see any more scenes and yet I would not have missed this for any consideration."[77] These same feelings would be famously expressed by Robert E. Lee on December 13, 1862, after the Battle of Fredericksburg: "It is well that war is so terrible! We should grow too fond of it!"[78]

In addition to its service as a training center, Fort Columbus also was a prison. On July 17 Smith was ordered to take custody of Edward Ruggles. "The Secretary of State having requested that Edward Seymour Ruggles now in custody by the superintendent of police in New York may be transferred to the care of the military authority the General-in-Chief directs that you receive him from the superintendent who has been instructed to deliver him on this order and confine him as in the case of Mr. Quillen."[79] Ruggles was arrested on June 24, 1861, on suspicion of treason. He was accused of trying to obtain information on how treasure from California was transported across Panama and the measures used to protect the shipments. When he was detained, he was carrying documents indicating his desire to enlist in the Confederate Army. He was also accused of recruiting General Albert S. Johnston and other military officers to join the Confederacy.[80] Smith had little to do with the case and only served as a temporary jailer for Ruggles. "Pursuant to the instructions of the General-in-Chief dated on the 17th instant I sent to the city of New York this morning and received from the superintendent of police as a prisoner Edward Seymour Ruggles. Shall I send him to Fort Lafayette?"[81]

Smith heard nothing from the War Department about a promotion or a transfer to the field, and the volunteers going off to war continued to arrive at Fort Columbus. On July 20, *The New York Times* reported, "A detachment of United States troops, enlisted in Rochester, arrived here yesterday, and were sent over to Col. Smith, at Fort Columbus, to be drilled and drafted for regimental service."[82]

Both sides thought the conflict would be over in a few months, but the perspectives on the war of rebellion soon changed. Near a small church in Manassas, Virginia, the cruel reality of war crashed down upon the citizens of the North and South. On July 21 blood was shed, and men were mutilated and killed. The boasts of a quick victory were trampled under the feet of the panicked Union soldiers fleeing to Washington. This would not be a three-month war, nor would it be a grand adventure.

Following the North's defeat at Bull Run or the South's victory at Manassas, Lincoln replaced General Irvin McDowell with General George B. McClellan. All of the troops around Washington were combined into the Division of the Potomac and placed under McClellan's command. McClellan was a young, egotistical West Pointer who believed that he had been summoned to save his country. He had always thought highly of Smith, as did most of the younger officers in the army, and he immediately asked to have Smith on his staff. This would have been an excellent opportunity for the colonel to distinguish himself in the closely watched campaign in the East. Unfortunately, for both men, McClellan's request was denied.[83]

Rumors surrounded Colonel Smith and *The New York Times* reported that he was "about to be put in an important position at the sea of war." The article went on to describe Smith as "one of the ablest tacticians in the Army, was twice [thrice] brevetted for distinguished service in the Mexican War, and [who] possesses in an eminent degree one of the best attributes of a successful General —- viz.: a thorough military education, enhanced by a lifetime of active experience." The *Times* concluded, "He is in the prime of life."[84]

When the *Times* announced on August 14 that the army had consolidated its operations at Fort Columbus, it seemed as if Smith would spend the war on Governor's Island. The paper noted, "It is quite likely that the business to be hence-forward transacted in connection with the Army here, will be done in the office of Col. Smith, the Superintendent-in-chief of all the recruiting offices in the old Department of the East."[85]

Fortunately, the gossip about Smith proved to be true. On August 19 the War Department relieved him of his duties at Fort Columbus and ordered him to "immediately repair to St. Louis, MO., and report for duty at the Headquarters of the Department of the West."[86] Seven days later Smith turned over command of the station to Colonel Loomis [Lumis] and prepared to leave for St. Louis.[87] This was his chance to contribute, and he planned to make the most of it.

16. "The war in Kentucky has commenced"

"Go to Cairo"

Smith was finally summoned to battle. He arrived in St. Louis in early September 1861 and was cordially received by his new commander, Major General John C. Frémont. Smith obtained a room in the Planter's Hotel and waited for Frémont's orders. Frémont had placed Smith's name before Congress on August 31 to approve his appointment as brigadier general[1] with the intention of putting Smith in charge of a division. In the meantime, Smith's assignment was "to go to Cairo (Illinois) at the junction of the Ohio & Mississippi" where his opponent was the "redoubtable Gideon F. Pillow."[2]

While Smith was en route to St. Louis, his good friend General Robert Anderson was facing a crisis in Kentucky. Anderson had been placed in charge of the Department of the Cumberland, which included the States of Kentucky and Tennessee, on August 15.[3] Anderson had not yet reached Kentucky when Indiana Governor O. P. Morton declared, "Civil war in Kentucky is inevitable."[4] Anderson arrived in Cincinnati on September 1 and informed Secretary of the Treasury Salmon P. Chase that several men from Louisville believed an "invasion from Tennessee was immediately threatened." Anderson asked to "have as many regiments as possible placed, subject to my orders and within call, in Ohio, Indiana, and Illinois."[5] The following day, Governor Morton warned, "the southern border is lined with Tennessee troops" and "If we lose Kentucky now, God help us."[6] On September 12, Governor Morton informed Secretary of War Cameron that "The war in Kentucky has commenced" and asked for troops to defend Indiana's border with Kentucky.[7]

Both sides recognized the strategic importance of controlling the Mississippi, Tennessee, and Cumberland rivers. The realization transformed the river ports of Columbus, Paducah, and Smithland into key targets. In early September, Major General Leonidas Polk, the Episcopal bishop in charge of the Confederate forces in western Tennessee, became convinced that federal troops were ready to seize these cities.[8] On September 4 Polk violated Kentucky's neutrality when he ordered Brigadier General Gideon Pillow to occupy Columbus. The strategic city was the terminus of the Mobile and Ohio Railroad and was located in a commanding position on high bluffs overlooking the Mississippi River. The Confederates strengthened the position by constructing Fort DeRussy, "The Gibraltar of the West," and arming it with 140 cannons. They also stretched an anchor chain across the river from Columbus to Belmont, Missouri, to control river traffic.[9]

"Competent to command"

When news of Lincoln's proclamation asking for 75,000 volunteers reached Galena, Illinois, the enraged citizens were "determined to avenge the insult to the national flag." Galena native and former army office, Ulysses S. Grant, was asked to preside over a meeting in April to raise volunteers for a company. Galena was located in Jo Daviess County, and the new company named themselves the "Jo Daviess Guards." Grant declined the request to be captain, but offered to help in any way he could. Grant organized the volunteers into squads and supervised their training. By April 25, the Galena infantry company was outfitted and drilled for the march to Springfield. The Jo Daviess Guards was mustered into service as a company in the Eleventh Illinois Volunteer Infantry. Governor Richard Yates believed that Grant's military experience would be very useful, and he asked Grant to remain in Springfield to serve in the Adjutant General's office.[10]

While in Springfield, Grant met his West Point classmate and fellow Mexican War veteran Brigadier General John Pope. Pope suggested that Grant "ought to go into the United States service" and offered to recommend Grant for a position. Grant declined the endorsement. After completing his duties in Springfield, Grant returned to Galena and wrote to the Adjutant General of the Army on May 24 offering his services.

> Having served for fifteen years in the regular army, including four years at West Point, and feeling it the duty of every one who has been educated at the Government expense to offer their services for the support of that Government, I have the honor, very respectfully, to tender my services, until the close of the war, in such capacity as may be offered. I would say, in view of my present age and length of service, I feel myself competent to command a regiment, if the President, in his judgment should see fit to entrust one to me.[11]

Grant did not receive a reply from his letter. He was disappointed at the rejection and asked for a one-week leave of absence in early June to visit his parents in Covington, Kentucky. While he was in the area, Grant decided to visit Major General George McClellan at the general's headquarters in Cincinnati. Grant knew McClellan at West Point and served with him in the Mexican War. He hoped that McClellan would offer him a position on his staff. Grant tried to see him several times but was unable to meet with the general. A disheartened Grant returned to Springfield.[12]

Grant had just left Covington when a telegram arrived from Governor Yates offering Grant the colonelcy of the Seventh District Regiment. Grant's appointment was a final effort to straighten out the rebellious regiment. The volunteers refused to re-enlist on June 15 for a new three-year term unless their current

The Invasion of Paducah (from Hall Allen, *Center of Conflict*).

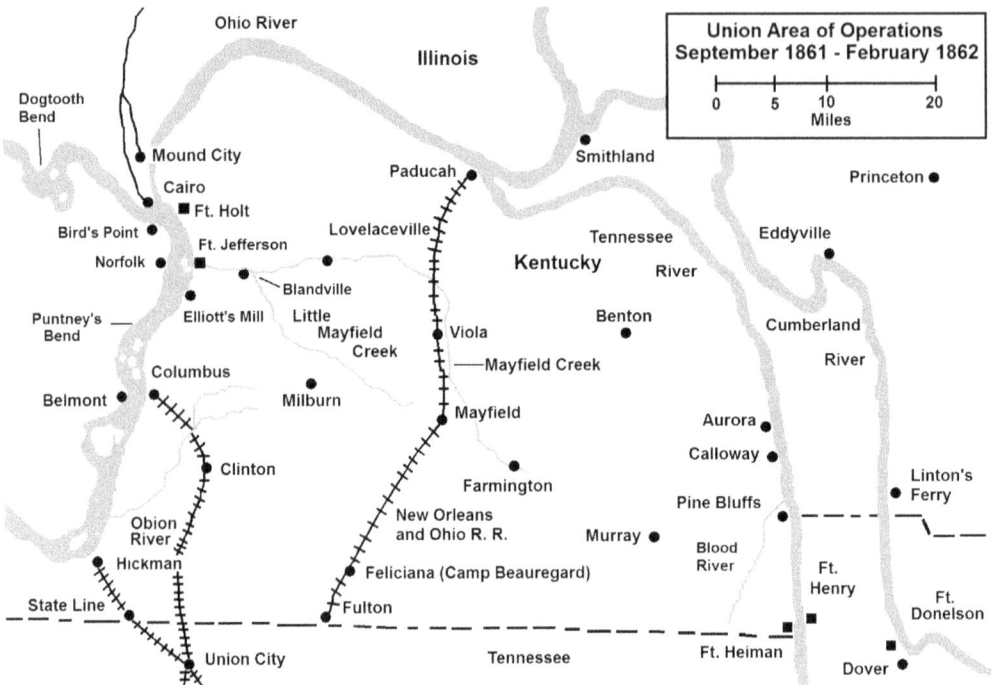

Union Area of Operations, September 1861–February 1862 (author's drawing based on Grant's Area of Operations in early 1862, courtesy *Papers of Ulysses S. Grant* and Ulysses S. Grant Association).

commander was replaced. The undisciplined men had earned the sobriquet, "Governor Yates's Hellions." The title was richly deserved as the men had mutinied over bad bread, burned the guardhouse, and spent their nights in nearby saloons. Half of the unit had deserted since May 15. Grant was desperate for a command and accepted Yates's offer.[13]

Lincoln's July 1 call for additional volunteers created new opportunities for Grant. The requirement for Illinois rose to 26,148 although 58,689 men were actually raised.[14] This meant that an addition four or five brigadier generals would be needed.[15] Within the month, Grant obtained one of these coveted positions.

On July 31, Grant was assigned to command a sub-district under General Pope. He was appointed a brigadier-general of volunteers on August 7, with the commission dated to May 17. Events moved rapidly following his new appointment and on August 28, he was assigned to the command of the District of Southeastern Missouri, embracing all the territory in Missouri south of St. Louis, and all southern Illinois. He arrived at his headquarters in Cairo, Illinois, on September 2[16] with orders from Major General John Frémont to assume leadership of all of the forces in the area, "take command of the combined forward movement," and "to occupy Columbus, Ky., as soon as possible."[17]

"I am here to defend you"

Grant learned that the Confederates had occupied Columbus and were planning to capture Paducah. He warned Frémont and announced that he "was taking steps to get off that night to be in advance of the enemy in securing that important point."[18] The former quartermaster obtained steamers and crews to transport his forces from Cairo. Frémont had not replied to Grant's first request, and Grant sent another message stating his intentions to "start for Paducah that night unless I received further orders."[19]

Grant's flotilla of two gunboats and three steamboats left Cairo at 10:30 p.m. on September 5. His forces were the Ninth Illinois under Brigadier General E. A. Paine, the Twelfth Illinois under Colonel John McArthur, and four pieces of light artillery under Lieutenant Willard. An accident with one of the steamers at Mound City forced Grant to transfer troops to another ship. During the delay, Grant was joined by Captain Foote of the United States Navy.

It was nearly dawn when Grant's fleet reached Tug Island in the middle of the Ohio River and across from Paducah. Grant planned to enter Paducah using a pontoon bridge from Tug Island. The bridge permitted Union troops to march into Paducah if they met little resistance and to escape to Tug Island if the Confederates attacked in force. Reports indicated that a 3,800-man Confederate Army was sixteen miles away. Grant's 5,000 troops were unloaded on the Illinois side of the island and prepared to march into Paducah.[20]

From Tug Island, Grant saw "numerous secession flags flying over the city in anticipation of the approach of the rebel army." When the Union forces arrived at Paducah at 8:30 a.m., Confederate Brigadier General Lloyd Tilghman, his staff, and a company of volunteers escaped southwest on the train. Grant's forces marched unopposed into the city and captured it without firing a shot.[21] The occupation of Paducah gave the Union control of the northern end of the New Orleans and Ohio Railroad and the mouth of the Tennessee River.

The arrival of federal troops in Paducah was an unwelcome surprise to the citizens since they had been expecting Confederate forces from Columbus. The Confederate flags that decorated the town were quickly removed before the Union troops entered the city. Stunned people stood on the sidewalks,[22] and "Men, women and children came out of their doors looking pale and frightened."[23]

At the railroad depot, Union troops seized a large number of rations and about two tons of leather destined for the Confederate Army. The troops took control of the telegraph office and railroad station where they found enemy letters and dispatches. Grant distributed his troops "so as best to command the city and least annoy peaceable citizens."[24] Later that morning, at Broadway and Water Streets near the bank of the Tennessee River, General Grant read a proclamation to the alarmed citizens.

September 1861
Paducah, Kentucky
PROCLAMATION.
To the CITIZENS OF PADUCAH:

I have come among you not as an enemy, but as your fellow citizen; not to maltreat or annoy you, but to enforce the rights of all loyal citizens. An enemy, in rebellion against our common government, has taken possession of and planted its guns on the soil of Kentucky, and has fired upon you. Columbus and Hickman are in its hands. He is moving upon your city. I am here to defend you against the enemy, to assist the authority and sovereignty of your government.

I have nothing to do with opinions and deal only with armed rebellion and its aiders and abettors. You can pursue your usual avocations without fear. The strong arm of government is here to protect its friends and punish its enemies. Whenever it is manifest that you are able to defend yourselves and maintain the authority of the government, I shall withdraw my command.

U. S. Grant
Brigadier General, U.S. Army, Commanding
PADUCAH, September 6, 1861[25]

Grant issued instructions "to take special care and precaution that no harm is done to inoffensive citizens; that the soldiers shall not enter any private dwelling nor make any searches unless by your [an officer's] orders, and then a detail shall be made for that purpose. Exercise the strictest discipline against any soldier who shall insult citizens or engage in plundering private property."[26] Grant placed the city under the command of General Paine and left at noon to return to Cairo.[27]

Before leaving Paducah, Grant sent a telegraph to the Kentucky legislature informing them of his actions. Governor Magoffin denounced both sides for violating the Commonwealth's neutrality and demanded that the Union and Confederate forces leave the state. However, a resolution drafted by the Kentucky General Assembly's only ordered withdrawal of the Rebel forces. Magoffin vetoed the proposal, but the legislature overrode his veto, and forced the governor to issue a proclamation condemning the Confederate invasion.[28]

Paducah's fears concerning the Union occupation were confirmed when Grant left General Paine in charge of the post. Paine disregarded Grant's orders, considered Paducah a conquered town, treated the pro–Confederate population harshly, and arrested a number of citizens. Paine's undisciplined, green, volunteer troops engaged in stealing, plundering, and vandalism. In response to the Union occupation, residents moved their property to safe locations outside the city, closed their stores, and abandoned their homes.

The citizens were hostile to the occupying Union forces. The *St. Louis Republican* said secessionists dominated the population. "On the streets people wear secession caps, and boast that before the week closes every Federal will be driven out." The residents also committed acts of sabotage, including poisoning some of the wells used by soldiers and cutting the telegraph lines through the town. In spite of their poor reception, some of the Union soldiers were "greatly impressed" with Paducah. An Illinois sergeant wrote, "I fell in love with Paducah while I was there, and I think I will settle there when the war is over. I never saw so many pretty women in my life. They hollered 'Hurrah for Jeff' at us ... but that's all right."[29]

A rumor spread that the Yankees hated Jews. Paducah had a substantial Jewish community, many of whom were respected merchants and businessmen. In response to the Union occupation, many Jewish merchants closed their stores and left for Illinois and Tennessee. When slaves from the surrounding areas learned that the "Yankee Saviors" were in Paducah, they escaped from their masters and sought protection at the Union post. Paine refused to provide them with food and shelter, which forced the runaways to steal to survive.

When Grant returned to Cairo he "found authority from department headquarters" for him to take Paducah. Although Frémont was pleased with Grant's capture of Paducah, he was not happy about Grant communicating with Kentucky authorities and he "warned against a repetition of the offense."[30] Frémont told Grant that the department commander would conduct any dealings between the military and state officials. He cautioned Grant not to get out of line or to overstep his authority. Frémont also notified Grant "to enable you to continue personally in command of our forces in Cairo, Bird's Point, Cape Girardeau and Ironton," he was sending Brigadier General Charles F. Smith to take charge at Paducah.[31]

Smith was placed in command of the District of Western Kentucky, which included the troops at Paducah and on the Kentucky side of the Mississippi and Ohio Rivers. The district had six volunteer regiments from Illinois, a battery of six field guns, and a gunboat. Smith departed St. Louis on a special train at 8:00 a.m. on September 7 and reached Cairo at 6 p.m.[32] From Cairo, Smith traveled by steamer on the Ohio River to Paducah. With Smith's arrival, General Paine was demoted to command a brigade.

Smith inherited the hostility that Paine had nurtured during the latter's brief time in charge. Although the new commander said the citizens were in "hot secession," he was better regarded by the residents. He treated them fairly, stopped pillaging and stealing, and dealt harshly with his soldiers who insulted women on the streets.[33]

On the morning of September 8, Smith rode around the town posting the troops. He believed that the city might be "attacked at any moment."[34] During Smith's first days at Paducah, Frémont sent orders to him through Grant at Cairo. Frémont instructed Smith to "throw up earthworks and plant guns at Paducah," but not advance. The department commander directed Smith to "occupy Smithland[35] with four companies if they can be spared." He asked how many heavy guns Smith required and promised to send "as many as you will require, not exceeding six."[36]

General Smith spent the first few days at Paducah in a flurry of activity as he organized his command and prepared the city's defense. Everyone was "exhorted to learn and discharge their duties," soldiers were ordered to "sleep on their arms," and the Provost Marshall was empowered "to arrest all persons absent from Camp without permission also citizens creating a disturbance."[37] Over the next six days, Smith issued ten General Orders and fourteen Special Orders.

Grant was pleased with Smith's posting and wrote, "General C. F. Smith, a most accomplished soldier, reported at Cairo and was assigned to the command of the post at the mouth of the Tennessee. In a short time, it was well fortified, and a detachment was sent to occupy Smithland."[38] Grant respected and admired his former West Point Commandant of Cadets, but now, by virtue of the date of his appointment to brigadier general, he was General Smith's superior in rank.

On September 9 Frémont informed Smith that General Gideon Pillow was marching toward Paducah with 7,000 men and artillery. The department commander warned, "The Tennesseans are going to make a forward movement to-night or to-morrow to Kentucky." Frémont asked if the reinforcements had arrived at Paducah and directed Smith to move towards Mayfield when he received the troops.[39] The following day, Frémont repeated his order to send four companies to occupy Smithland and to control the Cumberland River.[40] Frémont said the Eleventh Regiment Indiana Volunteers, with three companies of regular cavalry and one company of volunteer cavalry, was en route to Paducah.[41]

Charles wrote home that his men did not look "much like soldiers, but he thought they might prove to be excellent." He was waiting for his aide-de-camp, Lieutenant J. T. Price to arrive with their horses and servants. Smith complained that he had only two officers from whom he could expect assistance: Joseph D. Webster and E. A. Paine. Major Webster, a former Topographical Engineering officer, was laying out Paducah's defenses, and Paine, a 1839 West Point graduate, was "enjoying his recent promotion from Colonel to Brigadier General."[42]

He sent a note to his friend General Anderson, commander of the Department of the Cumberland, informing him of the size and nature of his command. "As I am operating within the limits of your department or at least believe so though I have not yet received the order I deem it proper to acquaint you with the fact that I am here with a force of (say) 4,300 men, 6 field guns and a gun boat heavily armed."[43]

Thanks to General Frémont, Smith was a brevet brigadier general responsible for commanding an important post on a strategically significant river in a pivotal border state. Unfortunately, Smith faced a superior enemy in a place unprepared for an attack.

"To lose Kentucky"

General Frémont was not pleased with Grant's conciliatory statement to the citizens of Paducah on September 6. The tenor was in contrast to the department commanders' August 31 proclamation placing Missouri under martial law and stating:

All persons who shall be taken with arms in their hands within these lines shall be tried by court-martial, and, if found guilty, will be shot. The property, real and personal, of all persons in the State of Missouri who shall take up arms against the United States, and who shall be directly proven to have taken active part with their enemies in the field, is declared to be confiscated to the public use; and their slaves, if any they have, are hereby declared free.[44]

After Grant captured Paducah, Frémont applied the terms of his Missouri decree to that city and all of Kentucky. The emancipation order set off a hailstorm that disrupted the Department of the West and threatened Kentucky's allegiance to the Union.

President Lincoln had strong reservations about two aspects of Frémont's Missouri proclamation, and he sent a special messenger to St. Louis on September 2 outlining his concerns. Lincoln objected to the order to shoot those taken with arms. The president feared that such action would lead to Confederate retaliation and ordered that no such action be taken without his consent.[45] Lincoln also asked Frémont to limit "emancipation to those slaves forced to take up arms or otherwise actively participate in the war on the Confederate side." Lincoln believed that confiscation and freeing of slaves "will alarm our Southern Union friends, and turn them against us—perhaps ruin our rather fair prospect for Kentucky." Lincoln asked Frémont to modify the proclamation to conform to the terms of the Confiscation Act, which allowed the Union, through legal actions, to confiscate and free those slaves helping Confederate forces.[46]

The president's fears were confirmed when he learned from General Anderson that a company of Union volunteers from Kentucky "had thrown down their arms and disbanded" in response to Frémont's edict. The president was also warned that Kentucky would go "over the mill dam" if the proclamation was not retracted.[47] Lincoln's friend Joshua Speed said Frémont's edict would "crush out every vestage [sic] of a union party in the state if not annulled."[48]

Frémont responded to Lincoln's concerns on September 8, and sent his wife Jessie to Washington to talk to the president. Frémont said he issued the proclamation with his "best judgment to serve the country and yourself" and was "perfectly willing to receive the amount of censure which should be thought due if I had made a false step." He described his decision "as much a movement in the war as a battle is" and asked Lincoln to order him "to make the correction."[49]

Jessie Frémont did not help her husband's case. President Lincoln recalled, "She sought an audience with me at midnight and taxed me so violently with many things that I had to exercise all the awkward tact I have to avoid quarreling with her."[50] Mrs. Frémont failed to convince Lincoln to alter his position. By September 10 Lincoln had had enough of the Frémonts, and the president "cheerfully" ordered the general to modify the order so it conformed to the Confiscation Act.[51] Lincoln recognized that removing the most objectionable parts of Frémont's proclamation was essential to keeping Kentucky in the Union.[52] Unfortunately, for Lincoln, the northern press, abolitionists, and even some members of his cabinet supported Frémont's proclamation.[53]

Lincoln's response to Frémont's edict had two significant effects. It clearly defined the boundaries for officers concerning slaves. They could be confiscated as property but not given their freedom as human beings. In answer to his critics, Lincoln described the status of slaves: "If the General needs them he can seize them, and use them; but when the need is past, it is not for him to fix their permanent future condition. That must be settled according to laws made by lawmakers, and not by military proclamations." The public and private responses provided Lincoln with extensive information that he would incorporate in his own Emancipation Proclamation.[54]

Smith learned from a St. Louis paper that "'Old Abe' has rapped Frémont on the knuckles for confiscating the negro." Charles told Francis, "His calling up is no doubt nigh, for Frémont acted in violation of law as well as expediency (so far as General Frémont is concerned) but the way that Frémont treated the question is what will have to be resolved to at least, and he used it as a big bid for the Presidency."[55]

The president's position also put commanding officers in a difficult position. Should Smith and other officers strictly adhere to the government's guidelines and risk public censure as a Southern sympathizer or defy the parameters by freeing, keeping, and protecting escaped slaves and face military censure and dismissal? While politically appointed officers would cater to public opinion, professional soldiers like Smith would obey their commander-in-chief's orders.

"This place is to be attacked"

On September 11, 1861, General Smith learned that the Kentucky legislature had asked the governor to order the Confederates to remove their forces from the State.[56] About the same time, Smith heard a rumor that "President Jeff Davis had ordered all of the Confederate troops from the State of Kentucky in consequence of the recent act of the legislature."[57] Smith was suspicious of the information because, "Davis must see at once that if his forces are withdrawn we will immediately advance and throw the field of strife farther south."[58]

The reports of enemy movements around Paducah continued to bedevil the post's commander and increase tension in the occupied city. On September 15 Smith learned that Confederate troops were assembling at the railroad station near Mayfield, Kentucky, approximately twenty-five miles south of Paducah. Intelligence indicated that the Rebels had a regiment of cavalry, two field batteries, and about 5,000 infantry at Mayfield. Other information indicated the force was to be increased to 15,000. Adding to the crisis was the news that Smith's friend, General Albert Sidney Johnston, was going to Mayfield to assume command. It seemed obvious that a Rebel attack was imminent. "If my men are staunch, as I hope they will prove, the struggle must be severe." Charles warned Francis, "I do not know if it is wise to tell you these things in advance but it is as well, perhaps, in the whole you should be prepared for all contingencies by knowing the facts."[59]

The Union forces were on a high state of readiness in anticipation of the rumored Rebel assault. Smith described the residents as "wild with affright." His warnings that they might be attacked at any time did little to ease their concerns.[60] Smith ordered the regiments to be formed at midnight September 18 and had the men sleep with their weapons. Their commander spent the night fully dressed and prepared to leap into action "as was his habit when in enemy country." The extension of the pontoon bridge from Tug Island across the Ohio River to the Illinois side was almost finished. The bridge would allow his command to escape from Paducah "if need be, though I have [had] not yet thought of taking that course."[61]

In the midst of this tense situation, Charles had some good news for his family. He learned from the Army Revenue Board that at least two officers above him in rank had retired. Because of the retirements, the only way to advance in the Regular Army, he would be promoted to colonel of either the Third or Fourth Infantry. He reminded Francis that when he accepted the position of brigadier general of volunteers he did not forfeit his position in the army and would "fall back in my colonelcy when the war is over."[62]

General Smith continued to prepare his troops for battle. "I am just in from my daily review of a portion of the troops and am tired enough. The men do very creditably, but the officers are lamentably deficient. However, I am working them up. They think me a little strict, but their good sense induces them to say it's all right."[63] Recent reports said Johnston was in Columbus with around 30,000 men and 100 guns. In response to the threat, Smith was "fortifying as well as I can with a view to an advance, when all is ready." Smith thought the army needed 100,000 men to attack and "crush them out." Charles continued to complain about performing "the duties of my perceived staff and playing the politics with all sorts of citizens." However, he was pleased to inform Francis that he would "be able in a few hours to talk with you by telegram from my bedside. I have had wires put up from here to Cairo and its terminus is at my elbow."[64]

As the month progressed, the command in the Department of the West still considered an attack on Paducah likely. On September 26 Frémont instructed Smith to send a regiment and two gunboats to Owensborough to scatter the enemy force. "After dispersing the enemy the force will return again to Paducah, as the latest movements of the enemy require the concentration of our troops as far as possible at that place."[65] On September 28 Smith sent two messages to Frémont. In the first, Smith warned, "Intimations from various quarters are that this place is to be attacked soon by a heavy force from Columbus." He asked for "24-pounder howitzers, with plenty of ammunition."[66] In Smith's second note later that day, he informed headquarters that the gunboat *Lexington* had not found any enemy forces in Owensborough. Smith ordered the gunboat *Conestoga* to remain at Owensborough in case the enemy appeared.[67]

The latest intelligence reports estimated that there were 70,000 soldiers at Columbus. Smith thought that the number was too high and probably included Confederate forces on the Missouri side of the Mississippi River. Previous estimates placed the enemy strength at Columbus at 40,000 men with many light and heavy guns. On September 28 Charles told Francis, "My orders are to act in the defensive, indeed I could not do otherwise." Although, a cavalry regiment was added to his command, it was "ten miles below on the opposite shore, and has neither swords or pistols—which are not at St. Louis, and I believe not nearer than Washington and so this body is of no use to me." He said that it was "uphill work" to "make good soldiers" out of the militia reserves. What Smith really wanted was 40,000 men "in the field ready for battle now." For the general, it was "the same old story of too late, too late."[68]

The troop buildup in Kentucky was raising fears in the bordering states. General Paine received a request from John Holloway in Indiana asking for "3,000 troops with gunboat" to defend Lock and Dam No. 1 on the Green River from a 4,500-man force led by General Buckner. Smith declined the request saying: "Can't be furnished. I don't know Mr. Holloway."[69]

On September 30 "a little lull in business" allowed Charles to "seize a sheet to scrawl a few lines" to his family. He grumbled, "Talking, explaining, scolding, trying to set people right actually makes my lips weary." He blamed his fatigue on the lack of "staff officers who had any experiences in the service" to lighten his labors. In spite of these irritations, Charles was making progress with Paducah's defenses.

> I have received three additional pieces of heavy artillery this morning but days elapse before they are in position. I have commenced this morning the construction of a redoubt enclosing the Marine Hospital—a large brick building, which will make a strong defense—one thousand men will be its garrison.
>
> Get a little time and we will be able to make a good fight against any number.[70]

Smith centered his defenses on the Marine Hospital.[71] The troops built earthworks around the building, and Smith christened the fortification Fort Anderson after his good friend General Anderson.

On September 30 General Grant met with Smith at Paducah. By virtue of his earlier appointment, Grant was now Smith's superior officer. This was an extremely awkward situation for Grant who respected and admired his old Commandant of Cadets. Smith's long and distinguished military career and age also complicated the relationship. Therefore, Grant was nervous about the meeting and shrank "like a modest schoolboy" in anticipation.

Their reunion was different from their first encounter twenty-two years ago on the Plain at West Point. Grant described the fifty-four-year-old officer as "tall, slender and ramrod-straight, with pink cheeks and clear blue eyes, and great white mustachios dropping down either side of his chin." Even though he outranked him, Grant said, "It does not seem quite right for me to give General Smith orders." However, the reversal in position never bothered Smith, who was proud of his former pupil.[72]

Smith "had a long consultation with him [Grant] about our plans of defense or attack as the case may be for the future." Grant agreed with Smith that the Confederates had 30,000 troops at Columbus and between 8,000 and 9,000 men and twenty-six pieces of artillery under General Hardee camped nearby on the opposite side of the river. Smith believed that if Hardee moved toward Paducah, Grant could attack him in the flank or rear from Cairo.[73] When their meeting was over, Grant's admiration and esteem increased because "there was not the slightest trace of jealousy or disappointment in General Smith's manner." Their future "private and personal conferences" increased their friendship.[74]

As the month ended, there were persistent "wild rumors" of an attack on Paducah, and Smith continued to send spies to get more accurate intelligence about the situation at Columbus.

Fort Anderson, Paducah, Kentucky (Library of Congress, LC-USZ62-105266).

Reports, with "small foundation," indicated that Paducah was "to be attacked tonight or tomorrow night by any number of thousands" and "the enemy have 75,000 at C [Columbus]."[75]

Smith had a broadside printed on October 1 for the Paducah community containing the proclamation by Governor Magoffin demanding that "the Confederate, or Tennessee troops ... be withdrawn from her soil unconditionally." Among the resolutions included in the proclamation was one that would be particularly important.

> Resolved, ... no citizen shall be molested on account of his political opinions; that no citizen's property shall be taken or confiscated because of such opinions, nor shall any slave be set free by any military commander; and that all peaceable citizens who remain at home and attend to their private businesses, until legally called into the public service, as well as their families, are entitled to and shall receive the fullest protection of the government in the enjoyment of their lives, their liberties, and their property.

The Kentucky General Assembly provided measures to enact the proclamation. The state called for "not less than forty thousand soldiers, residents and citizens of Kentucky, between the ages of eighteen and forty-five years, to be mustered into the service of the Commonwealth for any term of service not less than twelve months nor more than three years from the time they were mustered into service, unless sooner discharged."[76]

"Will make a good soldier"

Smith had scarcely assumed control of Paducah, when Colonel Lew Wallace and the Eleventh Indiana Regiment arrived at the wharf. Wallace's regiment disembarked on September 10 accompanied by his band playing the "Star-Spangled Banner" and the cheers of soldiers on the landing. Wallace said that the reception "signified welcome, and appreciation, and comradeship, and a real soldier somewhere about in command of the place."

Wallace went to report to General Smith. He knew of Smith's reputation as "the best all-around officer in the regular army—a disciplinarian, stern, unsympathetic, an ogre to volunteers, but withal [nevertheless] a magnificent soldier of the old school of Winfield Scott." Smith was quartered in a Southern mansion that served as both his residence and office.[77] Wallace reached headquarters and was escorted to Smith's office. The room was well furnished and warmed by a fire burning in a grate. A large table in the middle of the office was covered with books, writing material, a sword, sash, and gauntlet gloves.

Years later, Wallace recalled his first impression of his new commander.[78]

General Lewis Wallace (Wikipedia Commons).

He was very tall, erect, broad-shouldered, a symmetrical figure in a well-fitting uniform. He held his head high; long, white mustaches trailed below his chin shading his lower face; perfect health left its morning colors on his cheeks, and his blue eyes, bright with invitation, negatived [negated] the reputation he bore for sternness.

   This description is elaborate, I know; and if one asks wherefore, the answer is ready—the man before me was by odds the handsomest, stateliest, most commanding I had ever seen, the one who has since remained in memory my ideal of a general officer. Probably better cannot be done than to add that his appearance has always helped me to a perfect understanding of the impression Washington is said to have left upon all who came near him.[79]

Smith barely welcomed his new subordinate. "The general did not move from his place before the fire, or even bend his head; much less did he come forward and shake hands." Wallace was not offended and said he respected him more because Smith was "a soldier without a tincture of the politician." Smith asked if Wallace had just arrived and whether the colonel had been met at the landing by the quartermaster and wagons. Wallace said yes and thanked Smith for the arrangements at the wharf. The general told Wallace to "come round this evening" and ended the brief interview.[80]

Wallace returned after supper for a "purely social" visit. Smith "put his stateliness aside" and quizzed Wallace about his military knowledge and experience. When the colonel rose to leave, Smith walked him to the door and said, "Our situation here is somewhat precarious, and will be until the fort I have in process of construction is finished. Come again, tomorrow afternoon, and we will go over the map together."

When the men met the following day, the general spread a large map over the table. Smith pointed out how easily General Polk could march from Columbus and attack Paducah. General Smith said that Polk had "about ten thousand men, with additions coming in rapidly." Then he explained the reasons why the Confederates would want to capture the place. The general pointed to the Tennessee and Cumberland rivers on the map, and said, "These are lines leading into the heart of the seceding states, and, with Paducah fortified, you see how tight he locks them against us."

Wallace asked what prevented Grant from crossing the river from Cairo and cutting Polk off. Smith laughed, and replied, "To attempt that Grant must have a force sufficient to give Polk battle." Then Smith became serious and complained, "Frémont is too intent upon schemes of his own to think of strengthening us. I wonder he let your regiment come here."

The evening passed pleasantly with Smith leading the conversation and focusing it on the war. Several times Smith alluded mystically to some grand operation being planned that "when undertaken, would be worth a long, ordinary life to every one engaged in it." He did not tell Wallace about the plan, but Wallace saw that his commander was enthusiastic about the prospect. "Opportunities—opportunities—opportunities," Smith kept repeating, with the eagerness of a young man.[81]

Wallace was destined by virtue of his political connections to rise in the ranks, and paperwork for his promotion to brigadier general arrived soon after he reached Paducah. When the official communication arrived, he was astonished. The colonel had mixed feelings about the appointment. He did not want to leave his regiment, but "felt the urgencies of ambition." Compounding his decision, he "knew nothing of the duties of a brigadier" and was overwhelmed with the responsibilities of the position especially those in battle." He decided to obtain Smith's advice.

That evening Wallace found Smith sitting comfortably before the fire. Without rising, Smith said, "Bring up a chair. It's chilly outside." When the colonel was seated, Smith asked, "What is it? Anything I can do for you?"

Wallace showed him the papers confirming his appointment to brigadier general. Smith read it gravely, stood up, and asked, "Well, sir, what of it?"

Then Wallace stood up, and answered with the same directness, "Will you tell me if I ought to accept that appointment?"

"Why not?" Smith asked.

"Because I don't know anything about the duties of a brigadier-general," Wallace replied. Smith was surprised. After briefly looking at Wallace, he said, "This is extraordinary. Here have I been spending a long life to get an appointment like this one about which you are hesitating; and yet that isn't it—that you should confess your ignorance—good God! Who ever heard of the like?"

"Had you come here not doubting your sufficiency," he said, "I should have decided you meant a parade of your good-fortune; as it is, I say accept—accept by all means—and I will give you the benefit of what I know about the duties of the place, be it much or little. We can always make something of a man who is willing to admit that he don't know it all."[82]

General Smith selected a book from the mantel that Wallace recognized as the United States Army Regulations. Then Smith gave Wallace a "free-and-easy lecture" on the duties of a brigadier general.

> I divide the duties of a brigadier-general into two classes ... those owing to his immediate superior, and those owing to his command; and of the first....
>
> Obedience being the soul of military organization, I hold it the beginning and end of duty. It is the rein in hand by which the superior does his driving....
>
> The difference between a captain and a general with respect to duties is that the general is a captain with multiplied and extended relations....
>
> The chief duties of a general to his command may be classified—the enforcement of discipline—tactical instruction—care of the health of his men—and they are all important because tending to efficiency, the measure of which is the exact measure of his own efficiency....
>
> Government furnishes everything actually needful to the good condition of the army; and of us—you and me, for instance—it merely asks in return that we know how to get those things, and to help us to the knowledge it has furnished a system of formal requisitions which fools call 'red tape.' But I pronounce it the perfection of wisdom, since by it alone the government is enabled to keep accounts, prevent waste, and assert the principle of personal responsibility. Here is that system—in this book [U.S. Army Regulations], more indispensable to every officer than his sword, for even in battle he can make out with a riding-whip. As the preacher knows his Bible, as the lawyer knows his statutes, every general should know the regulations and articles of war. Here they are within these lids ... here he will find every duty relative to the care of his command defined and prescribed....
>
> It is not possible for a general always to see with his own eyes, or be in two places at the same time; hence the device of a staff—that is, an alter ego for every duty....
>
> Staff-officers should be men of aptitude and experience, not figure-heads or mere pretty men.
>
> In battle a general's duties, in so far as they are reducible to rule, are—first, to fight; second, to fight to the best advantage....
>
> Genius is determinable by the manner of obedience. A fort is to be taken; genius consists in finding a way to take it with the least appreciable loss. A campaign is to be planned; genius proves itself by devising the best plan; at the same time, strange as it seems, he [who is] the most capable in planning may be the most incapable in execution, making two different qualities. The great genius is he who possesses both the qualities....
>
> Battle is the ultimate to which the whole life's labor of an officer should be directed. He may live to the age of retirement without seeing a battle; still he must always be getting ready for it exactly as if he knew the hour of the day it is to break upon him. And then, whether it come late or early, he must be willing to fight—he must fight.[83]

After the lecture, Wallace returned to camp a grateful and wiser man. Smith's counsel was all he needed to accept the commission.

There was some confusion about Wallace's promotion. Smith was unaware that the appointment contained orders that relieved General Wallace from his duties at Paducah. Smith apologized for detaining Wallace, but he refused to excuse him from his current responsibilities until he received orders directing him to do so.[84] During their discussion on the matter, Smith, who was always a stickler for regulations, corrected General Wallace on several points of military protocol. Through his adjutant general, F. Tooth, the commander cited a violation of paragraph 457 of the General Regulations of the Army in sending communications addressed to him personally. Smith attributed the error to "a misconception of military usage." Smith's adjutant explained: "That directed to report by letter to Head Quarters of the Army is a customary formula which does not relieve from duty at this post." In addition, because General Smith had not received "any specific instructions respecting you," he was not authorized to relieve Wallace from duty" and therefore could not comply with his request. Tooth ended by writing that "Genl Smith also instructs me to say that he would regret to receive any instructions by which your services would be lost to this command."[85] Smith was firm in his interpretation of military procedure and Wallace was unable to persuade him to change his position.[86]

Charles knew that Wallace's pride was hurt by his procedural rebuke, and he wrote Francis about the reprimand. He said he had "no difficulty with General Wallace" and was "only putting him right on a point of duty." Smith thought that Wallace was "a clever man a lawyer and will make a good soldier," although he was "a little conceited." Charles explained to Francis, that Wallace could not be relieved from his position until Charles had received orders "concerning him." He said Wallace protested and foolishly implied that he would appeal Smith's decision. While Wallace thought that Smith was being difficult and jealous, Smith was merely acting as Wallace's tutor by giving him further instructions on the duties of an officer. Charles said the appeal had not gone through him, and, if Wallace communicated with Smith's superior, he had committed "a breach of military propriety."[87] Regrettably, this would not be the last difficulty Smith had with the new brigadier general.

"Hold this place at all hazards"

October began with rumors about Confederate troops mobilizing for an advance on Smith's command. Charles wrote to Francis about Rebel movements against his post. Frémont told him that Grant had sent "nearly all his forces to Cape Girardeau and Birds Point" in response to reports that Johnston had "sent a very large force across the Mississippi to attack these points." It was also reported that Pillow was advancing with 20,000 men to attack Paducah. Smith believed Pillow's force had probably gone in the opposite direction because Smith's cavalry pickets had not reported any Confederates marching towards Paducah. Charles restated, "My orders are, however, primarily to hold this place at all hazards: that I will do."[88]

Several days later Smith learned about additional Confederate troop movements and an imminent attack on Paducah. The latest account was "that the rebels are to eat their Sunday dinner in this city" which Smith dismissed as "doubtful." One of Smith's scouts managed to reach the enemy's pickets about eight miles from Columbus on the Blountville road. The rebels were quite communicative and revealed that some of their forces had "crossed the river to make a demonstration at Birds Point & Cape Girardeau" in Missouri while other troops had "gone to aid Buckner" in Kentucky. The scout also discovered three regiments of reinforced infantry (about 2,200 strong) and 150 cavalry about three miles below Mayfield. Thanks to this "valuable young man," Smith was able to obtain "the plans of attack on this place when it comes off and that is to approach in three directions; make a feint on the works in front and really attack in flank." Charles judged that the Rebel strategy was "a good idea."

General Smith's troops continued to fortify the approaches to Paducah. "A large number of axes wielded by brawny arms daily busy all around felling trees which is a very efficient defense in itself or rather a great obstacle to successful approach." Smith had 700 men "working on the trenches and cutting down the forest daily—Sunday not excepted." However, the progress was slow because "the vols [volunteers] hate work."[89]

The general received several telegrams from the mayors of Henderson, Kentucky, and Evansville, Indiana, asking him to send troops to their assistance because General Buckner "with from ten to twelve thousand was rapidly moving down Green River to Henderson." Smith refused the requests because "neither the aspect of affairs in this quarter, nor my instructions allow me to make detachments in force." However, he sent the gunboat *Conestoga* to Hendersonville to investigate the situation.[90]

Aside from the threats posed by the Confederates, Charles' chief complaint was the lack of a suitable staff. He did not bring any staff with him and, the staff he found was small and confused. While some of them were capable, others were "without the slightest knowledge of his duties." He had grown tired from trying to teach them "a smattering of military propriety." However, Frémont did send relief in the form of two engineers to assist him. Major Webster, a topographic engineer, came from Cairo and laid out the earthworks in front of the city. When Webster returned to Cairo, Frémont sent "an Austrian who had been on his staff, and since appointed a Captain in the 19th Infantry by the name of Rziha (pronounce it if you can) as an Engineer." Smith said, "Capt R (pronounced Riha)" was "an accomplished Engineer and is of great comfort."[91]

Smith was also having difficulty with his aide Lt. J. T. Price, who "got into one of his crazy fits" and wanted the general to let him go on a leave of absence so he could join Frémont. Smith refused to grant the leave and "tried to argue him out of his absurd notions." Finally, Smith agreed to relieve him from his duty and send him to St. Louis. However, he warned Price that, if he granted this request, the lieutenant "need never expect to join me again." This seemed to quiet the young man for the time.[92]

On October 8 Smith took a steamer to Smithland, twelve miles up the Ohio River at the mouth of the Cumberland, to inspect the works. He had assigned the 350-man garrison the task of preparing defenses and embrasures for their three heavy guns. Smith found the work was not proceeding as fast as he hoped for and decided to send two additional companies to help.[93]

In the meantime, the Confederate forces around his positions were getting bolder. On October 9 about 300 Rebel cavalry attacked six of his mounted pickets stationed about four or five miles from Paducah. The enemy killed one, wounded one, captured two, and two escaped. "The enemy made a bad business of it for themselves, in the darkness and confusion firing into each other, and doing much mischief." The general suspected that the picket was asleep. Prior to this event, four of Smith's civilian scouts met two Rebel officers who tried to take them prisoners. The scouts fought back, killed one, and mortally wounded the other. Smith said, "This firing upon pickets and sentinels is simply assassination." He planned to send out two postings that night that he hoped would "bag some game."[94]

Intelligence on enemy movements confirmed that Confederate forces planned to attack

Smith's post. Smith said that Hardee's force at Mayfield was "to attack me [Smith's forces] on the roads leading from that quarter," "the notorious Jeff Thompson" was to move on the Blandville road, and General Simon Buckner's troops were to travel down the Tennessee River. Smith estimated the Rebel force was around 20,000 men. "The day of attack is fixed for the 15th instant but these people like three Millerites,[95] have so often fixed the day of doom that I give little heed to the on dits [rumor or hearsay]. The occupation of Mayfield looks more suspicious than anything else about their intention to attack."[96] Opposing these Confederate forces, Smith had 6,821 troops at Paducah and Smithland, and Grant commanded 13,608 men at Cairo and vicinity.[97] While Union spies were unrelenting in their reports of Confederate movements toward Paducah, Smith thought that the Rebel forces were probably "quite apprehensive of an attack" from the combined Union forces at Cairo and Paducah. Although, the Rebels had troops below Mayfield and at Clinton, ten miles from Columbus, Smith said it was "idle to speculate on the probabilities of an attack from them."

Smith spent his time "well filled with business." He rode around the perimeter of the defenses daily, and he occasionally took a regiment with him "to see how much they don't know." The rest of his time was dedicated to seeing "all manner of people on matters that after all do not concern the public much." He had divided his force into two brigades under Brigadiers Paine and Wallace, which relieved him "from a vast deal of the routine military drudgery that at first fell to my lot."[98]

The general had initiated gunboat reconnaissance south of his position on the Tennessee River and learned that there were enemy troops at "Fort Henry on the Tennessee river" near the Tennessee State line. One of Smith's gunboats discovered that the fort was "quite well armed." On October 16 he transmitted the findings to Frémont in St. Louis. Captain Phelps, in command of the gunboat *Conestoga*, described it as "a respectable earthwork, mounting heavy guns, with outworks, and a garrison of probably 1,700 to 1,800 men." Several days later, Smith learned that fort had twenty guns and a garrison of 2,000 men. His sources also reported that the Confederates were building three iron-plated gunboats with heavy ordnance near the fort. It appeared that the Rebels planned to attack Paducah with "the old scheme" employing gunboats and land forces.[99]

Frémont was concerned about the threat of Confederate advances into Missouri and warned Smith about the safety of Ironton and St. Louis. He asked Charles to "apprise him at the earliest moment of your views as to the whole service thus likely to be affected, desiring you on any sudden emergency to act in Kentucky as in your judgment may seem to you best."[100]

On a more pleasant note, Smith's promotion to colonel of the Third Regiment of Infantry in the Regular Army was announced by the War Department on October 22, 1861. The promotion took effect on September 9 and was subject to the approval of the Senate.[101]

General Grant continued to alert Smith on enemy movements. On October 25, Grant warned Smith: "Just learned from a man from Columbus that the troops that marched out towards Paducah returned last night, he is one of Jeff Thompson's command. Hardee had not arrived at Columbus this morning."[102] The same day, Grant alerted Smith that "a regiment of cavalry is organizing at Princeton, Ky., for the Southern Confederacy." The 500-man mounted force was armed from weapons gathered from the local citizens. Grant's informant suggested that, if a cavalry detachment left Paducah at dark by steamers, the troops would reach Eddyville around midnight and could march the twelve miles east to Princeton in 2 to 2½ hours. Grant suggested that if Smith deemed it prudent, he could "take steps to secure these fellows."[103]

The situation in Kentucky was taking a toll on General Robert Anderson. By early October, Anderson's health had declined to the point where Winfield Scott ordered Brigadier General William T. Sherman to assume command of the Department of the Cumberland. In response to Scott's order, Anderson issued General Orders No. 6, in which he endorsed Sherman as his successor. Anderson hoped Sherman would be "the means of delivering this department from the marauding bands, who, under the guise of relieving and benefiting Kentucky, are doing all the injury they can to those who will not join them in their accursed warfare."[104]

"Hear the women rail at me"

Commanding a post among citizens with questionable loyalties meant dealing with complaints from the residents. Mindful of Lincoln's criticism of Frémont's emancipation decree, Grant's Paducah proclamation, and Kentucky's declaration, Smith was careful to maintain proper relations with the community. Unfortunately, it soon became apparent that the "conciliatory policy" he had adopted had ceased to be a "virtue." Therefore, on October 10 the frustrated commander announced that in the future he would "take such measures as the circumstances call for and justify." He indicated that these "measures" would develop over time. His first restriction was to forbid "the outposts to pass out any person without a written permission from these headquarters, which will only be given to persons of approved loyalty to the Government of the United States." Smith applied the same certification for "goods or stores of any description" leaving Paducah.[105]

Charles enclosed a copy of the proclamation in his letter to Francis and announced that he had changed his "tactics a little in regard to the inhabitants hereabouts as you will see by my wee bit of a proclamation (why should I not utter a *pronuncimento* [pronouncement] as well as another?) And have commenced arrests of secesshers, of whom I have several bad specimens in custody."[106]

Charles explained that his travel restriction was not sitting too well with the ladies of the city.

> It would also do you good to hear the women rail at me. First I ordered away the wife and family of every officer and soldier. Appeal to me was vain. There was a hubbub! The Secesh women who until recently were [coming] in and out giving aid to our enemies have been stopped from departing by the guards and outposts. I give no pass to anyone who is not vouched by someone well known to me as a Union man. This granting of passes I leave to one of my Staff who has general instructions on the subject. We refused a pass to several ladies so they put at me when I was standing looking over the fence into the street. A petulant old French woman said "I want to go out"; I replied "Madam you cannot go." Her companion a young woman begged to go, she had a child outside. I said "Madam when I say no I mean it, etc., etc." If I ever saw mad women I saw them there. I was invited to go to tea by a woman I don't know and whom I refused to see when she came for the purpose, but pleaded business, which is true; still I do not choose to be bored by such a chatterbox as this woman is. The staff amused themselves by telling me the abuse I get from your sex: "He is stiff, pompous, an icicle, rude," I scarcely know what else.[107]

On October 20 Frémont responded to problems caused by "depredations by individuals of the United States troops now marching southward" by issuing General Orders No. 23. Frémont wanted "to inspire confidence in the loyal inhabitants of this State, and to assure others of protection and immunity if they return to their allegiance." Frémont stated, "It is therefore strictly forbidden to take private property from any person, for any purpose whatever, except by authority of a general officer; to enter any dwelling occupied or unoccupied, unless accompanied by a commissioned officer; to fire a gun or pistol in camp or on the march, or to leave the ranks upon any pretense without the order or permission of the company commander." The major general held all commanding officers "responsible for the strict execution of this order."[108]

Several days later, Smith had to deal with another group of Paducah "ladies." He sent Grant a warning about their activities.

> Oct. 22nd
> To: U.S. Grant
> On the report of the Medical Director that a number of prostitutes were here giving disease to the troops I caused the Provost Marshall to notify them to leave here & not to return on penalty of being treated with certain indignity. He did notify some (27) twenty-seven of these persons and they were to have left here by ten of the clock last night: the greater part if not all have gone; whether to Cairo or other places I cannot say. Thinking it not unlikely that their friendships might pay Cairo town a visit I give you this notification.
> C. F. Smith[109]

Complicating Smith's governance of the community was the problem of dealing with runaway slaves, many of whom were the property of Union supporters. Regardless of the allegiance of their owners, slaves took the opportunity to escape bondage by seeking sanctuary in Union camps. With Lincoln trying to appease slaveholders in border states, requests from people to assist in the return of "property" became a difficult task for officers. Smith had learned from the fate of General Frémont what happened to officers who interfere with the president's policy. In late January 1862, Smith received a request to return a woman and her children to a Union woman. Louise Boyd said that on January 13, her "negro woman (Mariah) run away from home and went to the encampment of Genl Wallace." The next day, six cavalry soldiers went to Mrs. Boyd's home and seized Mariah's two boys "in the name, or by the authority of Genl Wallace." Mrs. Boyd said she learned that Mariah wanted to return home and asked Smith to do her "the kindness to have Mariah and her children returned to me."[110] General Wallace had failed to control his men and, as a result, they had clearly violated Lincoln's directives. Smith's believed that slavery should be addressed by politicians not soldiers. He explained his position in a letter to Grant in January 1862.

> I gave orders to the outposts not to allow fugitive slaves to enter the camps. With regard to the slaves of loyal masters or slaves of those of secession proclivities who are mere waiters upon providence I have neither interposed any obstacle to their being recovered tho' I cannot consent to act as the slave catcher myself unless it is made my duty by the law. Perhaps we do not differ about this matter.[111]

On October 16 Grant forwarded a request from General Sherman, now in command of the Department of the Cumberland, asking Grant and Smith to make a demonstration on Columbus. Grant said he was "ready to co-operate" with "any plan" that Smith had to propose.[112]

By October, President Lincoln had had enough of Frémont, and on October 24 Winfield Scott replaced Frémont with Major General David Hunter.[113] It took over a week for Frémont to acknowledge his dismissal.[114] Hunter's tenure lasted until November 9 when the command was reorganized. Under the provisions of General Orders No. 97, the department was divided into three new departments: Department of New Mexico consisting of the Territory of New Mexico commanded by Colonel E. R. S. Canby; Department of Kansas, including the State of Kansas, the Indian Territory west of Arkansas, and the Territories of

Nebraska, Colorado, and Dakota commanded by General Hunter; and Department of the Missouri, including the States of Missouri, Iowa, Minnesota, Wisconsin, Illinois, Arkansas, and that portion of Kentucky west of the Cumberland River commanded by Major General Henry W. Halleck.[115]

Following Halleck's appointment, the designation of Grant's command changed "from the District of Southeast Missouri to the District of Cairo." The small district commanded by General C. F. Smith, "embracing the mouths of the Tennessee and Cumberland rivers" was added to Grant's jurisdiction.[116] The designation of General Smith's command changed from the District of Paducah to the United States Forces at Paducah. Smith gracefully accepted the new reporting relationship. Although he was "now a subordinate," Smith said, "I know a soldier's duty." He told Grant, "I hope you will feel no awkwardness about our new relations."[117]

Charles continued to wait for approval of his generalship and complained bitterly about his own situation. His name appeared on the list of candidates for promotion to brigadier general of volunteers, but he was disgusted about those men who were placed ahead of him on the rolls. On a more positive note, Charles received official notice of his promotion to colonel. "I am now the Colonel of the Third Infantry where I shall stick for life, unless I find Aladdin's lamp by which to obtain a palace and reign."[118]

In a letter home, Charles described an expedition he sent up the Cumberland. The 300-man infantry force, escorted by the gunboat *Conestoga*, was sent "to capture or destroy some 200 rebel cavalry." The men landed, made a night march, and partially surprised the enemy. "A movement of the double quick and a charge with the bayonet made it an affair of but a few minutes." The enemy fled after losing seven men including their captain. A number of wounded Rebels were able to escape on their horses. The Union troops had three wounded. Smith's forces captured thirty horses, twelve mules, twenty-four prisoners, and "any quantity of saddles, bridals and rifles." The raid was helpful "in driving off the rebels who were organizing at different places just east of the Cumberland" and "harassing Union men," but otherwise he said it was "not worth recording."[119]

In addition to writing to Francis, Charles was also sending information about his activities to General McClellan in Washington. On November 2 McClellan asked for "a report on the number and position of troops." Smith replied several days later using the telegraph cable in his quarters.

> There are four companies of the Second Illinois Cavalry in camp at Old Fort Massac, badly armed with old carbines. The whole of this regiment was under my orders, but, at the request of Brigadier-General Grant, I attached six companies to him at Cairo.

Smith tried to get rifles for the regiment, but the Chief of the Ordnance Department was unable to supply them. Smith wanted the companies at Paducah, but he could not bring them there without proper arms. The men were currently "guarding the line of telegraph and stopping the passage of contrabands across the river."[120]

Smith had sent 300 men under Lieutenant Colonel Augustus Chetlain of the Twelfth Illinois Regiment to occupy Smithland at the mouth of the Cumberland.

> They have erected two respectable earthworks, which are protected with two 32-pounders and one 8-inch columbiad. Two field guns (a 6 and 12 pounder howitzer) are needed there, but I cannot spare them, and I see no probability of getting them from Saint Louis. I made a recent inspection of Smithland. The works are well constructed, and, although they will not be completed for a fortnight or so, can make a respectable defense. My orders are to hold Paducah and Smithland at all hazards.[121]

Chetlain said Smith was a favorite with all the soldiers of his command. "He was six feet tall, spare, straight, with a heavy white mustache and close cut gray hair. His personality was that of the ideal soldier, and his appearance on parade or elsewhere always elicited the applause of the soldiers." Smith visited the post often to check on its progress and Chetlain "became not only well acquainted with him, but much attached to him, and grew to have great admiration for his splendid soldierly qualities."[122]

In early November, Smith sent a sketch of Paducah and its vicinity showing the defenses and placement of troops to General McClellan. He described the area as: "a flat, wooded country, not much susceptible of defense at first, but by an unsparing use of the ax a very sufficient abatis, several hundred yards in width, renders all approaches, except by the roads, which are guarded by the earthworks, very difficult, if not impracticable." The line of defense was about two miles long from the redoubt at the Marine Hospital to the bridge over Island Creek. Smith explained that the redoubt around the Marine Hospital was the city's main defense with room for a 1,000-man garrison and an emplacement for an 8-inch Columbiad cannon.[123]

General Smith provided McClellan with an estimate of the size and disposition of Confederate forces in the area.

> At Columbus and its immediate vicinity, 10,000, General Pillow in command of the post: on the opposite shore, 2,000. The whole force in and around Columbus commanded by General Polk. At Feliciana (Camp Beauregard), south of Mayfield, towards the State line, is a battery of artillery, three companies of cavalry, and four regiments of infantry; in all probably 2,500 men, who are in a very sickly condition, the measles prevailing to a great extent and many deaths daily. At Trenton, on the State line, or a little south of it, a camp of instruction is being formed. At Memphis is a camp of instruction, under the State authorities, of, say, 3,000 men. Generals A. S. Johnston and Hardee are at Bowling Green. The force there is 40,000.[124]

Smith believed that the Confederates could concentrate probably 30,000 troops at Columbus in a very short time because they controlled the railways from Louisville and Columbus to Memphis.[125]

General Smith completed his report by attaching the field return of the troops at Paducah and its dependencies. He said that the sick list was large, but the medical director reported the general health of the command was improving.

> The men have plenty of food and are well clad. They are tolerably well instructed and the discipline is reasonably good. It would aid the administration of justice if I had the authority to appoint general courts-martial. This I can only do by this force being considered an army in the field, always, of course, subordinate to the commander of the department.[126]

Two days later, Smith forwarded an updated description of the works on the Tennessee and Cumberland Rivers. He said Fort Henry, located seventy-one miles up the Tennessee at the State line, was the more important fort.

> It is a strong earthwork, on the water front, but not nearly so strong on the land side. It has three 24 or 32 pounders, one or two 8-inch columbiads [sic], and the remainder of field guns, in all from 14 to 16; its garrison was two weeks since about 1,200. They have been under apprehension of attack from here for the two weeks.[127]

About eight miles above Fort Henry, the Confederates were converting river steamers into iron-plated gunboats. Unfortunately, Fort Henry prevented the Union gunboats from examining the shipbuilding operations. Smith noted that the gunboat *Conestoga*, "admirably commanded by Lieutenant Phelps, of the Navy," was Smith's "only security in this quarter." Phelps was constantly moving his vessel up and down the Tennessee and Cumberland

Rivers. When the *Conestoga* returned from a reconnaissance on the Cumberland up as far as Dover, Tennessee, Phelps reported that the Rebels had works at Dover. He said the fort was called: "Fort Gavock, or Fort MacGavock, or something else, usually called Fort Gavock."[128] General Smith would soon learn more about the earthworks and its correct name—Fort Donelson.

17. "Make demonstrations with your troops"

"'Skirmish'! Hell and damnation!"

In Paducah, Smith organized the defenses and prepared for an anticipated Confederate attack on the critical river port. In Cairo, Grant continued to receive reinforcements and by November 1 he had over 20,000 men. Grant spent the past two "uneventful" months training his restless troops for "the service which was sure to come."[1]

The boredom of constant drill was made even worse by the living conditions in the tent city near Cairo. The low and muddy land of the campsite was known as "Egypt"[2] for its terrain, flooding, and deadly pestilences.[3] The general believed his well-drilled troops were "ready to meet any equal body of men who, like themselves, had not yet been in an engagement." The men were eager to fight but had yet to experience a battle and "see the elephant." However, Grant was not allowed to attack Columbus because the city "was so strongly fortified that it would have required a large force and a long siege to capture it."[4]

On November 1 Grant received orders from Frémont, who remained in command in spite of his removal on October 24,[5] to "make demonstrations with your troops along both sides of the river towards Charleston, Norfolk, and Blandville, and to keep your columns constantly moving back and forward against these places without, however attacking the enemy."[6] Grant was "fitting out an expedition to menace Belmont" and asked Smith to make a simultaneous feint towards Columbus with part of his command. Grant hoped the ploy would prevent the Confederates from moving troops across the river and allow him to drive the Rebels out of Missouri. During the action, Smith's troops were to stop "a few miles from town to await further orders" from Grant. Grant explained that Smith's demonstration toward Columbus would "prevent the enemy from sending a force to fall in the rear of those now out from this command."[7] The next evening, Grant's command left Cairo on steamers and traveled nine miles below Cairo on the Mississippi River. The troops debarked on the Kentucky side of the river about six miles from Columbus, and Grant sent out pickets to contact Smith's forces from Paducah.[8]

Smith selected General Paine's First Brigade to support Grant's demonstration. The general directed Paine to lead his brigade "to Melvin 20 miles distant, from thence cross over to and return by the end of the third day from this by the Lovelaceville and Blandville road." He explained that the objective of the movement was to convince the enemy that Columbus was to be attacked. Smith's orders clearly stated that the First Brigade "will not attack" and that the "object is a demonstration merely."[9] His orders clearly reinforced Frémont's previous instructions "not to make fight unless attacked," not to attack Columbus, and "to make demonstrations against Columbus, with the view to deter any force being sent" from Columbus to add to those fighting Frémont in Missouri.[10]

Grant was operating under the same orders and had no intention of engaging the enemy. However, the commander was influenced by the excitement of the officers and men who "were elated at the prospect of at last having the opportunity of doing what they had volunteered to do—fight the enemies of their country."[11] About two o'clock in the morning, Grant learned that Confederate forces at Columbus had crossed the river and were planning to intercept the troops Grant sent under Colonel Oglesby towards New Madrid.[12] In response to the enemy's actions, Grant "speedily resolved to push down the river, land on the Missouri side, capture Belmont, break up the [enemy] camp and return."[13]

Grant's plan did not proceed as intended. After landing on the Missouri shore, the troops marched about a mile towards Belmont and formed a line of battle. The engagement began about 9 o'clock. Grant committed all of his troops except his reserve and drove the Rebels to their encampment on the riverbank. Grant's men charged through the abatis around the camp and forced the Confederates to run to their transports or find cover under the riverbank. Grant's men overran captured the camp and took everything that could be moved and destroyed the rest. The soldiers seized two artillery pieces, horses, and prisoners. As they prepared to leave the Rebel camp, the re-enforced Confederates appeared between Grant's troops and their transports to cut off their return. The Union troops charged the Confederates and defeated them again. Grant's men reached the ships and embarked. During the movement to the transports, the Twenty-Seventh Illinois took a different route and became separated. While waiting for the arrival of the lost regiment and retrieving some of the wounded from a nearby field hospital, the Rebel force and fresh troops from Columbus appeared on the riverbank and fired on the transports. The Union gunboats and men on the steamers returned the fire and forced the enemy to withdraw towards Belmont. The Twenty-Seventh finally appeared and were loaded aboard.

On November 7 Grant telegraphed Smith about the battle. "Attacked the rebels this morning at 9 o'clock; drove them out of Belmont and destroyed their encampment; loss heavy on both sides. They had eleven regiments against our 3,000 men." He asked Smith to inform General Paine that he had returned to Cairo.[14] The following day, Grant could hardly contain his enthusiasm, and he wrote Smith with the pride of a schoolboy who has completed a difficult assignment.

> We drove the rebels completely from Belmont, burned their tents, and carried off their artillery. For want of horses to draw them we had to leave all but two pieces on the field. The victory was complete. Our loss is not far from 250 killed, wounded, and missing. The rebel loss must have been from 500 to 600, including 130 prisoners brought from the field.[15]

In addition to informing Smith about the engagement, Grant seemed to be seeking approval or understanding from his former Commandant.

Smith sent his report to McClellan without any endorsement of Grant's actions at Belmont. General Smith had not heard from the force he sent to distract the Rebels at Columbus, but he expected it to arrive in Paducah that night. Smith enclosed Grant's telegram about the "affair at Belmont with reference to this demonstration."[16] While Grant was excited about his attack at Belmont, Charles was unenthusiastic in his letter to Francis. He wrote, "My own impression is that he did wrong to make the attack for it lead [led] to no result. He could not hold the place for it is directly under the heavy guns at Columbus."[17] Charles categorized the battle as "a shag affair." He labeled it a "Victory, though without results, and hence the attack should not have been undertaken without a sufficient object in view."

In spite of this opinion, Smith defended his former student whose justification was "he had to do it [to] protect and [that] part of his force which he had sent West or South West into Missouri, from being attacked and beaten by the force at Belmont." Charles' included an "anecdote attributed to "the Right Reverend General Bishop Polk, who was in command at Columbus."

> Grant sent an officer with a flag to get permission to bury the dead. In writing to Polk for this purpose he inadvertently spoke of the battle of Belmont (for it was a battle) as a skirmish; "In the recent skirmish between our forces at Belmont, etc." When Polk read this communication he threw it down with much indignation and said, "If General Grant call[s] that affair a skirmish what in hell does he call a battle?" A rather unclerical speech I should say, but perhaps he has a dispensation, or perhaps he thought he was in the pulpit—where parsons are allowed to swear, certainly to discuss their fellow creatures.[18]

Following the battle, Smith had more pressing concerns than to critique Grant's actions at Belmont.

"An unjustifiable departure from my orders"

General Smith's orders seemed clear enough. General Paine's First Brigade was to proceed twenty miles to Melvin, advance towards Columbus, and return by the end of the third day on the Lovelaceville and Blandville road. The object of this movement was to persuade the enemy that Union forces planned to attack Columbus. Paine was under strict orders not to attack the enemy.[19]

Paine's troops reached Mayfield Creek on the night of November 6 and made camp. The following day General Paine "heard firing at or near Columbus" and immediately changed direction, "leaving Melvin to their left and took the shortest road to Columbus." The brigade marched to Milburn, and Paine sent three messengers to the Mississippi River. The couriers were ordered to contact the officer in command of the federal forces and ask him to fire a signal gun. If the signal gun was fired, Paine intended to march on Columbus that night. The next morning, a messenger returned with news that the gunboats and federal forces had returned to Cairo. With the attack on Belmont-Columbus over, Paine ordered the brigade to return to Paducah.[20]

The march back to Paducah was filled with problems and bad conduct by Paine's men toward local citizens. In response to the behavior, Smith issued General Orders No. 32 complaining about "the conduct of a portion of the troops recently marched to Milburn, under command of Brig. Gen. E. A. Paine." The orders pointed out that "in returning, several regiments (the Ninth and Twelfth Illinois excepted) straggled home in parties without the semblance of military array—mere armed mob; and that the property of citizens was wantonly destroyed, and in some instances robbery by violence committed." The general said the conduct implied "a want of discipline that he can scarcely credit," and he directed the officers "to use their utmost endeavors to remedy such a state of things." He concluded by stating his intention to ask for an "investigation into the conduct of all concerned."[21]

Smith was angry about the unruly actions of troops under his command. The general understood the importance of discipline and strict adherence to orders, especially when dealing with volunteer troops. The behavior of Paine's brigade reflected badly on Smith and was in direct violation of McClellan's instructions to Halleck "to maintain thorough organization, discipline and economy throughout your department."[22] Smith was also furious at Paine's disregard of his specific instructions not to engage the enemy.

On November 11 Smith requested General Halleck to order "a court of inquiry at an early date to sift this whole matter." General Smith charged Paine with "transcending" his orders and those of Frémont and Grant. Smith felt that Paine's movement to Milburn and failure to return to Paducah by the Lovelaceville and Blandville road was "an unjustifiable departure from my orders." He also condemned Paine's assertion that "he would in a certain contingency have moved to the attack of Columbus." In Smith's view this attitude demonstrated Paine's intent "to gain notoriety without reference to the public interests or his plain duty as a soldier." The general concluded: "Had he by chance carried out his avowed purpose, I am satisfied, from what we know of the strength of the garrison and the inland defenses of Columbus, he would have been entirely unsuccessful and his command probably cut up in its retreat, thereby greatly imperiling the safety of this post, which is deemed of much importance." Smith also criticized the brigade's conduct on their return to Paducah. He described the command as "totally demoralized as a military body" with some of the regiments "straggling loosely along the road and committing great excesses." He blamed this behavior on the length of the detour to Milburn and "injudicious marching." Smith asked Halleck to investigate the conduct of General Paine, his regimental commanders, and the enlisted men accused of committing the excesses.[23]

Privately, Charles complained that Paine's troops "behaved shockingly in their return march committing great excesses and exasperating the inhabitants very much of course." Charles explained how Paine had disobeyed orders and put his command and the safety of Paducah at risk. He accused Paine of going "for a little of the Spread Eagle[24] glorification and notoriety regardless of its cost to the country and his plain duty." Charles said, "If I had any one about me to put in his place I should have arrested him." He warned Francis, "I speak of all of this because I do not doubt from reports I hear that Columbus would have fallen into our hands but for mismanagement on this side and also that blame will be attached to me."[25]

While waiting for General Halleck's decision on the court of inquiry, the commander of the Department of the Missouri sent Smith a report on Rebel movements. Halleck said, "General Hardee, with 8,000 men, is about to cross the Ohio between the Wabash and Cumberland, to destroy the Ohio and Mississippi and the Illinois Central Railroad." Other intelligence indicated Hardee was "to be re-enforced by General Polk and attack Paducah." The general asked Smith to keep him "advised of the enemy's movements."[26]

The next day, Smith informed the major general there were about 2,000 men at Princeton mainly involved in "running off hogs" and "plundering." Smith "sent the gunboat *Conestoga* to gain information and watch the Ohio." He advised Halleck on the possible Rebel strategy.

> One of the three points of attack to be made simultaneously on this place, it has always been understood, is to be by the Tennessee or Cumberland or both. The idea has military merit. What renders it probable (whenever the attack is to come off) is that the enemy is constructing one or more gunboats far up the Cumberland, and at Sandy Creek, up the Tennessee, some 8 miles beyond the State line, he has been converting river steamers (two or three) into iron-plated gunboats, to be heavily armed. This river side is my weak point.[27]

Halleck replied to Smith's letter with advice on the disposition of troops, employment of the Navy flotilla, and occupation of Shawneetown and Cave-in-Rock. The department commander thought it was critical to protect the Ohio River between the mouths of the Wabash and Tennessee to prevent Hardee's forces from crossing into Illinois. From Illinois the Rebels could attack Cairo, isolate Paducah, and obtain subsistence. With that possibility, Halleck recommended Smith concentrate his forces at Paducah and not disperse troops to

Shawneetown, Cave-in-Rock, and Golconda. The commander directed Smith to have his gunboats watch the river for attempted crossings and protect the bridgehead on the Illinois side of the Ohio. Halleck said Smith's gunboats would provide the main defense against Rebel vessels descending from the Tennessee or Cumberland Rivers. He left it to Smith's discretion how to deal with the Rebel scouting parties, but suggested Smith use cavalry scouts to break up marauding in the country east of the Tennessee River. The Rebel activities seemed focused on collecting hogs, and Halleck asked if Smith could "capture some of these droves so collected."[28]

Halleck notified Smith that a board would be organized to examine the officers of the volunteer units to remove those incompetent officers from the service.[29] This last item was certainly pleasing to Smith who had his fill of inept volunteer line and staff officers. Charles said his "command has a reputation of having more of discipline, as well as instruction than any volunteer force in the West." As pleasing as this accolade was to him, Charles said, "As a soldier I must say God help the others if that is so. I have taught them many things— they are not soldiers—and it is a grinding operation for me to have to all day dry nurse to staff officers and everybody around me all my life." He believed the army had "been outraged by the appointments made from first to last." He hoped, for the "sake of the Country," that "himself and all of our titular Generals may be successful everywhere, on all occasions, but it is rather much to expect."[30]

Unknown to Smith, his future situation was being discussed by Major General George McClellan in Washington and Brigadier General Don Carlos Buell in Louisville. McClellan instructed Buell to "protect our Union friends in Eastern Tennessee" and suggested that "if you possess the means, carry Nashville." McClellan promised to provide Buell with all the resources possible, including twelve regiments from West Virginia and additional artillery batteries. McClellan also offered to place Smith's command under Buell and replace them at Paducah with other troops. Unforeseen events at Paducah and Washington ended the possible transfer.[31]

Halleck refused Smith's request for a court of inquiry to examine the conduct of Paine's command and told Smith to conduct his own investigation. Smith replied that his own examination would be a "hopeless task" and only a "court of inquiry" could " ferret-out-the guilty and do full justice to this matter." Smith continued, "The people of the country through which the troops passed are exasperated to the last degree by the excesses committed by the soldiers, friends and foes were enraged most impartially." Smith blamed the infractions on the long march ordered by Paine, which "broke the men down and scattered the command along the road like a flock of geese." Even more damning in Smith's view was that Paine knew about these depredations but did not try to stop them. However, Smith did not foresee formal charges being brought against Paine, and that a "Trial by Court-Martial would involve trouble and expense and might result in failure."[32]

Smith desperately needed good officers, and in the absence of a suitable replacement, he was willing to let the matter end with the reprimand. Regrettably, Paine refused to learn from his mistakes. The chastised officer plotted to destroy Smith's reputation and replace him in command. Paine quickly put his plan into action and started causing trouble.

18. The Incident at the Tilghman House

Smith's brand of discipline was having an impact on the roughhewn volunteers. After two months of training, they realized that the general was teaching them the skills they needed to defeat the enemy. An old colonel told Smith, "The boys didn't like me much at first; thought you were too damned strict; but they think it all right now and say you are just the person they want to make them soldiers." Several of his officers circulated a petition to be sent to President Lincoln requesting that Smith be promoted to major general. Smith learned about the campaign and stopped it. He was amazed that the men took this action, because although he had "been very forbearing in my behavior to the Volunteers on account of their being new troops," he had "in many things been very rigid."[1]

However, new recruits would soon challenge Smith's authority and create the most difficult period in his military career. The situation arose as a simple expression of a citizen's sentiment and blossomed into a near mutiny. Although the accounts of the matter differed greatly, it was all over a flag.

According to the November 26 account from the *St. Louis Democrat*, a secessionist named Woolfolk hung a Rebel flag out of the window of his house[2] and, as Union troops were passing by, "hurrahed for Jeff Davis." Mr. Woolfolk had done this in the past to show his support for the Confederacy. The incident was reported to General Smith who refused to interfere. According to the paper, Smith's failure to stop this demonstration "caused great indignation among the troops, and doubts of his loyalty were freely expressed in Paducah."[3]

The *Democrat's* story said Woolfolk's actions were reported to General Wallace, who sent his aide-de-camp with a squad of men to order Woolfolk to take the "traitorous flag" down and "erect the Stars and Stripes over his house." Woolfolk refused to remove the flag and appealed to General Smith for assistance. Wallace's aide, Captain Frederick Knefler, "forcibly took down the Rebel flag and hoisted the Stars and Stripes." By this time, Wallace had reached Woolfolk's house to oversee the proceedings. Smith's aide, Lieutenant Price, arrived and ordered Wallace to take down the Union flag. "Wallace refused to obey the order, and sent word to Smith that the flag should not be taken down while there was a live man in his brigade." Captain Knefler said that Woolfolk should sleep under a loyal flag for at least one night, and Lieutenant Price replied he did not think that was any great honor. Knefler knocked down Price, and because Smith had no one but his "defeated lieutenant" to enforce his order, "the old flag still waves." Seizing the opportunity, General Paine agreed to support Wallace's actions. The *Democrat* concluded: "The affair has created intense excitement among the soldiers, and Wallace's insubordination is enthusiastically approved."[4]

The *Evansville Journal* provided more details on the Eleventh Indiana's actions. The newspaper reported that Wallace accompanied his old regiment to Woolfolk's house

The Tilghman House (author's photograph).

to remove the flag. The flag bearer led the procession, followed by the band, and then the whole regiment. The Eleventh gave three cheers and a tiger[5] as the U.S. flag was placed on the mansion. The *Journal* said, "The boys were in a frenzy of excitement." After the flag raising, General Wallace stood on a fence post and said, "Boys, the flag is floating now; go to your quarters, boys; you have done your duty, now go back." The soldiers started for camp, when an argument occurred between some of the Eleventh's officers and

General Smith's aide about placing the flag on the home. When the Missouri Eighth heard about the event, they started up town with a fire engine with plans to wash out Smith's quarters. Fortunately, Wallace convinced the Eighth to return to camp. The sentiment of many of the soldiers was "that if that flag came down, the house would come down with it."[6]

Another version of the incident attributed it to a visit by Confederate officers. "Once some of Smith's men descended on a house whose occupants had hoisted a Rebel flag, when some Confederate officers visited Paducah under a flag of truce, and prepared to take the place apart; Smith went around in person, dispersed the rioters, and the next day issued orders denouncing the whole business as a grave breach of duty, mutinous in spirit."[7] In this story, Smith gave the Confederates permission to enter the city under a flag of truce. The officers met at Woolfolk's home to conduct some unexplained business. General Wallace decided to drill a company of soldiers on the street in front of the Woolfolk home. He shouted commands and marched and counter marched them along Kentucky Avenue. It is doubtful that Wallace, a brigade commander, would be drilling a company of volunteers instead of a captain or lieutenant. Woolfolk was annoyed by the Union demonstration and responded by hoisting the Confederate flag and shouting "Hurrah for Jeff Davis." Wallace sent an aide into the house and demanded that the Rebel flag be removed, but Woolfolk refused to take it down. The officer called for reinforcements and the soldiers "ripped down the Confederate banner, tore it to shreds, and threw it in the midst of the Confederate officers." Then Wallace's aide ran up the American flag. As the soldier finished raising the flag, Woolfolk knocked the man onto the floor. The other Union soldiers jumped Woolfolk, and the Confederate officers joined in the fight. There was considerable "head-knocking" and the noise was heard in the street. Wallace sent one of his men to General Smith to complain about the problems Smith had created by allowing the Confederates into the city. Smith walked into the house, called the men to attention, and apologized to Woolfolk for the behavior of his soldiers. He ordered the men to report to quarters under arrest. The next day he issued an order deploring the whole business.[8]

One of Wallace's zouaves described Lieutenant Price's fight with Captain Knefler. Woolfolk "occasionally flew a Confederate flag from his house, and General Smith refused to order him to take it down." On November 25 three or four officers of the Eleventh Indiana took a Union flag to Woolfolk's house and informed Mrs. Woolfolk that they intended to fly it from the home. She sent word about the confrontation to Smith, who came to her home and ordered the officers away. After the officers returned to camp, their men became excited, and soon the whole regiment was marching to the home, led by the regimental band playing "The Marseillaise." The Eleventh raised the Stars and Stripes from the house as the band played a medley of patriotic music. General Wallace witnessed the affair on his way to Smith's quarters. He did not interfere with the flag raising and ordered his men back to camp. After the first attempt to raise the flag, Lieutenant Price returned to the house, condemned the act, and got into an argument with Captain Frederick Knefler. Price hit Knefler in the face, and Knefler responded by knocking Price into the mud. The fight escalated with cries of "kill him." One soldier tried to slash Price with a knife, and another kicked him before General Wallace intervened and rescued Price.[9]

In his version of events, Smith indicates that a "flag of truce arrived here," but he does not reveal the details of the truce. The flag might have been carried by the messenger who brought a proposal for a prisoner exchange. It seems most unlikely that a group of officers entered the city because on November 26 Smith refused a prisoner exchange with General Pillow. Smith informed the Confederate officer:

To do this would imply that the Government of the United States admits the existing civil war to be one between independent nations. This I can not admit; and must therefore decline making any terms or conditions in reference to those we naturally hold as prisoners taken in arrest without the orders of my government.

As an act of humanity, and until otherwise instructed I shall always treat those whom the fortunes of war places in my hands as prisoners of war.[10]

Other, possibly more accurate, explanations come from the key players. According to Wallace, he was at Smith's house when Captain Thomas Newsham reported that a mob was across the street at Mr. Woolfolk's home. General Smith told Newsham to disperse the crowd. Then an orderly reported that Eleventh Indiana and other men from Wallace's Second Brigade were taking down a secession flag from Woolfolk's house. Smith became excited, and Wallace assured him that he knew nothing about the affair, but would see about it and report. When Wallace reached the house, he found Captain Knefler and Captain Newsham fighting. Wallace separated the men, but soldiers from the Eleventh pursued Newsham with clubs and stones. After Wallace rescued him again, the general returned to Woolfolk's "just as the stars and stripes supplanted the stars and bars on his house." From a post of the front gate, the brigade commander ordered the men to return to camp and he reported the outcome to Smith. Smith was even more upset, and he said that such a thing had never happened to him in all his years of service. He threatened to make an example or the officers, but Wallace "finally got the old soldier calmed down." Then, in Wallace's version of events, Smith asked him to write a general order for the division. He quoted Smith as saying, "They are not soldiers yet—only politicians. You know them better than I do. Write."[11]

Wallace's account of events and his opinion of Smith were modified after the war. This story presents Wallace as a peacekeeper and voice of reason in stark contrast with other reports describing him as an insubordinate instigator. Wallace also says that the fight took place between Captain Knefler and Captain Newsham. Other accounts and Lieutenant Price's statements indicate that Newsham was not involved.

Later that month, General Smith presented his own description of events.

On the day on which a flag of truce arrived here I heard from one of my orderlies after it had gone that it was said by soldiers near by that Mr. Woolfolk ... had flaunted a secession flag from his window, and that the men were highly indignant. I sent for him immediately, he said he had not been at home and knew nothing about it; that he did not believe there was such a flag in his house. He left me and soon after returned to say that he had been mistaken, that a small sized secession flag—a child's plaything had been brought to his house and shaken out of the window by one of his children. This is the extent. A week [later] ... I saw a collection of soldiers standing in front of Mr. Woolfolk's house. I asked my aide-de-camp, Lt. Price, to ride forward and see what was the matter and then immediately followed myself. I saw several officers standing in the yard one of whom had a flag in his hand. Asking what all this meant, he said the officers of the 11th Indiana meant to put the flag up on the house. Regarding the proceeding as meant merely to annoy the family—the ladies only were present. I ordered the whole party away and they moved off quietly. I however soon afterwards sent for Genl Wallace who commands the brigade to which the regt [regiment] belongs to speak to the officers and point out the impropriety of such proceeding that I could not permit it; this he promised to do and did. Anticipating no further disturbance I thought no more of the matter until after retreat of the same day when the soldiers of the 11th Ind. [Indiana] marched to this house with music and with much shouting placed the flag on the roof. I sent for Genl Wallace and told him this must be stopped. He ordered them away and they went. My aide-de-camp went to the house without any instructions from me during the progress of the affair and got into a personal altercation with an officer. This is the whole affair. My order flowing from this occasion is enclosed herewith. (Mr. Woolfolk I understand is on good terms with the officers of the regt. several of whom visit his house and I suppose all feeling which gave rise to the occurrence has passed away).[12]

Smith's explanation agrees with the central elements of the event: a Rebel flag was displayed at the Woolfolk house, soldiers from Wallace's brigade pulled down the flag and replaced it with the Stars and Stripes, Wallace ordered his men from the home, and Price got into a fight with one of Wallace's officers.

Smith was dismayed at the flagrant insubordination. Not only did the officers refuse to obey his orders, but they also violated Grant's instructions "to take special care and precaution that no harm is done to inoffensive citizens" and "exercise the strictest discipline against any soldier who shall insult citizens or engage in plundering private property."[13] While Wallace may not have contributed to the events, he was clearly guilty of failing to control the officers and soldiers of his brigade and impress upon them the importance of Grant's orders. Wallace's claim of writing the proclamation seems self-serving. The language and comments are more consistent with Smith's treatment of wayward cadets than of political persuasion. The personal feelings of the Indiana volunteers were irrelevant. They had no more right to define political strategy in Kentucky than did Frémont or Wallace. General Wallace, in another test of leadership, failed to control his raw recruits and instill in them the critical importance of discipline and obedience of orders.

As a former West Point Commandant, General Smith was used to being obeyed without question. The actions and disobedience of the Indiana volunteers were close to mutiny. However, Smith realized that he needed to move quickly past this incident and prepare his men for the coming battles. He decided to use the disturbance as a teaching opportunity, and on November 27 he issued General Orders No. 36.

Head Quarters, U.S. Forces
Paducah, Ky., Nov. 27th, 1861.
General Orders No. 36
   On the afternoon of the 25th, inst., a grave breach of discipline was committed by a part this command, chiefly, if not altogether, by officers and soldiers of the 11th Ind. Regiment, in the raising of a flag over the house of a resident of this city, not, certainly, by the act of raising our flag, but by the manner of proceeding—the attendant circumstances.
   The Commanding General desires to address those engaged in this proceeding in a kindly spirit. He is aware they have subjected themselves to prosecution under the Articles of War. He is compelled to denounce the transaction as a great violation of good order and military discipline; but he is inclined to the belief that those engaged in it will, upon reflection, come to regard it in that light themselves. Had it been possible for him to have anticipated its occurrence it would have been his duty, by all means of his command and at every hazard, to have prevented it. The affair is more mortifying to him from the fact that, in a long military life, it is the first proceeding of a mutinous character that ever happened with troops under his immediate command: that, if his feelings were wounded by the transaction, as he admits they were, he is confident sensible, intelligent and generous men, such as he believes composes the command he more especially addresses, will make due allowance for the pride and sensibilities of an officer who has given nearly thirty-seven years of life to the service of his country in the army.
   Though the occurrence may subject him to criticism by those placed over him in authority, he is disposed to let it drop without investigation; less, however, for his own sake than that of the persons engaged in it. So disposed on his side, he trusts they will listen patiently to his remonstrances against like occurrences in the future.
   In this spirit the Commanding General appeals, then, to the intelligence of officers and soldiers. Although Kentucky is full of traitors, her Legislature left her one of the States of the Union; and our forces on her soil are charged with the high mission of protecting her people and sovereignty. More plainly, he desires every soldier, without regard to his position, to know that he is sent

here by the Government as the protector of a loyal State, which, though occupied by rebel armies, is not an enemy's country; and that success requires him by the patient exercise of moderation, obedience and charity to earn that character from both friends and foes. We charge the rebels with oppressions: is it policy to subject ourselves, our cause, or our flag to like charges? Our boast is we are fighting for a Government that never harmed a citizen: whose thanks we will earn if we are the first to rob ourselves of that boast?

The General has derived great satisfaction from the soldierly deportment of those he more particularly addresses; and it is hardly enough to say that it grieved him to see them manifest the slightest spirit of disorder. All his hopes for the triumph of our flag and its re erection in all rebellious States, are based upon the discipline of the army; and he feels every blow at that discipline as a blow to the common cause. Upon the restoration of peace, each soldier will go back to the civilian pursuits from which he came. How important that he should do so without reproach or shame! Property, Liberty, Government!—everything precious—has been committed to the army; when the army supplants the Commander, or turns from the path, or bursts the bands of discipline, it makes itself a thing of terror and ruin. Enthusiasm for the flag is a spirit to be encouraged; the General would do everything in his power to raise it to the highest pitch; yet he calmly asks each soldier to watch its fiery impulses lest, while fitting him for boldness in battle, they do not plunge him unguardedly into excesses.

In conclusion, the General asks the soldiers of his command, by their conduct in the future, their gentleness to friends, and their moderation towards unarmed enemies, living under the shadow of our flag, to give him reason to believe they admit the necessity of order and are willing to enforce it. If they will only exercise their intelligence, and not forget the observance of law which so becomes them as citizens will still more become them as soldiers, no complaint will ever be heard against them from any source.

By order of Brig. Gen'l C. F. Smith

J. T. Price, Lieut. and Aide-de-camp[14]

Lieutenant Price used the event to renew his request for a transfer near to his home and family. Price felt it was his obligation to exercise his "influence" in that vicinity. He believed it was "duty to sever the agreeable connection, with which your [Smith's] favor and kindness has honored me." Price was determined to leave Smith's command. "With great regret that circumstances over which I have no control induce me to part (tho perhaps temporarily only) from an officer and gentleman whom I have learned to love and whom I should proudly follow into the thickest of any battle; and with many thanks to you for taking by the hand a young soldier groping in total darkness, and leading him to a point where he begins to see a few faint glances of daylight." Behind the flowery language, Price wanted to be closer to home and to remove an object of ridicule and embarrassment from Smith's staff. Price ended his letter with a postscript apologizing for not writing the note himself because he had "sprained my thumb in the disgraceful riot which just occurred."[15]

While Wallace may have protested his innocence, Smith received a disturbing, anonymous letter from Indianapolis describing Wallace as a "most unscrupulous and insubordinate officer" and warning him to "keep your eye on Lew Wallace. Court-Martial him if you can for he will ruin you at any cost."[16]

Smith was obeying his orders, and his attitude toward residents was consistent with the army's overall policy toward civilians. Frémont's General Orders No. 23 forbade the army "to take private property from any person, for any purpose whatever, except by authority or a general officer; to enter any dwelling occupied or unoccupied, unless accompanied by a commissioned officer" and held all commanding officers "responsible for the strict execution of this order."[17] Smith also knew that Kentucky presented a difficult situation for the country and that Lincoln had removed Frémont for the latter's emancipation proclamation. Kentuckians had to be treated carefully, and abolitionists held in check to maintain the state's neutrality. At this point in the Western Theater, the political and military strategy was to win the hearts and minds of Southerners. General Grant said, "Up to that time [the battle of Shiloh] it had been the policy of our army, certainly of that portion commanded by me, to protect the property of the citizens whose territory was invaded, without regard to their sentiments whether Union or Secession."[18] Smith had no intention of losing his hard-won generalship by disobeying orders and inciting Southern sympathizers.

19. "They are false in every particular"

"Doubtlessly a Southern sympathizer"

Smith's war had developed into fighting enemies on two fronts: internal attacks on his loyalty by fellow officers and external threats on his command by Rebel forces.

On November 27 Congressman Lucian Anderson from Kentucky sent General Halleck a list of complaints "relative to the management and control of the Army of the U.S. at this place." Then Anderson and Mr. Bolinger presented their grievances in person to Halleck in St. Louis. They cited four examples of, what they believed were General Smith's mismanagement of his command.

The first complaint was that General Smith failed to send troops to rescue Mr. J. F. Conner who was imprisoned in Mayfield. Mr. Conner and his brother, M. M. Conner, had gotten into a fight with Mr. John Milliken who called them "black Republicans" and threatened to kill them. Milliken was killed in the fight and J. Conner was arrested. M. Conner was afraid that Rebel soldiers would seize J. Conner from prison and murder him. He asked Smith "to let him have a force sufficient to protect his brother." Generals Wallace and Paine asked Smith to "permit them to go with force sufficient to protect Conner from the band of murderers." He refused this request, but granted Conner a pass to leave the city to help his brother. Conner obtained men and horses and went to Mayfield, but was too late by one hour. The Confederate troops had broken into the jail and killed his brother. Anderson and Bolinger said that the life of an "innocent man" was taken through Smith's failure to act in time.

The second objection involved Smith's delay in confiscating wheat and hogs in Bullard County that were being sent to Confederate troops in Columbus. General Paine told Smith that a man near Lovelaceville had purchased large quantities of wheat and was grinding it up for the troops at Columbus. The man was also buying all the hogs in the county for sale to the Rebels. Smith refused to have the grain and hogs confiscated. Although Paine obtained an affidavit from a Union man from the area confirming the facts, Smith would not act unless the man was endorsed as "a true man" by a Union man in Paducah. After receiving the sanction, Paine went to confiscate the property and seized about 2,000 bushels of wheat and about 100 hogs. Paine had to leave about 2,000 bushels, and Confederate forces removed the rest before Smith authorized Paine to collect the remaining wheat.

A third grievance was that Smith refused to send out a force to confiscate hogs in Union County, which were being purchased by Confederate agents.

The last complaint concerned Smith's handling of the display of a secessionist flag by Mr. Woolfolk. Soldiers from General Wallace's brigade decided to remove the Stars and Bars and replace it with the Stars and Stripes. When the soldiers entered Woolfolk's house, Smith's adjutant ordered them to stop. "They refused and put up the Union flag and the cussed Smith's adjutant got a sound drubbing."

Anderson and Bolinger summed up their grievances by saying that Smith's Federal troops protected secessionists while Union men in the area were undefended and "left to the ravages of the Confederate troops." The men warned, "Unless some changes are made here, bad results will certainly flow, for the soldiers here are almost prepared to rise against the policy which has thus far been pursued."[1]

Unfortunately, the war would not wait for Smith to defend himself against these charges. Confederate troop movements near Cave-in-Rock produced an urgent call for help. On November 29, Captain John Seaton, commanding a company from the Twenty-Second Illinois Regiment, notified Smith that 600 to 1,000 Rebel troops were at Caseyville, five miles from Cave-in-Rock, and intended to cross the Ohio River into Illinois. Apparently, the enemy force planned to seize a steamboat and employ her to ferry men across the river.[2]

The news of other Confederate troop movements seemed to confirm an imminent attack on Paducah. The day after receiving Seaton's warning, Smith learned that the 2,000 troops at Princeton had gone to Hopkinsville. The Confederates were rumored to be marching toward Muldraugh Hill in central Kentucky. Smith ordered three companies of the Eighth Missouri Volunteers under Lieutenant Colonel James Peckham, to proceed to Cave-in-Rock, and "act as circumstances may require." General Smith also intended to send the gunship *Conestoga* to Caseyville when she returned from her mission up the Tennessee River. The *Conestoga* was watching a Rebel gunboat that was conducting reconnaissance below Fort Henry. Smith believed the Rebel movements were in preparation for an attack on Paducah, and he asked for another gunboat for added security.[3]

It soon became apparent that many of the enemy's movements were to capture hogs and not Paducah. Colonel Peckham's report of his expedition to Caseyville revealed that the town was a leading transit hub for sending goods to the Rebels in Nashville. Peckham said the Rebels did not intend to blockade the Ohio and the reason for their presence was to seize pigs. The colonel reported that a large business in salt was being conducted by the Confederates via Caseyville and Cave-in-Rock. He told Smith that vast quantities of goods were passing through Caseyville en route to Nashville.[4]

With one crisis under control, Smith could address Lucian Anderson's complaints. Halleck had forwarded the letter to Smith for his comments. The general scarcely had time to respond to the accusations when attacks began to appear in the papers. The first volley was fired by the *Chicago Tribune* on December 1 when it reported, "From all accounts, and these come to us from various sources, General Charles F. Smith, in command of the Federal forces at Paducah, has been making an ass of himself, which is stating the case mildly." The *Tribune* claimed that under Smith's weak rule, Union troops had openly been subjected to gross insults from disloyal residents, with no chance given to them to fight back. They reported that these occurrences had caused dissatisfaction among the officers and troops at Paducah.[5] On December 5 the *Chicago Tribune* reported that General Smith was "exceedingly unpopular both with the officers and men." The *Tribune* accused him "of sympathizing with the rebels, and refusing to aid Union men who have been driven from their homes, and whose property has been plundered by the secesh."[6]

While Smith's character was called into question, Anderson's was not. According to Charles, Lucian Anderson was considered a person of questionable character and "a shallow man ... generally found to be an ardent supporter of the Party in power be it Government or Rebellion." After Lincoln's proclamation calling for raising of troops, Anderson was reported to have made "violent and determined harangues against the Government of the United States, and proposed armed resistance to the passage of Federal Troops through the State of Kentucky."[7]

The accusations must be considered in the overall context of Smith's primary mission at Paducah. He was charged with defending the strategic city from anticipated Confederate attacks. The complaints mentioned were insignificant in Smith's view and intervention in them might compromise the defense of Paducah. Union officers were often subject to criticism because of power struggles between northern Democrats and Republican abolitionists. These battles often overflowed into the political makeup of volunteer and militia units. Governors appointed officers for volunteer regiments based on their political affiliations and support for abolition. These political appointees used their connections to advance their own careers at the expense of more capable but less well-connected fellow officers.[8]

A new attack was launched against Smith in an editorial in the *Cincinnati Commercial* blaming him for failing to capture Columbus during the battle of Belmont. The editorial also said, "in all the action of that General he favors Secession." The comments resulted in a highly critical letter from D. D. I. Benedict to Congressman John A. Gurley, who was an aide-de-camp to General Frémont. Benedict complained that Smith was still "allowed to hold an important command." The vicious attack continued:

> Now sir we are on the eve of another battle at Columbus Kentucky, would it not be well to examine this matter and see whether General Smith is safe to trust before he gets the privilege of defeating our army again. For me I think that he is not safe to trust. I, for one think he will surely defeat our army again if he gets the chance to do so and this is the opinion of three fourths of the citizens and soldiers in the west who know about that General.

Benedict's letter indirectly calls for Smith's removal, and the reference to Columbus suggests that Benedict was allied with Paine.[9]

The newspapers started to refer mockingly to Smith as "Paducah Smith." In the midst of these character assassinations, Smith received a note from Iowa City to tell him "how highly" he was "esteemed by thousands & tens of thousands of Northerners."[10]

Wallace was upset that the "trifling" affair caused him "an injury of long standing." He said the newspapers welcomed the event, gave him credit for the outbreak, complimented his patriotism, and denounced General Smith. The papers proclaimed that no one but a "traitor" would have objected to "the substitution of the flags." Thanks to the newspaper stories, the incident reached headquarters in Cairo and St. Louis. The articles blamed Wallace for the disturbance and labeled him a political agitator. Wallace complained to General Smith, who laughed at him. Wallace recalled his exchange with Smith.

> "Why," he said, "don't you see? If I can stand to be accused of disloyalty, what have you to grumble at?"
> In another interview he grew angry.
> "Disloyal—I? The scoundrels!"
> Suddenly he stopped.
> "What an ass I am making of myself! A few days more, and I'll have a chance to show if I am a traitor. It's their day now; it will be mine then."
> He stubbornly refused to allow me to card the papers in his behalf or my own.[11]

The attacks continued, and Charles warned Francis about "scurrilous and malignant articles" in the *Chicago Tribune* and the *St. Louis Democrat*.

> They are false in every particular and known to be so. Pay no heed to them. My friends—and I have some warm friends—made by my command have asked me to write, but I say "no." Still I see articles in different papers telling the truth. I'll send you all the squibs before long.[12]

As Charles indicated, not all the papers were calling for Smith's head. General Wallace sent Smith a note saying that the *Indianapolis Journal* had paid him a "handsome tribute." Wallace praised the writer for the peculiar manner of the article and called him a "damnation sharp chap."[13]

While Wallace was pretending to be Smith's loyal subordinate, his actions indicate that he was part of the cabal wanting Smith to be removed. On January 13, 1862, President Lincoln gave Secretary of War Cameron a petition bearing the names of Henry S. Lane of Indiana, Garrett Davis of Kentucky, and others, asking for Smith's removal. It is possible that Wallace may have had something to do with the petition. Lane was a fellow townsman of Wallace and his wife's brother-in-law. On January 8 Wallace wrote to Indiana Governor Oliver P. Morton, "Nothing new.' All quiet in Paducah.' *Gen. Smith is not removed.*" More evidence that Wallace was part of the effort is contained in a February 19 letter to his wife. "I am now in command of these forts (Henry and Heiman) with fourteen regiments. In other words, I am acting Major Genl commanding a division. All [of] which is not so satisfactory as the happy riddance of Gen. Smith, which is at last accomplished. He is at Donelson, I here. He left me behind on the marching of the troops, thro' jealousy."[14]

Charles knew that Paine was "at the bottom of this" and wanted "to supersede" him. Smith described his subordinate as a "weak crass man" and "of the proper material to be made a Senator of the U.S." who "wants to be made in some way a newspaper hero." Charles explained that Paine had enlisted the help of "a fellow—a Methodist parson and Chaplain of one of the regiments" to write to the *Chicago Tribune*. In response, some of Charles' friends, "the true soldiers of the camp," began a vigorous writing campaign to the newspapers on his behalf.[15]

While General Paine was leading the attack on Smith's loyalty, officers in Paine's brigade were engaging in behavior that would enrage most Northerners. Chaplain Henry C. McCook of the Forty-First Regiment Illinois Volunteers charged that certain officers in the regiment "brought into our camps fugitive slaves who had placed themselves under their protection at the pickets, and afterwards delivered them over to their masters receiving therefore sums varying from fifty to twenty dollars each." McCook believed this "trading in slaves to be a gross prostitution of the honor of officers and of the good name of the regiment." He tried to have the regiment's colonel dismiss the offenders, but the colonel refused to remove "the obnoxious parties." Faced with "the disgrace which doubt will fall upon the Regiment as well as upon the guilty," McCook submitted his resignation as Chaplain. He wrote, "I do not desire to be one of a Regiment [of] slave trading officers, [that] if deemed dishonorable, are not dealt with as such." His resignation was accepted by Colonel I. C. Pugh and General Paine.[16]

"Victim of a base conspiracy"

Finally, the complaints, accusations, and innuendos had their intended effect. Smith's confirmation as brigadier general was delayed in the Senate, and General Halleck was forced to investigate the situation. McClellan approved preliminary orders for Halleck to remove Smith from command if Halleck considered it necessary. Before acting on the orders, Halleck sent General Cullum, General Sturgis, Colonel Totten, and other officers to Paducah to inspect Smith's command and report on its condition. McClellan sent Inspector General Van Rensselaer to join the review. In order not to prejudice the men, Halleck did not indicate the subjects to be examined.

When the officers returned to the Department of the Missouri headquarters, Halleck asked them about the condition of Smith's command and reports of difficulties between

Smith and some of his officers. All of the officers said Smith's fortifications and his whole command were in infinitely better condition than any other volunteer artillery unit. The inspectors reported that Smith's command was "in the best discipline & order of any one in the department." The inspection team said that the problems between Smith and his subordinates was caused by others and not Smith. General Grant expressed the same opinion. The officers' judgments convinced Halleck that there were "no real grounds of complaint" against Smith and certainly none "sufficient to justify his withdrawal."

After receiving the initial reports, Halleck asked McClellan to suspend the removal order.

> Head Quarters Dept. of the Mo.
> St. Louis December 16th 1861
> Maj. Gen. Geo. B. McClellan.
> Washington, D.C.
> Unless your information is unquestionable I respectfully request that the order for the withdrawal of Gen. Smith may be suspended for the present. From all the information I can obtain Gen. S. is the victim of a base conspiracy among his own subordinates. I have sent officers of confidence to ascertain, if possible, the real state of the case. If these reports warrant it, I will immediately remove him; if not I will await your answer.
> Signed H. W. Halleck Maj. Genl.

> Washington, Dec 17th 1861
> Maj. Gen. Halleck
> The order concerning Gen. Smith may be suspended as you desire.
> Signed L. Thomas
> Adgt. Gen.[17]

Sadly, the defamations were having a serious impact on Charles. On December 17 he told Francis that he had "scarcely heart to take up a pen to write to you." He was depressed by the accusations that robbed his time and sapped his energy.[18] While Smith was exonerated by Halleck, no public statement clearing his name had been issued, and the newspaper attacks continued. On December 22 an obviously mentally exhausted Charles defended "a malignity quoted in your letter from a Philadelphia paper" that accused him of always being "in a somnolent and unmilitary condition." He said the allegation, in plain language, meant that he was "always drunk and unfitted for duty." Charles placed the assertion in the same category as the charge of disloyalty—"Both are falsehoods and calumnies of the worst type."

> This last accusation is a little too much [as] it affects my gentlemanly status. No one really believes me to be disloyal. If there is one man in the Country more than another who looks upon the course of South Carolina and the South generally in this most unnecessary and damnable rebellion with greater abhorrence and detestation than myself, I do not know him. I have ever been from the time I could think and reason on political matters an avowed and earnest advocate of the Government as against the ridiculous assertion of States rights which means no Government at all. I would crush this thing out with a strong hand.
> But unfortunately it is in a grand degree a political war. The dirty leaders in party aspire for favors by dirty means. I have been made almost a victim perhaps quite by the efforts of a paltry politician part by my constant and lately stinging rebukes for his want of military propriety and neglects. I have incurred an amount of hatred and vituperation you can scarcely conceive. The whole of the newspaper statements against me arose from this cause and my not choosing socially to recognize the female coterie he has around him. With the exception of a small clique of officers, soldiers and citizens, all in this place Army and Citizens are on my side.[19]

Charles did receive good news from Special Orders No. 78 that designated Grant's command as the District of Cairo and transferred General Paine to Cairo.[20] Grant's General

Order No. 22 assigned Paine to command the forces as Bird's Point.[21] "What a howling on one side what a rejoicing on the other," Charles noted with glee. He continued: "There never was a more crestfallen man in the world than when he [Paine] received the order to leave here and go to the Bird's Point."[22] Charles described the post as a "very hell hole." He was pleased that at the moment Paine and his "companions in iniquity" were reveling in the prospect of Paine replacing him at Paducah based on rumors from Washington, a "shell fell in their midst." Charles went on to describe the "active agent" in the attacks on him as the Reverend Ferrie who was the chaplain of Paine's old regiment. Ferrie had been absent without leave from Paducah for the past three weeks, and Smith had preferred charges against him. The chaplain was staying away to avoid a general court martial.[23]

These assaults left Charles confused and weary. He grumbled that he was "overworked [and] overtaxed in trying to do my duty." He rose early and went to bed late because he was forced to do the duty of his inexperienced staff officers who could not "write me a letter nor an order" when he explained the contents. In addition, he had been suffering from neuralgia and a bad cold, which had affected his eyes, teeth, and jaws.[24]

The rumors and accusations continued to plague Smith, and on December 26 he finally decided to write a formal reply to Lucian Anderson's charges. General Smith began by stating: "I very much regret that I am thus compelled to waste time that might be far more profitably employed in the public service than in noticing each statement made by such a person." Smith responded to each of the counts "in the indictment against" him.

> The first count in the indictment against me is that I failed to send a force to liberate Mr. J. F. Connor from the jail in Mayfield where he had been incarcerated by the civil authority charged with the murder of judge Jno. [John] Milliken. A person by the name of M. M. Connor came to me with a statement something like that set forth in his affidavit (herewith returned). I knew nothing of either Conner or Milliken, and regarding it as a private broil, did not choose to send a large force (prudence ever forbid sending a small one) to Mayfield to take J. F. Conner from the hands of civil authority on a supposition. Subsequent events show that J. F. Conner, the man taken from the jail and murdered, was the person who killed Milliken and not Mr. M. Conner, the brother who came to me, although the latter claims to have committed the homicide. (To dispose of this Mr. M. Connor at once I will state that both Mr. Andersen, the complainant and Mr. John Bolenger, who accompanied him on his mission to St. Louis, on being called on before a civil court on a former occasion to testify to Connor's character for truth and veracity, both made affidavit they would not believe him on oath). Neither Genls Paine nor Wallace importuned me to send out; but I did permit a small party of Kentucky Vols to go although I refused to mount them on government horses. Personal feuds—private quarrels—is so frequently the pretext in this part of the country for making complaints that one's neighbor is a secessionist—an enemy, that I have been frequently much deceived and for this reason I have for a long time past required everyone who came to make complaints to make affidavit to his statements and get some one to vouch for the character of the complainants.

In reply to the second allegation, Smith defended his refusal to act on General Paine's request to remove supplies intended for Rebel forces at Columbus until he could "get some proper grounds for action." Smith charged Paine with spending too much time investigating the loyalties of people in Paducah to the "neglect of his military duties." Many of the arrests based on Paine's assertions had to [be] discharged, which explained Smith's "course of action in this matter." General Smith also cited Paine's failure to obey orders to destroy a mill and bring the flour and grain to Paducah.

The third allegation was that Smith "failed to send and seize all the hogs in Union county Kentucky." He said that he did not have enough cavalry to send on such an expedition. He was prohibited from sending a large enough infantry force to round up the animals because it would weaken his defense at Paducah. He indicated that many people from Union County had made similar requests and "the people ... apparently ... seem to expect that a company of soldiers are to be stationed at each house to guard it." Smith added that there is a strong economic incentive to have troops in community, which is a "strong motive for raising a clamor to get them."

The next allegation was about Smith's involvement in the Eleventh Indiana's flag raising at the Woolfolk house. The general described the sad affair, which was "merely to annoy the family." He enclosed his order commenting on the Eleventh's behavior and explaining how the soldiers should conduct themselves.

The last allegation was that Smith protects secessionists and not unionists. He charged: "This imputation on my loyalty is an unmitigated calumny and falsehood." Then, the general charged that Lucian Anderson had "made violent and determined harangues ... against the government ... and proposed armed resistance to the passage of Federal forces through the state of Kentucky." Smith concluded by calling Anderson "a shallow man" who was "an ardent supporter of the party in power, be it Gov't or rebellion."

General Smith added the following postscript.

> I have no military ambition to subserve [promote]. I have but one feeling or thought connected with my profession; and that is to do my duty, as I have endeavored to do it according to my best lengths. It matters little to me where I am placed. If it is deemed expedient to remove me elsewhere well and good, I care not.[25]

The same day, General Cullum said the beleaguered officer enjoyed "the confidence of General Halleck and your old army friends here." Cullum reported that Halleck "defended your reputation and protected you against the political cabal in Kentucky and Washington." Halleck also said that Smith was the "victim of a base conspiracy" that resulted in the issue of Special Orders No. 78.[26]

Smith thanked General Halleck for "for his manliness and just appreciation" of him as Halleck demonstrated in his telegram to McClelland. Smith complained to Cullum about "the unworthy course pursued toward me by those in authority." He was outraged that he was condemned by "political tricksters" without the "slightest opportunity of self defense." He could hardly restrain his "indignation within the bounds of decency" at his treatment. "My military pride has been stricken down; how or why it is needless to inquire; but my attendance to duty to my country and to myself, will now as ever, carry me on in the straight path in whatever condition I am placed, without a murmur, however enraged I may feel."[27]

Although the order suspending Smith was withdrawn, no formal letter was sent to McClelland's Adjutant General until January 7. General Halleck suggested the attacks on Smith were due to his request for a court of inquiry of General Paine that was forwarded to McClellan's office for action by the president but "received no reply." Halleck stated that the attempt "to injure Genl. S. by newspaper attacks" was done in order to have him "removed to give place for another aspirant, who by all accounts, is totally unfit for any command." Halleck restated his satisfaction that there were "no real grounds of complaint" against General Smith and that his command was the best disciplined and most orderly of any one in the department. He also repeated that other officers in Smith's command and not Smith were responsible for the difficulties in the district. Halleck explained that he was not aware that he was expected to issue a formal report on this matter or he would have reported some time ago.[28]

The following day Charles responded to Francis' letter about assaults on her husband's loyalties. Charles believed the source of the "infamously false" accusations of "secession tendencies" came from his acquaintances in Washington who were "Southern sympathizers, as or were nineteen-twentieths (19/20) of the inhabitants." When he met them on the street, Smith greeted them as "old acquaintances, without the slightest reference to politics, and did not talk up on the subject, except generally to deprecate." Charles said he "only expressed my regret at the state of affairs" and did not sympathize with the "Southern side." He restated his opposition to "States Rights, which carried out in the shape of Secession is simply rebellion." Charles said there was no use in speculating on the reasons for the lies, and he must bear the consequences.[29]

On December 30 Charles sent copies of Halleck's telegram and Cullum's letter to Francis revealing that he was "almost made a victim" of a "base conspiracy." He said he had known for several weeks about the activities of this cabal to "report me and to put that froc [coarse], weak, vain, good for nothing thing as a soldier, Paine in my place." Fortunately, thanks to the "manliness of Halleck," Smith's "enemies were foiled ... and Paine was hoisted by his own petard." However, Charles was "both angry and dispirited" about the "worst feature in this transaction." He concluded that because of the "underhanded style of people who rule this country, no one, no matter what his conduct may be, is safe from the stab in the back."[30]

General Cullum acknowledged the receipt of Smith's official report rebutting Anderson's charges. Cullum explained that, while Halleck "did not attach any importance to such complaints," he wanted to give Smith "an opportunity of putting any thing you chose on file with charges against you, whether just or unjust, for your protection should a copy of the complaints be asked for by outside politicians with a statement of any action upon them." Cullum concluded by saying, "Your chief tormentor [Paine] having left you, I trust you will have but little more trouble."[31] With the receipt of Cullum's letter, Smith hoped he could put aside the attacks on his reputation and concentrate on the Rebel activities in Kentucky and Tennessee.

After New Year's Day, Charles informed Francis that the "base assertion of my want of loyalty is now making its appearance in Western Journals as coming from Washington." An officer showed Charles a paper containing the accusation and asked Charles for permission to respond to the charges. The officer said, "I am an old politician and understand this sort of thing!" He said that they all knew that this assertion was false but did not like seeing Smith "take it so genially." Charles told him to do as he pleased.[32]

From her home on the Hudson River, Mrs. Smith decided to take action on the assaults on her husband's character. On January 4, 1862, Francis asked Charles' cousin J. B. S. Todd, who represented the Dakota Territory in the House of Representatives, for assistance in rebuking the "cruel & unjust accusations" made against her husband. "I ask in the sight of right that the President of the United States those be made fully acquainted of this base conspiracy against General Smith & at the same time be convinced of the General's unblemished loyalty as a soldier & and unspotted integrity as a man."[33] Representative Todd's response soothed her fears: "the Dept understands the motives that induced the charges ... and now will not permit so great an outrage to be perpetrated against so gallant a soldier as Genl Smith, as was intended by his enemies."[34]

Next Francis appealed to President Lincoln for help in securing approval of Charles' nomination as a brigadier general.

> Your excellency:
> The New York papers of today included C. F. Smith's name amongst those whose confirmation as Brig. General is withheld by the Congress. I appeal at once to your Excellency's sense of justice (feeling assured that appeal will all sufficient) & ask you if you will allow such a slur to be cast

upon the loyalty & honor of one of the best, if not the very best of officers you have in the service. Trusting that I have over stepped no prescribed limits—in thus addressing your Excellency in your official capacity, I have the honor to be Very Respectfully,
Your obt. [obedient] sert. [servant]
Francis Mactier Smith
Jan. 20th 1862.[35]

At Halleck's suggestion, Smith asked Adjutant General Thomas "what allegations have been made against me."[36] General Smith protested: "I have long known that a base conspiracy was on foot in this place." He said the motive for this campaign was to remove him from command and place General Paine in charge. Smith said, "Truth was no obstacle with this party. Anything that would strike me down—that would ruin me was sufficient." Smith said the Reverend Ferrie, who was removed as chaplain of the Ninth Illinois Regiment, wrote derogatory articles in the *Chicago Tribune*. This "underbred, vulgar and impertinent fellow" was the first "dirty instrument." Smith called Lucien Anderson, the "author of certain articles of the worst type in Cincinnati papers," a small-minded man. The cabal sent delegations to St. Louis and Washington to present their allegations and recommend Paine replace Smith at Paducah.

> In all this time I have been quietly pursuing the even tenor of my way—doing my duty to the best of my ability; never noticing the attack upon me in the belief that if my past history, and reputation would [if] not shield me from base aspersions at least they would guarantee to me a fair hearing before I was stricken down. In this it seems I have been mistaken.[37]

Finally, the pent up rage burst forth, and Charles demanded "to be furnished with the allegations against me with copies of all correspondence." He declared that he deserved this information out of respect to his "age, past service and reputation—to justice—to charity."

> I request to be informed what allegations have been made against me for I am, entirely ignorant. The miscreants who have originated the cry against me continue to have insinuations inserted in the papers about my loyalty. Presuming this to be one of the allegations against me, I take this occasion to meet that issue at once; and to brand any one, be he who he may, who dares to say that I am not as loyal to my country as the most loyal, to be an unmitigated liar and scoundrel.
>
> I am not conscious of having done aught here or elsewhere at anytime—on any occasion, that could by the remotest chance induce any fair-minded person to suspect my loyalty. The charge [that] is made to the Gov't against me is an infamous falsehood and calumny.[38]

The next day Charles sent a copy of the letter to Francis. He expressed his determination to have the charges against him fully investigated. "If I am civilly refused satisfaction I shall pass them all by and lay my complaint before the throne of Abraham the 1st."[39]

By the end of January, Charles was able to write to his brother-in-law, William, that the efforts to destroy him had been defeated.[40] Cullum sent Smith a copy of Halleck's letter to Thomas which Cullum hoped would "prove satisfactory" to Smith.[41] Long after the war, General McClellan said, "he had the highest respect for Smith as a soldier and gentleman and had no recollection of his confidence in Smith being shaken."[42]

Smith had been deeply injured by the accusations and the army's response to them. While he had defeated his political enemies and was ready to move forward, the wounds were deep and the scars enduring.

> Until this Civil War is over I shall, to my best ability, serve in any capacity, under any commander, where chance may place me, but on its conclusion I shall certainly from a sense of self respect, retire from the service of a government where to be suspected merely is to be damned. I write under a strong sense of injury recd. both in Washington in April last and here. It is useless to dwell longer upon this.[43]

"For the benefit of loyal inhabitants"

In the midst of the attacks on his loyalty, Smith tried to focus his energies on military operations. At the end of December, Smith sent General Wallace on a reconnaissance mission towards Camp Beauregard and Viola, Kentucky. Wallace left on December 28 with 130 men from the Second Illinois Cavalry, Companies I and C, Regular Cavalry, and seventy men from Captain Christian Thielemann's dragoons. His orders were to proceed toward Camp Beauregard to gather intelligence on enemy strength and positions and to learn whether re-enforcements had left Camp Beauregard for Bowling Green. Wallace had permission "to attack and cut up" a corps of marauders led by a man named King.

Wallace's cavalry traveled to Mayfield and advanced to within six miles of Camp Beauregard. The Union troops encountered an enemy outpost guarded by about seventy-five men who "fled helter-skelter" on Wallace's approach. The general learned from a local farmer that all the troops at Camp Beauregard, except for a battery of artillery and King's marauders, had gone to Bowling Green. They were replaced by three or four regiments of "sixty-days' men" that were mostly unarmed, green troops. After determining the strength of the Rebel force, Wallace returned to Viola and bivouacked for the night.

About daybreak the next morning, one of Wallace's pickets reported "a heavy force of infantry and cavalry upon us and about to attack." The general ordered his men across Mayfield Creek and prepared for the assault. However, the enemy refused to engage the Union forces, and Wallace "drew off about a mile and a half on the Paducah road and fed the men and horses." Wallace sent an officer to report to General Smith and to request him to send five companies of infantry. Wallace planned to hold the Confederates in place until he heard from headquarters. He decided to return to Viola to skirmish with the Rebels, but they had retreated. Wallace remained across the creek and waited until 3 a.m. for orders. The general thought the enemy might return that night so he recrossed the creek and prepared to receive them. Early the next morning a group of Rebel cavalry appeared, but they left as soon as they saw the Union troops.

The report, while appearing straightforward, contains a number of noticeable sarcastic remarks directed at Smith.

> Knowing the general's disinclination to hazard any of his command I was exceedingly cautious, and would not have engaged the enemy in a serious fight until I was certain of their numbers. I also took every possible care to have my way of retreat open, for which purpose I kept parties in continual motion to and from Plumley's Station, at which point I ordered all re-enforcements dispatched to me to remain for orders. In obedience to his orders, I returned without loss of time to Paducah on Tuesday.

Wallace concluded by noting that it gave him "pleasure to say that my command behaved excellently. Excepting one piece of bacon, not an article of property belonging to a citizen was touched."[44]

On January 7 Smith issued General Orders No. 2 to accompany General Halleck's General Orders No. 24 to the citizens of Paducah, Cave-in-Rock, and Smithland. Under General Orders No. 2, Smith required every person of legal age who owned property "within a circuit of twenty-five miles from this place" to take a loyalty oath to the United States." Those who refused to take the oath would be assessed a tax "for the benefit of loyal inhabitants of Kentucky and Tennessee, who have been driven from their homes by those in rebellion."[45]

Smith attached a copy of Halleck's General Order No. 24 to these instructions. Halleck said that the suffering families that were driven by Rebels from southwestern Missouri to

St. Louis have been helped by voluntary contributions made by Union men. He said that the others who were on the way "must be supplied by the charity of men known to be hostile to the Union." The general authorized a ten thousand dollar contribution to be levied on them in the form of clothing, provisions, quarters, or money.[46]

At the end of December, the Woolfolks were in trouble again with the federal authorities. Mr. Woolfolk had been detained by Major Rziha in connection with General Polk's arrest of a citizen accused of killing a Rebel officer. Woolfolk was suspected of being involved in the man's apprehension, but statements made by John Calloway indicated that Woolfolk was not present. Mrs. Woolfolk and Mr. Calloway were allowed to go to Columbus to obtain information that would help release her husband. Smith instructed Rziha to release Woolfolk under the condition that he gave "his parole of honor to consider himself in arrest in his own house until further notice from me."[47]

Part Five

Fort Henry and Fort Donelson: February 1862

"Smith was the ideal soldier, whose shape was that of Apollo and whose disposition in peace was that of a lamb, while in battle was as fierce as a lion of the Jordan."—Henry W. Halleck[1]

The Attack on Fort Donelson by John S. Davis (Wikipedia Commons).

20. "Take and hold Fort Henry"

"He will attack one or both"

Confederate leaders recognized that control of the inland river systems was a key strategic goal. As a result, General Albert S. Johnston, commander of the Western Department, was committed to protecting the three major rivers in his district—the Mississippi, Tennessee, and Cumberland.[1] Loss of the Mississippi would cut the Confederacy in half, loss of the Tennessee would provide Union forces access to northern Alabama, and loss of the Cumberland would allow Union gunships and troop transports to attack Nashville. Johnston was especially concerned about Fort Henry and Fort Donelson that were protecting the Tennessee and Cumberland.[2] In spite of the importance of the inland river system, the construction of defenses of the rivers was not proceeding as well as required.

Fort Henry was a five-sided, open-bastioned[3] earthen structure covering ten acres on the eastern bank of the Tennessee River. In May 1861, the governor of Tennessee recognized the strategic importance of the Tennessee and Cumberland Rivers and appointed the state's attorney, Daniel S. Donelson, as a brigadier general.[4] The governor ordered Donelson to build fortifications on the rivers in the middle of the state. Unfortunately, the best sites for forts were in neutral Kentucky, and Donelson was forced to find locations in Tennessee. He found a site upriver just inside the Tennessee border on the Cumberland River. Colonel Bushrod Johnson of the Tennessee Corps of Engineers approved the site of the future Fort Donelson.[5]

After construction began on the fort to guard the Cumberland, Donelson traveled twelve miles west to the Tennessee River to select a location for a fort to protect that river. Since Fort Donelson was on the west bank of the Cumberland, he selected the east bank of the Tennessee for the second fort so that troops could be shifted between them. He named the post Fort Henry after Tennessee senator Gustavus Adolphus Henry, Sr.[6]

The location had both advantages and disadvantages. Donelson thought it was unlikely that both forts would be attacked simultaneously. Henry was only twelve miles away from Donelson, which allowed troops to be moved between them. Fort Henry had an unobstructed field of fire two miles downriver. The major disadvantage was that the location was on low, swampy ground that was subject to flooding if the Tennessee River rose too much in the spring. The other problem was the higher bank on the Kentucky side of the river from which enemy artillery could fire on Fort Henry. Despite these problems and objections from Donelson's engineers, Colonel Johnson approved the selection.[7]

Fort Henry was designed to restrict military and commercial traffic on the river and not to withstand land-based infantry assaults. Construction began in mid–June but work on the fort slowed down during the fall because defenses on the Mississippi River were given a higher priority. After Kentucky allied with the Union, the Confederates built a small fortification on the opposite side of the river and named it Fort Heiman. About the same time, General Tilghman assumed command of both forts. The garrison at Fort Henry was composed of 2,800–3,400 men organized in two brigades commanded by Colonels Adolphus Heiman and Joseph Drake.[8]

Sixteen guns were mounted in Fort Henry by the time of the Union attack. Eleven pieces were placed to cover the river and six pieces were positioned to defend against a land attack. When the river was at normal levels, the walls of the fort rose twenty feet above it. The walls were twenty feet thick at the base and sloped upward to about ten feet thick at the parapet.[9] However in early February, heavy rains had caused the river to rise, and most of the fort including the powder magazine was underwater. The Confederates had also constructed a minefield across the river. Several torpedoes, rigged to explode on contact with a ship's hull, were anchored below the surface in the main shipping channel. Unfortunately for the Rebels, the mines turned out to be useless because of high water levels and defective metal containers on the torpedoes.[10]

Fort Henry was the biggest problem because it was located on the wrong side of the Tennessee River. The site was originally selected to help maintain Kentucky's fragile neutrality.[11] By mid-October 1861, the walls at Fort Henry were in place, and nine artillery pieces were at the works. Unfortunately, only four of the guns were positioned to fire down the river. The ground on the bank opposite the fort was 170 feet above the river and only 1,500 yards away from Henry. However, the situation twelve miles away near the town of Dover was worse. On October 18, 1861, Colonel Adolph Heiman warned General Johnston: "The defenses on the Cumberland have so far been almost entirely overlooked." Additionally, the Tennessee and Cumberland Rivers were rising and there was "nothing to prevent the enemy from harassing us on this [the Cumberland] and the Tennessee Rivers, both of which are in fine boating order."[12]

The value of the inland river system was also apparent to the Union commanders. In May 1861 the Navy Department was ordered to examine establishing "a naval armament on the Mississippi Rivers [Tennessee and Cumberland Rivers], or either of them, with a view of blockading or interdicting communication and exchanges with the States that are in insurrection." By the middle of August three commercial steamboats, the *Lexington, Conestoga,* and *Tyler,* had been converted to gunboats and were on their way to Cairo for final outfitting.[13] The "timberclad" fleet was soon supplemented by a new design authorized by the War Department. A St. Louis shipbuilder was awarded the contract to construct seven shallow-draft "ironclad" gunboats. The "city class" gunboats were named for towns along the river—*Cairo, Carondelet, Cincinnati, Louisville, Mound City, St. Louis,* and *Pittsburgh.*[14] Captain Andrew Foote was placed in charge of "naval operations upon the Western waters" by Secretary of the Navy, Gideon Wells. Foote was a thirty-nine-year veteran, a staunch supporter of the abolitionist and temperance movements, and was "equally adept at preaching, fighting, or praying."[15]

The Union naval forces had begun reconnaissance on both rivers by mid–October. The USS *Conestoga* steamed up the Tennessee River to within sight of Fort Henry. Several days later, she traveled up the Cumberland to Eddyville about forty-five miles below Fort Donelson. These expeditions established that both forts were within the range of Union gunboats and infantry steamship transports. Regrettably, these river investigations provided inaccurate intelligence. Captain Phelps described Fort Henry "as respectable earthwork, mounting heavy guns, with outworks, and a garrison of probably 1,700 to 1,800 men." Based on information from three different sources, General Smith revised Phelps' estimate and reported "that the number of guns is 20 and the garrison 2,000; that they are constructing three gunboats, iron plated, to mount heavy ordnance, and expect to attack this place [Paducah], aided by a land force from different directions."[16] Confederate Colonel Heiman, commanding at Fort Henry, reported his actual strength as 330 men and nine guns. The Union command had no reliable information on Fort Donelson and was unaware of its "essentially defenseless condition."[17]

On November 17 General Lloyd Tilghman, who was in charge of Confederate troops around Hopkinsville, Kentucky, was ordered to "assume command of Forts Donelson and Henry and their defenses and the defenses of the intermediate country." Tilghman was directed to "push forward the completion of the works and their armament with the utmost activity" and "apply to the citizens of the surrounding country for assistance in labor."[18]

Fort Henry's vulnerability from the heights on the opposite shore of the Tennessee was finally addressed in early December. The Twenty-Seventh Alabama Regiment and 500 slave laborers began work on defenses on the high ground in Kentucky opposite Fort Henry. The works were named Fort Heiman in honor of Colonel Heiman.[19]

In early January, Halleck directed General Grant to make a demonstration towards Camp Beauregard and Murray to convince Rebel forces that an attack was planned on Nashville. Halleck cautioned Grant not to "advance far enough to expose your flank and rear to an attack from Columbus, and by all means avoid a serious engagement." He provided additional details on how to implement the ruse. "Make a great fuss about moving all your forces toward Nashville, and let it be so reported by the newspapers." The commander told Grant to represent his force as "merely the advanced guards" for the main column, which will have 20,000 to 30,000 men. Halleck warned his eager general to be very careful to avoid a battle because the army was not ready, but permitted Grant to "cut off detached parties and give your men a little experience in skirmishing." The major general suggested that if Foote could make a simultaneous gunboat demonstration it would assist with the deception.[20]

Grant prepared to implement Halleck's orders. The expedition and feint would be a joint operation with Commodore Foote's fleet. The navy would provide three gunboats at Cairo and two other gunboats to escort a transport carrying a battalion of infantry and one section of artillery up the Tennessee. General Smith's part of the plan was to move to Mayfield where his force would be supplemented by cavalry and two regiments of infantry from Cairo. From Mayfield the combined force would threaten Camp Beauregard and Murray to make it appear that Murray, Fort Donaldson, and Dover were in the greatest danger. Grant would move his current force, increased by re-enforcements from St. Louis, to occupy the area from Fort Jefferson to Blandville and to protect Smith's flank and rear. Grant cautioned Halleck that the continuous rains during the previous weeks had made the roads extremely bad and would slow their movement.[21]

The weather continued to hinder the operation, and Smith informed Grant on January 9 that the dense fog was prohibiting his movement. The delay would force Grant to postpone his movements so that the two forces could link at Mayfield. "As the matter now stands," Smith wrote, "the column leaving Paducah need not start until Saturday." He said he would telegraph Grant if there were further holdups.[22] Problems occurred with Grant's part of the operation. Reinforcements from St. Louis were delayed and a grounded steamer was blocking ships on the Tennessee River.[23] Smith was anxious to get back into action and wrote Grant, "The force at Camp Beauregard is represented by my latest advices so weak that I think I will run over them before morning in the direction of Murry. I want these men to say they have done something."[24] After these setbacks, the reconnaissance expedition finally got underway on January 14.

In spite of the bad press Smith was receiving, he did little to accommodate reporters. He told Francis that she would probably "see an account of my recent march around the country in *The New York Herald*" because one of their reporters was allowed to go with the command to Murray.

> With the impudence characteristic of his class this person, an entire stranger to me came to me on the evening before we started and proposed to accompany my H.Q., to which I gave a very prompt negative! Adding something to the effect of my deeming reporters little more than a nuisance. You may judge that I will not receive many puffs from Mr. C.
>
> General Grant [crossed out] had a whole corps of reporters about him and General McClernand made one of his A.D.C. for the occasion.[25]

A week later Charles wrote Francis from his "Camp on the Tennessee, 20 miles below Ft. Henry (or Calloway a town with one house)." He had been delayed by horrible roads the past two days and the provisions were nearly exhausted by the holdup. He concluded, "That during the season of rain which is expected to commence in a fortnight or so, the country south of Paducah is impassable for large trains." He thought that the newspapers would criticize the movement as "silly" and a "failure," and "abuse the different commanders for not doing something." He reminded Francis that the purpose of the mission was "to induce the supposition that Nashville was the point of attack." Charles said his "orders have been executed both on letter and in spirit," and he supposed "the other commanders did the same."[26]

By January 21, Smith's Second Division had reached Calloway, Kentucky. Captain Rziha described the town as a small place of three or four houses, one non-operating mill, and a poor landing place on the Tennessee River. The steamer *Wilson*, escorted by the gunboat *Lexington*, supplied the division with needed with forage and provisions.

The following day, while waiting for the stores to be distributed, General Smith, Brigade Surgeon Dr. Hewitt, and Captain Rziha went up the river on the *Lexington* "to have a look at Fort Henry." The recent rains had increased the water level of the river to fourteen feet above its very low stage the week before. Smith discounted rumors that the fort was abandoned. The *Lexington* got about 2½ miles below the fort and fired several shots. The two Rebel stern-wheel steamers that were at the fort moved away rapidly after the first shot. The *Lexington* shelled the fort, and the works fired one shot that fell half a mile short. Rziha reported that there was a zigzagged line of entrenchment on the north side of the fort armed with four 32-pounders. The three other sides were rectangular with two 64 and two 24-pounders. A redan was under construction in front of the entrenchments on the north side. There was a large camp south of the fort, and one regiment was encamped east of the works. Rziha said there was a good twelve-mile road that connected Fort Henry with Fort Donelson. There were two hills about ninety feet above Tennessee River on the Kentucky side opposite the fort. Henry was also protected by two and a half miles of abatis.[27]

General Smith judged that there were from 2,000 to 3,000 Confederates defending Fort Henry and estimated that "by the number of roofs seen in the fort it must cover considerable space." The fort appeared to match the rough sketch that Smith had in his quarters. Rziha concluded that Fort Henry was strongly built and well garrisoned. Smith believed that Henry could not be taken by a land assault, but "two iron-clad gunboats would make short work of Fort Henry."[28]

After the gunship returned to Calloway, Smith sent a brief report to Grant and made plans to begin the march to Paducah the following morning.[29] The *Lexington* and transport *Wilson* would depart at the same time with some sick men and the mail. During the division's return, the general learned that a large Confederate force had left Columbus. He thought the Rebel troops might attack his column near the town of Benton, which was only four miles from the line of march. "No enemy was heard of," and Smith's command arrived at their home base on January 25.

When Smith reached his quarters, he sat down without an overcoat and reviewed his mail. The room was damp because there had not been a fire during Smith's absence, and he developed "a chill in half an hour followed by fever at night." The fever broke the next day, but it left him "only good for nothing today with a vast deal to do." He wrote Francis about the attacks on his character, which he labeled "warfare upon one is only black guardism." He said it was "Democracy run riot, against the gentleman like element." He attributed the problems to the undisciplined troops and sometimes wished he "might be defeated in the Senate so as to get away from volunteers." Charles said his chief regret was that he "ever accepted the appointment."[30]

Overall, the mission went well except for "outrages committed by the men in killing hogs and poultry" despite precautions taken by Smith and his commanders. There were even attempts made to steal horses. Smith had the guilty parties arrested and planned to try them before a military tribunal. He believed that the reason for this behavior was that the company officers refused to enforce regulations and, in some cases, encouraged this conduct.[31]

Halleck was delighted with Smith's report to Grant, and he expressed "his great gratification with your complete and satisfactory performance of this duty, executed in your usual soldiery manner, and so fully laid before him by your explicit report & itinerary of march."[32] As desired by Halleck, the Union expedition down the Tennessee River was observed by the Rebels. On January 18 General Tilghman reported that Smith's force had landed at Eggner's Ferry and were camped six miles out on the road to Murray. Tilghman believed that the Union target was the railroad at Paris. He told General Polk that he would try to destroy the Wood's Creek Bridge to slow Smith's advance. The general also planned to move 600 men from Fort Donelson to increase the garrison at Fort Henry. The Confederates added a 10-inch gun at the fort and planned to have a 32-pounder in place by midnight.[33]

The next day, Tilghman warned Polk, "C.F. Smith is at Murray with, I think 7,500 men, including 1,000 cavalry and twelve field pieces." Tilghman said he had occupied the hill on the west bank opposite Fort Henry and was constructing fortifications. The general believed he could make the defenses "strong, if time is allowed."[34] Tilghman continued to watch Smith's movements and reported, "Smith tacked about at dark last night, and is now within 9 miles of Highland with [his] whole force."[35] At 6 p.m. on January 21 Tilghman learned that Smith's movements had only been a feint with just 1,000 men. Tilghman notified Confederate headquarters that the main body of the Union force had returned to their former position near Murray. Prophetically, Tilghman said, "I do not feel satisfied about [the] effect of high water on earthworks at Henry."[36] At 11 p.m., Tilghman informed General Polk, "He [Smith] must cross [the] river at that point [Highland, Kentucky], and has good road to Donelson and Henry. He will attack one or both."[37]

At 10:30 a.m. on the 23rd, General Tilghman said that his scout reported Smith's "movements down river to Eggner's Ferry," but Tilghman remained uncertain about Smith's intentions. He decided to send 950 cavalry and some artillery to harass the Union rear.[38] Tilghman's forces followed Smith's men to within twelve miles of Paducah, where the Confederates determined that the federals posed no immediate threat and returned to Fort Henry.[39]

On January 24 General Halleck asked Smith for "a full description of the road & country from Smithland to Dover & Fort Henry; also the road south of the Tennessee to Fort Henry & the means of crossing the river at different points above Paducah." The major general wanted to know if troops could be "sustained" by the gunboats.[40]

Several days later, Charles casually mentioned to Francis the possibility that, in a few days, "a large force will be moving up the Tennessee to attack Fort Henry." The assault on Henry would be "aided by sundry gunboats." He said the Rebels had increased the size of their forces at the fort to 6,000 "in anticipation of an attack from me." He had also received information that the garrison could be bolstered by an additional 8,000 or 9,000 troops. Charles concluded by writing, "I have no doubt the destination of a large force will in a few days be Fort Henry. I presume to say I shall be one of the party."[41]

"Fort Henry is ours"

Grant sent a telegram to General Halleck asking permission to come to St. Louis to discuss an important issue. Halleck reluctantly allowed him to leave his post, and, on January 23, Grant was waiting in Halleck's office to present his plans for an attack on Fort Henry. Halleck was recovering from a bout of measles and was in no mood to listen to strategic ideas from a junior officer. Grant had barely unfolded his maps when Halleck advised him that military strategy was the responsibility of the major general commanding the department. Halleck said that if he wanted Brigadier General Grant's advice, he would ask for it. The meeting was over.[42] Grant said Halleck acted "as if my plan was preposterous," and he "returned to Cairo very much crestfallen."[43]

The Battle of Fort Henry (Library of Congress, LC-DIG-pga-03975).

Halleck had a low opinion of Grant and was trying to remove him from command. The commander disliked Grant's scruffy appearance and past "intemperate behavior." Many officers and officials considered Grant's attack at Belmont a poor military decision and a costly battle that achieved nothing. These issues prejudiced Halleck's opinion of military advice from Grant.[44] Grant thought that Halleck rejected his proposal to attack Fort Henry because he found the idea preposterous. What Halleck really found preposterous was that an unimpressive subordinate would presume to advise him on anything.[45]

Fortunately for Grant, Smith and Foote supported his proposal to capture Henry, and they tried to convince Halleck on the merits of the operation. Encouraged by their support, Grant telegraphed Halleck for approval: "With permission, I will take Fort Henry, on the Tennessee, and establish and hold a large camp there."[46] The same day, Foote asked for permission to capture Henry. Foote wrote, "Commanding General Grant and myself are of opinion that Fort Henry, on the Tennessee River, can be carried with four ironclad gunboats and troops to permanently occupy. Have we the authority to move for that purpose when ready?"[47] On January 29 Grant sent a more persuasive telegram arguing for the attack.

> In view of the large force now concentrating in this district and the present feasibility of the plan I would respectfully suggest, the propriety of subduing Fort Henry, near the Kentucky and Tennessee line, and holding the position. If this is not done soon there is but little doubt but that

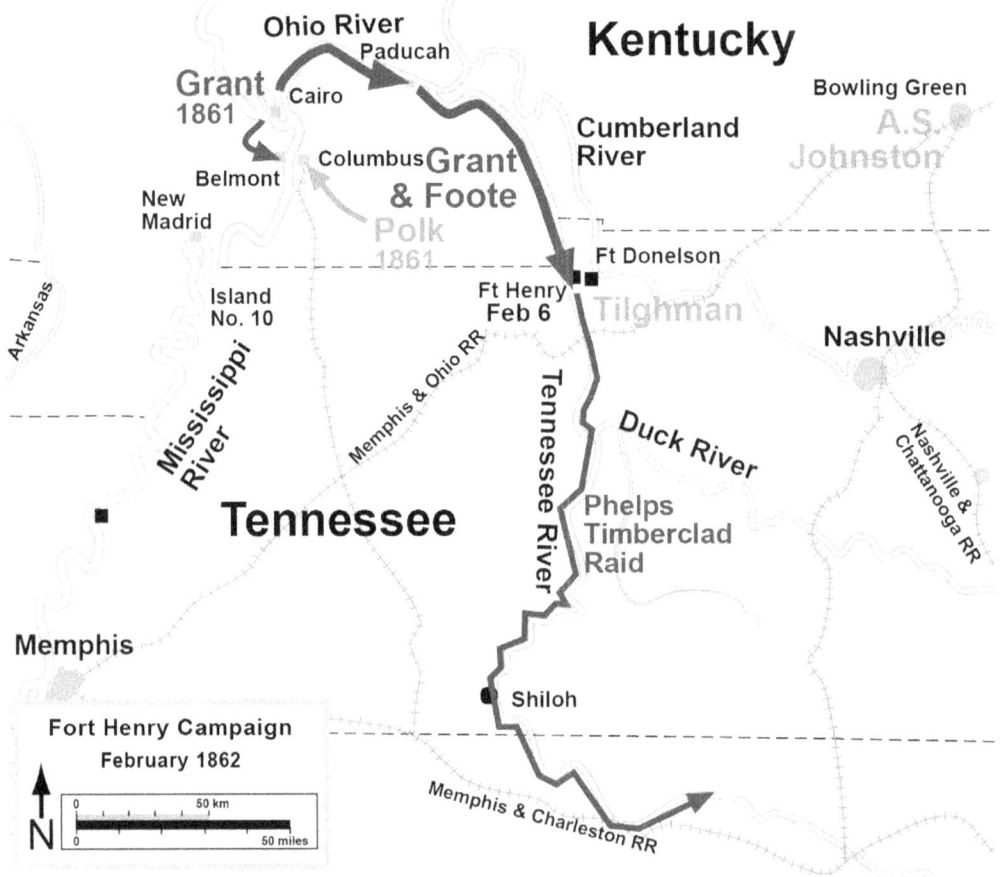

The Fort Henry Campaign (map by Hal Jespersen, www.cwmaps.com).

the defenses on both the Tennessee and Cumberland Rivers will be materially strengthened. From Fort Henry it will be easy to operate either on the Cumberland, only 12 miles distant, Memphis, or Columbus. It will, besides, have a moral effect upon our troops to advance them toward the rebel States. The advantages of this move are as perceptible to the general commanding as to myself, therefore further statements are unnecessary.[48]

Halleck was finally convinced and quickly approved the operation. On January 30 he telegraphed Grant to make "preparations to take and hold Fort Henry." Halleck's decision was aided when he learned that General P. G. T. Beauregard had left Manassas "with fifteen regiments for the line of Columbus and Bowling Green." Halleck wanted to cut that route before Beauregard arrived.[49]

Grant quickly got things moving. His invasion force consisted of 15,000 to 17,000 men in two divisions and the Western Flotilla. Brigadier General John A. McClernand commanded the First Division at Cairo, Brigadier General Charles F. Smith led Second Division at Paducah and Smithland, and U.S. Navy Flag Officer Andrew Hull Foote directed the Western Flotilla. The Western Flotilla had four "ironclad" gunboats (Foote's flagship USS *Cincinnati*, USS *Carondelet*, USS *St. Louis*, and USS *Essex*) commanded by the flag officer, and three "timberclad" gunboats (USS *Conestoga*, USS *Tyler*, and USS *Lexington*) under Lieutenant Seth L. Phelps.

Grant sent the following orders to Smith:

HEADQUARTERS DISTRICT OF CAIRO,
Cairo, January 31, 1862.

General C. F. SMITH,
Commanding U.S. Forces, Paducah. Ky.:

On Monday next I expect to start from Smithland, Paducah, and this place some 15,000 men for Fort Henry, to take and occupy that position. Full instructions will be received from General Halleck in the morning. At the present I am only in possession of telegraphic orders to take and hold it.

If my instructions contain nothing to change the plan I would adopt, I will want a brigade from Paducah, and all the command from Smithland, except the Fifty-second Illinois, and one battalion to be designated by yourself. These troops will take with them all their baggage, but no baggage train; these being left, to be taken up afterwards.

I do not regard over a squadron of cavalry being necessary for the whole command in taking the position. All that might afterwards be required can be sent from here.

The troops going from your command may take with them such rations as they have on hand at the time of starting, not less than two days' supply, however, preparation being made here for issuing at the place of debarkation. A supply of ammunition will also be taken from here, but every regiment should take with them all they have on hand, and not less than 40 rounds.

Should I not be able to write more definitely by tomorrow's boat, I will telegraph during the day if a change from the above is necessary. But very little preparation is necessary for this move; and, if possible, the troops and community should be kept from knowing anything of the design. I am well aware, however, that this caution is entirely unnecessary to you.

It is impossible to spare a boat just now to run exclusively between Paducah and Smithland; but until one can be sent, the steamer from here can continue her trips to the latter place upon your order as often as necessary.

U. S. GRANT,
Brigadier-General, Commanding.[50]

The following day, Grant's Assistant Adjutant General John Rawlins sent instructions to Smith to "take all available forces, including Cavalry, which can be spared from Paducah and Smithland, leaving only such forces as may absolutely be necessary to hold these places against attack." Grant directed Smith to "organize your forces at Paducah & Smithland into brigades." General Grant assigned the Seventh Illinois Regiment under Colonel John Cook to Smith's command and recommended that Cook be given command of a brigade.[51]

On February 4, General McClernand's troops were loaded on steamships and landed eight miles below Fort Henry on the Tennessee side. Grant wanted them as near as possible to the fort so the men would not have to march through the wilderness to attack the Confederate garrison. Their landing position would depend on how close the transports could approach without coming under fire of Fort Henry's cannons. To test the range of these guns, Grant boarded the ironclad *Essex* and asked its commander, William Porter, to draw fire from the Confederate batteries. The *Essex* moved toward the fort and fired a few rounds. Although Fort Henry had eleven guns facing down the river, the *Essex* was out of the range of seven of the guns, and there was no ammunition for two of them. The 10-inch Columbiad and a 24-pound rifled gun were the only guns available, and the fort returned fire with the rifled gun. At two and a half miles, the Rebel gun crew fired its first shot that raked some trees on a riverbank near the gunboat. The second round narrowly missed Grant and Porter on the stern deck, tore through the captain's cabin, and splashed into the water.[52]

When the federal attack began on February 4, Colonel Heiman was in command of the works because General Tilghman was inspecting construction at Fort Donelson. The Confederates fired rockets to alert Tilghman of the Union assault. Fort Henry's garrison of 2,600 troops was scattered with two regiments at Fort Heiman and two up the river at Paris Landing. Colonel Heiman waited for Tilghman's orders to consolidate the dispersed troops. When Tilghman heard the artillery exchange that morning and learned that Union troops had landed below the fort that afternoon, he placed Colonel John W. Heard in command at Donelson and left for Henry. Tilghman ordered Colonel Heard to form a reserve force and station it halfway between the two forts in case it was needed at Fort Henry. Tilghman and his escort reached Fort Henry around 11:30 p.m. on February 4.

The next day, Tilghman ordered the evacuation of Fort Heiman except for two companies of Alabama cavalry and the forty Kentucky men of Padgett's Spy Company. This small force was instructed to harass Union forces on the Kentucky side of the river. The

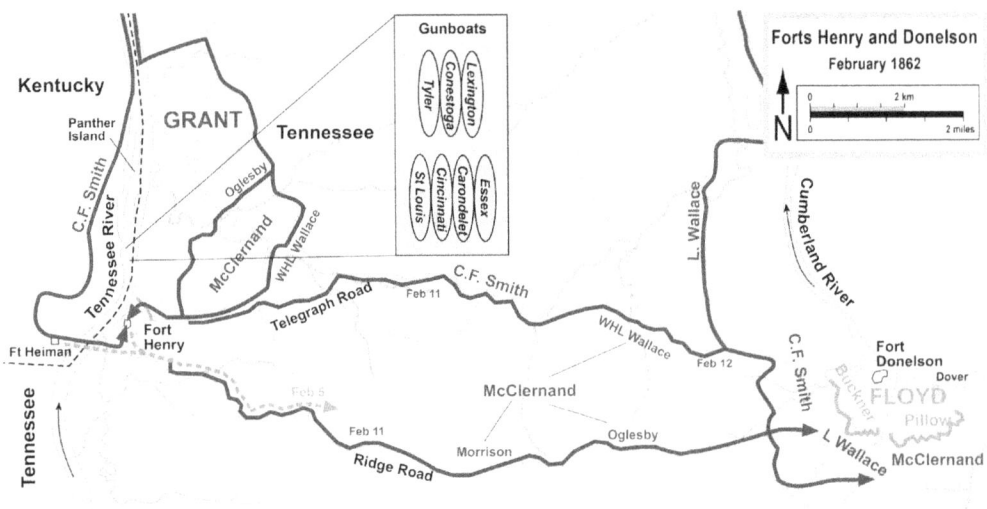

The Attack on Fort Henry and Movement to Fort Donelson (map by Hal Jespersen, www.cwmaps.com).

Fifteenth Arkansas Regiment and Twenty-Seventh Alabama Regiment crossed the river and joined their comrades at Fort Henry.

Smith's Second division arrived on the scene. Two brigades landed on the Kentucky side and one brigade on the Tennessee side. It was after 11:00 p.m. on February 5 before all of Grant's army was in position. Tilghman knew he was outnumbered and regretted "the wretched military position of Fort Henry and the small force" at his disposal.[53]

The attack began at dawn on February 6. While Union gunboats were bombarding Fort Henry, General Smith's troops advanced to Fort Heiman. The remaining Confederates quickly left Heiman when they saw Smith's troops. The Rebels abandoned the fort so fast that they left their recently prepared dinner. Smith and General Wallace enjoyed a meal of a block of pork "done to a turn" and cornbread. Across the river, they saw the United States flag flying over Fort Henry.[54]

In the time it had taken for Smith's forces to reach Fort Heiman, Foote's seven-gunboat flotilla had bombarded Fort Henry into submission. Foote deployed the four ironclads in a line abreast, followed by the three wooden ships. The "timber clad" gunboats were kept away from the fort and fired from long-range on the works. The flagship USS *Essex* opened fire at 1,700 yards, and the artillery battle began. The other gunboats started shelling the fort, and Henry's guns returned fire. The gunships slowly approached the fort until they were within 600 yards of the Rebel batteries when "the fire both from the gunboats and fort increased in rapidity and accuracy of range." About twenty minutes before the fort surrendered, the *Essex* "received a shot in her boilers, which resulted in wounding, by scalding, 29 officers, and men, including commander Porter." The disabled *Essex* was forced out of the line. The firing continued with "unabated rapidity and effect upon the three gunboats" as they "continued to approach the fort with their destructive fire until the rebel flag was hauled down, after a very severe and closely contested action of one hour and fifteen minutes." General Tilghman had no choice except to surrender, and he sent a boat containing his adjutant general and captain of engineers to request a meeting with the flag officer. The fort was so badly flooded that a small boat was able to sail through the sally port[55] to pick up Tilghman for the surrender ceremony on the *Cincinnati*. The evacuating force left all of its artillery and equipment behind. Foote reported taking "the general, his staff and 60 or 70 men as prisoners,[56] and a hospital ship containing 60 invalids, together with the fort and its effects, mounting twenty guns, mostly of heavy caliber, with barracks and tents capable of accommodating 15,000 men, and sundry articles." Flag Officer Foote commented, "The excessively muddy roads and high stage of water" altered the army's role in the attack and "prevented the Army reaching the rear of the fort to make a demonstration simultaneously with the Navy" until after Foote had taken possession of the fort.[57]

The Union victory was mostly due to the flooded condition of the fort. The low elevation of the Rebel guns only allowed their shells to hit the ships where their armor was strongest. As Foote pointed out in his report to General Halleck, except for skirmishes the day before and pursuit of the fleeing Confederates, it was a victory won by the Union navy. While the flag officer and the new city class gunboats claimed the victory, both the army and navy were proud of the successful amphibious operation.

Buoyed by the easy victory, Grant sent a triumphant dispatch to Halleck:

HEADQUARTERS DISTRICT OF CAIRO,
Fort Henry, February 6, 1862.
 Fort Henry is ours. The gunboats silenced the batteries before the investment was completed. I think the garrison must have commenced the retreat last night. Our cavalry followed, finding two guns abandoned in the retreat.

> I shall take and destroy Fort Donelson on the 8th and return to Fort Henry.
> U. S. GRANT,
> Brigadier-General.
> Maj. Gen. H. W. HALLECK, Saint Louis, Mo.[58]

Even though the army had little to do with the victory, Grant quickly added the capture of Fort Henry to his resume. Halleck wired Washington: "Fort Henry is ours. The flag is reestablished on the soil of Tennessee. It will never be removed."[59]

> HEADQUARTERS DEPARTMENT OF THE MISSOURI,
> Saint Louis, February 7, 1862.
>
> Fort Henry was taken yesterday, with seventeen heavy guns, General Lloyd Tilghman and staff, and 60 men, after a bombardment of one hour and a quarter by gunboats. General Grant's cavalry and gunboats in pursuit of the remainder of the garrison, who have abandoned artillery on the road. Our loss, killed, wounded, and scalded by destruction of boiler of the Essex, 44. Captain Porter is badly but not dangerously scalded. General C. F. Smith has possession of the enemy's redan on the western bank of the Tennessee. General Grant's infantry and artillery have gone to attack Fort Donelson at Dover, on the Cumberland. The gunboats not disabled are moving up the Tennessee. Commodore Foote, with disabled gunboats, has returned to Cairo—gunboats for repairs; will soon return to the field. Enemy's loss not known.
> H. W. HALLECK,
> Major-General, Commanding.
> Major-General McClellan.[60]

The New York Times proclaimed the Union triumph as "Another Great Victory" and included comments from Halleck and Foote. Foote summed up the battle by writing: "At precisely forty minutes past one, the enemy struck his colors—and such cheering, such wild excitement, as seized the throats, arms, or caps, of the four or five hundred sailors of the gunboats can be imagined. After the surrender, which was made to Flag Officer Foote by Gen. Lloyd Tilghman, who defended the fort in a most determined, manner, we found that the rebel infantry encamped outside the fort, numbering four or five thousand, had cut and run, leaving the rebel artillery company in command of the fort." The article reported, "General Smith, on the west, and General Grant on the east side of the Tennessee River, are pursuing the retreating rebels." In Washington, "the news from Fort Henry has diffused general joy, and stimulated the openly expressed desire for additional victories."[61] General Tilghman complained bitterly that Fort Henry was in a "wretched military position.... The history of military engineering records no parallel to this case."[62]

The northern population, anxious for a Union battlefield success, celebrated Fort Henry as a glorious victory. On February 7 the gunboats *Cincinnati*, *St. Louis*, and *Essex* returned to Cairo with whistles blowing and Confederate flags flying upside down. The *Chicago Tribune* declared that the battle was "one of the most complete and signal [sic] victories in the annals of the world's warfare."[63]

21. "I shall take and destroy Fort Donelson"

"We should move without the loss of a day"

In St. Louis General Halleck struggled with the Union victory. While happy about the army's success, Halleck maintained a low opinion of and little confidence in Grant and continued to look for someone to replace him. Halleck tried to supervise operations from St. Louis and sent daily orders to Grant, many of which had little or no relation to the actual situation at Fort Henry. Grant's success created a new problem. Halleck became jealous of his subordinate and started to regard him as a potential rival instead of a troublesome officer. However, in spite of his concerns and petty envy, Halleck continued to send Grant all of the available supplies and reinforcements. "Old Brains" was smart enough to realize that Grant's success would reflect favorably on him.[1]

The fall of Fort Henry presented the Confederate command with a more difficult predicament. When the news reached General Johnston, he held a meeting with Generals Beauregard and Hardee in Bowling Green to decide the fate of Fort Donelson. After some discussion, "it was determined that, Fort Henry, on the Tennessee River, having fallen yesterday into the hands of the enemy, and Fort Donelson, on the Cumberland River, not being long tenable, preparation should at once be made for the removal of this army to Nashville."[2] With this decision, the defense of Fort Donelson became a delaying action. Johnston hoped that the garrison could hold out for a few days and then escape to Nashville. Unfortunately, Johnston did not execute his plans effectively. The force at Donelson was too small to effectively defend the fort but too large to easily escape. The command structure that Johnston created led to confusion and resulted in seven changes in leadership over the next eight days.[3]

After General Tilghman was captured at Fort Henry, Colonel Heiman assumed command at Fort Donelson. Major Jeremy Gilmer, Johnston's chief engineer, organized work teams to build an outer line of defenses surrounding the fort. Over the next few days, the teams cut trees and brush for abatis, dug rifle pits, and placed artillery batteries.[4]

While the Confederates were improving the fortifications, Grant was conducting reconnaissance. On February 7 he took his staff and cavalry on a scouting mission to within "about a mile of the outer line of works at Donelson."[5] On February 9 seventy-six men from Company C of the Second Cavalry Regiment and Company I of the Fourth United States Cavalry Regiment skirmished with Confederate cavalry. Grant's troops defeated the Confederates and captured twenty-three men and a number of horses. On February 11 the Second Cavalry rode to Fort Donelson and examined the fort's works. As they returned to Fort Henry, they were surrounded by a large force of Rebel cavalry and infantry, but they cut their way through the enemy and reached the Union lines. Subsequent scouting missions probed Donelson's defenses and selected positions for artillery batteries.[6]

Grant appreciated Smith's contributions and did not want to lose the able commander. On February 10 an obviously frustrated Grant wrote Congressman Washburne, "For God's sake get the Senate to reconsider Gen Smith's Confirmation. There is no doubt of his loyalty & efficiency. We Cant spare him now."[7] Other officers added their endorsements. Colonel Augustus Chetlain wrote Washburne, "Why was not Gen C F Smith not confirmed by the Senate?—He is one of the best officers in the army." Halleck telegraphed Senator Milton S. Latham of California, "Don't permit C. F. Smith's nomination to be rejected. He is the best officer in my command, and there is not the slightest ground for suspecting his loyalty."[8] Grant and the Union needed Smith, and his generalship was finally confirmed four days after Grant's letter.

On the morning of February 11, a staff officer delivered a brief message to each division and brigade commander: "General Grant sends his compliments, and requests to see you this afternoon on his boat." In his stateroom aboard the *New Uncle Sam*, Grant met with Smith, McClernand, and Wallace to discuss capturing Fort Donelson. General Wallace described Grant's demeanor at the meeting.

> From the first his silence was remarkable. He knew how to keep his temper. In battle, as in camp, he went about quietly, speaking in a conversational tone: yet he appeared to see everything that went on, and was always intent on business. He had a faithful assistant adjutant-general, and appreciated him; he preferred, however, his own eyes, word, and hand. His aides were little more than messengers. In dress he was plain, even negligent; in partial amendment of that his horse was always a good one and well kept. At the council—calling it such by grace—he smoked, but never said a word. In all probability he was framing the orders of march which were issued that night.[9]

All of his officers urged Grant to attack. Smith said, "There is every reason why we should move without the loss of a day." McClernand proposed a plan with his First Division taking the lead. Wallace added that the Union forces should invest Fort Donelson as soon as possible.[10]

Wallace described Smith as "a person of superb physique, very tall, perfectly proportioned, straight, square-shouldered, ruddy-faced, with eyes of genuine blue and long snow-white mustaches."

> He seemed to know the army regulations by heart, and caught a tactical mistake, whether of command or execution, by a kind of mental coup doily [stroke of the eye]. He was naturally kind, genial, communicative, and never failed to answer when information was sought of him; at the same time he believed in "hours of service" regularly published by the adjutants as a rabbi believes in the ten tables, and to call a court-martial on a "bummer" was in his eyes a sinful waste of stationery. On the review he had the look of a marshal of France. He could ride along a line of volunteers in the regulation uniform of a brigadier-general, plume, chapeau, epaulets and all, without exciting laughter—something nobody else could do in the beginning of the war.[11]

While Wallace praised Smith long after the war, he did not have any good words for Smith after Fort Henry. In accordance with Grant's instructions, Smith ordered Wallace to remain at Fort Heiman with 2,500 men to hold that area. Wallace's admiration for his commander had already been dwindling because of his association with the problems in Paducah. In a letter to his wife, Wallace blamed Smith for leaving him behind.

> The whole force, except my brigade, marched this morning to attack Fort Donelson. Through old Smith, I am left command of this Fort and Fort Henry. Nice arrangement! My patience with old Smith is now played out! I have been too modest and patient. I will change policy—in fact, have done so.[12]

The morning of February 12 was sunny and unseasonably warm as Grant's forces approached the fort via the Cumberland River, Telegraph Road, and Ridge Road. He had "15,000 men including eight batteries and part of a regiment of cavalry."[13] General McClernand's First Division started at 8:00 a.m. with one brigade advancing on the Telegraph Road to the north and the other two marching on Ridge Road to the south. Smith's Second Division followed on Telegraph Road. The USS *Carondelet*, commanded by Captain Henry Walke, proceeded from Fort Henry on the Cumberland River ahead of Foote's flotilla of gunboats and transports.[14]

"We took nothing with us"

On the day of their departure, General Smith's Second Division consisted of five brigades: First Brigade under Colonel John McArthur, Third Brigade commanded by Colonel John Cook, Fourth Brigade directed by Colonel Jacob G. Lauman, and the Fifth Brigade under Colonel Morgan L. Smith. Wallace's Second Brigade remained at Fort Henry to hold the submerged works. The First Brigade was composed of the Ninth, Twelfth, and Forty-First Illinois Regiments. Cook's Third Brigade was made up of the Seventh and Fiftieth Illinois Regiments, Fifty-Second Indiana Regiment, Fourteenth Iowa Regiment, Thirteenth Missouri Regiment, and Batteries D, H, and K of the First Missouri Light Artillery Battery. The Twenty-Fifth Indiana Regiment, the Seventh and Fourteenth Iowa Regiments, and Birge's Sharpshooters were in Colonel Lauman's Fourth Brigade. Colonel Morgan Smith's Fifth Brigade consisted of the Eighth Missouri and Eleventh Indiana Regiments.

First Sergeant F. F. Kiner of the Fourteenth Iowa Regiment in the Third Brigade remembered the march.

> About ten o'clock on the 12th, we took up our line of march for this fort. The day was beautiful and warm and the distance about fifteen miles. We took nothing with us but our blankets and haversacks, three days of rations of crackers and boiled pork; our muskets and cartridges completed our load. On our journey we rested several times as we had not been used to marching we tired very easily.[15]

Some of the men abandoned their blankets and overcoats along the road to Donelson.

Just before noon, the troops approaching Donelson heard firing from the USS *Carondelet*. The ironclad was shelling the fort from long-range to locate enemy batteries and announce the flotilla's arrival to Grant. In the early afternoon, McCler-

Col. Jacob G. Lauman, Fourth Brigade (Library of Congress).

nand's First Division units began moving into position on the left sector of the Confederate defenses. Smith's Second Division arrived near the outer works later that afternoon and started to invest the right sector of the Confederate fortifications. Later that day they extended their positions to their south.[16]

Colonel John Cook's Third Brigade left Fort Henry at 8 a.m. on the 12th and arrived within a mile and a half of Fort Donelson at 3 p.m. Cook said that the twelve-mile road was in excellent condition. He thought that the position assigned to the brigade was "well chosen, being a high ridge of nearly 1 mile in length, and almost overlooking the enemy's works on his right." His troops spent the night in "fine spirits, with full assurance of success" and "prepared for an attack should a sally be made from the fort."[17]

Lauman's Fourth Brigade reached Fort Donelson that evening. After arriving, Smith ordered Colonel Lauman to move the Seventh Iowa Infantry to the front to support a battery of Major Cavender's rifled 20-powder Parrott guns, which were located "to command a portion of the rebel works." Lauman received Smith's permission "to associate the regiment of Birge's sharpshooters in the movement" and he positioned the two regiments for the night.[18]

The same morning Colonel McArthur's First Brigade left Fort Heiman, arrived about three miles from their line of operations at 6 p.m., and encamped. Around 10:30 p.m., McArthur moved the brigade a mile and a half nearer the enemy and made camp for the rest of the night.[19] Because it was the last to arrive, the brigade was held in reserve.

Smith placed Lauman's Fourth Brigade on the left and Cook's Third Brigade on the right to close the line with McClernand's First Division. An artillery battery was placed on the road leading to Dover and Fort Donelson.[20] Colonel M. L. Smith's brigade was later placed next to the Third Brigade. When General Wallace was summoned on February 14 to Fort Donelson to command the newly formed Third Division, the First and Fifth Brigades were detached from Smith's division and assigned to Wallace's command.[21]

That evening General Grant established his headquarters and lodgings in a small house owned by a widow named Crisp. Grant took the feather bed near the fireplace, and his staff slept in makeshift beds.[22]

The weather changed dramatically that night. The warm, pleasant day turned into a cold, miserable night. The rain changed into sleet, and the soldiers bivouacking in the lines suffered without the protection of the blankets and overcoats they had discarded on the march from Fort Henry. Wilbur F. Crummer of the Forty-Fifth Illinois described the conditions.

> The night was very chilly and cold. Our boys had left their knapsacks two miles to the rear and were without blankets. Cold, hungry and disappointed, we shivered during that long dreary night.... It was our first experience, and we knew nothing about making ourselves comfortable. We learned better after a while and always carried our blankets with us ... during the night it rained and turned very cold. We were forbidden to leave the lines, hence we could not go back for our blankets.[23]

"The investment was extended"

In his official report to General Halleck, Grant wrote, "The following day, owing to the non-arrival of the gunboats and re-enforcements sent by water, no attack was made but the investment was extended on the flanks of the enemy and drawn closer to his works, with skirmishing all day."[24] His memoirs sum up the day with a single sentence. "The investment on the land side was made as complete as the number of troops engaged would admit of."[25] The men of Grant's First and Second Divisions remembered February 13 differently.

The actions that cold February day were much more than occasional exchanges of cannon and musket fire by a few batteries and skirmishers. Grant organized reconnaissance operations to probe for weaknesses in the Confederate defenses. He ordered the USS *Carondelet* to move up the river and shell the fort. The gunboat attack was designed to learn more about the enemy's positions and strengths on the Cumberland River. In conjunction with the naval demonstration, Grant asked his commanders to conduct a reconnaissance in force to probe for weaknesses in the enemy's land defenses using "as many skirmishers as possible, well supported by their regiments."[26]

Sometime after 9:00 a.m., the *Carondelet* began to fire on the fort in hopes of creating a diversion for Smith's and McClernand's troops.[27] General Smith described the actions in the rough draft of his report.

> Early on the following morning (13th) the regiments were posted in order of investment in easy cannon-range of the enemy's line of defence from the west—his extreme right—to the south, a somewhat central position with reference to that line, going as far as possible to the left of the First Division. The ground covered by the division was thickly wooded and exceedingly hilly and broken. The enemy's works were on the highest ground in the vicinity. He had an infantry breast-work in front of his main line (vaguely called rifle pits), crested with logs, from under which they fired, the whole strengthened by a wide abatis from felled timber of large size. Ignorant of the ground, we had to feel our way cautiously. As soon as the regiments were measurably in position, orders were given to brigade commanders to cover our front of attack with as many skirmishers as possible, well supported by their regiments, keeping a strong reserve; to press forward as steadily and rapidly as the ground would admit, and, if the opportunity offered, to assault with the bayonet.[28]

Around 10:00 a.m., Colonel Lauman moved the left wing of his brigade, consisting of Colonel William T. Shaw's Fourteenth Iowa and Colonel James C. Veatch's Twenty-Fifth Indiana, from their camp towards the enemy entrenchments about a mile away. The regiments advanced steadily and "in as good an order as the ground permitted" until they reached the ravine at the base of the hill below the Rebel fortifications. The units paused in the gully to reform their ranks before they continued to advance.[29]

The Second Kentucky was waiting for them on the crest of the hill. The 600-man Confederate regiment, led by Colonel Roger Hanson, was "well-entrenched in rifle pits with logs along the top." The Twenty-Fifth Indiana moved steadily up the hill towards the works "under a most galling fire of musketry and grape, until their onward progress was obstructed by the fallen timber and brush-wood." Hanson's men anxiously waited for the order to fire. When the Union forces were almost upon them, the Kentuckians let loose a barrage of musket fire. On the Union right, Captain Tom Potter's Rebel battery swept the valley and hillside with shell and canister.[30]

A soldier in the Fourteenth Iowa described the scene:

> The air seemed literally full of flying bullets … they screamed through the air above our heads and ploughed through our ranks…. We returned fire as best we could but all the advantage was with the Rebels. They were behind breastworks and were little exposed while we were in plain view.[31]

The Twenty-Fifth Indiana stopped after "gaining an advantageous position," which they held "unflinchingly for more than two hours" until ordered to fall back out of range of the enemy's fire.[32] The regiment lost fourteen killed and sixty-one wounded.[33]

The Fourteenth Iowa advanced at the same time and reached a spot across a ravine on the right where they "did good execution." While these two regiments were taking these places, the Seventh Iowa Infantry under Lieutenant Colonel James C. Parrott "came up in fine style and took a position in the center between the Twenty-Fifth Indiana and the Fourteenth Iowa." Lieutenant Colonel H. S. Compton's First Regiment Sharpshooters Western Division, the Western Sharpshooters-Fourteenth Missouri Volunteers,[34] were posted on the hill to the extreme right except for a detachment of about sixty who were deployed as skirmishers. The sharpshooters on the hill "rendered most effective service in that capacity and proving by their deadly aim that they are a most valuable arm of the service." The Fourteenth Iowa suffered two killed and fourteen wounded in the action. Lauman's men held their position until night, when they returned to the ridgeline they occupied in the morning.[35]

After his men had enjoyed a hearty breakfast, Colonel Cook moved his Third Brigade up the Dover Road to a point about one-half mile from the enemy's outer works. Cook sent out a line of skirmishers from the Seventh Illinois on the right and Fifty-Second Indiana on the left. The brigade "moved steadily forward through the dense timber, crossing the deep ravine without resistance" until Lieutenant Colonel Andrew J. Babcock's Seventh Illinois advanced inside the range of a hidden Confederate battery. The enemy artillery opened a destructive fire that killed Captain Mendel of Company I and wounded several others. The dense timber prevented the troops from moving into position. The regiment retreated beyond the range of the Rebel guns and went to support Captain Henry Richardson's battery from the First Missouri Light Artillery that was getting into place. Cook led his other four regiments to the summit of a ridge overlooking the fort and about 600 yards away. He stopped there because "the immensity of the abatis covering the whole precluding [precluded] the possibility of proceeding farther but by an unwarranted destruction of life" by enemy fire from the earthworks on the opposing ridge. The Confederates, "concealed in his rifle pits and behind his palisades," continued their fire which was "answered by sharpshooters and skirmishers from our side." The Third Brigade held their new position during the night with "the men resting on their arms without fires and without blankets, everything but arms and ammunition having been cast aside on approaching the fort."[36]

Colonel McArthur's First Brigade was held in reserve and used to support Major Cavender's artillery batteries that were located opposite the center of the enemy's works. At 4 p.m., the brigade moved around to the left of General McClernand's division. That night a part of the command constructed two small earthworks with two 20-pounder and two 10-pounder guns "to operate against the left of the enemy's center." At 11.30 p.m., McClernand ordered the Ninth and Forty-First from McArthur's First Brigade to move about a quarter of a mile nearer to his left where they remained "under arms all night without fires in the midst of a heavy snow-storm."[37]

Smith concluded his report of the day's events by praising the actions of Cavender's batteries.

> During this time Major Cavender's batteries [Batteries D, H, and K of 1st Missouri Artillery Regiment], by sections or pieces, were posted to the best apparent advantage, well supported, with orders to open on the enemy. This was handsomely done and quick response made. Our pieces were shifted from time to time, and served with good effect, better, as we afterward knew from the enemy, than was suspected; their long ranges sending shells into the fort and causing sharp loss and great moral effect. Our casualties were numerous on this day. The reports of the different commanders, partially confirmed by my personal observations, satisfied me that an assault on almost any part of the entire front covered by us was not practicable without continuous sacrifice of life. At nightfall the skirmishers were recalled and the troops ordered to remain in position, but from necessity without fires, as the night was very inclement—rainy, snow, sleet, and cold—and the discomfort of the men was very great.[38]

The havoc wreaked on the Union troops terminated General Smith's "reconnaissance." It took some of his men the rest of the day to return behind the ridgeline. The division lost about seventeen killed and 142 wounded in their investigation of the Rebel defenses. The cost was high, but Smith found out that the Confederates in his front were there in force and held an excellent position.[39]

The second night at Fort Donelson was brutal. The temperature dropped, and the rain turned into sleet. In most places along the line, the opposing forces were so close that fires were not allowed. The Union troops were still without blankets and overcoats. Without fires, blankets, and overcoats, the troops on the exposed ridgelines suffered from the elements. Their clothes were soaked from the rain, and the plunging temperatures soon froze the uniforms to their bodies.[40]

Grant did not achieve the hoped for results. In addition to Smith's problems, General McClernand's division also ran into difficulty as he extended his lines to the east to invest the fort and town of Dover.[41] Grant now realized that capturing Donelson would be much tougher than Henry. While his troops suffered in freezing weather, Grant fell asleep to the sounds of rain and sleet in his feather bed in the warm farmhouse kitchen.[42]

"A gallant attack was made"

Weather conditions at Fort Donelson continued to degrade during the night, and on February 14 the men awoke to a below freezing temperature of 12 °F. and three inches of snow on the ground.[43] Neither side was thinking about love or romance that frigid Valentine's Day morning.

As Colonel Cook reported: "On the Fourteenth, after a long and weary night of watching, the men being unprovoked [not provided] with tents or blankets and our immediate proximity to the enemy's works and batteries precluding the possibility of building fires, knowing that the light would draw his fire from his two strong redoubts, under which we lay, the troops under my command arose at an early hour, shook the thick covering of snow from their overcoats, partook of a meager breakfast, and cheerfully resumed their old position under the entrenchments."[44]

While the men on the line struggled to keep warm, Grant rose from the comfort of his bed near the fireplace in the Crisp House. With yesterday's disappointments, Grant hoped that the Navy might produce a victory as they did at Fort Henry. Grant planned a two-phase attack with Foote's gunboats destroying Donelson's water batteries and McClernand's division sweeping in from the Union right and capturing the fortifications and possibly the town of Dover.[45] Smith's division was assigned to prevent the Confederate garrison from escaping.[46]

As Grant's forces were investing Donelson, General Halleck was sending additional troops to his support. During the night, Flag Officer Foote arrived with the ironclads *St. Louis*, *Louisville* and *Pittsburg* and the wooden gunboats *Tyler* and *Conestoga*.[47] Troopships delivered Colonel John M. Thayer's Third Brigade and Colonel Charles Cruft's First Brigade to near the Hickman Creek staging area. General Wallace, whom Grant had ordered over from Fort Henry, arrived about the same time with the Eleventh Indiana and Eighth Missouri regiments from the Second Brigade of General Smith's division. These regiments were restored to Smith's division, and Wallace was assigned to lead a new division composed of Thayer's and Cruft's brigades. The Second Brigade did not have a commander and its four regiments were attached to Thayer's Third Brigade. Wallace's division was sent to the center of the line to fill a mile-long gap in the lines between General Smith and General McClernand.[48] Colonel Morgan L. Smith, assumed command of Wallace's former brigade following the reorganization.[49]

That morning the Confederate commanders met in Dover and decided that they needed to escape from Grant's trap or be captured. The plan was for General Gideon Pillow to lead an attack by the Left Wing Division on the right side of the federal line, secure the Charlotte Road out of Dover, and escape to Nashville. General Buckner volunteered to have his Right Wing Division act as the rear guard and defend the escape.[50]

On February 14 Smith's division continued "the same system of annoyance," but to a more limited extent in accordance to Grant's orders.[51] General Smith "had contented himself with allowing Buckner no rest, keeping up a continual sharp-shooting." Early in the morning, Smith "made a demonstration of assault with three of his regiments, and though he purposely withdrew them, he kept the menace standing, to the great discomfort of his *vies-à vies*."[52] During the gunboat attack, Smith rode through his command and grimly joked with the men. According to Wallace, "He who never permitted the slightest familiarity from a subordinate, could yet indulge in fatherly pleasantries with the ranks when he thought circumstances justified them."[53]

Colonel Cook said, "Though suffering from the snow and rain of the previous night, they [the Third Brigade] returned during the whole of the day the enemy's fire, doing him no little damage."[54] That night "all the advance parties were recalled as before." The day's casualties were less than the previous day. Smith conducted a personal reconnaissance of the ground to the extreme left of his position and decided, "The only apparent practicable point of assault was in that quarter, the enemy's extreme right being protected by an impassable slough." He passed on his conclusions to Grant and prepared to endure another uncomfortable, inclement night.[55]

By 3 p.m., Foote's fleet was ready and steamed toward the water batteries. The ships advanced slowly, pouring a "constant fire … from every gun that could be brought to bear upon the fort." However, as the ironclads closed on the batteries, they were systematically disabled by the Confederate guns. The flagship gunboat *St. Louis* was hit about sixty times resulting in severe destruction to the ship and numerous casualties including Flag Officer Foote. The *Louisville* was also damaged, and both ships "drifted helplessly down the river." The *Pittsburg* and *Carondelet* were also wrecked and "the whole fleet followed [down the river after the disabled *St. Louis* and *Louisville*] and the engagement closed for the day."[56] Foote reported, "The enemy must have brought over twenty heavy guns to bear upon our boats from the water batteries and the main fort on the side of the hill, while we could only return the fire with twelve bow guns from the four boats." The hour and a half engagement disabled the fleet, resulted in fifty-four casualties, and ended naval support.[57]

Colonel McArthur's Third Brigade spent the day "under arms, awaiting orders." At 5 p.m., they were directed to move to a place on the extreme right of Second Division's lines. The brigade reached the new position "a little after dark (about 7 p.m.) having been hotly shelled by the enemy's batteries on the way." They "encamped for the night without instructions" and "without adequate knowledge of the nature of the ground in front and on our right."[58]

The other phase of the attack also failed when McClernand's and Wallace's assault on the right was repulsed. Grant explained, "After these mishaps I concluded to make the investment of Fort Donelson as perfect as possible, and partially fortify and await repairs to the gunboats."[59]

The pain of the Valentine's Day disaster was eased somewhat for Smith when he received a telegram from Halleck announcing the approval of his promotion to brigadier general. The major general informed Smith, "The Senate today confirmed your appointment unanimously. The commission of major general awaits you. The fight has been a hard one and its victory complete. You will not disappoint your friends."[60]

At the end of the day, Smith's reconstituted command was composed of the Third Brigade made up of the Seventh Illinois, Fiftieth Illinois, Twelfth Iowa, and Fifty-Second Indiana; the Fourth Brigade made-up of the Seventh Iowa, Second Iowa, Fourteenth Iowa, Twenty-Fifth Indiana, and the Fourteenth Missouri or Western Sharpshooters; and the Second Battalion, First Missouri Light Artillery consisting of three batteries with four Parrott guns each.[61] The First and Fifth Brigades were detached for duty with Wallace's Third Division.

The Union forces surrounding Donelson had grown to around 27,500 men facing an estimated Confederate army of 17,500.[62] Grant's army encircled the Confederate defenses around Fort Donelson and Dover except for Hickman Creek on the west and the swamps northeast of Dover. That night "the troops fell back for rest and such refreshments as could under the circumstances be had, reasons before mentioned preventing the building of fires."[63]

Colonel Cook's picket line, on Smith's right, was held by companies selected from the Fiftieth Illinois, Fifty-Second Indiana, and Twelfth Iowa, supported by the Thirteenth Missouri. Because of their proximity to the enemy's lines, these troops were not permitted to make campfires. It snowed again that night exposing the troops, especially those on outpost duty, to another terrible night in the hostile elements. Colonel Crafts J. Wright, the commander of the Thirteenth Missouri reported:

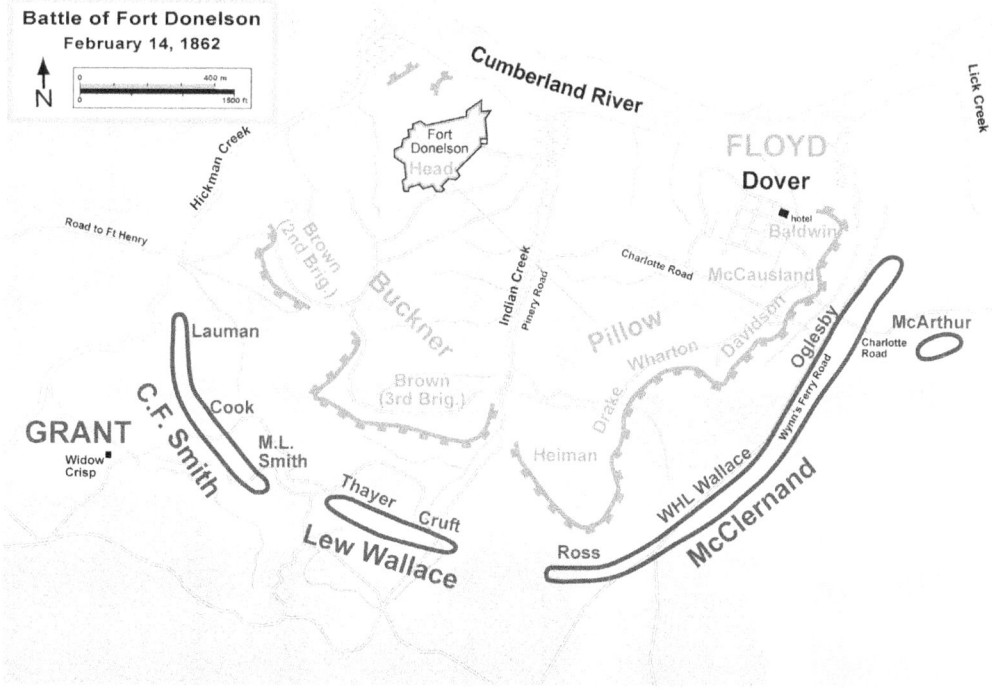

Positions on the evening of February 14, 1862 (map by Hal Jespersen, www.cwmaps.com).

We remained in this position [on the ridge opposite the Confederate rifle pits] without fires during the storm of rain, hail, and snow. The clothes of the men were drenched and frozen upon then. I sat upon a log wrapped in my blanket until 3 o'clock, when permission was given to go back half a mile and build fires to dry the men.[64]

Colonel Lauman asked his regimental commanders to select companies to hold his brigade's advance position. After these units had occupied his line of outposts on the windswept ridge, Lauman withdrew the remainder of his troops to the shelter provided by the hollows overlooking Hickman Creek. Once in the hollows, the men started campfires to heat coffee, cook rations, and dry clothes.

Lauman's brigade had been strengthened by the addition of one regiment. The transport, *McGill*, with the Second Iowa aboard, had reached the Fort Donelson area about 11 a.m. The Second Iowa's commander, Colonel James M. Tuttle, was ordered to form his regiment on the brigade's extreme left. The regiment took position to the left of the Twenty-Fifth Indiana where they spent a "cold and disagreeable night, without tents or blankets."[65]

Colonel Morgan L. Smith, in command of Wallace's Fifth Brigade, reported to General Smith for orders. In consideration of the late hour and the limited space available, Smith decided to hold the brigade in reserve. Colonel Smith's troops bivouacked the night on either side of the Ridge Road, several hundred yards east of Mrs. Crisp's house.[66]

That night Smith patiently waited Grant's pleasure "knowing that when the time came he would be called upon." He never doubted the courage of his volunteers, and he believed if they were properly led, "they would storm the gates of his Satanic Majesty."[67]

22. "You must take Fort Donelson"

"All has failed on our right"

At daybreak on February 15, the Confederates launched a powerful attack on the Union right. The Rebel plan was for Pillow's Left Wing Division to push McClernand's First Division out of the way and for Buckner to move his Right Wing Division across Wynn's Ferry Road and act as rear guard while the remainder of the army escaped and moved east. When the attack began east of Indian Creek, five of Grant's eight brigades were west of the creek. Two of Smith's brigades, Lauman and Cook, and both of Wallace's brigades, Thayer and Cruft manned the line of outposts on the ridges opposite the Confederate rifle pits. Colonel Morgan L. Smith's brigade was held in reserve.[1]

Before the attempted breakout, the Confederate defenses opposite Smith and Wallace were held by the six regiments from Buckner's division. The escape plan called for stripping

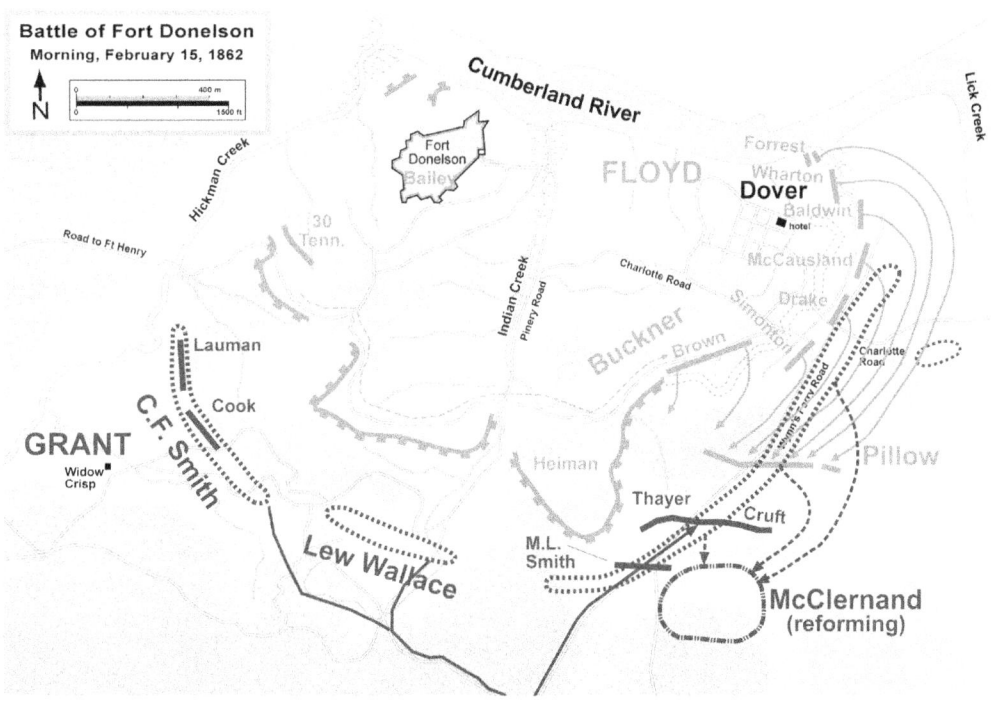

Confederate Breakout Attempt, morning February 15, 1862 (map by Hal Jespersen, www.cwmaps.com).

Buckner's troops from this line to support Pillow's attack on the Union right. The line could not be left unprotected, and Colonel John W. Head's Thirtieth Tennessee Regiment, which was stationed within the fort's earthworks, was sent to man the defenses. It was a risky decision by the Confederate command because it dramatically weakened the three-quarters of a mile of rifle pits previously occupied by Buckner's 3,600 troops. Now the defenses would be manned by approximately 450 officers and men. The Confederate leaders were willing to take the chance because they believed Grant's forces would focus their attention and manpower on Pillow's assault on the Union right and would not be able to capitalize on the weakly held line on the federal left. Three Confederate batteries, composed of sixteen guns, were also withdrawn to support the breakout.[2]

At dawn Lauman's and Cook's troops returned to their positions on the ridge facing the Confederate rifle pits. Colonel Lauman's brigade was deployed on the left flank with the following regiments from left to right: the Second Iowa, Twenty-Fifth Indiana, Seventh and Fourteenth Iowa, and Fourteenth Missouri. Colonel Cook placed four of his regiments in line on the right flank from left to right: the Twelfth Iowa, Fiftieth Illinois, Thirteenth Missouri, and Fifty-Second Indiana. Cook's fifth regiment, the Seventh Illinois, continued to support Battery D of the First Missouri Light Artillery. During the night, Captain Henry Richardson's Battery K relocated two of their Parrott rifles to a position on the ridge near Captain Edward McAllister's Battery D's 24-pounder howitzers.[3]

The action on February 15 began in the same fashion as the previous day. Smith's division continued "to keep up the annoyance by skirmishers and slow artillery fire."[4] Shortly after Smith's troops had returned to their battle stations, the men heard the sound of artillery and small arms fire from the right of their line. The noise became louder during the morning as the battle moved closer. Smith's men listened to the din "with bated breath and clasped muskets waiting orders which would send them to the help of their comrades."[5] A soldier in the Seventh Illinois recalled the conditions:

> It snowed again last night, but this morning the sky is clear; the clouds have disappeared, and the sunlight is seen again on the Cumberland hills. How cheeringly does it fall around the weary soldiers. It is indeed a blessing sent from heaven, for Grant and his army. But hark! we hear the rattle of musketry. It comes from the right wing. Soon we learn that [Wallace's], McArthur's, and Oglesby's brigades are engaged. The battle is now raging furiously.[6]

From their position on the ridge, Richardson's Parrott rifles started firing eastward across the Indian Creek valley at Pillow's attacking Confederate forces. The rounds from the Union guns were effective in spite of being 1¼ miles away. The Thirteenth Missouri were sent to protect both artillery sections.[7]

About the same time General Wallace heard the "full-throated roar of battle" from the northeast and he ordered the "long roll" beaten.[8] As soon as Wallace had mustered his new division, the regimental commanders led them to the front. The officers formed their men into line of battle and covered their fronts with a strong line of skirmishers. Wallace initially thought that McClernand had launched the attack. However, instead of beginning the battle, McClernand's First Division was bearing the brunt of the Confederate assault. The Rebel advance started well, and, after two hours of heavy fighting, Pillow's Division had pushed McClernand out of the way and opened the escape route.[9]

Grant was just starting his day when the attack began. A courier arrived at Mrs. Crisp's house with a message from Flag Officer Foote requesting a meeting on his ironclad. Foote said his injury, suffered during the navy's attack on the Water Batteries, prevented him from leaving his gunship to visit the general. Grant instructed Captain Rawlins to inform the division commanders that he was meeting with Foote. Grant also had Rawlins "instruct them to do nothing to bring on an engagement until they received further orders." Then Grant left to confer with Foote on board the *St. Louis*.[10]

By 8:00 a.m., McClernand, "seeing the issue hanging in the balance," sent an aide to request help from Wallace, Smith, and Grant.[11] Wallace wondered what to do. Although he was under specific orders not to engage the enemy, he was worried about the safety of his own division. He assumed that a courier was en route with orders to support McClernand, and about 8:30 a.m. he decided to send Colonel Cruft's brigade.[12]

Around 9 a.m., Smith learned that Wallace had sent Cruft's Brigade to reinforce McClernand. This movement left Captain Richardson's two Parrott rifles without support. Smith was concerned that the Rebels might attack his left flank near Hickman Creek. The general thought that if an assault was made it would come from the rifle pits to the northeast of the Eddyville Road. Smith did not know that the Confederate defenses were only manned by the Thirtieth Tennessee, and there was no danger of a Rebel assault on his flank. To guard against this suspected danger, Smith instructed Colonel Cook to assign two regiments from his brigade to strengthen the defenses. Cook sent the Thirteenth Missouri to support Richardson's First Missouri guns and the Fifty-Second Indiana to cover Colonel Lauman's left flank. This left Cook with only the Fiftieth Illinois and Twelfth Iowa to defend the right side of Smith's line.[13]

Smith completed his defense by deploying the Fourteenth Missouri in front of his line as skirmishers. He placed one battalion from the regiment in front of Lauman's brigade and the other forward of Cook's forces. Companies were also taken from Cook's and Lauman's brigades to strengthen the skirmish line. From their position at the bottom of the ravine near the edge of the abatis, the skirmishers and sharpshooters "blazed away, whenever some reckless Confederate exposed himself outside the protection of the rifle pits." This sporadic shooting continued until noon when the Thirtieth Tennessee stopped returning the Union fire.[14]

Around 11:00 a.m. Grant returned to shore after meeting with Foote. The general was greeted by a concerned Captain Charles T. Hillyer from his staff. Hillyer told Grant that a powerful Confederate force from the left side of Fort Donelson's defenses was "rolling up the Union right." Grant hurried to the Crisp House for a brief consultation with his staff. Then Grant and his entourage rode to McClernand's sector. On the way, he stopped at Smith's headquarters where he instructed Smith to send Colonel M. L. Smith's brigade to solidify the Union right.[15]

Sometime after noon, Wallace saw the remnants of the defeated Union units retreating on the Wynn's Ferry Road into his lines. Wallace realized that this was "a disaster in the making." Colonel W. H. L. Wallace, who was retreating with 400 or 500 men from his battered brigade, advised General Wallace to form his men into line of battle because the Confederates were just over the hill and would be along shortly. General Wallace placed his nine regiments[16] across Wynn's Ferry Road and prepared for the Rebel assault. For the next hour, Wallace's men held their position against three Confederate attacks.[17] Finally about 1:30 p.m. the Confederates stopped the attack. Wallace's new division had prevented the breakout and stabilized the right side of the federal line.

The battle reached its critical point between 1:30 and 1:45 p.m. General Buckner's forces had arrived and were in place to maintain the escape route along Wynn's Ferry Road and Forge Road. Buckner's men brought their knapsacks and rations, prepared to be a rear guard for Pillow's troops and then escape to Nashville. Instead, the soldiers from the Confederate Right Wing were shocked to see Pillow's men withdrawing from their hard-won positions to the lines they had occupied before the breakout attempt. Pillow decided that his exhausted troops, who were nearly out of ammunition, could not continue the attack, and he ordered the men back to their earthworks. He planned to allow his men to rest and escape that night.[18]

By the time Grant reached the Wynn's Ferry Road, the Confederate advance had stopped, and the battlefield was quiet. Both sides seemed to be "catching their breath and waiting for their opponent's next move." Grant found "the men standing in knots talking in the most excited manner." He observed, "No officer seemed to be giving any directions. The soldiers had their muskets, but no ammunition, while there were tons of it close at hand."[19]

Grant ordered McClernand and Wallace "to retire their commands to the heights out of cannon range, and throw up works." The commanding general said, "Re-enforcements were en route, and it was advisable to await their coming." Wallace and McClernand explained "the mishap to the First Division," and that "the road to Charlotte was open to the foe."[20] This information helped Grant understand the comments from some of the men. The soldiers reported that the enemy troops had attacked "with knapsacks and haversacks filled with rations." The men thought, "This indicated a determination on ... [the Rebels'] part to stay-out and fight just as long as the provisions held out." Grant decided that although some of his men were badly demoralized, "the enemy must be more so, for he has attempted to force his way out, but has fallen back; the one who attacks first now will be victorious and the enemy will have to be in a hurry if he gets ahead of me." The energized commander ordered Wallace and McClernand to retake "the position on the right" and left to meet with Smith.[21]

Grant decided to have General Smith attack the entrenchments opposing the Second Division on the Confederate right. He believed that the Confederates had committed their whole garrison, except for a few pickets, to break through McClernand's lines. Grant concluded that that the "enemy had started to march out with his entire force," and, if Smith could attack "on the left before the enemy could redistribute his forces along the line, he would find but little opposition except from the intervening abatis."[22] As he passed Wallace's and McClernand's men en route to Smith's headquarters, Grant had Colonel Webster order the men to "Fill your cartridge-boxes quick, and get into line; the enemy is trying to escape, and he must not be permitted to do so." According to Grant, "This acted like a charm. The men only wanted someone to give them a command."[23]

It was between 1:45 and 2:00 p.m. when Grant and his staff reached Smith's command post. They found General Smith and Captain Newsham sitting at the base of a large tree on the ridge facing the Confederate rifle pits. Grant explained the dire situation. "General Smith, all has failed on our right," said Grant. "You must take Fort Donelson." Smith jumped to his feet, brushed his mustache with his right hand, and announced confidently, "I will do it."[24]

"No flinching now"

In his report on the battle, Smith recorded Grant's request matter-of-factly and noted that he "received the general's personal order to assault the enemy's right, a half mile or more from my habitual position."[25] While Grant was briefing him on the tactical situation, Smith sent Captain Newsham to alert the brigade and regimental commanders. Grant's plans were simple. He wanted Smith's division to charge the Confederate works on the ridge opposing Cook's and Lauman's brigades. Grant advised Smith that "he would find

The Attack on Fort Donelson by Kurz and Allison (Wikipedia Commons).

nothing but a very thin line to contend with."[26] Grant's "confidence in Smith as a soldier was so strong that he had not the slightest doubt about the success of the charge General Smith, by his command, was to make at Fort Donelson."[27] Smith might have considered the assault routine, but Lew Wallace wrote, "Their hour of trial was now come"[28] and Frederick Grant called it "the decisive charge at the battle."[29]

Smith decided to make the main attack with Lauman's brigade on the left flank and have Cook's brigade on the right feign a supporting attack on the Confederate rifle pits. If the assault went according to his plans, Cook's ruse would hold the Confederates in position while Lauman's troops captured the Rebel defenses.[30]

In accordance with the general's instructions, Colonel Cook strengthened his skirmish line. The colonel sent detachments from the Fiftieth Illinois and Twelfth Iowa down from the ridge to the edge of the timber in front of the abatis. The soldiers joined the line of skirmishers and sharpshooters who had been harassing the Confederate line that morning. The units found positions, and the "men went cheerfully to the work assigned them, and kept up a warm fire on the enemy."[31] When Cook learned the guns that the Seventh Illinois had been supporting had been ordered to the right, he instructed Lieutenant Colonel Andrew J. Babcock to move his regiment to the front.[32]

While Cook prepared his command for their ruse, Captain Newsham alerted Colonel Lauman to prepare his brigade to attack. The Second Iowa had arrived on the 14th, and the fresh troops were selected to lead the attack. It was a dubious honor for Colonel Tuttle and his 600 men, but it was a chance to recover their tarnished reputation. The Second Iowa had left St. Louis under disgrace. Some of the men had vandalized property when they were billeted at McDowell Medical College, and the regiment was punished by leaving

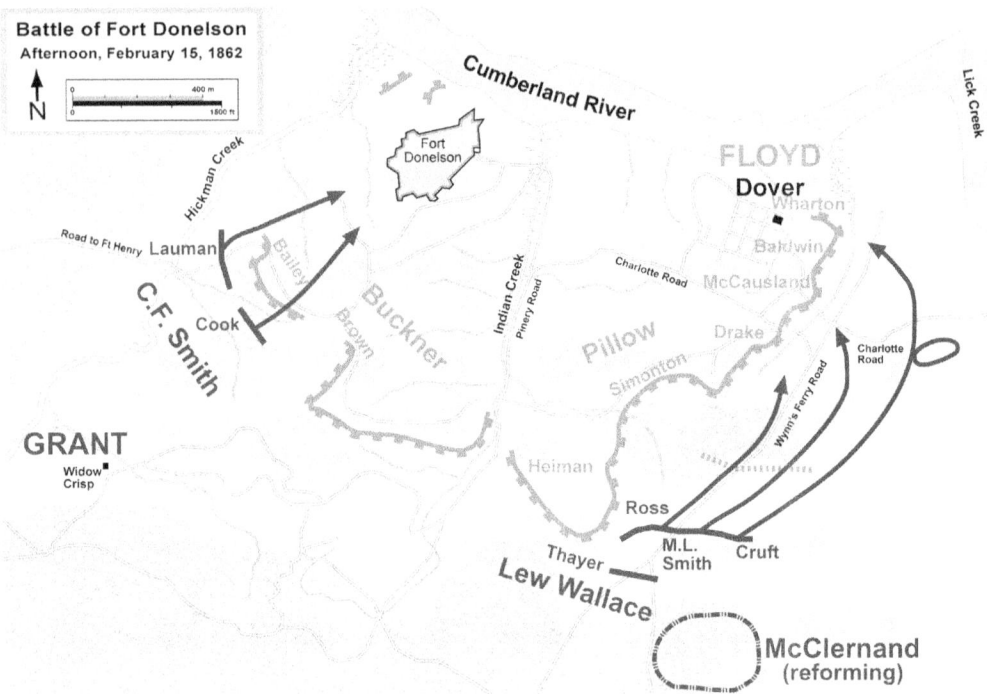

The Battle of Fort Donelson, afternoon February 15, 1862 (map by Hal Jespersen, www.cwmaps.com).

St. Louis with its flags cased and drums silent. Tuttle considered the assignment a chance to redeem the regiment's honor.[33]

Tuttle formed his troops into a double line of battle with the left battalion composed of five companies in front and the right battalion with the remaining five companies following in support. Colonel Tuttle planned to lead the advance battalion with Lieutenant Colonel James Baker in command of the other. The Second Iowa would be covered on the left by the Fifty-Second Indiana and on the right by the Twenty-Fifth Indiana. Before the advance, Colonel James C. Veatch, commanding the Twenty-Fifth Indiana, deployed Company B as skirmishers. Colonel Lauman placed the Seventh Iowa and Fourteenth Iowa on the Twenty-Fifth Indiana's right. Then Lauman redeployed the Fourteenth Missouri as skirmishers to protect the flanks of his brigade during the assault.[34]

General Smith rode up as Tuttle finished forming his command. Smith asked Captain Newsham the name of the regiment, and his chief of staff replied, "The 2d Iowa." Smith turned to the soldiers and said, "Second Iowa, you must take the fort—take the caps off your guns—fix bayonets and I will support you."[35] The general took his battle station between the two battalions and led the Second Iowa forward.[36]

Smith directed the artillery "to open heavily" and instructed the brigade commanders "to press forward with large numbers of skirmishers, and make a dash at any available opening, whilst the Second Iowa supported by the Fifty-second Indiana…, Twenty-fifth Indiana, Twelfth Iowa, &c., was ordered to lead the assault." Smith reminded the Second Iowa "to rely on the bayonet and not to fire a shot until the enemy's ranks were broken."[37]

After Pillow stopped the breakout attack, Buckner hurried his division back to their previous positions to defend against a possible attack on Colonel Head's outnumbered Thirtieth Tennessee regiment. On the Union right, Wallace and McClernand were happy to see the Confederates withdraw to their defensive works and decided not to pursue them. This allowed Buckner to disengage his division without any difficulty. After reaching the fortifications on the west side, Buckner's exhausted troops still had from one to one and half miles to go before they reached their former places on the line. The Confederate troops moved quickly and all of Buckner's units, except the Second Kentucky and Fourteenth Mississippi, reached their previous places before Smith's attack began. Captain Thomas Porter's and Captain Rice Graves' artillery batteries also managed to return to their original emplacements. Unfortunately for the Confederates, the Second Iowa was advancing toward the rifle pits that were originally held by the Second Kentucky but were only defended now by three companies from the Thirtieth Tennessee under Major James J. Turner.[38]

As Cook's feint began on the right, Lauman's brigade prepared to launch their attack. Tuttle examined the difficult terrain facing his regiment as they waited on the ridgeline for the order to advance. They had to move down from the ridge into a valley and then climb a hill on the other side through an abatis of brush and logs to reach the Confederate line.

A little after two o'clock, General Smith gave the word and the Second Iowa began to descend the timber covered eastern face of the hollow. Colonel Tuttle's battalion was in the vanguard followed by about 150 yards by Colonel Baker's battalion led by General Smith. On the right of the Second Iowa, the skirmishers from Company B of the Twenty-Fifth Indiana unintentionally started to advance at the same time.[39]

Four of the five other regiments composing Lauman's attacking force advanced *en echelon*[40] on the right and left of the Second Iowa. The Fifty-Second Indiana was on Tuttle's left, and the Twenty-Fifth Indiana, Seventh and Fourteenth Iowa were on his right. The sharpshooters of the Fourteenth Missouri were deployed as skirmishers to cover Lauman's flanks.

Tuttle's battalion crossed the small stream at the bottom of the hollow and entered the abatis on the western face. The colonel urged his men through the abatis and up the slope toward the Confederate rifle pits. The other battalion, with Smith in the lead, followed in the wake of Tuttle's vanguard. Waving his sword, Smith led the men forward, down the slope, and into the abatis. "The light reflected off their bayonets as the determined Iowa regiment gradually moved up the hill toward the Confederate earthworks."[41]

The brave Iowa men advanced up the slope led by the regimental color guard. One by one, five members of the color guard fell as they carried the flag. Finally, Corporal Voltaire E. Twombly took the colors. Twombly was knocked down by a spent ball, but he got up, struggled back into position, and carried the colors until the end of the battle. Twombly received the Medal of Honor for this achievement.[42]

Tuttle's lead battalion steadily advanced through the abatis toward the Rebel works. The left wing "proceeded in line of battle steadily up the hill until we reached the fortifications without firing a gun."[43] The Thirtieth Tennessee waited patiently in the rifle pits until Tuttle's men were within twenty paces from the earthworks. Then the Confederates opened fire with "double barreled shot guns loaded with buckshot" and ripped several gaps in the Union line.[44] As Smith described it, "The left wing of the regiment ... moved steadily over the open space, down the ravine, and up the rough ground, covered with heavy timber, in unbroken line, regardless of the fire poured into it, and paused not until the enemy broke and fled."[45]

From Smith's position in the middle of the regiment at the head of the second battalion, he urged the men up the slope through the abatis.

> Occasionally he turned in the saddle to see how the alignment was kept. For the most part, however, he held his pace steadily toward the enemy. He was of course, a conspicuous object for sharpshooters in the rifle pits. The air around him twittered with minnie-bullets. Erect as if on review he rode on, timing the gait of his horse with the movement of his colors.[46]

Schematic representation of the attack by Lauman's Brigade on February 15, 1862 (author's diagram).

    Smith was a conspicuous figure on his horse as he shouted, cursed, and urged the raw Iowa volunteers forward. He waved his sword toward the rifle pits and called out to the men, "No flinching now, my lads!—Here—this is the way!" Come on!" One soldier remembered, "I was nearly scared to death, but I saw the old man's white mustache over his shoulder, and went on."[47]

    Some soldiers hesitated and were reluctant to advance into the Rebel guns. Tuttle's regiment was new to Smith, and he "blasphemed them into better acquaintance."[48]

> "Damn you, gentlemen. I see skulkers. I'll have none here. Come on, you volunteers, come on. This is your chance. You volunteered to be killed for love of your country and now you can be. You are only damned volunteers. I am only a soldier and I don't want to be killed, but you came to be killed and now you can be."[49]

    As the advance proceeded, Smith called to his division surgeon, "Hewitt, my god, my friend. If you love me, go back and bring up another regiment of these damned volunteers. You'll find them behind the bushes."[50]

"Go forward and consummate the work"

    The Second Iowa "charged into the rebel's works, driving the enemy before him and planting his colors on their fortifications."[51] Tuttle's men found that most of Turner's Tennesseans had quickly abandoned their rifle pits after the first shot. The colonel said, "On reaching the works we found the enemy fleeing before us, except a few who were promptly put to the bayonet."⁵² Lauman noted, "In this engagement the Iowa 2nd suffered terribly, Captains Slayman [Slaymaker] and Clantman [Cloutman] fell just as they entered the fortification. Clantman [Cloutman] was instantly killed; Slayman [Slaymaker] died gallantly shouting to his men to go forward and consummate the work."⁵³

After the bayonet charge captured the rifle pits, Tuttle ordered his men to shoot at the fleeing Tennesseans. The soldiers fired several enthusiastic volleys "with fatal precision" at the retreating Rebels until the right wing with Colonel Baker and General Smith "reached the captured works.⁵⁴ The skirmishers from Company B of the Twenty-Fifth Indiana successfully captured the enemy rifle pits a little to the right of the Second Iowa's breakthrough. Smith wasted no time in celebrating and acted quickly to exploit the opportunity. One staff officer wrote, "And so the old cock led then with a mixture of oaths and entreaties over the breastwork."⁵⁵ He ordered Tuttle to redeploy his regiment and continue the attack.⁵⁶ Then the Second Iowa "formed in line of battle, again under a galling fire, and charged on the encampment across the ravine in front, the enemy still retreating before us."⁵⁷ Smith recalled that "the united body pursuing [pursued] the enemy through their encampment and toward the enemy's works just above, where they skirmished for a considerable time." The general said, "Right gallantly was the duty performed,"⁵⁸ and he later reported, "The movement of this regiment was a very handsome exhibition of soldierly conduct."⁵⁹

The supporting regiments (Fifty-Second Indiana, Twenty-Fifth Indiana, Seventh Iowa, and Fourteenth Iowa) on either side of the Second Iowa crossed the small stream, entered the abatis, and advanced to the captured works. As Tuttle was reforming the Second Iowa into a line of battle, the other regiments from Lauman's brigade reached the captured rifle pits. The Fifty-Second Indiana arrived on the left of Tuttle's regiment. Unfortunately, the Indiana regiment reached the Confederate works in "confusion" due to the rugged terrain and the lack of tactical experience of the regiment's new officers. Smith instructed the Fifty-Second to regroup and support the Second Iowa's pursuit.⁶⁰ General Smith described the circumstances.

> The Fifty-second Indiana, ordered to follow and support the Second Iowa, from the nature of the ground and want of tactical knowledge, instead of going to the left, as I had intended, came up [in] confusion, and instead of moving forward, remained behind the earth work just taken, from where, and from some unexplained cause, fired a number of fatal shots into their friends in front. They remained in this position until ordered to reform in the rear.⁶¹

As the Twenty-Fifth Indiana climbed the hill, they veered to the left and entered the Confederate works where the Second Iowa had placed its colors. Smith ordered the Twenty-Fifth to support the Second Iowa's advance. On the right of the Twenty-Fifth Indiana, the Seventh and Fourteenth Iowa also reached the earthworks, but only the Seventh Iowa joined the attack on the retreating Confederates. By the time the Seventh and Fourteenth Iowa regiments arrived at the rifle pits, Captain Thomas Porter's Tennessee Battery had "started to pound the area with canister and shell." The Eighteenth Tennessee under Colonel Joseph Palmer opened fire on the Seventh and Fourteenth Iowa regiments from a commanding position on a knoll several hundred yards southwest of the breakthrough. Smith was concerned that this artillery barrage might be the start of a Confederate counterattack on the exposed right flank of Lauman's brigade. The general directed Colonel Shaw's Fourteenth Iowa to hold and defend the eastern portion of the captured rifle pits. Meanwhile, skirmishers from the Fourteenth Missouri continued to protect the flanks of Lauman's brigade.⁶²

As soon as the rifle pits were secured, Smith ordered Captain Newsham to hurry to the rear and bring up artillery. Smith planned to use the guns to support the attack on the new line of defense that the Confederates were frantically trying to establish on the next ridge located 400 yards to the east. Newsham quickly contacted the officer in charge of Battery K of the First Missouri Artillery, who ordered Lieutenant John O'Connell to move two 10-pounder Parrotts forward. After they reached the earthworks, the Missourians quickly unlimbered their pieces and opened fire. Colonel Shaw redeployed the Fourteenth Iowa to provide cover for his troops and support to the gun crews.[63]

When Newsham reached the front with O'Connell's Parrotts, Smith told him "the guns were too light," and asked him to find some heavier ordnance. Newsham returned to the Ridge Road where he met Captain Welker in charge of Battery H of the First Missouri Light Artillery. Newsham instructed Welker to take his guns to General Smith. The battery hurried to the rifle pits and unlimbered their three pieces (two 20-pounders and one 10-pounder Parrott rifle) on the left of O'Connell's Parrott guns. The Union artillery began to exchange rounds with the Confederate field pieces firing from the opposite side of the hollow.[64]

After sending Battery H to Smith, Newsham met General Grant who asked the aide if "Smith wanted anything." Without Smith's instructions, the captain said that the general "wanted some of his old regiments." Grant immediately sent Captain Rawlins across Indian Creek to order Colonel McArthur's brigade to report to Smith.[65]

The Second, Seventh, and Fourteenth Iowa and Twenty-Fifth Indiana continued to exploit their breakthrough and drove back the newly arrived Second Kentucky. The Kentuckians were forced back "in confusion" to the position held by the Eighteenth Tennessee, where Colonel Hanson and General Buckner rallied the regiment.

After Cook saw that Lauman's Fourth Brigade had taken the rifle pits, Cook wanted permission to commit his brigade to the attack. With General Smith managing the attack on the captured ridge, Cook sent a staff officer to request authorization from General Grant to join the assault. Cook wanted to pursue the fleeing Confederates and capture Porter's and Graves' batteries that were firing on the Fourteenth Iowa in the captured rifle pits. While waiting for the messenger to return, Cook learned the "Stars and Stripes" was flying from the Confederate works containing Porter's battery. Cook ordered his men to hold their fire while he verified that the battery had been taken. The colonel quickly discovered that the Confederates had raised the Union flag to decoy the federal troops into an ambush.[66]

When the staff officer returned with Grant's approval, Cook prepared to move his brigade forward. By this time, Colonel Babcock's Seventh Illinois Regiment had joined the brigade on the ridge and taken position on the right of the Fiftieth Illinois. Cook's brigade advanced on the double with the Twelfth Iowa on the left, Fiftieth Illinois in the center, and Seventh Illinois on the right. The three regiments descended the slope, crossed the small stream at the bottom, and climbed through the abatis up the opposite slope.[67]

Cook's regiments advanced against the left flank of the detached line of seized rifle pits. As the units from the Third Brigade climbed through the abatis, Porter's battery fired down the right flank of the columns. Fortunately, Cook's men had no trouble reaching the rifle pits. The colonel said, "The distance being short, the discharges caused but little damage, overshooting us just enough to tear into shreds the colors of the Seventh Illinois." Cook's troops entered the detached earthworks to the right of the breakthrough by Lauman's brigade, seized the rifle pits, and prepared to cover Lauman's troops.[68]

After reforming their lines, Lauman's Fourth Brigade resumed the attack led by the Second Iowa. Tuttle's regiment descended the hill in line of battle, with their flanks covered by skirmishers from the Fourteenth Missouri, until they reached the bottom of the ravine that separated the Confederate's former position from the new defense they were trying to form. Then the Iowans and Missourians began climbing the ridge. The Confederate fire slowed the Iowa regiment as they crawled up the very steep and wooded slope. The rugged terrain and enemy guns finally stopped the regiment before it reached the top of the ridge. Tuttle ordered his men to lie down and return the enemy's fire. The Iowans continued to fire at the Rebels "for over an hour" from this location.[69]

The Fifty-Second Indiana moved cautiously forward on Tuttle's left. The regiment, which had reached the rifle pits in "confusion," became even more disorganized. Many of the men refused to continue their advance and tried to seek shelter in the earthworks. Those soldiers from the Fifty-Second, who obeyed Smith's order, and the skirmishers from the Fourteenth Missouri continued to advance. The men reached the bottom of the hollow and started to climb the slope toward the new Confederate defensive position until their progress was also stopped by the Rebel defenders.[70]

Smith employed all of his efforts to urge the reluctant soldiers from the Fifty-Second Indiana to continue their advance. Smith sensed an opportunity and wanted to drive the Confederates from their new line before it was stabilized. Although he was a highly visible target, he was willing to take the risk to capture the next ridge.

> In getting these brave men, but poor soldiers to assault the only really practicable point for such a purpose, I had to expose myself greatly. I prayed, exhorted, urged and damned these men until I was too hoarse to speak—all to get them after taking the first breastwork to induce them to advance to the second point, which I could have carried in ten minutes, but all to no purpose.[71]

The men from the Fifty-Second, who remained in the rifle pits, began shooting at the Confederates on the opposite ridge. However, the distance was too great and the volleys fell short striking the Second Iowa troops in front of the Confederate line. The Iowans suffered severely from the Indiana regiment's "friendly fire." As Colonel Tuttle caustically commented:

> In the mean time the enemy were being re-enforced, and one of our regiments poured a disastrous fire upon us in the rear.... I am not able to name the regiment which fired upon our rear, but I do know that the greater part of the casualties we received at that point was from that source, for I myself saw some of our men fall who I know were shot from the hill behind us.[72]

When he realized what was happening, General Smith returned to the rifle pits, stopped the haphazard firing, and ordered the Indianans to remain where they were.[73]

On the right of the Second Iowa, the Twenty-Fifth Indiana and Seventh Iowa from the Fourth Brigade, with skirmishers from the other battalion of the Fourteenth Missouri, joined the attack. The lines for the two regiments had become "somewhat broken" as they descended the steep slope from the rifle pits. The officers halted the advance at the bottom of the ravine and reformed their ranks.[74]

Although the Second Iowa was stalemated in their advance, they held their position. Tuttle was finally forced to withdraw when his men ran out of ammunition. The regiment was able to disengage without any interference from the Confederates. The Second Iowa's heroics came at a heavy cost with forty-one killed and 157 wounded in the attack. While the regiment withdrew from their position, the Twenty-Fifth Indiana and Seventh Iowa regiments remained in the bottom of the hollow and covered their retreat.[75]

Eventually, the Union forces left the ravine and returned to the captured rifle pits, where they continued to exchange fire with the Confederates. Shortly after the Second Iowa arrived at the earthworks, Colonel Tuttle was injured when a Rebel cannon round struck the log on which he was standing. The impact knocked the colonel to the ground, injured his back, and sprained his wrist. Colonel Baker assumed command of the regiment. After the Second Iowa was established in the rifle pits, the Twenty-Fifth and Seventh slowly climbed the slope backward, facing the enemy, to the earthworks. After reaching the captured position, the two regiments took position on the Second Iowa's right. Colonel Veatch's Twenty-Fifth Indiana had forty wounded men and Colonel Babcock's Seventh Illinois suffered three killed and nineteen wounded men.[76]

After the reorganized Rebel line stopped the Second Division's assault, General Smith ordered Lauman and Cook to hold the captured rifle pits. Lauman's troops were redeployed from left to right: the Second Iowa, Twenty Fifth Indiana, Seventh Iowa, Fourteenth Missouri, and Fourteenth Iowa. Colonel Cook's brigade occupied the earthworks on Lauman's right. Colonel Shaw's Fourteenth Iowa continued to support Lieutenant O'Connell's 10-pounder Parrott rifles. Smith pulled the disorganized and destructive Fifty-Second Indiana out of the line.[77] Smith's forces held the captured rifle pits despite repeated Confederate counterattacks over the next two hours. The Second Division was now poised to seize Fort Donelson when the fighting resumed the next morning.[78]

Shortly before the Second Iowa was forced to withdraw, General Smith rode to Colonel Babcock's Seventh Illinois command post to praise their advance under the artillery fire from Porter's battery.

> I never saw a regiment make such grand movements under such a fire in all my military life as yours has just made. Colonel, I thank God for your command at this moment. Charge that rebel battery! Charge it with your steel and silence its work of death![79]

Colonel Babcock quickly formed his regiment into a line of battle. However, before the colonel could begin his attack on Porter's battery, Smith looked west, saw that the sun was setting, and stopped the assault. Smith countermanded "the order given you [Babcock] to charge the battery. It is now too late; I will leave that work for you to do tomorrow."[80]

The Fifty-Second Indiana and the Thirteenth Missouri, which had been supporting the four guns on the ridge southwest of the Crisp house, reported to Colonel Cook. The rifle pits occupied by Cook's command were not extensive and, to prevent overcrowding, Cook decided to place the Fifty-Second Indiana and Thirteenth Missouri in reserve on the western slope of the ridge. This left the Seventh and Fiftieth Illinois and Twelfth Iowa regiments in the captured earthworks.[81]

McArthur's brigade had been badly battered during the Confederate attack on the Union right. The brigade had been withdrawn into the upper part of Bufford Hollow where they were provided rations and ammunition. When Rawlins rode up at 4 p.m. to direct the First Brigade to return to Smith, McArthur was ready to redeploy his brigade. The brigade moved out with the Twelfth Illinois in the lead. It was dark and the day's fighting was over by the time McArthur's troops reached the hollow south of the Crisp House. Before going further, McArthur stopped the brigade and sent a staff officer to inform General Smith of their arrival. McArthur was directed to send one of his regiments to the front and hold the other two in reserve. McArthur selected the Twelfth Illinois to strengthen Smith's line. In the darkness the regiment climbed the abatis covered slope and reached the captured rifle pits. Smith sent the Twelfth Illinois to a position on the left of the Second Iowa. After the Illinois was in position, Welker's Battery H of three Parrott rifles assigned to the First Division was shifted from the Union right to Smith's sector in the area occupied by the Twelfth Illinois. The section of guns belonging to Battery D, First Missouri Light Artillery, which had been ordered to the Wynn's Ferry Road sector during the afternoon, was also directed to rejoin General Smith.[82]

Smith's battle report described the actions and positions as darkness ended the day's fighting.

The Twenty-fifth Indiana, following in order, moved in advance to the support of the Second Iowa, and covered it when that regiment, for want of cartridges, retired behind the entrenchments just taken from re-enforcements of the enemy. As soon as the out-work [outer works] was taken I sent for a section of Stone's battery, which soon arrived and opened upon the enemy with happy effect silencing a heavy gun (24-pounder). Meantime the regiments of the Third (Cook's) Brigade arrived, but as it was getting late I deemed it better to dispose of the troops for the night and be in readiness for a renewed assault on the morrow, the crest of the enemy's work being only some 400 yards distant and the ground more or less favorable. Increasing the artillery on the ground just taken by a couple of 20-pounder Parrott guns, the Fourth Brigade was disposed to guard the position, with the Third Brigade in reserve several hundred yards in rear. The Ninth and Twelfth Illinois (First Brigade) having reported at this time, the latter was thrown forward around the base of the hill toward the enemy's main work, the Ninth remaining in reserve. The night [was] very cold, but without the cruel storm.[83]

General Smith inspected and approved Cook's and Lauman's troop dispositions. Following the general's instructions, the brigade commanders had protected their fronts with a strong line of outposts. Before retiring to his headquarters, on the opposite ridge, Smith told Cook and Lauman to "hold the position obtained during the night and immediately prepare for a continued assault the following morning."[84]

Then Smith rode to the bottom of the hollow, west of the captured rifle pits. There he saw "a regiment drawn up in line of battle with about fifty men with bandages on their arms and legs." Smith turned to Captain Newsham and inquired what unit the men were from. Newsham replied the Ninth Illinois. Smith asked, "What those white bandages were on the men for?" The captain answered, "They were on men who when they heard that he wanted them had left the field hospital and joined the regiment to do and die for him." By this time, Smith and his staff had reached the Ninth Illinois' right flank. Then, Newsham recalled, "The grand old hero at once took off his cap and rode down the front of the regiment bareheaded. The officers and men stood silent until he had passed, and then a cheer from their full hearts broke forth that told him how they appreciated the mark of respect he had paid them."[85]

When they reached their field headquarters, Smith and his staff discovered that their tents had been converted into hospitals. Displaced from their lodging, the officers built a large campfire at "the foot of white oak tree." The officers gathered around the warm fire and discussed the day's accomplishments and the unfinished work facing them in the morning. Then they lay down in the snow and tried to sleep.

Except for sporadic exchanges along the picket line, the Union troops spent a quiet night in the captured rifle pits. Although the soldiers were required to remain under arms, they were permitted to build campfires which allowed "them to rest more comfortably" for tomorrow's battle.[86]

23. "Unconditional and immediate surrender"

"Ungenerous and unchivalrous terms"

The reward for the Second Division's successful attack that afternoon was to spend the night bivouacked in the cold. The men of Lauman's Fourth Brigade and McArthur's Twelfth Illinois Regiment spent a restless night waiting for the anticipated Confederate counterattack. At least there was no rain or sleet, and the men were permitted to have fires.

The situation at the Confederate headquarters in Dover was warmer but much less comfortable. After the day's engagements had ended, the Rebel troops were assembled for the escape from Fort Donelson. Before launching the second breakout attempt, General Floyd ordered a reconnaissance of the federal lines. The intelligence report was not good. Grant's forces "had not only reoccupied their former ground, but extended their lines still farther to our left."[1]

Faced with this situation, the three Confederate commanders, Floyd, Pillow, and Buckner, considered their options. Sometime after midnight, the officers decided that there was no alternative but surrender. General Buckner concluded that anything else would be a needless slaughter of brave men.

> The troops had been worn down with watching, with labor, with fighting. Many of them were frosted by the intensity of the cold; all of them were suffering and exhausted by their incessant labors. There had been no regular issue of rations for a number of days and scarcely any means of cooking. Their ammunition was nearly expended. We were completely invested by a force fully four times the strength of our own. In their exhausted condition they could not have made a march. An attempt to make a sortie would have been resisted by a superior force of fresh troops, and that attempt would have been the signal for the fall of the water batteries and the presence of the enemy's gunboats sweeping with the fire at close range the positions of our troops, who would thus have been assailed on their front, rear, and right flank at the same instant. The result would have been a virtual massacre of those troops, more disheartening in its effects than a surrender.[2]

Following their decision, General Floyd announced he would leave "with such portions of his division as could be transported in two small steamers." Then General Pillow remarked that he thought there were "no two persons in the confederacy whom the Yankees would prefer to capture than himself and General Floyd" and decided to leave as well. Then the command was quickly passed from Floyd to Pillow to Buckner. Floyd said to Pillow, "I turn the command over, sir," to which Pillow replied, "I pass it," to which Buckner responded, "I assume it. Give me a pen, ink, and paper and send for a bugler."[3] Buckner regarded capitulation "as a necessity of our position" and was determined to remain with his men.[4]

It was nearly daylight after these deliberations. Buckner ordered the troops back to their positions in the entrenchments and composed a note to General Grant asking for terms. "In consideration of all the circumstances governing the present situation of affairs at this station I propose to the commanding officers of the Federal forces the appointment of commissioners to agree upon terms of capitulation of the forces and post under my command, and in that view suggest an armistice until 1 o'clock today."[5] Buckner assigned the unpleasant task of delivering the message to Colonel John C. Brown whose brigade was opposite General Smith's division. Colonel Brown was wounded and he delegated the mission to Major Nathaniel F. Cheairs, commander of the Third Tennessee. "Cheairs and a bugler went to the line and after a considerable time, in which the bugler blew every tune he knew, they finally managed to get the attention of the Union forces."[6]

On the Union side of the sector, Colonel Lauman heard the sound of a bugle and saw the Rebels waving a white flag. Lauman immediately sent Colonel Parrott from the Seventh Iowa to "ascertain the intent of it." Parrott reported that a Confederate officer wished to see the officer in charge. Lauman hurried to meet Major Cheairs, who presented the offer of capitulation.[7] Lauman brought Cheairs to Smith who read Buckner's proposal. Smith bluntly told Cheairs: "I make no terms with Rebels with arms in their hands—my terms are unconditional and immediate surrender!"[8] Then Smith escorted Cheairs to the Crisp House.

General Grant was asleep in bed in the kitchen, and Surgeon John H. Brinton was curled up on the floor near the fire. An orderly entered with General Smith, who, according to Brinton, "seemed very cold, indeed half frozen." Smith immediately walked to the open fire on the hearth and briefly warmed his feet. Then he turned his back to the fire and faced General Grant who had gotten out of bed and was quickly putting on his outer clothes.[9]

"There's something for you to read, General Grant," said Smith, handing him the letter. As Smith passed the letter to Grant, he asked Brinton for something to drink. Brinton knew what Smith required, and the doctor reached into his medical bag and retrieved a flask. Smith took the container and "helped himself in a soldier-like manner." The surgeon remembered Smith as "erect, manly, every inch a soldier, standing in front of the fire, twisting his long white moustache and wiping his lips." While Grant read the note, Smith extended his feet and said, "See how the soles of my boots burned; I slept last night with my head in the saddle, and with my feet too near the fire: I've scorched my boots."[10]

Grant looked up at Smith and asked, "What answer shall I send to this, General Smith?" Smith did not hesitate and spoke plainly.

"No terms to the damned rebels," replied Smith.

Grant laughed and asked for some writing paper. An excited and flustered aide placed some poor-quality legal-sized paper on the table. For about three minutes, hardly a sound was heard as Grant considered and wrote. Finally, he leaned back in his chair and announced, "This is what I am writing, General Smith." Then he read his response, "Yours of this date, proposing armistice and appointment of Commissioners to settle terms of capitulation, is just received. No terms except an unconditional and immediate surrender can be accepted. I propose to move immediately upon your works."[11] Smith gave a short emphatic "Hm" and remarked, "It's the same thing in smoother words." Then Smith left the farmhouse and gave the letter to Major Cheairs.[12]

Cheairs was escorted back to his lines to deliver Grant's surrender demand. Buckner was angry and embarrassed at the bluntness and boldness of Grant's reply. He thought of resisting but realized that his forces either must surrender or be slaughtered. Accordingly, he accepted the terms of Grant's ultimatum.[13] "The distribution of the forces under my command incident to an unexpected change of commanders and the overwhelming force under your command compel me, notwithstanding the brilliant success of the Confederate arms yesterday, to accept the ungenerous and unchivalrous terms which you propose."[14]

News of the surrender reached the Union forces as the men were eating a "scanty breakfast" and being resupplied with ammunition for the anticipated attack on the Confederate works. Colonel Cook said "the woods around were made to ring with loud and enthusiastic cheers from the troops under the command of Colonel Lauman and myself, announcing the unconditional surrender of Fort Donelson, giving us uninterrupted ingress into and peaceful possession of its entire rebel contents."[15]

Since his brigade had spearheaded the assault on the Confederate rifle pits, Colonel Lauman asked General Smith to have the honor of entering the works first. Smith approved the request, and Lauman prepared his command to enter the works.[16]

Later that day Grant sent his report of the victory to General Halleck. The first paragraph was all Halleck needed to read. "I am pleased to announce to you the unconditional surrender this morning of Fort Donelson, with 12,000 to 15,000 prisoners, at least forty pieces of artillery, and a large amount of stores, horses, mules, and other public property." Grant's report also praised Smith for his "most brilliantly executed" attack.[17]

The fall of Fort Donelson opened the Tennessee and Cumberland Rivers for transportation of Union troops and material. As General Grant had envisioned, Donelson's capture forced the Confederate forces at Columbus to withdraw from the city and Western Kentucky. Grant's forces had momentum, and he "intend[ed] to keep the ball moving as lively as possible."[18]

"Three cheers and a tiger"

The capture of Forts Henry and Donelson, along with the Union victory at Belmont, gave Grant a national reputation and earned him a major generalship. It also won praise for General Smith. Grant wrote to General C. W. Cullum on February 16. "I ordered a charge upon the left—enemies right—with the division under General C. F. Smith which was most brilliantly executed and gave to our arms full assurance of victory."[19] *The New York Times* reported, "The whole operation was exceedingly brilliant, and reflects high credit upon General Smith, who personally superintended the operation, exposed himself precisely as if he had been a private soldier, and was among the first to mount the breastwork."[20] Even the enlisted men and volunteers were impressed with Smith's performance, as one soldier wrote, "By his presence and heroic conduct he led the green men to do things that no other man could have done."[21]

The northern press was hungry for good news about the government's effort to put down the rebellion and preserve the Union. If Fort Henry had whetted the public's appetite, Grant's triumph at Donelson provided a long-awaited feast. On February 17 newspapers, legislatures, and citizens erupted in a glorious celebration of national and regional pride. *The New York Times* reported how the victory was welcomed in the nation's capital.

> The news of the fall of Fort Donelson was received with extraordinary demonstrations in Congress today. In the Senate the gallery rose en masse and gave three enthusiastic cheers. In the House this was improved on the floor by three cheers and a tiger. Both Houses adjourned at an early hour, and a general jubilee reigns in the city. Salvos of artillery are heard from every camp within sound of Washington.

The *Times* announced that the Secretary of War had submitted Grant's name to the president for nomination to the Senate as a major general, as a reward for his gallant services.[22]

The news of the capture of Fort Donelson spread around the country as regional papers applauded the victory and described the role that their local regiments had played in the success. The West Chester paper wrote, "Great demonstrations are making here today in honor of the capture of Fort Donelson. The bells are ringing and cannons firing. All countenances are beaming with joy, except those of a few sympathizers with the Rebels." The people in Cincinnati were "crazy with excitement over the news of the capture of the Rebel army. The streets are crowded with men hurrahing, and flags are being run up at all points and salutes are fired." New Yorkers were "jubilant" and there was "every demonstration of joy." In upstate New York, the cities of Auburn, Geneva, Troy, Poughkeepsie, Rochester, and Utica celebrated by firing cannon and ringing bells tributes. State legislatures passed resolutions and members stood, threw their hats, clapped their hands, and cheered for the Union triumph.

In Chicago, the people claimed "the honor of the victory for Illinois" because twenty-five infantry regiments and four cavalry regiments from the state took part in the battle. Dispatches from Maine, New Hampshire, and Vermont announced the "general manifestation of enthusiasm and thanksgiving for the glorious result." In Burlington, Vermont, residents fired "all the guns she has left at home and rings all her bells in token of her great rejoicing over the feats of valor performed by the men of the West." Boston newspapers reported there "has not been so much joy manifested in Boston since the days of the old Revolution." The city planned "a hundred gun salute, ringing all the bells in the city, and a five hundred gun signal by the citizens."

The Indianapolis papers responded soberly, "The greatest excitement prevails here, increased by the terrible anxiety of the friends of the soldiers engaged in the struggle." In response, the city sent a special train "with physicians, twenty-five volunteer nurses and a large quantity of hospital stores" to care for the wounded. A citizens' meeting was held to organize care of the wounded sent to the city.[23]

The victories at Fort Henry and Fort Donelson brought attention to the Western Theater of Operations and its critical role in defeating the Confederacy. However, not all the news reports were positive especially from abolitionists. The Democratic *Cincinnati Commercial* boasted that Grant "certainly had never shown a symptom of anti-slaveryism" and that C. F. Smith was "rather proslavery than otherwise." Although Grant and Smith were regarded as indifferent to slavery, they helped win two significant battles, which helped broaden Lincoln's war coalition.[24]

In the days following the battles, Grant's roles in the victories were diminished in favor of Foote at Fort Henry and Smith at Fort Donelson. Correspondents learned that Grant had not entrenched at Donelson and was not present on the battlefield when the Confederate attack began. Several journalists omitted Grant's name from press accounts and gave Smith the credit for the Donelson victory. One reporter, probably Frank Chapman of *The New York Herald*, went so far as to spread a false rumor that Grant was so drunk before the battle that he had to be helped onto his horse.[25] However, Grant's biggest threat was not from northern journalists or General Johnston's Confederates, but from General Halleck's jealousies.

"General Smith for us"

On February 17 a correspondent for the *Missouri Democrat* described Smith's role in the victory at Fort Donelson. The lavish praise was in stark contrast to Smith's

Brigadier General Charles F. Smith from the *Philadelphia Inquirer* (courtesy Kurt Wille).

previous treatment by the press. In fact, the papers now seemed to be overly generous in applauding Smith in an effort to compensate for their past shabby treatment. In describing the assault, a *Missouri Democrat* journalist created a heroic portrait of Smith leading the storming party. He wrote that the general was "a most magnificent sight" as he directed the troops up the hill through "the perfect storm of bullets which rained about him." He pictured Smith "in the front and center of the line" motioning with "his hat on the point of his sword" and inspiring "them with furore [fury] there was no withstanding."[26]

The poetic newspaper account was in contrast to the matter-of-fact account Charles sent to Francis the day after the victory. He wrote, "The ultimate success is said to be due to myself. I let others speak of that."

> With but a few minutes to write in the midst of pressing duties, I announce our complete success after three days of fight. Our casualties I suppose will reach 500. [The Second Division's casualties were 987 with 478 in the First and Second Brigades.] My command—5 brigades—3 splendid batteries—some 15,000 men occupying all of the enemies extensive fortifications.... My loss was over one hundred at that place. However, this first success compelled the enemy to give up by unconditional surrender. My horse was hit and so was I, but I was not conscious of the fact until this morning when on stripping to bathe I found a contused wound, not breaking the skin, just below the stomach some two inches in diameter. It now causes me a little uneasy sensation but amounts to nothing.[27]

Charles said that his division was without his "old regiments" that had been detached to support General McClernand. "All of the regiments were new to me but I blasphemed them into better acquaintance and have received numerous congratulations from these very men."[28]

The next day Charles added a few more comments on the battle and referred Francis to the newspapers for details. He said they had taken 11,000 prisoners and sixty-six pieces of artillery. There were at least a dozen reporters covering the battle, but they kept "shy of me knowing my aversion to that class of animals." The other generals, except Grant, "feed them and make much of them for a purpose." Charles was surprised that his "personal exposure" impressed his raw recruits and said, "They now swear by me and wish to stick to me." He said that Grant told him that he owed "his success emphatically to me" and included "the remark for what is worth."[29]

Smith's hometown paper, *The Philadelphia Inquirer*, presented a brief account of the Second Division's heroics.

> General GRANT having in command of the division, driven the enemy back with reinforcements and gained the lost ground, at once ordered an advance by General SMITH on the left.
> Charging under a hot fire up the steep hill on which was located the outer redoubt, our troops

gained the high breastworks, and with hardly a pause went over them, planting the stars and stripes over the walls under a most galling fire.

They then formed, charged and drove the enemy back until he fell into a new position behind some batteries.[30]

When the newspaper accounts reached Charles, he rejected the glamorized stories published in the northern press.

> My blood runs cold when I read such stuff as that I put my cap on my sword etc. I did no such ridiculous thing. I certainly did use my sword in waving people on, etc. & would like to have used it extensively on those who went back; but not the cap business. I was ridiculous enough to curse and damn those most heartily who seemed to feel a reluctance to move and expose their precious persons as I thought ought to have been; and this an energetic way of revival had a salutary effect then and since.[31]

In an effort to ease his wife's concerns and to correct a published account, he clarified his place during the battle.

> I certainly was not the first in the enemy's entrenchments but followed the storming partly close to direct. Several prisoners of a Mississippi regiment on the next line of entrenchments said that they fired at the old gentleman on horseback with the white moustache repeatedly with their rifles, the Devil thank them.[32]

From his camp at Fort Donelson, Charles told Francis, "with the exception of a cold I am as I always am when living in camp in fine health with the appetite of a boa-constrictor." He had just talked with one of the medical officers who came to congratulate him on his "victory over the new men I command in consequence of my conduct in leading them." His "old Paducah force had gotten over the notions of my disloyalty—but the new men all came with the person instilled by the vile newspapers." However, the doctor told Smith these new men were convinced of his ability, and "they now cry General Smith for us." Charles said he was "glad of this purely for the success of the cause."[33]

In addition to being cheered in the press, Smith was also commended by his superiors. Grant wrote to Senator Washburne, "I want to call your attention to General C. F. Smith. It is a pity that our service should lose so fine a soldier from a first command. If major generals are to be made, a better selection could not be made than to appoint C. F. Smith."[34] Halleck joined the chorus and asked McClellan to promote Smith to major general.

> Brig. Gen. Charles F. Smith, by his coolness and bravery at Fort Donelson when the battle was against us, turned the tide and carried the enemy's outworks. Make him a major-general. You can't get a better one. Honor him for this victory and the whole country will applaud.[35]

Several days later Halleck told Smith about the recommendation.

> As soon as I ascertained the part taken by you at Fort Donelson I telegraphed your name to Genl McClellan for a Major Generalcy. I have not heard officially, but I see in the newspapers that the nomination was sent in. If so my friends say it will be immediately confirmed. I have no doubt it has before this time.[36]

In spite of the press' reversal of opinion, Smith continued to have no use of reporters. The general had always refused to play up to the reporters, but now he went as far as pack off a score or two of them. As Halleck reported, "He made a clean sweep, and since that the gallant old General sleeps well o'nights, and carries his plans undisturbed."[37]

Perhaps the best tribute to General Smith was written nearly a year later by Colonel William H. Morgan of the Twenty-Fifth Illinois Volunteer Infantry. At the time of the battle, Morgan was a lieutenant colonel of the regiment and was placed in charge "by Genl. Smith's verbal order" when the colonel was relieved. Morgan "followed him [Smith] into the rebel works and was with him at their capitulation." Colonel Morgan wrote, "He was the best officer, the most gallant soldier I have ever seen. It is the proudest boast of my life that I served under him at Donelson. I saw him often during those eventful three days, and no man was greater than he on that field."[38]

Over a month after the victory, Smith drafted his official report on the battle from Pittsburg, Tennessee. In this commentary, Smith praised the troops under his command and made a special mention on the performance of his units under detached service. He noted that Colonel McArthur's First Brigade "did gallant service; and as no official notice has been taken of this, so far as I am aware, I take pleasure in transmitting herewith the reports of the regimental commanders." He added, that according to reports by General Wallace, the Second Brigade, commanded by Colonel Morgan L. Smith, "performed most distinguished service." He was also gratified to mention that Captain Farrand's and Lieutenant Powell's cavalry companies did "gallant and effective service" and commended "both officers to the favorable notice of the Government."[39]

Finally, after months of delay in the Senate over the slanderous accusations of disloyalty, Smith received official notice of his promotion from Adjutant General's office. On February 19 Smith thanked Halleck "most heartily for your manliness and just appreciation of me." Charles pledged, "So far as it in me lies I will do my utmost not to disappoint the expectations of yourself and other friends have been pleased to express in regard to me."[40]

In addition to earning praise for his actions at Donelson, Smith received congratulations on his promotion to brigadier general. The confirmation was long overdue because as Congressman Thomas Harris wrote, "There was a strong effort to defeat you & for some months the military committee refused to report your name." Harris advanced the approval after an endorsement from Captain Rziha. Harris "resolved to instruct the committee to report & make that motion." He said the "triumph of the merits of your case & all of the slander against you were soon departed into thin air. Everybody was satisfied that all of the charges were mischief and now, since the news from Fort Donelson has been received almost all of the Senators have been here to congratulate me upon your gallantry ... for command, supposing that I have in some way a ... interest in you." Harris concluded by congratulating Smith on his "achievements in arms" and noting that the efforts of his enemies to malign him had "only served to elevate you in the opinion of all here & to degrade those who conspired against you."[41]

It must have been especially gratifying for Charles to receive Adjutant General Thomas' complementary letter. Thomas acknowledged the receipt of Smith's letter of January 10 requesting details of the charges against him and dispatches on the "fine state of discipline of your command at Paducah."

> I need hardly say that your subsequent confirmation by the Senate as Brig. Genl. of Volunteers, and the flattering notice of your own gallantry and that of the troops so efficiently prepared by you for success at Fort Donelson, afford the most positive refutation of the charges which had been brought by individuals not of the mily. [military] service, against you. Your letter would have been answered before, and a copy of the communication you asked for, furnished you, but that the letter had been mislaid in some of the offices. It is hoped at a time of less pressure from public business it will come to light, when a copy will be sent to you. Please acknowledge the receipt of this.[42]

Smith acknowledged Thomas' letter and asked to receive copies of the accusations when they "turn up." Charles ended by expressing his indignation over his treatment. "I am compelled to remark that Justice appears to have been little consulted when my removal from an important command was ordered on Allegations affecting my character without affording me the least opportunity for disproof."[43] Thomas, who may have had some part in delaying Smith's nomination to brigadier general, tried to erase the accusations against Charles. Thomas and others hoped that their past treatment of Smith along with Smith's "mislaid" request letter might be forgotten during the "pressure from public business." In early March Charles sent a copy of Thomas' letter to Francis. The "precious document" he received from the Adjutant General of the Army failed to satisfy him.[44]

Republican senator James W. Grimes of Iowa congratulated Smith for his "achievement at the storming of Fort Donaldson [sic]" and added his support for Smith's promotion to major general. Senator Grimes also praised "the soldiers of my own beloved state of Iowa that so many of them were permitted to serve under your command" and said they had "reflected renown and glory upon the other." Grimes observed that the men who were willing and anxious to reject Smith's promotion were now supporting his "conduct and services." The senator said that the Iowa delegation met with the Secretary of War and asked him to make Smith a major general. The Secretary assured the men that it was going to be done.[45]

Smith's old friend from the Utah Territory, Judge D. R. Eckels, commended Charles for his "noble and gallant conduct" at Fort Donelson. Judge Eckels said the country was indebted to Smith for the victory. Eckels hoped that Charles would be rewarded with the office of major general for the "good of the service" and "the success of her armies." The judge recalled how impressed he was with Smith's conduct as an officer, worth as a citizen, and personal kindness during the Utah expedition.[46] Another friend, Judge Henry Crosby, sent his and the Tenth Infantry Regiment's congratulations from the Utah Territory on "the brilliant manner in which you carried the day at Ft. Donelson." Crosby said the men of the Tenth Regiment "were perfectly crazy with excitement about our 'Col. Charley' as they call you" and all of them regretted the regiment "was not there under you." Crosby offered his services as a volunteer aide. He added a congratulatory postscript, "Just seen your promotion. I drink to the health of the Major General. Wish it was Commanding."[47]

The newspapers that a few months ago had accused Smith of being a southern sympathizer were now announcing that he was to be made a major general "for gallantry and meritorious service." His friends in Grant's command "rejoiced" at his success, and General Grant recommended to "strong friends of his who were influential politicians" Smith's promotion to major general.[48]

Part Six

Triumph and Turmoil: March–July 1862

"I can bear honest testimony to his great worth as a soldier and friend."—U. S. Grant[1]

Major General U. S. Grant (Library of Congress, LC-USZ62-59650).

24. "Take command of the expedition"

"It is a beautiful place"

Flag Officer Andrew Foote left Cairo on February 18 on board the *Conestoga* to conduct a reconnaissance up the Cumberland River toward Clarksville. When the *Conestoga* approached Fort Defiance, Foote found the works deserted and proceeded to Clarksville where he met with city officials. He learned that the Rebel troops and about two-thirds of the citizens had gone to Nashville. The flag officer found the city "in a state of the wildest commotion from the rumors that we would not respect the citizens in their persons or their property." Foote sent word to Grant that the city and its surrounding forts were now under his control.[1]

Grant wired Halleck that he was now in possession of Clarksville and would send "no force there except General Smith's division until he heard from General Halleck." He suggested that Halleck follow up the success at Fort Donelson by seizing Nashville because "white flags are flying from here [Donelson] to Clarksville, and rumor says the same thing extends to Nashville."[2]

On February 20 Charles notified Francis announcing that he was about to move to Clarksville with part of his division. He said she could read the details in the newspapers because the reporters' accounts saved him the trouble of explaining the events to her. On that point, Charles included a "*Chicago Times* filled with all sorts of stuff about our operations."[3] He had not heard about Foote's capture of Clarksville and wondered if the Confederate forces would fight there or continue to Nashville. "Will the rebels stand? If they do not the great battle of Armageddon will come off at Nashville."[4]

The next day, Smith received formal orders to "proceed to Clarksville, Tenn., with so much of your command, as transportation is now ready for, and occupy ground about the forts on the north bank of the river." Grant had no specific directions for Smith except "keeping the men from going into private houses and annoying the citizens generally." He also said that the mayor would turn over a large quantity of army stores.[5] Grant did not believe that a large garrison was required and only sent "four small regiments to Clarksville." Smith reached the city on February 24 and began its occupation. He described Clarksville as "a beautiful place of some 6000 inhabitants" with many houses that "are palatial in size and appearance." Smith made his headquarters and residence in a grand home located in the center of the city. "It is very large elegantly furnished has every modern appliance of comfort, and is full of old house servants." The home's former owner was "an Irish Presbyterian, a banker and a bitter Secessionist."

> As he was a member of the convention held at Nashville to form the bogus provisional government, he is beyond the pale of recognition as a loyal citizen of the U.S. and hence fled our approach to Nashville taking his wife and six fledges with him. As General Buell is now in possession of that

place I suppose Mr. has kept "moving"; indeed I heard yesterday that he had gone to New Orleans. I rejoice exceedingly that Mr. [illegible] has been so naughty, for it has enabled me to [illegible] my [illegible] in pleasant places and I should not object to the establishment as a heritage.[6]

Smith said that most of the men had left the city and observed that the women who remained were angry, spiteful, and uncharitable toward the Union occupiers. He related an incident at a Rebel hospital.

Two days since I took my Medical Director and went to inspect the rebel hospital where there are about one hundred of their sick and wounded. There were some 12 or 15 ladies of the place present ministering to their friends and it would have amused you as it did me to see the way in which the young and pretty ones jerked themselves about and tried to look spiteful as I passed gravely among the wounded. But I applied the universal solvent of your sex (flattery) to one of them and she relented like snow in the sun.[7]

No sooner had Smith arrived, than he received a dispatch from General Buell requesting his "services against the enemy." Smith believed that Buell did not need his troops but planned on leaving for Nashville "as soon as the steamer gets sufficient wood on board."[8] On March 1 Grant informed Halleck that Buell had ordered Smith's five regiments and artillery to join him at Nashville.[9]

Halleck was displeased when he learned that Smith had been sent to Clarksville. He directed Grant not to forward more forces to Clarksville and to recall Smith's division to "Fort Henry or a point higher up the Tennessee River." Halleck was even more upset when he learned Smith had gone to Nashville and asked who ordered the move. The movement of *his* troops under Buell's orders did not set well with Halleck, and he immediately ordered Smith's division to return to Fort Henry.[10] Unfortunately, the order did not reach Smith in time to prevent his movement to Nashville.

Smith left Clarksville on February 27 with 2,000 men, two artillery batteries, and a cavalry squadron by steamer for Nashville. The move to Nashville proved unnecessary as Smith believed it would be and his force returned to Clarksville two days later. Buell had secured Nashville and occupied the city with a large force. Acknowledging the unnecessary movement of Smith's troops, Buell telegraphed Halleck that he had sent Smith back to Clarksville and thanked Halleck for his "readiness to assist" him.[11] Smith returned to his lavish quarters in Clarksville and said, "The darkeys are charmed to see us back again." However, he did not expect to remain in Clarksville too long and believed his "force will soon be sent on the Tennessee" and expected "orders on that point daily."[12]

After the tumult of the past four months, Charles finally had some good news for his family. He wrote Fanny, "I have had numerous letters of congratulation on my success (charge at Fort Donn [Donelson]) some from persons who had almost faded from my membrances [memory]."

But the main feature is all you will care about—that I will probably receive the Commission of Major Genl and with that an independent command. Will your mother want to break up housekeeping: live in a small house but never think of boarding—the idea produces in me a cold chill—a shiver * * * but no boarding house with the smell of roast mutton pervading the establishment all the time—faugh—I hope you are making fine progress in your studies.[13]

"Why do you not obey my orders"

While Smith was traveling between Fort Donelson and Nashville, a political battle was underway between his superiors. Halleck decided to use the triumphs at Henry and

Major General Henry W. Halleck (Library of Congress, LC-DIG-cwpb-06956).

Donelson to advance his career. On February 17 he asked McClellan to "make Buell, Grant, and Pope major-generals of volunteers, and give me command in the West."[14] However, while Halleck was submitting Grant's and Buell's names for promotion, he was trying to have Grant removed from command and have Buell's plans rejected in favor of his own. Halleck asked McClellan to replace Grant with General Ethan Allen Hitchcock and wrote, "Hitchcock will take command here as soon as he gets his orders." Halleck also promised to "split secession in twain in one month" if he was given command in the west.[15]

The following day Halleck was more demanding.

> I must have command of the armies in the West. Hesitation and delay are losing us the golden opportunity. Lay this before the President and Secretary of War. May I assume the command? Answer quickly.[16]

Secretary of War Edwin M. Stanton received Halleck's plan "very favorably."[17] This good news was followed by a telegram from McClellan complaining that he was "embarrassed" by the lack of information from Halleck and Buell.[18] Halleck's proposed re-organization was rejected, Hitchcock refused the position, and Lincoln only submitted Grant's name for promotion. Grant's advancement meant that the new major general was the highest-ranking officer in Halleck's command. A defeated Halleck responded to Secretary Stanton: "If it is thought that the present arrangement is best for the public service, I have nothing to say. I have done my duty in making the suggestions, and leave it to my superiors to adopt or reject them."[19]

Adding to Halleck's disdain was another telegram from McClellan complaining about communications: "What more have you from Columbus? You do not report either often or fully enough. Unless you keep me fully advised, you must not expect me to abandon my own plans for yours."[20] Halleck had to censure someone, and there were several good candidates. First, he blamed the officers of his department for being "negligent or ignorant of their duties in this respect." Then the general condemned his predecessor, General Frémont, for allowing the officers to become "negligent ... of all law, regulations, and orders." Lastly, he asked for more time to improve the situation because he was "doing everything in my [his] power to effect it."[21]

Although their relationship was strained, Grant and Halleck worked together to organize the Union offensive up the Tennessee River. Halleck wanted Grant to destroy railroad connections south of Paducah along the river and recommended that "General C. F. Smith or some very discrete officer" to accomplish the work. The principal targets were the railroad bridge over Bear Creek near Eastport, Mississippi, and the rail connections at Corinth, Jackson, and Humboldt. General Halleck believed that "strong detachments of Cavalry and Light Artillery supported by infantry" could "reach these points from the River without any very serious opposition." He cautioned Grant to avoid "general engagements with strong forces" and emphasized that it would "be better to retreat than to risk a general battle." After destroying as many of the railroad targets as possible, Grant was directed to attack Paris.[22]

Frustrated in his attempts to have Grant replaced and his command enlarged, Halleck launched a campaign to discredit his new major general. Halleck blamed Grant for the lack of information.

> I have had no communication with General Grant for more than a week. He left his command without any authority and went to Nashville. His army seems to be as much demoralized by the victory of Fort Donelson as was that of the Potomac by the defeat of Bull Run. It is hard to censure a successful general immediately after a victory, but I think he richly deserves it. I can get no returns, no reports, no information of any kind from him. Satisfied with his victory, he sits down and enjoys it without any regard to the future. I am worn out and tired with this neglect and inefficiency. C. F. Smith is almost the only officer equal to the emergency.[23]

Smith confirmed Halleck's comments on the conditions of the forces at Fort Donelson in a letter to Francis. "This whole force is utterly demoralized by victory. There seems to be neither head nor tail. The utter want of discipline seems to me to be something marvelous."[24] McClellan quickly responded to Halleck's telegram and said, "The future success of our cause demands that proceedings such as Grant's should at once be checked." He authorized Halleck to place Grant under arrest "if the good of the service requires it" and replace him with Smith.[25]

On March 4 Charles wrote Francis from Clarksville explaining that he was "again on the wing, having received orders last night to go to Fort Donelson." He was to organize another command from the troops left at Forts Henry and Heiman. Grant would travel "far up the Tennessee even into Mississippi," and Smith would leave Donelson three or four days later and move to Davis, Tennessee. Charles was unwilling to reveal the object of the movement, but he indicated that the Union forces "are restrained from bringing on a general engagement with larger forces—to fall back rather than do so." He did not like that "part of the programme" but noted it was "part of a general scheme of course."[26]

Halleck decided to add more incriminating evidence and informed Washington that Grant had "resumed his former bad habits."

> If so, it will account for his neglect of my often-repeated orders. I do not deem it advisable to arrest him at present but have placed General Smith in command of the expedition up the Tennessee. I think Smith will restore order and discipline.[27]

On March 4 Halleck telegraphed Grant at Fort Henry. His order was brief and specific: "You will place Maj. Gen. C. F. Smith in command of expedition, and remain yourself at Fort Henry. Why do you not obey my orders to report strength and positions of your command?"[28]

"Assigned to the command of the expedition"

Grant acknowledged receipt of Halleck's order and confirmed that the troops would be "sent, under command of Major-General Smith, as directed."[29] Grant informed Halleck that when the gunboat convoy arrived all of the transports would be loaded and sent up the river. He managed to get a slight dig at Halleck when he noted that the transports would not be able take all the troops ready to move and blamed the problem on his removal from command.[30]

General Grant instructed Smith "to take command of the expedition which I designed commanding in person" and ordered Smith to leave Clarksville and return as fast as possible to Fort Henry.[31] Grant informed Smith that he had arranged for embarking the troops and was allocating "three regiments from Clarksville and all the troops at Donelson except Oglesby's brigade" for the mission. Grant said, "I will be here when you arrive and give you all the information I am in possession of concerning the status of the expedition."[32]

> Headquarters District of West Tennessee,
> Fort Henry, March 5, 1862.
> Maj. Gen. C. F. Smith,
> Fort Henry, Tenn.:
>
> By directions from headquarters Department of the Missouri you have been assigned to the command of the expedition up the Tennessee River. For instructions, see enclosed letter from Major-General Halleck.
>
> Information that seems to be reliable places the rebel forces at Eastport and Corinth at 20,000 men, with rolling stock between the two places sufficient to throw all the troops to either place in a short time.
>
> If this should prove true, I can hardly say what course should be pursued to carry out the instructions. A general engagement is to be avoided, while the bridges are to be destroyed, if possible. The idea probably is there must be no defeat, and rather than risk one it would be better to retreat.
>
> I will remain at Fort Henry and throw forward all the troops that can be provided with transportation. The commissary of subsistence is directed to take along 300,000 rations, and all the forage here is to go. It will probably be necessary to procure forage on the road.
>
> Allow me to congratulate you on your richly-deserved promotion, and to assure you that no one can feel more pleasure than myself.
> U. S. Grant,
> Major-General, Commanding.[33]

Smith received Grant's order at Fort Donelson on March 5. He wrote Francis that General Halleck had designated him "to prepare for a movement against the enemy which was to be conducted by General Grant." Charles noted that the order was addressed to "Major General Smith." This was his "first intimation that I have been confirmed by the Senate" and he "suppose[d] it is so."

Smith was somewhat surprised by his new orders. Since Fort Donelson he had been led on a merry chase with instructions from Grant, Buell, and Halleck. It is no wonder that the new major general was "a little puzzled in this matter." On March 5 he

Major General Charles Ferguson Smith (courtesy C. F. Smith Collection, U.S. Military Academy Library, Special Collections).

acknowledged receipt of Grant's orders and said he would leave for Fort Henry the next day. Halleck's telegram to Grant was confusing, and Smith asked for an "interpretation" of what he was expected to do when he reached Paris.[34] Smith wondered if he was to destroy the rail bridge at Paris and return to Fort Heiman, remain at that place for Grant, or wait for further orders[35]

In spite of his removal from command, tensions escalated between Grant and Halleck. Halleck continued to chastise Grant and blamed others for this harassment.

> General McClellan directs that you report to me daily the number and positions of the forces under your command. Your neglect of repeated orders to report the strength of your command has created great dissatisfaction and seriously interfered with military plans. Your going to Nashville without authority, and when your presence with your troops was of the utmost importance, was a matter of very serious complaint at Washington, so much so that I was advised to arrest you on your return.[36]

Two days later Halleck telegraphed McClellan that he had "not yet received any returns whatever from General Grant showing the number and position of his forces."[37]

During this time Grant responded to all Halleck's inquiries and tried to defend himself from the accusations. He summarized the situation: "Thus in less than two weeks after the victory at Donelson, the two leading generals in the army were in correspondence as to what disposition should be made of me, and in less than three weeks I was virtually in arrest and without a command."[38] Grant protested that he had done all he could to provide Halleck with information on the strength of his command. He said that it was not his fault if Halleck had not received his letters. Grant explained that had sent daily reports to his "chief of staff, who must have failed to keep you properly posted." Finally, he asked to be removed from command if his performance was unsatisfactory. Instead of blaming Halleck, Grant alluded to enemies between them who were causing problems.[39]

Halleck said Grant was mistaken, and there were no enemies between the men. Halleck said that he had had no information from Grant since the capture of Fort Donelson and requested the "number and position of your command." Halleck said McClellan was "out of all patience waiting for it."[40] The following day, Grant sent two messages to Halleck. The first repeated Grant's desire "to be relieved from further duty."[41] The second provided a detailed account of the disposition of Grant's forces at Fort Henry, Fort Donelson, and Clarksville.[42]

Halleck finally received Grant's letter of March 5. However, rather than moving forward, the department commander delivered another scolding. Halleck said Grant's failure to report "certainly indicated a great want of order and system in your command, the blame of which was partially thrown on me, and perhaps justly, as it is the duty of every commander to compel those under him to obey orders and enforce discipline." He warned Grant not to "let such neglect occur again, for it is equally discreditable to you and to me." He said he was "ashamed" to be "unable to give the strength of your command" to Washington.[43]

Charles remained concerned about the undisciplined troops at Fort Donelson and was worried about taking them deep into Confederate territory. He made it clear he would not tolerate any breach in discipline. "But of one thing I am resolved, if they flinch I will make others fire into them—they shall make their election to be fired upon by their enemies or by their friends."

Charles continued to be amazed about the excitement about his heroics at Fort Donelson.

> Don't get upset by all this nonsense about me. It does not give me an emotion except to stamp the lie upon the base aspersions on my character as a man of honor—as a soldier.

I don't comprehend all this furor about me. Bah! I thought nothing about it; except that I only prayed for 500 of my old men to go with me. Much I find is expected of me. Several of my old army friends just from St. Louis say they were excited much by my doings and that I am a person looked up to. If I had but the proper loots to work with! I move tomorrow early by land for the Tennessee.

You shall hear a good account of me or my death.[44]

As plans developed for the move up the Tennessee River, Union command received intelligence about Rebel movements. Halleck telegraphed the War Department that General Beauregard had 20,000 men at Corinth and was fortifying the city. Halleck criticized Buell for not sending forces up the Tennessee to join forces with Smith's expedition and capture Corinth. He said Smith had gone to do it, but he feared it was too late and that his command was too small.[45] Assistant Secretary of War Thomas Scott warned Halleck that the Confederates had 15,000 to 20,000 men at Corinth, 10,000 men at Henderson, and 8,000 troops at Bear Creek and were "receiving re-enforcements constantly from Columbus and Louisiana." Scott said that Buell could send 10,000 or 20,000 men to support him.[46]

With the buildup of Rebel forces at Corinth, the Union command rushed troops to Smith. General Sherman confirmed Grant's report that there were 20,000 Rebels fortifying their positions at Eastport and Corinth. Sherman was eager to assist his old Commandant of Cadets and told Halleck that he would send "all the Paducah garrison" to Savannah and asked permission to go with Smith's column.[47] He warned Grant: "General Smith must advance with great caution. If the enemy is in force at Corinth or Eastport, our landing must be below." Halleck did not express displeasure with Grant and, in a rare concession, agreed with Grant's recommendation that "water batteries at Fort Donelson should be dismounted and captured artillery sent to Paducah or Cairo."[48]

Smith received official notice of his promotion to brigadier general on March 7. He acknowledged the confirmation and renewed his oath of allegiance.

Fort Henry, Tenn.
March 7, 1862
The Adjt. Genl. of the Army
Washington, D.C.
Sir:
  On this date I rec'd my confirmation as a Brigadier General of Volunteers in the service of the United States which I accept.
  I return herein properly filled up my renewed oath of Allegiance to the Government. There being no civil magistrate available the oath was administered by Capt. Wm. McMichael asst. Adjt. General.
  You will find on file in your Office my Oath of Allegiance subscribed on receiving the appointment of Brigadier.
  Very respectfully
  Your Obt. Servt.
  C. F. Smith
  Brig. Genl. & Col. 3d Inf.

  I was born in Pennsylvania and am very nearly Fifty Five years of age; and had no fixed place of residence when appointed, being in the army, but I have never given up my birthright as a citizen of Penna. [Pennsylvania]
  C. F. Smith
  Brig. Genl.[49]

The same day, Special Orders No. 19 placed Smith officially in "command of the expedition now about moving up the Tennessee River."[50] Sherman had "sent up the Tennessee eleven regiments and one battery and enough boats to transport 20,000 men."[51] He proposed to leave Paducah that night with "two regiments of infantry and eight companies of cavalry" to join General Smith.[52]

Halleck suggested to McClellan, who was still in command on March 8, that Smith land troops at Savannah, Tennessee, because the place was "near the railroad and between Corinth and Henderson." Indicative of Halleck's cautious approach, he sent "entrenching tools" and was pushing "forward enforcements as rapidly as possible."[53] The next day Halleck pressed Grant to send all of the troops "up the Tennessee as rapidly as possible" and advised Grant to "hold yourself in readiness to take the command."[54]

Grant and Smith met on board the *Tigress* before Smith left for Savannah. Dr. John Brinton observed their discussions and commented that Grant "in one sense stilt [sic] looked up to him in the memory of his old office." However, Brinton felt and noticed "an unconscious deference on the part of Smith to Grant as a soldier. It was apart from rank: it seemed indescribable: but it was there, it was the recognition of the master." Brinton wrote, "On the evening before the expedition sailed, as the two walked up and down the guards of the boat, the last walk they ever took together, this relationship seemed to me stronger than ever."[55]

While the major generals organized, complained, and somehow managed to forward troops up the Tennessee, General Smith traveled on the steamer *Continental* toward the designated embarkation point. He issued General Orders No. 2 formally declaring, "the point of rendezvous of this expedition will be Savannah, Tenn."[56] Smith reached Savannah at noon on March 11 and remained on the *Continental* to coordinate the deployment of troops.

"Restored to command"

Finally, President Lincoln demanded evidence of General Grant's misconduct. Adjutant General Thomas conveyed the president's wishes through Secretary Stanton. "By direction of the President the Secretary of War desires you to ascertain and report whether General Grant left his command at any time without proper authority, and, if so, for how long; whether he has made to you proper reports and returns of his force; whether he has committed any acts which were unauthorized or not in accordance with military subordination or propriety, and, if so, what."[57] This put Halleck on notice that he needed to either clarify the situation and bring formal charges against Grant or drop the matter entirely.

However, on March 11 Lincoln changed the game by removing McClellan from overall command and granting Halleck's wish to direct operations in the West. Under the President's War Order No. 3, Lincoln ordered that "the two departments now under the respective commands of Generals Halleck and Hunter, together with so much of that under General Buell as lies west of a north and south line indefinitely drawn through Knoxville, Tenn., be consolidated and designated the Department of the Mississippi, and that until otherwise ordered Major-General Halleck have command of said department."[58]

Now that Halleck had what he wanted, he began to soften the criticism of his victorious general. On March 13 the new department commander restored Grant to power and ordered him to Savannah.

> You cannot be relieved from your command. There is no good reason for it. I am certain that all which the authorities at Washington ask is that you enforce discipline and punish the disorderly. The power is in your hands; use it, and you will be sustained by all above you. Instead of

relieving you, I wish you as soon as your new army is in the field to assume the immediate command and lead it on to new victories.[59]

Smith was caught in the middle of the argument between Grant and Halleck. On one side was Grant, his superior officer and former student who respected and admired him, and on the other was Halleck, who had defended Smith from accusations and supported his promotion. Smith chose a middle ground in defending Grant and rationalizing that Halleck corrected the misunderstanding when he learned the facts. As Charles explained to Francis,

> The public are all astray about General Grant; his habits (drink) are unexceptionable; his absence during the engagement [Fort Donelson] to see Flag Officer Foote he explained to the satisfaction of General Halleck and his going to Nashville was perfectly proper if he thought fit to go. The reason why both Halleck and McClellan were down on him was they had no information from him for two weeks, although he always wrote once and sometimes twice or thrice a day, and sent daily reports of the strength of his force. Why these reports and letters were not received is not known, but the moment Halleck had Grant's explanation he was restored to command. Grant is a very modest person. From an old awe of me—he was one of my pupils from 1838 to 1844 [actually 1839 to 1842] (I think)—he dislikes to give me an order—and says I ought to be in his place. Fancy his surprise when he received no communication from General Halleck for two weeks after the fall of Donelson and then that ... telegram of bitterest rebuke.
>
> He showed it to me in utter astonishment, wondering the cause, as well he might.[60]

Grant was now "restored to command" and was "very grateful" to Halleck for "his interposition that had set me right with the government."[61] Halleck followed his telegram to Grant with a response to Thomas' inquiry. Halleck withdrew his complaints and softened his protests. The major general explained that Grant went to Nashville in response to Buell's request to have Smith's division sent to that city. Halleck believed that Grant "deemed it his duty to go there in person" and his actions were taken "from good intentions and from a desire to subserve the public interests." He also explained that the problems with Grant's forces at Fort Donelson were in violation of Grant's orders. Halleck concluded by reporting that all the "irregularities have now been remedied," and Grant has been directed to return to command.[62]

Sometime after the war, General Grant learned the truth about Halleck's campaign.

> General Halleck unquestionably deemed General C. F. Smith a much fitter officer for the command of all the forces in the military district than I was, and, to render him available for such command, desired his promotion to antedate mine and those of the other division commanders. It is probable that the general opinion was that Smith's long services in the army and distinguished deeds rendered him the more proper person for such a command. Indeed I was rather inclined to this opinion myself at that time, and would have served as faithfully under Smith as he had done under me. But this did not justify the dispatches which General Halleck sent to Washington, or his subsequent concealment of them from me when pretending to explain the action of my superiors.[63]

Grant noted that when he arrived in Savannah, Smith "was delighted to see me and was unhesitating in his denunciation of the treatment I had received."[64]

25. "Hold his position"

"I raked the whole of my right leg"

After Smith reached Savannah, he received a telegram from Grant urging him to "send back steamers as rapidly as possible, to enable me to forward [the] balance of troops."[1] On the morning of March 12, Smith directed General Sherman "to cut the Charleston and Memphis Railroad at a point between Corinth and Iuka." Sherman planned "to run up the river nearly to Eastport and Chickasaw, which is fortified; then to drop back to Tyler's Landing, above the mouth of Yellow Creek; there to disembark the whole command, march back about 7 miles on the road to Iuka, then halt, and send the cavalry to the railroad, about 7 miles off, destroy it, and then return to the boats."[2]

General Wallace reached Savannah that day aboard the *John J. Roe* at the head of a flotilla of ships carrying his division. The shoreline was cluttered with full and empty steamboats. On the Savannah side of the river Wallace noticed a fine mansion on a bluff overlooking the river that was flying the Union flag. The home belonged to a loyal Union man named W. H. Cherry. Although Mrs. Cherry was an ardent Southerner, her husband granted the use of the house to General Smith as his headquarters and residence.[3] However, Smith chose to remain on board the *Continental* to coordinate the disposition of arriving troops.

Just after sundown, Smith took a yawl to visit Wallace. Smith startled Wallace as he walked into his cabin.

"I am on business," Smith announced. "Are you alone?"

The cabin was immediately cleared for the two generals.

Smith asked Wallace for a map which Wallace quickly provided. Smith unfolded it and continued:

"Down in Paducah, you may remember, I once told you of Corinth as a place of strategic importance. Well, I think we are going there now just as quick as we can dispose of a couple of preliminaries. There are not more than 10,000 Confederates keeping it. Give me your attention."

"I am following you," Wallace acknowledged.

"One of the preliminaries is to cut the railroad connecting Corinth and Columbus on the north; the other is to cut the railroad from Corinth to Decatur and Chattanooga on the east. This last I have given to Sherman; the first is to be yours, and for that you are to go on up to Crump's Landing, four miles above Savannah, from which there is a road, said to be good, leading to Purdy."

Smith bent over the map and traced the road with his finger.

"You understand? Very well. Now, how to do the thing. I might have sent you an order, and left you to your own devices, but knowing it [is] a business new to you, I have come over to try and help you with suggestions."[4]

The Cherry Mansion (author's photograph).

Wallace thanked Smith, who continued with his careful instructions. Smith explained that Wallace should send his cavalry ahead to disable the rail line. He told Wallace to select a place at a convenient distance and remain there with his infantry to support his cavalry. The location could also be used as a rallying point in case of trouble. Smith cautioned Wallace that Confederate General Cheatham was seen at Pittsburg Landing, about six miles above Crump's Landing with a force reported to be larger than Wallace's division.

"But here," Smith said, "see this creek—Snake Creek. It is out of its banks, and Cheatham [is] on the other side with but one bridge by which he can possibly get at you—and that"—he looked at Wallace with a twinkle in his eye—"is called Wallace's Bridge. You must keep it well watched."

After Smith finished his instructions, Wallace accompanied him down to the small boat waiting to ferry Smith back to his headquarters. They shook hands and said goodnight. As Smith stooped to get into the yawl, he lost balance in the darkness, fell forward, and scraped his leg on the sharp edge of a seat. It was a deep laceration all the way to the bone on the shin of his right leg from the ankle to the knee. One of the boatmen helped lift the general onto the seat. Wallace saw it was "a frightful hurt" and urged Smith to stay that night and be cared for by his surgeon.

Through his clenched teeth, Smith groaned: "No—too much business."

As they rowed away into the darkness, Smith shouted a "Good-night" to Wallace and returned to his cabin on the *Continental* where he received medical attention.[5]

On March 13 Charles paused from his work to reply to a letter from Francis. He was still on board the *Continental* confined to his cabin and living like a "Prince on a steamer as my headquarters with a ponderous staff." Grant and McClellan had sent officers to help Smith. He told Francis he had 30,000 men at Savannah, which was "far in the interior say 200 miles above Ft. Henry." There were 10,000 more troops at Fort Henry waiting for transportation, and General Halleck was sending a large force from Missouri. Charles thought, "Halleck will be this way before long." Charles said he had a "delicate mission to accomplish to do a certain thing which requires fighting; without fighting on a large scale."[6]

Back in St. Louis, Halleck had no information on the progress of the expeditionary force and asked Grant to inform him "as early as possible where General Smith has landed."[7] The following day, Grant received a note from Smith and wired Halleck that Smith had debarked at Savannah. Grant suggested that the "landing there would indicate fortifications and the enemy in force above."[8]

Later on March 14, Grant received Smith's report and manpower statement by a steamer returning to Fort Henry and telegraphed Halleck. Smith's men had discovered a battery of a dozen or more pieces at Eastport. The expedition commander thought that Corinth would "have to be let alone for the present" but planned to learn more and send information on the next steamer. Smith also told Grant that he was sending an expedition from Pittsburg Landing toward the east of Corinth.[9]

> Please say to the Genl. [Grant] that I arrived here at noon two days since. With the view of returning steamers I have ordered Genl. McClernand's division to disembark and occupy this place [Savannah]. I sent yesterday Genl. Wallace's division to Crump's landing about 3½ miles above on the west bank to make a dash with a battalion of Cavalry (4 troops) south of Purdy to cut the communication. It is about 17 miles. The cavalry will be supported by Infantry, Arty [Artillery] and a Gun Boat. I expect to hear from this force tonight. I went up yesterday with the gun boat Tyler to look at Pittsburgh [Pittsburg Landing] on the west bank from whence the road leads directly to Corinth say 19 miles off. It is a good place to hold and from whence to operate. On the same day the gun boats went up and engaged the enemies batteries at Eastport, some dozen guns or more—two of them rifled 24 or 32 pounders—to draw their fire and convey the impression that that was the point of attack. I am unable to speak of the strength of the enemy at Corinth, but shall know more tonight. I am organizing an expedition from Pittsburgh [Pittsburg Landing] in the direction of Corinth but east of it. In view of the restrictive nature of my orders I think that I shall have to cut the rails as I have indicated and [leave] Corinth alone.[10]

Smith was pleased to report that Wallace's "expedition to injure the Railway Communication north of Purdy has been successful." He explained that he was sending Sherman on an "expedition on the same principle ... to operate between Corinth and Eastport, at a point about 12 miles from the river, in the neighborhood of Burrsville." The general regretted that he had been unable to obtain the desired information on the strength of the enemy, but the Confederates appeared to have 50,000 to 60,000 men "from Jackson through Corinth, Eastport and farther East." With the main Rebel force at Corinth, Smith decided not to try to cut communications there and risk a major engagement. A more distressing situation was the increasing number of sick men. The hospital ship, *Memphis*, was nearly full of soldiers suffering with diarrhea caused by drinking water from the Tennessee River. Smith ordered the steamer "to get rid of her freight and then to return" to Fort Henry with the ailing soldiers.[11]

Smith spent the next several days limping from chair to chair in his cabin. Despite his pain, he continued to assemble forces for the attack on Corinth and order reconnaissance missions to learn the enemy's positions and strengths. On March 14, Charles informed his wife and daughter about the extent of his injury. He complained, "Do you know I fear I shall not be able to take the field soon, not being able to sit a horse or in fact walk about the cabin of this steamer without great pain." He remarked on the praise being showered on him.

It is so natural that you all join me the laudations of others on me that I will not say you are all a little crazy, but it reads like it. People in this world usually set up their idols and then knock them down. I have so just an appreciation of human nature in this respect that I do not feel at all elated by the newspaper compliments, a few of which only I have seen.
Thank the dear children for their notes. They must not be too elated at Papa's success.[12]

Smith believed that Grant would come up the river soon to take charge. He asked the commander of the District of West Tennessee for instructions on troop dispositions.

I would be glad to have the General's direction in regard to sending back steamers. Genl. McClernand's division, as I have heretofore reported, occupies this place and its surroundings, hence I have been enabled to send back the transports of his command. Am I to disembark more troops? or keep them in hand for expeditions? I have now Wallace's division with its transportation at Crumps landing about 3½ miles up; Hurlbut's division with its transportation at Pittsburgh some 9 miles up watching Genl. Cheatham and to prevent his moving against Genl. Sherman, as Sherman's division with its transportation is at Cooks landing still farther up (see my letter of yesterday). This is all [illegible] of keeping the transports with the troops. The gunboats are with Sherman and Hurlbut, I have not had time to hear from Sherman's attempt, indeed he did not. I suppose arrive at his point of landing before last night; and as it rained hard all day yesterday and partly during the night I think he cannot make much progress during the day. One other point in the matter of transportation occurs to me. There are no buildings in the town suitable for storing our supplies hence they are kept afloat and the steamer remains as a matter of course.[13]

Grant sent a second telegram on March 15, reporting that Wallace's expedition had cut one-half mile of railroad trestle north of Purdy and had located a Rebel force of from 12,000 to 18,000 men on his left.[14] Halleck responded by reminding Grant that his instructions "not to advance so as to bring on an engagement must be strictly obeyed." Halleck ordered Grant to have Smith "hold his position without exposing himself by detachments until we can strongly re-enforce him." He explained that General Buell was moving toward Savannah and hoped to send 10,000 or 15,000 more troops from Missouri. Lastly, he cautioned Grant: "We must strike no blow until we are strong enough to admit no doubt of the result."[15]

The directive was designed to keep Grant in check, for as soon as Grant rejoined his army at Savannah he began to drop hints about advancing on Corinth. This was a familiar pattern, and Halleck tried to make sure that his eager subordinate waited for orders. Grant reported that the Confederate army gathering in Corinth was in low spirits and predicted that the town would be easier to capture than Fort Donelson. Halleck told him to stay where he was, wait for Buell, and fortify before moving forward. These instructions limited reconnaissance south of the Union encampment to learn more about Confederate deployment, strength, and intentions.[16]

General Halleck encouraged Buell to move his "forces by land to the Tennessee as rapidly as possible." Halleck wired Buell in Nashville that 60,000 Rebel troops were at Eastport and Corinth. He told Buell to rendezvous in Savannah where Grant was concentrating the Army of the Tennessee[17] and warned Buell to direct his "march on that point, so that the enemy cannot get between us" because the Confederates still controlled Island No. 10.[18]

"I have just arrived"

Shortly after Smith and Sherman arrived in Savannah, they decided to disembark the waiting and arriving troop ships on the west bank of the Tennessee River. The generals selected a relatively open area near Pittsburg Landing as an ideal place to land forces and assemble an army for the planned twenty-mile advance against Corinth, Mississippi. The landing was located about midway down a twelve-mile loop in the Tennessee River. The place, which was named for "Pitts" Tucker who ran a tavern on the site before the war, contained one or two log cabins located on a forty to fifty-foot high bluff overlooking the river.[19] The plateau from Pittsburg Landing provided dry ground and enough room for an entire army to camp. The landing provided easy access to the Union line of supply via Tennessee River, and the bluff was high enough to be above the spring floodwaters. Owl Creek protected its western flank, Lick Creek formed its southern border, and the Tennessee River guarded the eastern access. Another steamboat landing, Crump's Landing, was six miles downriver, where the loop turned eastward toward Savannah.

Smith sent two brigades under General Steven A. Hurlbut to occupy Pittsburg Landing on March 14 and four brigades under General Sherman on the river past the landing to attack the Memphis & Charleston Railroad. Unfortunately, the spring floods forced Sherman to abandon the mission, and Smith had them join Hurlbut at Pittsburg Landing on March 15. Smith ordered Sherman to move out into the countryside and secure an area large enough to encamp the whole army.

With his injured leg, Smith was especially happy to have Grant returned to command.

> I wrote you yesterday to say how glad I was to find from your letter of the 11th, that you were to resume your old command from which you so unceremoniously stricken down. I greatly fear your coming here will be a matter of necessity in consequence of my lameness. I cannot mount a horse. I hope for the best but it with great difficulty that I limp thro' the cabin from one chair to another.[20]

Bad news greeted Grant when he arrived in Savannah on March 17. Smith was still suffering from his injured leg, Sherman's expedition to Yellow Creek was a failure, and the number of men on the sick list was growing daily. Sherman said it was impossible to "cut the Charleston and Memphis road, without a general or serious engagement" because the ground was "well watched and a dash cannot be made."[21]

Grant forwarded Sherman's report on the expedition and Smith's latest intelligence on enemy strength to Halleck. One of Smith's scouts reported the Rebels were "very strong from Chickasaw to Corinth" with 150,000 troops of which 50,000 were at Corinth. Grant thought the number was "very much exaggerated," but the news that General Johnston was at Corinth was "very much against my expectations." Grant advised Halleck that the country was so flooded that "but few roads can be traveled, and all are most impassable for artillery." He hoped that a change in the weather and a few dry days would improve the situation.[22]

As soon as Grant arrived at the front, he acquainted himself with the army's location. Grant trusted the site selected by Smith and Sherman and continued to assemble his forces at Pittsburg Landing. Before visiting the site, he wrote Halleck, "Having full faith in the judgment of General Smith who located the present point of debarkation. I do not expect any change will be made."[23] He established his headquarters at Savannah and waited for the arrival of General Buell's 35,000-man Army of the Ohio. Grant expected Buell's forces to reach Savannah soon because the lead columns were just sixty miles away on March 20. When the two armies joined at Pittsburg Landing, General Halleck planned to assume command of the combined force and lead the offensive against General Johnston's forces protecting the railroad junction at Corinth.

Grant assumed the Confederates would wait patiently at Corinth for the Union attack. He was so anxious to move forward that he did not consider what might happen if the Confederates struck first. He agreed with Sherman and Smith's decision not to entrench and decided that training the new regiments would be a better use of the time. This was a significant concern because Sherman's and Prentiss's raw recruits had never been in combat.

The new soldiers might hide behind entrenchments and run if their line was breached. Grant and Smith's experience with volunteers during the Mexican War suggested that recruits were unreliable in their first battle. With his offensive mindset and Halleck's warnings not to bring on a general engagement, Grant was reluctant to send scouting patrols south of Lick Creek. Instead, Grant relied on second hand reports and rumors. Meanwhile, the Army of the Ohio was making slow progress to Savannah. Halleck tried to hurry Buell along while he restrained Grant from attacking Corinth. Grant thought that a Confederate offensive would try to split the two armies and Crump's Landing was the likely place. He decided to keep Wallace's division at the landing. However, Halleck and Grant believed that the Rebels would remain on the defensive because of the rumored fragile morale of their army.

Grant continued training the raw recruits at Pittsburg Landing. In spite of the delays, untested soldiers, and recent problems with Halleck, the commander of the Army of the Tennessee was optimistic. "What you may look for is hard to say, possibly a big fight," he told Julia. "I have already been in so many that it begins to feel like home to me." As March ended, he said, "A big fight may be looked for someplace before a great while which it appears to me will be the last in the West."[24]

Hindsight following the battle of Shiloh suggested that Grant should have built entrenchments. However, before the Rebel attack, the Union commanders believed earthworks were an unnecessary luxury. Instead of fearing an attack, General Smith invited an assault. "By God," Smith declared, "I ask nothing better than to have the Rebels to come out and attack us! We can whip them to hell. Our men suppose we have come here to fight, and if we begin to spade it will make them think we fear the enemy." When Grant arrived, he expected to march on Corinth in a few days when Buell's forces reached Pittsburg Landing. Under this assumption, Grant "had no expectation of needing fortifications, though this subject was taken into consideration." Grant "had no idea that the enemy would leave strong entrenchments to take the initiative when he knew he would be attacked where he was if he remained."[25] Sherman seemed to be the only officer concerned and warned, "We are in danger here." He did not caution Grant because "oh, they'd call me crazy again." Eventually, even Sherman became complacent and assured Grant that he did not expect "anything like an attack."[26]

With Grant shuttling back and forth between Savannah and Pittsburg Landing, Sherman quickly took charge of the troops around the landing. Sherman sent reconnaissance parties to determine the location of Rebel forces.[27] Buell's forces continued their slow movement to Savannah. On March 18 Buell suggested that General Smith "had better commence the telegraph line to meet us."[28] Smith's veteran Second Division with 8,500 troops arrived on March 19 and was placed in reserve about a mile north of Pittsburg Landing. Grant's army at Pittsburg Landing had grown to 34,500 men and 102 guns.[29]

In a rare criticism of General Smith, Grant took exception to his subordinate's failure to obey Halleck's order for a gunboat patrol on the Tennessee. Grant told Halleck that he would "go in person ... to execute your perfectly-feasible order."[30]

On March 20 Grant started organizing the advance on Corinth. He instructed Smith to "hold all the command at Pittsburg subject to marching orders at any time."[31] Three days later, Grant approved Smith's plans to move the army south to Pea Ridge and occupy and partially fortify the position.[32] Grant became concerned about the delays and told Smith, "I am clearly of the opinion that the enemy are gathering strength at Corinth quite as rapidly as we are here, and the sooner we attack the easier will be the task of taking the place."[33]

Over the next week, Grant consolidated his forces and organized his divisions. In Special Orders No. 36 he designated Smith to command Pittsburg Landing "during the continuance of headquarters of the district at this place [Savannah] or until properly relieved." Grant assigned General Prentiss to command the unattached troops at Pittsburg Landing, which would eventually be formed into brigades in the new Sixth Division.[34]

Grant's appointment of Smith to the command at Pittsburg Landing was more form than substance. Smith's injury was taking its toll, and he was now confined to bed at the Cherry Mansion.

> In jumping into a yawl I raked the whole of [my] right leg—the shin and calf—with the seat. The doctor fears injury to the bone. Although it is greatly better I still limp about the cabin of the steamer and cannot put on a boot. Super-added and immediately after I was prostrated by sickness, against which I had been fighting ever since Ft. Donelson. But I had no time to be sick. At length I had to go bed. Now I am well tho' weak.[35]

General McClernand objected to Smith being placed in charge and complained that the order was "evidently founded upon the idea that Genl Smith is my senior, and hence ranks me." McClernand noted that both men were major generals and said he would only recognize Smith as his superior if his "promotion gives him seniority." McClernand said if Smith's promotion did not make him senior, "I cannot recognize him as my superior in rank or command; and no earthly power can make me do so." The general demanded "the legitimate, determinate facts, upon which it is founded." He said that until the issue is resolved, he would "consider, and execute, such orders as may come from Genl Smith, as included within your own, and coming from yourself; he being the official medium through whom you think proper to convey them to me." The irate officer told Grant: "I say this with all respect for General Smith, whom I regard as a gallant, experienced, and skillful commander, and whom under proper circumstances, if left to me, I would probably choose, as such."[36] Grant had no time for such squabbling and referred the issue to General Halleck. Halleck said he knew "nothing about it, except that General McClellan directed me to place General Smith in command of the expedition until you [Grant] were ordered to join it." Halleck refused to deal with the issue and passed it on to the Secretary of War for resolution.[37]

News of Smith's nomination and expected Senate approval to major general began to circulate among the Union camps. Captain Rziha sent his "sincerest congratulations to your honors [sic] promotion, as Major General of the U.S. Army." He thanked Smith "for all the kindness you have shown me and my best wishes for my most honored Commander's personal welfare."[38] Smith's friend, Captain Seth L. Phelps, sent his best wishes from the USS *Benton* near Island No. 10. Phelps said it gave him "unqualified pleasure." The captain said the promotion was "pleasing beyond the mere gratification of my friendly feelings as it is a triumph of right truth of worth & professional skill and gallantry over favoritism and political corruption of the vilest and meanest type, and over secret stabbing through the means of a licentious press." He said, "It gives a consolatory hope that all of honor is not yet dead among us as a people."

> I believe that on the Cumberland victory or defeat hung upon your safety at a time when your life—to use an assurance expression—was not worth a minute's purchase. The nation believes it—that part of it whose belief is worth anything. We hope that in the decisive battle to be fought by your forces ere long you will be where your campaign turns the tide of battle in our favor.

Phelps ended his letter with a hopeful prediction. "I think your next battle will settle the war if you soundly thrash Mr. Beauregard and, as I believe you will."[39]

Major George Mason praised his commander, "Beloved by his whole command, he rivaled the commanding general himself in the confidence of his men. It was even said that Grant relied on him for advice and counsel."[40]

26. "Does not set easy on me yet"

"They may spring upon us suddenly"

Smith's condition continued to decline, forcing Grant to consider replacing his most experienced division commander. On March 22 Grant discussed the situation with Brigadier General William H. L. Wallace. The forty-one-year-old former Illinois lawyer had just received his brigadier's commission the previous day.[1]

Events swirled around Smith after his March 14 letter to Francis. As Grant's army at Pittsburg Landing and Savannah waited for Buell's forces to arrive, Smith tried to perform his duties while battling infection and fever on board the *Continental*, but he finally asked Sherman to "give the necessary directions for encamping the troops as they arrive."[2] On March 27, Charles revealed to Francis just how sick he had been.

> Since I last wrote to you, on the 15th [14th] I believe, I have been quite sick. From going into an open barn of a house after the fall of Ft. Donelson I took a shocking cold, and for several weeks after that I was battling against disease—fever, [illegible], etc., yet having no time to be sick. But I was obliged to yield at last. For a week I was very sick, and this joined the pain of my injured leg did not make me the most amiable of mortals. Still I was compelled to be up, more or less to attend to duty. My general health is restored but the injury to my leg is more severe than was at first anticipated. The injury is deeply seated in the bone, which the doctors fears may exfoliate.[3] I shall have to ride to the battlefield in an ambulance; for although I can limp about the cabin of the steamer, in which I make my headquarters, I cannot stand up for more than a few minutes without great pain and damage to the aggrieved part. Of course sitting on a horse is the same thing but pain or no pain I'll have to do it.[4]

Smith managed to limp his way onto the gunboat *Tyler* to travel up the river thirty-five miles for a personal reconnaissance of a Rebel battery at Chickasaw. The ship got within range and fired several shells at them but "elicited no reply." Then just as the gunboat was turning around, two one-gun batteries opened fire. For a few moments, they "had quite a lively time of it." The shots flew all around them, but none hit the ship. The *Tyler* returned the fire briefly and, after learning about the fortifications, the gunboat backed out gracefully. Smith thought, "The enemy wanted to beguile us as far up as possible to get us in a bad scrape."[5]

The anticipated arrival of Buell's army from Nashville was delayed another week because they had to construct a bridge at Columbia. Smith told Francis that the combined force would contain 75,000–80,000 men and then it would be "old Nick take the hindmost!" He expected that Halleck would come to Pittsburg Landing to take personal charge of the march to Corinth. Charles believed the Rebel force was much larger and noted, "All the great rebel dignitaries in the military line were at Corinth many days since—Jeff Davis, Sydney Johnston, Bragg, Beauregard, and other lesser lights—but better soldiers." Charles concluded by cautioning Francis, "At the present moment I see no likelihood of active operation in large force for a week or more, but they may spring upon us suddenly."[6]

Smith continued to receive congratulations on his achievement at Fort Donelson and his promotion. He told Francis that he had received over fifty letters and copies of newspaper stories over the past three days.

> You have no idea of the strange variety of correspondents there is suddenly sprung upon me, many, nay most of them, entire strangers. Some want my autograph—a matter easily disposed of; some to recommend themselves or their friends for office; others inquiring after their friends in the true Irish style without giving me a clue of their whereabouts; others again to get their husbands discharged or to make sons, husbands or brothers send them a part of their pay. I try by means myself or staff to give all a civil answer, but [it] is a great bore.[7]

As sick as he was, Smith remained in command of the Second Division on March 29. His division was composed of three brigades of infantry and three batteries of artillery comprising 9,629 men of which 7,887 were present for duty. The First Brigade was led by Colonel Lauman, Second Brigade by Colonel McArthur, and Third Brigade by Colonel Thomas W. Sweeny. Major J. S. Cavender was in charge of three artillery batteries with twelve guns.[8]

On March 31 Grant decided to move the headquarters of the District of West Tennessee to Pittsburg Landing. In order to liaison with General Buell's forces, he maintained his command center at Savannah. The office would also serve as the official communications center because it provided easier access than Pittsburgh Landing[9] especially with wires being laid from Nashville to Savannah.[10] In General Orders No. 43, Grant transferred newly promoted Brigadier General J. G. Lauman from Smith's division to Hurlbut's Fourth Division. Grant assigned W. H. L. Wallace to command Lauman's First Brigade in the Second Division."[11]

The new regiments, which had been drilled since their arrival, were assigned to brigades and the brigades to divisions. Grant held a review on April 2 to evaluate their readiness, and the commander was pleased with their progress. Like Smith, Grant expected that Halleck would come to Pittsburg Landing to assume command of the two armies. Waiting for Buell's troops to arrive was trying Grant's patience. Every day that Buell was delayed meant that additional Rebel forces were gathering at Corinth. The Confederates were also getting restless, and there were reports of enemy troops conducting reconnaissance south of Pittsburg Landing. This increased Grant's concern that Wallace's division at Crump's Landing might be attacked. However, Grant's confidence increased when he heard rumors about the low morale of the Confederate troops, and he felt as "unconcerned about it as if nothing more than a review was to take place." He knew that "a terrible sacrifice of life must take place" and was "concerned for my army and their friends at home."[12]

On April 3[13] General Smith was moved from his cabin on the *Continental* to a second floor bedroom at the Cherry Mansion. Use of the home had been offered to Smith when he first landed at Savannah, but he chose to remain on the ship to coordinate troop placements and reconnaissance missions. When Grant arrived, he took advantage of the offer and selected the mansion for his headquarters and residence. The military shared the house with the Cherry family. Grant made his headquarters on the first floor and occupied a bedroom adjoining Smith's on the second floor. The commanding general divided his time between Pittsburg Landing and Savannah. Grant decided to remain on the other side of the river so he could coordinate troop disposition with General Buell when the Army of the Ohio arrived from Nashville.

It was now obvious that Smith was too sick to lead his division, and Grant placed General W. H. L. Wallace in command. Wallace told his wife about his new position. "I have just been ordered to assume command of General Smith's division, he being sick—I suppose this is merely temporary, but it may be otherwise. The division consists of fourteen regiments of infantry, four batteries, and two battalions of cavalry." Wallace accepted his new responsibility with a mixture of awe and fear. He thought it was "a compliment to be placed in such a command," however; he felt "a good deal of embarrassment in attempting to fill the place of such a man as General Smith." Wallace recognized the great responsibility he had been given and observed it "does not set easy on me yet."[14]

Grant visited Pittsburg Landing on April 4 to evaluate reports of enemy movements. His officers assured him that all was calm. As he rode back to the steamboat landing in a rainstorm, his horse slipped, tripped over a log, and fell. Grant was thrown to the ground and severely injured his ankle. He returned to the Cherry Mansion where he joined Smith in nursing non-combat injuries.[15]

That day Charles sent a troubling letter to Francis about his failing health.

Last Saturday a week ago tomorrow—my lame leg took as the Doctors phrased it an erysipeltic[16] turn and forced me to be mad with pain from whence I have not yet emerged. I write this on a book as best I may. From the effect of this pain which lasted some 18 hours, my previous general debility and the sickly atmosphere (I have been living on the river for many weeks) I just sank down and felt as if I did not care whether I lived or died. I eat nothing; I could not eat. I seemed to have no positive disease and I told the Doctor so.

He said I was right; it was purely the exhaustion of my vital energy produced by long continued exertion in a bad climate where I had been subjected to much exposure; [Illegible] too, to my period of life. That all I needed was rest, proper food and change of air to recover, having a constitution that ought then to carry me along for 20 years. He at once began to dose me with all sorts of poisons in the pill form: Strychnine to arouse the brain, Quinine for one purpose, Persulphate of Iron for another, Nitrate of Silver and Opium for another all of which pleasant little affairs I take repeatedly every day with decided benefit to my health and strength. Then too I came down here yesterday and occupy a fine airy room in Genl. Grant's quarters. I enjoy my meals and eat considerably but the leg is the drawback. As soon as the erysipelas made its appearance the Doctor told me he would have to make a long incision down to the bone, a painful affair. He brought the [sic] me Chloroform but I might as well have sniffed at a dry pocket handkerchief. I told him it was of no use that I always felt my nervous organization would resist the influence of Chloroform and that he might cut away. And cut away he did until I howled with pain. Some minor puncturings were performed and now my leg is although a great deal of trouble and will not allow me to get out of bed, decidedly on the mend. I think I might in a week be well enough to be carried about a battlefield on a hand litter.[17]

Charles explained that the federal forces were "powerful now in numbers" in artillery and cavalry, and he expected "within the next four or five days" they would "be largely increased by four divisions of Buell's army the advance of which is near the town." He said, "Bully Nelson," who commanded the advance, came to see him that morning. "This is a curious sort of metamorphosis, to convert a Lieut. of the Navy into a Brigr. [Brigadier] Genl. of the Army. Don't you remember him? He knows everybody." Charles thought that the army would begin "active operations in a week" and hoped his "poor leg will let me take part in the same. This writing on my back is very tiresome."[18]

"No fight at Pittsburg Landing"

On the eve of the battle of Shiloh, Smith's Second Division had changed from the one he led at Fort Donelson. The most significant change was that Smith was no longer in charge and his duties were now in the hands of General W. H. L. Wallace. At Donelson, Smith's division was composed of four brigades led by Colonel McArthur, Colonel Cook, Colonel Lauman, and Colonel Smith. The unit that Wallace directed at Shiloh was made up of three brigades, three cavalry, and four artillery companies. Colonel Tuttle, General McArthur, and Colonel Sweeney led the brigades. Although the division was reduced from its size in early February, it still contained a strong core of veterans trained by Smith.

On April 5 Grant received reports of skirmishes outside the Union lines at Pittsburg Landing. Sherman discounted these incidents in spite of his observation that "the rebel cavalry in our front was getting bolder and more saucy."[19] Sherman informed Grant "the enemy was in some considerable force at Pea Ridge" and had a "brigade of two regiments of infantry, one regiment of cavalry, and one battery of field artillery" five miles away.[20] Even with this knowledge, Sherman and Grant did not believe the Rebels were planning an attack on their camp but were waiting at Corinth. Grant wired Halleck that he had "scarcely the faintest idea of an attack (general one) being made upon us, but will be prepared should such a thing take place." If an attack should occur, Grant was confident that he could repel the assault until Buell arrived. He informed his commander that General Nelson's Fourth Division had reached Savannah.[21] As soon as the rest of Buell's army arrived, they would be transported across the river and assembled for the advance on Corinth.

Nelson told Grant that Buell would reach Savannah the following day. The Fourth Division commander was surprised Grant did not send him immediately to Pittsburg Landing. Instead, Grant "ordered him to move up the east bank of the river, to be in a position where he could be ferried over to Crump's landing or Pittsburg as occasion required."[22] Nelson asked Grant if he was concerned about a Confederate attack, and the commander nonchalantly replied that he had more troops than he did at Fort Donelson and that he could hold his own.[23] General Smith reassured Nelson, "They're [the enemy are] all back at Corinth, and, when our transportation arrives, we have got to go there and draw them out, as you would draw a badger out of a hole."[24]

Grant's friend, Colonel Jacob Ammen was in charge of the Tenth Brigade in Nelson's Division. Ammen's brigade encamped "on the southwest side of the town about half to three-fourths of a mile from the brick house on the river." About 3 p.m., Grant and Nelson came to Ammen's tent and Grant informed the officers, "There will be no fight at Pittsburgh Landing; we will have to go to Corinth, where the rebels are fortified." Grant said he would send boats to transport the men to Pittsburgh Landing on Monday or Tuesday. Because the brigade was scheduled to remain at Savannah for several days, Ammen made plans to review and inspect the troops the following day.[25]

On Sunday morning, Grant got up, reviewed his mail, and finalized plans to move his headquarters to Pittsburg Landing. It was essential to be on the other side of the river because the recent promotion of General McClernand to major general meant that a man he did not trust was now the senior commander at the encampment. As Grant began breakfast at six o'clock "heavy firing was heard in the direction of Pittsburg landing."[26] Grant rose from the table and announced, "Gentlemen, the ball is in motion. Let's be off." He ordered Nelson to move to the landing at Savannah and sent a message to Buell about the attack. "I have been looking for this, but did not believe the attack could be made before Monday or Tuesday." Grant and his staff quickly boarded the *Tigress*, left Savannah, and headed to Pittsburgh Landing.[27]

In Colonel Ammen's camp, his men were "putting their guns in order and brushing their uniforms for the parade." The peaceful morning was interrupted by the sounds of cannon from the direction of Pittsburg Landing. The noise did not surprise Ammen because cannon fire was often heard near a large army. However, soon "the reports are more numerous and the intervals less, and soon there is almost a continuous roar of artillery; distant, it is true, but as it continues and increases without any cessation, all conclude that a battle has commenced and is raging." Plans for the parade and review were abandoned, and the officers and men prepared to march. Nelson ordered Ammen "to be ready to proceed to the assistance of the Army of the Tennessee at Pittsburg Landing." After his command was ready to depart, Ammen went to the Cherry Mansion where he met Buell and Nelson. Both officers were anxiously waiting for the troop ships to return to Savannah from the battlefield.

Ammen learned that his friend General Smith was bedridden upstairs and was given permission to see him.

> He was in fine spirits; laughed at me for thinking that a great battle was raging; said it was only a skirmish of pickets, and that I was accustomed to small affairs. He said it was a large and hot picket skirmish. As there was no cessation, no diminution, and the sounds appeared to be coming nearer and growing more distinct, he said a part of the army might be engaged.

As the men were discussing the size of the engagement, an orderly came to the door and said Nelson wanted to see Ammen. The colonel said goodbye to Smith and joined Nelson, who was preparing to board his division on an arriving steamer.[28]

As the *Tigress* passed Wallace's command at Crump's Landing, Grant saw that Wallace was not under attack and ordered him to be ready to march at a moment's notice. Grant reached Pittsburg Landing at nine o'clock and found that "the attack on Pittsburg was unmistakable."[29] The situation was confusing and chaotic and the raw recruits were running away from the front lines to escape the Confederate onslaught. Some stragglers wandered about in a daze while others ran in a mad dash to the landing. Men huddled around the bluff above the landing waiting to leave on the next troopship. The entire army seemed to be in full retreat.

Grant moved quickly to stabilize his forces and halt the Rebel assault. He forwarded ammunition to the front, sent a staff officer to hurry Wallace's division to Pittsburg Landing, and tried to reorganize the terrified units into a line of defense. Grant met with his division commanders to assess the situation and encouraged the officers to hold their positions. Although Grant was concerned about the attack, he "bore no evidence of excitement or trepidation" and maintained his "coolness & bravery" under fire. Thankfully, the initial momentum of the attack had slowed because the Confederate troops stopped to salvage the Union camp and encountered resistance from veteran Union soldiers.[30]

Sherman and McClernand's divisions retreated across the Hamburg-Purdy Road. Prentiss' division had withdrawn to near an abandoned road that connected the Hamburg-Purdy and the Hamburg-Savannah roads. General W. H. L. Wallace's and General Hurlbut's divisions held the ground on either side of Prentiss' forces. Grant realized that his lines would continue to fall back, and he began organizing a defensive position and rallying point along the Pittsburg Landing Road. Grant directed Colonel Webster to form an artillery line in front of the road.

As resistance failed on the Union right, Grant observed that opposition had stiffened along the left side where Wallace, Prentiss, and Hurlbut held a strong defensive position along the Duncan's farm road connecting the Corinth and River roads.[31] Grant needed time for Sherman's and McClernand's forces to regroup, Lew Wallace's division to reach Pittsburg Landing, and Buell's army to cross the Tennessee River from Savannah. The fate of his army might depend on the bravery of the Union defenders along the sunken road.

27. "The devils own day"

"Gallantly stood their ground"

On April 6 General W. H. L. Wallace's Second Division awoke to begin, what they hoped would be, an uneventful Sunday morning. The men thought the sounds of firing in the distance were just more skirmishes between pickets. The Second Iowa Regiment had assembled for the morning inspection when the alarm sounded. Two men from the Fourteenth Iowa were washing dishes and wondered if the Rebels would leave them alone until their chore was finished. Then the men heard the beat of the long roll being from the Second Iowa camp. As they listened to the drumbeats and scrubbed the dishes, the alarm sounded in their own camp. In a few minutes, the two dishwashers were formed into a line and moving forward at the double-quick.[1]

Ann Wallace had just arrived at Pittsburg Landing and was planning to walk to her husband's headquarters when she heard firing. An officer on the steamer told her it was only an exchange between pickets. The captain offered to locate General Wallace to see how far it was to his headquarters. In less than thirty minutes, the officer returned with news that a major battle was beginning and that her husband had taken his division forward to meet the attacking Confederates.[2] The battle of Shiloh had begun, and C. F. Smith's former command was destined to play a critical role in the day's events.

General Wallace's division was composed of three brigades with 419 officers, 8,289 men, and twenty-four artillery pieces. Tuttle's First Brigade consisted of the Second, Seventh, Twelfth and Fourteenth Iowa Regiments. McArthur commanded the Second Brigade composed of the Ninth and Twelfth Illinois, Eighty-First Ohio, and Thirteenth and Fourteenth Missouri Regiments. Sweeney's Third Brigade contained the Eighth Iowa and the Seventh, Fiftieth, Fifty-Second, Fifty-Seventh and Fifty-Eighth Illinois Regiments. The division also included several unattached cavalry units and artillery batteries. Wallace marched his forces to the "sunken," abandoned road that ran diagonally from the northwest to the southeast and intersected the three roads from Corinth. The old wagon road ran from the Duncan Field where it met the road from Purdy then west across the Eastern Corinth Road to near a peach orchard where it ended at the Hamburg-Savannah Road.[3]

The Second Division was placed in the woods northeast along the road with Sweeny's Seventh Illinois and Fifty-Eighth Illinois at the front and to the left of the Eastern Corinth Road. The Fifty-Second Illinois and Fifty-Seventh Illinois were held in reserve. Colonel Tuttle's First Brigade formed across the Eastern Corinth Road with the Second, Seventh, Twelfth, and Fourteenth Iowa and the Eighth Iowa from Sweeny's Third Brigade. The Eighty-First Ohio was sent to secure the Snake Creek Bridge for Lew Wallace's Third Division. Prentiss' Sixth Division consisting of the Twenty-First Missouri, Eighteenth Missouri, Twelfth Michigan, Eighteenth Wisconsin, and Twenty-Third Missouri occupied the next portion along the "sunken" road. Regiments from Lauman's Third Brigade of Hurlbut's Fourth Division were next on the line. McArthur's Second Brigade was east of the Hamburg-Savannah Road with the Ninth Illinois and Twelfth Illinois from his brigade followed by the Fiftieth Illinois from Sweeny's Third Brigade.[4]

Tuttle formed his brigade and prepared to receive the Confederate attack. The brigade had only been in line a few moments before the enemy appeared and assaulted the left wing defended by the Twelfth and Fourteenth Iowa regiments. The Iowans "gallantly stood their ground and compelled the assailants to retire in confusion." The Confederates reformed and renewed the attack on Tuttle's line, but the First Brigade repulsed the assault. The Rebels advanced two more times, but each time they were "baffled and completely routed" by the rifle and cannon fire from the Union positions.[5]

The Seventh Iowa commanded by Colonel Parrott was in the center of the line formed by the First and Third Brigades. Around 9:00 a.m., the regiment advanced from the woods to the edge of Duncan Field.

> It then moved forward by the flank until within a short distance of the advancing rebels, where it was thrown into line of battle, being in heavy timber, when it advanced to the edge of a field, from which position we got a view of a portion of the rebel forces. I [Parrott] ordered my men to lie down and hold themselves in readiness to resist any attack, which they did, and remained in that position until ordered to fall back at about 5 p.m., holding the rebels in check and retaining every inch of ground it had gained in the morning, being all the time under a galling fire of canister, grape, and shell, which did considerable execution in our ranks, killing several of my men and wounding others.[6]

Around 8:30 a.m., the Fourteenth Iowa formed on the left of the Twelfth Iowa about 500 yards from the Rebel artillery. After the regiment was in line, the enemy guns began a severe fire on the Iowans. The Union batteries responded and an hour-long artillery duel started. The Confederate infantry appeared and advanced across the Duncan Field. Colonel W. T. Shaw of the Fourteenth Iowa realized that his brigade was not lined up parallel with the Confederate infantry and was "inclined to it at an angle of about 45 degrees" with the left portion "in advance." This exposed the Fourteenth's left flank to the enemy "some distance in advance of General Prentiss' line, upon which it should have rested, and about two hundred yards from his extreme right." Shaw discussed the alignment with Colonel Woods of the Twelfth Iowa, and both officers decided to move the Fourteenth and the left wing of the Twelfth back to bring their portion of the line parallel to the advancing enemy and in line with Prentiss' division. The adjustments still failed to connect with Prentiss' line and left an opening of about 200 yards. However, the realignment allowed the regiments to be partially protected by the ridge instead of being exposed to the enemy's artillery on top of it. The Rebels advanced steadily in two lines about 200 yards apart. Shaw ordered his men to lie down and hold their fire until the enemy was within thirty paces. When the men were ordered to fire, the Twelfth and Fourteenth "opened directly in their faces," destroyed the enemy's first line, and inflicted high casualties on Colonel Williams Stephens' Second Brigade. Only a few men returned the fire, and the survivors fled in every direction.[7]

After the Rebel attack was repulsed, the Fourteenth and the left wing of the Twelfth advanced toward the fleeing Confederates. The Iowans passed "almost without opposition over the ground which had been occupied by the [Rebel] first lines." The Union forces attacked and drove the second Rebel line back "for some distance" until Shaw recalled the men to protect his left flank. Shaw caustically noted, "No part of General Prentiss' division having advanced with us." The men of the Fourteenth and Twelfth returned to their former position in the line of battle. Colonel James L. Geddes, of the Eighth Iowa, moved his regiment

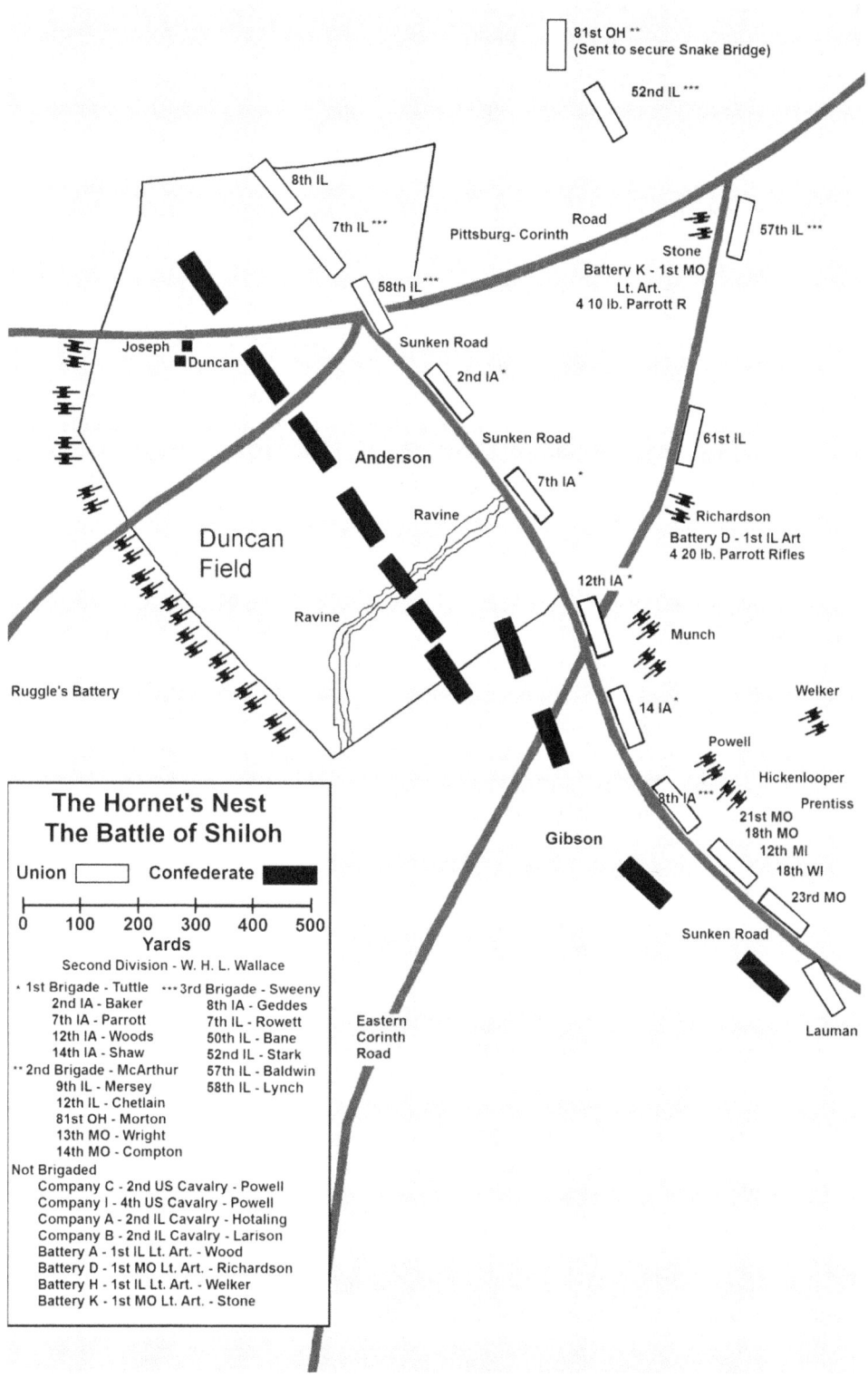

Units along the Sunken Road at Shiloh (author's diagram).

in line with and to the left of the Fourteenth and filled the gap between Shaw's regiment and the Twenty-First Missouri from Prentiss' division.[8]

> Colonel J. J. Woods' Twelfth Iowa Regiment was placed to the left of the Seventh Iowa and right of the Fourteenth Iowa regiments along the "sunken" road. Colonel Randall L. Gibson's First Brigade of Brigadier General Daniel Ruggles' Confederate First Division began the first of their three attacks on the Union strongpoint. Woods said that Gibson's men commenced "a bold attack on us, but met with a warm reception, and soon we repulsed him." The enemy forces assaulted the position repeatedly "trying vainly to drive us from our position." Woods boasted that the Rebels "failed to move us one inch from our position" as the regiment "repulsed every attack of the enemy and drove him back in confusion."[9]

The Confederates were disconcerted by the stiff resistance offered by the Union forces in the woods north of the abandoned wagon road. The Southerners felt as if they had run into a nest of stinging, bothersome insects and soon named the place "The Hornet's Nest." The Army of Mississippi stubbornly continued the infantry attacks throughout the morning and afternoon. According to Colonel Shaw, as the fighting continued, Prentiss' and Hurlbut's divisions "materially changed" their positions with their "left falling back repeatedly, until the line of these two divisions had swung around almost at right angles to us."[10]

Shaw saw "a large force of the enemy approaching from the left and front," and requested "a couple of brass[11] [bronze] 6-pounders." The guns were quickly moved into position in time to fire on the attacking Rebels. The Confederates "advanced with the most desperate bravery" and directed the brunt of their attack on the Eighth Iowa "by whom it was most gallantly borne." The fighting continued "with great severity" for about an hour, during which the Union troops repelled three separate Rebel assaults on the center of the line. Shaw believed with "good authority ... that the firm resistance of the center at that time was the chief means of saving our whole army from destruction."[12]

After the last assault, Colonel Geddes withdrew the Eighth Iowa a short distance from the line to care for his wounded and reform the regiment. When Shaw moved the Fourteenth to occupy the Eighth's "more important and exposed" position, the adjustment created an opening on his right between the Fourteenth and the Twelfth. After reforming his regiment, Geddes moved the Eighth Iowa to the right of Prentiss' forces and fought there the rest of the day.[13]

Around 3:00 p.m., General Beauregard assumed command of the Army of Mississippi following General Johnston's death. Beauregard ordered Ruggles' First Division to attack the left and center of the Hornet's Nest and General Braxton Bragg's Second Army Corps to assault the right. The failed attacks convinced Ruggles that the infantry needed additional artillery support to take the position. The general ordered all of the cannon on the army's left to be brought to the western side of the Duncan Field. From about 3:30 to 4:30 p.m., he assembled a collection of 12-pounder howitzers, 6-pounder smooth bored cannons, 12-pounder rifled cannons, and 3-inch rifles into a 52–53-gun battery[14] that stretched over 1,000 feet. Then the guns began to pound the Union position 500 yards away at a rate of 180 rounds per minute.[15]

The artillery bombardment forced the Union batteries to fall back. Hurlbut's Fourth Division was driven from the line and withdrew toward Pittsburg Landing. When General Grant visited the front, he instructed Prentiss and Wallace to hold the position "at all hazards." Grant desperately needed more time to establish a strong defensive line along the Pittsburgh Landing and Savannah-Hamburg roads.[16]

By this time, Tuttle reported that the Confederate attack on the left had forced Prentiss' line to swing around "to be almost parallel with ours [the Fourteenth Iowa Infantry], and back to back with us, about 150 yards in our rear, at our end of the two lines." In this deployment, a large body of the enemy from the left attacked Prentiss' forces. Wallace, Sweeney, and Tuttle continued to hold their positions. Tuttle reported, "It became evident that our forces on each side of us had given way, so as to give the enemy an opportunity of turning both our flanks."

> At this critical juncture General Wallace gave orders for my [Col. Tuttle's] whole brigade to fall back, which was done in good order. The Second and Seventh Regiments retired through a severe fire from both flanks and reformed, while the Twelfth and Fourteenth, who were delayed by their endeavors to save a battery which had been placed in their rear, were completely cut off and surrounded and were compelled to surrender.[17]

As Wallace moved through the crossfire, he "fell mortally wounded." With Wallace and McArthur wounded, Tuttle became the senior officer, assumed command, and rallied the remainder of his brigade.[18]

> The regiment, when ordered, fell back in good order and passed through a most galling flank fire from the enemy. When it gained cover of the timber it rallied in good style and helped to hold the enemy in check for some time, when it was again ordered to fall back upon the main river road, and there it bivouacked for the night exposed to a heavy rain of several hours' duration.[19]

The Twelfth and Fourteenth Iowa were unable to escape the enveloping Rebel forces. Colonel Woods noted that around 4 p.m., "it became evident, by the firing on our left, that the enemy were getting in our rear." An aide-de-camp directed Woods "to face to the rear and fall back" and informed him that he "would receive orders as to the position I was to occupy."

> The Second and Seventh Iowa had already gone to the rear, and on reaching the high ground between our position and General Hurlbut's headquarters we discovered that we were already surrounded by the enemy, caused by no fault of our own, but by the troops at a distance from us on our right and left giving way before the enemy. Seeing ourselves surrounded, we nevertheless opened a brisk fire on that portion of the enemy who blocked our passage to the Landing, who, after briskly returning our fire for a short time, fell back. A brisk fire from the enemy on our left (previous right) was going on at the same time. Seeing the enemy in front falling back, we attempted by a rapid movement to cut our way through, but the enemy on our left advanced rapidly, coming in behind us, pouring into our ranks a most destructive fire. The enemy in front faced about and opened on us at short range, the enemy in our rear still closing in on us rapidly.[20]

The Rebels had "already so closely surrounded us that their balls which missed our men took effect in their ranks beyond us." Woods reasoned that holding "out longer would have been to suffer complete annihilation" and "determined to surrender the regiment as prisoners of war."[21]

About 4:45 p.m., Tuttle ordered Shaw's Fourteenth Iowa "to about-face and proceed to engage the same body of the enemy." After Shaw moved his men, the regiment fought the enemy for "the third time that day." After less than half an hour, Shaw's Iowans repulsed them and made a short advance, which revealed the circumstances of their position. The center of the Confederate force had taken the ground that the regiment had previously defended and was now attacking the rear of their position. The right and left wings of the Confederate forces "had advanced so far as to form a junction between us [Fourteenth Iowa] and Pittsburg Landing." The situation was desperate because Prentiss had surrendered his command on the Fourteenth's left. This placed the Fourteenth "in advance of all that remained, but completely enclosed, receiving the enemy's fire from three directions."

> The regiment still kept its ranks unbroken and held its position facing the enemy, but the men were almost completely exhausted with a whole day of brave and steady fighting and many of them had spent their whole stock of ammunition. It was therefore useless to think of prolonging

a resistance which could only have wasted their lives to no purpose, and at about a quarter to six p.m. I surrendered them and myself prisoners of war.[22]

Tuttle formed a new defensive line composed of his brigade, the Thirteenth Iowa under Colonel Marcellus M. Crocker, Colonel Mersey's Ninth Illinois, the Twelfth Illinois commanded by Lieutenant Colonel Augustus L. Chetlain, and fragments of several other regiments. The defense "held the enemy in check until the line was formed that resisted the last charge just before dark of that day."[23]

The Second Division also performed well on other parts of the field. About 8:00 a.m. Sunday morning, Colonel Crafts J. Wright's Thirteenth Missouri, attached to General McArthur's Second Brigade, marched to a position on the Purdy Road about two miles from Pittsburg Landing and reported to General Sherman. The regiment formed a line of battle and "for some twenty minutes we were able to rally to ours fragments of three regiments and form them on the left of our own." About nine o'clock, Sherman ordered the regiment to the left of his division to resist the Rebel attack near the junction of the Hamburg-Purdy Road and Corinth Road. After they formed their battle line, the Thirteenth Missouri began "firing and advancing." Sherman's forces gradually gained the ground that had been lost. However, the Confederates renewed their advance with additional fresh troops and forced the Union troops to fall back to their initial position. The Thirteenth suffered severely during this engagement and lost ten of its officers and seventy-one of its enlisted men. Colonel Wright noted, "The officers and men did their whole duty, and had the regiment been supported we should have captured the battery which fired so destructively." After advancing and falling back several times, the regiment was finally forced to retire along with the rest of Sherman's command to the Hamburg-Savannah Road. The men bivouacked that night under a torrential rain, without fires, and tried to sleep in their bed of mud and water. They awoke the next morning "as weary ... as they had been the evening before."[24]

The Second Division lost 2,749 men during the battle with the First Brigade having 858 casualties, the Second Brigade 580, and the Third Brigade 1,247. Nearly half of the casualties were listed as captured or missing with the First Brigade suffering 676 and the Third Brigade 619. The division suffered 270 men killed and 1,173 wounded. In actions at the Hornet's Nest, the Second and Fourth Divisions lost a total 3,400 men, which was a third of the Army of the Tennessee's casualties.[25]

In spite of the heroics of General Wallace's Second Division,[26] General Grant reserved his praise for Prentiss' troops.

> The division of W. H. L. Wallace, as much from the disorder arising from changes of division and brigade commanders, under heavy fire, as from any other cause, had lost its organization and did not occupy a place in the line as a division. Prentiss' command was gone as a division, many of its members having been killed, wounded or captured; but it had rendered valiant services before its final dispersal, and had contributed a good share to the defence of Shiloh.[27]

Grant might not have recognized the division's contributions, but General Smith must have been pleased with the performance of his former command.

"Not beaten yet by a damn sight"

Following the collapse of the Hornet's Nest, Grant's forces rallied around the artillery batteries along the Pittsburg Landing Road. By the end of the day, Wallace was on the Hamburg-Savannah Road, Sherman and McClernand formed the right side of the Union defense, Hurlbut was positioned on the left, and Nelson's division anchored the extreme left near the landing. The gunships USS *Tyler* and *Lexington* were up river from Pittsburg Landing.[28]

Any hope the Confederates had of driving Grant's forces into the river faded with the cannon fire from Colonel Webster's batteries in front of the Pittsburg Landing Road, shells from the Union gunships, and rough terrain between Dill Branch and Pittsburg Landing. Among those batteries destroying the Confederate attack were three from the Second Division: Captain Frederick Welker's Battery H First Illinois Light Artillery, Captain Henry Richardson's Battery D First Missouri Light Artillery, and Captain George Stone's Battery K First Missouri Light Artillery. Even with their division badly mauled from the day's fighting, the Second still managed to play an important role in the Union defense.[29]

The Confederate attack was over, and both sides anticipated that the following morning would bring success and destruction of the opponent's forces. Behind his line, Grant considered the situation and declared he was "not beaten yet by a damn sight." Unfazed by the near disaster, Grant began planning for the next day's battle. "They can't force our lines around these batteries tonight," he remarked, "it is too late." He ordered Sherman to prepare to attack in the morning. Grant boldly remarked, "Tomorrow we shall attack them with fresh troops and drive them, of course." Grant had good reason to be confident with the arrival of the rest of Buell's army and Lew Wallace's Division. These fresh troops added about 25,000 men to the exhausted Union forces.[30]

Both of the armies spent an unpleasant night in the heavy rain trying to sleep while serenaded by the moans of the wounded and the dying and roused by the sounds of artillery fire. It was especially difficult for Grant who spent the night under a tree.[31] Sherman met Grant and stated the obvious: "Well, Grant, we've had the devil's own day, haven't we?" Grant was not interested in rehashing the day's events and replied, "Yes. Lick 'em tomorrow, though."[32]

Early on April 7 Grant and Buell ordered their men to advance. The Confederates fell back during the morning but rallied by midday along Sherman's and Prentiss' old campsites. By mid-afternoon, Beauregard had seen enough, and the Rebels began to withdraw. Late that afternoon, Grant sent his report to Halleck.

> Yesterday the rebels attacked us here with an overwhelming force, driving our troops in from their advanced position to near the Landing. General Wallace was immediately ordered up from Crump's Landing and in the evening one division of General Buell's army and General Buell in person arrived. During the night one other division arrived, and still another to-day. This morning, at the break of the day, I ordered an attack, which resulted in a fight which continued until late this afternoon, with severe loss on both sides, but a complete repulse of the enemy. I shall follow to-morrow far enough to see that no immediate renewal of an attack is contemplated.[33]

Grant considered pursuing the Confederate forces but decided his men were too exhausted. Although his troops were relatively fresh, Buell refused to take the initiative and order his men to chase Beauregard's Confederates. Grant was also aware that the cautious Halleck would not approve another engagement. The following day, Grant reported, "enemy badly routed and fleeing towards Corinth" pursued by cavalry supported by infantry.[34] Sherman's pursuit was unenthusiastic and ended a few miles south of Shiloh. The beaten Confederates returned unmolested to Corinth.[35]

"The battle of Armageddon came off"

The victorious commander issued General Orders No. 34 in which he congratulated "the troops who so gallantly maintained, repulsed, and routed a numerically superior force of the enemy, composed of the flower of the Southern Army, commanded by their ablest generals, and fought by them with all the desperation of despair." Grant said, in terms of "numbers engaged, no such contest ever took place on this continent; in importance of results, but few such have taken place in the history of the world." He made "special notice of the brave wounded and those killed upon the field" noting, "they have won a nation's gratitude and undying laurels, not to be forgotten by future generations, who will enjoy the blessings of the best government the sun ever shone upon, preserved by their valor."[36]

Following the death of General William Wallace, Grant placed General McArthur in acting command and assigned General Smith to the temporary "command of the post of Savannah."[37] On April 14 Brigadier General Thomas A. Davies was assigned command of the Second Division.[38] Any faint hope Smith had of regaining command of his troops was gone. His focus turned to getting well enough to return to the war.

As the casualty reports from Shiloh were published, Smith's family became concerned about him. On April 11 Fanny wrote to her Uncle William Mactier,

> Momma has just received your note and with it came a letter from Papa who has been very ill and judging from that he could not have been in this terrible battle for he had an operation performed on his leg which would keep him confined to his bed for two or three days & Papa says if the battle should take place in a week's time then he would be able to in a hand liter. His letter was written the 4th instant. We were in an awful state all yesterday, & Momma telegraphed to the Secretary of War to know the particulars. He did not know, but promised to find out by telegraphing to different points & then sending us word.[39]

From his bed in the Cherry Mansion, Charles described the Union victory to his wife.

> The battle of Armageddon came off at and in the vicinity of Pittsburg Landing on Sunday and Monday last. The place is by water only 9 miles from Pittsburg, whilst in a direct line to the battle ground which extended over several miles, it is at the nearest point only six.
> Imagine if it be possible my feelings—but no that is impossible— lying here bedridden with my injured leg and excessive bodily weakness listening for two days to the sounds of battle—the roar of artillery the rattle of muskets, without being able to take my proper part in it.
> The enemy made a judicious calculation though it failed. Their object was to attack and defeat Grant's force of about 60,000 with their 90,000 before the reinforcements under Genl. Buell (some 40,000).[40]

After the battle, General Halleck became concerned about the condition of the Union forces, and hurried to Pittsburg Landing to assume control. Halleck directed Grant to, "Avoid another battle if you can 'till all arrive, we shall then be able to beat them without fail." Halleck was very pleased with Sherman and recommended his promotion to major general. While Sherman was praised, Grant was criticized. The second-guessing and condemnation of the commander started immediately after publication of the casualty reports. The Army of the Tennessee lost 10,868 officers and enlisted men and the Army of the Ohio suffered 2,179 casualties. Someone had to be blamed for the losses, and Grant was the obvious choice. When Halleck arrived at Pittsburg Landing on April 11, he noted, "This army is undisciplined and very much disorganized." He warned Grant: "Immediate and active measures must be taken to put your command in condition to resist another attack by the enemy."[41]

Over the next several weeks, Grant and his division generals established measures to instill discipline and restore order to the encampment. Meanwhile, Halleck paused to contemplate the army's next move. Just as he had done after Fort Donelson, Halleck began a campaign to minimize Grant's role and criticize his conduct. The general soon complained that Grant did not comply "with the promptness of the commanders of the other Army

Corps." A soldier saw Halleck aboard a steamer, "pacing back and forth, and scolding in a loud and haughty manner" while Grant "sat there, demure, with red face, hat in lap, covered with the mud of the field, and undistinguishable from an orderly."[42]

After his experience following Fort Donelson, Grant was aware of the possible attacks and alerted Julia, "I will come in again for heaps of abuse from persons who were not here." He was correct about criticism from outsiders, but he also had detractors who fought at Shiloh. "Never was an Army more thoroughly & completely surprised," remarked one Union officer. While another officer admitted, "There can be no doubt of our army being surprised ... it was worse we were astonished." Throughout the country, relatives of the dead and wounded, citizens, politicians, and journalists discussed Grant's responsibility for the debacle.[43]

On April 23 Stanton telegraphed Halleck that Lincoln wanted to know "whether any neglect or misconduct of General Grant or any other officer contributed to the sad casualties that befell our forces on Sunday." Halleck might not have been happy with Grant, but by now, he had heard enough from Sherman and others, to dismiss newspaper reports of the battle. According to one of Grant's staff officers, the conduct of the battle and all the details met his entire approbations. Instead, Halleck blamed poor performances by some regimental officers, rejected reports that Grant had been surprised, and reminded Stanton that battles inevitably led to casualties.[44]

Although Grant claimed that his forces were not surprised, his defense indicated that he was not prepared as well as possible. Once more, in his eagerness to attack the enemy, he had overlooked the possibility that the enemy might attack him. In his memoirs, Grant described the battle as "more persistently misunderstood" than any other engagement during the rebellion.[45]

When not degrading Grant, Halleck made organizational changes to his forces. He consolidated Buell's Army of the Ohio with John Pope's Army of the Mississippi and placed Pope in command. Grant's Army of the Tennessee was merged with the division commanded by Major General George Thomas and placed under Thomas. McClernand received command of a reserve of three divisions. Grant was named second in command to Halleck so "Old Brains" could keep him under close observation and control.

> Although next to him in rank, and nominally in command of my old district and army, I was ignored as much as if I had been at the most distant point of territory within my jurisdiction; and although I was in command of all the troops engaged at Shiloh I was not permitted to see one of the reports of General Buell or his subordinates in that battle, until it was published by the war Department long after the event.[46]

Pope and Thomas were pleased with the new arrangement, but Buell and McClernand were outraged. Grant was dejected as well and complained to Halleck. Halleck charged him with ingratitude and replied, "For the past three months I have done everything in my power to ward off the attacks that were made upon you." Smith's health eliminated him from any command.[47] Halleck now had fifteen divisions with 120,000 men and 200 guns crawling towards Corinth.

28. "His great worth as a soldier and friend"

"Lost one of its brightest ornaments"

While Grant was battling for his career, Smith was fighting for his life. Smith failed to respond to the treatments and procedures administered by his friend, medical director Dr. Henry Hewitt. Confined to his bed, Smith prepared his last letter to his daughter. He indicated how a check from the government was to be distributed and cautioned Fanny not to "let a fashionable school inoculate you with false ideas of economy and of fashion in dress." Charles complained, "I am good for nothing—no appetite—my nervous power wanting. My health will be no better until I can get out of bed—out of the house. My leg is improving slowly."[1]

However, Smith's condition did not improve, and General Halleck allowed his dying general to return home. On April 16 Halleck directed Smith to "repair to Fort Columbus, New York Harbor, and from there report by letter to the Adjutant General of the Army for further orders."[2] Smith thanked Halleck for "permitting me to make the effort to recover my broken down health in a more congenial climate." Smith discussed when he might be leaving Savannah and asked Halleck for another favor.

> I do not know when I shall start, but probably not for several days. I am about to remind you of your promise to aid me in a certain way to add to my comfort. Next to the mere fact of change of climate producing beneficial results, I regard the presence and watchfulness of a skillful medical officer as of equal importance in my being able to start the journey. Allow me in this connection to name my friend as Medical Adviser Brigadier General H. S. Hewitt who is thoroughly conversant with my case in all its bearings and who apart from this has his strict attention to duty at all times and frequently under very discouraging circumstances has earned no little claim to indulgence. One special reason why I name him is, that he is now worn out and exhausted from duties professional and nonprofessional at the Battle of Pittsburg [Shiloh] and subsequently. See if you can [get] this accomplished and add another to my obligations to you.[3]

Halleck allowed Dr. Hewitt to continue to care for Smith for "as long as may be necessary." Halleck ordered the medical director to have a comfortable steamer available to take Smith to Cincinnati as soon as the general was ready to travel. General Cullum, writing on behalf of Halleck, hoped that Smith would "soon be able to join his friends in the East and once there be returned to health." Cullum said that they would miss Smith's "heroic sword" in the coming "desperate battle."[4]

Smith realized that he would not be returning soon to active duty and began arranging for his departure. On April 18 he informed Lieutenant J. F. Worth that he was "compelled to dispense with his services" as one of his aides-de-camp. Smith explained he was "relieved from duty with the troops" and was "about to proceed to the East on account of ill health."[5]

The following day Smith released Lieutenant John R. Miller from his staff.[6] In an unspecified Special Order, he instructed six privates from the Second Regiment Cavalry, who served as his orderlies, to return to duty with their companies. On April 21 Halleck agreed to allow Private John Sullivan to escort Smith to Fort Columbus.[7] Three days later Smith's service status was confirmed when he was notified that "no detail of body guard has been made, and probably none will be made."[8]

His separation from the war was assured, and the end of his military career was probable. From his bed on the second floor of the Cherry Mansion, he dictated a last letter to his commander and former student, Ulysses Grant.

> Savannah, Tenn.
> April 21st, 1862
> My dear Sir;
>   I shall leave here in a few days and doubt if the accidents of life shall throw us together again. But I trust you will believe to the fullest extent my sense of appreciation of the kindness and consideration I have ever received at your hands during our service together in this land of Egyptian darkness.[9]
>   I do not know that I should attempt to express myself thus if I did not think I perceived in the Newspaper press a studied attempt on the part of other politicians to strike down your well deserved honors. I do not know what your aspirations for the future may be; but there is evidently a class of political intriguers who joined to some of your friends, thinking you an available candidate for the Presidency, would seek to place you in that office. I must confess I think too well of you as a modest christian gentleman to run the gauntlet for the office; still success attend you in that or any other line you may desire.
>   Yours, most truly
>   C. F. Smith
>   Maj. Gen'l.[10]

Even on his sickbed, Smith remained Grant's mentor and teacher.

Next, Smith sent his thanks to Halleck.

> Savannah, Tenn.
> April 21st, 1862
> Major Genl. H. W. Halleck
> U.S. Army
> My dear General,
>   If I am not too feeble I trust in a few more days to move to the only climate where I have the least hope of recovery.
>   Before going I would again assure you of my sense of the kindness and consideration with which you have uniformly treated me, and more expressly for the manliness with which you stepped to the relief of my reputation in its days of more than Egyptian darkness; a thousand thanks for such conduct.
>   At my period of life I can scarcely anticipate the strength necessary for active service in many months, which is the subject of great regret that I cannot lend a helping hand to entirely crush this rebellion whose days are over or so evidently numbered.
>   God bless you,
>   C. F. Smith
>   Major General[11]

Instead of recovering sufficiently to travel, Smith's condition worsened. He observed his fifty-fifth birthday on his deathbed. On April 25 Grant sent Dr. John H. Brinton to Savannah to check on the general. Brinton found Smith "unconscious and moribund," and he died at 4 p.m. that afternoon.

Later that day, Halleck issued General Orders No. 21 to announce Smith's death.

Headquarters Dept. of the Miss
Pittsburgh Landing Tenn April 25, 1862
General Orders No. 21

    The Major General commanding announces, with deep regret, to the troops of this Department the death of Major General Chas. F. Smith who at 4 o'clock P.M. departed this life at Savannah on the Tennessee River.

    General Smith had been in the service of his country for more than Forty years, and had passed through all the Military Grades from Cadet to Major General. He has fought with distinction in nearly all the battles in Mexico, and by his gallantry and skill, had gained imperishable laurels at the seige [sic] of Fort Donelson.

    He combined the qualities of a faithful officer, an excellent disciplinarian, an able commander, and a modest and courteous gentleman.

    In his death the Army has lost one of its brightest ornaments, and the country a General whose place it will be difficult to supply.

    By Command of Maj. General Halleck
And C. Kemper
A. A. Gen'l[12]

General Grant mourned when he learned of Smith's death and declared, "A better soldier or truer man does not live." Grant's son, Frederick Dent Grant, said, "During the war father was saddened often over the death of many who had been associates either at West Point or in the army, but I think his greatest grief, and perhaps his greatest disappoint [sic], were occasioned by the accidental death of General Smith."[13] The following day, Grant informed Smith's widow of the general's death and of his "great worth as a soldier and friend."

Pittsburg Landing, Ten.
April 26th, 1862
Mrs. C. F. Smith
No. 191 East 4th St. New York

    It becomes my painful duty to announce to you the death of your lamented husband, Major General Charles F. Smith. He died at 4 o'clock P.M. yesterday at Savanna [sic] Tennessee.

In his death the nation has lost one of its most gallant and most able defenders.

    It was my fortune to have gone through West Point with the Gen. then Captain, as Commandant of Cadets, and to have served with him in all his battles in Mexico, and in this rebellion, and I can bear honest testimony to his great worth as a soldier and friend. Where an entire nation consoles with you in your bereavement no one can do so with more heartfelt grief than my self.

    Very truly yours,
U. S. Grant
Major General[14]

Smith's last letter deeply touched Grant. He sent the letter to Julia with instructions to save it. "Gen. Smith was my old Commandant whilst a Cadet and a better soldier or truer man does not live."[15]

    Halleck telegraphed Secretary of War Edwin Stanton about Smith's death. He noted that Smith's "remains have been sent to Saint Louis, where they will be buried with military honors." Halleck asked for permission to allow military honors at Pittsburg Landing,[16] and Stanton granted "Military honors be paid to his memory."[17] Halleck ordered a salute fired at every post and aboard every warship in the department.

    Several days later General Nelson wrote to Charles' brother-in-law, Navy Captain William Jeffers, expressing the grief felt by the armies at Shiloh.

The deplorable event of the death of Gen. C. F. Smith your brother in law, has cast a glom [sic] over the whole Army or rather the three armies now united here.

He was the Agamemnon of the Army of the Tennessee. Had he been in health, the awful battle of Shiloh need never have been fought and such a price would have been impossible with him in the field. The whole army mourns him.[18]

In his memoirs, Dr. Brinton related a late-night discussion between Dr. Hewitt and General Smith on theology and Purgatory.

The utility of such a state was stoutly challenged by the General. "Why, Doctor," he said, "do you mean to say that I shall ever go to Purgatory?" "General," was the answer, "the time will come when you will die, will go up to Heaven's gate, and claim admittance." 'Who comes?' St. Peter will demand. 'I, Charles F. Smith, Major General of the United States Army.' 'Have you passed a proper stage?' 'No, I come direct, and plead my mortal life and claims.' 'General,' will be St. Peter's answer, 'I know you well; I know your life; you have been a spotless citizen, an obedient son, a kind and loving father, an affectionate and tender husband; you have been a brave soldier, a true patriot, a gallant and distinguished general; but General, you, of all others, should know that discipline must be preserved, and that you must spend a few days in Purgatory.'" As this climax was reached, the General in surprise and admiration drew himself up against the door of the stateroom, which yielded to his weight, and he stumbled backwards, landing in his berth, muttering strangely, "So discipline must be preserved, and I must spend a few days in Purgatory; St. Peter thinks so."[19]

The Forgotten Soldier

General Smith's obituary notice in the April 27 edition of the *New York Times* praised him as "an officer of unsurpassed courage and skill." The article noted, "His loss at the present time will be a great blow to the army of the Southwest, by the men of which he was beloved as was no other commanding officer." The *Times* concluded, "The country and the army, as well as his own family, will suffer a great and deplorable loss in the death of this truly gallant and distinguished soldier."[20] *The Philadelphia Inquirer* said it best: "There was no better soldier in the army than General Smith."[21]

Smith's body was transported to Philadelphia for the military funeral and internment at Laurel Hill Cemetery. Smith's remains arrived in Philadelphia on the afternoon of Saturday May 3. They were received by military officials and escorted to Independence Hall where his body lay in state. On Monday, the Hall was opened for public viewing until the funeral on the following afternoon. The May 6 funeral was attended by "civil functionaries of the city, naval and army officers, and the military of Philadelphia, under the command of General Alfred Pleasanton." General Robert Anderson, Smith's friend and defender of Fort Sumter, served as a pallbearer.[22]

Smith's family was offered several plots for the general's burial including one in the graveyard attached to the Third Presbyterian Church. Charles' paternal and maternal grandfathers were buried in the cemetery, and he was baptized in the church.[23] Mrs. Smith decided to use the family lots 438 and 440 in section x at the Laurel Hill Cemetery. According to a diagram, the three plots were designated for Charles, Francis, and Margaret F. Smith. The perpetual care agreement indicated that there would be two marble headstones and three marble footstones.[24]

On April 8, 1862, the City Council of Philadelphia awarded a sword to General Smith for his achievement at Fort Donelson. The sword was presented to his family on January 21, 1863, in a private ceremony.

Presentation of a sword to the family of Major General Charles F. Smith," he began. "The presentation of the sword voted by the City Council several months since to Major General Charles

F. Smith, took place on Monday evening. The weapon was presented to the family. The affair was entirely private. It occurred at the house of the General's family. The presentation speech was made by Mayor Henry, supported by Mr. Theodore L. Cuyler of Select Council. His remarks were brief and to the point. The sword was received by Mrs. Smith, in person. She acknowledged, with much grace, the honor conferred upon the memory of her deceased husband, and offered her thanks.

The sword is a fine piece of workmanship. The hilt is covered in diamonds and finely set with enamel, amethysts and pearls. On one side of the scabbard is the national and municipal emblems; on the other, a representation of General Smith, leading the desperate charge for which he was noted. On a fine enameled band the following inscription, written by Mayor Henry, is attached:—

"The City of Philadelphia, April 8th, 1862, to Brig. General Charles Ferguson Smith, in recognition of his signal valor and success while upholding the flag of his country and advancing it to the overthrow of the Rebellion at the memorable capture of Fort Donelson."[25]

General Smith received several honors after his death. On May 30, 1863, Brigadier General J. G. Barnard, Chief Engineer of Defense of the Department of Washington, recommended that "the new fort immediately north of Fort De Kalb, and near the Potomac, be called Fort C. F. Smith, after the late Maj. Gen. C. F. Smith, who died at Savannah, Tenn., of disease contracted in the service, and who greatly distinguished himself at the battle of Fort Donelson."[26] The remains of the fort exist today as part of a Virginia State Park.[27]

A second Fort C. F. Smith served as a military post in the Powder River country in the Montana Territory. The fort was originally called Fort Ransom, but was renamed Fort C. F. Smith on August 12, 1866, in honor of General Smith. The post was established by Colonel Henry B. Carrington as part of a three-fort chain that included Fort Phil Kearny and Fort Reno. The posts were built to protect travelers on the Bozeman Trail that connected the Montana gold fields with the Oregon Trail. Fort C. F. Smith was composed of a 125-foot-square adobe and wood stockade and bastions. Two companies of the Eighteenth Infantry Regiment with 90 to 100 officers and men were stationed at Fort Smith during 1866. The garrison was increased to 400 men from the Twenty-Seventh Infantry in 1867. In the Hayfield Fight, a large party of Sioux attacked workers cutting hay near the fort

Fort C. F. Smith marker (author's photograph).

who were guarded by twenty soldiers, but the Indians were driven off. The army abandoned Fort C. F. Smith as a condition of the Fort Laramie Treaty of 1868.[28] Today, the only trace of the fort is a small flat stone on private property.

In November 1891, a portrait of Major General Smith was presented to The United States Military Academy. The painting was commissioned by Henry Carey Baird and executed by T. Henry Smith, a leading American portrait painter. According to Baird, "it is regarded by the family of General Smith, and by those friends who knew him towards the close of his life, as a faithful likeness as well as a fine composition."[29]

> Philadelphia, November 14, 1891
> Colonel John M. Wilson, U.S. Engineers
> Supt. U.S. Military Academy, West Point, N.Y.
>
> By express this day, I have the honor to forward to your address a portrait of Major General Charles Ferguson Smith, of which I beg your acceptance for the Military Academy.
>
> This picture has been painted for me by Mr. T. Henry Smith, of this city, who is one of the best portrait painters in the country: and it is regarded by the family of General Smith, and by those friends who knew him, towards the of his life, as a faithful likeness as well as a fine composition.
>
> Not only did the battles of Palo Alto, Resaca de a Palma, and Monterey, under General Taylor; the campaign of General Scott, in Mexico; and that of Fort Donelson, under General Grant, prove his prowess on many a well-fought field, but it has, I believe, long been conceded by those who were familiar with the personnel of the army, before the opening of the late war, that he was so nearly the ideal soldier as to be considered almost peerless.
>
> Accordingly it seems fitting that his portrait should have a place alongside of the portraits of the other great soldiers which adorn the walls of the United States Military Academy, whence they and he were graduated, and who, while serving their country so faithfully and well, conferred enduring honor on their alma mater.
>
> Trusting that the painting itself may in some slight degree be found worthy of so grand a subject, I am,
>
> Very respectfully, your obedient servant,
>
> Henry Carey Baird[30]

Colonel John M. Wilson thanked Baird for his "generosity in presenting the portrait of another of the distinguished officers of our army." Superintendent Wilson called Smith "the knightly soldier, the skilled leader of men, the chivalric and accomplished gentleman." Wilson quoted from the biographic sketch written by General George W. Cullum:

> On the twenty fifth of April 1862, this brave and noble paladin, who was intrepid as Ney, as chivalric as Murat,

Portrait of Smith given to West Point (courtesy West Point Museum Collection, U.S. Military Academy).

and as rock-fast as Macdonald, breathed his last. The Army could boast no better general. His stately and commanding presence inspired his soldiers with respect and almost fear. In his rigid disciple [discipline], though severe, he was always just, requiring no greater subordination from inferiors than he was ready to yield to superiors.

The call of duty was to him a magic sound for which he was always ready to make every sacrifice and endure any fatigue.

He was the very model of a soldier, calm, prudent, self-poised, yet in the hour of danger, bold almost to rashness.

Had he lived, he would have held a high niche in the temple of fame, whose doors were already opened to him.

Smith's portrait was placed in Grant Hall next to those of his colleagues: Grant, Sherman, Sheridan, and Meade.

Side by side, I believe, these noble soldiers are enjoying immortal life in that blessed land where peace and happiness are the rewards of those who are welcomed with the glorious words, "Well done, good and faithful servant, thou hast been faithful over a few thing, I will make thee ruler over many things, enter thou into the joy of thy Lord."[31]

Philadelphia's *Evening Telegraph* reported the event, but incorrectly referred to General Smith as "Baldy Smith," which was the nickname of General William Farrar Smith. Baird sent the article to Mr. Leslie Oliver, Smith's grandson, and said the error would be corrected and it would "be made quite clear who C. F. Smith was and what he did."[32]

Baird sent a copy of his correspondence with West Point to General George Cullum. Cullum thanked Baird saying, it was "a most grateful tribute from the son of an early graduate of the renowned institution which has produced such heroes as General Smith." Cullum referred Baird to his biographical sketch in the military academy register as a testament of his "high appreciation of the General as man and a soldier."[33]

Mrs. Smith and her family returned to their home in Fishkill Landing, New York. She was granted a pension on Jun 27, 1862 for her relief through an Act of Congress.[34] Mrs. Smith lived only four years after her husband and died on May 26, 1866, in Philadelphia and was buried in the family plot at Laurel Hill Cemetery.[35] Shortly after her death, her son, Allen, was made a 2nd lieutenant at the request of General Grant. Grant's letter to Edwin Stanton asked for the position "as due to the memory of his father Maj. Gen. C. F. Smith, who died in Savannah, Tenn. in 1863 [actually 1862]." Grant based his request on the recent death of Mrs. Smith, which left Allen and his sisters "full orphans to get through the world almost destitute of means." After obtaining Allen's commission, General Grant sent the following note to Miss Fanny Smith:

Washington, D.C.
July 21st, 1866
My Dear Miss Smith,

I am very happy to be able to inform you that I have this day succeeded in getting the order for your brother Allen's appointment of 2d Lieut. in the Army. I need scarcely assure you of the great pleasure it affords me to be able to serve in any way within my power the family of one who I so highly respected, I might say loved, as your father. My great respect for him commenced when he was Commandant of Cadets and I a plebe. This respect increased as I knew him better in later years.

My very kindest regards for yourself and assurances that it will always afford me the greatest pleasure to have you call on me for anything within my control to grant.

Yours truly
U. S. Grant[36]

On May 27, 1887, Allen Smith informed Colonel DeLancey Floyd-Jones that he had been elected to the Aztec Club to succeed his father. Captain Smith asked to be sent his certificate of membership and gold medal.[37] Allen had a forty-year career in the army, most of which was served at posts in the West in connection with Indian outbreaks. He rose to the rank of brigadier general before retiring in 1905.[38] He also took part in subduing the Coeur d'Alene mining strike of 1899 in the Idaho panhandle that was organized by the Western Federation of Miners against the Mine Owners Association.[39] Allen Smith married Julia Stephens on June 2, 1874, and the couple had four children: Allen, Charles, Margaret, and Susan. After his retirement, Allen lived in Spokane, Washington, where he was president of the Spokane Amateur Athletic Club.[40] Allen died on October 30, 1927, in Spokane.[41]

Allen's son, Charles F. Smith, entered the Military Academy in 1899 and was commissioned a 2nd lieutenant in the Thirteenth Infantry on June 11, 1903, after graduating last in his class. He was with Company K of the regiment on Angel Island, California, where he served as battalion quartermaster and commissary. He was removed from this position in May 1904 and transferred to Company H. Following his assignment, he was absent without leave and subsequently placed under arrest and held at the Presidio of San Francisco for trial by general court-martial. He was convicted and dismissed from the service on September 15, 1904. His service record dishonored the name he bore.[42]

Miss Fanny Smith married Marshall Oliver on June 16, 1874, at St. James Church in New York City.[43] Captain Oliver was a mathematics professor at the United States Naval Academy. Fanny and Marshal had three children: Miriam, Marshall, and Leslie. Professor Oliver held academic positions as instructor in the Department of Mathematics and Department of Marine, Engineering and Naval Construction and served as the Academy's librarian. He died suddenly on November 26, 1890, of apoplexy. Mrs. Oliver was unsuccessful in her efforts to have a biography written about her father. Fanny moved to New York where she died on April 30, 1918.[44]

Henrietta Smith married Charles M. Campbell, who was an attorney in Denver. In a letter to Marshall Oliver in 1889, Mr. Campbell wrote that he planned to close his law office and expressed his appreciation of the "kindness and attention" shown by Marshall and Fanny during Henrietta's visit to Annapolis.[45]

Marker at Fort Donelson of Smith's attack on February 15, 1862 (author's photograph).

On January 9, 1936, the Military Academy Museum refused to accept documents offered by Mr. Leslie Allen Oliver, Smith's grandson, saying "all of this data is of record at the Military Academy and we have no facilities in the Museum for display of documentary material."[46] However, the following month the Library of Congress was pleased to accept documents relating to Smith's graduation from West Point and his military commissions.[47]

In the over 150 years since his triumph at Fort Donelson, Charles Ferguson Smith has become the "Forgotten Soldier." There is no monument at Fort Donelson in his honor. The remains of Fort C. F. Smith in Washington still exist as a reminder of the chain of forts that once protected the Union capital. The post in Montana is remembered not for Smith but for its role in settling the West. The swords that were bestowed on him are not on display in museums, and, if they exist, are in the hands of private collectors. A repaired headstone marks Smith's grave. He lies there with his wife and mother joined in death after a lifetime of separation. His picture no longer hangs on the wall at the Military Academy he served so well. Today, the portrait lays in "deep storage" among the dusty relics of the West Point Museum. Smith's part in the Civil War is marginalized to nearly a footnote with virtually no acknowledgement of his contributions as instructor and role model for many of the Civil War's senior commanders. While forgotten by history, his legacy lives on as the *beau ideal* soldier, steadfast patriot, loving father, and respected teacher.

Appendices

Grave memorial for C. F. Smith at Laurel Hill Cemetery, Philadelphia, Pennsylvania (courtesy Find a Grave).

A. Biographical Sketch from the Cullum *Register*

Major-General Charles F. Smith was born, April 24, 1807, in Philadelphia, Pa. He was a grandson of a Colonel of the Continental Army, and son of Asst. Surgeon Samuel B. Smith, of the U.S. Army. Upon his graduation from the Military Academy in a distinguished class, of which the great scientist, Alexander D. Bache, was the head, Smith was promoted to the Artillery. After four years doing garrison duty, he was detailed, June 25, 1829, as an Asst. Instructor of Infantry Tactics at the Military Academy. After the lapse of over threescore years, how vividly can I recall the tall, graceful, and handsome Lieutenant drilling our company of cadets in marches and the manual of arms, and two years later as the soldierly Adjutant of the great Superintendent, Colonel Thayer! This latter position of exacting details Smith efficiently filled for nearly seven years, when he became the Commandant of Cadets. After thirteen years of service at the Academy, where he won the golden opinions of all over and under him, he, having been promoted to be Captain, took command of his company.

Difficulties with Mexico, in 1845, took Smith to the field. In command of a Battalion of Artillery, he led the advance across the Colorado; won his brevet of Major by his gallantry at Palo Alto and Resaca-de-la-Palma; for the brilliant storming of Federation Hill, at Monterey, was brevetted a Lieut.-Colonel; and, transferred to General Scott's army, took a conspicuous part in the varied operations of that daring invasion from Vera Cruz to the enemy's capital. In the Valley of Mexico he commanded the Light Infantry Battalion, with signal ability and characteristic intrepidity, at the Capture of San Antonio, Battle of Churubusco, Storming of Chapultepec, and Assault of the City of Mexico, receiving· his third brevet,— that of Colonel,—as his well-merited reward in this short war. The citizens of his native city, who appreciated the value of disciplined courage, military instruction, and skilled leadership, at the close of this war presented him with a Sword of Honor.

Soon after the termination of hostilities, Smith was placed upon the Board to devise a "Complete System of Instruction for Siege, Garrison, Seacoast, and Mountain Artillery." Promoted, Nov. 25, 1854, Major 1st Artillery, and, March. 3, 1855, appointed Lieut.-Colonel of the new Tenth Infantry, he took command, in 1856, of an expedition to the Red River of the North, and the following year against the Mormons in Utah, remaining in charge, till 1861, of the Department of Utah.

When the Rebellion began, Smith was called by his old Chief, General Scott, who appreciated his merits, to the command of the Department of Washington, embracing Maryland and the District of Columbia, in which was the defenseless capital of the Nation. In Sep., 1861, as Brigadier-General of Volunteers, he took charge of the District of Western Kentucky, headquarters Paducah, at the mouth of the Tennessee River, a post of great importance, which soon became the base of operations against the Confederate first line of defense. At once he put the place in a good condition of defense against any attack in front or flank. Engaged day and night preparing to resist the foe without, he was suddenly assailed by a secret and unscrupulous enemy within, who, aided by some scurrilous newspapers, was untiringly trying to supplant Smith in his command. Fortunately a gentleman and a soldier was at the head of the Department of the Missouri, who, knowing Smith's worth, and the falsity of the accusations against him through Halleck's Chief of Staff, who had just visited Paducah, supported the General against his demagogic adversary, and thus retained in command a hero soon to show his brilliant leadership against a nobler and more open foe.

After various expeditions to deceive, and prevent the concentration of, the Confederate forces, General Smith moved his command up the Tennessee, and captured Fort Heiman, at the same time that Fort Henry surrendered. Marching next across the narrow strip between the Tennessee and Cumberland rivers, Fort Donelson, with its numerous batteries, strong entrenchments, and large garrison confronted the Union forces. We cannot go into a full description of this well-known battle. Suffice it to say that the assault of the enemy's lines on our right having failed, General Smith was ordered to storm those on our left. Instantly mounting his superb steed, the General, the impersonation of another Mars, rode along the front of his brigades, and, with brow knit in stern resolve, told the men to be ready; then, placing himself before the center as for review, with McPherson at his side, cool and self-possessed, commanded to charge at double quick with fixed bayonets. Onward his volunteers advanced with the utmost intrepidity through the tempest of iron and leaden hail, opening wide gaps in the serried ranks, soon filled by other brave men. Forward they sped to the thick abatis, which seemed impassable under the deadly fire. Their knightly leader, turning in his saddle and brandishing his sword, cried out in a loud voice: "No flinching now, my lads! Here,—this is the way! Come on, my brave boys!" Threading his path through the felled timber, his noble example inspired his followers, who swarmed in after him as best they could. Then, reforming their ranks, they rushed after their gallant chiefs into the very jaws of death. Upward, through the smoke of battle, they climbed till the perilous goal was reached; a lodgment was made in the enemy's works, the defenders fled, the day was won, and the battle ended with "unconditional and immediate surrender." The hero of the fight, though such a conspicuous target to the sharpshooters, fortunately escaped with only a contusion below the stomach.

Grant generously acknowledged to Smith "that he owed his success at Donelson emphatically to him." Halleck, the Commander of the Department, at once telegraphed to McClellan: "Brig.-General Charles F. Smith, by his coolness and bravery at Fort Donelson when the battle was against us, turned the tide and carried the enemy's outworks; make him a Major-General. You can't get a better one. Honor him for this victory, and the country will applaud." The appointment was at once made, and unanimously confirmed by the Senate; and the municipal authorities of Philadelphia voted Smith at Sword of Honor.

Shortly after the capture of Donelson, our troops were in possession of Clarksville and Nashville. Smith, March 7, 1862, was assigned to the command of the expedition then moving up the Tennessee River, of which he says: "This whole force is utterly demoralized by victory. There seems to be neither head nor tail. The utter want of discipline seems to me to be something marvelous, and yet I have to go far into the bowels of the earth with these men"; but he adds, "You shall hear a good account of me or of my death."

When the expedition had arrived at Savannah, Ten., Smith, in jumping from his steamer into a yawl, missed his foothold and badly injured the bone of the lower part of his right leg, which greatly distressed him, not so much for the pain he had to endure, but because, as he writes, "he could not; take the field soon, not being able to sit at horse, or in fact walk," which would compel him "to ride to the battlefield in an ambulance." Notwithstanding the agony he suffered, he made a reconnaissance of the river up to Chickasaw Bluff. Before the end of March the General had to take to his bed, where he was obliged to submit to a severe surgical operation. This, with his debility caused by a cold taken at Donelson, continued harassing exertion, bad climate, supervening erysipelas, and poisonous drugs, completely sapped his vital energy. To the last moment he hoped to be well enough "to be carried about the expected battlefield in a hand litter." This was denied him, and like a caged lion he chafed, hearing the tumult of Shiloh a few miles distant. "Imagine," says he, "if it be possible, my feelings,—but no, that is impossible—lying here bedridden with my injured leg, and excessive bodily weakness, listening for two days to the sounds of battle, the roar of artillery, the rattle of musketry, without being able to take my proper part in it." Ten days later I saw him on his death-bed. Though resigned to the inevitable, his soldier soul was all aglow with the anticipated success of the Union cause, in which his loyal heart was so much bound up.

On the 25th of April, 1862, this brave and noble paladin, who was as intrepid as Ney, as chivalric as Murat, and as rock-fast as Macdonald, breathed his last. The Army could boast of no better general. His stately and commanding presence inspired his soldiers with respect and almost fear. In his rigid discipline, though severe, he was always just, requiring no greater subordination from inferiors than he was ready to yield to superiors. The call of duty was to him a magic sound for which he was always ready to make every sacrifice and endure any fatigue. He was the very model of a soldier, calm, prudent, and self-poised, yet, in the hour of danger, bold almost to rashness. Had he lived he would have held a high niche in the Temple of Fame, whose doors were already opened to him. Sherman said that, "had C. F. Smith lived, Grant would have disappeared to history after Donelson."

We cannot better terminate this brief sketch of this knightly soldier than in the words of General Halleck's Obituary Order, issued from his headquarters at Pittsburg Landing on the day of Smith's death: "He had been in the service of his country for more than forty years, and had passed through all the military grades from Cadet to Major-General. He had fought with distinction in nearly all the battles of Mexico, and by his gallantry and skill had gained imperishable laurels at the Siege of Ft. Donelson. He combined the qualities of a faithful officer, an excellent disciplinarian, an able commander, and a modest, courteous gentleman. In his death the army has lost one of its brightest ornaments, and the country a general whose place it will be difficult to supply."

General Smith's remains were borne to Laurel Hill Cemetery, in his native city, with the highest military and civic honors. Peace to his sacred dust![1]

B. Notable Cadets During Smith's Term as Commandant

Cullum Number	Class	Name	Army	Rank
986	1839	Isaac I. Stevens	Union	Maj. Gen. U.S. Vol.
988	1839	Henry W. Halleck	Union	Maj. Gen. Chief of Staff
989	1839	Jeremy F. Gilmer	Confederate	Maj. Gen. Chief Eng.
1001	1839	James B. Ricketts	Union	Bvt. Maj. Gen. U.S. Army
1002	1839	Edward O. C. Ord	Union	Bvt. Maj. Gen. U.S. Army
1004	1839	Henry J. Hunt	Union	Bvt. Maj. Gen. U.S. Army
1009	1839	Eleazer A. Paine	Union	Brig. Gen. U.S. Vol.
1015	1839	Edward R. S. Canby	Union	Brig. Gen. U.S. Army
1017	1840	Paul O. Herbert	Confederate	Brig. Gen.
1022	1840	William T. Sherman	Union	Maj. Gen. U.S. Army
1028	1840	George H. Thomas	Union	Maj. Gen. U.S. Army
1029	1840	Richard E. Ewell	Confederate	Lt. Gen.
1031	1840	George W. Getty	Union	Bvt. Brig. Gen. U.S. Army
1034	1840	William Hays	Union	Bvt. Brig. Gen. U.S. Army
1039	1840	Bushrod R. Johnson	Confederate	Maj. Gen.
1059	1841	Zealous B. Tower	Union	Bvt. Maj. Gen. U.S. Vol.
1060	1841	Horatio G. Wright	Union	Bvt. Maj. Gen. U.S. Army
1063	1841	Amiel W. Whipple	Union	Bvt. Maj. Gen. U.S. Army
1064	1841	Josiah Gorgas	Confederate	Brig. Gen. Chief of Ordinance
1065	1841	Thomas J. Rodman	Union	Bvt. Brig. Gen. U.S. Army
1066	1841	Albion P. Howe	Union	Bvt. Maj. Gen. U.S. Vols.
1069	1841	Nathaniel Lyon	Union	Brig. Gen. U.S. Vols.
1080	1841	Joseph B. Plummer	Union	Brig. Gen. U.S. Vols.
1081	1841	John M. Brannan	Union	Bvt. Maj. Gen. U.S. Army
1082	1841	Schuyler Hamilton	Union	Brig. Gen. U.S. Vols.
1083	1841	James Totten	Union	Brig. Gen. U.S. Army
1084	1841	John F. Reynolds	Union	Maj. Gen. U.S. Vols.
1085	1841	Robert S. Garnett	Confederate	Brig. Gen.
1087	1841	Richard B. Garnett	Confederate	Brig. Gen.
1090	1841	Don Carlos Buell	Union	Maj. Gen. U.S. Vols.
1092	1841	Alfred Sully	Union	Bvt. Maj. Gen. U.S. Vols.
1096	1841	Israel B. Richardson	Union	Maj. Gen. U.S. Vols.
1104	1841	William T. H. Brooks	Union	Brig. Gen. U.S. Vols.
1111	1842	Henry L. Eustis	Union	Brig. Gen. U.S. Vols.
1112	1842	John Newton	Union	Bvt. Maj. Gen. U.S. Army
1115	1842	Williams S. Rosecrans	Union	Bvt. Maj. Gen. U.S. Army
1117	1842	Barton S. Alexander	Union	Bvt. Brig. Gen. U.S. Army
1118	1842	Gustavus W. Smith	Confederate	Maj. Gen.
1127	1842	John Pope	Union	Maj. Gen. U.S. Army
1132	1842	Charles L. Kilburn	Union	Bvt. Brig. Gen. U.S. Army

Cullum Number	Class	Name	Army	Rank
1133	1842	Seth Williams	Union	Bvt. Maj. Gen. U.S. Army
1134	1842	Abner Doubleday	Union	Bvt. Maj. Gen. U.S. Army
1139	1842	Napoleon J. T. Dana	Union	Maj. Gen. U.S. Vols.
1147	1842	Ralph W. Kirham	Union	Bvt. Brig. Gen. U.S. Army
1149	1842	George Sykes	Union	Bvt. Maj. Gen. U.S. Army
1158	1842	Lafayette McLaws	Confederate	Maj. Gen.
1161	1842	Samuel B. Hayman	Union	Bvt. Brig. Gen. U.S. Vols.
1162	1842	Earl Van Dorn	Confederate	Maj. Gen.
1164	1842	James Longstreet	Confederate	Lt. Gen.
1167	1843	William B. Franklin	Union	Bvt. Maj. Gen. U.S. Army
1171	1843	William F. Raynolds	Union	Bvt. Brig. Gen. U.S. Army
1174	1843	John J. Peck	Union	Maj. Gen. U.S. Vols
1176	1843	Joseph J. Reynolds	Union	Brig. Gen. U.S. Vols.
1177	1843	James A. Hardie	Union	Bvt. Maj. Gen. U.S. Army
1178	1843	Henry F. Clarke	Union	Bvt. Maj. Gen. U.S. Army
1180	1843	Samuel G. French	Confederate	Maj. Gen.
1182	1843	Christopher C. Auger	Union	Bvt. Maj. Gen. U.S. Army
1183	1843	Franklin Gardner	Confederate	Maj. Gen.
1187	1843	Ulysses S. Grant	Union	Lt. Gen. U.S. Army
1188	1843	Joseph H. Potter	Union	Brig. Gen. U.S. Vols.
1192	1843	George S. Hamilton	Union	Maj. Gen. U.S. Vols
1196	1843	Frederick Steele	Union	Bvt. Maj. Gen. U.S. Army
1198	1843	Rufus Ingalls	Union	Bvt. Maj. Gen. U.S. Army
1199	1843	Frederick T. Dent	Union	Brig. Gen. U.S. Vols.
1200	1843	John C. McFerran	Union	Bvt. Brig. Gen. U.S. Army
1201	1843	Henry M. Judah	Union	Brig. Gen. U.S. Vols.
1212	1844	Alfred Pleasanton	Union	Bvt. Maj. Gen. U.S. Army
1216	1844	Simon B. Buckner	Confederate	Lt. Gen.
1223	1844	Winfield S. Hancock	Union	Maj. Gen. U.S. Army
1225	1844	Alexander Hays	Union	Brig. Gen. U.S. Vols.
1231	1845	William H. C. Whiting	Confederate	Maj. Gen.
1234	1845	William F. Smith	Union	Bvt. Maj. Gen. U.S. Army
1235	1845	Thomas J. Wood	Union	Bvt. Maj. Gen. U.S. Army
1236	1845	Thomas G. Rhett	Confederate	Major
1237	1845	Charles P. Stone	Union	Brig. Gen. U.S. Vols.
1238	1845	Fitz-John Porter	Union	Maj. Gen. U.S. Vols.

Cashiered/Reinstated

1247	1845	John P. Hatch	Union	Bvt. Maj. Gen. U.S. Army
1255	1845	Edmund K. Smith	Confederate	Lt. Gen.
1257	1845	John W. Davidson	Union	Bvt. Maj. Gen. U.S. Army
1262	1845	Delos B. Sacket	Union	Brig. Gen. Staff U.S. Army
1263	1845	Barnard B. Bee	Confederate	Brig. Gen.
1265	1845	Gordon Granger	Union	Bvt. Maj. Gen. U.S. Army
1266	1845	Henry B. Clitz	Union	Bvt. Brig. Gen. U.S. Army
1268	1845	David A. Russell	Union	Bvt. Maj. Gen. U.S. Army
1270	1845	Marshall G. Pitcher	Union	Bvt. Brig. Gen. U.S. Army

C. Fort Donelson Union Order of Battle[1]

Division	Brigade	Regiment	Commander
District of Cairo			Brig. Gen. U. S. Grant
			Col. J. D. Webster[a]
			Col. J. B. McPherson[b]
1st Division			Brig. Gen. J. A. McClernand
	1st Brigade		Col. R. J. Oglesby
		8th Illinois	Lt. Col. F. L. Rhoads
		18th Illinois	Col. M. K. Lawler
		29th Illinois	Col. J. S. Reardon
		30th Illinois	Lt. Col. E. S. Dennis
		31st Illinois	Col. J. A. Logan
		Battery D	Cap. T. Larrison
		2nd IL Cavalry Cos. A & B	Cap. J. Hotaling
		2nd U.S. Cavalry, Co. C	
		4th U.S. Cavalry, Co. I	Lt. J. Powell
		IL Cavalry Co.	Cpt. E. Carmichael
		IL Cavalry Co.	Cap. J. Dollins
		IL Cavalry Co.	Cpt. M. J. O'Harnett
	2nd Brigade		Col. W. H. L. Wallace
		11th Illinois	Lt. Col. T. E. G. Ransom
		20th Illinois	Col. C. C. Marsh
		45th Illinois	Col. John E. Smith
		48th Illinois	Col. I. N. Haynie
		Battery B, 1st IL Lt. Art.	Cap. E. Taylor
		Battery D, 1st IL Lt. Art.	Cpt. E. McAllister
		4th IL Cavalry	Col. T. L. Dickey
	3rd Brigade		Col. W. R. Morrison (w)
			Col. L. F. Ross
		17th Illinois	Col. L. F. Ross
			Maj. F. M. Smith
		49th Illinois	Lt. Col. P. Pease
		Battery H, 1st MO Art.	
		Battery K, 1st MO Art.	
2nd Division			Brig. Gen. C. F. Smith
	1st Brigade		Col. J. McArthur
		9th Illinois	Lt. Col. J. J. Phillips
		12th Illinois	Lt. Col. A. L. Chetlain
		41st Illinois	Col. I. C. Pugh
	3rd Brigade		Col. J. Cook
		7th Illinois	Lt. Col. A. J. Babcock
		50th Illinois	Col. M. M. Bane
		52nd Illinois	Col. T. W. Sweeny

Division	Brigade	Regiment	Commander
		12th Iowa	Col. J. J. Wood
		52nd Indiana	Col. J. M. Smith
		13th Missouri	Col. C. J. Wright
		Battery D, 1st MO Art.	Capt. H. Richardson
	4th Brigade		Col. J. G. Lauman
		2nd Iowa	Col. J. Tuttle
		7th Iowa	Lt. Col. J. Parrott
		14th Iowa	Col. W. T. Shaw
		25th Indiana	Col. J. C. Veatch
		14th Missouri Sharpshooters	Col. J. M. Burke
	5th Brigade		Col. M. L. Smith
		11th Indiana	Col. G. F. McGinnis
		8th Missouri	Maj. J. McDonald
3rd Division			Brig. Gen. L. Wallace
	1st Brigade		Col. C. Cruft
		31st Indiana	Lt. Col. J. Osborn
		44th Indiana	Col. H. B. Reed
		17th Kentucky	Col. J. H. McHenry, Jr.
		25th Kentucky	Col. J. M. Shackelford
	2nd Brigade		Attached to 3rd Brigade
		46th Illinois	Col. J. A. Davis
		57th Illinois	Col. S. D. Baldwin
		58th Illinois	Col. W. F. Lynch
		20th Ohio	Col. C. Whittlesey
	3rd Brigade		Col. J. M. Thayer
		1st Nebraska	Lt. Col. W. McCord
		58th Ohio	Lt. Col. F. F. Rempel
		68th Ohio	Col. S. H. Steedman
		76th Ohio	Col. W. B. Woods
	Unattached	Battery A, 1st IL Light Art.	Lt. P. P. Wood
		32nd IL, Co. A	Cpt. H. Davidson
Western Flotilla			Flag Officer A. H. Foote (w)
City Class Ironclad			
		USS *St. Louis*	Lt. L. Paulding
		USS *Carondelet*	Com. H. Walke
		USS *Louisville*	Com. B. M. Dove
		USS *Pittsburgh*	Lt. E. Thompson
Timberclad			
		USS *Tyler*	Lt. Com. W. Gwin
		USS *Conestoga*	Lt. Com. S. L. Phelps
		USS *Lexington*	Lt. J. W. Shirk

Notes
[a] Chief of Staff
[b] Chief of Engineers

Military Rank
  Lt. = 1st Lieutenant
  Capt. = Captain
  Maj. = Major
  Lt. Col. = Lieutenant Colonel
  Col. = Colonel
  Brig. Gen. = Brigadier General
  Com. = Commander
  Lt. Com. = Lieutenant Commander

D. Chronology

Date	Event
April 24, 1807	Charles Ferguson Smith is born in Philadelphia, PA, the son of Assistant Surgeon Samuel B. Smith and Mary Ferguson Smith.
July 1, 1820	Smith admitted to West Point.
June 1821	Smith fails and is forced to repeat first year.
July 1, 1825	Smith graduates 19th in a class of 37 and is appointed 2nd lieutenant in the Second Artillery Regiment.
1825–1827	Smith is posted at Fort Delaware, DE.
1827–1829	Smith is stationed at Augusta Arsenal, GA.
May 30, 1832	Smith promoted to 1st lieutenant.
June 25, 1829	Smith appointed Assistant Instructor of Infantry Tactics at U.S. Military Academy.
September 1, 1831	Smith promoted to Military Academy Adjutant under Superintendent Thayer.
April 1, 1838	Smith selected as Commandant of Cadets and Instructor of Infantry Tactics at Military Academy.
July 7, 1838	Smith promoted to captain in the Second Artillery Regiment.
June 14, 1839	U. S. Grant enters West Point.
March 24, 1840	Smith marries Francis Mactier in Baltimore, MD.
September 1, 1842	Smith is relieved as Commandant of Cadets.
July 28, 1843	U. S. Grant graduates 21st in a class of 39 and is appointed brevet 2nd lieutenant in the Fourth Infantry Regiment.
March 1, 1843	Smith stationed at Fort Columbus, NY.
July 11, 1844	Smith sent to Frankford Arsenal, PA.
September 25, 1844	Smith's eldest child, Fanny Mactier Smith is born at Frankford Arsenal, PA.
August 26, 1845	Smith returns to Fort Columbus, NY.
October 13, 1845	Smith leaves Fort Columbus for Corpus Christi, TX.
1845–1846	Smith and Grant in military occupation of Texas.
March 20, 1846	Smith leads advance across the Colorado River.
April 23, 1846	Mexico declares war on United States.
May 8, 1846	Battle of Palo Alto.
May 9, 1846	Battle of Resaca-de-la-Palma. Smith receives brevet to major for gallant and distinguished conduct at Palo Alto and Resaca-de-la-Palma.
May 13, 1846	United States declares war on Mexico.
September 21–23, 1847	Battle of Monterey.
	Smith commands storming party at Federation Hill.
September 23, 1846	Smith receives brevet to lieutenant colonel for actions at Monterey.

Date	Event
January 9–23, 1847	Smith transferred from Gen. Taylor's force to Gen. Scott's army.
March 9–29, 1847	Siege of Veracruz.
April 17–18, 1847	Battle of Cerro Gordo.
May 1–November 3, 1847	Smith in command of the light battalion.
August 20, 1847	Battle of Churubusco.
August 20, 1847	Smith receives brevet to colonel for his actions at Contreras and Churubusco.
September 13, 1847	Smith leads troops in storming of Chapultepec.
September 1847–June 4, 1848	Smith in command of the Police Guard of the City of Mexico.
October 13, 1847	The Aztec Club of 1847 is established.
February 2, 1848	Peace treaty of Guadalupe Hidalgo ends war.
June 12, 1848	Gen. Worth's division leaves Mexico City.
January–September 1849	Smith is stationed at Ft. Marion, FL.
April 12, 1849	Smith's son, Allen, is born in St. Augustine, FL.
September 1, 1849–November 1851	Smith is member of a board to devise system of instruction for Siege Garrison Sea Coast and Mountain Artillery.
September 7, 1852–April 3, 1855	Smith serves in Washington, D.C., as president of board of claims for supplies furnished by Col. Frémont in 1846 to California volunteers.
October 15, 1853	Smith's second daughter, Henrietta, is born in Washington, D.C.
November 25, 1854	Smith promoted to major of First U.S. Artillery Regiment.
March 3, 1855	Smith promoted to lieutenant colonel of Tenth Infantry Regiment at Carlisle Barracks, PA.
July–November 1856	Smith leads expedition to the Red River of the North in Minnesota Territory.
1857–1861	Smith serves under A. S. Johnston in expedition against the Mormons in Utah Territory.
February 29, 1860–February 28, 1861	Smith commands Department of Utah.
November 6, 1860	Lincoln wins election and southern states begin to secede.
February 1861–April 1861	Smith posted at Fort Crittenden in Utah.
March 4, 1861	Lincoln inaugurated as 16th president.
April 10–28, 1861	Smith commands the Department of Washington.
April 12, 1861	Civil War begins with the Confederate attack on Fort Sumter, SC.
April 15, 1861	Lincoln calls for 75,000 volunteers.
April 28–August 19, 1861	Smith serves as Superintendent of General Recruiting Service at Fort Columbus, NY.
July 1, 1861	Congress asks for 300,000 volunteers.
July 21, 1861	Confederates defeat Union forces at Manassas (First Bull Run).
August 31, 1861	Maj. Gen. Frémont appoints Smith a brigadier general of volunteers in the Western Department.
September 6, 1861	Grant occupies Paducah, KY.
September 8, 1861–January 31, 1862	Smith commands District of Western Kentucky from headquarters at Paducah, KY.
September 9, 1861	Smith promoted to colonel of Third U.S. Infantry Regiment in the Regular Army.
September 12, 1861	Previously neutral Kentucky joins the Union.
November 7, 1861	Battle of Belmont.
November 25, 1861	Smith upset by flag-raising incident at the Woolfolk/Tilghman House.

D. Chronology

Date	Event
February 6, 1862	Naval forces under Flag Officer Foote capture Fort Henry and Smith occupies Fort Heiman.
February 13, 1862	Grant's troops invested Fort Donelson.
February 14, 1862	Confederate river batteries repulse Flag Officer Foote's gunboat assault.
February 15, 1862	Confederates breakout fails and Smith leads attack on the federal left and captures Rebel defenses.
February 16, 1862	Grant demands terms of "unconditional surrender" and attributes victory at Donelson to Smith.
March 7, 1862	Halleck relieves Grant from command and appoints Smith to command expedition up the Tennessee River to Savannah, TN.
March 12, 1862	Smith meets with Wallace on steamer and seriously injures his leg.
March 17, 1862	Grant is restored to command and arrives at Savannah where he waits for Gen. Buell's Army of the Ohio.
March 21, 1862	Smith is promoted to major general of volunteers and awarded a sword by City of Philadelphia.
April 6, 1862	Battle of Shiloh—Day One—Confederate forces attack the Union position. A stubborn defense at the Hornets' Nest by Smith's Second Division allows Grant to organize a defensive position.
April 7, 1862	Battle of Shiloh—Day Two—Aided by Buell's and Wallace's reinforcements, Grant drives the Confederates from the field.
April 11, 1862	Halleck takes personal command of the army and begins slow movement to Corinth.
April 25, 1862	Smith dies in Savannah, TN.

Chapter Notes

Epigraph

1. Lew Wallace, *Lew Wallace: An Autobiography* (New York: Harper & Brothers Publishers, 1906), vol. I, 343–345.

Preface

1. Stephen E. Ambrose, *Duty, Honor, Country: A History of West Point* (Baltimore: Johns Hopkins University Press, 1996) quoting Oliver E. Wood, *The West Point Scrapbook*, New York, 1871, 289, 136.
2. Please see "Notable Cadets During Smith's Term as Commandant" in Appendices.
3. Ambrose, *Duty, Honor, Country*, 136.
4. General Orders No. 21, issued by Major General Halleck, Headquarters Department of the Mississippi, Pittsburg Landing, TN, April 25, 1862, C. F. Smith Papers.
5. Grant to Julia, April 25, 1862 as quoted in Jean Edward Smith, *Grant* (New York: Simon & Schuster, 2001), 658.
6. Ulysses S. Grant, *Personal Memoirs* (New York: The Modern Library, 1885), 17.
7. U. S. Grant, Letter to Mrs. Fanny M. Smith, 26 April 1862, C. F. Smith Papers.
8. Grant, *Personal Memoirs*, 173.
9. Holland, "An Anecdote of General Grant Related by His Son," February 1909–1912, *New News of Yesterday*. Interview with Frederick Dent Grant by Holland in 1899 just before he sailed for the Philippines to take a military command.
10. W. T. Sherman, Letter to Colonel R. N. Scott. September 6, 1885. General J. T. Fry referenced this quote in "An Acquaintance with Grant" which appeared in the December 1885 issue of the *North American Review*. This quote was denied by General Sherman who suggested that it might have been fabricated by General J. T. Fry. General Fry in "An Open Letter" to the editor of the *North American Review*, says that Sherman asked Allen Thorndike Rice "to repudiate the sentiment attributed to him." This disagreement is described a January 30, 1886, article in *The New York Times* titled "Authority for Gen. Sherman."
11. Cullum, *Biographical Register*, 355–357.
12. Lew Wallace, *Lew Wallace: An Autobiography* (New York: Harper & Brothers Publishers, 1906), vol. I, 446.
13. Smith's height is described as from six feet to six feet four inches.
14. John H. Brinton, *Personal Memoirs of John H. Brinton* (New York: The Neal Publishing Company, 1914), 130.
15. Shelby Foote, *The Civil War: A Narrative, Vol. 2: Fort Donelson to Memphis* (Alexandria: Time-Life Books, 1958), 32.
16. War Department Letter to Marshall Oliver, January 5, 1897, and Charles M. Campbell, Letter to William F. Smith, 10 November 1885, C. F. Smith Papers.
17. Henry R. Crosby, Letter to Mrs. Fanny Oliver. April 20, 1885, C. F. Smith Papers.

Part One

1. George W. Cullum, *Biographical Register of the Officers and Graduates of the U.S. Military Academy at West Point, N.Y. from Its Establishment, in 1802 to 1890 with the Early History of the United States Military Academy* (New York: Houghton, Mifflin and Company, 1891) Third Edition, Vol. I, Nos. 1 to 1000, 355–357.

Chapter 1

1. Jack Hurst, *Men of Fire* (New York: Basic Books, 2007), 291–292.
2. James M. Tuttle, Report of Col. James M. Tuttle, February 18, 1862, *The War of the Rebellion: A Compilation of the Official Records of the Union and Confederate Armies* (Washington: Government Printing Office, 1882), ser. 1, vol. 7, 230.
3. C. F. Smith, Letter to Miss Fanny M. Smith, February 11, 1862, C. F. Smith Papers.
4. Cullum, *Biographical Register*, 355.
5. Robert Smith, Virtual American Biographies, http://famousamericans.net/robertsmith/, Accessed November 24, 2013.
6. Samuel B. Smith, Letter to John C. Calhoun, December 1819, Archives, U.S. Military Academy Library. U.S. Military Academy, West Point, NY.
7. A common or vulgar fraction, such as ½, ⅖, ¾, that consists of an integer numerator and a non-zero integer denominator.
8. "Annual Report of the Board of Visitors to the United States Military Academy Made to Congress and the Secretary of War for the Year 1819," *Annual Report of the Board of Visitors (1819–2002)*, Special Collections & Archives, Archives, United States Military Academy Library, 8.
9. *The Centennial of the United States Military Academy at West Point, New York, 1802–1902, Volume I Addresses and Histories* (Washington: Government Printing Office, 1904), 226.
10. Francis H. Smith, "West Point Fifty Years Ago," an address delivered before the Association of Graduates of

the U.S. Military Academy, West Point, at the annual reunion, June 12, 1879, Annual Reunion of the Association of Graduates (1870–1916), U.S. Military Academy Library, Archives, 112.

11. Francis H. Smith, "West Point Fifty Years Ago," an address delivered before the Association of Graduates of the U.S. Military Academy, West Point, at the annual reunion, June 12, 1879, Annual Reunion of the Association of Graduates (1870–1916), Archives, 112.

12. An encampment is the place where a camp is established. The word is especially used to describe a military camp, http://dictionary.reference.com/browse/encampment, Accessed November 20, 2013.

13. Ambrose, *Duty, Honor, Country*, 83–84.

14. Ambrose, *Duty, Honor, Country*, 83.

15. George Ochoa and Melinda Corey, eds., *West Point in the Making of America* (Irvington: Hydra Publishing, 2002), 17.

16. Robert Cowley and Thomas Guinzburg, *West Point—Two Centuries of Honor and Tradition, The Bicentennial Book of the United States Military Academy* (New York: Warner Books, 2002), 33.

17. Cowley, *West Point*, 231.

18. Cowley, *West Point*, 230.

19. Kevin M. Klopcic, "Come Fill Your Glasses Fellows, But Why?" December 14, 2000, Tactical Officer Education Program Papers, Special Collections, Special Collections & Archives, U.S. Military Academy Library, 2–3.

20. A first-year student at the U.S. Military Academy was called plebe, which was short for plebian, which was used in ancient Rome to denote the common or lower class.

21. The system of designating classes at West Point can be confusing. The first-year cadets (freshman) are in the fourth class, the second-year cadets (sophomores) are in the third class, the third-year cadets (juniors) are in the second class, and the fourth-year cadets (seniors) are in the first class.

22. According to the class records for 1821, C. F. Smith was listed as 14 years and 3 months at his July 1, 1820, date of admission. "Register of the Officers and Cadets of the U.S. Military Academy, June, 1821," *Official Records of the Officers and Cadets 1818-1966*, Special Collections & Archives, Archives, United States Military Academy Library.

23. *Centennial*, Vol. I, 227.

24. Ambrose, *Duty, Honor, Country*, 70.

25. *The Centennial of the United States Military Academy at West Point, New York, 1802-1902, Volume II—Statistics and Bibliographies* (Washington: Government Printing Office, 1904), 80.

26. A "coatee" is a close fitting short coat especially one with tails or short flaps.

27. Henry Perkins, *A Sketch of the History and Topography of West Point and the U.S. Military Academy* (Philadelphia: Roswell Park, 1840), 103–104.

28. Ambrose, *Duty, Honor, Country*, 39.

29. "Register of the Officers and Cadets of the U.S. Military Academy, June 1821," Academic Staff, *Official Records of the Officers and Cadets*.

30. On the Road to Professionalism, 3.

31. John G. Waugh, *The Class of 1846* (New York: Warner Books, 1994), 19.

32. Edward Charles Boynton, *History of West Point* (Bedford: Applewood Books, 1864), 267.

33. Made by Harpers Ferry Armory and Springfield Armories. Circa 1816–1844 Harpers Ferry Armory made over 350,000. Circa 1816–1840, Springfield Armory made over 325,000. 42" round .69 caliber smoothbore barrel. No front or rear sight. Bayonet lug on top of barrel at muzzle. Steel ramrod with button shaped head. Three barrel bands retained with barrel band retaining springs. Iron mountings. Metal parts finished bright. Walnut stock. Variations of this basic musket were produced. Civil War Era Firearms, http://www.edsmart.com/jz/guns.htm, Accessed April 8, 2011.

34. Ambrose, *Duty, Honor, Country*, 81.

35. Sidney Forman, ed., "Cadet Life Before the Mexican War," Bulletin No. 1, The Library, United States Military Academy, USMA Library Publications, U.S. Military Academy, Special Collections, 8–9.

36. *Centennial*, Vol. II, 81.

37. "Annual Report of the Board of Visitors to the United States Military Academy Made to Congress and the Secretary of War for the Year 1821," *Annual Report of the Board of Visitors (1819–2002)*, 29–30.

38. *Centennial*, Vol. II, 65.

39. Regulations for commons, 1815, Alden Partridge Papers, USMA Library, as quoted in Ambrose, *Duty, Honor, Country*, 47–48.

40. Ambrose, *Duty, Honor, Country*, 76.

41. *Centennial*, Vol. I, 231.

42. Ambrose, *Duty, Honor, Country*, 73.

43. Ambrose, *Duty, Honor, Country*, 74.

44. Ambrose, *Duty, Honor, Country*, 90.

45. *Centennial*, Vol. I, 315.

46. *Centennial*, Vol. I, 317.

47. *Centennial*, Vol. I, 319.

48. *Centennial*, Vol. I, 322.

49. *Centennial*, Vol. I, 461–464.

50. Cullum, *Biographical Register*, Vol. I, 319–337.

51. Leonne M. Hudson, *The Odyssey of a Southerner: The Life and Times of Gustavus Woodson Smith* (Macon: Mercer University Press, 1998), chapter one.

52. *Centennial*, Vol. II.

53. Robbins, *Last in Their Class*, 10.

54. Ambrose, *Duty, Honor, Country*, 67–68.

55. Ambrose, *Duty, Honor, Country*, 80.

56. "Register of the Officers and Cadets of the U.S. Military Academy, June, 1821," *Official Register of the Officers and Cadets of the United States Military Academy (1818–1966)*, 13.

57. Eric A. Dubelier, "Charles F. Smith: The Forgotten Soldier" (Honors Thesis, Tulane University, 1977), 3.

58. Ambrose, *Duty, Honor, Country*, 81–82.

59. *Centennial*, Vol. II, 82.

60. *Centennial*, Vol. I, 377–378.

61. Post Order Book, October 15, 1821, *Post Orders 1834–1904*, Archives, U.S. Military Academy Library.

62. Ambrose, *Duty, Honor, Country*, 149–150.

63. "Register of the Officers and Cadets of the U.S. Military Academy, June, 1822," *Official Register of the Officers and Cadets of the United States Military Academy (1818–1966)*, 14.

64. "Annual Report of the Board of Visitors to the United States Military Academy Made to Congress and the Secretary of War for the Year 1821," *Annual Report of the Board of Visitors (1819–2002)*, 29; Forman, "Cadet Life Before the Mexican War," 4.

65. Ambrose, *Duty, Honor, Country*, 90.

66. Dubelier, "The Forgotten Soldier," 4.
67. "Annual Report of the Board of Visitors to the United States Military Academy Made to Congress and the Secretary of War for the Year 1821," *Annual Report of the Board of Visitors (1819–2002)*, 29.
68. Merit Roll of the 2nd Class in Philosophy, January 18, 1824, Archives, U.S. Military Academy Library.
69. Merit Roll of the 2nd Class in Chymistry [sic], January 20, 1824. Archives, U.S. Military Academy Library.
70. Merit Roll of the 2nd Class in Drawing, January 23, 1824. Archives, U.S. Military Academy Library; "Cadet Life Before the Mexican War," 4.
71. *Centennial*, Vol. II, 85.
72. Merit Roll of the Second Class as established at the General Examination, 27 June 1824. *Register of the Officers and Cadets of the U.S. Military Academy June 1824*, Archives, United States Military Academy Library at West Point, http://digital-library.usma.edu/libmedia/archives/oroc/v1824.pdf.
73. Orders, June 29, 1824, Archives, U.S. Military Academy Library West Point, NY.
74. *Centennial*, Vol. II, 82.
75. Battalion Orders, August 21, 1824, Archives, U.S. Military Academy Library.
76. Post Order No. 156, September 14, 1824, *Post Orders 1834–1904*, Archives, U.S. Military Academy Library.
77. Post Order No. 175, October 15, 1824, *Post Orders 1834–1904*, Archives, U.S. Military Academy Library.
78. Ambrose, *Duty, Honor, Country*, 90.
79. First Class according to merit in Engineering, January 23, 1825, Archives, U.S. Military Academy Library West Point, NY.
80. First Class according to merit in Geography, January 23, 1825. Archives, U.S. Military Academy Library West Point, NY.
81. First Class according to merit in Mineralogy, January 23, 1825. Archives, U.S. Military Academy Library West Point, NY.
82. "Register of the Officers and Cadets of the U.S. Military Academy, June, 1825," *Official Register of the Officers and Cadets of the United States Military Academy (1818–1966)*, 6.
83. "Annual Report of the Board of Visitors to the United States Military Academy Made to Congress and the Secretary of War for the Year 1821," *Annual Report of the Board of Visitors (1819–2002)*, 29.
84. Dubelier, "The Forgotten Soldier," 4.
85. "Merit Roll of the First Class as Determined at the General Examination in June 1825," Archives, U.S. Military Academy Library, West Point, NY. The discrepancy in class ranking is based on two different reports.
86. Battalion Orders No. 54, May 30, 1825, Archives, U.S. Military Academy Library.
87. "Register of the Officers and Cadets of the U.S. Military Academy, June, 1826," *Official Register of the Officers and Cadets of the United States Military Academy (1818–1966)*, 11 & 12.
88. Battalion Orders No. 65, June 25, 1825, Archives, U.S. Military Academy Library.
89. D. L. Gabel, "Leadership or Management: The Cadet Chain of Command and the West Point Class of 1915," December 4, 1989, Tactical Officer Education Program papers, Special Collections, U.S. Military Academy Library, 5–6.
90. In the military chain of command, communications from junior officers to a superior were delivered to that officer's adjutant. It was inappropriate for a junior officer to communicate in writing directly to his superior. Likewise, superior officers issued orders through their adjutants.
91. Battalion Order No. 70, 5 July 1825, Orders No. 84, Extract, 10 July 1825, Mess Orders 3, 31 July 1825, Orders No. 84, Extract, 10 July 1825, Mess Orders 3, 31 July 1825, Archives, U.S. Military Academy Library.
92. Battalion Orders, August 1, 1825, Battalion Orders No. 96, August 22, 1825, Battalion Orders No. 66, June 26, 1825, Battalion Orders No. 76, July 5, 1825, Battalion Orders No. 94, August 13, 1825, Archives, U.S. Military Academy Library.
93. Battalion Detail & Countersign, August 7, 1825, Archives, U.S. Military Academy Library.
94. Orders No. 96, August 4, 1825, Orders, Archives, U.S. Military Academy Library.
95. Hudson, *The Odyssey of a Southerner*, chapter one.
96. Orders No. 54, July 11, 1825, Orders, Archives, U.S. Military Academy Library.
97. *Centennial*, Vol. II, 84.
98. *Centennial*, Vol. II, 86; Orders No. 18, 5 April 1824, Archives, U.S. Military Academy Library.
99. W. A. Simpson, "The Second Regiment of Artillery," in Theo. F. Rodenbough and William L. Haskin, eds., *The Army of the United States: Historical Sketches of Staff and Line with Portraits of Generals-in-Chief* (New York: Maynard, Merrill & Co., 1896, 314.
100. The fort's problems included a fire in February 1831 and a decade-long legal battle over island ownership, which halted construction. The fort was finally built between 1848 and 1859 and was the largest fort in the United States at the time. Fort Delaware, http://en.wikipedia.org/wiki/Ft._Delaware, Accessed November 6, 2013.
101. The Rev. Moses Shipley, "Gen. C. F. Smith's Body Servant," *Philadelphia Inquirer*, March 14, 1893.
102. "U.S. Arsenal in Augusta," U.S. History, http://www.u-s-history.com/pages/h3114.html, Accessed October 17, 2013.
103. "Augusta Arsenal (1826)," Augusta State University, http://www.aug.edu/public_relations/history/arsenal.html, Accessed October 17, 2013.
104. "Augusta Arsenal (1826)," Augusta State University, http://www.aug.edu/public_relations/history/arsenal.html, Accessed May 11, 2011.
105. History of Augusta, Georgia, http://en.wikipedia.org/wiki/History_of_Augusta,_Georgia, Accessed May 11, 2011.
106. Simpson, "The Second Regiment of Artillery," 314.
107. Ambrose, *Duty, Honor, Country*, 143; Cullum, *Biographical Register*, Class of 1825, numbers 392–428.

Chapter 2

1. Ambrose, *Duty, Honor, Country*, 84.
2. Ambrose, *Duty, Honor, Country*, 122.
3. Ambrose, *Duty, Honor, Country*, 116–117.
4. Notes on Charles F. Smith's life, C. F. Smith Papers. Other accounts place his height at six feet four inches. Brinton, *Personal Memoirs*, 130.
5. *Centennial*, Vol. II, 102.
6. Ambrose, *Duty, Honor, Country*, 79.

7. Laureen M. Barone, "Evolution of the Cadet Disciplinary System: From Confusion to Clarity (1802–1833)," U.S. Military Academy, December 4, 1990, Tactical Officer Education Program papers, Special Collections, U.S. Military Academy Library, 9.

8. Forman, "Cadet Life Before the Mexican War," 9–10.

9. Cullum, *Biographical Register*, Vol. I, 355.

10. C. F. Smith, Letter to John H. Eaton, March 22, 1839, Officers Letters, Archives, U.S. Military Academy Library.

11. William F. Hecker, ed., *Private Perry and Mister Poe*, The West Point Poems, 1831, Facsimile Edition (Baton Rouge: Louisiana State University Press, 2005), Introduction xvii–xviii.

12. Robbins, *Last in Their Class*, 20.

13. *Centennial*, Vol. II, 76.

14. Stanley P. Tozeski, *Preliminary Inventory of the Records of the United States Military Academy* (Washington: General Services Administration, 1976), 43.

15. Ambrose, *Duty, Honor, Country*, 107–108.

16. Ambrose, *Duty, Honor, Country*, 106–107.

17. Barone, "Evolution of the Cadet Disciplinary System," 11, 36, 37.

18. William Frazer, Letter to his brother, June 21, 1833, Misc. MSS, USMA Library as quoted in Ambrose, *Duty, Honor, Country*, 109–110.

19. Ambrose, *Duty, Honor, Country*, 108.

20. Ambrose, *Duty, Honor, Country*, 108.

21. *Centennial*, Vol. II, 91.

22. Robbins, *Last in Their Class*, 25.

23. Ambrose, *Duty, Honor, Country*, 110.

24. Ambrose, *Duty, Honor, Country*, 110–111.

25. *Centennial*, Vol. II, 92.

26. *Centennial*, Vol. II, 94.

27. Ambrose, *Duty, Honor, Country*, 120–121.

28. C. F. Smith, Letter to Mrs. Margaret F. Smith, April 18, 1834, C. F. Smith Papers.

29. John Todd (John B. S.) was the oldest son of Dr. John Todd and Charles' cousin. Charles' aunt, Elizabeth Fisher Blair Smith, married Dr. John Todd on July 1, 1813. This union made her aunt to Mary Todd. John Todd was a brigadier general in command of Missouri troops. He took a leave of absence from the army to stand for election as a delegate to Congress from the Dakota Territory. John G. Turner and Linda Levitt Turner, *Mary Todd Lincoln: Her Life and Letters* (New York: Fromm International, 1987), 18 & 105. *Biographical and Genealogical History of the State of Delaware*, vol. I (Chambersburg: J. M. Runk, 1899), 149.

30. Cullum, *Biographical Register*, Vol. I, 691.

31. "Register of the Officers and Cadets of the U.S. Military Academy, June, 1837," Official Register of the Officers and Cadets of the United States Military Academy (1818–1966), Archives, U.S. Military Academy Library, 24.

32. *Centennial*, Vol. II, 96.

33. *Centennial*, Vol. II, 95.

Chapter 3

1. Battalion Order No. 29, March 31, 1838, Archives, U.S. Military Academy Library.

2. *Centennial*, Vol. I, 393.

3. Ambrose, *Duty, Honor, Country*, 136. Quoting Oliver E. Wood, *The West Point Scrapbook*, New York, 1871, 289.

4. Battalion Order No. 30, April 1, 1838, Archives, U.S. Military Academy Library.

5. Battalion Orders No. 34, April 6, 1838, Archives, U.S. Military Academy Library.

6. Battalion Orders No. 44, May 14, 1838, Archives, U.S. Military Academy Library.

7. *The Centennial of the United States Military Academy at West Point 1802–1902, Volume II Statistics and Bibliographies* (Washington: Government Printing Office, 1904), Vol. II, 88.

8. The Congress approved and recognized that title and created the Department of Tactics by a law approved on June 12, 1858. Tozeski, *Preliminary Inventory of the Records of the United States Military Academy*, 31.

9. Ambrose, *Duty, Honor, Country*, 87.

10. "Register of the Officers and Cadets of the U.S. Military Academy, June, 1840," "Register of the Officers and Cadets of the U.S. Military Academy, June, 1839," *Official Register of the Officers and Cadets of the United States Military Academy (1818–1966)*; Winfield Scott, *Rules and Regulations for the Exercise and Maneuvers of the United States Infantry* (New York: H. W. Mercein, 1815), https://archive.org/details/cu31924030756666, Accessed December 17, 2013.

11. Battalion Orders No. 15, February 17, 1840, Archives, U.S. Military Academy Library.

12. Orders No. 18, March 15, 1840, Orders, Archives, U.S. Military Academy Library.

13. Orders No. 54, July 20, 1840. Orders, Archives, U.S. Military Academy Library.

14. C. F. Smith, Letter to R. Delafield, September 2, 1840, Officers Letters, Archives, U.S. Military Academy Library.

15. Battalion Orders No. 29, April 6, 1839, Archives, U.S. Military Academy Library.

16. Battalion Orders No. 49, May 31, 1839, Archives, U.S. Military Academy Library.

17. Battalion Orders No. 36, April 28, 1839, Archives, U.S. Military Academy Library.

18. The Board of Visitors was composed of senior military officers and distinguished citizens "whose duty it shall be to visit the Academy at the times of examination of the Cadets, for the purpose of ascertaining the progress and improvement of the Cadets, and of examining into, and reporting everything connected with the management and Police of the Institution." Annual Report of the Board of Visitors to the United States Military Academy Made to Congress and the Secretary of War for the Year 1819, *Annual Report of the Board of Visitors (1819–2002)*, Archives, U.S. Military Academy Library, 8.

19. Ambrose, *Duty, Honor, Country*, 134–135.

20. C. F. Smith, Letter to I. McDowell, June 15, 1842, C. F. Smith Papers.

21. Klopcic, "Come Fill Your Glasses Fellows, But Why?" 4–5.

22. Freeman Cleaves, *Rock of Chickamauga: The Life of General George H. Thomas* (Norman: University of Oklahoma Press, 1948), 11.

23. Robbins, *Last in Their Class*, 68.

24. Klopcic, "Come Fill Your Glasses Fellows, But Why?" 5.

25. Orders No. 28, May 22, 1841, Orders, Archives, U.S. Military Academy Library.

26. Orders No. 76, September 11, 1840, Orders, Archives, U.S. Military Academy Library.
27. C. F. Smith, Letter to R. Delafield, May 31, 1839, Officers Letters, Archives, U.S. Military Academy Library.
28. M. S. Culbertson, Note to C. F. Smith, December 26, 1838, Officers Letters, Archives, U.S. Military Academy Library.
29. C. F. Smith, Letter to R. Delafield, November 9, 1838, Officers Letters, Archives, U.S. Military Academy Library.
30. R. Delafield, Note to C. F. Smith, November 9, 1838, Officers Letters, Archives, U.S. Military Academy Library.
31. Gilmer Note to C. F. Smith, January 14, 1839, Officers Letters, Archives, U.S. Military Academy Library.
32. C. F. Smith, Letter to R. Delafield, December 23, 1838, Officers Letters, Archives, U.S. Military Academy Library.
33. *Centennial*, Vol. II, 97.
34. *Centennial*, Vol. II, 97.
35. *Centennial*, Vol. II, 97.
36. *Centennial*, Vol. II, 101.
37. *Centennial*, Vol. II, 103.
38. Forman, "Cadet Life Before the Mexican War," 1.
39. In his communications with his wife, Charles addressed her as Fanny. This was also the name that would be given to his daughter. In order to avoid confusion, Mrs. Smith will be referred to as Francis.
40. *Historic Structures Inventory United States Military Academy West Point, New York* (Washington: National Park Service Department of the Interior, 1984), Historic Structures Inventory, Archives, U.S. Military Academy Library, Vol. 1, National Landmark Historic District, 6.
41. Simpson, "The Second Regiment of Artillery," 317.
42. Orders No. 30, May 29, 1841, Orders, Archives, U.S. Military Academy Library.
43. "Register of the Officers and Cadets of the U.S. Military Academy, June, 1841," *Official Register of the Officers and Cadets of the United States Military Academy (1818-1966)*, 6 & 22.
44. Orders No. 29, July 5, 1842, Orders, Archives, U.S. Military Academy Library.
45. Battalion Orders No. 24, July 13, 1838, Archives, U.S. Military Academy Library.
46. Battalion Orders No. 67, July 30, 1839, Archives, U.S. Military Academy Library.
47. Battalion Orders No. 84, July 31, 1838, Archives, U.S. Military Academy Library.
48. *Centennial*, Vol. II, 97.
49. Forman, "Cadet Life at West Point Before the Mexican War," 11.
50. Robbins, *Last in Their Class*, 77.
51. Forman, "Cadet Life at West Point Before the Mexican War," 11.
52. Barone, "Cadet Disciplinary System," 6.
53. Ambrose, *Duty, Honor, Country*, 78.
54. Dubelier, "The Forgotten Soldier," 7-8.
55. Henry Coppee, *Grant and His Campaigns* (New York: Charles Richardson, 1866), 72.
56. Robbins, *Last in Their Class*, 7.
57. Hudson, *The Odyssey of a Southerner*, chapter one.
58. Barone, "Cadet Disciplinary System," 9-10.
59. Barone, "Cadet Disciplinary System," 11.
60. Jeffrey D. Wert, *General James Longstreet: The Confederacy's Most Controversial Soldier* (New York: Simon & Schuster, 1993), 29.

61. John M. Moore, C. McKenna, and H. Raugh, "From Disorder to Discipline: The Origins of the Thayer Disciplinary System," 4 December 1990, Tactical Officer Education Program, Special Collections, Special Collections & Archives, United States Military Academy, 12.
62. The honor code was simply that an officer's word was his bond. This meant "a cadet will not lie, cheat, steal, or tolerate those who do." Cadet Honor Code, http://en.wikipedia.org/wiki/Cadet_Honor_Code#The_U.S._Military_Academy_at_West_Point, Accessed April 6, 2013.
63. C. F. Smith, Note to G. G. Waggaman, May 1839, Officers Letters, Archives, U.S. Military Academy Library.
64. Robbins, *Last in Their Class*, 9.
65. *Centennial*, Vol. II, 100-101.
66. Orders No. 57, July 28, 1840, Archives, U.S. Military Academy Library.
67. Battalion Orders No. 30, April 14, 1838, Archives, U.S. Military Academy.
68. Battalion Orders No. 53, May 30, 1838, Archives, U.S. Military Academy Library.
69. Battalion Orders No. 79, July 23, 1838, Archives, U.S. Military Academy Library.
70. Battalion Orders No. 80, July 24, 1838, Archives, U.S. Military Academy Library.
71. Battalion Orders No. 82, July 31, 1838, Archives, U.S. Military Academy Library.
72. Battalion Orders No. 77, October 2, 1839, Archives, U.S. Military Academy Library.
73. C. F. Smith, Note to R. Delafield, February 5, 1839, Officers Letters, Archives, U.S. Military Academy Library.
74. C. F. Smith, Letter to R. Delafield, January 6, 1839, Officers Letters, Archives, U.S. Military Academy Library.
75. *Centennial*, Vol. II, 97.
76. C. F. Smith, Note to G. G. Waggaman, June 11, 1839, Officers Letters, Archives, U.S. Military Academy Library.
77. Officers Letters, September 1840, Officers Letters, Archives, U.S. Military Academy Library.
78. Officers Letters, October 1840, Officers Letters, Archives, U.S. Military Academy Library.
79. Pledge of 168 Cadets, May 13, 1840, Archives, U.S. Military Academy Library.
80. Pledge of Cadets Letter, May 12, 1840, Archives, U.S. Military Academy Library.
81. C. F. Smith, Note to R. Delafield, October 10, 1838, Archives, U.S. Military Academy Library.
82. R. Delafield, Note, October 1838, C. F. Smith Papers.
83. C. F. Smith, "S. G. Jones vs. Couts" to R. Delafield, October 10, 1838, Officers Letters, Archives, U.S. Military Academy Library.
84. C. F. Smith, Letter to G. G. Waggaman, September 2, 1840, Officers Letters, Archives, U.S. Military Academy Library.
85. C. F. Smith, Letter to G. G. Waggaman, February 16, 1840, Officers Letters, Archives, U.S. Military Academy Library.
86. Hudson, *The Odyssey of a Southerner*, chapter one.
87. Edward G. Longacre, *The Man Behind the Guns: A Biography of General Henry Jackson Hunt* (New York: A. S. Barnes & Company, 1977), 29.
88. C. F. Smith, Memorandum, May 1, 1840, Officers Letters, Archives, U.S. Military Academy Library.
89. C. F. Smith, Note to R. Delafield, January 1, 1840, Officers Letters, Archives, U.S. Military Academy Library.

90. C. F. Smith, Letter to R. Delafield, October 31, 1841, Officers Letters, Archives, U.S. Military Academy Library.
91. C. F. Smith, Letter to J. McDowell, July 8, 1842, Officers Letters, Archives, U.S. Military Academy Library.
92. McDowell Note to C. F. Smith, April 6, 1842, Officers Letters, Archives, U.S. Military Academy Library.
93. Orders No. 26, April 26, 1840, Officers Letters, Archives, U.S. Military Academy Library.
94. Orders No. 2, January 11, 1841, Officers Letters, Archives, U.S. Military Academy Library.
95. A. C. Darne, Note to C. F. Smith, June 27, 1840, Archives, U.S. Military Academy Library.
96. The terms "light" and "dark" prison refer to rooms either with or without a window. The "dark" windowless room was used for more serious offenses.
97. C. F. Smith, Note to G. G. Waggaman, June 29, 1840, Officers Letters, Archives, U.S. Military Academy Library.
98. C. F. Smith, Letter to G. G. Waggaman, November 2, 1840, Officers Letters, Archives, U.S. Military Academy Library.
99. C. F. Smith, Letter to J. G. Totten, May 23, 1842, Officers Letters, Archives, U.S. Military Academy Library.
100. C. F. Smith, Complaint of informality by Adjutant of Military Academy, October 24, 1839; M. Knowlton, Note to C. F. Smith, October 24, 1839; C. F. Smith, Letter to Major Delafield, October 24, 1839, Officers Letters, Archives, U.S. Military Academy Library.
101. C. F. Smith, Letter to I. McDowell, November 1, 1841, Officers Letters, Archives, U.S. Military Academy Library.
102. C. F. Smith, Note to Richard Delafield, December 22, 1838, C. F. Smith Papers.
103. G. G. Waggaman, Letter to R. Delafield, May 8, 1840, Officers Letters, Archives, U.S. Military Academy Library.
104. M. Knowlton, Letter to R. Delafield, November 11, 1839, Officers Letters, Archives, U.S. Military Academy Library.
105. C. F. Smith, Letter to I. McDowell, March 14, 1842, Officers Letters, Archives, U.S. Military Academy Library.
106. C. F. Smith, Report to R. Delafield, September 22, 1840, Officers Letters, Archives, U.S. Military Academy Library.
107. C. F. Smith, Letter to R. Delafield, September 22, 1840, Officers Letters, Archives, U.S. Military Academy Library.
108. Joseph Howard Parks, *General Edmund Kirby Smith, C.S.A.* (Baton Rouge: Louisiana State University Press, 1954), 19–20.

Chapter 4

1. Grant, *Personal Memoirs*, 17.
2. Frederick T. Dent, Notes on U. S. Grant at West Point, Ulysses S. Grant Homepage, http://www.granthomepage.com/intdent.htm, Accessed July 30, 2011.
3. Lloyd Lewis, *Captain Sam Grant* (Boston: Little, Brown and Company, 1950), 61–62.
4. Lewis, *Captain Sam Grant*, 62.
5. The complete list of conditions includes the following ailments: (1) Feeble constitution and muscular tenuity: unsound health from whatever cause: indications of former disease: glandular swellings, or other symptoms of scrofula; (2) Chronic cutaneous affections, especially of the scalp, or any disorder of an infectious character; (3) Severe injuries of the bones of the head: convulsions; (4) Impaired vision from whatever causes: inflammatory affections of the eyelids; immobility or irregularity of the iris: fistutla lachrymalis, etc., etc.; (5) Deafness; copious discharge from the ears; (6) Loss of many teeth, or the teeth generally unsound; (7) Impediment of speech; (8) Want of due capacity of the chest, and any other indication of a liability to a pulmonic disease; (9) Impaired or inadequate efficiency of one or both of the superior extremities on account of fractures, especially of the clavicle, contraction of a joint, extenuation, deformity, etc., etc.; (10) An unusual excurvature or incurvature of the spine; (11) Hernia; (12) A varicose state of the veins of the scrotum or spermatic cord (when large), sarcocele, hydrocele, hemorrhoids, fistulas; (13) Impaired or inadequate efficiency of one or both of the inferior extremities on account of varicose veins, fractures, malformation (flat feet, etc.), lameness, con traction, unequal length, bunions, overlying or supernumerary toes, etc. etc.; (14) Ulcers, or unsound cicatrices of ulcers likely to break out afresh. *Guide to West Point and the U.S. Military Academy* (New York: D. Van Nostrand, 1867), 79–81.
6. In Arithmetic they had to be able to perform "with facility examples under the four ground rules," and hence must be familiar with the tables of addition, subtraction, multiplication, and division: and must be able to perform examples in reduction and vulgar fractions. In English Grammar, they were required to exhibit a "familiarity" with the nine parts of speech and the rules in relation thereto, and must be able to parse any ordinary sentence which may be given them, and generally they must understand those portions of the subject usually taught in the higher academies and schools throughout the country, comprehended under the heads of Orthography, Etymology, Syntax, and Prosody. In Descriptive Geography they were required to name, locate, and describe the natural grand and political divisions of the earth, and be able to delineate any one of the States or Territories of the American Union, with its principal cities, rivers, lakes, seaports, and mountains. In History they had to name the periods of the discovery and settlement of the North American continent, of the rise and progress of the United States, and of the successive wars and political administrations through which the country has passed. *Guide to West Point and the U.S. Military Academy* (New York: D. Van Nostrand, 1867), 84–87.
7. Lewis, *Captain Sam Grant*, 68–69.
8. Forman, "Cadet Life Before the Mexican War," 7.
9. Grant, *Personal Memoirs*, 15.
10. Grant, *Personal Memoirs*, 15.
11. The term "policing the grounds" entails picking up trash and "anything that doesn't grow."
12. *Guide to West Point and the U.S. Military Academy*, 56.
13. Grant, *Personal Memoirs*, 15.
14. "Register of the Officers and Cadets of the U.S. Military Academy, June, 1840," *Official Register of the Officers and Cadets of the United States Military Academy (1818-1966)*, 5.
15. Grant, *Personal Memoirs*, 15.
16. Hudson, *The Odyssey of a Southerner*, chapter one.
17. The scents were not the exotic fragrances of Arabia.
18. Robbins, *Last in Their Class*, 67–68.

19. "At West Point Together—Grant's Courtship—The War and Afterwards," Confederate General James Longstreet discusses his friendship with Grant, *New York Times*, July 24, 1885.
20. Lloyd Lewis, *Captain Sam Grant*, 61-62.
21. "Register of the Officers and Cadets of the U.S. Military Academy, June, 1843," *Official Register of the Officers and Cadets of the United States Military Academy (1818-1966)*, 21.
22. Lewis, *Captain Sam Grant*, 75.
23. Grant, *Personal Memoirs*, 15.
24. Max L. Heyman, *Prudent Soldier: A Biography of Major General E.R.S. Canby* (Glendale: The Arthur Clarke Company, 1959), 30.
25. Jeffrey D. Wert, *General James Longstreet: The Confederacy's Most Controversial Soldier* (New York: Simon & Schuster, 1993), 31.
26. H. S. Grant, Letter to M. Griffith, September 22, 1839; John Y. Simon, ed., *The Papers of Ulysses S. Grant: Vol. I 1837-1861* (Carbondale: Southern Illinois University Press, 1967), 7.
27. "Register of the Officers and Cadets of the U.S. Military Academy, June, 1840," *Official Register of the Officers and Cadets of the United States Military Academy (1818-1966)*, 16-17.
28. "Register of the Officers and Cadets of the U.S. Military Academy, June, 1840," *Official Register of the Officers and Cadets of the United States Military Academy (1818-1966)*, 16 & 23.
29. *Centennial*, Vol. II, 98.
30. Grant, *Personal Memoirs*, 15.
31. *Centennial*, Vol. II, 99.
32. *Centennial*, Vol. II, 100.
33. Holland, "An Anecdote of General Grant Related by His Son," February 1909-1912, *New News of Yesterday*, Interview with Frederick Dent Grant by Holland in 1899 just before he sailed for the Philippines to take a military command.
34. Robbins, *Last in Their Class*, 72.
35. Lewis, *Captain Sam Grant*, 82.
36. "Register of the Officers and Cadets of the U.S. Military Academy, June, 1841," *Official Register of the Officers and Cadets of the United States Military Academy (1818-1966)*, 13, 14, & 20.
37. Grant, *Personal Memoirs*, 17.
38. Grant, *Personal Memoirs*, 16.
39. "Register of the Officers and Cadets of the U.S. Military Academy, June, 1842," *Official Register of the Officers and Cadets of the United States Military Academy (1818-1966)*, 9, 10, & 21.
40. Lewis, *Captain Sam Grant*, 73-74.
41. J. W. Bankhead, Letter to C. F. Smith, April 23, 1842, C. F. Smith Papers.
42. F. W. Stewart, Note to C. F. Smith, June 14, 1842, C. F. Smith Papers.
43. J. G. Totten, Letter to C. F. Smith, July 7, 1842, C. F. Smith Papers.
44. Winfield Scott, Special Orders No. 56, July 9, 1842, Archives, U.S. Military Academy Library.
45. Winfield Scott, Special Orders No. 60, July 18, 1842, Archives, U.S. Military Academy Library.
46. Kurt Wille, Descendants of Dr. Samuel Blair Smith, MD, USA, Information compiled from records at Virginia Historical Society, Pennsylvania Historical Society, and Delaware Historical Society, October 22, 2011.

Chapter 5

1. C. F. Smith, "Memorandum of the Military Services of Captain C. F. Smith, 2nd Artillery from Sept. 1, 1842 to October 13, 1845," C. F. Smith Papers.
2. Jacob Dolson Cox, *Military Reminiscences of the Civil War Vol. I* (New York: Charles Scribner & Sons, 1900), 166.
3. Frankford Arsenal, http://en.wikipedia.org/wiki/Frankford_Arsenal, Accessed April 18, 2012.
4. James J. Farley, *Making Arms in the Machine Age* (University Park: Pennsylvania State University, 1994), 42.
5. Farley, *Making Arms*, 43.
6. E. D. Townsend, Letter to C. F. Smith, July 16, 1844, C. F. Smith Papers. Edward D. Townsend graduated from the U.S. Military Academy in 1837. He served in the Florida War and on the Northern Frontier during Canada Border Disturbances. At the time of this letter, Townsend was at Fort Columbus, NY. He later went on to serve as Assistant Adjutant General in the Adjutant General's Office, Washington, D.C. He was twice brevetted for service during the Civil War. Cullum, *Biographical Register*, Vol. I, 673-674.
7. I. McDowell, Letter to C. F. Smith, March 3, 1843, C. F. Smith Papers.
8. Returns are reports prepared on a monthly basis on the state of the officers' command. They include the number of men fit for duty, new recruits, discharges, and provisions.
9. C. F. Smith, Journal entry of December 12, 1844, Public Letters of Capt. C. F. Smith, 2nd Artillery, Commenced at Frankford Arsenal, PA November 18, 1844 and Finished in the City of Mexico, October 1, 1849, C. F. Smith Papers.
10. Farley, *Making Arms*, 43.
11. C. F. Smith, Journal entry of November 18, 1844, Public Letters of Capt. C. F. Smith, November 18, 1844-October 1, 1849, C. F. Smith Papers.
12. C. F. Smith, Journal entry of November 30, 1844, Public Letters of Capt. C. F. Smith, 2nd Artillery, Commenced at Frankford Arsenal, PA November 18, 1844 and Finished in the City of Mexico, October 1, 1849, C. F. Smith Papers.
13. C. F. Smith, Journal entry of January 10, 1845, Public Letters of Capt. C. F. Smith, November 18, 1844-October 1, 1849, C. F. Smith Papers.
14. C. F. Smith, Journal entry of December 25, 1844, Public Letters of Capt. C. F. Smith, November 18, 1844-October 1, 1849, C. F. Smith Papers.
15. C. F. Smith, Journal entry of January 2, 1845, Public Letters of Cap. C. F. Smith, 18 November 1844-1 October 1849, C. F. Smith Papers.
16. C. F. Smith, Journal entry of January 15, 1845, Public Letters of Capt. C. F. Smith, November 18, 1844-October 1, 1849, C. F. Smith Papers.
17. C. F. Smith, Letter to Bankhead, January 20, 1845, Public Letters of Capt. C. F. Smith, November 18, 1844-October 1, 1849, C. F. Smith Papers.
18. C. F. Smith, Journal entry of January 22, 1845, Public Letters of Capt. C. F. Smith, November 18, 1844-October 1, 1849, C. F. Smith Papers.
19. C. F. Smith, Journal entry of November 28, 1844, Public Letters of Capt. C. F. Smith, November 18, 1844-October 1, 1849, C. F. Smith Papers.

20. C. F. Smith, Journal entry of July 7, 1845, Public Letters of Capt. C. F. Smith, November 18, 1844–October 1, 1849, C. F. Smith Papers.
21. C. F. Smith, Journal entry of December 7, 1844, Public Letters of Capt. C. F. Smith, November 18, 1844–October 1, 1849, C. F. Smith Papers.
22. C. F. Smith, Journal entry of February 1, 1845, Public Letters of Capt. C. F. Smith, November 18, 1844–October 1, 1849, C. F. Smith Papers.
23. C. F. Smith, Journal entry of May 25, 1845, Public Letters of Capt. C. F. Smith, November 18, 1844–October 1, 1849, C. F. Smith Papers.
24. C. F. Smith, Journal entry of February 9, 1845, Public Letters of Capt. C. F. Smith, November 18, 1844–October 1, 1849, C. F. Smith Papers.
25. C. F. Smith, Journal entry of April 23, 1845, Public Letters of Capt. C. F. Smith, November 18, 1844–October 1, 1849, C. F. Smith Papers.
26. C. F. Smith, Journal entry of December 15, 1844, Public Letters of Capt. C. F. Smith, November 18, 1844–October 1, 1849, C. F. Smith Papers.
27. C. F. Smith, Journal entry of May 12, 1845, Public Letters of Capt. C. F. Smith, November 18, 1844–October 1,1849, C. F. Smith Papers.
28. C. F. Smith, Journal entry of November 30, 1844, Public Letters of Capt. C. F. Smith, November 18 1844–October 1, 1849, C. F. Smith Papers.
29. C. F. Smith, Journal entry of April 8, 1845, Public Letters of Capt. C. F. Smith, November 18, 1844–October 1, 1849, C. F. Smith Papers.
30. C. F. Smith, Journal entry of December 18, 1844, Public Letters of Capt. C. F. Smith, November 18, 1844–October 1, 1849, C. F. Smith Papers.
31. C. F. Smith, Journal entry of February 8, 1845, Public Letters of Capt. C. F. Smith, November 18, 1844–October 1, 1849, C. F. Smith Papers.
32. C. F. Smith, Journal entry of January 12, 1845, Public Letters of Capt. C. F. Smith, November 18, 1844–October 1, 1849, C. F. Smith Papers.
33. Farley, *Making Arms*, 42–43.

Part Two

1. Henry Coppee, *Grant and His Campaigns* (New York: Charles Richardson, 1866), 72.

Chapter 6

1. Adrian N. Anderson, et al., *Texas and Texans* (New York: Macmillan/McGraw-Hill, 1993), 173–188.
2. Anderson, *Texas and Texans*, 221–222.
3. Anderson, *Texas and Texans*, 240.
4. Anderson, *Texas and Texans*, 244–246.
5. Anderson, *Texas and Texans*, 259–263.
6. Anderson, *Texas and Texans*, 273.
7. Texas Annexation, http://en.wikipedia.org/wiki/Texas_Annexation, Accessed July 11, 2011.
8. The Nueces River rises northwest of San Antonio and flows south through the Texas Hill Country approaching to within 35 miles of the Rio Grande on the border with Mexico. East of Carrizo Springs it turns to the east, flowing through the scrub plains of South Texas, across rural Dimmit, La Salle, and McMullen counties. In central Live Oak County it is joined from the northwest by the Frio River, then flows southeast along the coastal plain past Mathis, where it is impounded to form the Lake Corpus Christi reservoir. It enters Corpus Christi Bay on the Gulf of Mexico at Corpus Christi, Nueces River, http://en.wikipedia.org/wiki/Nueces_River, Accessed December 8, 2012.
9. Message from the President of the United States, relative to an invasion and commencement of hostilities by Mexico, May 11, 1846, House Executive Document No. 60, "Messages of the President of the United States with the Correspondence, Therewith Communicated Between the Secretary of War and other Officers of the Government on the Subject of The Mexican War" (Washington: Wendell and Van Benthuysen, 1848), Library of Congress, 6–7.
10. Simpson, "The Second Regiment of Artillery," 316; C. F. Smith, Journal entry of October 1, 1845, Public Letters of Captain C. F. Smith, November 18, 1844–October 1, 1849, C. F. Smith Papers.
11. Texas Annexation, http://en.wikipedia.org/wiki/Texas_Annexation, Accessed July 11, 2011.
12. Anonymous, *Complete History of Late Mexican War* (New York: 128 Nassau Street, 1851), 19.
13. Joseph Wheelan, *Invading Mexico: America's Continental Dream and the Mexican War, 1846–1848* (New York: Carroll & Graf, 2007), 81–82.
14. Spencer C. Tucker, ed., *The Encyclopedia of the Mexican-American War* (Santa Barbara: ABC-CLIO, 2013), vol. I, 1010.
15. Wheelan, *Invading Mexico*, 82.
16. W. A. Croffut, ed., *Fifty Years in Camp and Field Diary of Major-General Ethan Allen Hitchcock, U.S.A.* (New York: G. P. Putnam's Sons, 1909), 204; Cullum, *Biographical Register*, Vol. I, 167–179.
17. Richard Bruce Winders, *Mr. Polk's Army: The American Military Experience in the Mexican War* (College Station: Texas A&M University Press, 1997), 18.
18. George Winston Smith and Charles Judah, *The Chronicles of the Gringos: The U.S. Army in the Mexican War, 1846–1848—Accounts of Eyewitnesses & Combatants* (Albuquerque: University of New Mexico Press, 1968), 275–276.
19. Smith and Judah, *The Chronicles of the Gringos*, 310.
20. Winders, *Mr. Polk's Army*, 84.
21. W. L. Marcy, Order to Z. Taylor, January 13, 1846, House Executive Document No. 60, 90–91.
22. Z. Taylor, Letter to the Adjutant General of the Army, February 4, 1846, House Executive Document No. 60, 116.
23. David A. Clary, *Eagles and Empire: The United States, Mexico, and the Struggle for the Continent* (New York: Bantam Books, 2009), 82.
24. Bauer, *The Mexican War*, 37.
25. Greenberg, *A Wicked War*, 100.
26. Grant, *Personal Memoirs*, 31.
27. Justin H. Smith, *The War with Mexico* (Gloucester, Peter Smith, 1963), vol. I, 146–147.
28. Clary, *Eagles and Empire*, 83.
29. One soldier described chaparral "as an irregular, impenetrable mass of 'scraggly, scrubby, crooked, infernally illegitimate and sin-begotten bushy trees loaded with millions of thorn pins'—that is to say chaparral." J. Smith, *The War with Mexico*, vol. I, 148.
30. Clary, *Eagles and Empire*, 83.
31. Bauer, *The Mexican War*, 39.

32. E. Kirby Smith, Letter to his Wife, March 17, 1846, Emma Jerome Blackwood, ed. E. Kirby Smith, *To Mexico with Scott: Letters of Captain E. Kirby Smith to His Wife* (Cambridge: Harvard University Press, 1917), 30.

33. Z. Taylor, to the Adjutant General of the Army, March 21, 1846, House Executive Document No. 60, "Messages of the President of the United States with the Correspondence, Therewith Communicated Between the Secretary of War and other Officers of the Government on the Subject of the Mexican War" (Washington: Wendell and Van Benthuysen, 1848), Library of Congress, 124.

34. C. F. Smith, Letter to L. Smith, March 21, 1846, C. F. Smith Papers.

35. Mark Crawford, *Encyclopedia of the Mexican-American War* (Santa Barbara: ABC-CLIO, 1999), 174; Gary F. Kurutz, ed., Major John Corey Henshaw, *Recollections of the War with Mexico* (Columbia: University of Missouri Press, 2008), 47–48; and John E. Weems, *To Conquer a Peace* (College Station: Texas A&M University Press, 1974, 110.

36. Anonymous, *Complete History of the Mexican War*, 20.

37. R. T. Feldman, *The Mexican-American War* (Minneapolis: Lerner, 2004), 43; D. Nevin, *The Mexican War* (Alexandria: Time Life Books, 1978), 27–28; G. Meade, *The Life and Letters of George Gordon Meade, Major-General, United States Army* (New York: Charles Scribner's & Sons, 1913), vol. 1, 54; A. S. Greenberg, *A Wicked War: Polk, Clay, Lincoln, and 1846 U.S. Invasion of Mexico* (New York: Vintage Books, 2012), 203–204.

38. Crawford, *Encyclopedia of the Mexican-American War*, 90–91.

39. Z. Taylor, to the Adjutant General of the Army, April 26, 1846, House Executive Document No. 60, 141.

40. Weems, *To Conquer a Peace*, 122–123.

Chapter 7

1. Ambrose, *Duty, Honor, Country*, 139–140.
2. Crawford, *Encyclopedia of the Mexican-American War*, 207.
3. Grant, *Personal Memoirs*, 43.
4. John S. D. Eisenhower, *Zachary Taylor* (New York: Times Books, 2008), 47.
5. Dubelier, "The Forgotten Soldier," 14.
6. Grant, *Personal Memoirs*, 44.
7. Grant, *Personal Memoirs*, 44.
8. Zachary Taylor, Official Report of the Battle of Palo Alto to Roger Jones, May 16, 1846, http://www.dmwv.org/mexwar/documents/paloalto.htm, Accessed May 5, 2012.
9. Zachary Taylor, Official Report of the Battle of Palo Alto to Roger Jones, May 16, 1846, http://www.dmwv.org/mexwar/documents/paloalto.htm, Accessed May 5, 2012.
10. Grant, *Personal Memoirs*, 45.
11. Zachary Taylor, Official Report of the Battle of Palo Alto to Roger Jones, May 16, 1846, http://www.dmwv.org/mexwar/documents/paloalto.htm, Accessed May 5, 2012.
12. Zachary Taylor, Official Report of the Battle of Palo Alto to Roger Jones, 16 May 1846, http://www.dmwv.org/mexwar/documents/paloalto.htm, Accessed May 5, 2012.
13. A resaca is the dry channel or the former often marshy course of a stream. The word is derived from the Spanish word *resacar* meaning to draw back. http://www.merriam-webster.com/dictionary/resaca, Accessed December 8, 2012.
14. J. Frost, *The Mexican War and Its Warriors* (New Haven: H. Mansfield, 1850), 46.
15. Frost, *The Mexican War and Its Warriors*, 47–48.
16. Grant, *Personal Memoirs*, 45. McCall reported the size of his force as 220 men.
17. G. A. McCall, Report to W. S. Bliss, May 13, 1846, C. F. Smith Papers.
18. C. F. Smith, Report to G. A. McCall, May 13, 1846, C. F. Smith Papers.
19. C. F. Smith, Report to G. A. McCall, May 13, 1846, C. F. Smith Papers.
20. G. A. McCall, Report to W. W. S. Bliss, May 13, 1846, C. F. Smith Papers.
21. Zachary Taylor, official report of the battle of Resaca de la Palma to Roger Jones, May 17, 1846, http://www.dmwv.org/mexwar/documents/resaca.htm, Accessed May 10, 2012.
22. This promotion was awarded on May 9, 1846. It was probably backdated because Robert Anderson wrote in spring 1847 that Smith had "not even received notice of an empty brevet." Cullum, *Biographical Register*, vol. 1, 354.
23. M. Deltast, Letter to C. F. Smith, May 27, 1846, C. F. Smith Papers.
24. Grant, *Personal Memoirs*, 30.
25. Frost, *The Mexican War and Its Warriors*, 54–56.
26. Z. Taylor, to the Adjutant General, May 20, 1846, House Executive Document No. 60, 299.
27. Grant, *Personal Memoirs*, 48.
28. Bauer, *The Mexican War*, 83.
29. Irving W. Levinson, *Wars Within Wars: Mexican Guerrillas, Domestic Elites, and the United States of America 1846-1848* (Self-published in Canada, 2005), 31.
30. "Volunteers," July 25, 1846, *Niles National Register*, www.archive.org, 325.
31. A dragoon described the Rangers as, "A more reckless, devil-may-care set, it would be impossible to find this side of the Infernal Regions. Some wore buckskin shirts black with grease and blood, some wore red shirts, their trousers thrust into high boots; all were armed with Revolvers and huge Bowie knives. Take them altogether, with their uncouth costumes, bearded faces, lean and brawny forms, fierce wild eyes, and swaggering manners, they were fit representatives of the outlaws which make up the population of the Lone Star State." David Lavender, *Climax at Buena Vista* (Philadelphia: University of Pennsylvania Press, 1966), 36.
32. Walter P. Weber, *The Texas Rangers in the Mexican War* (Austin: Jenkins Garrett Press, 1975), 8–9; Crawford, *Encyclopedia of the Mexican-American War*, 22.
33. Winders, *Mr. Polk's Army*, 144.
34. Bauer, *The Mexican War*, 83.
35. Winders, *Mr. Polk's Army*, 13.
36. Crawford, *Encyclopedia of the Mexican-American War*, 71.
37. Z. Taylor, A Proclamation by the General Commanding the Army of the U.S. of America to the People of Mexico, House Executive Document No. 60, 167.
38. Eisenhower, *Zachary Taylor*, 55.
39. Martin Dugard, *The Training Ground: Grant, Lee, Sherman, and Davis in the Mexican War, 1846-1848* (New York: Little, Brown, 2008), 112–123.

Chapter 8

1. Crawford, *Encyclopedia of the Mexican-American War*, 302.
2. General William Worth was Commandant of Cadets at West Point from 1820 to 1828 during C. F. Smith's time as a cadet from 1820 to 1825.
3. C. F. Smith, Letter to W. L. Mactier, May 1846, C. F. Smith Papers.
4. C. F. Smith, Letter to E. D. Fordent, June 6, 1846, C. F. Smith Papers.
5. John L. Smith, Letter to C. F. Smith, June 11, 1846, C. F. Smith Papers.
6. Z. Taylor, Report No. 50 to the Adjutant General, June 6, 1846, House Executive Document No. 60, 305–306.
7. Nevin, *The Mexican War*, 60–61.
8. C. F. Smith, Correspondence of July 27, 1846, and July 29, 1846, C. F. Smith Papers.
9. Wheelan, *Invading Mexico*, 162.
10. E. J. Nichols, *Zachary Taylor's Little Army* (Garden City: Doubleday, 1963), 128.
11. W. W. Bliss, Orders No. 105, August 24, 1846, House Executive Document No. 60, 500.
12. Feldman, *The Mexican-American War*, 31.
13. Weems, *To Conquer a Peace*, 197; Crawford, *Encyclopedia of the Mexican-American War*, 249; Frost, *The Mexican War and Its Warriors*, 200.
14. John S. D. Eisenhower, *So Far from God: The U.S. War with Mexico 1846–1848* (New York: Anchor Books, 1989), 116.
15. Wheelan, *Invading Mexico*, 182, 184–185.
16. Frost, *The Mexican War and Its Warriors*, 66.
17. C. F. Smith, Journal entry of September 15, 1846, C. F. Smith Papers.
18. C. F. Smith, Journal entry of September 16, 1846, C. F. Smith Papers.
19. Smith and Judah, *Chronicles of the Gringos*, 78.
20. C. F. Smith, Journal entry of September 19, 1846, C. F. Smith Papers.
21. Frost, *The Mexican War and Its Warriors*, 95.
22. Weems, *To Conquer a Peace*, 220.
23. J. Smith, *The War with Mexico*, 121 & 134.
24. Eisenhower, *Zachary Taylor*, 59; Crawford, *Encyclopedia of the Mexican-American War*, 189.
25. Feldman, *The Mexican-American War*, 34; Weems, *To Conquer a Peace*, 222.
26. C. F. Smith, Journal entry of September 20, 1846, C. F. Smith Papers.
27. Light artillerymen manned the small caliber guns and howitzers.
28. C. F. Smith, Report to J. C. Pemberton, September 30, 1846, C. F. Smith Papers.
29. C. F. Smith, Journal entry of September 21, 1846, C. F. Smith Papers.
30. Z. Taylor, Report to the Adjutant General, October 9, 1846, House Executive Document No. 60, 83.
31. A forlorn hope is a group of soldiers chosen to take the leading part in a military operation, such as an assault on a defended position, where the risk of casualties is high. http://en.wikipedia.org/wiki/Forlorn_Hope#Etymology. Accessed May 6, 2013.
32. *New Orleans Daily Picayune*, No. 216, Sunday, October 4, 1846, as referenced in Dubelier, "The Forgotten Soldier," 20.
33. J. Smith, *The War with Mexico*, vol. I, 244–245.
34. C. F. Smith, Report to J. C. Pemberton, September 30, 1846, C. F. Smith Papers.
35. J. Smith, *The War with Mexico*, 244–245.
36. J. Smith, *The War with Mexico*, 244–245.
37. John J. Jenkins, *History of the War Between the United States and Mexico* (Auburn: Derby, Miller & Co., 1849), 167.
38. C. F. Smith, Report to J. C. Pemberton, September 30, 1846, C. F. Smith Papers.
39. Smith and Judah, *Chronicles of the Gringos*, 87.
40. C. F. Smith, Report to J. C. Pemberton, September 30, 1846, C. F. Smith Papers.
41. C. F. Smith, Journal entry of September 21, 1846, C. F. Smith Papers.
42. C. F. Smith, Report to J. C. Pemberton, September 30, 1846, C. F. Smith Papers.
43. *New Orleans Daily Picayune*, No. 216, Sunday, October 4, 1846, as referenced in Dubelier, "The Forgotten Soldier, 22.
44. J. B. Grayson, Letter to C. F. Smith, October 27, 1846, C. F. Smith Papers.
45. C. F. Smith, Journal entry of September 22, 1846, C. F. Smith Papers.
46. Smith also received a brevet to major dated to May 9, 1846, for "gallant and distinguished conduct in the battles of Palo Alto and Resaca-de-la-Palma, Tex." The brevet to lieutenant colonel was awarded on September 23, 1846, for "gallant conduct in the several battles at Monterrey, Mex." the brevets were probably backdated because Robert Anderson wrote in spring 1847 that Smith had "not even received notice of an empty brevet." Cullum, *Officers and Graduates of the U.S. Military Academy*, Vol. 1, 354.
47. Grant, *Personal Memoirs*, 56–57.
48. C. F. Smith, Journal entry of September 24, 1846, C. F. Smith Papers.
49. Grant, *Personal Memoirs*, 57.
50. C. F. Smith, Journal entry of September 25, 1846, C. F. Smith Papers.
51. Crawford, *Encyclopedia of the Mexican-American War*, 302; Henshaw, *Recollections of the War with Mexico*, 208.
52. Grant, *Personal Memoirs*, 57.
53. R. Anderson, Letter to Eliza B. C. Anderson, March 30, 1847, Robert Anderson, *An Artillery Officer in the Mexican War* (New York: Knickerbocker Press, 1911), 108.
54. *Senate Report*, 41st Congress, 2nd session, No. 34, February 14, 1870, as referenced in Dubelier, "The Forgotten Soldier," 26.
55. The date of Worth's nomination is unclear. It was probably in November or December, because General Scott refers to Brevet Lieutenant Colonel Smith in General Orders No. 170 on January 8, 1847. W. Scott, General Orders No. 170, January 8, 1847, C. F. Smith Papers.

Chapter 9

1. Grant, *Personal Memoirs*, 58.
2. Grant, *Personal Memoirs*, 59.
3. W. Scott, Letter to Z. Taylor, November 25, 1846, House Executive Document No. 60, 373.
4. Frost, *The Mexican War and Its Warriors*, 101; Smith, vol. I, 264.
5. Eisenhower, *So Far from God*, 171.

6. C. F. Smith, Letter to J. Cashman, December 12, 1846, C. F. Smith Papers.
7. C. F. Smith, Letter to E. McGwin, January 6, 1847, C. F. Smith Papers.
8. Bauer, *The Mexican War*, 106–109.
9. Grant, *Personal Memoirs*, 60.
10. Simpson, "The Second Regiment of Artillery," 317.
11. W. Scott, General Orders No. 170, January 8, 1847, C. F. Smith Papers.
12. C. F. Smith, Letters, January 20–21, 1847, C. F. Smith Papers.
13. Grant, *Personal Memoirs*, 61.
14. Grant, *Personal Memoirs*, 61.
15. Grant, *Personal Memoirs*, 62.
16. Frost, *The Mexican War and Its Warriors*, 129–130.
17. A gig boat is a small boat that was used as personal vessel by the ship's captain.
18. Woodworth, *Manifest Destinies*, 240.
19. Nevin, *The Mexican War*, 139; J. Smith, *The War with Mexico*, vol. I, 26.
20. Grant, *Personal Memoirs*, 61–62.
21. Bauer, *The Mexican War*, 106–109.
22. Grant, *Personal Memoirs*, 61–62.
23. Dugard, *The Training Ground*, 301–303.
24. Greenberg, *A Wicked War*, 169–170.
25. Simpson, "The Second Regiment of Artillery," 317.
26. W. Scott, Report to William L. Marcy, March 29, 1847, www.dmwv.org/mexwar/documents/veracru2.htm, Accessed December 11, 2013.
27. Grant, *Personal Memoirs*, 63–64.
28. Smith and Judah, *Chronicles of the Gringos*, 203–204.
29. Eisenhower, *So Far from God*, 278–279.
30. Of the 1,653 regular U.S. Army officers and 3,131 U.S. volunteer officers who served during the Mexican-American War, 454 received brevets for gallantry in action. Another 33 officers received brevet promotions for meritorious or distinguished service while serving in the country of the enemy. All but two of those merit promotions were conferred by an order issued on May 30, 1848. The largest number of brevet promotions awarded for a single battle was 184 for Churubusco. One hundred forty-seven officers received two brevet promotions during the war, and nine officers received three brevet promotions: Braxton Bragg, James Duncan, Joseph Hooker, Benjamin Huger, Robert E. Lee, Joseph Mansfield, Charles A. May, Charles F. Smith, and Zealous B. Tower. Spencer C. Tucker, ed., *The Encyclopedia of the Mexican-American War* (Santa Barbara: ABC-CLIO, 2013), vol. I, 1010.
31. Robert Anderson, *An Artillery Officer* (New York: Knickerbocker Press, 1911), 126.
32. Worth Orders No. 8, April 11, 1847, C. F. Smith Papers.
33. Simpson, "The Second Regiment of Artillery," 318.
34. Eisenhower, *So Far from God*, 278–279.
35. W. Scott, Report on the events following the capture of Vera Cruz and the battle at Cero Gordo. Probably to W. Marcy, April 19, 1847, C. F. Smith Papers.
36. Winfield Scott, Report on the events following the capture of Vera Cruz and the battle at Cero Gordo. Probably to W. Marcy, April 19, 1847, C. F. Smith Papers.
37. W. Worth, Orders No. 16, April 24, 1847, C. F. Smith Papers.
38. J. B. Scott, Letter to C. F. Smith, May 7, 1847, C. F. Smith Papers.
39. Woodworth, *Manifest Destinies*, 258.
40. Greenberg, *A Wicked War*, 206–208.
41. Eisenhower, *So Far from God*, 305–306.

Chapter 10

1. Woodworth, *Manifest Destinies*, 261.
2. J. Smith, *The War with Mexico*, vol. II, 93.
3. Feldman, *The Mexican-American War*, 58.
4. J. Smith, *The War with Mexico*, vol. II, 93–95.
5. Timothy J. Henderson, *A Glorious Defeat: Mexico and Its War with the United States* (New York: Hill and Wang, 2007), 165.
6. J. Smith, *The War with Mexico*, vol. II, 94.
7. W. J. Worth, Report to H. L. Scott, August 23, 1847, C. F. Smith Papers.
8. J. L. Mason, Report to W. Worth, August 24, 1847, C. F. Smith Papers.
9. C. F. Smith, Report of the Light Battalion Attack on Mexican *tête-de-pont* on August 20, 1847 to W. W. MacKall, August 23, 1847, C. F. Smith Papers.
10. W. J. Worth, Report to H. L. Scott, August 23, 1847, C. F. Smith Papers.
11. Woodworth, *Manifest Destinies*, 268.
12. Frost, *The Mexican War and Its Warriors*, 170 & 172.
13. C. F. Smith, Report of the Light Battalion Attack on Mexican *tête-de-pont* on August 20, 1847, to W. W. MacKall, August 23, 1847, C. F. Smith Papers.
14. Smith and Judah, *Chronicles of the Gringos*, 245.
15. Woodworth, *Manifest Destinies*, 272–273.
16. J. Smith, *The War with Mexico*, vol. II, 118; Nevin, *The Mexican War*, 181 & 192; Clary, *Eagles and Empire*, 354; Crawford, *Encyclopedia of the Mexican-American War*, 80; Otis A. Singletary, *The Mexican War* (Chicago: University of Chicago Press, 1960), 91.
17. There are two E. Kirby Smiths. The one under Colonel Smith is Ephraim Kirby Smith, who died in the Mexican War, and his brother, who became a Civil War general, is Edmund Kirby Smith.
18. C. F. Smith, Report of the Light Battalion Attack on Mexican *tête-de-pont* on August 20, 1847, to W. W. MacKall, August 23, 1847, C. F. Smith Papers.
19. Frost, *The Mexican War and Its Warriors*, 181.
20. Cullum, *Officers and Graduates of the U.S. Military Academy*, Vol. 1, 354.
21. Frost, *The Mexican War and Its Warriors*, 182.
22. E. Kirby Smith, Letter to his wife, August 22, 1847, Emma Jerome Blackwood, ed. E. Kirby Smith, *To Mexico with Scott: Letters of Captain E. Kirby Smith to His Wife* (Cambridge: Harvard University Press, 1917), 208.
23. Frost, *The Mexican War and Its Warriors*, 185.
24. Frost, *The Mexican War and Its Warriors*, 188.
25. Frost, *The Mexican War and Its Warriors*, 140 & 143.
26. Timothy D. Johnson, *A Gallant Little Army: The Mexico City Campaign* (Lawrence: University Press of Kansas, 2007), 202–203.
27. Joseph Howard Parks, *General Edmund Kirby Smith, C.S.A.* (Baton Rouge: Louisiana State University Press, 1954), 62.
28. Eisenhower, *So Far from God*, 335.
29. W. J. Worth, Report of Engagement at Molina del Rey to Scott, September 10, 1847, C. F. Smith Papers.
30. Parks, *General Edmund Kirby Smith*, 63.
31. Bauer, *The Mexican War*, 110.

32. J. Smith, *The War with Mexico*, vol. II, 147
33. J. B. Scott, Letter to C. F. Smith, January 12, 1848, C. F. Smith Papers.
34. Woodworth, *Manifest Destinies*, 281.
35. Woodworth, *Manifest Destinies*, 284.
36. Frost, *The Mexican War and Its Warriors*, 190 and 200.
37. Johnson, *A Gallant Little Army*, 216.
38. W. J. Worth, "Report of the Capture of Garita San Cosme and Entrance into Mexico City" to Scott, September 16, 1847, C. F. Smith Papers.
39. Weems, *To Conquer a Peace*, 407.
40. Johnson, *A Gallant Little Army*, 224
41. Nevin, *The Mexican War*, 209; Smith, *The War with Mexico*, vol. II, 385.
42. Frost, *The Mexican War and Its Warriors*, 197–198.
43. Woodworth, *Manifest Destinies*, 289.
44. Woodworth, *Manifest Destinies*, 289.
45. Alameda is the Spanish word for poplar. In the sense that it is used here, it probably refers to a poplar grove or an avenue lined with poplars. Alameda, http://en.wiktionary.org/wiki/alameda. Accessed February 6, 2014.
46. Bauer, *The Mexican War*, 319–320.

Chapter 11

1. Grant, *Personal Memoirs*, 76–77.
2. W. Scott, Report to W. L. Marcy, September 18, 1847, C. F. Smith Papers.
3. Grant, *Personal Memoirs*, 77–78.
4. W. J. Worth, Report of the Capture of Garita San Cosme and Entrance into Mexico City to W. Scott, September 16, 1847, C. F. Smith Papers.
5. W. J. Worth, Report of the Capture of Garita San Cosme and Entrance into Mexico City to W. Scott, September 16, 1847, C. F. Smith Papers.
6. W. J. Worth, Report of the Capture of Garita San Cosme and Entrance into Mexico City to W. Scott, September 16, 1847, C. F. Smith Papers.
7. W. Scott, Report to W. L. Marcy, September 18, 1847, C. F. Smith Papers.
8. W. J. Worth, Report of the Capture of Garita San Cosme and Entrance into Mexico City to W. Scott, September 16, 1847, C. F. Smith Papers.
9. W. J. Worth, Report of the Capture of Garita San Cosme and Entrance into Mexico City to W. Scott, September 16, 1847, C. F. Smith Papers.
10. Eisenhower, *So Far from God*, 342.
11. Eisenhower, *So Far from God*, 346.
12. W. Scott, Report to W. L. Marcy, September 18, 1847, C. F. Smith Papers.
13. W. Worth, Orders No. 101, September 16, 1847, C. F. Smith Papers.
14. Bauer, *The Mexican War*, 326.
15. Johnson, *A Gallant Little Army*, 55.
16. Bauer, *The Mexican War*, 326.
17. W. S. Scott, General Orders No. 296, September 22, 1847, C. F. Smith Papers.
18. H. R. Crosby, Letter to Mrs. Fanny Oliver, April 20, 1885, C. F. Smith Papers
19. H. R. Crosby, Letter to Mrs. Fanny Oliver, April 20, 1885, C. F. Smith Papers.
20. H. R. Crosby, Letter to Mrs. Fanny Oliver, April 20, 1885, C. F. Smith Papers.
21. Weems, *To Conquer a Peace*, 442.
22. Grant, *Personal Memoirs*, 86.
23. Petition of Officers of the United States Army in Mexico, December 20, 1847, 30th Congress, 1st Session, "The passage of a law providing for the retirement of old and disabled officers." "Congress passed enlisted retirement legislation for the first time in 1885. The act authorized voluntary retirement at thirty years and a retirement pay of 75 percent of active duty pay." John Whiteclay Chambers II, ed., *American Military History* (New York: Oxford University Press, 1999), 102.
24. Petition of Officers of the United States Army in Mexico, December 20, 1847, 30th Congress, 1st Session, "An amendment of the pension law for widows and orphans of officers and soldiers of the army."
25. History of its Founding, The Aztec Club of 1847, http://www.aztecclub.com/, Accessed August 26, 2010.
26. History of its Founding, The Aztec Club of 1847, http://www.aztecclub.com/, Accessed August 26, 2010.
27. History of its Founding, The Aztec Club of 1847, http://www.aztecclub.com/, Accessed August 26, 2010.
28. G. D. Ramsay, Letter to C. F. Smith, November 6, 1849, C. F. Smith Papers.
29. P. H. Galt, Orders No. 17, November 3, 1847, C. F. Smith Papers.
30. W. Worth, Orders No. 122, November 3, 1847, C. F. Smith Papers.
31. J. A. Grayson, Letter to C. F. Smith, March 12, 1852, C. F. Smith Papers.
32. History of its Founding, The Aztec Club of 1847, http://www.aztecclub.com/, Accessed August 26, 2010.
33. Simpson, "The Second Regiment of Artillery," 318.
34. Casualty Report of Company K Second Artillery Regiment, unknown date, C. F. Smith Papers.
35. Orders No. 25, June 3, 1848, C. F. Smith Papers.
36. W. J. Worth, Orders No. 71, June 4, 1848, C. F. Smith Papers.
37. J. Smith, *The War with Mexico*, vol. II, 251; vol. I, xxi.
38. C. F. Smith, Journal Entries from May through July 1848, C. F. Smith Papers.
39. "Benny Havens, Oh!" Words by: Lucius O'Brien, John T. Metcalfe (USMA 1838), Ripley A. Arnold (USMA 1838), et al. http://www.west-point.org/greimanj/west_point/songs/bennyhavens.htm. Accessed May 3, 2013.

Part Three

1. Henry Coppee, *Grant and His Campaigns* (New York: Charles Richardson, 1866), 72.

Chapter 12

1. C. F. Smith, Journal Entries from July through August 1848, C. F. Smith Papers.
2. C. F. Smith, Journal Entries from August through September 1848, C. F. Smith Papers.
3. W. Scott, Special Orders No. 8, September 23, 1848, C. F. Smith Papers.
4. D. H. Mahan, Letter to C. F. Smith, September 5, 1848, C. F. Smith Papers.
5. Robert E. Lee and Joseph Johnston. I. McDowell, Letter to C. F. Smith, January 24, 1849, C. F. Smith Papers.
6. M. W. Chapman, Letter to C. F. Smith, February 10, 1849, C. F. Smith Papers.

7. Simpson, "The Second Regiment of Artillery," 318.
8. James W. Covington, *The Seminoles of Florida* (Gainesville: University Press of Florida, 1993), 109–112.
9. Possibly "Cottage O Rose" or "Rose Cottage."
10. H. Campbell, Letter to C. F. Smith, January 26, 1849, C. F. Smith Papers. Campbell might have been U.S. district attorney in the Dakota Territory (1877–85). Campbell wrote *The State: How It May Be Formed from the Territory in 1883*, http://openlibrary.org/books/OL24467619M/The_state._How_it_may_be_formed_from_the_territory.
11. I. McDowell, Letter to C. F. Smith, March 8, 1849, C. F. Smith Papers.
12. G. D. Ramsay, Letter to C. F. Smith, April 3, 1849, C. F. Smith Papers.
13. G. D. Ramsay, Letter to C. F. Smith, February 8, 1849, C. F. Smith Papers.
14. John B. Scott was an 1821 graduate of the U.S. Military Academy who served with Smith in the Mexican-American War. He fought in the Battle of Palo Alto, Battle of Resaca-de-la-Palma, and Battle of Monterey. He was brevetted a major for gallant conduct at Palo Alto and Resaca-de-la-Palma. During 1847–48, he was in command at the mouth of the Rio Grande. Cullum Number 274. Cullum, *Biographical Register*, Vol. I, 270–271.
15. J. B. Scott, Letter to C. F. Smith, November 11, 1849, C. F. Smith Papers.
16. G. D. Ramsay, Letter to C. F. Smith, May 4, 1849, C. F. Smith Papers.
17. L. Thomas, Letter to R. Swann, May 18, 1849, C. F. Smith Papers.
18. R. Swann, Letter to C. F. Smith, May 15, 1849, C. F. Smith Papers.
19. R. Swann, Letter to J. Bankhead, May 1849, C. F. Smith Papers.
20. Brooks probably refers to Brevet Major William T. H. Brooks. Cullum, *Biographical Register*, Vol. II, 105–106.
21. S. S. Anderson, Letter to C. F. Smith, June 15, 1849, C. F. Smith Papers.
22. J. W. Bankhead, Letter to C. F. Smith, May 17, 1849, C. F. Smith Papers.
23. J. W. Bankhead, Letter to Adjutant General, July 22, 1849, C. F. Smith Papers.
24. S. S. Anderson, Letter to C. F. Smith, June 15, 1849, C. F. Smith Papers.
25. J. W. Bankhead, Letter to G. W. Crawford, July 10, 1849, C. F. Smith Papers.
26. W. A. Nichols, Letter to C. F. Smith, July 10, 1849, C. F. Smith Papers.
27. Major McCall was on leave of absence in Europe in 1848–1849 and finally was promoted to colonel and Inspector General on June 10, 1850. Cullum, *Biographical Register*, Vol. I, 294.
28. W. A. Nichols, Letter to C. F. Smith, August 6, 1849, C. F. Smith Papers.
29. Covington, *The Seminoles of Florida*, 114–116.
30. C. F. Smith, Letter to Assistant Adjutant General, July 17, 1849, C. F. Smith Papers.
31. Covington, *The Seminoles of Florida*, 116.
32. R. Jones, Letter to C. F. Smith, August 27, 1849, C. F. Smith Papers.
33. R. Jones, Letter to C. F. Smith, September 27, 1849, C. F. Smith Papers.
34. Covington, *The Seminoles of Florida*, 116–117.
35. W. G. Freeman, General Orders No. 12 to C. F. Smith, July 27, 1849, C. F. Smith Papers.
36. R. Jones, Letter to C. F. Smith, August 1, 1849, C. F. Smith Papers.
37. R. Jones, Letter to C. F. Smith, August 24, 1849, C. F. Smith Papers.
38. W. G. Freeman, General Orders No. 12 issued by W. Scott, July 27, 1849, C. F. Smith Papers.
39. John Phelps was a captain in the Fourth Artillery. He resigned in 1859 and rejoined the Army as a colonel of the First Vermont Volunteers. He served as brigadier general with Commodore Farragut in the capture of Forts Jackson and St. Philip. Cullum, *Biographical Register*, Vol. I, 646–647.
40. I. McDowell, Letter to C. F. Smith, August 9, 1849, C. F. Smith Papers.
41. W. A. Nichols, Letter to C. F. Smith, January 8, 1851, C. F. Smith Papers.
42. J. L. Reno, Letter to C. F. Smith, September 17, 1849, C. F. Smith Papers.
43. B. Huger, Letter to C. F. Smith, October 6, 1849, C. F. Smith Papers.
44. H. A. Stinnecke, Letter to C. F. Smith, July 13, 1850, C. F. Smith Papers.
45. B. Huger, Letter to W. G. Freeman, August 23, 1850, C. F. Smith Papers.
46. W. Scott, Special Orders No. 83, August 31, 1850, C. F. Smith Papers.
47. R. Jones, Letter to C. F. Smith, December 2, 1850, C. F. Smith Papers.
48. "Instruction for Heavy Artillery; Prepared by a Board of Officers for the Use of the Army of the United States" (Washington: Gideon and Co. Printers, 1851), Table of Contents. http://books.google.com/. Accessed June 6, 2013.
49. "Instruction for Heavy Artillery," Table of Contents.
50. L. Thomas, Letter to C. F. Smith, November 9, 1850, C. F. Smith Papers.
51. R. Jones, General Orders No. 48 to C. F. Smith, December 31, 1850, C. F. Smith Papers.
52. G. D. Ramsay, Letter to C. F. Smith, December 12, 1850, C. F. Smith Papers.
53. F. J. Porter, Letter to C. F. Smith, May 18, 1851, C. F. Smith Papers.
54. F. J. Porter, Letter to C. F. Smith, June 15, 1851, C. F. Smith Papers.
55. F. J. Porter, Letter to C. F. Smith, September 8, 1851, C. F. Smith Papers.
56. F. Taylor, Letter to C. F. Smith, September 5, 1851, C. F. Smith Papers.
57. S. Thayer, Letter to C. F. Smith, September 27, 1851, C. F. Smith Papers.
58. R. Jones, Special Orders No. 134, 3 November 1851, C. F. Smith Papers.
59. L. Thomas, Special Orders No. 1, 4 January 1852, C. F. Smith Papers.
60. Congressional Edition, Report of Board of Claims is published in Executive Document No. 13 (House of Representatives), 2d session, 33d Congress, Vol. 825, 41.
61. Dubelier, "The Forgotten Soldier," 35.
62. Although Smith was a brevet colonel, he was paid at his actual rank of captain.
63. Wille, Descendants of Dr. Samuel Blair Smith, MD.
64. Report of Board of Claims, Executive Document No. 13, 2d session, 33d Congress, Vol. 825, 41.

65. Report of Board of Claims, Executive Document No. 3, 2d session, 33d Congress, Vol. 825, 41.
66. Report of Board of Claims, Executive Document No. 13, 2d session, 33d Congress, Vol. 825, 60-61.
67. "John C. Fremont: 'Is He Honest? Is He Capable?'" Campaign Literature. Publisher and Publication Date are Unknown, Internet Archives, 6-8. Accessed July 14, 2014.
68. R. E. Lee, Letter to C. F. Smith, October 28, 1852, United States Military Academy, Superintendent's Letter Book No. 2 and No. 3, "The Daily Correspondence of Brevet Colonel Robert E. Lee, Superintendent United States Military Academy, September 1, 1852 to March 24, 1855, Transcribed and Edited by Major Charles R. Bowery, Jr., and Major Brian D. Hankinson, Department of History, USMA, United States Military Academy Library Occasional Papers #5, West Point, NY, 2003, 297.
69. Cullum, *Biographical Register*, Vol. I, 354.

Chapter 13

1. S. Y. Seyburn, "The Tenth Regiment of Infantry" in *The Army of the United States: Historical Sketches of Staff and Line with Portraits of Generals-in-Chief*, edited by T. F. Rodenbough and W. L. Haskin (New York: Maynard, Merrill & Co., 1896), 532.
2. *Chasseurs-a-pied* were developed in response to new French tactical thinking about light infantry. The military wanted a specialist light infantry unit, which could act as skirmishers and the advance or flank guards for an army on the march. French Crimean Army, *Chasseurs a Pied*, https://sites.google.com/site/frenchcrimeanarmy/chasse, Accessed November 12, 2013.
3. Seyburn, "The Tenth Regiment of Infantry," 532.
4. Seyburn, "The Tenth Regiment of Infantry," 532.
5. Wille, Descendants of Dr. Samuel Blair Smith, MD.
6. C. F. Smith, Letter to Miss Fanny M. Smith, December 18, 1855, C. F. Smith Papers.
7. C. F. Smith, Letter to Miss Fanny M. Smith, January 4, 1856, C. F. Smith Papers.
8. C. F. Smith, Letter to Miss Fanny M. Smith, January 25, 1856, C. F. Smith Papers.
9. C. F. Smith, Letter to Mrs. Margaret F. Smith, February 5, 1856, C. F. Smith Papers.
10. Pembina is a town in the far northeast of North Dakota. Until 1823, both the United States and Canada believed the community of Pembina was in Canadian territory. That year United States Army Major Stephen H. Long's survey of the 49th parallel revealed Pembina's location south of the Canada–United States border. In 1851, the United States established its first post office in North Dakota in Pembina. The city was an important trade center in the fur industry in the Red River of the North Valley. Pembina was the origin of a 471-mile cart trail that ended at St. Louis. City of Pembina, ND, History and Links, http://pembina.govoffice.com/index.asp?Type=B_BASIC&SEC={8E987F94-7051-4F71-AF15-449A0D02C4B6}, Accessed November 19, 2011.
11. C. F. Smith, Letter to Miss Fanny M. Smith, February 14, 1856, C. F. Smith Papers.
12. Seyburn, "The Tenth Regiment of Infantry," 534.
13. C. F. Smith, Letter to Miss Fanny M. Smith, April 6, 1856, C. F. Smith Papers.
14. C. F. Smith, Letter to Miss Fanny M. Smith, April 20, 1856, C. F. Smith Papers.
15. Seyburn, "The Tenth Regiment of Infantry," 534.
16. W. Scott, General Orders No. 5, June 9, 1856, C. F. Smith, "Report of an expedition of Companies B and F, 10th regiment of infantry, to the Red River of the North, in 1856," *Message from the President of the United States to the Two Houses of Congress at the Commencement of the Second Session of the Thirty-Fifth Congress* (Washington: James B. Steedman, 1858), 435.
17. Its original name, or rather that given to it by the early French hunters and trappers, is understood to be "*Bois de Chien*," from the quantity of dogwood that fringes its banks. Smith's notes from his report, Smith, "Report of an Expedition to the Red River of the North," 426.
18. Smith, "Report of an Expedition to the Red River of the North," 426.
19. Smith, "Report of an Expedition to the Red River of the North," 427.
20. C. F. Smith, Letter to Miss Fanny M. Smith, June 22, 1856, C. F. Smith Papers.
21. Smith, "Report of an Expedition to the Red River of the North," 438.
22. Pontoon wagons were drawn by mules and used for river crossings.
23. Smith, "Report of an Expedition to the Red River of the North," 438.
24. Smith, "Report of an Expedition to the Red River of the North," 428–429.
25. C. F. Smith, Letter to Miss Fanny M. Smith, July 24, 1856, C. F. Smith Papers.
26. The French term *terres tremblantes* or *terre tremblante* refers to trembling, unstable, shaky, unsteady, or uneven earth or soil such as marshes. Google Translate, http://translate.google.com/#fr/en/terres%20tremblantes, Accessed October 24, 2013.
27. Smith, "Report of an Expedition to the Red River of the North," 429.
28. Smith, "Report of an Expedition to the Red River of the North," 430.
29. Smith, "Report of an Expedition to the Red River of the North," 429.
30. Smith, "Report of an Expedition to the Red River of the North," 429.
31. Smith, "Report of an Expedition to the Red River of the North," 440–441.
32. Smith, "Report of an Expedition to the Red River of the North," 433.
33. The Red River Colony (or Selkirk Settlement) was a colonization project set up by Thomas Douglas, 5th Earl of Selkirk in 1811 on 120,000 square miles of land granted to him by the Hudson's Bay Company under what is referred to as the Selkirk Concession. The colony along the Red River of the North was never very successful. Changes during the development of Canada in the 19th century led to the colony's forming the basis of what is today Manitoba, although much of its original territory is now part of the United States. Selkirk Settlement, http://en.wikipedia.org/wiki/Selkirk_Settlement, Accessed August 22, 2012.
34. Smith, "Report of an Expedition to the Red River of the North," 454.
35. Charles N. Bell, "Some Red River Settlement History," Manitoba Historical Society, http://www.mhs.mb.ca/docs/transactions/1/redriverhistory.shtml, Accessed May 14, 2010.
36. Bell, "Some Red River Settlement History," http://

www.mhs.mb.ca/docs/transactions/1/redriverhistory.shtml, Accessed May 14, 2010.

37. Bell, "Some Red River Settlement History," http://www.mhs.mb.ca/docs/transactions/1/redriverhistory.shtml, Accessed May 14, 2010.

38. Bell, "Some Red River Settlement History," http://www.mhs.mb.ca/docs/transactions/1/redriverhistory.shtml, Accessed May 14, 2010.

39. C. F. Smith, Letter to Miss Fanny M. Smith, September 3, 1856, C. F. Smith Papers.

40. Smith, "Report of an Expedition to the Red River of the North," 444–445.

41. Smith, "Report of an Expedition to the Red River of the North," 445.

42. C. F. Smith, Letter to Miss Fanny M. Smith, 24 September 1856, C. F. Smith Papers.

43. Smith, "Report of an Expedition to the Red River of the North," 447.

44. Smith, "Report of an Expedition to the Red River of the North," 448.

45. Smith, "Report of an Expedition to the Red River of the North," 449.

46. Smith, "Report of an Expedition to the Red River of the North," 449–450.

47. Smith, "Report of an Expedition to the Red River of the North," 449–451.

48. Smith, "Report of an Expedition to the Red River of the North," 452.

49. Smith, "Report of an Expedition to the Red River of the North," 453.

50. Smith, "Report of an Expedition to the Red River of the North," 430.

51. Smith, "Report of an Expedition to the Red River of the North," 434.

52. Smith, "Report of an Expedition to the Red River of the North," 434.

53. C. F. Smith, Letter to Miss Fanny M. Smith, June 22, 1856, C. F. Smith Papers.

54. C. F. Smith, Letter to Miss Fanny M. Smith, December 14, 1856, C. F. Smith Papers.

55. C. F. Smith, Letter to Miss Fanny M. Smith, January 1, 1857, C. F. Smith Papers

56. C. F. Smith, Letter to Miss Fanny M. Smith, February 1, 1857, C. F. Smith Papers.

57. C. F. Smith, Letter to Miss Fanny M. Smith, February 10, 1857, C. F. Smith Papers.

58. C. F. Smith, Letter to Miss Fanny M. Smith, March 8, 1857, C. F. Smith Papers.

59. Seyburn, "The Tenth Regiment of Infantry," 536.

60. The Spirit Lake Massacre (March 8-12, 1857) was an attack by a *Wahpetuke* band of Santee Sioux on scattered Iowa frontier settlements during a severe winter. Suffering a shortage of food, the renegade chief Inkpaduta (Scarlet Point) led 14 Sioux against the settlements near Okoboji and Spirit lakes in the northwestern territory of Iowa near the Minnesota border. The Sioux killed 35–40 settlers in their scattered holdings, took four young women captive, and headed north. The youngest captive, Abbie Gardner, was kept a few months before being ransomed in early summer. http://en.wikipedia.org/wiki/Spirit_Lake_Massacre, Accessed 19 August 2012.

61. C. F. Smith, Letter to Miss Fanny M. Smith, June 2, 1857, C. F. Smith Papers.

62. C. F. Smith, Letter to Miss Fanny M. Smith, June 12, 1857, C. F. Smith Papers.

Chapter 14

1. Norman F. Furniss, *The Mormon Conflict 1850–1859* (New Haven: Yale University Press, 1960), vii.

2. Furniss, *The Mormon Conflict*, 67.

3. Furniss, *The Mormon Conflict*, 82.

4. Furniss, *The Mormon Conflict*, 90–91.

5. Furniss, *The Mormon Conflict*, 95.

6. Furniss, *The Mormon Conflict*, 99.

7. Otis G. Hammond, ed., "Letters of Capt. Jesse A. Gove, 10th Inf., U.S.A., of Concord, N.H., to Mrs. Gove, and special correspondence of *The New York Herald*," *The Utah Expedition 1857-18 58* (Concord: New Hampshire Historical Society, 1928), 5.

8. Seyburn, "The Tenth Regiment of Infantry," 536.

9. The term *posse comitatus* refers to the authority of a law officer to conscript any able-bodied males to assist him, http://en.wikipedia.org/wiki/Posse_comitatus, Accessed December 12, 2011.

10. Robert W. Coakley, *The Role of Federal Military Forces in Domestic Disorders 1789-1878* (Washington: U.S. Government Printing Office, 1988), 198.

11. Coakley, *The Role of Federal Military Forces*, 199.

12. Hammond, *The Utah Expedition*, 6.

13. Hammond, *The Utah Expedition*, 15.

14. Coakley, *The Role of Federal Military Forces*, 199.

15. "The Utah War," Preparations, http://en.wikipedia.org/wiki/Utah_War, Accessed July 18, 2014.

16. Coakley, *The Role of Federal Military Forces*, 203.

17. Coakley, *The Role of Federal Military Forces*, 203.

18. The phrase "war to the knife" refers to mortal combat or a "conflict carried to the last extremity," http://www.thefreedictionary.com/War+to+the+knife, Accessed February 16, 2013.

19. C. F. Smith, Letter to Miss Fanny M. Smith, August 26, 1857, C. F. Smith Papers.

20. Coakley, *The Role of Federal Military Forces*, 198–199.

21. Leroy R. Hafen and Ann W. Hafen, eds., *Mormon Resistance: A Documentary Account of the Utah Expedition, 1857–1858* (Lincoln: University of Nebraska Press, 2005), 39–40.

22. "Captain Van Vliet," Utah War, http://en.wikipedia.org/wiki/Utah_War#Captain_Van_Vliet, Accessed February 16, 2013.

23. Coakley, *The Role of Federal Military Forces*, 202.

24. "Martial Law," Utah War, http://en.wikipedia.org/wiki/Utah_War#Captain_Van_Vliet, Accessed February 16, 2013.

25. Gerard Patterson, "The Mormon Confrontation," *American History Illustrated*, December 1972, Vol. VII No. 8, 14–17.

26. C. F. Smith, Letter to Miss Fanny M. Smith, September 5, 1857, C. F. Smith Papers.

27. C. F. Smith, Letter to Miss Fanny Smith, September 23, 1857, C. F. Smith Papers.

28. C. F. Smith, Letter to Miss Fanny M. Smith, September 27, 1857, C. F. Smith Papers.

29. Hammond, *The Utah Expedition*, 66.

30. Hammond, *The Utah Expedition*, 67.

31. Hammond, *The Utah Expedition*, 68–69.

32. Coakley, *The Role of Federal Military Forces*, 203.

33. Coakley, *The Role of Federal Military Forces*, 204.

34. Coakley, *The Role of Federal Military Forces*, 204.

35. Coakley, *The Role of Federal Military Forces*, 204–205.
36. C. F. Smith, Letter to Miss Fanny M. Smith, October 13, 1857, C. F. Smith Papers.
37. Coakley, *The Role of Federal Military Forces*, 205.
38. Albert Sydney Johnston, "Letter Book" (Special Papers, Howard Tilton Memorial Library, Tulane University, New Orleans), vol. 31, November 5, 1857, 47 as referenced in Dubelier, "The Forgotten Soldier," 39.
39. C. F. Smith, Letter to Miss Fanny M. Smith, November 30, 1857, C. F. Smith Papers.
40. Coakley, *The Role of Federal Military Forces*, 206.
41. Coakley, *The Role of Federal Military Forces*, 206.
42. Seyburn, "The Tenth Regiment of Infantry," 537.
43. Coakley, *The Role of Federal Military Forces*, 206–207.
44. In fortification, a lunette was originally an outwork of half-moon shape; later it became a redan with short flanks, in trace somewhat resembling a bastion standing by itself without curtains on either side. The gorge was generally open. Lunette (fortification), http://en.wikipedia.org/wiki/Lunette_(fortification), Accessed February 16, 2013.
45. C. F. Smith, Letter to Miss Fanny M. Smith, November 30, 1857, C. F. Smith Papers.
46. C. F. Smith, Letter to Miss Fanny M. Smith, November 30, 1857, C. F. Smith Papers.
47. C. F. Smith, Letter to Miss Fanny M. Smith, December 25, 1857, C. F. Smith Papers.
48. Coakley, *The Role of Federal Military Forces*, 207.
49. C. F. Smith, Letter to Miss Fanny M. Smith, November 30, 1857, C. F. Smith Papers.
50. Coakley, *The Role of Federal Military Forces*, 207–208.
51. Coakley, *The Role of Federal Military Forces*, 208.
52. Coakley, *The Role of Federal Military Forces*, 209.
53. C. F. Smith, Letter to Miss Fanny M. Smith, December 25, 1857, C. F. Smith Papers.
54. Boston Whist is an 18th century trick-taking card game, http://en.wikipedia.org/wiki/Boston_whist#American_Boston, Accessed October 19, 2011.
55. C. F. Smith, Letter to Miss Fanny M. Smith, December 25, 1857, C. F. Smith Papers.
56. C. F. Smith, Letter to Miss Fanny M. Smith, February 27, 1858, C. F. Smith Papers.
57. C. F. Smith, Letter to Miss Fanny M. Smith, February 27, 1858, C. F. Smith Papers.
58. Coakley, *The Role of Federal Military Forces*, 211.
59. Coakley, *The Role of Federal Military Forces*, 211.
60. Traveling companion.
61. C. F. Smith, Letter to Miss Fanny M. Smith, April 14, 1858, C. F. Smith Papers.
62. Coakley, *The Role of Federal Military Forces*, 212.
63. Coakley, *The Role of Federal Military Forces*, 210.
64. Coakley, *The Role of Federal Military Forces*, 211.
65. Coakley, *The Role of Federal Military Forces*, 212–213.
66. Coakley, *The Role of Federal Military Forces*, 213.
67. Coakley, *The Role of Federal Military Forces*, 214.
68. Coakley, *The Role of Federal Military Forces*, 214.
69. Hammond, *The Utah Expedition*, 232.
70. Coakley, *The Role of Federal Military Forces*, 214–215.
71. Coakley, *The Role of Federal Military Forces*, 215.
72. C. F. Smith, Letter to Miss Fanny M. Smith, June 3, 1858, C. F. Smith Papers.
73. Coakley, *The Role of Federal Military Forces*, 215.
74. Hammond, *The Utah Expedition*, 175.
75. Coakley, *The Role of Federal Military Forces*, 215–216.
76. Coakley, *The Role of Federal Military Forces*, 218.
77. "The Utah War, " The Move South, http://en.wikipedia.org/wiki/Utah_War, Accessed July 18, 2014.
78. C. F. Smith, Letter to Miss Fanny M. Smith, June 3, 1858, C. F. Smith Papers.
79. C. F. Smith, Letter to Miss Fanny M. Smith, June 11, 1858, C. F. Smith Papers.
80. William P. MacKinnon, "Causes of the Utah War," *Ford Douglas Vedette*, Newsletter of the Fort Douglas Military Museum Association, Spring 2007.
81. C. F. Smith, Letter to Miss Fanny M. Smith, July 7, 1858, C. F. Smith Papers.
82. Coakley, *The Role of Federal Military Forces*, 217.
83. C. F. Smith, Letter to Miss Fanny M. Smith, July 7, 1858, C. F. Smith Papers.
84. C. F. Smith, Letter to Miss Fanny M. Smith, June 11, 1858, C. F. Smith Papers
85. C. F. Smith, Letter to Miss Fanny M. Smith, July 7, 1858, C. F. Smith Papers.
86. Coakley, *The Role of Federal Military Forces*, 217–218.
87. C. F. Smith, Letter to Miss Fanny M. Smith, August 1, 1858, C. F. Smith Papers.
88. William L. Krecht and Peter L. Crowley, eds., *History of Brigham Young* (Berkeley: Mass Col Associates, 1964), 241.
89. Coakley, *The Role of Federal Military Forces*, 218–219.
90. C. F. Smith, Letter to Miss Fanny M. Smith, August 1, 1858, C. F. Smith Papers.
91. Seyburn, "The Tenth Regiment of Infantry," 537.
92. C. F. Smith, Letter to Miss Fanny M. Smith, September 19, 1858, C. F. Smith Papers.
93. C. F. Smith, Letter to Miss Fanny M. Smith, September 19, 1858, C. F. Smith Papers.
94. Seyburn, "The Tenth Regiment of Infantry," 537.
95. C. F. Smith, Letter to Miss Fanny M. Smith, November 11, 1858, C. F. Smith Papers.
96. This is a reference to the Aesop fable "The Frogs Who Desired a King." The story concerns a group of frogs who called on the great god Zeus to send them a king. He threw down a log, which fell in their pond with a loud splash and terrified them. Eventually one of the frogs peeped above the water and, seeing that it was no longer moving, soon all hopped upon it and made fun of their king. Then the frogs made a second request for a real king and were sent a water snake, later changed to a stork, that started eating them. Once more the frogs appealed to Zeus, but this time he replied that they must face the consequences of their request. The fable is a political lesson. Initially it was that people feel the need of laws but are impatient of personal restraint. Later the lesson was that the people are uneasy without a ruler, but they are never satisfied with either situation. Another view was expressed by Martin Luther when he alludes to this fable to illustrate how humanity deserves the rulers it gets: "frogs must have their storks." http://en.wikipedia.org/wiki/The_Frogs_Who_Desired_a_King, Accessed November 1, 2011.

97. C. F. Smith, Letter to Miss Fanny M. Smith, January 6, 1859, C. F. Smith Papers.
98. C. F. Smith, Letter to Miss Fanny M. Smith, January 6, 1859, C. F. Smith Papers.
99. A writ of *habeas corpus* is a summons, with the force of a court order, sent to custodian, such as a prison official, that demands that a prisoner be taken before the court, and that the custodian present proof of authority, allowing the court to determine whether the custodian has lawful authority to detain the person. If the custodian does not have authority to detain the prisoner, then he must be released from custody. http://en.wikipedia.org/wiki/Habeas_corpus, Accessed November 2, 2011.
100. C. F. Smith, Letter to Miss Fanny M. Smith, January 6, 1859, C. F. Smith Papers.
101. C. F. Smith, Letter to Miss Fanny M. Smith, January 6, 1859, C. F. Smith Papers.
102. C. F. Smith, Letter to Miss Fanny M. Smith, January 6, 1859, C. F. Smith Papers.
103. C. F. Smith, Letter to Miss Fanny M. Smith, January 6, 1859, C. F. Smith Papers.
104. C. F. Smith, Letter to Miss Fanny M. Smith, January 6, 1859, C. F. Smith Papers.
105. One gill is equivalent to four ounces.
106. Albert Tracy, "The Journal of Albert Tracy," *Utah Historical Quarterly*, Utah State Historical Society, Vol. 13, 1945, 54–56, Accessed August 19, 2014.
107. Coakley, *The Role of Federal Military Forces*, 219.
108. Coakley, *The Role of Federal Military Forces*, 219.
109. Coakley, *The Role of Federal Military Forces*, 220.
110. Coakley, *The Role of Federal Military Forces*, 222.
111. James L. Morrison, Jr., ed., *The Memoirs of Henry Heth* (Westport: Greenwood Press, 1974), 145–146.
112. Coakley, *The Role of Federal Military Forces*, 223.
113. Michael S. Durham, "The Utah War," *MHQ: The Quarterly Journal of Military History*, Spring 1998, Volume 10, Number 3, 32.
114. Durham, "The Utah War," 33.
115. Durham, "The Utah War," 33.
116. Morrison, *The Memoirs of Henry Heth*, 144–145.
117. Dubelier, "The Forgotten Soldier," 42.
118. Coakley, *The Role of Federal Military Forces*, 224.
119. Coakley, *The Role of Federal Military Forces*, 224.
120. Coakley, *The Role of Federal Military Forces*, 225–226.
121. Coakley, *The Role of Federal Military Forces*, 226.
122. Morrison, *The Memoirs of Henry Heth*, 147–148.
123. C. F. Smith, Letter to Miss Fanny M. Smith, March 10, 1860, C. F. Smith Papers.
124. Morrison, *The Memoirs of Henry Heth*, 137–138.
125. Henry R. Crosby, Letter to Mrs. Fanny Oliver, April 20, 1885, C. F. Smith Papers.
126. Dubelier, "The Forgotten Soldier," 44.
127. C. F. Smith, Letter to Miss Fanny M. Smith, March 10, 1860, C. F. Smith Papers.
128. General Orders No. 10, April 16, 1860, C. F. Smith Papers.
129. C. F. Smith, Letter to Miss Fanny M. Smith, June 8, 1860, C. F. Smith Papers.
130. C. F. Smith, Letter to Miss Fanny M. Smith, June 8, 1860, C. F. Smith Papers.
131. Seyburn, "The Tenth Regiment of Infantry," 538.
132. C. F. Smith, Letter to Miss Fanny M. Smith, June 8, 1860, C. F. Smith Papers.
133. C. F. Smith, Letter to Miss Fanny M. Smith, January 23, 1861, C. F. Smith Papers.

Part Four

1. Wallace, *An Autobiography*, 338.

Chapter 15

1. United States presidential election, 1856. http://en.wikipedia.org/wiki/United_States_presidential_election,_1856, Accessed August 27, 2012.
2. Morrison, *The Memoirs of Henry Heth*, 148.
3. Bowman, *The Civil War*, 22–24.
4. C. F. Smith, Letter to Miss Fanny M. Smith, January 23, 1861, C. F. Smith Papers.
5. C. F. Smith, Note to Miss Fanny Smith, February 24, 1861, C. F. Smith Papers.
6. Special Orders No. 80, March 15, 1861, C. F. Smith Papers.
7. Morrill Anti-Bigamy Act, http://en.wikipedia.org/wiki/Morrill_Anti-Bigamy_Act, Accessed November 22, 2013.
8. Dubelier, "The Forgotten Soldier," 47.
9. R. A. Anderson, Report No. 11 to S. Cooper, December 26, 1860, *Official Records*, Ser. 1, Vol. 1, 2.
10. C. R. Woods, Report to H. L. Scott, January 13, 1861, *Official Records*, Ser. 1, Vol. 1, 9–10.
11. G. T. Beauregard, Letter to R. Anderson, April 11, 1861, *Official Records*, Ser. 1, Vol. 1, 13.
12. R. Anderson, Letter to P. G. T. Beauregard, April 11, 1861, *Official Records*, Ser. 1, Vol. 1, 13.
13. J. Chestnut and S. D. Lee, to R. Anderson, April 12, 1861, *Official Records*, Ser. 1, Vol. 1, 14.
14. R. A. Anderson, Report to S. Cameron, April 18, 1861, *Official Records*, Ser. 1, Vol. 1, 12.
15. Michael Burlingame, *Abraham Lincoln: A Life* (Baltimore: Johns Hopkins University Press, 2008), vol. 2, 132–133.
16. John Lockwood and Charles Lockwood, *The Siege of Washington: The Untold Story of the Twelve Days That Shook the Union* (New York: Oxford University Press, 2011), 40.
17. Theodore B. Gates, *The War of the Rebellion* (New York: P. F. McBreen, 1884), 17.
18. Lockwood, *The Siege of Washington*, 6.
19. Burlingame, *Abraham Lincoln*, 137.
20. Lockwood, *The Siege of Washington*, 28.
21. Special Orders No. 58, *Official Records*, Ser. 1, Vol. 51 (Part I)—Correspondence, 320.
22. Elizabeth Todd Grimsley was the daughter of Dr. John Todd and wife of Harrison Grimsley of Springfield. She was John Todd's sister and Charles' cousin. Mrs. Grimsley spent six months at the White House helping her cousin Mary Todd Lincoln get settled in Washington. Turner, *Mary Todd Lincoln*, 82 & 84.
23. C. F. Smith, Letter to Mrs. Fanny M. Smith, April 7, 1861, C. F. Smith Papers.
24. General Orders No. 102, April 11, 1861, *Official Records*, Ser. 1, Vol. 51 (Part I)—Correspondence, 323–324.
25. General Orders No. 1, April 10, 1861, *Official Records*, Ser. 1, Vol. 51 (Part I)—Correspondence, 322.
26. "Probable Attempt to Seize Washington," *New York Times*, April 15, 1861, Harold B. Holzer and Craig L.

Symonds, eds., *The New York Times—The Complete Civil War* (New York: Black Dog & Leventhal Publishers, 2010).

27. Winfield Scott to Abraham Lincoln, Tuesday, April 15, 1861, Abraham Lincoln Papers, Series 1. General Correspondence. 1833–1916. Library of Congress.

28. Special Orders No. 2, April 14, 1861, *Official Records*, Ser. 1, Vol. 51 (Part I)—Correspondence, 325.

29. General Orders No. 4, April 16, 1861, *Official Records*, Ser. 1, Vol. 51 (Part I)—Correspondence, 326.

30. Lockwood, *The Siege of Washington*, 60.

31. Winfield Scott to Abraham Lincoln, Tuesday, April 16, 1861, Abraham Lincoln Papers, Series 1, General Correspondence, 1833–1916, Library of Congress.

32. Lockwood, *The Siege of Washington*, 14.

33. C. F. Smith, Letter to Mrs. Fanny M. Smith, April 16, 1861, C. F. Smith Papers.

34. Madeliene Vinton Dahlgren, *Memoir of John A. Dahlgren, Rear-Admiral United States Navy* (Boston: John R. Osgood, 1882), 330.

35. General Orders No. 3, April 19, 1861, *Official Records*, Ser. 1, Vol. 2, 579.

36. R. Patterson, Telegram to W. Scott, April 19, 1861, *Official Records*, Ser. 1, Vol. 2, 579.

37. Burlingame, *Abraham Lincoln*, 146.

38. Lockwood, *The Siege of Washington*, 174.

39. William E. Gulick, Washington D.C., to John E. Ellis, April 21, 1861, in Noble J. Tolbert, ed., *Papers of John W. Ellis* (Raleigh: State Department of Archives and History, 1964), vol. 2, 648.

40. Henry Villard, *Memoirs of Henry Villard, Journalist and Financier, 1835–1900* (Boston: Houghton, Mifflin and Company, 1904), vol. 1, 166.

41. Winfield Scott to Abraham Lincoln, April 22, 1861, Abraham Lincoln Papers, Series 1. General Correspondence. 1833–1916. Library of Congress.

42. Special Orders No. 19, April 23, 1861, *Official Records*, Ser. 1, Vol. 51 (Part I), 322; Special Orders No. 22, April 22, 1861, *Official Records*, Ser. 1, Vol. 51 (Part I), 355; Special Orders No. 19, April 23, 1861, *Official Records*, Ser. 1, Vol. 51 (Part I), 355; Special Orders No. 32, April 27, 1861, *Official Records*, Ser. 1, Vol. 51 (Part I), 337.

43. *Philadelphia Inquirer*, April 25, 1861, 4.

44. "From Washington to New York—Notes and Observations on the War—Sentiment of the People in Maryland," *New York Times*, April 25, 1861, Holzer and Symonds, *The New York Times—Complete Civil War*.

45. *Baltimore Sun*, April 25, 1861, 1.

46. L. A. Williams, Note to McDowell, April 23, 1861, *Official Records*, Ser. 1, Vol. 51 (Part 1), 335. Major McDowell was on the staff of General-in-Chief Totten and was assigned to Capitol Hill. *Official Records*, Ser. 1, Vol. 2, 603.

47. Lockwood, *The Siege of Washington*, 215.

48. Lockwood, *The Siege of Washington*, 216.

49. Doris Kearns Goodwin, *Team of Rivals: The Political Genius of Abraham Lincoln* (New York: Simon & Schuster, 2005), 355.

50. W. Scott, General Orders No. 4, April 26, 1861, *Official Records*, Ser. 1, Vol. 2, 602.

51. "What Gen. Scott Says," *New York Times*, April 27, 1861, Holzer and Symonds, *The New York Times—Complete Civil War*.

52. C. F. Smith, Letter to Mrs. Fanny M. Smith, April 26, 1861, C. F. Smith Papers.

53. "News from the Seat of the War. The War Measures of the Administration," *The New York Herald*, April 30, 1861, Accessed by Michael K. Shafer and provided to the author on December 14, 2011.

54. General Orders No. 12, April 27, 1861, *Official Records*, Ser. 1, Vol. 2, 607.

55. General Orders No. 8, April 28, 1861, *Official Records*, Ser. 1, Vol. 51 (Part I), 341.

56. Cox, *Military Reminiscences of the Civil War*, 45.

57. William Swinton covered the Civil War for the *New York Times*, during which he became the personal gadfly of Ulysses S. Grant. Grant reports that he discovered Swinton crouched behind a tree stump eavesdropping on a conversation between the general and a confidant. Later, Union General Ambrose Burnside arrested Swinton and ordered him shot for reporting too freely on Union movements or lack of movement. One of Swinton's *Times* pieces told how Burnside had gotten an entire Union regiment stuck in the mud. Grant countermanded Burnside and had Swinton released, but only on the condition he be expelled from Union lines. "William Swinton, the Original Radical," *Illuminations*, University of California, Berkeley, February 2005, Accessed January 27, 2012.

58. Cox, *Military Reminiscences of the Civil War*, 45.

59. Bruce Catton, *Grant Moves South* (Boston: Little, Brown, 1960), 51.

60. The Indictment of Samuel Mactier involved in the Baltimore "Riot" of 1861, 04/19/1861, National Archives. OPA—Online Public Access, http://research.archives.gov/description/278862, Accessed September 3, 2012.

61. C. F. Smith, Letter to Mrs. Fanny M. Smith, April 28, 1861, C. F. Smith Papers.

62. C. F. Smith, Letter to Mrs. Fanny M. Smith, December 31, 1861, C. F. Smith Papers.

63. C. F. Smith, Letter to Mrs. Fanny M. Smith, November 1, 1861, C. F. Smith Papers.

64. Hammond, *The Utah Expedition*, 194–196.

65. "The Great Rebellion—Military and Naval Movements," *New York Times*, May 3, 1861, Holzer and Symonds, *The New York Times—Complete Civil War*.

66. C. F. Smith, Note to Unknown, May 6, 1861, C. F. Smith Papers.

67. C. F. Smith, Letter to Mrs. Fanny M. Smith, May 3, 1861, C. F. Smith Papers.

68. Letter from Simon Cameron to the governors of Maine, New Hampshire, Vermont, Connecticut, New York, New Jersey, Pennsylvania, Maryland, Virginia, Michigan, Tennessee, Missouri, Indiana, Ohio, Minnesota, Illinois, and Wisconsin, April 15, 1861, *Official Records*, Ser. 3, Vol. 2, 68–69.

69. New York City in the American Civil War, http://en.wikipedia.org/wiki/New_York_City_in_the_American_Civil_War#Military_recruitment_in_New_York_City, Accessed July 20, 2011.

70. "Military and Naval Movements," *New York Times*, May 7, 1861, Holzer and Symonds, *The New York Times—Complete Civil War*.

71. "Military and Naval Movements," *New York Times*, May 10, 1861, Holzer and Symonds, *The New York Times—Complete Civil War*.

72. "Military and Naval Movements," *New York Times*, June 6, 1861, Holzer and Symonds, *The New York Times—Complete Civil War*.

73. "Military and Naval Movements," *New York Times*, June 7, 1861, Holzer and Symonds, *The New York Times—Complete Civil War*.

74. "Military and Naval Movements," *New York Times*, July 2, 1861, Holzer and Symonds, *The New York Times—Complete Civil War*.
75. F. M. Oliver, Note on her father's state of mind during the summer at Fort Columbus, C. F. Smith Papers.
76. Letter from Abraham Lincoln to the governors of Maine, New Hampshire, Vermont, Connecticut, New York, New Jersey, Pennsylvania, Maryland, Virginia, Michigan, Tennessee, Missouri, Indiana, Ohio, Minnesota, Illinois, and Wisconsin, and the President of the Military Board of Kentucky, July 1, 1861, *Official Records*, Ser. 3, Vol. 2, 187–188.
77. John D. Wright, ed., *The Oxford Dictionary of Civil War Quotations* (Oxford: Oxford University Press, 2006), 31.
78. Wright, *Civil War Quotations*, 194.
79. E. D. Townsend, Letter to C. F. Smith, July 17, 1861, *Official Records*, Ser. 2, Vol. 2, 363.
80. Case of Edward Seymour Ruggles, *Official Records*, Ser. 2, Vol. 2, 358–359.
81. C. F. Smith, Note to Assistant Adjutant General, July 19, 1861, *Official Records*, Ser. 2, Vol. 2, 363.
82. "Military and Naval Movements," *New York Times*, July 20, 1861, Holzer and Symonds, *The New York Times—Complete Civil War*.
83. G. B. McClellan, Letter to W. F. Smith, [illegible] 24, 1885, C. F. Smith Papers.
84. "Military and Naval Movements," *New York Times*, August 6, 1861, Holzer and Symonds, *The New York Times—Complete Civil War*.
85. "Military and Naval Movements," *New York Times*, August 14, 1861, Holzer and Symonds, *The New York Times—Complete Civil War*.
86. Special Orders No. 222, August 19, 1861, C. F. Smith Papers.
87. "Military and Naval Movements," *New York Times*, August 27, 1861, Holzer and Symonds, *The New York Times—Complete Civil War*.

Chapter 16

1. According to Dave Eicher, this was the official lengthy procedure to be followed in the U.S. Army, for promotions in both the Regular and Volunteer forces: (1) Proposal by superior officer, Congressman, Governor or other influential officer or citizen; (2) Approbation by officers senior to the candidate; (3) Endorsement by the General-in-Chief (Commander-in-Chief); (4) Appointment by the Secretary of War or his delegate; (5) Acceptance by the candidate; (6) Nomination by the President; (7) Approval in a report by the Senate Committee on Military Affairs and the Militia; (8) Confirmation by a vote on advice and consent by the Senate; (9) Engrossment and registration of the appointment by the Adjutant General; (10) Appointment signed and sealed by the Secretary of War and the President.
Steps 1–3 were routine and could be bypassed on occasion, while steps 4, 5, 7, and 9 were usually followed. The most important steps were 6, 8 and 10, which were legal requirements for an appointment. U.S. Civil War Generals FAQ, http://sunsite.utk.edu/civil-war/FAQ.html, Accessed February 22, 2012.
2. C. F. Smith, Letter to Mrs. Fanny M. Smith, September 5, 1861, C. F. Smith Papers.
3. General Orders No. 57, *Official Records*, Ser. 1, Vol. 4, 254.
4. O. P. Morton, Letter to Thomas A. Scott, August 29, 1861, *Official Records*, Ser. 1, Vol. 4, 255.
5. R. Anderson, Letter to Secretary Chase, September 1, 1861, *Official Records*, Ser. 1, Vol. 4, 255–256.
6. O. P. Morton, Letter to Thomas A. Scott, September 2, 1861, *Official Records*, Ser. 1, Vol. 4, 256.
7. O. P. Morton, Letter to Simon Cameron, September 12, 1861, *Official Records*, Ser. 1, Vol. 4, 257.
8. Lowell Harrison, *The Civil War in Kentucky* (Lexington: University Press of Kentucky, 1975), 12.
9. Lonnie E. Manes, "Columbus: The Gibraltar of the West," *Journal of the Jackson Purchase Historical Society*, Volume 10, 30.
10. Grant, *Personal Memoirs*, 117–118.
11. Grant, *Personal Memoirs*, 121.
12. Grant, *Personal Memoirs*, 122.
13. Lewis, *Captain Sam Grant*, 427–428.
14. Letter from Abraham Lincoln to the governors of Maine, New Hampshire, Vermont, Massachusetts, Rhode Island, Connecticut, New York, Pennsylvania, New Jersey, Delaware, Maryland, Virginia, North Carolina, Tennessee, Arkansas, Kentucky, Missouri, Illinois, Indiana, Ohio, Michigan, Wisconsin, Iowa, and Minnesota, July 1, 1861, *Official Records*, Series 3, Volume 2, 188.
15. Letter from Simon Cameron to the governors of Maine, New Hampshire, Vermont, Connecticut, New York, New Jersey, Pennsylvania, Maryland, Virginia, Michigan, Tennessee, Missouri, Indiana, Ohio, Minnesota, Illinois, and Wisconsin, April 15, 1861, *Official Records*, Series 3, Volume 2, 68–69.
16. U. S. Grant, Letter to J. C. Frémont, September 2, 1861, *Official Records*, Series I, Volume 3, 145–146.
17. J. C. Frémont, Orders from to U. S. Grant, August 28, 1861, *Official Records*, Series I, Volume 3, 141–142.
18. Grant, *Personal Memoirs*, 135.
19. Grant, *Personal Memoirs*, 135–136.
20. Hall Allen, *Center of Conflict* (Paducah: The Paducah Sun-Democrat, 1961), 22.
21. U. S. Grant, Report to J. C. Frémont, September 6, 1861, *Official Records*, Ser. 1, Vol. 4, 197.
22. Bruce Catton, *Grant Moves South*, 49.
23. Grant, *Personal Memoirs*, 136.
24. U. S. Grant, Report to J. C. Frémont, September 6, 1861, *Official Records*, Ser. 1, Vol. 4, 197.
25. U. S. Grant, Proclamation to the Citizens of Paducah, September 6, 1861, *Official Records*, Ser. 1, Vol. 52 (Part I), 189.
26. U. S. Grant, Orders to E. A. Paine, September 6, 1861, *Official Records*, Ser. 1, Vol. 4, 198.
27. U. S. Grant, Report to J. C. Frémont, September 6, 1861, *Official Records*, Ser. 1, Vol. 4, 197.
28. Harrison, *The Civil War in Kentucky*, 13.
29. Benny F. Craig, "Northern Conquerers [sic] and Southern Deliverers: The Civil War Comes to the Jackson Purchase," *The Register of the Kentucky Historical Society*, Vol. 73, No. 1, 29–30, http://www.jacksonpurchasehistory.org/wp-content/uploads/2011/04/Craig2.pdf, Accessed February 2, 2012.
30. Grant, *Personal Memoirs*, 136–137.
31. Allen, *Center of Conflict*, 28.
32. C. F. Smith, Letter to Mrs. Fanny M. Smith, September 8, 1861, C. F. Smith Papers.
33. Allen, *Center of Conflict*, 29.

34. C. F. Smith, Letter to Mrs. Fanny M. Smith, September 8, 1861, C. F. Smith Papers.
35. Smithland is located in Kentucky where the Ohio and Cumberland rivers meet about nineteen miles from Paducah. Smithland, Kentucky, http://en.wikipedia.org/wiki/Smithland,_Kentucky, Accessed September 19, 2014.
36. W. S. Hillyer, Letter to C. F. Smith, September 7, 1861, *Official Records*, Ser. 1, Vol. 4, 57.
37. C. F. Smith, Letter to Troops, September 8, 1861, C. F. Smith Papers.
38. Grant, *Personal Memoirs*, 136.
39. J. C. Frémont, Order to U. S. Grant, September 8, 1861, *Official Records*, Ser. 1, Vol. 3, 480.
40. J. C. Frémont, Order to U. S. Grant, September 9, 1861, *Official Records*, Ser. 1, Vol. 3, 481.
41. J. C. Frémont, Order to U. S. Grant, September 10, 1861, *Official Records*, Ser. 1, Vol. 3, 484.
42. C. F. Smith, Letter to Mrs. Fanny M. Smith, September 10, 1861, C. F. Smith Papers.
43. C. F. Smith, Letter No. 1 to Brig. Genl. Anderson, 9 September 1861, C. F. Smith Papers.
44. "The Beginning of the End," *Harper's Weekly*, September 14, 1861, 578.
45. Richard Carwardine, *Lincoln* (New York: Alfred A. Knopf, 2006), 179.
46. Carwardine, *Lincoln*, 178.
47. Carwardine, *Lincoln*, 179.
48. J. C. Frémont and Missouri, Mr. Lincoln and Freedom, The Lincoln Institute, Civil War, http://www.mrlincolnandfreedom.org/inside.asp?ID=31&subjectID=3, Accessed July 26, 2011.
49. J. C. Frémont and Missouri, Mr. Lincoln and Freedom, The Lincoln Institute.
50. "J. C. Frémont and Missouri" from Michael Burlingame and John R. Turner Ettlinger, eds., *Inside Lincoln's White House: The Complete Civil War Diary of John Hay* (Carbondale: Southern Illinois University Press, 1997), December 9, 1863 entry, 133.
51. The Confiscation Act of 1861 was an act of Congress during the early months of the Civil War permitting court proceedings for confiscation of any of property being used to support the Confederate independence effort, including slaves. Confiscation Act of 1861, http://en.wikipedia.org/wiki/Confiscation_Act_of_1861, Accessed September 19, 2014.
52. Carwardine, *Lincoln*, 179.
53. J. C. Frémont and Missouri, Mr. Lincoln and Freedom, The Lincoln Institute.
54. J. C. Frémont and Missouri, Mr. Lincoln and Freedom, The Lincoln Institute.
55. C. F. Smith, Letter to Fanny M. Smith, September 18, 1861, C. F. Smith Papers.
56. Action of the Kentucky Legislature, Frankfort, KY, September 11, 1861, *Richmond Times Dispatch*, September 13, 1861, Accessed July 26, 2011.
57. C. F. Smith, Letter to Mrs. Fanny M. Smith, September 18, 1861, C. F. Smith Papers.
58. C. F. Smith, Letter to Mrs. Fanny M. Smith, September 18, 1861, C. F. Smith Papers.
59. C. F. Smith, Letter to Mrs. Fanny M. Smith, September 16, 1861, C. F. Smith Papers.
60. C. F. Smith, Letter to Mrs. Fanny M. Smith, September 17, 1861, C. F. Smith Papers
61. C. F. Smith, Letter to Mrs. Fanny M. Smith, September 25, 1861, C. F. Smith Papers.
62. C. F. Smith, Letter to Mrs. Fanny M. Smith, September 18, 1861, C. F. Smith Papers.
63. C. F. Smith, Letter to Mrs. Fanny M. Smith, September 25, 1861, C. F. Smith Papers.
64. C. F. Smith, Letter to Mrs. Fanny M. Smith, September 25, 1861, C. F. Smith Papers.
65. J. C. Frémont, Letter to C. F. Smith, September 26, 1861, *Official Records*, Ser. 1, Vol. 4, 275.
66. C. F. Smith, Letter to Assistant Adjutant General, September 28, 1861, *Official Records*, Ser. 4, Vol. 4, 279.
67. C. F. Smith, Letter to Assistant Adjutant General, September 28, 1861, *Official Records*, Ser. 4, Vol. 4, 279.
68. C. F. Smith, Letter to Mrs. Fanny M. Smith, September 28, 1861, C. F. Smith Papers.
69. J. G. Holloway, Letter to E. A. Paine, September 30, 1861, *Official Records*, Ser. 1, Vol. 4, 283.
70. C. F. Smith, Letter to Mrs. Fanny M. Smith, September 20, 1861, C. F. Smith Papers.
71. The Marine Hospital was originally built as part of the Marine Hospital Service. The Service was the first federal-level system to provide public health care and disease prevention in America. The hospitals were constructed at key river and seaports to provide medical services for merchant marine sailors and to monitor and control pathogenic diseases. The Paducah hospital was built in 1853 and had beds for fifty patients. U.S. Marine Hospital, Historical Marker Database, http://www.hmdb.org/Marker.asp?Marker=48505, Accessed January 28, 2012.
72. *Military Essays and Recollections*, Vol. 1, 22, as referenced in Dubelier, "The Forgotten Soldier," 51.
73. C. F. Smith, Letter to Mrs. Fanny M. Smith, September 30, 1861, C. F. Smith Papers.
74. Holland, "An Anecdote of General Grant Related by His Son," February 1909–1912, *New News of Yesterday*, Interview with Frederick Dent Grant by Holland in 1899 just before he sailed for the Philippines to take a military command.
75. C. F. Smith, Letter to Mrs. Fanny M. Smith, September 30, 1861, C. F. Smith Papers.
76. General Orders No. 17, 1 October 1861, *Official Records*, Ser. 1, Vol. 4, 287–289.
77. Wallace, *An Autobiography*, 338.
78. Wallace, *An Autobiography*, 339.
79. Wallace, *An Autobiography*, 339.
80. Wallace, *An Autobiography*, 340.
81. Wallace, *An Autobiography*, 340–341.
82. Wallace, *An Autobiography*, 342–343.
83. Wallace, *An Autobiography*, 343–345.
84. F. Tooth, Note to L. Wallace, October 30, 1861, C. F. Smith Papers.
85. F. Tooth, Note to L. Wallace, October 30, 1861, C. F. Smith Papers.
86. F. Tooth, Note to L. Wallace, November 1, 1861, C. F. Smith Papers.
87. C. F. Smith, Letter to Mrs. Fanny M. Smith, November 7, 1861, C. F. Smith Papers.
88. C. F. Smith, Letter to Mrs. Fanny M. Smith, October 1, 1861, C. F. Smith Papers.
89. C. F. Smith, Letter to Mrs. Fanny M. Smith, October 6, 1861, C. F. Smith Papers.
90. C. F. Smith, Letter to Mrs. Fanny M. Smith, October 4, 1861, C. F. Smith Papers.
91. C. F. Smith, Letter to Mrs. Fanny M. Smith, October 6, 1861, C. F. Smith Papers.

92. C. F. Smith, Letter to Mrs. Fanny M. Smith, October 4, 1861, C. F. Smith Papers.
93. C. F. Smith, Letter to Mrs. Fanny M. Smith, October 8, 1861, C. F. Smith Papers.
94. C. F. Smith, Letter to Mrs. Fanny M. Smith, October 10, 1861, C. F. Smith Papers.
95. Millerites refers to followers of William Miller, who predicted in 1833 the second coming of Jesus Christ for the year 1843. Smith's reference here may refer to three Millerites who were admitted to the Taunton State Lunatic Hospital in Massachusetts including one described as "on old and nearly hopeless" case, who presented "the sad spectacle of a promising man blasted in the mind and prospects by a foolish and wicked delusion." EllenWhite-Exposed.com, Millerite Insanity, http://www.ellenwhiteexposed.com/egw64.htm and Millerism, http://en.wikipedia.org/wiki/Millerism, Accessed October 10, 2012.
96. C. F. Smith, Letter to Mrs. Fanny M. Smith, October 11, 1861, C. F. Smith Papers.
97. Abstract from statement of troops in Western Department, October 10, 1861, *Official Records*, Ser. 1, Vol. 3, 530.
98. C. F. Smith, Letter to Mrs. Fanny M. Smith, October 15, 1861, C. F. Smith Papers.
99. C. F. Smith, Letter to Assistant Adjutant General, October 16, 1861, *Official Records*, Ser. 1, Vol. 4, 308–309.
100. J. H. Eaton, Letter from to C. F. Smith, October 19, 1861, *Official Records*, Ser. 1, Vol. 3, 539.
101. Simon Cameron to C. F. Smith, October 22, 1861, C. F. Smith Papers.
102. U. S. Grant, Telegram to C. F. Smith, October 25, 1861, C. F. Smith Papers.
103. U. S. Grant, Letter to C. F. Smith, October 25, 1861, *Official Records*, Ser. 1, Vol. 3, 556.
104. General Orders No. 6, October 8, 1861, *Official Records*, Ser. 1, Vol. 4, 296–297.
105. C. F. Smith, Proclamation, October 10, 1861, *Official Records*, Ser. 1, Vol. 4, 302.
106. C. F. Smith, Letter to Mrs. Fanny M. Smith, October 11, 1861, C. F. Smith Papers.
107. C. F. Smith, Letter to Mrs. Fanny M. Smith, October 15, 1861, C. F. Smith Papers.
108. General Orders No. 23, October 20, 1861,*Official Records*, Ser. 1, Vol. 3, 539–540.
109. C. F. Smith, Note to U. S. Grant, October 22, 1861, C. F. Smith Papers.
110. Louise Boyd, Letter to C. F. Smith, January 31, 1861, C. F. Smith Papers.
111. C. F. Smith, Letter to U. S. Grant, January 4, 1862, John Y. Simon, ed., *The Papers of U. S. Grant* (Carbondale: Southern Illinois University Press, 1970), vol. 3, 431.
112. U. S. Grant, Letter to C. F. Smith, October 16, 1861, *Official Records*, Ser. 1, Vol. 3, 536.
113. General Orders No. 18, October 24, 1861, *Official Records*, Ser. 1, Vol. 3, 553.
114. General Orders No. 28, November 2, 1861, *Official Records*, Ser. 1, Vol. 3, 559.
115. General Orders No. 97, November 9, 1861, *Official Records*, Ser. 1, Vol. 3, 567.
116. Grant, *Personal Memoirs*, 146–147.
117. Jean Edward Smith, *Grant* (New York: Simon & Schuster, 2001), 121.
118. Simon Cameron, Letter to C. F. Smith, October 22, 1861; C. F. Smith, Letter to Mrs. Fanny M. Smith, November 1, 1861, C. F. Smith Papers.
119. C. F. Smith, Letter to Mrs. Fanny M. Smith, November 1, 1861, C. F. Smith Papers.
120. C. F. Smith, Letter to Adjutant-General of the Army, November 6, 1861, *Official Records*, Ser. 1, Vol. 4, 339.
121. C. F. Smith, Letter to Adjutant-General of the Army, November 6, 1861, *Official Records*, Ser. 1, Vol. 4, 339.
122. Augustus Louis Chetlain, *Recollections of Seventy Years* (Galena: The Gazette Publishing Company, 1899), 82–83.
123. C. F. Smith, Report to Adjutant General of the Army, November 6, 1861, *Official Records*, Ser. 1, Vol. 4, 339–340.
124. C. F. Smith, Report to Adjutant General of the Army, November 6, 1861, *Official Records*, Ser. 1, Vol. 4, 340.
125. C. F. Smith, Report to Adjutant General of the Army, November 6, 1861, *Official Records*, Ser. 1, Vol. 4, 340.
126. C. F. Smith, Report to Adjutant General of the Army, November 6, 1861, *Official Records*, Ser. 1, Vol. 4, 340.
127. C. F. Smith, Report to Adjutant General of the Army, 6 November 1861, *Official Records*, Ser. 1, Vol. 4, 345–346.
128. C. F. Smith, Report to Adjutant General of the Army, 6 November 1861, *Official Records*, Ser. 1, Vol. 4, 345–346.

Chapter 17

1. Grant, *Personal Memoirs*, 138.
2. Southern Illinois was known as Egypt by its residents who called themselves Egyptians. According to Rhonda Kohl: "The people who had settled southern Illinois hailed principally from Virginia, Kentucky, the Carolinas, and Tennessee. Many migrants feared freed Southern blacks would move north, disrupting the labor system, as well as initializing integration through marriage. Racism was integral to the region's history, culture, and development. So homogeneous was the culture and belief system that the area became known as Egypt." Rhonda M. Kohl, *The Prairie Boys Go to War* (Carbondale: Southern University Press, 2013), 1 & 3.
3. James R. Knight, *The Battle of Fort Donelson* (Charleston: The History Press, 2011), 47–48.
4. Grant, *Personal Memoirs*, 138.
5. General Orders No. 18, October 24, 1861, *Official Records*, Ser. 1, Vol. 3, 553.
6. Chauncey McKeever, Letter of November 1, 1861, to U. S. Grant, included in Grant's report No. 1, November 17, 1861, *Official Records*, Ser. 1, Vol. 3, 267.
7. U. S. Grant, Letter to C. F. Smith, November 5, 1861, *Official Records*, Ser. 1, Vol. 3, 273.
8. Grant, *Personal Memoirs*, 139.
9. T. J. Newsham, General Smith's Order to E. A. Paine, November 6, 1861, *Official Records*, Ser. 1, Vol. 3, 301.
10. T. J. Newsham, General Smith's Order to E. A. Paine, November 6, 1861, *Official Records*, Ser. 1, Vol. 3, 301.
11. Grant, *Personal Memoirs*, 139.
12. U. S. Grant, Report No. 1 to S. Williams, November 17, 1861, *Official Records*, Ser. 1, Vol. 3, 269.
13. Grant, *Personal Memoirs*, 139.

14. U. S. Grant, Note to C. F. Smith, November 7, 1861, *Official Records*, Ser. 1, Vol. 4, 346.
15. U. S. Grant, Note to C. F. Smith, November 8, 1861, *Official Records*, Ser. 1, Vol. 4, 346.
16. C. F. Smith, Letter to the Assistant Adjutant General, November 8, 1861, *Official Records*, Ser. 1, Vol. 4, 346.
17. C. F. Smith, Letter to Mrs. Fanny M. Smith, November 9, 1861, C. F. Smith Papers.
18. C. F. Smith, Letter to Mrs. Fanny M. Smith, November 14, 1861, C. F. Smith Papers.
19. T. A. Newsham, Instructions to E. A. Paine, November 6, 1861, *Official Records*, Ser. 1, Vol. 3, 301.
20. E. A. Paine, Report to T. A. Newsham, November 9, 1861, *Official Records*, Ser. 1, Vol. 3, 302–303.
21. General Orders No. 32, November 11, 1861, *Official Records*, Ser. 1, Vol. 3, 303.
22. G. B. McClellan, Orders to H. W. Halleck, November 11, 1861, *Official Records*, Ser. 1, Vol. 3, 568–569.
23. C. F. Smith, Letter to the Assistant Adjutant General, November 11, 1861, *Official Records*, Ser. 1, Vol. 3, 299–300; C. F. Smith, Letter to Mrs. Fanny M. Smith, November 14, 1861, C. F. Smith Papers.
24. Dictionary.com, Spread-eagleism. Spread-eagleism refers to boastfulness or bombast, especially in the display of patriotic or nationalistic pride in the U.S.; flag-waving, http://dictionary.reference.com/browse/spread eagleism, Accessed August 16, 2011.
25. C. F. Smith, Letter to Mrs. Fanny M. Smith, November 14, 1861, C. F. Smith Papers.
26. H. W. Halleck, Letter to C. F. Smith, November 22, 1861, *Official Records*, Ser. 1, Vol. 7, 444.
27. C. F. Smith, to Assistant Adjutant General, November 23, 1861, *Official Records*, Ser. 1, Vol. 7, 445–446.
28. H. W. Halleck, Letter to C. F. Smith, November 22, 1861, *Official Records*, Ser. 1, Vol. 7, 448–449.
29. H. W. Halleck, Letter to C. F. Smith, November 22, 1861, *Official Records*, Ser. 1, Vol. 7, 448–449.
30. C. F. Smith, Letter to Mrs. Fanny M. Smith, November 17, 1861, C. F. Smith Papers.
31. G. B. McClellan, Letter to D. C. Buell, November 29, 1861, *Official Records*, Ser. 1, Vol. 7, 457–458.
32. C. F. Smith, Letter to H. W. Halleck, 25 November 1861, C. F. Smith Papers.

Chapter 18

1. C. F. Smith, Letter to Mrs. Fanny M. Smith, November 14, 1861, C. F. Smith Papers.
2. The home referred to is the Lloyd Tilghman house or the Tilghman-Woolfolk house. The Greek Revival house was built in 1852 by Robert Woolfolk on the behalf of Lloyd Tilghman, who had just moved with his family to Paducah that year. Tilghman was a West Point graduate, having finished 46th out of 49 in his class, but spent less than a year as a second lieutenant. He moved to Paducah, then a community of 3,000 people, due to being assigned there by his employer, the New Orleans and Ohio Railroad, as a railroad civil engineer for the first railroad to connect Paducah to major cities to the south. Tilghman did not purchase the house; Woolfolk remained the owner of the property. Tilghman and his wife, seven children, and five slaves called the residence home until 1861, although Tilghman spent much of his time working on a railroad in the Isthmus of Panama. At the time of his departure from the home, he was one of two colonels of the Kentucky State Guard whose stated purpose was to defend the state's neutrality. He officially left Paducah in June of 1861, delaying his departure to prevent more pro–Union officers from leading the state militia in Paducah.

Woolfolk's family then moved into the home. When Federal troops finally arrived in Paducah, their headquarters were directly across from the Woolfolk home. Woolfolk was pro–Southern and flew a Confederate flag in response, sparking a riot in November 1861 that included Union soldiers, particularly those of the 11th Indiana Regiment.

Woolfolk was banished from Paducah and the United States to Canada on August 1, 1864, by Union Brigadier General Eleazer A. Paine. Two weeks later his wife and family were also banished to Canada, which resulted in eight of Woolfolk's household, four others from Paducah, and eleven from Columbus, Kentucky, following Woolfolk into exile. These acts infuriated the Kentucky governor, and Paine was removed from command in Paducah after only ninety days. Lloyd Tilghman House, http://en.wikipedia.org/wiki/Lloyd_Tilghman_House, Accessed July 27, 2010.

3. "Great Excitement in Paducah—Quarrel Among Generals," from Correspondence of the *St. Louis Democrat*, *Philadelphia Inquirer*, November 28, 1861. http://archive.olivesoftware.com/Default/Scripting/ArticleWin.asp?From=Search&Key=PHQ/1861/12/05/2/Ar00203.xml&CollName=PHILADELPHIA_INQUIRER&DOCID=49582&Keyword=%28%3Cmany%3E%3Cstem%3ESmith%29&skin=CivilWarNB&AppName=2&ViewMode=HTML&GZ=T, Accessed July 27, 2010.
4. "Great Excitement in Paducah—Quarrel Among Generals," from Correspondence of the *St. Louis Democrat*, *Philadelphia Inquirer*, November 28, 1861.
5. A roar that often accompanied cheers.
6. "Great Excitement in Paducah—Quarrel Among Generals," from Correspondence of the *Evansville Journal*, *Philadelphia Inquirer*, November 28, 1861. http://archive.olivesoftware.com/Default/Scripting/ArticleWin.asp?From=Search&Key=PHQ/1861/12/05/2/Ar00203.xml&CollName=PHILADELPHIA_INQUIRER&DOCID=49582&Keyword=%28%3Cmany%3E%3Cstem%3ESmith%29&skin=CivilWarNB&AppName=2&ViewMode=HTML&GZ=T, Accessed July 27, 2010.
7. Catton, *Grant Moves South*, 87.
8. Allen, *Center of Conflict*, 29–30.
9. Thomas W. Durham, *Three Years with Wallace's Zouaves* (Macon: Mercer University Press, 2003), 61.
10. C. F. Smith, Letter to G. J. Pillow, November 26, 1861, C. F. Smith Papers.
11. Wallace, *An Autobiography*, 350–351.
12. C. F. Smith, Letter to G. W. Cullum, December 26, 1861, C. F. Smith Papers.
13. U. S. Grant, Orders to E. A. Paine, September 6, 1861, *Official Records*, Ser. 1, Vol. 4, 198.
14. C. F. Smith, General Orders No. 36, November 27, 1861, C. F. Smith Papers.
15. J. T. Price, Note to C. F. Smith, November 25, 1861, C. F. Smith Papers.
16. Unknown person from Indianapolis Letter to C. F. Smith, December 2, 1861, C. F. Smith Papers.
17. General Orders No. 23, October 20, 1861, *Official Records*, Ser. 1, Vol. 3, 539–540.
18. Grant, *Personal Memoirs*, 193–194.

Chapter 19

1. Lucian Anderson, Letter to H. W. Halleck, November 27, 1861, C.F. Smith Papers.
2. J. Seaton, Note to C. F. Smith, November 29, 1861, *Official Records*, Ser. 1, Vol. 7, 462.
3. C. F. Smith, Note to Assistant Adjutant General, November 30, 1861, *Official Records*, Ser. 1, Vol. 7, 462.
4. James Peckham, Report to C. F. Smith, December 2, 1861, *Official Records*, Ser. 1, Vol. 7, 6.
5. *Chicago Tribune*, Vol. 15, December 1, 1861, 1 as referenced in Dubelier, "The Forgotten Soldier," 56–57.
6. Gen. Smith, of Paducah—His Loyalty, December 5, 1861, *Chicago Tribune*, http://pqasb.pqarchiver.com/chicagotribune/access/581874012.html?FMT=ABS&FMTS=ABS:AI&type=historic&date=Dec+5%2C+1861&author=-&pub=Chicago+Tribune+(1860-1872)&edition=&startpage=0_1&desc=Gen.+Smith%2C+of+Paducah—His+Loyalty, Accessed August 23, 2011.
7. Unknown source comment on Anderson, C. F. Smith Papers.
8. Kohl, *The Prairie Boys Go to War*, 4.
9. D. D. I. Benedict, Letter to John A. Gurley, December 6, 1861, C. F. Smith Papers.
10. Unknown sender from Iowa City Letter to C. F. Smith, January 5, 1862, C. F. Smith Papers.
11. Wallace, *An Autobiography*, 350–351.
12. C. F. Smith, Letter to Mrs. Fanny M. Smith, December 6, 1861, C. F. Smith Papers.
13. Lewis Wallace, Note to C. F. Smith, December 7, 1861, C. F. Smith Papers.
14. H. W. Halleck, Letter to L. Thomas, January 21, 1862, Simon, *The Papers of U. S. Grant*, Vol. 4, 191.
15. C. F. Smith, Letter to Mrs. Fanny M. Smith, December 9, 1861, C. F. Smith Papers.
16. H. C. McCook, Letter to J. C. Kelton, December 12, 1861, C. F. Smith Papers.
17. H. W. Halleck, Letter to G. B. McClellan, December 16, 1861, with response of December 17, 1861, from L. Thomas, C. F. Smith Papers.
18. C. F. Smith, Letter to Mrs. Fanny M. Smith, December 17, 1861, C. F. Smith Papers.
19. C. F. Smith, Letter to Mrs. Fanny M. Smith, December 17, 1861, C. F. Smith Papers.
20. Special Orders No. 78, December 20, 1861, *Official Records*, Ser. 1, Vol. 52, 201.
21. General Orders No. 22, December 23, 1861, *Official Records*, Ser. 1, Vol. 7, 515.
22. Bird's Point is an unincorporated community in Mississippi County, Missouri. It lies on an island or former island in the Mississippi River near the confluence of the Ohio and Mississippi Rivers and is situated directly across the Mississippi River from Cairo, Illinois. Bird's Point was a strategic site during the Civil War. The Battle of Charleston occurred in the vicinity on August 19, 1861. Union cavalry under David P. Jenkins guarded the region for the early part of the war, deterring Confederate attempts to regain control of the vital supply routes. Once secure from enemy threat, Bird's Point was transformed into an important supply and repair site, as well as a training camp and military post, for the Union army and navy. Bird's Point, Missouri, http://en.wikipedia.org/wiki/Bird%27s_Point,_Missouri, Accessed November 29, 2013.
23. C. F. Smith, Letter to Mrs. Fanny M. Smith, December 30, 1861, C. F. Smith Papers.
24. C. F. Smith, Letter to Mrs. Fanny M. Smith, December 22, 1861, C. F. Smith Papers.
25. C. F. Smith, Letter to G. W. Cullum, December 26, 1861, C. F. Smith Papers.
26. G. W. Cullum, Letter to C. F. Smith, December 26, 1861, C. F. Smith Papers.
27. C. F. Smith, Letter to G. W. Cullum, December 31, 1861, C. F. Smith Papers.
28. H. W. Halleck, Letter to S. Thomas, January 7, 1862, C. F. Smith Papers.
29. C. F. Smith, Letter to Mrs. Fanny M. Smith, December 27, 1861, C. F. Smith Papers.
30. C. F. Smith, Letter to Mrs. Fanny M. Smith, December 30, 1861, C. F. Smith Papers.
31. G. W. Cullum, Letter to C. F. Smith, December 31, 1861, C. F. Smith Papers.
32. C. F. Smith, Letter to Mrs. Fanny M. Smith, January 2, 1862, C. F. Smith Papers.
33. F. M. Smith, Letter to J. B. S. Todd, January 4, 1862, C. F. Smith Papers.
34. J. B. S. Todd, Letter to Mrs. F. M. Smith, January 11, 1862, C. F. Smith Papers.
35. F. M. Smith, Letter to Abraham Lincoln, January 20, 1862, C. F. Smith Papers.
36. G. W. Cullum, Letter to C. F. Smith, January 1862, C. F. Smith Papers.
37. C. F. Smith, Letter to Adjutant General of the Army, January 10, 1862, C. F. Smith Papers.
38. C. F. Smith, Letter to Adjutant General of the Army, January 10, 1862, C. F. Smith Papers.
39. C. F. Smith, Letter to Mrs. Fanny M. Smith, January 11, 1862, C. F. Smith Papers.
40. C. F. Smith, Letter to W. L. Mactier, January 31, 1862, C. F. Smith Papers.
41. G. W. Cullum, Letter to C. F. Smith, February 1, 1862, C. F. Smith Papers.
42. G. B. McClellan, Letter to W. F. Smith, [illegible] 24, 1885, C. F. Smith Papers.
43. C. F. Smith, Letter to G. W. Cullum, December 31, 1861, C. F. Smith Papers.
44. Lewis Wallace, Report on Expedition to Camp Beauregard and Viola, Ky., January 1, 1862, *Official Records*, Ser. 1, Vol. 7, 66–68.
45. C. F. Smith, General Order No. 2, January 7, 1862, C. F. Smith Papers.
46. H. W. Halleck, General Orders No. 24, December 12, 1861, C. F. Smith Papers.
47. C. F. Smith, Note to J. Rziha, December 30, 1861, C. F. Smith Papers.

Part Five

1. William Conant Church, *Ulysses S. Grant* (New York: G. P. Putnam's Sons, 1897), 115–116.

Chapter 20

1. Knight, *Fort Donelson*, 29–30.
2. Knight, *Fort Donelson*, 30.
3. A bastion is an angular structure projecting outward from the curtain wall of an artillery fortification. The fully developed bastion consists of two faces and two flanks with fire from the flanks being able to protect the curtain wall and the adjacent bastions. Bastion, http://

en.wikipedia.org/wiki/Bastion, Accessed November 16, 2013.

4. General Donelson had graduated with Smith in the class of 1825 from West Point but had resigned his commission several months later.

5. Knight, *Fort Donelson*, 15–16.
6. Knight, *Fort Donelson*, 16.
7. Knight, *Fort Donelson*, 16.
8. Estimates of the size of the garrison vary from 2,800 to 3,400 depending on the source. Battle of Fort Henry, http://en.wikipedia.org/wiki/Battle_of_Fort_Henry, Accessed March 31, 2011.
9. A parapet (or breastwork) is a wall of stone, wood or earth on the outer edge of a defensive wall or trench, which shelters the defenders. They could be provided with embrasures for the fort's guns to fire through, and a banquette or fire-step so that defending infantry could shoot over the top. The top of the parapet often slopes towards the enemy to enable the defenders to shoot downwards. http://en.wikipedia.org/wiki/Parapet, Accessed 15 October 2012.
10. Hurst, *Men of Fire*, 116–117.
11. Knight, *Fort Donelson*, 33.
12. Knight, *Fort Donelson*, 54.
13. Knight, *Fort Donelson*, 34–35.
14. Knight, *Fort Donelson*, 36.
15. Knight, *Fort Donelson*, 37–38.
16. C. F. Smith, Letter to Assistant Adjutant General, October 16, 1861, *Official Records*, Ser. 1, Vol. 7, 308–309.
17. Knight, *Fort Donelson*, 55.
18. W. W. Mackall, Orders to L. Tilghman, November 17, 1861, *Official Records*, Ser. 1, Vol. 7, 560.
19. Knight, *Fort Donelson*, 59.
20. H. W. Halleck, Orders to U. S. Grant, January 6, 1862, *Official Records*, Ser. 1, Vol. 7, 533–534.
21. U. S. Grant, Letter to H. W. Halleck, January 8, 1862, *Official Records*, Ser. 1, Vol. 7, 537–538.
22. C. F. Smith, Letter to U. S. Grant, January 9, 1862, *Official Records*, Ser. 1, Vol. 7, 541–542.
23. U. S. Grant, Letter to C. F. Smith, January 10, 1862, *Official Records*, Ser. 1, Vol. 7, 543.
24. C. F. Smith, Note to U. S. Grant, January 13, 1862, Simon, *The Papers of U.S. Grant*, vol. 4, 51.
25. C. F. Smith, Letter to Mrs. Fanny M. Smith, January 30, 1862, C. F. Smith Papers.
26. C. F. Smith, Letter to Mrs. Fanny M. Smith, January 21, 1862, C. F. Smith Papers.
27. J. Rziha, Journal of the march of the First and Second Brigades of the United States forces from Paducah, Ky. to Callaway, on the Tennessee River, and back. January 21 & 22, 1862, *Official Records*, Ser. 1, Vol. 7, 73.
28. C. F. Smith, Letter to Mrs. Fanny M. Smith, January 22, 1862, C. F. Smith Papers.
29. C. F. Smith, Letter to Assistant Adjutant General, January 22, 1862, *Official Records*, Ser. 1, Vol. 7, 561.
30. C. F. Smith, Letter to Mrs. Fanny M. Smith, January 27, 1862, C. F. Smith Papers.
31. C. F. Smith, Report to U. S. Grant, January 27, 1862, *Official Records*, Ser. 1, Vol. 7, 72.
32. G. W. Cullum, Letter to C. F. Smith, February 1, 1862, C. F. Smith Papers.
33. L. Tilghman, Report to General Polk, January 18, 1862, 11 p.m., *Official Records*, Ser. 1, Vol. 7, 74.
34. L. Tilghman, Report to W. W. Mackall, January 19, 1862, *Official Records*, Ser. 1, Vol. 7, 74.
35. L. Tilghman, Report to General Polk, January 19, 1862, *Official Records*, Ser. 1, Vol. 7, 74.
36. L. Tilghman, Report to General Polk, January 21, 1862, 6 p.m., *Official Records*, Ser. 1, Vol. 7, 75.
37. L. Tilghman, Report to General Polk, January 21, 1862, 11 p.m., *Official Records*, Ser. 1, Vol. 7, 75.
38. L. Tilghman, Report to General Polk, January 23, 1862, 10:30 p.m., *Official Records*, Ser. 1, Vol. 7, 75.
39. L. Tilghman, Report to General Polk, January 25, 1862, 3 p.m., *Official Records*, Ser. 1, Vol. 7, 75.
40. H. W. Halleck, Letter to C. F. Smith, January 24, 1862, C. F. Smith Papers.
41. C. F. Smith, Letter to Mrs. Fanny M. Smith, 30 January 1862, C. F. Smith Papers.
42. Knight, *Fort Donelson*, 64.
43. Grant, *Personal Memoirs*, 147.
44. Knight, *Fort Donelson*, 63.
45. Knight, *Fort Donelson*, 65.
46. U. S. Grant, Telegram to H. W. Halleck, January 28, 1862, *Official Records*, Ser. 1, Vol. 7, 121.
47. A. H. Foote, Telegram to H. W. Halleck, January 28, 1862, *Official Records*, Ser. 1, Vol. 7, 120.
48. U. S. Grant, Telegram H. W. Halleck, January 29, 1862, *Official Records*, Ser. 1, Vol. 7, 120.
49. Knight, *Fort Donelson*, 70.
50. U. S. Grant, Orders to C. F. Smith, January 31, 1862, *Official Records*, Ser. 1, Vol. 7, 575.
51. J. Rawlins, Note to C. F. Smith, February 1, 1862, C. F. Smith Papers.
52. Knight, *Fort Donelson*, 72.
53. Knight, *Fort Donelson*, 73.
54. Knight, *Fort Donelson*, 80.
55. A sally port is a secure, controlled entryway of a fortification. Sally port, http://en.wikipedia.org/wiki/Sally_port, Accessed 15 October 2012.
56. Other accounts say 12 officers and 82 men surrendered with 15 men killed and 20 wounded.
57. A. H. Foote, Report to H. W. Halleck, February 7, 1862, *Official Records*, Ser. 1, Vol. 7, 122–124.
58. U. S. Grant, Note to H. W. Halleck, February 6, 1862, *Official Records*, Ser. 1, Vol. 7, 124.
59. H. W. Halleck, Telegram to G. B. McClellan, February 7, 1862, *Official Records*, Ser. 1, Vol. 7, 590.
60. H. W. Halleck, Telegram to G. B. McClellan, February 7, 1862, *Official Records*, Ser. 1, Vol. 7, 120.
61. "Another Great Victory: The Capture of Fort Henry on the Tennessee River," *New York Times*, February 8, 1862, Holzer and Symonds, *The New York Times—Complete Civil War*.
62. L. Tilghman, Report of the bombardment of Fort Henry to S. Cooper, February 12, 1862, *Official Records*, Ser. 1, Vol. 7, 138–139.
63. Battle of Fort Henry, http://en.wikipedia.org/wiki/Battle_of_Fort_Henry, Accessed March 31, 2011.

Chapter 21

1. Knight, *Fort Donelson*, 87.
2. Knight, *Fort Donelson*, 89.
3. Knight, *Fort Donelson*, 90.
4. Knight, *Fort Donelson*, 90.
5. Grant, *Personal Memoirs*, 152.
6. J. Powell, Report to Assistant Adjutant General of 2nd Division U.S. Forces, March 25, 1862, C. F. Smith Papers.

7. U. S. Grant, Telegram to E. B. Washburne, February 10, 1862, Simon, *The Papers of U. S. Grant*, Vol. 4, 188.
8. A. L. Chetlain, Letter to E. B. Washburne, February 10, 1862, Simon, *The Papers of U. S. Grant*, Vol. 4, 189.
9. Lew Wallace, "The Capture of Fort Donelson" in *Battles and Leaders of the Civil War* (New York: The Century Company, 1887), vol. 1, 404–405.
10. Knight, *Fort Donelson*, 95.
11. Wallace, *Battles and Leaders of the Civil War*, 405.
12. Lew Wallace, Letter to Mrs. Susan Wallace, February 11, 1862, Simon, *The Papers of U. S. Grant*, Vol. 4, 192–193.
13. Grant, *Personal Memoirs*, 155.
14. Knight, *Fort Donelson*, 99.
15. Knight, *Fort Donelson*, 99.
16. Knight, *Fort Donelson*, 101.
17. J. Cook, Report of Third Brigade, March 6, 1862, *Official Records*, Ser. 1, Vol. 7, 220.
18. J. G. Lauman, Report of Fourth Brigade Second Division, February 18, 1862, *Official Records*, Ser. 1, Vol. 52 (Part I), 9.
19. J. McArthur, Report of First Brigade, February 20, 1862, *Official Records*, Ser. 1, Vol. 7, 215.
20. C. F. Smith, "true copy of original pencil draft of General C. F. Smith's report, unfinished and unsigned," March 29, 1862, *Official Records*, Ser. 1, Vol. 52 (Part II), 7.
21. Smith, "Draft of Smith's Report," *Official Records*, Ser. 1, Vol. 52 (Part I), 7.
22. Knight, *Fort Donelson*, 102.
23. Knight, *Fort Donelson*, 102.
24. U. S. Grant, Report to H. W. Halleck, February 16, 1862, *Official Records*, Ser. 1, Vol. 7, 175.
25. Grant, *Personal Memoirs*, 157.
26. Smith, "Draft of Smith's Report," *Official Records*, Ser. 1, Vol. 52 (Part I), 8.
27. Knight, *Fort Donelson*, 104.
28. Smith, "Draft of Smith's Report," *Official Records*, Ser. 1, Vol. 52 (Part I), 7.
29. J. G. Lauman, Report of Fourth Brigade Second Division, February 18, 1862, *Official Records*, Ser. 1, Vol. 52 (Part I), 9.
30. Knight, *Fort Donelson*, 105–106.
31. Knight, *Fort Donelson*, 106.
32. J. G. Lauman, Report of Fourth Brigade Second Division, February 18, 1862, *Official Records*, Ser. 1, Vol. 52 (Part I), 10.
33. J. C. Veatch, Report to J. G. Lauman, February 18, 1862, *Official Records*, Ser. 1, Vol. 7, 228.
34. The regiment was raised by General Frémont at St. Louis' Benton Barracks. Members were recruited from Ohio, Michigan, Illinois, and Missouri. They were the only Federal unit completely armed with "sporting rifles." The sharpshooters were used as skirmishers and scouts and to a lesser extent as snipers. These elite troops were well equipped and trained, and placed at the front of any column to first engage the enemy. Marksman, http://en.wikipedia.org/wiki/Sharpshooters#Union_Army, Accessed December 19, 2013.
35. J. G. Lauman, Report of Fourth Brigade Second Division, February 18, 1862, *Official Records*, Ser. 1, Vol. 52 (Part I), 10.
36. J. Cook, Report of Third Brigade, March 6, 1862, *Official Records*, Ser. 1, Vol. 7, 219–222.
37. J. McArthur, Report of First Brigade, February 20, 1862, *Official Records*, Ser. 1, Vol. 7, 215–216.
38. Smith, "Draft of Smith's Report," *Official Records*, Ser. 1, Vol. 52 (Part I), 7–8.
39. Knight, *Fort Donelson*, 106.
40. Knight, *Fort Donelson*, 107.
41. Knight, *Fort Donelson*, 106–107.
42. Robert Leckie, *None Died in Vain: The Saga of the American Civil War* (New York: HarperCollins, 1990), 245.
43. Knight, *Fort Donelson*, 107.
44. J. Cook, Report of Third Brigade, March 6, 1862, *Official Records*, Ser. 1, Vol. 7, 219–222.
45. Knight, *Fort Donelson*, 109.
46. James Hamilton, *The Battle of Fort Donelson* (New York: A. S. Barnes, 1968), 125–129.
47. Knight, *Fort Donelson*, 107.
48. Grant, *Personal Memoirs*, 156; Knight, *Fort Donelson*, 110.
49. Edwin C. Bearss, "General C. F. Smith's Attack on Rebel Right," December 1959, Fort Donelson National Military Park Service, Research Project #10, 8.
50. Knight, *Fort Donelson*, 108.
51. C. F. Smith, "Draft of Smith's Report," *Official Records*, Ser. 1, Vol. 52 (Part I), 8.
52. One that is face to face with or opposite to one another.
53. Lew Wallace, "Capture of Fort Donelson," Harold Holzer, ed., *Hearts Touched by Fire* (New York: Modern Library, 2011), 231–232.
54. J. Cook, Report of Third Brigade, March 6, 1862, *Official Records*, Ser. 1, Vol. 7, 219–222.
55. C. F. Smith, "Draft of Smith's Report," *Official Records*, Ser. 1, Vol. 52 (Part I), 8.
56. Grant, *Personal Memoirs*, 156.
57. A. H. Foote, Report to H. W. Halleck, February 15, 1862, *Official Records*, Ser. 1, Vol. 7, 166.
58. John McArthur, Report of the First Brigade, February 20, 1862, *Official Records*, Ser. 1, Vol. 7, 215–216.
59. U. S. Grant, Report to H. W. Halleck, February 16, 1862, *Official Records*, Ser. 1, Vol. 7, 159.
60. H. W. Halleck, Note to C. F. Smith, February 14, 1862, C. F. Smith Papers.
61. Smith, "Draft of Smith's Report," *Official Records*, Ser. 1, Vol. 52 (Part I), 7.
62. Leckie, *None Died in Vain*, 246.
63. J. Cook, Report of Third Brigade, March 6, 1862, *Official Records*, Ser. 1, Vol. 7, 219–222.
64. C. J. Wright, Report of Thirteenth Missouri Infantry, February 17, 1862, *Official Records*, Ser. 1, Vol. 7, 224.
65. Bearss, "Smith's Attack on Rebel Right," 8–9.
66. Bearss, "Smith's Attack on Rebel Right," 8.
67. Holzer, *Hearts Touched by Fire*, 232.

Chapter 22

1. Bearss, "Smith's Attack on Rebel Right," 1.
2. Bearss, "Smith's Attack on Rebel Right," 1–2.
3. Bearss, "Smith's Attack on Rebel Right," 19.
4. Smith, "Draft of Smith's Report," *Official Records*, Ser. 1, Vol. 52 (Part I), 8.
5. Bearss, "Smith's Attack on Rebel Right," 20.
6. Bearss, "Smith's Attack on Rebel Right," 21.
7. Bearss, "Smith's Attack on Rebel Right," 21–22.

8. The long roll is a prolonged roll of the drums, as the signal of an attack by the enemy, and for the troops to arrange themselves in line. http://www.thefreedictionary.com/Long+roll, Accessed November 22, 2012.

9. Bearss, "Smith's Attack on Rebel Right," 9–10.
10. Bearss, "Smith's Attack on Rebel Right," 11–12.
11. Hamilton, *The Battle of Fort Donelson*, 187.
12. Hamilton, *The Battle of Fort Donelson*, 193.
13. Bearss, "Smith's Attack on Rebel Right," 21.
14. Bearss, "Smith's Attack on Rebel Right," 22–23.
15. Bearss, "Smith's Attack on Rebel Right," 19.
16. The regiments were from Wallace's Second and Third Brigades and the unattached Thirty-Second Illinois. Colonel Cruft's First Brigade was already involved in the battle.
17. Knight, *Fort Donelson*, 120.
18. Knight, *Fort Donelson*, 120.
19. Grant, *Personal Memoirs*, 159.
20. Bearss, "Smith's Attack on Rebel Right," 23–24.
21. Holzer, *Hearts Touched by Fire*, 231.
22. Grant, *Personal Memoirs*, 159.
23. Bearss, "Smith's Attack on Rebel Right," 25.
24. Bearss, "Smith's Attack on Rebel Right," 25.
25. Smith, "Draft of Smith's Report," *Official Records*, Ser. 1, Vol. 52 (Part I), 8.
26. Bearss, "Smith's Attack on Rebel Right," 25.
27. Holland, "An Anecdote of General Grant Related by His Son," February 1909–1912, *New News of Yesterday*, Interview with Frederick Dent Grant by Holland in 1899 just before he sailed for the Philippines to take a military command.
28. Holzer, *Hearts Touched by Fire*, 232.
29. Holland, "An Anecdote of General Grant Related by His Son," February 1909–1912, *New News of Yesterday*, Interview with Frederick Dent Grant by Holland in 1899 just before he sailed for the Philippines to take a military command.
30. Bearss, "Smith's Attack on Rebel Right," 27.
31. Bearss, "Smith's Attack on Rebel Right," 27.
32. Bearss, "Smith's Attack on Rebel Right," 28.
33. Hamilton, *The Battle of Fort Donelson*, 46.
34. Bearss, "Smith's Attack on Rebel Right," 28.
35. Smith had the men remove the caps from their muskets to prevent them from firing and reloading until they reached the trench line. This would prevent the attack from bogging down and allow the regiment to reach the enemy trenches as fast as possible.
36. Bearss, "Smith's Attack on Rebel Right," 28–29.
37. Smith, "Draft of Smith's Report," *Official Records*, Ser. 1, Vol. 52 (Part I), 8.
38. Bearss, "Smith's Attack on Rebel Right," 29–30.
39. Bearss, "Smith's Attack on Rebel Right," 30.
40. *En echelon* is a military formation in which members are arranged diagonally. Each member is stationed behind and to the right (a "right echelon"), or behind and to the left ("left echelon"), of the member ahead. The name of the formation comes from the French word *échelle*, meaning ladder, which describes the staircase effect that this formation has when viewed from above or below, Echelon formation, http://en.wikipedia.org/wiki/Echelon_formation, Accessed November 25, 2012.
41. Bearss, "Smith's Attack on Rebel Right," 31.
42. Following the Confederate surrender, the Second Iowa is chosen to lead the army into the fort. Twombly is chosen to raise the flag upon Donelson's flagpole. Twombly is awarded the Medal of Honor on March 12, 1897. The citation reads: "Took the colors after three of the color guard had fallen, and although most instantly knocked down by a spent ball, immediately arose and bore the colors to the end of the engagement." (Twombly later recalled that five members of the color guard had fallen: Sgt. H. B Doolittle, Corp. G. S. Page, Corp. J. H. Churcher, Corp. H. E. Weaver, and Corp. J. W. Robinson.) Date and place: Feb. 15, 1962, at Fort Donelson, Tennessee. Issued: March 12, 1897. State Historical Society of Iowa, Iowa Medal of Honor Heroes, Corporal Voltaire P. Twombly, http://www.iowahistory.org/museum/exhibits/medal-of-honor/sf-02-twombly-cw/index.htm, Accessed March 29, 2014.

43. J. M. Tuttle, Report of Second Iowa Infantry, February 18, 1862, *Official Records*, Ser. 1, Vol. 7, 229.
44. Bearss, "Smith's Attack on Rebel Right," 33.
45. Smith, "Draft of Smith's Report," *Official Records*, Ser. 1, Vol. 52 (Part I), 8.
46. Wallace, *Battles and Leaders of the Civil War*, 423.
47. Holzer, *Hearts Touched by Fire*, 232.
48. C. F. Smith, Letter to Mrs. Fanny M. Smith, February 17, 1862, C. F. Smith Papers.
49. Catton, *Grant Moves South*, 169–170.
50. Bruce Catton, *This Hallowed Ground* (New York: Doubleday & Co., 1956), 97.
51. J. G. Lauman, Report of Fourth Brigade Second Division, February 18, 1862, *Official Records*, Ser. 1, Vol. 52 (Part I), 10.
52. J. M. Tuttle, Report of Second Iowa Infantry, February 18, 1862, *Official Records*, Ser. 1, Vol. 7, 229.
53. J. G. Lauman, Report of Fourth Brigade Second Division, February 18, 1862, *Official Records*, Ser. 1, Vol. 52 (Part I), 10.
54. J. M. Tuttle, Report of Second Iowa Infantry, February 18, 1862, *Official Records*, Ser. 1, Vol. 7, 229.
55. Catton, *This Hallowed Ground*, 97.
56. Bearss, "Smith's Attack on Rebel Right," 33.
57. James M. Tuttle, Report to J. G. Lauman, February 18, 1862, *Official Records*, Ser. 1, Vol. 7, 229.
58. Smith, "Draft of Smith's Report," *Official Records*, Ser. 1, Vol. 52 (Part I), 8.
59. Smith, "Draft of Smith's Report," *Official Records*, Ser. 1, Vol. 52 (Part I), 8.
60. Bearss, "Smith's Attack on Rebel Right," 34.
61. Smith, "Draft of Smith's Report," *Official Records*, Ser. 1, Vol. 52 (Part I), 9.
62. Bearss, "Smith's Attack on Rebel Right," 34–35.
63. Bearss, "Smith's Attack on Rebel Right," 35.
64. Bearss, "Smith's Attack on Rebel Right," 50.
65. Bearss, "Smith's Attack on Rebel Right," 52.
66. Bearss, "Smith's Attack on Rebel Right," 40–41.
67. Bearss, "Smith's Attack on Rebel Right," 41.
68. J. Cook, Report of Col. John Cook, Seventh Illinois Infantry, March 6, 1862, *Official Records*, Ser. 1, Vol. 7, 221.
69. Bearss, "Smith's Attack on Rebel Right," 42.
70. Bearss, "Smith's Attack on Rebel Right," 43.
71. C. F. Smith, Letter to Mrs. Fanny M. Smith, February 17, 1862, C. F. Smith Papers.
72. J. M. Tuttle, Report of Second Iowa Infantry, February 18, 1862, *Official Records*, Ser. 1, Vol. 7, 229–230.
73. Bearss, "Smith's Attack on Rebel Right," 43.
74. Bearss, "Smith's Attack on Rebel Right," 44.
75. Bearss, "Smith's Attack on Rebel Right," 44.
76. Bearss, "Smith's Attack on Rebel Right," 48–49.

77. Bearss, "Smith's Attack on Rebel Right," 49.
78. Bearss, "Smith's Attack on Rebel Right," 56.
79. Bearss, "Smith's Attack on Rebel Right," 51.
80. Bearss, "Smith's Attack on Rebel Right," 51.
81. Bearss, "Smith's Attack on Rebel Right," 51.
82. Bearss, "Smith's Attack on Rebel Right," 52–53.
83. Smith, "Draft of Smith's Report," *Official Records*, Ser. 1, Vol. 52 (Part I), 9.
84. Bearss, "Smith's Attack on Rebel Right," 55.
85. Bearss, "Smith's Attack on Rebel Right," 55–56.
86. Bearss, "Smith's Attack on Rebel Right," 56.

Chapter 23

1. S. B. Buckner, Report of Operations of Second Division of the Central Army of Kentucky, August 11, 1862, *Official Records*, Ser. 1, Vol. 7, 333.
2. S. B. Buckner, Report of Operations of Second Division of the Central Army of Kentucky, August 11, 1862, *Official Records*, Ser. 1, Vol. 7, 334.
3. Knight, *Fort Donelson*, 125.
4. S. B. Buckner, Report of Operations of Second Division of the Central Army of Kentucky, August 11, 1862, *Official Records*, Ser. 1, Vol. 7, 334.
5. S. B. Buckner, Note to U. S. Grant, February 16, 1862, *Official Records*, Ser. 1, Vol. 7, 166.
6. Knight, *Fort Donelson*, 126.
7. Hamilton, *The Battle of Fort Donelson*, 313.
8. Catton, *Grant Moves South*, 174.
9. Brinton, *Personal Memoirs*, 129.
10. Brinton, *Personal Memoirs*, 129.
11. Grant, *Personal Memoirs*, 161.
12. Brinton, *Personal Memoirs*, 130.
13. Hamilton, *The Battle of Fort Donelson*, 318–319.
14. S. B. Buckner, Note to U. S. Grant, February 16, 1862, *Official Records*, Ser. 1, Vol. 7, 161.
15. J. Cook, Report of Third Brigade, March 6, 1862, *Official Records*, Ser. 1, Vol. 7, 219–222.
16. Edwin C. Bearss, "Unconditional Surrender—The Fall of Fort Donelson," Reprinted from *Tennessee Historical Quarterly*, March & June 1962, Vol. XXI, Nos. 1 & 2, Part II, 28–29.
17. U. S. Grant, Report to G. W. Cullum, February 16, 1862, *Official Records*, Ser. 1, Vol. 7, 160.
18. U. S. Grant, Letter to Mary Grant, February 9, 1862, Simon, *The Papers of U. S. Grant*, Vol. 4, 179.
19. U. S. Grant, Letter to G. W. Cullum, February 16, 1862, Simon, *The Papers of U. S. Grant*, Vol. 4, 224.
20. "The Siege of Fort Donelson," *New York Times*, February 22, 1862, Holzer and Symonds, *The New York Times—Complete Civil War*.
21. Catton, *Grant Moves South*, 170.
22. "The Fall of Fort Donelson," *New York Times*, February 17, 1862, Holzer and Symonds, *The New York Times—Complete Civil War*.
23. "Gen. Grant Gives the Union Its Second Major Victory: The Battle of Fort Donelson," NewsinHistory.com, http://www.newsinhistory.com/feature/gen-grant-gives-union-its-second-major-victory-battle-fort-donelson, Accessed January 4, 2013.
24. Larry J. Daniel, *Shiloh: The Battle That Changed the Civil War* (New York: Simon & Schuster, 1997), 38.
25. Daniel, *Shiloh*, 51.
26. Bearss, "Smith's Attack on Rebel Right," Notes viii from *Source Book*, 773–774.
27. C. F. Smith, Letter to Mrs. Fanny M. Smith, February 17, 1862, C. F. Smith Papers.
28. C. F. Smith, Letter to Mrs. Fanny M. Smith, February 17, 1862, C. F. Smith Papers.
29. C. F. Smith, Letter to Mrs. Fanny M. Smith, February 18, 1862, C. F. Smith Papers.
30. "The Fort Donelson Victory!—Further Details," *Philadelphia Inquirer*, February 19, 1862, 1, Courtesy of Kurt S. Wille.
31. C. F. Smith, Letter to Mrs. Fanny M. Smith, February 26, 1862, C. F. Smith Papers.
32. C. F. Smith, Letter to Mrs. Fanny M. Smith, February 20, 1862, C. F. Smith Papers.
33. C. F. Smith, Letter to Mrs. Fanny M. Smith, February 19, 1862, C. F. Smith Papers.
34. U. S. Grant, Letter to E. B. Washburne, February 21, 1862, Simon, *The Papers of U. S. Grant*, Vol. 4, 264.
35. H. W. Halleck, Letter to G. B. McClellan, February 19, 1862, *Official Records*, Ser. 1, Vol. 7, 637.
36. H. W. Halleck, Letter to C. F. Smith, February 24, 1862, C. F. Smith Papers.
37. "General Halleck's Department," *New York Times*, February 12, 1862, Holzer and Symonds, *The New York Times—Complete Civil War*.
38. William H. Morgan, Letter to Fanny Smith, October 1, 1863, C. F. Smith Papers.
39. Smith, "Draft of Smith's Report," *Official Records*, Ser. 1, Vol. 52 (Part I), 7.
40. C. F. Smith, Letter to H. W. Halleck. February 19, 1862, C. F. Smith Papers.
41. T. W. Harris, Letter to C. F. Smith, February 18, 1862, C. F. Smith Papers.
42. L. Thomas, Letter to C. F. Smith, February 24, 1862, C. F. Smith Papers.
43. C. F. Smith, Letter to Adjutant General of the Army, 3 March 1862, C. F. Smith Papers.
44. C. F. Smith, Letter to Mrs. Fanny M. Smith, March 4, 1862, C. F. Smith Papers.
45. J. W. Grimes, Letter to C. F. Smith, February 24, 1862, C. F. Smith Papers. Iowan James Grimes served in the U.S. Senate throughout the Civil War and into the Reconstruction period. In 1861 he participated in the Peace Convention in Washington, D.C., which ultimately failed to prevent the Civil War. As chairman of the Committee on Naval Affairs, Grimes proposed a naval service award that became the model of the Medal of Honor established by Congress in 1863. Presented by the president, in the name of Congress, the Medal of Honor recognizes "non-commissioned officers and privates as shall most distinguished themselves by their gallantry in action, and other soldier like qualities." Perhaps most famously, Grimes became one of the seven Republican senators who broke with their party and voted with twelve Democratic senators to acquit President Andrew Johnson in his 1868 impeachment trial. http://www.senate.gov/pagelayout/history/h_multi_sections_and_teasers/CivilWar_Biographies.htm and James W. Grimes, http://en.wikipedia.org/wiki/James_W._Grimes, Accessed February 15, 2013.
46. D. R. Eckels, Letter to C. F. Smith, February 25, 1862, C. F. Smith Papers.
47. Henry R. Crosby, Letter to C. F. Smith, March 2, 1862, C. F. Smith Papers.
48. C. F. Smith, Letter to Mrs. Fanny M. Smith, February 26, 1862, C. F. Smith Papers.

Part Six

1. U. S. Grant, Letter to Mrs. Fanny M. Smith, April 26, 1862, C. F. Smith Papers.

Chapter 24

1. A. H. Foote, Report to U. S. Grant, February 20, 1862, *Official Records*, Ser. 1, Vol. 7, 423.
2. U. S. Grant, Note to H. W. Halleck, February 21, 1862, *Official Records*, Ser. 1, Vol. 7, 423–424.
3. C. F. Smith, Letter to Mrs. Fanny M. Smith, February 20, 1862, C. F. Smith Papers.
4. C. F. Smith, Letter to Mrs. Fanny M. Smith, February 19, 1862, C. F. Smith Papers.
5. U. S. Grant, Order to C. F. Smith, February 21, 1862, *Official Records*, Ser. 1, Vol. 7, 649.
6. C. F. Smith, Letter 1 to Mrs. Fanny M. Smith, February 26, 1862, C. F. Smith Papers.
7. C. F. Smith, Letter 1 to Mrs. Fanny M. Smith, February 26, 1862, C. F. Smith Papers.
8. C. F. Smith, Letter 2 to Mrs. Fanny M. Smith, February 26, 1862, C. F. Smith Papers.
9. U. S. Grant, Letter to H. W. Halleck, March 1, 1862, *Official Records*, Ser. 1, Vol. 7, 675.
10. G. W. Cullum, Note to U. S. Grant via W. T. Sherman, March 2, 1862, *Official Records*, Ser. 1, Vol. 7, 677.
11. D. C. Buell, Telegram to H. W. Halleck, March 1, 1862, *Official Records*, Ser. 1, Vol. 7, 675.
12. C. F. Smith, Letter to Mrs. Fanny M. Smith, March 1, 1862, C. F. Smith Papers.
13. C. F. Smith, Letter to Miss Fanny M. Smith, March 3, 1862, C. F. Smith Papers.
14. H. W. Halleck, Telegram to G. B. McClellan, February 17, 1862, 1 p.m., *Official Records*, Ser. 1, Vol. 7, 628.
15. H. W. Halleck, Telegram to G. B. McClellan, February 19, 1862, 4 p.m., *Official Records*, Ser. 1, Vol. 7, 636.
16. H. W. Halleck, Telegram to G. B. McClellan, February 20, 1862, 8 p.m., *Official Records*, Ser. 1, Vol. 7, 641.
17. E. M. Stanton, Note to H. W. Halleck, February 21, 1862, *Official Records*, Ser. 1, Vol. 7, 648.
18. A. V. Colburn, Telegram to J. B. Fry, February 21, 1862, *Official Records*, Ser. 1, Vol. 7, 650.
19. H. W. Halleck, Telegram to E. M. Stanton, February 24, 1862, *Official Records*, Ser. 1, Vol. 7, 660.
20. G. B. McClellan, Telegram to H. W. Halleck, February 21, 1862, *Official Records*, Ser. 1, Vol. 7, 646.
21. H. W. Halleck, Letter to G. B. McClellan, February 21, 1862, *Official Records*, Ser. 1, Vol. 7, 647.
22. H. W. Halleck, Telegram to U.S. Grant, March 1, 1862, *Official Records*, Ser. 1, Vol. 7, 674.
23. H. W. Halleck, Telegram to G. B. McClellan, March 3, 1862, *Official Records*, Ser. 1, Vol. 7, 679–680.
24. C. F. Smith, Letter to Mrs. Fanny M. Smith, March 5, 1862, C. F. Smith Papers.
25. G. B. McClellan, Telegram to H. W. Halleck, March 3, 1862, 8 p.m., *Official Records*, Ser. 1, Vol. 7, 680.
26. C. F. Smith, Letter to Mrs. Fanny M. Smith, March 4, 1862, C. F. Smith Papers.
27. H. W. Halleck, Telegram to G. B. McClellan, March 4, 1862, *Official Records*, Ser. 1, Vol. 7, 682.
28. H. W. Halleck, Telegram to U. S. Grant, March 4, 1862, *Official Records*, Ser. 1, Vol. 10 (Part II), 3.
29. U. S. Grant, Letter to H. W. Halleck, March 5, 1862, *Official Records*, Ser. 1, Vol. 10 (Part II), 4–5.
30. U. S. Grant, Letter to H. W. Halleck, March 6, 1862, *Official Records*, Ser. 1, Vol. 10 (Part II), 9–10.
31. U. S. Grant, Letter to C. F. Smith, March 5, 1862, *Official Records*, Ser. 1, Vol. 10 (Part II), 5–6.
32. U. S. Grant, Letter to C. F. Smith, March 5, 1862, *Official Records*, Ser. 1, Vol. 10 (Part II), 6.
33. U. S. Grant, Letter to C. F. Smith, March 5, 1862, *Official Records*, Ser. 1, Vol. 10 (Part II), 6.
34. Paris, Tn., is northwest of Nashville about 86 miles.
35. C. F. Smith, Letter to Assistant Adjutant General, March 5, 1862, C. F. Smith Papers.
36. H. W. Halleck, Telegram to U. S. Grant, March 6, 1862, *Official Records*, Ser. 1, Vol. 10 (Part II), 15.
37. H. W. Halleck, Telegram to G. B. McClellan, March 8, 1862, 10:30 a.m., *Official Records*, Ser. 1, Vol. 10 (Part II), 20.
38. Grant, *Personal Memoirs*, 173.
39. U. S. Grant, Telegram to H. W. Halleck, March 7, 1862, *Official Records*, Ser. 1, Vol. 10 (Part II), 15.
40. H. W. Halleck, Telegram to U. S. Grant, March 8, 1862, *Official Records*, Ser. 1, Vol. 10 (Part II), 21.
41. U. S. Grant, Telegram to H. W. Halleck, March 9, 1862, *Official Records*, Ser. 1, Vol. 10 (Part II), 21.
42. U. S. Grant, Telegram to H. W. Halleck, March 9, 1862, *Official Records*, Ser. 1, Vol. 10 (Part II), 21.
43. H. W. Halleck, Telegram to U. S. Grant, March 9, 1862, *Official Records*, Ser. 1, Vol. 10 (Part II), 22.
44. C. F. Smith, Letter to Mrs. Fanny M. Smith, March 5, 1862, C. F. Smith Papers.
45. H. W. Halleck, Telegram to T. A. Scott, March 6, 1862, *Official Records*, Ser. 1, Vol. 10 (Part II), 10.
46. T. A. Scott, Telegram to H. W. Halleck, March 6, 1862, *Official Records*, Ser. 1, Vol. 10 (Part II), 10.
47. W. T. Sherman, Telegram to H. W. Halleck, March 6, 1862, *Official Records*, Ser. 1, Vol. 10 (Part II), 12.
48. H. W. Halleck, Telegram to W. T. Sherman and U. S. Grant, March 6, 1862, *Official Records*, Ser. 1, Vol. 10 (Part II), 12.
49. C. F. Smith, Letter to Adjutant General of the Army, March 7, 1862, C. F. Smith Papers.
50. J. A. Rawlins, Special Orders No. 19, March 7, 1862, *Official Records*, Ser. 1, Vol. 10 (Part II), 17.
51. W. T. Sherman, Telegram to H. W. Halleck, March 6, 1862, *Official Records*, Ser. 1, Vol. 10 (Part II), 12.
52. W. T. Sherman, Telegram to G. W. Cullum, March 8, 1862, *Official Records*, Ser. 1, Vol. 10 (Part II), 12.
53. H. W. Halleck, Telegram to G. B. McClellan, March 8, 1862—10:30 a.m., *Official Records*, Ser. 1, Vol. 10 (Part II), 20–21.
54. H. W. Halleck, Telegram to U. S. Grant, March 9, 1862, *Official Records*, Ser. 1, Vol. 10 (Part II), 22.
55. Brinton, *Personal Memoirs*, 149–150.
56. C. F. Smith, General Orders No. 2, March 10, 1862, *Official Records*, Ser. 1, Vol. 10 (Part II), 20.
57. L. Thomas, Telegram to H. W. Halleck, March 10, 1862, *Official Records*, Ser. 1, Vol. 7, 683.
58. A. Lincoln, President's War Order No. 3, March 11, 1862, *Official Records*, Ser. 1, Vol. 10 (Part II), 28–29.
59. H. W. Halleck, Telegram to U. S. Grant, March 13, 1862, *Official Records*, Ser. 1, Vol. 10 (Part II), 32.
60. C. F. Smith, Letter to Mrs. Fanny M. Smith, March 27, 1862, C. F. Smith Papers.
61. Grant, *Personal Memoirs*, 173.
62. H. W. Halleck, Telegram to L. Thomas, March 15, 1862, *Official Records*, Ser. 1, Vol. 7, 683–684.

63. Grant, *Personal Memoirs*, 173.
64. Grant, *Personal Memoirs*, 173.

Chapter 25

1. U. S. Grant, Message to C. F. Smith, March 11, 1862, *Official Records*, Ser. 1, Vol. 10 (Part II), 29.
2. W. T. Sherman, Message to Commanders of Brigades, March 12, 1862, *Official Records*, Ser. 1, Vol. 10 (Part II), 31.
3. Wallace, *An Autobiography*, 443.
4. Wallace, *An Autobiography*, 444.
5. Wallace, *An Autobiography*, 445.
6. C. F. Smith, Letter to Mrs. Fanny M. Smith, March 13, 1862, C. F. Smith Papers.
7. H. W. Halleck, Telegram to U. S. Grant, March 13, 1862, *Official Records*, Ser. I, Vol. 10 (Part II), 32-33
8. U. S. Grant, Telegram to H. W. Halleck, March 14, 1862, *Official Records*, Ser. I, Vol. 10 (Part II), 35.
9. U. S. Grant, Telegram to H. W. Halleck, March 14, 1862, *Official Records*, Ser. I, Vol. 10 (Part II), 35.
10. C. F. Smith, Letter to Assistant Adjutant General, March 13, 1862, C. F. Smith Papers.
11. C. F. Smith, Letter to Assistant Adjutant General, March 14, 1862, C. F. Smith Papers.
12. C. F. Smith, Letter to Mrs. Fanny M. Smith, March 14, 1862, C. F. Smith Papers.
13. C. F. Smith, Letter to Assistant Adjutant General, March 15, 1862, C. F. Smith Papers.
14. U. S. Grant, Telegram to H. W. Halleck, March 15, 1862, *Official Records*, Ser. 1, Vol. 10 (Part II), 40.
15. H. W. Halleck, Telegram to U. S. Grant, March 16, 1862, *Official Records*, Ser. 1, Vol. 10 (Part II), 41.
16. Simpson, *Ulysses S. Grant*, 128–129.
17. The designation "Army of the Tennessee" was first used on March 11, 1862, when the name "Army of West Tennessee" was renamed. John H. Eicher and David J. Eicher, *Civil War High Commands* (Stanford: Stanford University Press, 2001), 857.
18. H. W. Halleck, Telegram to D. C. Buell, March 16, 1862, *Official Records*, Ser. 1, Vol. 10 (Part II), 42.
19. Charles E. Shedd, Jr., "A History of Shiloh National Military Park Tennessee," United States Department of the Interior, National Park Service, 1954, 9.
20. C. F. Smith, Letter to U. S. Grant, March 14. 1862, Simon, *The Papers of U. S. Grant*, Vol. 4, 343.
21. W. T. Sherman, Report to J. A. Rawlins, March 17, 1862, *Official Records*, Ser. 1, Vol. 10 (Part I), 26–27.
22. U. S. Grant, Telegram to H. W. Halleck, March 17, 1862, *Official Records*, Ser. 1, Vol. 10 (Part II), 42–43.
23. U. S. Grant, Letter to H. W. Halleck, March 18, 1862, Simon, *The Papers of U. S. Grant*, Vol. 4, 387.
24. Daniel, *Shiloh*, 81.
25. Grant, *Personal Memoirs*, 175.
26. Leckie, *None Died in Vain*, 278.
27. W. T. Sherman, Report to W. McMichael, March 17, 1862, *Official Records*, Ser. 1, Vol. 10 (Part II), 25.
28. D. C. Buell, Note to H. W. Halleck, March 18, 1862, *Official Records*, Ser. 1, Vol. 10 (Part II), 44.
29. Daniel, *Shiloh*, 106.
30. U. S. Grant, Note to H. W. Halleck, March 19,1862, *Official Records*, Ser. 1, Vol. 10 (Part II), 49.
31. U. S. Grant, Note to C. F. Smith, March 20, 1862, *Official Records*, Ser. 1, Vol. 10 (Part II), 52.
32. Pea Ridge was approximately halfway between Pittsburg Landing and Corinth at the point the Purdy and Corinth Roads meet. William T. Sherman, *Memoirs* (New York: Barnes & Noble Publishing, 2005), 217.
33. U. S. Grant, Note to C. F. Smith, March 23, 1862, *Official Records*, Ser. 1, Vol. 10 (Part II), 62.
34. U. S. Grant, Special Orders No. 36, March 26, 1862, *Official Records*, Ser. 1, Vol. 10 (Part II), 67.
35. C. F. Smith, Letter to W. Mactier, March 26, 1862, C. F. Smith Papers.
36. John A. McClernand, Letter to U. S. Grant, March 27, 1862, C. F. Smith Papers.
37. H. W. Halleck, Letter to U. S. Grant, March 31, 1862, *Official Records*, Ser. 1, Vol. 10 (Part II), 82.
38. John Rziha, Letter to C. F. Smith, March 24, 1862, C. F. Smith Papers.
39. S. L. Phelps, Letter to C. F. Smith, March 28, 1862, C. F. Smith Papers.
40. *Military Essays and Recollections*, Military Order of the Loyal Legion of the United States, Illinois Commandery, Chicago 1891, Vol.1, 103.

Chapter 26

1. Daniel, *Shiloh*, 109.
2. W. T. Sherman, Letter to Colonel Lauman, March 20, 1862, *Official Records*, Ser. 1, Vol. 10 (Part II), 53.
3. Come off in a very thin piece.
4. C. F. Smith, Letter to Mrs. Fanny M. Smith, March 27, 1862, C. F. Smith Papers.
5. C. F. Smith, Letter to Mrs. Fanny M. Smith, March 27, 1862, C. F. Smith Papers.
6. C. F. Smith, Letter to Mrs. Fanny M. Smith, March 27, 1862, C. F. Smith Papers.
7. C. F. Smith, Letter to Mrs. Fanny M. Smith, March 27, 1862, C. F. Smith Papers.
8. Abstract from field return of the Second Division of United States forces, commanded by Maj. Gen. Charles F. Smith, March 29, 1862, *Official Records*, Ser. 1, Vol. 10 (Part II), 79.
9. J. A. Rawlins, General Orders No. 30, March 31, 1862, *Official Records*, Ser. 1, Vol. 10 (Part II), 84.
10. C. F. Smith, Letter to Mrs. Fanny M. Smith, March 27, 1862, C. F. Smith Papers.
11. J. A. Rawlins, General Orders No. 43, April 21, 862, *Official Records*, Ser. 1, Vol. 10 (Part II), 87–88.
12. Simpson, *Ulysses S. Grant*, 129–130.
13. According to Charles' letters to Francis, he was on the steamship *Continental* around March 27. He writes Francis on April 4 that "I came down here yesterday and occupy a fine airy room in Genl Grant's quarters." C. F. Smith, Letter to Mrs. Fanny M. Smith, April 4, 1862, C. F. Smith Papers.
14. Isabel Wallace, *The Life and Letters of General W. H. L. Wallace* (Chicago: R. R. Donnelley & Sons, 1909), 180–181.
15. Grant, *Personal Memoirs*, 176.
16. Erysipelas is an acute streptococcus bacterial infection. Patients typically develop symptoms including high fevers, shaking, chills, fatigue, headaches, vomiting, and general illness within 48 hours of the initial infection. The infection usually affects the extremities. The erythematous skin lesion enlarges rapidly and has a sharply demarcated raised edge. It appears as a red, swollen, warm, hardened and painful rash, similar in consistency to an orange peel. More severe infections can result in vesicles,

blisters, and purple spots, and death of skin cells leading to gangrene. For this reason, it is often necessary to remove the dead tissue surgically with a process known as debridement. Depending on the severity, treatment involves either oral or intravenous antibiotics such as penicillin, clindamycin or erythromycin. There is a risk that the infection will spread to other areas of body through the bloodstream. Erysipelas. http://en.wikipedia.org/wiki/Erysipelas, Accessed August 22, 2013.

17. C. F. Smith, Letter to Mrs. Fanny M. Smith, April 4, 1862, C. F. Smith Papers.

18. C. F. Smith, Letter to Mrs. Fanny M. Smith, April 4, 1862, C. F. Smith Papers.

19. Sherman, *Memoirs*, 215.

20. W. T. Sherman, Report to U. S. Grant, April 5, 1862, *Official Records*, Ser. 1, Vol. 10 (Part I), 90.

21. U. S. Grant, Telegram to H. W. Halleck, April 5, 1862, *Official Records*, Ser. 1, Vol. 10 (Part I), 89.

22. Grant, *Personal Memoirs*, 177.

23. Col. Jacob Ammen's diary of march to and battle at Pittsburg Landing, Tenn. April 5, 1862, entry, *Official Records*, Ser. 1, Vol. 10 (Part I), 330–331.

24. Daniel, *Shiloh*, 140.

25. Col. Jacob Ammen's diary of march to and battle at Pittsburg Landing, Tenn., *Official Records*, Ser. 1, Vol. 10 (Part I), 331.

26. Grant, *Personal Memoirs*, 177.

27. Brooks D. Simpson, *Ulysses S. Grant: Triumph Over Adversity* (New York: Houghton Mifflin, 2000), 130–131.

28. Col. Jacob Ammen's diary of march to and battle at Pittsburg Landing, Tenn., *Official Records*, Ser. 1, Vol. 10 (Part I), 330–332.

29. Grant, *Personal Memoirs*, 177.

30. Simpson, *Grant*, 131.

31. Map of the Battle of Shiloh April 6 a.m., http://www.cwmaps.com/freemaps/Shiloh_Battle_Apr6am png.

Chapter 27

1. James Lee McDonough, *Shiloh—In Hell Before Night* (Knoxville: University of Tennessee Press, 1977), 93.

2. McDonough, *Shiloh—In Hell Before Night*, 95.

3. Organization of the Union forces and return of casualties at the battle of Pittsburgh Landing, or Shiloh, Tenn., April 6–7, 1862, *Official Records*, Ser. 1, Vol. 10 (Part I), 101–102.

4. Troop placement from various sources including Daniel, *Shiloh*, 205; Map of the Battle of Shiloh by Hal Jespersen, www.cwmaps.com; Maps of Shiloh, Tennessee (1862), Civil War Trust, http://www.civilwar.org/battlefields/shiloh/maps/shilohmap.html; and Map of the Battle of Shiloh, April 6 & 7, 1862, Library of Congress, http://www.loc.gov/item/85690890.

5. James M. Tuttle, Report of Second Iowa Infantry, Second Division, and Second Brigade, April 10, 1862, *Official Records*, Ser. 1, Vol. 10 (Part I), 149.

6. James C. Parrott, Report of the Seventh Iowa Infantry, April 10, 1862, *Official Records*, Ser. 1, Vol. 10 (Part I), 150.

7. William T. Shaw, Report of Fourteenth Iowa Infantry, October 26, 1862, *Official Records*, Ser. 1, Vol. 10 (Part I), 153.

8. William T. Shaw, Report of Fourteenth Iowa Infantry, October 26, 1862, *Official Records*, Ser. 1, Vol. 10 (Part I), 153.

9. J. J. Woods, Report of Twelfth Iowa Infantry, April 1862, *Official Records*, Ser. 1, Vol. 10 (Part I), 151.

10. William T. Shaw, Report of Fourteenth Iowa Infantry, October 26, 1862, *Official Records*, Ser. 1, Vol. 10 (Part I), 153.

11. While these guns were described as "brass," the current understanding is that they were made of bronze. The guns were cast in bronze, but when highly polished they looked like brass and the incorrect metallurgy stuck. Some naval cannons were made of the lighter brass although some say these guns were made from cast iron. It has also been suggested that some brass cannons might have been used in light artillery batteries because of their lower weight. "Were Cannons Ever Made Out of Brass?" Askville, http://askville.amazon.com/cannons-made-brass-HMS-Victory-USS-Constitution/AnswerViewer.do?requestId=6434497, Accessed January 6, 2014.

12. William T. Shaw, Report of Fourteenth Iowa Infantry, October 26, 1862, *Official Records*, Ser. 1, Vol. 10 (Part I), 153–154.

13. William T. Shaw, Report of Fourteenth Iowa Infantry, October 26, 1862, *Official Records*, Ser. 1, Vol. 10 (Part I), 154.

14. Prior to the battle the Confederate Army of Mississippi had 62 guns, but around 10 were lost before General Ruggles organized the combined battery for the assault on the Hornet's Nest.

15. McDonough, *Shiloh—In Hell Before Night*, 162.

16. B. M. Prentiss, Report of Brig. Gen. B. M. Prentiss, U.S. Army, commanding Sixth Division, November 17, 1862, *Official Records*, Ser. 1, Vol. 10 (Part I), 278.

17. James M. Tuttle, Report of Second Iowa Infantry, Second Division, and Second Brigade, April 10, 1862, *Official Records*, Ser. 1, Vol. 10 (Part I), 149.

18. James M. Tuttle, Report of Second Iowa Infantry, Second Division, and Second Brigade, April 10, 1862, *Official Records*, Ser. 1, Vol. 10 (Part I), 149.

19. James M. Tuttle, Report of Second Iowa Infantry, Second Division, and Second Brigade, April 10, 1862, *Official Records*, Ser. 1, Vol. 10 (Part I), 149.

20. J. J. Woods, Report of Twelfth Iowa Infantry, April 1862, *Official Records*, Ser. 1, Vol. 10 (Part I), 151–152.

21. J. J. Woods, Report of Twelfth Iowa Infantry, April 1862, *Official Records*, Ser. 1, Vol. 10 (Part I), 152.

22. William T. Shaw, Report of Fourteenth Iowa Infantry, October 26, 1862, *Official Records*, Ser. 1, Vol. 10 (Part I), 154.

23. James M. Tuttle, Report of Second Iowa Infantry, Second Division, and Second Brigade, April 10, 1862, *Official Records*, Ser. 1, Vol. 10 (Part I), 149.

24. Crafts J. Wright, Report of Thirteenth Missouri Infantry, Unknown Date, *Official Records*, Ser. 1, Vol. 10 (Part I), 159.

25. Organization of the Union forces and return of casualties at the battle of Pittsburgh Landing, or Shiloh, Tenn., April 6–7, 1862, *Official Records*, Ser. 1, Vol. 10 (Part I), 100–108.

26. Mr. Timothy Smith in an article "Battle of Shiloh: Shattering Myths" published in *America's Civil War Magazine* and presented on Civil War Trust web site, comments on Benjamin Prentiss as the hero of Shiloh. Smith says: "Prentiss was not the key defender of the Hornet's

Nest." "His division began the day with roughly 5,400 men, only to dwindle to 500 by 9:45 that morning. When Prentiss took his position in the Sunken Road, his numbers were nearly doubled by an arriving regiment, the 23rd Missouri. Prentiss had lost almost his entire division, and could not have held his second line without the veteran brigades of Brig. Gen. W. H. L. Wallace's division. It was primarily Wallace's troops who held the Hornet's Nest."

"Prentiss was in an advantageous position to become a hero after the battle, however. Although he remained a prisoner for six months, he was able to tell his story. Peabody and Wallace were both dead from wounds received at Shiloh. Thus Prentiss took credit for their actions and became the hero of the fight. Prentiss never even mentioned Peabody in his report, except to say that he commanded one of his brigades. Likewise, Wallace was not around to set the record straight as to whose troops actually defended the Sunken Road and Hornet's Nest. Prentiss, the only Federal officer who could get his own record out, thus benefited from public exposure. In the process, he became the hero of Shiloh." Civil War Trust, Timothy B. Smith, "Battle of Shiloh: Shattering Myths," http://www.civilwar.org/battlefields/shiloh/shiloh-history-articles/battle-of-shiloh-shattering.html. Accessed August 13, 2013. Timothy B. Smith's forthcoming book *The Untold Story of Shiloh: The Battle and the Battlefield* (Knoxville: University of Tennessee Press, 2008.)

27. Grant, *Personal Memoirs*, 182.
28. Troop placement from various sources including Daniel, *Shiloh*, 205; Map of the Battle of Shiloh by Hal Jespersen, www.cwmaps.com; Maps of Shiloh, Tennessee (1862), Civil War Trust, http://www.civilwar.org/battlefields/shiloh/maps/shilohmap.html; and Map of the Battle of Shiloh, April 6 & 7, 1862, Library of Congress, http://www.loc.gov/item/85690890.
29. Based on Map 12 Grant's Last Line 4:30–6:00 p.m., Daniel, *Shiloh*, 247.
30. Catton, *Grant Moves South*, 238.
31. Grant, *Personal Memoirs*, 183–184.
32. Catton, *Grant Moves South*, 242.
33. U. S. Grant, Telegram to H. W. Halleck, April 7, 1862, *Official Records*, Ser. I, Vol. 10 (Part II), 108.
34. U. S. Grant, Telegram to H. W. Halleck, April 8, 1862, *Official Records*, Ser. I, Vol. 10 (Part II), 108.
35. McDonough, *Shiloh*, 208–210.
36. U. S. Grant, General Orders No. 34, April 8, 1862, *Official Records*, Ser. I, Vol. 10 (Part II), 111–112.
37. J. A. Rawlins, General Orders No. 49, April 9, 1862, *Official Records*, Ser. 1, Vol. 10 (Part II), 100–101.
38. J. A. Rawlins, General Orders No. 54, April 14, 1862, *Official Records*, Ser. 1, Vol. 10 (Part II), 106.
39. F. M. Smith, Letter to W. Mactier, April 11, 1862, C. F. Smith Papers.
40. F. M. Smith, Letter to W. Mactier, April 9, 1862, C. F. Smith Papers.
41. H. W. Halleck, Letter to U. S. Grant, April 14, 1862, *Official Records*, Ser. 1, Vol. 10 (Part II), 105–106.
42. Simpson, *Grant*, 136.
43. Simpson, *Grant*, 136.
44. Simpson, *Grant*, 136–137.
45. Grant, *Personal Memoirs*, 194.
46. Grant, *Personal Memoirs*, 194.
47. Leckie, *None Died in Vain*, 348.

Chapter 28

1. C. F. Smith, Letter to Miss Fanny M. Smith, April 13, 1862, C. F. Smith Papers.
2. Special Field Orders No. 9, April 16, 1862, C. F. Smith Papers.
3. C. F. Smith, Letter to G. Cullum, April 18, 1862, C. F. Smith Papers.
4. G. W. Cullum, Letter to C. F. Smith, April 18, 1862, C. F. Smith Papers.
5. C. F. Smith, Letter to J. W. Worth, April 18, 1862, C. F. Smith Papers.
6. C. F. Smith, Letter J. R. Miller, April 19, 1862, C. F. Smith Papers.
7. Special Field Orders No. 19, April 21, 1862, C. F. Smith Papers
8. A. Kemper, Note to C. F. Smith, April 21, 1862, C. F. Smith Papers.
9. Egyptian darkness is a reference to Exodus X.21-2: "Yahweh then said to Moses, 'Stretch out your hand towards heaven, and let darkness, darkness so thick that it can be felt, cover Egypt.' So Moses stretched out his hand towards heaven, and for three days there was thick darkness over the whole of Egypt," http://en.wiktionary.org/wiki/Egyptian_darkness, Accessed November 16, 2011.
10. C. F. Smith, Letter to U. S. Grant, April 21, 1862, C. F. Smith Papers.
11. C. F. Smith, Letter to H. W. Halleck, April 21, 1862, C. F. Smith Papers.
12. General Orders No. 21, issued by Major General Halleck, Headquarters Department of the Mississippi, Pittsburgh Landing, TN, April 25, 1862, C. F. Smith Papers.
13. Holland, "An Anecdote of General Grant Related by His Son," February 1909–1912, *New News of Yesterday*, Interview with Frederick Dent Grant by Holland in 1899 just before he sailed for the Philippines to take a military command.
14. U. S. Grant, Letter to Mrs. Fanny M. Smith, April 26, 1862, C. F. Smith Papers.
15. U. S. Grant, Note to Julia Grant, April 25, 1862, as quoted in Jean Smith, *Grant*, 658.
16. H. W. Halleck, Telegraph to E. M. Stanton, April 27, 1862, *Official Records*, Ser. 1, Vol. 10 (Part II), 132.
17. E. M. Stanton, Telegraph to H. W. Halleck, April 27, 1862, *Official Records*, Ser. 1, Vol. 10 (Part II), 132.
18. W. Nelson, Letter to W. Jeffers, April 29, 1862, C. F. Smith Papers.
19. Brinton, *Personal Memoirs*, 159–160.
20. "Death of General C. F. Smith," *New York Times*, April 27, 1862, Holzer and Symonds, *The New York Times—Complete Civil War*.
21. Jean Smith, *Grant*, 208.
22. Probably General Alfred Pleasanton who was a cadet at West Point from 1840 to 1844, fought in the Mexican War, and rose to major general of volunteers in the Civil War. Cullum, *Biographical Register*, Vol. II, 196–197.
23. "The Remains of Gen. C. F. Smith," *New York Times*, May 4, 1862, Holzer and Symonds, *The New York Times—Complete Civil War*.
24. Report on Burial Lot for a Fund for its Perpetual Care, Mrs. Marshall Oliver, March 21, 1914, and Laurel Hill Cemetery Deed 2128, Lots. 438 & 440, May 5, 1862, C. F. Smith Papers. Following her death in 1866, Francis

was buried on May 28, 1866. Charles' mother, Margaret Ferguson Smith, was buried there on December 6, 1901. Personal information from Laurel Hill Cemetery, September 30, 2014.

25. "Presentation of a Sword to the Family of Major-General Charles F. Smith," *Philadelphia Inquirer*, January 21, 1863.

26. J. G. Barnard, Letter to S. P. Heintzelman, May 30, 1863, *Official Records*, Ser. 1, Vol. 25 (Part II), 569.

27. Arlington Parks and Recreation, Arlington, VA. "History of Fort C. F. Smith." http://www.fortcfsmith.com/.

28. Fort C. F. Smith (Fort Smith, Montana), http://en.wikipedia.org/wiki/Fort_C._F._Smith_(Fort_Smith,_Montana), Accessed October 1, 2013.

29. H. C. Baird, Letter to J. M. Wilson, November 14, 1891, C. F. Smith Papers.

30. H. C. Baird, Letter to J. M. Wilson, November 14, 1891, C. F. Smith Papers.

31. Portrait of Major General C., F. Smith for the U. S. Military Academy, Correspondence to John M. Wilson from Henry Carey Baird, November 14, 1891 and to Henry Carey Baird from John M. Wilson, November 17, 1891, C. F. Smith Papers.

32. Henry Carey Baird, Note with Newspaper Clipping to Mr. Oliver, October 10, 1891, C. F. Smith Papers.

33. George W. Cullum, Letter to Henry Carey Baird, November 25, 1891, C. F. Smith Papers.

34. The Library of Congress, Bills and Resolutions, 37th Congress, 2nd Session, A Bill for the Relief of Fanny Mactier Smith (S. 371).

35. Obituary Notice, *New York Times*, June 1, 1866.

36. U. S. Grant, Letter to Miss Fanny M. Smith, July 21, 1866, C. F. Smith Papers.

37. Allen Smith, Letter to DeLancey Floyd-Jones, Union Club New York, May 27, 1887, Army Heritage and Education Center files, Carlisle, PA.

38. "From Long Line of Fighters Gen. Allen Smith has Military Poise," *Spokesman Review*, May 7, 1928.

39. The Coeur d'Alene, Idaho, labor confrontation of 1899, http://en.wikipedia.org/wiki/Coeur_d%27Alene,_Idaho_labor_confrontation_of_1899, Accessed October 31, 2012.

40. "From Long Line of Fighters Gen. Allen Smith has Military Poise," *Spokesman Review*, May 7, 1928.

41. Wille, Descendants of Dr. Samuel Blair Smith, MD, USA.

42. Cullum, *Biographical Register*, 714.

43. New York Marriages—June 18, 1874, DistantCousin.com, *New York Times*, June 18, 1874, http://distantcousin.com/marriage/ny/1800/1874/jun/18.html, accessed August 18, 2011.

44. Obituary notice for Professor Marshall Oliver, provided by Betsy Miller.

45. Charles M. Campbell, Letter to Marshall Oliver, April 4, 1889, C. F. Smith Papers.

46. S. B. Buckner, Jr., Letter to Leslie A. Oliver, January 7, 1936, C. F. Smith Papers.

47. Leslie Allen Oliver, to Library of Congress, February 10, 1936, C. F. Smith Papers.

Appendix A

1. Cullum, *Biographical Register*, 355–357.

Appendix C

1. Knight, *Fort Donelson*, 146–148.

Bibliography

Abraham Lincoln Papers, Series 1. General Correspondence. 1833–1916. Library of Congress.

"Action of the Kentucky Legislature, Frankfort, KY, September 11, 1861." *Richmond Times Dispatch,* September 13, 1861.

Allen, Hall. *Center of Conflict.* Paducah: The Paducah Sun-Democrat, 1961.

Ambrose, Stephen E. *Duty, Honor, Country: A History of West Point.* Baltimore: Johns Hopkins University Press, 1996.

Anderson, Adrian N., et al. *Texas and Texans.* New York: Macmillan/McGraw-Hill, 1993.

Anderson, Robert. *An Artillery Officer in the Mexican War.* New York: Knickerbocker Press, 1911.

Annual Report of the Board of Visitors (1812–2002). 1819 and 1821. Archives. U.S. Military Academy Library.

Anonymous. *Complete History of Late Mexican War.* New York: 128 Nassau Street, 1851.

Arlington Parks and Recreation, Arlington, VA. "History of Fort C. F. Smith." http://www.fortcfsmith.com/.

Army Heritage and Education Center. Carlisle, PA. Allen Smith, Letter to DeLancey Floyd-Jones, Union Club New York, May 27, 1887.

"At West Point Together—Grant's Courtship—The War and Afterwards." *New York Times,* July 24, 1885.

"Augusta Arsenal (1826)." Augusta State University. http://www.aug.edu/public_relations/history/arsenal.html.

"Authority for Gen. Sherman." *New York Times,* January 30, 1886.

Barone, Laureen M. "Evolution of the Cadet Disciplinary System: From Confusion to Clarity, (1802–1833)," U.S. Military Academy, 4 December 1990, Tactical Officer Education Program Papers, Special Collections, U.S. Military Academy Library.

Battalion Orders. August 21, 1824, to August 13, 1825, and April 6, 1838, to February 17, 1840. Archives. U.S. Military Academy Library.

Battles and Leaders of the Civil War. Vol. 1. New York: Century, 1887.

Bauer, K. Jack. *The Mexican War, 1846–1848.* New York: Macmillan, 1974.

Bearss, Edwin C. "General C. F. Smith's Attack on Rebel Right." Fort Donelson National Military Park Service. Research Project #10, December 1959.

_____. "Unconditional Surrender—The Fall of Fort Donelson." Reprinted from *Tennessee Historical Quarterly* Vol. XXI, Nos. 1 & 2, Part II, March & June 1962.

"The Beginning of the End." *Harper's Weekly,* September 14, 1861.

Bell, Charles N. "Some Red River Settlement History." Manitoba Historical Society, http://www.mhs.mb.ca/docs/transactions/1/redriverhistory.shtml.

"Benny Havens, Oh!" Words by: Lucius O'Brien, John T. Metcalfe (USMA 1838), Ripley A. Arnold (USMA 1838), et al. http://www.west-point.org/greimanj/west_point/songs/bennyhavens.htm.

Biographical and Genealogical History of the State of Delaware, vol. I. Chambersburg: J. M. Runk, 1899.

Bowery, Charles R., Jr., and Brian D. Hankinson, eds. "Superintendent's Letter Books No. 2 and No. 3." "The Daily Correspondence of Brevet Colonel Robert E. Lee, Superintendent United States Military Academy, September 1, 1852, to March 24, 1855." Special Collections, United States Military Academy.

Bowman, John S. *The Civil War: The Definitive Reference Including a Chronology of Events, an Encyclopedia and the Memoirs of Grant and Lee.* East Bridgewater: World Publications Group, 2006.

Boynton, Edward Charles. *History of West Point.* Bedford: Applewood Books, 1864.

"Brigadier-General Charles F. Smith." *Philadelphia Inquirer,* February 19, 1862.

Brinton, John H. *Personal Memoirs of John H. Brinton: Major and Surgeon U.S.V. 1861–1865.* New York: Neale, 1914.

Bulletin 1. "Cadet Life Before the Mexican War." West Point: United States Military Academy Library, 1945.

Burlingame, Michael. *Abraham Lincoln—A Life,* vol. 2. Baltimore: Johns Hopkins University Press, 2008.

Carwardine, Richard. *Lincoln.* New York: Alfred A. Knopf, 2006.

Catton, Bruce. *Grant Moves South.* New York: Little, Brown, 1960.

_____. *This Hallowed Ground.* New York: Doubleday, 1956.

The Centennial of the United States Military Academy at West Point, New York, 2 Vols. Washington: GPO, 1904.

Chambers, John Whiteclay II, ed. *American Military History.* New York: Oxford University Press, 1999.

"Charles Ferguson Smith Family Papers 1840–1896." U.S. Military Academy Library Special Collections, West Point, NY.

Chetlain, Augustus Louis. *Recollections of Seventy Years.* Galena: Gazette Publishing, 1899.

Church, William Conant. *Ulysses S. Grant.* New York: G. P. Putnam's Sons, 1897.

Civil War Era Firearms. http://www.edsmart.com/jz/guns.htm.

Clary, David A. *Eagles and Empire: The United States, Mexico, and the Struggle for the Continent.* New York: Bantam Books, 2009.

Cleaves, Freeman. *Rock of Chickamauga: The Life of General George H. Thomas.* Norman: University of Oklahoma Press, 1948.

Coakley, Robert W. *The Role of Federal Military Forces in Domestic Disorders 1789–1878.* Washington: U.S. Government Printing Office, 1988.

Coppee, Henry. *Grant and His Campaigns.* New York: Charles Richardson, 1866.

Covington, James W. *The Seminoles of Florida.* Gainesville: University Press of Florida, 1993.

Cowley, Robert, and Thomas Guinzburg. *West Point— Two Centuries of Honor and Tradition: The Bicentennial Book of the United States Military Academy.* New York: Warner Books, 2002.

Cox, Jacob Dolson. *Military Reminiscences of the Civil War Vol. I.* New York: Charles Scribner & Sons, 1900.

Craig, Benny F. "Northern Conquerers [sic] and Southern Deliverers: The Civil War Comes to the Jackson Purchase." The Register of the Kentucky Historical Society. Vol. 73, no. 1. http://www.jacksonpurchasehistory.org/wp-content/uploads/2011/04/Craig2.pdf.

Crawford, Mark. *Encyclopedia of the Mexican-American War.* Santa Barbara: ABC-CLIO, 1999.

Croffut, W. A., ed. *Fifty Years in Camp and Field Diary of Major-General Ethan Allen Hitchcock, U.S.A.* New York: G. P. Putnam's Sons, 1909.

Cullum, George W. *Biographical Register of the Officers and Graduates of the U.S. Military Academy at West Point, N.Y. from Its Establishment, in 1802 to 1890 with the Early History of the United States Military Academy.* Third Edition, Vol. I, Nos. 1 to 1000. Vol. II, Supplement, Vol. V, 1900–1910. Houghton, Mifflin, 1891.

Dahlgren, Madeliene Vinton. *Memoir of John A. Dahlgren, Rear-Admiral United States Navy.* Boston: John R. Osgood, 1882.

Daniel, Larry J. *Shiloh—The Battle That Changed the Civil War.* New York: Simon & Schuster, 1997.

Descendants of Mexican War Veterans. May 8, 1846: Battle of Palo Alto. http://www.dmwv.org/mexwar/documents/paloalto.htm.

_____. May 9, 1846: Battle of Resaca de la Palma. http://www.dmwv.org/mexwar/documents/resaca.htm.

_____. Taylor, Mar. 9–29, 1847: Siege of Vera Cruz. http://www.dmwv.org/mexwar/documents/veracru2.htm.

Dubelier, Eric A. "Charles F. Smith: The Forgotten Soldier." Diss. Tulane University, 1977.

Dugard, Martin. *The Training Ground: Grant, Lee, Sherman, and Davis in the Mexican War, 1846–1848.* New York: Little, Brown, 2008.

Durham, Michael S. "The Utah War," *MHQ: The Quarterly Journal of Military History.* Spring 1998, Vol. 10, Number 3.

Durham, Thomas W. *Three Years with Wallace's Zouaves.* Macon: Mercer University Press, 2003.

Eicher, John H., and David J. Eicher. *Civil War High Commands.* Stanford: Stanford University Press, 2001.

Eisenhower, John S. D. *So Far from God: The U.S. War with Mexico 1846–1848.* New York: Anchor Books, 1989.

Eisenhower, J. S. D. *Zachary Taylor.* New York: Times Books, 2008.

EllenWhiteExposed.com. Millerite Insanity. http://www.ellenwhiteexposed.com/egw64.htm.

Farley, James J. *Making Arms in the Machine Age: Philadelphia's Franklin Arsenal, 1816–1870.* University Park: Pennsylvania State University Press, 1994.

Feldman, R. T. *The Mexican-American War.* Minneapolis: Lerner, 2004.

Find a Grave. Find a Grave Memorial for Charles Ferguson Smith. http://www.findagrave.com/cgi-bin/fg.cgi?page=gr&GRid=8049.

Foote, Shelby. *The Civil War: A Narrative, Volume 2: Fort Donelson to Memphis.* Alexandria: Time-Life Books, 1958.

Forman, Sidney, ed. "Cadet Life Before the Mexican War." Bulletin No. 1. The Library. United States Military Academy. USMA Library Publications. U.S. Military Academy. Special Collections. U.S. Military Academy Library.

"The Fort Donelson Victory!—Further Details." *Philadelphia Inquirer,* February 19, 1862.

"From Long Line of Fighters Gen. Allen Smith Has Military Poise." *Spokesman Review,* May 7, 1928.

Frost, J. *The Mexican War and Its Warriors.* New Haven: H. Mansfield, 1850.

Furniss, Norman F. *The Mormon Conflict 1850–1859.* New Haven: Yale University Press, 1960.

Gabel, D. L. "Leadership or Management: The Cadet Chain of Command and the West Point Class of 1915." December 4, 1989. Tactical Officer Education Program Papers, Special Collections. U.S. Military Academy Library.

Gates, Theodore B. *The War of the Rebellion.* New York: P. F. McBreen, 1884.

"Gen. Smith, of Paducah—His Loyalty." *Chicago Tribune,* December 5, 1861. http://pqasb.pqarchiver.com/chicagotribune/access/581874012.html?FMT=ABS&FMTS=ABS:AI&type=historic&date=Dec+5%2C+1861&author=&pub=Chicago+Tribune+(1860–1872)&edition=&startpage=0_1&desc=Gen.+Smith%2C+of+Paducah—His+Loyalty.

Goodwin, Doris Kearns. *Team of Rivals: The Political Genius of Abraham Lincoln.* New York: Simon & Schuster, 2005.

Grant, Ulysses S. *Personal Memoirs.* New York: The Modern Library, 1885.

"Great Excitement in Paducah—Quarrel Among Generals." From Correspondence of the *St. Louis Democrat. Philadelphia Inquirer,* November 28, 1861.

Greenberg, A. S. *A Wicked War: Polk, Clay, Lincoln, and 1846 U.S. Invasion of Mexico.* New York: Vintage Books, 2012.

Guide to West Point and the U.S. Military Academy. New York: D. Van Nostrand, 1867.

Hafen, Leroy R., and Ann W. Hafen, eds. *Mormon Resistance: A Documentary Account of the Utah Expedition, 1857–1858.* Lincoln: University of Nebraska Press, 2005.

Hamilton, James J. *The Battle of Fort Donelson.* New York: A. S. Barnes, 1968.

Hammond, Otis G., ed. *The Utah Expedition 1857–1858—Letters of Capt. Jesse A. Gove, 10th Inf. U.S.A. of Concord, N.H., to Mrs. Gove, and Special Correspondence of the New York Herald.* Concord: New Hampshire Historical Society, 1928.

Harrison, Lowell. *The Civil War in Kentucky.* Lexington: University Press of Kentucky, 1975.

Hecker, William F., ed. *Private Perry and Mister Poe. The West Point Poems, 1831, Facsimile Edition.* Baton Rouge: Louisiana State University Press, 2005.

Henderson, Timothy J. *A Glorious Defeat: Mexico and Its War with the United States.* New York: Hill and Wang, 2007.

Henshaw, Major John Corey. *Recollections of the War with Mexico.* Edited by Gary F. Kurutz. Columbia: University of Missouri Press, 2008.

Heyman, Max L. *Prudent Soldier: A Biography of Major General E.R.S. Canby.* Glendale: The Arthur Clarke Company, 1959.

Historic Structures Inventory United States Military Academy West Point, New York. Washington: National Park Service Department of the Interior, 1984.

Historical Marker Database. U.S. Marine Hospital. Historical Marker Database. http://www.hmdb.org/Marker.asp?Marker=48505.

History of Its Founding. The Aztec Club of 1847. http://www.aztecclub.com/.

Holland. "An Anecdote of General Grant Related by His Son." *New News of Yesterday.* February 1909–1912.

Holzer, Harold, ed. *Hearts Touched by Fire.* New York: Modern Library, 2011.

Holzer, Harold B., and Craig L. Symonds, eds. *The New York Times—The Complete Civil War.* New York: Black Dog & Leventhal, 2010.

House Executive Document No. 60. "Messages of the President of the United States with the Correspondence, Therewith Communicated Between the Secretary of War and Other Officers of the Government on the Subject of the Mexican War." Washington: Wendell and Van Benthuysen, 1848, Library of Congress.

Hudson, Leonne M. *The Odyssey of a Southerner: The Life and Times of Gustavus Woodson Smith.* Macon: Mercer University Press, 1998.

Hurst, Jack. *Men of Fire: Grant, Forest, and the Campaign That Decided the Civil War.* New York: Basic Books, 2007.

Illuminations. University of California, Berkeley. February 2005.

"Instruction for Heavy Artillery; Prepared by a Board of Officers for the Use of the Army of the United States." Washington: Gideon and Co. Printers, 1851. Table of Contents. http://books.google.com/.

"J. C. Frémont and Missouri." In *Inside Lincoln's White House: The Complete Civil War Diary of John Hay,* Michael Burlingame and John R. T. Ettlinger, eds. Carbondale: Southern Illinois University Press, 1997.

"J. C. Frémont and Missouri, Mr. Lincoln and Freedom." The Lincoln Institute. Civil War. http://www.mrlincolnandfreedom.org/inside.asp?ID=31&subject-ID=3.

Jenkins, John J. *History of the War Between the United States and Mexico.* Auburn: Derby, Miller, 1849.

"John C. Fremont: 'Is He Honest? Is He Capable?'" Campaign literature. Publisher and publication date unknown.

Johnson, Timothy D. *A Gallant Little Army: The Mexico City Campaign.* Lawrence: University Press of Kansas, 2007.

Klopcic, Kevin M. "Come Fill Your Glasses Fellows, But Why?" 14 December 2000, Tactical Officer Education Program Papers, Special Collections, U.S. Military Academy Library.

Knight, James R. *The Battle of Fort Donelson.* Charleston: The History Press, 2011.

Kohl, Rhonda M. *The Prairie Boys Go to War.* Carbondale: Southern University Press, 2013.

Krecht, William L., and Peter L. Crowley, eds. *History of Brigham Young.* Berkeley: Mass Col Associates, 1964.

Lavender, David. *Climax at Buena Vista.* Philadelphia: University of Pennsylvania Press, 1966.

Leckie, Robert. *None Died in Vain: The Saga of the American Civil War.* New York: HarperCollins, 1990.

Levinson, Irving W. *Wars Within Wars: Mexican Guerrillas, Domestic Elites, and the United States of America 1846–1848.* Self-published in Canada, 2005.

Lewis, Lloyd. *Captain Sam Grant.* Boston: Little, Brown, 1950.

The Library of Congress, Bills and Resolutions, 37th Congress, 2nd Session, A Bill for the Relief of Fanny Mactier Smith (S. 371).

Lockwood, John, and Charles Lockwood. *The Siege of Washington: The Untold Story of the Twelve Days That Shook the Union.* New York: Oxford University Press, 2011.

Longacre, Edward G. *The Man Behind the Guns: A Biography of General Henry Jackson Hunt.* New York: A. S. Barnes, 1977.

MacKinnon, William P. "Causes of the Utah War," *Ford Douglas Vedette,* Newsletter of the Fort Douglas Military Museum Association, Spring 2007.

Manes, Lonnie E. "Columbus: The Gibraltar of the West." *Journal of the Jackson Purchase Historical Society* Vol. 10.

McDonough, James Lee. *Shiloh—In Hell Before Night.* Knoxville: University of Tennessee Press, 1977.

Meade, G. *The Life and Letters of George Gordon Meade, Major-General, United States Army,* vol. 1. New York: Charles Scribner's Sons, 1913.

Merit Rolls of the First Class (January 1825 and June 1825) and Second Class (January 1824 and June 1824). *Register of the Officers and Cadets of the U.S. Military Academy.* Archives. U.S. Military Academy Library.

Military Essays and Recollections. Vol. 1. Chicago: Military Order of the Loyal Legion of the United States, Illinois Commandery, 1891.

Minnesota Historical Society. Notes and Documents. The Red River Trails. http://collections.mnhs.org/MNHistoryMagazine/articles/6/v06i03p278–282.pdf.

Moore, John M., C. McKenna, and H. Raugh. "From Disorder to Discipline: The Origins of the Thayer Disciplinary System," December 4, 1990, Tactical Officer Education Program, Special Collections, United States Military Academy.

Morrison, James L., Jr., ed. *The Memoirs of Henry Heth.* Westport: Greenwood Press, 1974.

National Archives. OPA—Online Public Access. "The Indictment of Samuel Mactier Involved in the Baltimore 'Riot' of 1861." April, 19, 1861. http://research.archives.gov/description/278862.

Nevin, D. *The Mexican War*. Alexandria: Time Life Books, 1978.

"New York Marriages." *New York Times*, June 18, 1874.

"News from the Seat of the War. The War Measures of the Administration." *New York Herald*. April 30, 1861.

NewsinHistory.com. "Gen. Grant Gives the Union Its Second Major Victory: The Battle of Fort Donelson." http://www.newsinhistory.com/feature/gen-grant-gives-union-its-second-major-victory-battle-fort-donelson.

Nichols, E. J. *Zachary Taylor's Little Army*. Garden City: Doubleday, 1963.

Niles National Register, www.archive.org.

Ochoa, George, and Melinda Corey, eds. *West Point in the Making of America*. Irvington: Hydra, 2002.

Officers Letters. From October 1838 to July 1842. Archives. U.S. Military Academy Library

Official Register of the Officers and Cadets of the United States Military Academy (1818-1966). June 1821 to June 1825. Archives. U.S. Military Academy Library.

Park, Roswell. *A Sketch of the History and Topography of West Point and the U.S. Military Academy*. Philadelphia: Henry Perkins, 1840.

Parks, Joseph Howard. *General Edmund Kirby Smith, C.S.A.* Baton Rouge: Louisiana State University Press, 1954.

Patterson, Gerard. "The Mormon Confrontation." *American History Illustrated*. December 1972. Vol. VII No. 8.

Pembina, North Dakota, City of. History and Links. http://pembina.govoffice.com/index.

Post Orders. From October 15, 1821, to October 15, 1824. *Post Orders 1834-1904*, Archives. U.S. Military Academy Library.

"Presentation of a Sword to the Family of Major-General Charles F. Smith." *Philadelphia Inquirer*, January 21, 1863.

Report of Board of Claims. Executive Document No. 13, 2d session, 33d Congress. Vol. 825.

Robbins, James S. *Last in Their Class: Custer, Picket and the Goats of West Point*. New York: Encounter Books, 1962.

Scott, Winfield. *Rules and Regulations for the Exercise and Maneuvers of the United States Infantry*. New York: H. W. Mercein, 1815.

_____. Special Orders No. 56. July 9, 1842. Archives. U.S. Military Academy Library.

_____. Special Orders No. 60. July 18, 1842. Archives. U.S. Military Academy Library.

Seyburn, S. Y. "The Tenth Regiment of Infantry" in *The Army of the United States: Historical Sketches of Staff and Line with Portraits of Generals-in-Chief*. Edited by T. F. Rodenbough and W. L. Haskin. New York: Maynard, Merrill, 1896.

Shedd, Charles E., Jr. "A History of Shiloh National Military Park Tennessee." United States Department of the Interior, National Park Service, 1954.

Sherman, William T. *Memoirs*. New York: Barnes & Noble, 2005.

Shipley, The Rev. Moses. "Gen. C. F. Smith's Body Servant." *Philadelphia Inquirer*, March 14, 1893.

Simon, John Y., ed. *The Papers of U. S. Grant*. 5 vols. Carbondale: Southern Illinois University Press, 1970, and the Ulysses S. Grant Association.

Simpson, Brooks D. *Ulysses S. Grant: Triumph Over Adversity*. New York: Houghton Mifflin, 2000.

Simpson, W. A. "The Second Regiment of Artillery." In *The Army of the United States: Historical Sketches of Staff and Line with Portraits of Generals-in-Chief*, Theo. F. Rodenbough and William L. Haskin, eds. New York: Maynard, Merrill, 1896.

Singletary, Otis A. *The Mexican War*. Chicago: University of Chicago Press, 1960.

Smith, C. F. "Report of an expedition of Companies B and F, 10th regiment of infantry, to the Red River of the North, in 1856." *Message from the President of the United States to the Two Houses of Congress at the Commencement of the Second Session of the Thirty-Fifth Congress*. Washington: James B. Steedman, 1858.

Smith, E. Kirby. *To Mexico with Scott—Letters of Captain E. Kirby Smith to His Wife*. Ed. Emma Jerome Blackwood. Cambridge: Harvard University Press, 1917.

Smith, Francis H. "West Point Fifty Years Ago," An Address Delivered Before the Association of Graduates of the U.S. Military Academy, West Point, at the annual reunion, June 12, 1879, *Annual Reunion of the Association of Graduates (1870-1916)*. Archives. U.S. Military Academy Library.

Smith, George Winston, and Charles Judah. *The Chronicles of the Gringos: The U.S. Army in the Mexican War, 1846-1848—Accounts of Eyewitnesses & Combatants*. Albuquerque: University of New Mexico Press, 1968.

Smith, Jean Edward. *Grant*. New York: Simon & Schuster, 2001.

Smith, Justin H. *The War with Mexico*. Vols. I & II. Gloucester: Peter Smith, 1919.

Smith, Robert. Virtual American Biographies, http://famousamericans.net/robertsmith/.

Smith, Timothy B. "Battle of Shiloh: Shattering Myths." Civil War Trust. http://www.civilwar.org/battlefields/shiloh/shiloh-history-articles/battle-of-shiloh-shattering.html.

State Historical Society of Iowa. Iowa Medal of Honor Heroes. Corporal Voltaire P. Twombly. http://www.iowahistory.org/museum/exhibits/medal-of-honor/sf-02-twombly-cw/index.htm.

Tolbert, Noble J., ed. *Papers of John W. Ellis*, vol. 2. Raleigh: State Department of Archives and History, 1964.

Tozeski, Stanley P. *Preliminary Inventory of the Records of the United States Military Academy*. Washington: General Services Administration, 1976.

Tracy, Albert. "The Journal of Albert Tracy." *Utah Historical Quarterly*. Utah State Historical Society. Vol. 13, 1945, 54–56.

Tucker, Spencer C., ed. *The Encyclopedia of the Mexican-American War* Vol. I. Santa Barbara: ABC-CLIO, 2013.

Turner, John G., and Linda Levitt Turner. *Mary Todd Lincoln: Her Life and Letters*. New York: Fromm International, 1987.

Ulysses S. Grant Homepage. "Frederick T. Dent Notes on U S Grant at West Point." http://www.granthomepage.com/intdent.htm.

"U.S. Arsenal in Augusta." U.S. History, http://www.u-s-history.com/pages/h3114.html.

Villard, Henry. *Memoirs of Henry Villard, Journalist and Financier, 1835–1900*. Boston: Houghton, Mifflin, 1904.

Wallace, Isabel. *The Life and Letters of General W. H. L. Wallace*. Chicago: R. R. Donnelley & Sons, 1909.

Wallace, Lew. "The Capture of Fort Donelson." In *Hearts Touched by Fire*. New York: Modern Library, 2011.

Wallace, Lew. *Lew Wallace: An Autobiography*. Vol. I. New York: Harper & Brothers, 1906.

"The War in Kentucky—In and About Paducah." Sketched by J. C. Beard and Bill Travis. *Harper's Weekly*, October 26, 1861.

The War of the Rebellion: A Compilation of the Official Records of the Union and Confederate Armies. 8 Vols. Washington: Government Printing Office, 1882.

Waugh, John G. *The Class of 1846*. New York: Warner Books, 1994.

Weber, Walter P. *The Texas Rangers in the Mexican War*. Austin: Jenkins Garrett Press, 1975.

Weems, John E. *To Conquer a Peace*. College Station: Texas A&M University Press, 1974.

Wert, Jeffrey D. *General James Longstreet: The Confederacy's Most Controversial Soldier*. New York: Simon & Schuster, 1993.

Wheelan, Joseph. *Invading Mexico: America's Continental Dream and the Mexican War, 1846-1848*. New York: Carroll & Graf, 2007.

Wille, Kurt. Descendants of Dr. Samuel Blair Smith, MD, USA. Information compiled from records at Virginia Historical Society, Pennsylvania Historical Society, and Delaware Historical Society. October 22, 2011.

Winders, Richard Bruce. *Mr. Polk's Army: The American Military Experience in the Mexican War*. College Station: Texas A&M University Press, 1997.

Woodworth, Steven E. *Manifest Destinies: America's Westward Expansion and the Road to the Civil War*. New York: Alfred A. Knopf, 2010.

Wright, John D., ed. *The Oxford Dictionary of Civil War Quotations*. Oxford: Oxford University Press, 2006.

Index

abatis 163, 166, 193, 201, 205, 206, 213–215, 217, 219–220, 222, 275
adjutant 177, 202, 274, 281
adjutant general 183, 185, 197, 199, 202, 230–231, 241, 264
USS *Alabama* 91
Alexander, E.B. 102–103, 110, 112–116, 123
Ammen, Jacob 17, 253–254
Ampudia, Pedro de 53, 64, 66–67, 69
Anderson, Lucian 177–178, 182–185
Anderson, Robert 11, 13, 26–27, 55, 69, 73, 90, 98, 153, 267; Department of the Cumberland 144, 149–150, 160; Fort Sumter 133–134
Anderson, Samuel S. 96
Annapolis, Maryland 20, 94, 99, 103, 109, 138–140, 271
Arista, Mariano 53–56, 59
Army of Invasion 72–73, 75, 84, 87
Army of Mississippi 258
Army of Observation 47
Army of Occupation 47–49, 52–53, 60, 64, 71, 90
Army of the Mississippi 263
Army of the Ohio 247–248, 251, 262–263, 283
Army of the Tennessee 246, 248, 254, 260, 262–263, 267
Army of Utah 112–113, 115–119, 127
Arroyo Colorado, Texas 51–52, 60
assistant instructor of infantry tactics 1, 9, 17, 281
Augusta Arsenal, Georgia 14, 281
Austin, Moses 46
Aztec Club of 1847 89–90, 271, 282

Babcock, Andrew J. 206, 215, 220, 222, 279
Bailey, Jacob 28
Baird, Henry Carey 269–270
Baker, James 216–217, 219, 221
Baker-Fancher wagon train 126
Baltimore & Ohio Railroad 135

Bankhead, James M. 38–39, 41, 43, 63, 95–96
Barnard, J.G. 268
Battery A, First Illinois Volunteer Light Artillery, Second Division, Army of the Tennessee 280
Battery D, First Missouri Volunteer Light Artillery, Second Division, Army of the Tennessee 261
Battery D, First Missouri Volunteer Light Artillery, Third Brigade, Second Division, District of Cairo 212, 222, 280
Battery H, First Illinois Volunteer Light Artillery, First Division, Army of the Tennessee 261
Battery H, First Illinois Volunteer Light Artillery, Second Brigade, First Division, District of Cairo 220, 222, 279
Battery K, First Missouri Volunteer Light Artillery, First Division, Army of the Tennessee 261
Battery K, First Missouri Volunteer Light Artillery, Second Brigade, First Division, District of Cairo 212, 220, 279
Battle of Belmont 165–167, 179, 196, 226, 282; *see also* Belmont, Missouri
Battle of Bull Run (Manassas) 143, 237, 282
Battle of Cerro Gordo 73, 75–76, 282
Battle of Chapultepec 82–84, 87, 89, 274, 282; *see also* Castle of Chapultepec
Battle of Churubusco 78–81, 85, 91, 274, 282
Battle of Contreras 78, 80, 87, 89, 282
Battle of Fort Donelson 200–226, 283; Confederate breakout (February 15) 211–214; gunboat attack (February 14) 207–210; investment extended (February 13) 204–207; march (February 12) 203–204; praise for Smith 226–231, 234–235, 237–240, 242, 246, 251–253, 262–263, 266–269, 271–272, 275; Smith's attack (February 15) 214–223; unconditional surrender 224–226; Union Order of Battle 279; *see also* Fort Donelson, Tennessee
Battle of Fort Henry 196–200; *see also* Fort Henry, Tennessee
Battle of Monterrey 65, 66, 67, 69, 71, 73; *see also* Monterrey, Mexico
Battle of Palo Alto 48, 52, 54–56, 60, 72–73, 269, 274, 281
Battle of Resaca de la Palma 48, 54, 56–60, 73, 274, 281
Battle of Shiloh (Pittsburg Landing) 176, 248, 252–255, 260–264, 266–267, 276, 283
Bear Creek, Mississippi 237, 240
Bear River, Utah Territory 121–122
Bear River valley, Utah Territory 116
Beauregard, P.G.T. 197, 201; at Battle of Fort Sumter 134–135; at Battle of Shiloh 240, 249–250, 258, 261; Mexican War 75, 90; siege of Washington, DC 138; West Point 20
Bee, Barnard E. 1, 27, 90; Tenth Infantry 102, 118
Belén Causeway, Mexico City, Mexico 85
Belén Gate, Mexico City, Mexico 86
Belknap, William G. 49
Belmont, Missouri 144, 165; *see also* Battle of Belmont
Benedict, D.D.I. 179
Benny Havens 17, 18, 26, 91
USS *Benton* 249
Benton, Kentucky 194
Berard, Claudius 10, 33
Bibb, Lucien J. 17
Bird's Point, Missouri 148, 182
Birge's Western Sharpshooters (Fourteenth Missouri Sharp-

323

shooters), Fourth Brigade, Second Division, District of Cairo 203–204, 206, 209, 212–213, 216–217, 219–222, 280
Birge's Western Sharpshooters (Fourteenth Missouri Sharpshooters), Second Brigade, Second Division, Army of the Tennessee 255
Bishop's Palace, Monterrey, Mexico 64, 66–67, 69
Black's Fork, Utah Territory 116
Bladensburg, Maryland 139
Blair, Seth M. 123
Blandville, Kentucky 165, 192
Blandville Road, Kentucky 159, 165, 167–168, 192
Blountville Road, Tennessee 157
Board of Visitors 7, 11, 24, 38
Bolinger (Bollinger) 177–178
Bowlegs, Billy 97
Bowling Green, Kentucky 163, 186, 197, 201
Bragg, Braxton 20, 250, 258
brevet promotion 1, 13–14, 16, 48, 54, 60, 69–70, 72–73, 76, 81, 91, 100, 118, 124, 143, 274, 281–282
Brinton, Dr. John H. 225, 241, 265, 267
Brown, John C. 225
Buchanan, James 111–113, 118–121, 126, 132–134
Buckner, Simon: Battle of Fort Donelson 208, 211–213, 216–217, 220, 224–225; Civil War 152, 158–159; Mexican War 90; West Point 1, 6, 27, 278
Buell, Don Carlos: Battle of Shiloh 253–254, 261–263, 283; Civil War 169, 234–236, 238, 240–242, 246–248, 250–252; West Point 1, 21, 25, 27, 31, 277
Buffalo River, Minnesota Territory 108
Burton, Elizabeth Ferguson 39, 103
Butler, B.F. 139

cadet 1–2, 5–39, 84–85, 99, 101, 174, 266, 270, 274, 276–277
Cadet Mess Hall 8–10, 13, 17–18, 25, 28, 32
Cairo, Illinois 144, 146–149, 152–153, 155, 158–159, 161–162, 165–168, 179, 181, 191–192, 195, 197, 199–200, 234, 240
Calhoun, John C. 7, 19
California Board of Claims 100–101
California Gold Rush 111
Calloway, John 187
Camargo, Mexico 64
Cameron, Simon 137, 141–142, 144, 180
Camp Beauregard, Kentucky 163, 186, 192

Camp Biddle, US Military Academy, Summer 1840 27
Camp Clinton, US Military Academy, Summer 1820 8–9
Camp Fenwick, US Military Academy, Summer 1839 27
Camp Floyd, Utah Territory 122–129, 132–133
Camp Fowle, US Military Academy, Summer 1838 27
Camp Scott, Wyoming Territory 117–118, 120–122
Camp Spencer, US Military Academy, Summer 1842 27
Camp Tyler, US Military Academy, Summer 1841 27
Camp Walbach, Wyoming Territory 112
Campbell, Charles M. 271
Campbell, Hugh 95
Campbell, Reuben P. 126–127
Canby, Edward R.S.: Civil War 161; Mormon War 128; Tenth Infantry Regiment 102–103, 109–110; West Point 1, 20, 27, 31, 277
Cape Girardeau, Missouri 148, 157
Carlisle Barracks, Pennsylvania 102, 282
USS *Carondelet* 191, 197, 203, 205, 208, 280
Carrington, Henry B. 268
Carson Valley, Utah Territory 128
Casa de la Mata, Mexico City, Mexico 82
Casey, John 97
Caseyville, Illinois 178
Cashman, John 71
Cass, Lewis 19
Castle of Chapultepec (Chapultepec Castle), Mexico City, Mexico 81–85; *see also* Battle of Chapultepec
Castle Pinckney, South Carolina 134
Catholic Church 40, 53, 61
Cave-in-Rock, Illinois 168–169, 178, 186
Cavender, J.S. 204, 206, 251
Cedar City, Utah Territory 126–127
Cedar Valley, Utah Territory 122
Cerralvo, Mexico 64
Cerro Gordo, Jalapa, Mexico 73, 75, 76, 282; *see also* Battle of Cerro Gordo
Chapman, Frank 227
Chapman, W.N. 94
Charleston, Kentucky 165
Charleston and Memphis Railroad 243
Charleston Arsenal, South Carolina 134

Charlotte Road, Tennessee 208
Chase, Salmon P. 144
Chattanooga, Tennessee 243
Cheairs, Nathaniel F. 225
Cheatham, Benjamin F. 244, 246
Cherry, William H. 243, 251
Cherry Mansion, Savannah, Tennessee 244, 249, 251–252, 254, 262, 265
Chetlain, Augustus L. 162–163, 202, 260, 279
Chicago Tribune 178–180, 185, 200
Chickasaw, Tennessee 243, 247, 250, 276
Child, Thomas 67
Chippewas 105, 107
Churubusco, Mexico City, Mexico 78; *see also* Battle of Churubusco
Churubusco River, Mexico 80
Cincinnati Commercial 179, 227
City Council of Philadelphia 267
City Guards, Mexico City 88
Clarke, H.F. 56, 278
Clarke, Newman S. 77–78, 82, 84, 86
Clarksville, Tennessee 234–235, 237–239, 275
Clinton, James 8
Clinton, William 108
Clinton, Kentucky 159
Collado Beach, Veracruz, Mexico 72–73
Columbia, Tennessee 250
Columbus, Kentucky 144, 146–147, 152–155, 157, 159, 161, 163, 165–168, 177, 179, 182, 187, 192–193, 197, 226, 236, 240, 243
commandant of cadets, US Military Academy 1–2, 6–7, 13, 17, 21–22, 27, 29, 37–38, 63, 149, 153, 240, 266, 270, 274, 281
Compton, H.S. 206
USS *Conestoga* 152, 158–159, 162–164, 168, 178, 191, 197, 207, 234, 280
Confiscation Act 150
Conner, J.F. 177, 182
Conner, M.M. 177, 182
Conrad, C.M. 100
USS *Continental* 241, 243–244, 250–251
Contreras, Mexico 78; *see also* Battle of Contreras
Convent of San Mateo, Mexico City, Mexico 78–80
Cook, John P. 198, 203–204, 206–209, 211–215, 217, 220, 222–223, 226, 253, 279
Cooke, Philip St. George 114, 116–117
Coppee, Henry 29, 45, 90
Corinth, Mississippi 2, 237–238, 240–241, 243, 245–248, 250–251, 253–255, 261–263, 283

Corinth Road, Tennessee 255, 260
Corps of Cadets 8, 11–13, 19, 21–22, 32, 36–37, 39, 63, 88
Corpus Christi, Texas 45, 47–49, 281
Covington, Kentucky 145
Cox, Jacob 140
Cradlebaugh, John 125–127
Crane 94
Crawford, George W. 95–97
Crisp House, Battle of Fort Donelson, Tennessee 204, 207, 210, 212–213, 222, 225
Crocker, Marcellus M. 260
Crosby, Henry R. 3, 88, 128, 231
Cross, Truman 53
Cruft, Charles 207, 211, 213, 280
Crummer, Wilbur F. 204
Crump's Landing, Tennessee 243–245, 247–248, 251, 253–254, 261
Cullum, George W.: Civil War 180, 183–185, 226, 264; tributes to Smith 269–270, 274; West Point 2, 5, 17, 28
Cumberland River, Tennessee 144, 149, 155, 162–163, 169, 190–191, 197, 201, 203, 205, 226, 234, 275
Cummings, Alfred 118–123, 127

Davies, Thomas A. 262
Davis, Garrett 180
Davis, Jeff 151, 170, 172, 250
Davis, Tennessee 237
Deas, George B. 68, 72, 90
Decatur, Alabama 243
Delafield, Richard 21, 25–26, 31–32
Deltast, M.H. 60
demerits 11, 12, 14, 17, 19, 21, 29–31, 33, 36–37
Democratic Party 46, 71, 132, 179, 227
Dent, Frederick 34
Department of the Cumberland 144, 149, 160–161
Department of the Mississippi 241
Department of the Missouri 162, 168, 180, 200, 238, 275
Department of the West 143, 150, 152
Department of Washington 134, 137, 138, 139, 268, 274, 282
DeRussy, René E. 20, 40
Dialectic Society 31, 37
Dill Branch, Pittsburg Landing, Tennessee 261
discharge form 42–43
discipline 2, 7, 9, 14, 22, 29, 39, 40–43, 49, 60–62, 124, 128, 140–141, 146, 148, 156, 163, 167, 169–170, 174–175, 181, 183, 194, 230,

237, 239, 241, 262, 267, 270, 274–276
District of Cairo 162, 181, 197, 199, 279
District of Columbia 137–139, 274; *see also* Washington
District of Paducah 162
District of Southeast Missouri 162
Division of the Potomac 143
Donelson, Daniel S.: Civil War 190; West Point 6, 11, 13
Dover, Tennessee 164, 191–192, 195, 200, 204, 207–209, 224
Dover Road, Tennessee 206
Drake, Joseph 191
Duncan, James 47, 51, 59, 67, 77, 82, 84–85, 89, 94, 96
Duncan Field, Battle of Shiloh, Tennessee 255–256, 258

Eastern Corinth Road, Tennessee 255
Eastport, Mississippi 237, 238, 240, 243, 245–246
Eaton, John H. 17
Echo Canyon, Utah Territory 114–116
Eckels, Delana 118, 231
Eckelsville, Wyoming Territory 118
Eddyville, Kentucky 159, 191
Eddyville Road, Kentucky 213
Eggner's Ferry, Kentucky 194
Egyptian darkness (Egypt) 165, 265
Eighteenth Missouri Volunteer Infantry Regiment, Second Brigade, Sixth Division, Army of the Tennessee 255
Eighteenth Tennessee, Third Brigade, Right Wing, Army of Central Kentucky 219
Eighteenth Wisconsin Volunteer Infantry Regiment, Not Brigaded, Sixth Division, Army of the Tennessee 255
Eighth Iowa Volunteer Infantry Regiment, Third Brigade, Second Division, Army of the Tennessee 255–256, 258
Eighth Missouri Volunteer Infantry Regiment, Fifth Brigade, Second Division, District of Cairo 172, 178; at Battle of Fort Donelson 203, 207, 280
Eighty-First Ohio Volunteer Infantry Regiment, Second Brigade, Second Division, Army of the Tennessee 255
Eleventh Indiana Volunteer Infantry Regiment, Fifth Brigade, Second Division, District of Cairo 154; at Battle of Fort Donelson 203, 207, 280;

Tilghman House 170, 172, 173, 183
emancipation 150, 160, 175
Emancipation Proclamation 150, 175

Federation Hill, Monterey, Mexico 65–66, 68–69, 274, 281
Feliciana (Camp Beauregard), Kentucky 163
Ferguson, Ebenezer 7
Ferguson, Margaret 7, 20, 103, 140, 272
Ferrie, Reverend 182, 185
Fifteenth Arkansas Regiment, Third Brigade, Left Wing, Army of Central Kentucky 199
Fifth Infantry Regiment Mexican War 55, 64, 79; Mormon War 112–113, 115, 125
Fiftieth Illinois Volunteer Infantry Regiment, Third Brigade, Second Division, Army of the Tennessee 256
Fiftieth Illinois Volunteer Infantry Regiment, Third Brigade, Second Division, District of Cairo 203, 209, 212–213, 215, 220, 222, 279
Fifty-Eighth Illinois Volunteer Infantry Regiment, Third Brigade, Second Division, Army of the Tennessee 255
Fifty-Second Illinois Volunteer Infantry Regiment, Third Brigade, Second Division, Army of the Tennessee 255
Fifty-Second Illinois Volunteer Infantry Regiment, Third Brigade, Second Division, District of Cairo 197, 279
Fifty-Second Indiana Volunteer Regiment, Third Brigade, Second Division, District of Cairo 203, 206, 209, 212–213, 216–217, 219, 221–222, 279
Fifty-Seventh Illinois Volunteer Infantry Regiment, Third Brigade, Second Division, Army of the Tennessee 255
First Artillery Regiment 101
First Brigade, Army of Occupation 49, 51, 52, 66, 67; First Brigade, Army of Invasion 77, 84, 86, 90
First Brigade, Second Division, Army of the Tennessee 251, 255–256, 258, 260
First Brigade, Second Division, District of Cairo 165, 167; at Battle of Fort Donelson 203–204, 206–207, 222–223, 230, 279
First Class, West Point 9, 12, 13, 23, 27, 31, 38

Index

First Division, Army of Invasion 72, 75, 76, 77, 78, 91
First Division, District of Cairo 197, 202, 203, 204, 205, 211, 212, 214, 222, 279
First Division, Second Army Corps, Army of the Mississippi 258
First Missouri Light Artillery 206
Fishkill Landing, New York 110, 270
Floyd, John B. 121, 122, 127, 133, 224
Floyd-Jones, DeLancey 271
Foote, Andrew 147, 191–192, 196–197, 199–200, 203, 207–208, 212–213, 227, 234, 242, 280, 283
Fort Anderson, Paducah, Kentucky 153
Fort Bridger, Wyoming Territory 116–117, 119
Fort Brown, Texas 61
Fort C.F. Smith, Montana Territory 268–269
Fort C.F. Smith, Virginia 268, 272
Fort Columbus, New York 40–43, 47, 63, 72, 94, 133, 139, 141–143, 264–265, 281–282
Fort Crawford, Wisconsin 102–104
Fort Crittenden, Utah Territory 129, 133, 282
Fort Defiance, Tennessee 234
Fort De Kalb, Virginia 268
Fort Delaware, Delaware 7, 14, 281
Fort DeRussy, Missouri 144
Fort Diablo (Devil's Fort), Monterrey, Mexico 66
Fort Donelson, Tennessee 164, 190–194, 198; *see also* Battle of Fort Donelson
Fort Garland, New Mexico Territory 128
Fort Hamilton, New York 94
Fort Heiman, Kentucky 191, 192, 198, 199, 202, 204, 239, 275, 283
Fort Henry, Tennessee 159, 163, 178, 189–195; *see also* Battle of Fort Henry
Fort Jefferson, Kentucky 192
Fort Jessup, Louisiana 47
Fort Kearney, Nebraska Territory 115
Fort Laramie, Wyoming Territory 114–117, 120, 128, 269
Fort Laramie Treaty of 1868 269
Fort Leavenworth, Kansas 102, 110, 112, 114, 120
Fort Marion, Florida 94, 96
Fort McHenry, Maryland 95–96
Fort Moultrie, South Carolina 39, 134

Fort Phil Kearny (Kearney), Nebraska Territory 115, 268
Fort Randall, South Dakota 110
Fort Ransom, Montana Territory 268
Fort Reno, New Mexico Territory 268
Fort Ripley, Minnesota Territory 102–103, 108
Fort Snelling, Minnesota Territory 102–110, 112
Fort Soldado, Monterrey, Mexico 66–69
Fort Texas, Texas 53–54, 60
Fort Washington, Maryland 100–101, 135, 137–139
Forty-Fifth Illinois Volunteer Infantry Regiment, Second Brigade, First Division, District of Cairo 204, 279
Forty-First Illinois Volunteer Infantry Regiment, First Brigade, Second Division, District of Cairo 203, 279
Fourteenth Iowa Volunteer Infantry Regiment, First Brigade, Second Division, Army of the Tennessee 255–256, 258–259
Fourteenth Iowa Volunteer Infantry Regiment, Fourth Brigade, Second Division, District of Cairo 203, 205, 206, 209, 212, 216–217, 219–220, 222, 280
Fourth Class, West Point 8–9, 13, 23, 28, 31, 35, 38
Fourth Infantry Regiment, Army of Occupation 55–56, 72, 151, 281
Fourth United States Cavalry Regiment 201
Frankford Arsenal, Philadelphia, Pennsylvania 40–41, 281
Frazer, William 18–19
Freeman, W.G. 33, 98
Frémont, John C. 100–101, 132, 144, 146, 148–152, 155, 157–161, 165–166, 168, 174–175, 179, 236, 282

Galena, Illinois 102, 145
Galt, P.H. 90
Garland, John 82, 84, 86–87
Geddes, James L. 256, 258
General Orders No. 8, Composition of the Army of Utah, Mormon War 112
General Orders No. 48, Board to revise the uniform dress of the Army 99
General Orders No. 43, Grant transferred Lauman to Hurlbut's Fourth Division, Civil War 251

General Orders No. 4, Defense of Washington, Civil War 137
General Orders No. 97, Division of the Department of the West, Civil War 161
General Orders No. 111, Attack on La Atalaya, Mexican War 75
General Orders No. 170, Brevet promotion to Lt. Col. for Smith, Mexican War 72
General Orders No. 6, Anderson recommends Sherman, Civil War 160
General Orders No. 10, Orders for reassignment of troops from Camp Floyd, Mormon War 128
General Orders No. 34, Grant congratulates troops at Shiloh, Civil War 261
General Orders No. 36, Smith in response to conduct at Tilghman House, Civil War 174
General Orders No. 32, Smith complaint on conduct of Paine's troops, Civil War 167
General Orders No. 12, Military Department of Washington, Civil War 139
General Orders No. 12, System of instruction for siege, garrison, seacoast, and mountain artillery 98
General Orders No. 25, Smith relieved of duties as Chief of Police, Mexican War 91
General Orders No. 24, Halleck's orders to the citizens of Paducah, Cave-in-Rock, and Smithland, Civil War 186
General Orders No. 21, Halleck announces Smith's death, Civil War 265–266
General Orders No. 23, Frémont's orders on army's treatment of citizens, Civil War 160, 175
General Orders No. 22, Grant assigned Paine to Bird's Point, Civil War 182
General Orders No. 2, Smith declares that Savannah, Tennessee will be the rendezvous of expedition up the Tennessee River, Civil War 241
General Orders No. 2, Smith requires citizens to taker loyalty oath, Civil War 186
General Orders No. 296, Scott warns troops about conspiracy to murder officers and men, Mexican War 88
General Orders, Smith at Paducah, Kentucky, Civil War 149
Gentile 111, 114, 116, 122, 126
Gibson, Randall L. 258
Gilmer, Jeremy 1, 26, 201, 277

Golconda, Illinois 169
Gove, Jesse A. 102, 112, 115, 117, 121, 141
Governor's Island, New York 38, 141–143
Grant, Elihu 34
Grant, Frederick Dent 215, 266
Grant, Ulysses S. 1–3, 269, 276; at Battle of Belmont 165–167; at Battle of Fort Donelson 6, 200–205, 207–210, 279, 283; at Battle of Fort Henry 195–200; at Battle of Shiloh 240, 243, 245–254, 258, 260–263, 283; capture of Paducah 146–148, 150, 282; Civil War 142, 145–146, 155, 227–228, 231, 233; death of General Smith 264–266, 270; February 15 at Fort Donelson 211–215, 220, 227–229, 275; Mexican War 49–50, 54–56, 60–61, 64, 69, 71–74, 86–87, 90; problems with Halleck 234–239, 241–242, 283; Smith at Paducah 149, 153, 157, 159–162, 168, 174, 176, 181, 192–194; unconditional surrender 224–226, 283; West Point 27, 31, 34–38, 278, 281
Graves, Rice 217, 220
Grayson, John B. 69, 90
Great Salt Lake, Utah Territory 111–112
Green River, Kentucky 152, 158
Green River, Wyoming Territory 113, 115–116
Grimes, James W. 231
Guadalupe Hidalgo Peace Treaty 90, 282
Gulick, William 138
Gurley, John A. 179

Halleck, Henry W.: Battle of Fort Donelson 201–202, 204, 207, 209, 226, 275; Battle of Fort Henry 195–197, 199–200; Battle of Shiloh 237, 240–241, 245–251, 253, 261, 263; Civil War 2, 162, 167–169, 177–178, 180–181, 183–186, 189, 192, 194, 230, 262, 275, 283; death of General Smith 264–266, 276; removal of Grant 227, 229, 234–239, 241–242, 263, 283; West Point 1, 20, 27, 277
Hamburg-Purdy Road, Tennessee 254, 260
Hamburg-Savannah Road, Tennessee 254–256, 260
Hamer, Thomas L. 34
Hamilton, Edmund 68
Hamilton, Fowler 50–51
Ham's Fork, Wyoming Territory 113, 115–116
Hanson, Roger 205, 220

Hardee, William J. 1, 20, 90, 153, 159, 163, 168, 201
Harney, William S. 75, 112, 114, 116, 120
Harris, Nathaniel S. 17
Harris, Thomas 230
Haskin, J.A. 137
Havens, Benny 17–18, 26, 91
Hawes, Albert Gallatin 20
Hay, Jack 67–69
Hayfield Fight 268
Head, John W. 212
Heard, John W. 198
Heiman, Adolphus 191–192, 198, 201
Henderson, Kentucky 158, 240–241
Henry, Gustavus Adolphus Henry, Sr. 190
Heth, Henry 102, 126–128, 132
Hewitt, Dr. Henry S. 193, 218, 264, 267
Hickman, Kentucky 147
Hickman Creek, Tennessee 207, 209–210, 213
Highland, Kentucky 194
Hill, A.P. 38
Hill, D.H. 49
Hillyer, Charles T. 213
Hitchcock, Ethan Allen 17–18, 48, 64, 236
Holloway, John G. 152
Hopkinsville, Kentucky 178
The Hornet's Nest, Battle of Shiloh 258, 260
Hudson River, New York 11, 18, 25–26, 28, 110, 184
Hudson's Bay Company 107
Huger, Benjamin 11, 82, 83, 98
Humboldt, Mississippi 237
Humboldt Route, Utah Territory 128
Hunt, Henry Jackson: Mexican War 86–87, 90; West Point 1, 20, 27, 31–32, 277
Hunter, David 161–162, 241
Hurlbut, Steven A. 246–247, 251, 254, 256, 258–260

Illinois Central Railroad 168
Independence Hill, Monterey, Mexico 64–67, 69
Indian Creek, Tennessee 211–212, 220
Indianapolis Journal 179
infantry tactics (tactics) 1, 8, 10, 13, 16–17, 21–24, 27, 38–39, 56, 114, 116, 119, 160, 274, 281
Ingalls, Rufus 36–37, 278
Ironton, Missouri 148, 159
Island No. 10, Mississippi River 246, 249
Iuka, Mississippi 243

Jackson, Andrew 18–20
Jackson, Thomas "Stonewall" 1, 28, 87

Jackson, Mississippi 237, 245
Jalapa, Mexico 73, 75
Jeffers, Ann Burton ("Annie") 103
Jeffers, Lucie LeGrand Smith 103
Jeffers, William Nicholson 103, 266
Jo Daviess Guards 145
USS *John J. Roe* 243
Johnson, Bushrod West Point 1, 21, 27, 277; Civil War 190
Johnston, Albert Sydney Mormon War 114, 116–124, 126–128, 282; Civil War 6, 142, 151–152, 157, 163, 190–191, 201, 227, 247, 250, 258
Johnston, Joseph E. 13, 94
Jones, Gerald R. 42, 97, 99

Kane, Thomas J. 113, 119, 121
Kansas-Nebraska Act 132
Kearney, Phil 91
Kemper, And C. 266
Kentucky General Assembly 148
Kinner, F.F. 203
Knefler, Frederick 170, 172–173
Knowlton, Miner 27

La Atalaya, Mexico 73, 75
La-kik-wa-nel (Green Feather), Chief 105, 107
La Veronica Causeway, Mexico City, Mexico 82, 86
Lake Chicot, Minnesota Territory 105
Lake Mini-Waken (Devil's Lake), Minnesota Territory 104, 107–108
Lane, Henry S. 180
Latham, Milton S. 202
Lauman, Jacob G.: at Battle of Fort Donelson march on February 12 203–204; at Battle of Shiloh 251, 253, 256; Confederate breakout on February 15 211–213; gunboat attack on February 14 210; investment extended on February 13 205–206; Smith's attack of February 15 214–220, 222–223, 280; unconditional surrender 224–226
Laurel Hill Cemetery, Philadelphia, Pennsylvania 267, 270, 273, 276
Lee, A.T. 58
Lee, John D. 126–127
Lee, Richard B. 100
Lee, Robert E. 1, 13, 73, 75, 87, 90, 94, 99, 101, 142
USS *Lexington* 47
USS *Lexington* (gunboat) 152, 191, 193, 197, 261, 280
Lick Creek, Tennessee 247–248
Light Battalion (Mexican War) 56, 59, 75, 77–79, 83–85, 87, 282

Lincoln, Abraham 132–133, 282; Civil War 142–143, 145–146, 227; Fort Sumter crisis 134; Frémont 150, 160–161; removal of Grant 236, 241, 263; removal of Smith 180, 184; siege of Washington 135, 137–138; Tilghman House 170, 175, 178
Lincoln-Douglas Debates 132
Little Jordan River, Utah Territory 122
Locke, Joseph L. 17–18
Lockwood, H.H. 99
Longstreet, James 1, 27, 31, 36, 58, 90, 275
USS *Louisville* 191, 207–208, 280
Lovelaceville, Kentucky 177
Lovelaceville Road, Kentucky 165, 167–168

Mactier, William 63, 262
Magoffin, Beriah 148, 154
Magruder, John B. 17, 87, 90
Mahan, Dennis H. 10, 32, 94
Manassas, Virginia 142–143, 197, 282
Mansfield, J.K.F. 139–140
Marcy, R.B. 117, 120
Marcy, William L. 60, 73, 87, 94
Marin, Mexico 65
Marine Hospital, Paducah, Kentucky 152–153, 163
Mason, George 249
Mason, J.L. 77–78
USS *Massachusetts* 72
Matamoros (Matamaras), Mexico 47, 49, 51–54, 56, 58–61, 63–64, 71–72
Mayfield, Kentucky 149, 151, 158–159, 163, 177, 182, 186, 192
Mayfield Creek, Kentucky 167, 186
McAllister, Edward 212, 279
McArthur, John: at Battle of Fort Donelson 147, 203–204, 206, 208, 212, 220, 222, 224, 230, 279; at Battle of Shiloh 251, 253, 255–256, 259–260, 262
McCall, George 57–59, 96
McClellan, George B. 38, 54, 87, 143, 145, 162–163, 166–167, 169, 180–181, 183, 185, 200, 229, 236–237, 239, 241–242, 245, 249, 275
McClernand, John A. 193, 197–198, at Battle of Fort Donelson 202–208, 211–214, 216, 228, 279; at Battle of Shiloh 245–246, 249, 253–254, 260, 263
McCook, Henry C. 180
McCulloch, Ben 120–121
McDowell, Irvin 41, 94, 95, 98, 138, 143; West Point 20, 31, 32
USS *McGill* 210
McGwin, Ellen 72
McIntosh, James S. 49
McMichael, William 240

Mejia, Francisco 51–53, 64
Melvin, Kentucky 165, 167
USS *Memphis* 245
Memphis, Tennessee 163, 197
Memphis & Charleston Railroad 247
Mersey, August 260
Mexican War (U.S.–Mexican War) 2- 3, 45, 47, 49, 60, 71, 89, 94–95, 99, 100, 104, 111, 120, 143, 145, 248
Mexico City (City of Mexico), Mexico 45, 47, 74, 76, 77, 78, 79, 81, 82, 86, 87, 88, 89, 90, 91, 274, 282
Middle River, Minnesota Territory 107
Milburn, Kentucky 167–168
Miles, Dixon S. 68
Military Department of Utah 114, 120
Miller, John R. 265
Millerites 159
Milliken, John 177, 182
Min-e-ha-ha falls, Minnesota Territory 105
Minnesota River (St. Peters River) 103
Mississippi River 135, 144, 152, 165, 167, 190–191
Missouri Democrat 227–228
Missouri River 112
Molina del Rey, Mexico 81–82, 87, 91
Monterrey, Mexico 64, 65, 66, 67, 69, 71, 73; *see also* Battle of Monterrey
Morales, Juan 73
Morgan, William H. 229–230
Mormon (Church of Latter Day Saints, Saints) 1, 61, 111–129, 132–133, 274, 282
Mormon War (Mormon Expedition, Mormon Rebellion, Utah Expedition, Utah War) 1, 110, 111, 112, 113, 122, 132, 282
Morrill Anti-Bigamy Act of 1862 133
Morton, Oliver P. 144, 180
Moseley, William D. 95
Mound City, Illinois 147, 191
Mountain Meadows massacre 126
Muldraugh Hill, Kentucky 178
Murray, Kentucky 192–194

Nashville, Tennessee 169, 178, 190, 192–193, 201, 208, 213, 234–235, 237, 239, 242, 246, 250–251, 275
National Palace, Mexico City, Mexico 87–88
National Road, Mexico 73
Nauvoo Legion 113–114, 120–121
Nelson, William "Bully" 252–254, 261, 266

New Madrid, Missouri 166
New Orleans and Ohio Railroad 147
New Orleans Daily Picayune 67, 69, 89
USS *New Uncle Sam* 202
New York, New York 7, 11, 20, 26, 34, 38–40, 72, 94, 98, 103, 133–134, 140–142, 184, 264, 266, 271
The New York Herald 122, 139, 193, 227
The New York Times 112, 137, 139–143, 200, 226, 267
Newsham, Thomas 173, 214–216, 219–220, 223
Nichols, William A. 96, 98
Niles National Register 49, 61
Ninth Illinois Volunteer Infantry Regiment, First Brigade, Second Division, District of Cairo 147, 185, 223, 279
Ninth Illinois Volunteer Infantry Regiment, Second Brigade, Second Division, Army of the Tennessee 256, 260
Norfolk, Kentucky 165
Nueces River, Texas 46–47, 53

O'Connell, John 220, 222
Oglesby, Richard J. 166, 238, 279
Ohio and Mississippi Railroad 168
Ohio River 147–148, 151, 158, 168, 178
Old Fort Massac, Illinois 162
Oliver, Leslie Allen 270, 272
Oliver, Marshal 270–271
Oriziba, Mexico 73
Owensborough, Kentucky 152
Owl Creek, Tennessee 247

Pacific Springs, Wyoming Territory 116
Padgett's Spy Company, Army of Central Kentucky 198
Paducah, Kentucky 131, 144–155, 157–163, 165–170, 172, 174, 177–180, 182–183, 185–186, 192–195, 197, 202, 229–230, 236, 240–241, 243, 274–275, 282
Paine, E.A.: Civil War 147–149, 152, 159; conspiracy against Smith 170, 177, 179–185; demonstration at Columbus 165–169; West Point 20, 31, 277
Palmer, Joseph 219
Paris, Tennessee 194, 237, 239
Parrott, James C. 206, 225, 256, 280
Parrott, Robert P. 10
Parrott guns (rifles) 204, 209, 212–213, 220, 222–223
Partridge, Alden 10
Patterson, Robert 40; Civil War 138–140; Mexican War 72–73, 75

Index

Pea Ridge, Tennessee 248, 253
Peckham, James 178
Pemberton, John C. 20, 58, 87
Pembina, Minnesota Territory 103–109
Phelps, John W. 98, 112–113, 115
Phelps, Seth L. 159, 163–164, 191, 197, 249, 280
The Philadelphia Inquirer 138, 228, 267
Pillow, Gideon F.: at Battle of Fort Donelson 208, 211–213, 216, 224; Civil War 6, 144, 149, 157, 163, 172; Mexican War 75–76, 81–82, 84, 89
USS *Pittsburg* 191, 207–208, 280
Pittsburg Landing, Tennessee 244–255, 258–262, 266, 276
Pittsburg Landing Road, Tennessee 260
Platte River, Wyoming Territory 115
Pleasanton, Alfred 1, 27, 58, 267, 278
plebe 8–9, 11, 17, 27, 35–36, 270
Plumley's Station, Kentucky 186
Poe, Edgar Allan 17–18
Point Isabel, Texas 49, 52, 54, 61
Polk, James K. 46–49, 53–54, 60–61, 64, 71, 89, 94–95
Polk, Leonidas 144, 155, 163, 167–168, 187, 194
polygamy 111, 113
Pony Express 129, 132
Pope, John 1, 27, 145–146, 236, 263, 277
Porter, David 53
Porter, Fitz John 1, 27, 90, 99, 278
Porter, Thomas 217, 219–220, 222
Porter, William 198–200
posse comitatus 112, 114, 121, 124, 127
Potomac River 135
Potter, Tom 205
Powell, Lazarus W. 120–121
Prentiss, Benjamin M. 247, 249, 254–256, 258–261
President's War Order No. 3, Lincoln designates the Department of the Mississippi 241
Price, John T. 149, 158, 170, 172–175
Princeton, Kentucky 159, 168, 178
Provo, Utah Territory 119, 122, 126
Puebla, Mexico 75–76
Pugh, Isaac C. 180, 279
Purdy, Tennessee 243, 245–246, 255
Purdy Road, Tennessee 254, 260

Quitman, John A. 76, 84–90

Ramsay, George D. 40, 42, 90, 95, 99
Rawlins, John A. 197, 212, 220

Red Lake River, Minnesota Territory 107
Red River of the North (Red River), Minnesota Territory 104–105, 107–109, 274, 282
Reno, Jesse L. 98, 112
Richardson, Henry 206, 212–213, 261, 280
Richardson, Israel B. 1, 21, 27, 277
Ridge Road, Tennessee 203, 210, 220
Ridgely, Randolph 58–59
Ringgold, Samuel 51, 55–56, 58
Rio del Plan, Mexico 73, 75
Rio Grande River 46–47, 49, 51–52, 56, 60, 64, 72
Rivière aux Marais, Minnesota Territory 108
Ruggles, Daniel 87, 258
Ruggles, Edward Seymour 142
Rules and Regulations for the Exercise and Maneuvers of the United States Infantry 23, 27
Rziha, John 158, 187, 193, 230, 249

St. Augustine, Florida 94–95, 97–98, 282
St. Joseph, Minnesota Territory 105, 107–108
USS *St. Louis* 191, 197, 200, 207–208, 213, 276, 280
St. Louis, Missouri 143–144, 146, 148, 150–152, 158–159, 162, 177, 179, 181–182, 185, 187, 191–192, 195, 200–201, 215–216, 240, 245, 266
St. Louis Democrat 170, 179
St. Louis Republican 148
Saltillo, Mexico 64–65, 67, 71
San Agustin, Mexico 77
San Antonio, Mexico 46, 77–78, 274
San Cosmé Causeway, Mexico City, Mexico 85–86
San Cosmé Church 86
San Cosmé Gate, Mexico City, Mexico 86–87
San Juan d'Ulloa, Veracruz, Mexico 73
Sand Hill River, Minnesota Territory 108
Sandy Creek, Tennessee 168
Santa Anna, Antonio López de 46, 64, 71, 73, 76–78, 81–82, 87
Santa Catarina River, Monterey, Mexico 66, 68
Savannah, Tennessee 240–243, 245–251, 253–254, 262, 264–266, 268, 270, 275, 283
Savannah-Hamburg Road, Tennessee 255–256, 258, 260
School of the Soldier 9, 23
Scott, John B. 59, 67
Scott, Thomas 240
Scott, Winfield 2, 17, 19, 23, 27, 37, 39, 42, 94, 95, 98, 131, 269, 274; Civil War 134–135, 137–139, 142, 154, 160–161; Mexican War 48, 63, 71–73, 75–76, 78, 80–91, 282; Mormon War 112, 116, 133
Seaton, John 178
Second Army Corps, Army of the Mississippi 258
Second Artillery Regiment 15, 27, 38–41, 47, 49, 56, 63–64, 69, 72, 75, 78, 90, 94, 98, 281
Second Brigade, Army of Occupation 49, 51, 66–69; Army of Invasion 77, 84, 86
Second Brigade, Second Division, Army of the Tennessee 251, 255–256, 260
Second Brigade, Second Division, District of Cairo 173, 203, 207, 230, 279
Second Class, West Point 12, 23, 28, 31
Second Dragoons, Army of Occupation 58
Second Dragoons (Second United States Cavalry), Army of Utah 112, 114, 116, 201
Second Illinois Cavalry, First Brigade, First Division, District of Cairo 162, 186, 279
Second Iowa Volunteer Infantry Regiment, First Brigade, Second Division, Army of the Tennessee 255
Second Iowa Volunteer Infantry Regiment, Fourth Brigade, Second Division, District of Cairo 209–210, 212, 215–223, 280
Second Kentucky Infantry Regiment, Second Brigade, Right Wing, Army of Central Kentucky 205, 217, 220
Seminoles 95–97, 112
Seventh District Regiment (Governor Yates's Hellions) 145–146
Seventh Illinois Volunteer Infantry Regiment, Third Brigade, Second Division, Army of the Tennessee 255
Seventh Illinois Volunteer Infantry Regiment, Third Brigade, Second Division, District of Cairo 198, 206, 209, 212, 215, 220, 222, 279
Seventh Iowa Volunteer Infantry Regiment, First Brigade, Second Division, Army of the Tennessee 256, 258–259
Seventh Iowa Volunteer Infantry Regiment, Fourth Brigade, Second Division, District of Cairo 204, 206, 209, 216, 219, 221–222, 225, 280
Seventh Regiment of New York 139

Seward, William 134
Shaw, William T. 205, 219–220, 222, 256, 258–259, 280
Shawneetown, Illinois 168–169
Shayenne River, Minnesota Territory 105, 108
Sherman, Thomas W. 30, 109
Sherman, William T. 1–3, 93, 276; at the Battle of Shiloh 240, 243, 245–248, 250, 253–254, 260–263, 270; Civil War 142, 160–161; Mexican War 90; at West Point 20, 27, 30–31, 33, 36, 277
Siege of Veracruz 73, 282; *see also* Veracruz
Simpson, Sir George 107
Sinclair, Charles 125
Sixth Division, Army of the Tennessee 249, 255
Slidell, John 47
Smith, Allen 95, 103–104, 110, 270–271, 282
Smith, Edmund Kirby 1, 27, 33, 51, 75, 80–83, 278
Smith, Fanny Mactier (Oliver) 3, 6, 26, 41; Civil War 235, 245, 262, 264, 270–271, 281; Fort Marion 94–95; Mexican War 69; Tenth Infantry Regiment 103–104, 107, 109–110, 116, 119, 123–124
Smith, Francis Mactier 26, 39–41; after General Smith's death 266–268, 270, 281; Civil War 137, 139–141, 151–152, 157, 160, 162, 166, 168, 179, 181, 183–185, 193–195, 228–229, 231, 234, 237–238, 242, 244–245, 250–252; Fort Marion 94–95, 99–100; Mexican War 60, 65, 69, 76, 91; Tenth Infantry Regiment 103, 110, 124
Smith, Henrietta Laurens 100, 271, 282
Smith, Henry Mactier 26
Smith, John Blair 7
Smith, John L. 63
Smith, Joseph 126
Smith, Lucie LeGrand 103
Smith, Mary (Margaret) Ferguson 20, 281
Smith, Morgan L. 203, 208, 210, 213, 230, 252, 280
Smith, Persifor F. 66–69, 85, 90, 120
Smith, Robert 7
Smith, Samuel B. 7, 14, 281
Smith, Sidney 87
Smith, T. Henry 269
Smith, William Farrar 1, 27, 270, 278
Smithland, Kentucky 144, 149, 158–159, 162, 186, 195, 197
Snake Creek, Tennessee 244, 255
South Pass, Wyoming Territory 114, 116

Southern, John 25
Special Orders No. 80, Smith appointed Superintendent of Eastern Department, Civil War 133
Special Orders No. 58, Smith assigned command of troops in Washington and Fort Washington, Civil War 135
Special Orders No. 19, Smith placed in-charge of expedition up the Tennessee River, Civil War 240
Special Orders No. 107, Smith relieved from command of Department of Utah, Mormon War 129
Special Orders No. 102, Smith placed in command of ten companies of militia, Civil War 137
Special Orders No. 78, Designated Grant's command as the District of Cairo, Civil War 181, 183
Special Orders No. 36, Grant designates Smith to command forces at Pittsburg Landing, Civil War 248
Speed, Joshua 150
Spirit Lake, Minnesota Territory 110
Spirit Lake Massacre 110
Springfield, Illinois 145
Staniford, Thomas 66
Stanton, Edwin M. 236, 241, 263, 266, 270
USS *Star of the West* 134
Stephens, Williams 256
Stinnecke, Dr. Henry A. 98
Stone, Charles P. 137, 278
Stone, George 223, 261
Sturgis, Samuel Davis 180
Sullivan, John 265
Sunken road (abandoned road), Battle of Shiloh 254, 256–258
Sutter's Mill, California 111
Swann, Ann ("Anna") 103
Swann, Carolina Laurens ("Carry") 103
Swann, Richard 95–96, 103
Swann, Thomas Laurens 103
Sweeny, Thomas W. 251, 255–256, 279
Sweet Water River, Wyoming Territory 113, 116
Swinton, William 140

tactical officers ("tacs") 7, 17–18, 30
Talbot, Theodore 137
Taos, New Mexico 117
Taylor, Francis 98–99
Taylor, Zachary 47–49, 51–56, 59–61, 63–66, 69, 71–72, 89–90, 269, 282

Telegraph Road, Tennessee 203
Tennessee Corps of Engineers 190
Tennessee River 147, 159, 169, 178, 190–194, 196, 200–201, 235–236, 238, 240, 245–247, 254, 266, 274–275, 283
Tenth Infantry Regiment 102, 111, 113, 231, 282
terres tremblantes 105
Texas Rangers 58, 67–68
Thayer, John M. 207, 211, 280
Thayer, Sylvanus 6–14, 18–19, 25, 29, 39, 100, 274, 281
Thielemann, Christian 186
Third Brigade, Army of Occupation 49
Third Brigade, Second Division, Army of the Tennessee 251, 255–256, 260
Third Brigade, Second Division, District of Cairo 203–204, 206–209, 220, 223, 279
Third Class, West Point 9, 12, 23, 28, 31, 34, 37
Third Division, Army of Invasion 73
Third Division, Army of the Tennessee 255
Third Division, District of Cairo 204, 209, 280
Third Presbyterian Church, Philadelphia 267
Thirteenth Iowa Volunteer Infantry Regiment, First Division, Army of the Tennessee 260
Thirteenth Missouri Volunteer Infantry Regiment, Second Brigade, Second Division, Army of the Tennessee 260
Thirteenth Missouri Volunteer Infantry Regiment, Third Brigade, Second Division, District of Cairo 203, 209, 212–213, 222, 280
Thirtieth Tennessee Regiment, Fourth Brigade, Fort Donelson Garrison, Left Wing, Army of Central Kentucky 212–213, 216–217
Thomas, Charles 100
Thomas, George H. 1–2, 21, 27, 263, 273
Thomas, J.A. 39
Thomas, Lorenzo 95, 96, 101, 181, 185, 230–231, 241–242
Thompson, Jeff 159
USS *Tigress* 241, 253–254
Tilghman, Lloyd 20, 147, 171, 191, 192, 194, 282; at the Battle of Fort Henry 198–201
Todd, John Blair Smith 21, 137, 184
Tooth, F. 157

Totten, James 30, 32, 180
Totten, Joseph 38–39
Tracy, Albert 125
Treaty of Guadalupe Hidalgo, Mexican War 90, 282
Trenton, Tennessee 163
Trist, Nicholas 90
Tucker, "Pitts" 247
Tug Island, Ohio River 147, 151
Turner, James J. 217–218
Tuttle, James M.: at Battle of Fort Donelson 210, 215–221, 280; at Battle of Shiloh 253, 255–256, 258–260
Twelfth Illinois Volunteer Infantry Regiment, First Brigade, Second Division, District of Cairo 147, 162, 167, 203, 222–224, 279
Twelfth Illinois Volunteer Infantry Regiment, Second Brigade, Second Division, Army of the Tennessee 255–256, 260
Twelfth Iowa Volunteer Infantry Regiment, First Brigade, Second Division, Army of the Tennessee 255–256, 258–259
Twelfth Iowa Volunteer Infantry Regiment, Third Brigade, Second Division, District of Cairo 209, 212–213, 215–216, 220, 222, 280
Twelfth Michigan Volunteer Infantry Regiment, First Brigade, Sixth Division, Army of the Tennessee 255
Twenty-Fifth Indiana Volunteer Infantry Regiment, Fourth Brigade, Second Division, District of Cairo 203, 205–206, 209–210, 212, 216–217, 219–223, 229, 280
Twenty-First Missouri Volunteer Infantry Regiment, First Brigade, Sixth Division, Army of the Tennessee 255, 258
Twenty-Second Illinois Volunteer Infantry Regiment, Detached 178–179
Twenty-Seventh Alabama Regiment, First Brigade, Left Wing, Army of Central Kentucky 192, 199
Twenty-Third Missouri Volunteer Infantry Regiment, Not Brigaded, Sixth Division, Army of the Tennessee 255
Twiggs, David E. 48–50, 72–73, 75–76, 79, 97
Twombly, Voltaire E. 217
USS *Tyler* 191, 197, 207, 245, 250, 261, 280
Tyler's Landing, Tennessee 243

unconditional surrender 120, 221, 226, 228, 283
United States Military Academy *see* West Point
Utah Territory 111–112, 115, 128, 231, 282

Van Rensselaer, Henry Bell 180
Van Vliet, Stewart 20–21, 69, 114, 116
Veatch, James C. 205, 216, 222, 280
Veracruz, (Vera Cruz) 71–73, 91; *see also* Siege of Veracruz
Viola, Kentucky 186

Waggaman, George G. 34
Waite, Gilbert 113
Walke, Henry 203, 280
Walker, Leroy Pope 134
Walker, Sam 58
Wallace, Ann 255
Wallace, Lew 2, 131, 154–157, 159, 161; at Battle of Fort Donelson 202–204, 207–210, 280; at Battle of Shiloh 243–246, 248, 254–255, 260–261, 283; Confederate breakout (February 15) 211–216; conspiracy against Smith 177, 179–180, 182; at Fort Heiman 199; injury to Smith 244, 283; reconnaissance towards Camp Beauregard 186; Tilghman House 170–175
Wallace, William H.L. 213, 250–255, 258–260, 262, 279
Wallace's Bridge 244
Washburne, Elihu B. 202, 229
Washington: Mexican War 51, 53, 60–61, 64, 73; Civil War 132–135, 143, 150, 152, 155, 162, 169, 200, 226, 240, 270, 272; Fort C.F. Smith 268; Grant removal 237, 239, 241–242; Mormon War 114, 127–129; removal of Smith 181–185; Siege of 135, 137–141, 274, 282; Smith on boards in 94–96, 99–100, 102–103, 282; *see also* Department of Washington; District of Columbia
Weber Canyon, Utah Territory 115
Weber River Valley, Utah Territory 122
Webster, Joseph D. 149, 158, 214, 254, 261, 279
Welker, Frederick 220, 222, 261
Wells, Gideon 191
West Point 1, 2, 5–8, 10–13, 15, 40–41, 91, 97–101, 110, 281; Civil War 134, 142–143, 145, 149, 153, 174, 266; Grant as Cadet 34–38; Mexican War 47–48, 54, 88, 91; Smith as commandant of cadets 23, 26, 27, 29, 33, 39; Smith as officer 16–21; Smith's honors 269, 270, 272; *see also* U.S. Military Academy
Western Department, Confederate States Army 190
Western Department, United States Army 282
Whig Party 71, 132
USS *Whiteville* 72
Wild Rice River, Minnesota Territory 108
The Willard Hotel 135–136, 140
USS *Wilson* 193
Wilson, John M. 269
Wood Road, Minnesota Territory 108
Woods, Joseph J. 256, 258–259
Woods, Samuel 104
Woolfolk, Robert 170, 172–174, 177, 183, 187, 282
Worth, J.F. 264
Worth, William C.: Mexican War 48–49, 51–52, 63–64, 66–73, 75–79, 81–87, 89–91, 282; West Point 6–10, 13–14
Wright, Crafts J. 209, 260, 280
Wright, George 82–83, 141
Wynn's Ferry Road, Tennessee 211, 213–214, 222

Yates, Richard 145–146
Yellow Creek, Tennessee 243, 247
Yellow Fever (*vomito*) 9, 64, 73
Young, Brigham 111, 113–115, 118–121, 126–128, 133

www.ingramcontent.com/pod-product-compliance
Lightning Source LLC
Chambersburg PA
CBHW081537300426
44116CB00015B/2666